Langenscheidt
Dicionário Universal

Inglês

Inglês – Português
Português – Inglês

Langenscheidt

Langenscheidt
Universal Dictionary

Portuguese

Portuguese – English
English – Portuguese

Langenscheidt

Original edition compiled by Claudina Marques Coelho

1. Auflage 2018 (1,02 - 2021)

www.langenscheidt.com

Print: Druckerei C. H. Beck, Nördlingen
Printed in Germany

ISBN 978-3-12-514034-9

Contents
Índice

Abbreviations
Abreviaturas 4

Portuguese Pronunciation
A pronúncia portuguesa 5

English Pronunciation
A pronúncia inglesa 8

Portuguese – English
Português – Inglês 11

English – Portuguese
Inglês – Português 169

Numerals
Numerais 416

Abbreviations
Abreviaturas

The sign of repetition (~) or, with capital initial letter (♀), replaces either the whole headword: **abandon** (…) **~ed** = **abandoned** or that part of it which precedes the vertical bar (|): **abbreviat|e** (…) **~ion** = **abbreviation**; **alp** (…) the **♀s** = the **Alps**.

O til (~, com inicial alterada ♀) substitui o título inteiro ou a parte dele que precede o traço vertical (|); p.ex. civil: **~idade** = **civilidade**; **abert|o** (…) **~ura** = **abertura**; **natal** adj: ♀ = **Natal** *m*

a and, *e*
abbr abbreviation, *abreviatura*
adj adjective, *adje(c)tivo*
adv adverb, *advérbio*
ANAT anatomy, *anatomia*
ARCH architecture, *arquite(c)tura*
art article, *artigo*
AUTO automobilism, *automobilismo*
AVIAT aviation, *aviação*
BOT botany, *botânica*
Braz Brazilian, *brasileiro*
CHEM chemistry, *química*
COM commerce, *comércio*
COMP computing, *computação*
conj conjunction, *conjunção*
contr contraction, *contra(c)ção*
dem demonstrative, *demonstrativo*
ECCL ecclesiastical, *eclesiástico*
ELECT electricity, *ele(c)tricidade*
f feminine, *feminino*
fam familiar, *familiar*
fig figurative, *figurativo*
GB Great Britain, *Grã-Bretanha*
GEOL geology, *geologia*
GRAM grammar, *gramática*
int interjection, *interjeição*
JUR juridical, *jurídico*
m masculine, *masculino*
MAR maritime, *marítimo*
MEC mechanical, *mecânico*
MED medical, *medicinal*
MIL military, *militar*
MIN mineralogy, *mineralogia*
MUS music, *música*
NAUT nautical, *náutica*
pers personal, *pessoal*
pl plural, *plural*
poss possessive, *possessivo*
pres present, *presente do indicativo*
pron pronoun, *pronome*
prp preposition, *preposição*

s substantive, *substantivo*
sg singular, *singular*
TEL telecommunications, *telecomunicação*
THEAT theatre, *teatro*
US United States, *Estados Unidos*
v/aux auxiliary verb, *verbo auxiliar*
v/i intransitive verb, *verbo intransitivo*
v/r reflexive verb, *verbo reflexivo*
v/t transitive verb, *verbo transitivo*
ZOO zoological, *zoológico*

Portuguese Pronunciation

1. Vowels

			nearest English equivalent
a	unstressed:	o	as in *mother*
	stressed:	a	as in *father*
e	ê – closed:	—	
	é – open:	e	as in *get*
	weak stress:	a	as in *about*
i		i	as in *city*
o	closed		resembles English *aw* in *law*, but closer and short
	ó – open:	o	as in *not*
u		oo	as in *book*

All vowels may be nasalized, as for example in American *long*, *language*, French *rendezvous*.
Diphthongs: each of the two vowels in a diphthong retains its independent quality.
Nasalized diphthongs: the stressed first element and the unstressed second element are nasalized as one sound.

2. Consonants

			nearest English equivalent
b		b	as in *but*
c	before a, o, u:	c	as in *come*
	before e and i:	s	as in *sing*
ç	(only before a, o, u)	s	as in *song*
ch		sh	as in *shine*
d		d	as in *door*
f		f	as in *first*
g	before a, o, u:	g	as in *give*
	before e and i:	s	as in *pleasure*
gu	before e and i:	g	as in *gate*
h	silent		
j		s	as in *measure*
l		l	as in *silver*
lh		—	
m		m	as in *mean*
n		n	as in *night*
nh			—
p		p	as in *people*
qu	before a:	qu	as in *frequent*
	before e and i:	c	as in *cat*
r			as Scottish rolled r
s	at the beginning of a word or syllable:	s	as in *sail*
	in medial position between vowels:	s	as in *used*
	in final position	sh	as in *ship*

			nearest English equivalent
x			as in *shoe, lazy race, box*
z	in initial and medial position: in final position:	z s	as in *zero* as in *usual*

Peculiarities of Brazilian pronunciation

Before the nasal consonants *m* and *n* the vowels *e* and *o* in the tonic syllable are closed (as opposed to being open in Portugal) and bear a circumflex (ˆ) as opposed to an acute accent (´):

Portuguese	género antónimo	*Brazilian*	gênero antônimo

A pronúncia inglesa

1. Vogais e ditongos

símbolos	pronúncia	
	som semelhante em português	exemplo inglês
ɑː	c**a**ro	father
ø	c**a**ma	mother
æ	t**e**nho	fat
ɛə	—	care
ai	v**ai**	my
au	m**au**	cloud
e	f**é**	get
ei	l**ei**te	name
ə	d**e**pois	about
əː	—	bird
əu	v**ou**	boat
i	part**i**	city
iː	aqu**i**	tea
iə	t**ia**	fear
ɔ	n**ó**	not
ɔː	far**o**l	law
ɔi	b**ói**a	point
u	p**o**rque	book
uː	fáci**l** (Braz)	few
uə	**u**va	poor

2. Consoantes

símbolos	pronúncia som semelhante em português	 exemplo inglês
b	**b**ebedeira	but
d	**d**ar	dear
f	**f**eira	food
g	**g**ato	give
h	—	ahead
j	**i**ate	yes
k	**c**omo	come
l	qua**l**	call
m	**m**ão	mean
n	**n**ão	night
p	**p**asta	top
r	—	right
s	**s**entir	song
t	**t**omar	take
v	**v**i	of
w	**ué!** (Braz)	wait
z	**z**ebra	rose
ŋ	—	bring
ʃ	**ch**á	she
tʃ	**t**eatro (Braz)	rich
dʒ	a**dj**etivo	join
ʒ	**j**á	usual
θ	—	think
ð	—	lather

O acento tónico (ˈ) é sempre indicado antes da sílaba tónica: por exemplo about [əˈbaut]

Sílabas finais sem transcrição fonética

Por falta de espaço, não se inseriram no vocabulário alfabético a transcrição fonética das terminações seguintes:

-ability [-əbiliti]
-able [-əbl]
-age [-idʒ]
-al [-əl]
-ally [-əli]
-an [-ən]
-ance [-əns]
-ancy [-ənsi]
-ant [-ənt]
-ar [-ə]
-ary [-əri]
-ation [-eiʃən]
-cious [-ʃəs]
-cy [-si]
-dom [-dəm]
-ed [-d; -t; -id]*
-edness [-dnis; -tnis; -idnis]*
-ee [-iː]
-en [-n]
-ence [-əns]
-ent [-ənt]
-er [-ə]
-ery [-əri]
-ess [-is]
-fication [-fikeiʃən]
-ful [-ful]
-fy [-fai]
-hood [-hud]
-ial [-əl]
-ian [-iən; -jən]
-ible [-əbl]
-ic(s) [-ik(s)]
-ical [-ikəl]
-ily [-ili]
-iness [-inis]
-ing [-iŋ]
-ish [-iʃ]
-ism [-izəm]
-ist [-ist]
-istic [-istik]
-ite [-ait]
-ity [-iti]
-ive [-iv]
-ization [-aizeiʃən]
-ize [-aiz]
-izing [-aiziŋ]
-less [-lis]
-ly [-li]
-ment(s) [-mənt(s)]
-ness [-nis]
-oid [-ɔid]
-or [-ə]
-ory [-əri]
-our [-ə]
-ous [-əs]
-ry [-ri]
-ship [-ʃip]
-(s)sion [-ʃən]
-sive [-siv]
-some [-səm]
-ties [-tiz]
-tion [-ʃən]
-tious [-ʃəs]
-trous [-trəs]
-try [-tri]
-y [-i]

* [-d] quando segue vogais e consoantes sonoras; [-t] quando segue consoantes surdas; [-id] quando segue d e t finais.

A

a *art f* the; *pers pron* her, it; *dem pron* that, the one, her; *prp* to, at, in, on, by; **~ custo** with difficulty; **~ direito** straight on; **~ pé** on foot; **~ que horas?** at what time?

à *contr of prp* **a** *and art f* **a**; **~ esquerda** on the left; **~s escuras** in the dark; **~ meia-noite** at midnight; **~ pressa** in haste

aba *f* brim, edge; tail

abacate *m* avocado (pear)

abacaxi *m* ananas; *Braz* mess

abad|e *m* abbot; **~essa** *f* abbess; **~ia** *f* abbey

abafado *adj* sultry

abafar *v/t, v/i* choke; suffocate; smother

abaixar *v/t* lower; humble

abaixo down, below, under

abalar *v/t, v/i* affect; go off; shock; shake

abalo *m* shock; disturbance

abalro|amento *m* collision; **~ar** *v/t* collide

abanar *v/t* fan, shake; winnow

abandon|ar *v/t* abandon; **~o** *m* abandonment; desertion

abarrotar *v/t* fill (up), glut

abast|ado rich, well off; **~ança** *f* wealth, easy circumstances

abastecer *v/t* supply, provide

abastecimento *m* supply; refuel(l)ing

abat|er *v/t, v/i* abate; decrease; cast down; fell; **~ido** downcast, dejected; faint; **~imento** *m* allowance, discount; dejection

abdica|ção *f* abdication; renunciation; **~r** *v/t, v/i* abdicate

abdómen *m* abdomen

abeirar *v/r* approach

abelha *f* bee

abençoar *v/t* bless

aberta *f* opening, gap

abert|o *adj* open; **~ura** *f* opening; aperture; MUS overture

abeto *m* fir

abismo *m* abyss

abje(c)ção *f* abjection

abje(c)to abject, base

abjudicar *v/t* oust, dispossess

abjurar *v/t* abjure

abnega|ção *f* abnegation; **~r** *v/t* abnegate, renounce

abóbada *f* vault

abóbora *f* pumpkin

abol|ição *f* abolition; **~ir** *v/t* abolish

abominar *v/t* abominate, detest, abhor

abominável abominable

abonado *adj Braz* wealthy, well-off

abon|ar *v/t* answer for; guarantee; **~o** *m* warranty; **~o de família** family allowance
abordar *v/t* board; accost; **~ um assunto** broach a subject
aborrec|er *v/t, v/r* bore; weary; disgust; displease; **~ido** wearisome; bored; weary; **~imento** *m* bore(dom); nuisance; weariness
abort|ar *v/i* abort, miscarry; fail; **~o** *m* abortion
abotoar *v/t* button (up), fasten
abraç|ar *v/t* embrace; **~o** *m* embrace, hug
abrandar *v/t, v/i* soften; relent; appease; slacken
abranger *v/t* include, comprise
abras|ador burning, scorching; **~ar** *v/t* burn, scorch
abre-latas *m* tin/can opener
abrevi|ação *f* abridg(e)ment; **~ar** *v/t* abbreviate; abridge; **~atura** *f* abbreviation
abrig|ar *v/t, v/r* shelter, protect; **~gar-se** *v/r* look for shelter; **~o** *m* shelter, protection, cover; **ao ~o de** under (the) cover of; **~o antiaéreo** air-raid shelter
Abril *m* April; **1º de ~** All Fool's Day
abrir *v/t, v/i, v/r* open; unfold; unfasten; **~ os olhos a alguém** open someone's eyes **~se com alguém** unbosom oneself to someone
abrunho *m* sloe
absolut|amente absolutely, quite; **~o** *adj* absolute
absolv|er *v/t* absolve; **~ição** *f* absolution
absor|ção *f* absorption; **~to** absorbed; **~ver** *v/t, v/r* absorb
abstenção *f* abstention
abster *v/t, v/r* **(de)** abstain (from)
abstinência *f* abstinence
abstra|(c)ção *f* abstraction; **~(c)to** *adj* abstract; absent-minded; **~ir** *v/t* abstract, separate; **~ir-se** *v/r* collect one's thoughts
absurdo *m* absurdity; *adj* absurd
abund|ância *f* abundance; **~ante** abundant; **~ar (em)** *v/i* abound (in)
abusar (de) *v/t, v/i* abuse, misuse
abuso *m* abuse, misuse
abutre *m* vulture
acabado *adj* finished; worn--out, old; perfect, faultless
acabar *v/t, v/i* finish, end, conclude; complete; **~ de ...** have just ...
acabrunhado downcast
acabrunhar *v/t* deject, distress
acácia *f* acacia
academia *f* academy
açaime *m* muzzle
acalentar *v/t* lull, rock
acalmar *v/t, v/i* calm; *v/i* chill out
acamar *v/t* lay, dispose in layers
açambarc|ador *m* monopolizer; **~ar** *v/t* monopolize
acampamento *m* camp
acampar *v/i* camp

acanhado bashful, shy, timid; narrow, close
acanhar *v/t*, *v/r* intimidate; narrow, make tight
acariciar *v/t* fondle, caress, stroke
acaso *m* chance, hazard; **ao ~** at random; **por ~** by chance
acatar *v/t* respect, revere, venerate
acautel|ado cautious, wary; **~ar** *v/t*, *v/r* beware of; caution, warn; be on one's guard
a(c)ção *f* action, deed; COM stock, share
a(c)cionista *m*, *f* shareholder
aceder *v/i* accede, comply
aceitação *f* acceptance
aceitar *v/t* accept
aceler|ador *m* accelerator; **~ar** *v/t* accelerate
acenar *v/i* nod; beckon; **~ com a mão** wave one's hand
acend|edor *m* lighter; **~er** *v/t* light, kindle; switch on
aceno *m* nod; wave
acent|o *m* accent; **~uação** *f* accentuation; **~uar** *v/t* accentuate
acepção *f* meaning, sense
acepipe *m* dainty, titbit; **~s** *m/pl* hors d'œuvre
acerbo tart, bitter; harsh
acerca de about, with regard to
acercar-se de *v/r* approach
acertar *v/t*, *v/i* set right; hit the mark; guess right; adjust; **~ em cheio** hit the nail on the head
aceso lighted, lit, on; excited, hot
acessível accessible
acesso *m* access; fit, attack
acessório *m* accessory, appendage; *adj* accessory
achado *m* find, discovery; **não se dar por ~** pretend to ignore
achaque *m* ailment; defect
achar *v/t* find, hit on; think; **~-se** be; find oneself
achatar *v/t* flatten, squash
acident|ado *adj* uneven; **~al** accidental; **~e** *m* accident
acidez *f* acidity
ácido *adj* acid, sour, tart; *m* acid
acima above; up; **~ de** above; beyond; over; **~ de tudo** above all; **pela rua ~** up the street
acinte *m* spite, malice
aclam|ação *f* acclamation; **~ar** *v/t* acclaim
aclarar *v/t*, *v/i* clear up; make clear, clarify
aclima(ta)r *v/t*, *v/r* acclimatize
aço *m* steel
acobardar *v/t*, *v/r* discourage, intimidate
acocorar-se *v/r* squat; crouch
açodar *v/t* incite; hurry
acolá there; **~ adiante** over there
acolchoar *v/t* wad, quilt
acolh|er *v/t*, *v/r* welcome; shelter; take refuge; **~ida** *f*, **~imento** *m* reception, welcome; shelter
acometer *v/t* attack, assault, assail
acomodar *v/t*, *v/r* accommodate; fit, suit; arrange

acompanh|amento *m* accompaniment; **~ar** *v/t* accompany; keep company
acondicionamento *m* packing
acondicionar *v/t* condition; pack, box
aconselhar *v/t*, *v/r* advise; **~-se com o travesseiro** sleep on a thing/question
acontec|er *v/i* happen; **~imento** *m* happening, event
açor *m* goshawk
açorda *f* bread panada
acordar *v/t*, *v/i* awake, wake(n)
acordo *m* agreement; **de ~!** it's agreed!; **de ~ com** in accordance with; **chegar a (um) ~** come to terms
acorrer *v/i* run to help
acossar *v/t* harass
acostar *v/t*, *v/i* run ashore; join; **~-se a** lean on/against
acostumar (a) *v/t*, *v/r* accustom; get used (to), get accustomed (to)
acotovelar *v/t* elbow, jostle
açougue *m* slaughterhouse, abattoir
acre *adj* acrid, tart; mordant
acredit|ado accredited; credible; **~ar** *v/t* believe; accredit
acrescentar *v/t* add
acrescer *v/t*, *v/i* grow, increase
acréscimo *m* addition, increase
acroba|cia *f* acrobatics; **~ta** *m*, *f* acrobat
a(c)ta *f* record; **~s** *f/pl* minutes *s/pl*
a(c)tiv|ar *v/t* activate; **~idade** *f* activity; **~o** *adj* active
a(c)to *m* act, deed, action
a(c)t|or *m* actor; **~riz** *f* actress
a(c)tual present, current; **~idade** *f* (the) present moment; **~idades** *f/pl* news
a(c)tuar *v/t* actuate; act
açúcar *m* sugar
açucar|ar *v/t* sugar, sweeten; **~eiro** sugar-basin
açude *m* dam, sluice, weir
acudir *v/i* run to help
acuidade *f* acuity, sharpness
açular *v/t* incite, set on
acumular *v/i*, *v/r* accumulate
acus|ação *f* accusation; **~ado** *m* accused; **~ar** *v/t* accuse; **~ a recepção de** acknowledge the receipt of
acústica *f* acoustics
adágio *m* adage; adagio
adapt|ação *f* adaptation; **~ar** *v/t* adapt; **~ável** adaptable
adega *f* (wine) cellar
adej|ar *v/i* flutter; **~o** *m* flutter
adelgaçar *v/t* make thin, make slender
adentro indoors; inward(s)
adepto *m* adept; **~** *m* **de sofá** couch potato
adequado adequate, suitable
adereç|ar *v/t* adorn, attire; **~o** *m* attire, finery
ader|ência *f* adherence; **~ente** *adj*, *m*, *f* adherent; **~ir** *v/i* adhere
aderno *m* BOT privet
ades|ão *f* adhesion; **~ivo** *adj* adhesive; *m* sticking-plaster
adestrar *v/t* instruct, train

adeus *int*, *s* good-bye; **~inho!** cheerio!, bye-bye!
adiamento *m* postponement
adiantado *adj* fast; advanced
adiant|amento *m* progress, improvement; advance; advancement; **~ar** *v/t* advance; put on/forward; **isso não adianta** that is no good
adiante *adv* forward(s), onward(s); *int* go on!
adiar *v/t* postpone; put off
adi|ção *f* addition; supplement; appendix; **~cionar** *v/t* add up, tot up
adido *m* attaché
aditamento *m* addition, supplement
adivinh|a *f* riddle, puzzle; **~ar** *v/t* guess; **~o** *m* fortune-teller
adjac|ência *f* contiguity; **~ente** adjacent
adje(c)tivo *m* adjective
adjudic|ação *f* adjudication; **~ar** *v/t* adjudicate
adjunto *m* adjunct; assistant
adjurar *v/t* adjure
administr|ação *f* administration; **~ de empresas** business management; **~ador** *m* **executivo** CEO; **~ar** *v/t* administer
admir|ação *f* admiration; surprise; **~ar** *v/t*, *v/r* admire; wonder; **não admira** no wonder
admirável admirable
admiss|ão *f* admission; **~ível** admissible
admitir *v/t* admit; concede
adoção *f child* adoption, *idea* adoption, taking over
adoçar *v/t* sweeten; assuage, soften
adocicado sweetish
adocicar *v/t* sweeten
adoecer *v/i* become ill, fall sick
adoentado seedy, unwell
adoentar *v/t* make ill, sicken
adolescência *f* adolescence
adolescente *adj*, *m*, *f* adolescent
ado(p)|ção *f* adoption; **~tar** *v/t* adopt
ador|ação *f* adoration; worship; **~ar** *v/t* adore; worship
adormecer *v/t*, *v/i* put to sleep; fall asleep
adormecido asleep, sleeping
adornar *v/t* adorn
adquirir *v/t* acquire
adro *m* churchyard
adstringente *adj*, *s m* astringent
aduana *f* custom-house
adub|ar *v/t* fertilize; **~o** *m* manure, fertilizer
adula|ção *f* adulation; **~dor** *m* flatterer; **~r** *v/t* flatter
adulter|ador *m* adulterer; **~ar** *v/t* adulterate
adultério *m* adultery
adulto *adj*, *m* adult; grown-up
adunco hooked, crooked
advent|ício *adj* adventitious; **~o** *m* advent; ECCL Advent
advérbio *m* adverb
advers|ão *f* opposition; **~ário** *m* adversary; **~idade** *f* adversity; **~o** adverse
advert|ência *f* warning; re-

mark; **~imento** *m* warning; **~ir** *v/t* warn
advogado *m* lawyer, advocate
advogar *v/t* advocate
aéreo aerial
aerodinâmica *f* aerodynamics
aeródromo *m* aerodrome
aeromoça *f* stewardess
aeronáutica *f* aeronautics
aeronave *f* airship
aeroplano *m* aeroplane, airplane
aeroporto *m* airport
afã *m* anxiety; eagerness
afabilidade *f* affability
afadigar *v/t, v/r* fatigue, tire
afag|ar *v/t* caress, stroke, pat, fondle; **~o** *m* caress, pat
afamado renowned
afanar *v/i, v/r* toil, labour
afastado remote, distant
afast|amento *m* remoteness; removal; separation; **~ar** *v/t* remove; separate
afável affable
afazer *v/t, v/r* accustom; **~es** *m/pl* business, affairs
afe(c)t|ação *f* affectation; affectedness; **~ado** affected; conceited; **~ar** *v/t, v/r* affect; pretend; **~o** *m* affection; **~uoso** affectionate
afeição *f* affection
aferir *v/t* check; gauge
aferrolhar *v/t* bolt, lock
afiançar *v/t* guarantee
afiar *v/t* sharpen
afigurar *v/t, v/r* shape; imagine
afilhado *m* godson
afim *adj* akin; *m* relative
afinação *f* refining; tuning
afinal after all; at last; finally
afinar *v/t, v/i* get angry; refine; tune
afirm|acão *f* affirmation; **~ar** *v/t, v/i* affirm, aver
afivelar *v/t* buckle
afixar *v/t* affix, stick
afli|ção *f* affliction; grief; **~gir** *v/t, v/r* afflict; grieve; **não se aflija!** don't worry!
afluência *f* affluence; crowd, concourse
afluente *adj* affluent; abundant
afluir *v/i* flow; abound
afogar *v/t, v/r* choke, stifle; drown
afoit|ado bold; **~ar** *v/t* encourage; **~eza** *f* boldness
afora *adv, prp* except, save; excluding
afortunado fortunate
afreguesado frequented
africano African
afro-americano Afroamerican
afronta *f* insult, affront
afrontar *v/t* insult, affront
afrouxar *v/t* slacken, loosen
afugentar *v/t* put to flight, scare away
afundar *v/t, v/r* sink; deepen
agachar-se *v/r* squat; crouch; cower
agarrar *v/t, v/r* clasp, grip; grasp; seize
agasalh|ar *v/t, v/r* wrap up; lodge, shelter; **~o** *m* shelter, lodging; warm clothes
agência *f* agency; bureau; of-

fice; ~ **de informações** information bureau; ~ **de viagens** travel agency/bureau; ~ **funerária** funeral parlo(u)r
agenda *f* notebook; ~ **de bolso** pocket diary; ~ **eletrônica** palmtop
agente *m* agent; ~ **marítimo** shipping agent; ~ **provocador** agent provocateur
ágil agile
agilidade *f* agility
agir *v/i* act
agita|ção *f* agitation; **~do** excited, agitated; rough; restless; **~r** *v/t*, *v/r* shake; agitate
aglomer|ação *f* agglomeration; **~r** *v/t* agglomerate
agoni|a *f* agony; **~ado** seasick, sick; **~ar** *v/t*, *v/r* nauseate, sicken; afflict; **~zar** *v/t*, *v/i* agonize; be in agony
agora now
Agosto *m* August
agour|ar *v/t* forebode, augur; **~o** *m* augury, omen
agraciar *v/t* invest with, award
agradar *v/t*, *v/r* like; please
agradável pleasant
agradec|er *v/t*, *v/i* thank; **~ido** grateful; **~imento** *m* thanks
agrado *m* pleasure, liking; satisfaction
agravamento *m* aggravation
agrav|ar *v/t*, *v/r* insult aggravate; **~o** *m* offence, injury
agre|dir *v/t* attack; **~ssão** *f* aggression; **~ssivo** aggressive; **~ssor** *m* aggressor
agreste rural; rustic
agrião *m* water-cress
agrícola *adj* agricultural
agricultor *m* agricultur(al)ist, farmer
agricultura *f* agriculture
agrupamento *m* grouping; group
agrupar *v/t* group
água *f* water; ~ **mineral** mineral water; ~ **potável** drinking water
aguaceiro *m* shower
água-de-colónia *f* (eau de) cologne
aguardar *v/t* wait for, await
aguardente *f* brandy, aqua vitae
aguarela *f* water colo(u)r
aguçar *v/t* sharpen
agud|eza *f* sharpness; acuity; **~o** sharp; acute
aguentar *v/t* suffer, bear; endure
águia *f* eagle
aguilhão *m* goad
agulha *f* needle; **~das** *f/pl* MED stabbing pain
ai *m* groan, moan; *int* ah!; **num** ~ instantly
aí there; ~ **tens!** there you are!
ainda still; yet; even; ~ **bem** fortunately; ~ **assim** nevertheless; even so; ~ **não** not yet; ~ **por cima** into the bargain; ~ **que** although; even if
aipim *m* cassava
aipo *m* celery
airbag *m* airbag
ajeitar *v/t*, *v/i* adapt; arrange
ajoelhar *v/t*, *v/i* kneel (down)

ajud|a *f* aid, help; **~ar** *v/t* aid, help, assist
ajuizado sensible
ajuizar *v/t* judge; estimate
ajunt|amento *m* assembly; **~ar** *v/t* assemble; add
ajustar *v/t* adjust; agree on, settle; **~ (as) contas** account for, settle accounts; **~ contas com** *fig* get even with
ajuste *m* agreement, settlement
ala *f* wing
alagar *v/t, v/r* overflow; inundate
alameda *f* alley, lane
álamo *m* poplar
alargar *v/t, v/i, v/r* enlarge (on); spread out; widen
alarido *m* outcry
alarm|ante alarming; **~ar** *v/t, v/r* frighten; alarm; **~e** *m* alarm
alastrar *v/i* spread
alavanca *f* lever; crowbar
albatroz *m* albatross
alberg|ar *v/t* lodge; harbo(u)r; **~ue** *m* shelter, refuge; **~ue** *m* **da juventude** youth hostel
alcachofra *f* artichoke
alcançar *v/t, v/i* obtain; attain; reach
alcance *m* reach; range; **ao ~ da mão** within reach
alcaparra *f* caper
alçar *v/t* raise
alcatifa *f* carpet
alcatrão *m* tar
álcool *m* alcohol
alcoolismo *m* alcoholism
alcunha *f* nickname
aldeão *m* villager
aldeia *f* village
aldrabão *m* liar, fibber
alecrim *m* rosemary
alegar *v/t* allege
ategoria *f* allegory
atualiza|ção *f* COMP update; **~r** *v/t* COMP update
alegr|ar *v/t, v/r* cheer up; gladden; **~e** joyful, glad, gay; tipsy; **~ia** *f* joy, gladness
aleij|ado *adj* crippled; *m* cripple; **~ão** *m* deformity; **~ar** *v/t* cripple; hurt
além *adv* beyond; (over) there; **~ disso** besides
alemão *adj, m* German
além-mar *adv* overseas
alentado courageous; vigorous
alento *m* breath; courage; vigo(u)r; **dar ~ a** encourage
alerta *m* alert
aletria *f* vermicelli
alface *f* lettuce
alfaiate *m* tailor
alfândega *f* customs; custom-house
alfazema *f* lavender
alfinete *m* pin
algarismo *m* figure, cypher
algazarra *f* uproar, hubbub
algemas *f/pl* handcuffs
algibeira *f* pocket; **andar de mãos nas ~s** idle (away)
álgido chilly, cold
algo *adv* rather, somewhat; *pron* something
algodão *m* cotton; **~ em rama** cotton wool

algoz *m* hangman
alguém somebody, someone; anyone, anybody
algum, **~a** some; any; **~ tanto** somewhat; **~ dia** one day
alguns, **algumas** some; any; a few
algures *adv* somewhere
alheio belonging to another; alien
alho *m* garlic
ali there
alia|do *m* ally; *adj* allied; **~r** *v/t*, *v/r* unite; ally; **~nça** *f* alliance
aliás *adv* besides; by the way; otherwise
alibi *m* alibi
alicate *m* pliers
alicerce *m* foundations
aliciar *v/t* allure
aliena|ção *f* alienation; **~do** *adj* alienated
alienar *v/t* alienate
aligeirar *v/t* lighten; hasten, speed up
aliment|ação *f* nourishment; **~ar** *v/t* feed; *adj* nourishing
alimento *m* food
alindar *v/t* embellish
alínea *f* paragraph
alinh|ar *v/t* align; **~o** *m* neatness
alisar *v/t* smooth
alistar *v/t*, *v/r* enlist
aliviar *v/t*, *v/i* lighten; alleviate; relieve
alívio *m* relief; alleviation
alma *f* soul
almejar *v/t* covet, long for
almirante *m* admiral
almoçar *v/t*, *v/i* have lunch, lunch
almoço *m* lunch
almofada *f* cushion; pillow
almôndega *f* meat ball
alocução *f* address
alojamento *m* lodging
alojar *v/t* lodge; billet
alongar *v/t* prolong, lengthen
alperc(h)e *m* apricot
alpinismo *m* mountaineering
alta *f* COM rise, boom; discharge
altaneiro arrogant, haughty
altar *m* altar; **~-mor** *m* high altar
altear *v/t*, *v/i* raise; rise
alteração *f* alteration, change
alterar *v/t* alter, change
alternar *v/t* alternate
alternativa *f* alternative
altiv|ez *f* haughtiness; pride; **~o** haughty; proud
alto *int* stop!, halt!; *adv* loudly; *m* height; summit; *adj* high, tall; loud; **alta noite** in the dead of the night; **em voz alta** aloud; **por ~** superficially
alto-falante *m* loudspeaker
altruísmo *m* altruism
altura *f* height; altitude; occasion, time; **à ~ da situação** equal to the occasion
aludir *v/i* allude to, hint at
alug|ar *v/t* hire; let; rent; **~uer** *m* hire; rent
aluir *v/t*, *v/i* shake; crumble
alumiar *v/t* illuminate
alumínio *m* aluminium
aluno *m* pupil
alusão *f* allusion
alva *f* dawn

alvejar *v/t* aim at
alvíssaras *f/pl* reward
alvitr|ar *v/t* suggest, propose; **~e** *m* suggestion
alvo *adj* white; *m* target; aim, intent
alvorada *f* dawn
alvoroço, **alvoroto** *m* excitement; agitation; tumult
ama *f* governess, mistress; nurse
amabilidade *f* kindness
amada *f* darling
amador *m* amateur
amadurecer *v/t*, *v/i* ripen; mature
âmago *m* heart, core
amainar *v/i* abate
amaldiçoar *v/t* curse
amálgama *m* amalgam
amamentar *v/t* suckle
amanhã *adv* tomorrow
amanhecer *v/i* dawn; *m* daybreak
amanho *m* cultivation, tillage
amansar *v/t* tame; mitigate
amante *m*, *f* lover
amar *v/t*, *v/i* love
amarar *v/i* AVIA land on water
amarel|ado yellowish; **~ecer** *v/t*, *v/i* yellow; **~o** *adj*, *m* yellow
amarfanhar *v/t* wrinkle; ill--treat
amarg|ar *v/t*, *v/i* taste bitter; make bitter; **~o** *adj* bitter; **~ura** *f* bitterness; **~urar** *v/t* embitter
amarr|a *f* hawser; **~ar** *v/t* make fast, moor; fasten, tie
amarrotar *v/t* crumple
amassar *v/t* knead
amável kind
âmbar *m* amber
ambição *f* ambition
ambici|onar *v/t* hanker after; **~oso** ambitious
ambiente *adj* surrounding; *m* surroundings; atmosphere; environment
ambíguo ambiguous
âmbito *m* ambit; scope
amb|os, **~as** both
ambulância *f* ambulance
ameaça *f* threat; **~dor** threatening; **~r** *v/t*, *v/i* threaten
amealhar *v/t* save
amedrontar *v/t*, *v/i* frighten
ameia *f* battlement
amêijoa *f* cockle
ameix|a *f* plum; **~(i)eira**, **~(o)eira** *f* plum-tree
amêndoa *f* almond
amendo|eira *f* almond-tree; **~im** *m* ground-nut, peanut
ameno pleasant
americano *adj*, *m* American
amesquinhar *v/t*, *v/r* belittle, disparage
amestrar *v/t* train, break in
amical amicable
amig|a *f* (girl) friend; **~ável** friendly, amicable; COMP user-friendly; **~o** *m* friend; *adj* fond of; **~o de ambiente** environmentally friendly; **~o-da--onça** *m*, **~ de Peniche** fair--weather friend; **ter cara de poucos ~os** have an unfriendly look; **tornar-se ~o de** make friends with

amimar *v/t* pet, spoil
amiúde often
amizade *f* friendship
a(m)nistia *f* amnesty
amo *m* master
amolar *v/t, v/i, v/r* brood over; grind; harass; *Braz* annoy, bother
amolecer *v/t, v/i* soften; mollify
amolgar *v/t* squash, crush
amontoar *v/t* heap up
amor *m* love
amora *f* mulberry
amordaçar *v/t* gag
amorfo amorphous
amornar *v/t* warm; make lukewarm
amoroso *adj* loving; lovable, sweet
amor-perfeito *m* pansy
amortecedor *m* shock-absorber; damper
amortecer *v/t, v/i* damp; absorb; deaden; weaken
amortiz|ação *f* amortization; **~ar** *v/t* amortize
amostra *f* sample
amotinar *v/t, v/r* mutiny
ampar|ar *v/t* support; prop; protect; **~o** *m* shelter; protection
ampli|ação *f* enlargement; **~ar** *v/t* amplify, enlarge
amplific|ador *m* amplifier; **~ar** *v/t* amplify
amplitude *f* amplitude
amplo ample, spacious
ampola *f* blister
amuar *v/i, v/r* sulk
amurada *f* NAUT rail
anais *m/pl* annals
analisar *v/t* analyse
análise *f* analysis
analogia *f* analogy
análogo *m* analogous
ananás *m* pineapple
anão *m* dwarf
anca *f* haunch, hip
anchova *f* anchovy
ancião *m* old man
ancinho *m* rake
âncora *f* anchor
ancorar *v/t, v/i* anchor
andaime *m* scaffold(ing)
andamento *m* course, proceeding; MUS measure
andar *v/t, v/i* go; walk; *m* stor(e)y, floor, gait
andas *f/pl* stilts
andebol *m* handball
andorinha *f* ZOO swallow
andrajo *m* rag; **~so** ragged
anedota *f* anecdote
anel *m* ring; curl
anel|ar *v/t* long for; **~o** *m* desire, longing
anemia *f* an(a)emia
anémico an(a)emic
anestesia *f* an(a)esthesia
anestésico *m* an(a)esthetic
anex|ação *f* annexation; **~ar** *v/t* annex; **~o** *adj* included; *m* annex(e)
angariar *v/t* canvass; obtain
angular angular
ângulo *m* angle; corner
angústia *f* anguish
anho *m* lamb
animação *f* animation
animal *m, adj* animal

animar *v/t*, *v/r* cheer up; animate
ânimo *m* courage; mind; *int* come on!; cheer up!
aninhar *v/t*, *v/r* nestle; snuggle
aniquilamento *m* annihilation
aniquilar *v/t* annihilate
aniversário *m* anniversary; **~ natalício** birthday
anjo *m* angel
ano *m* year; **~ bissexto** leap year; **quando fazes ~s?** when is your birthday?; **ter dez ~s** be ten years old
anoitecer *v/i* grow dark; *m* nightfall; **ao ~** at nightfall
anomalia *f* anomaly
anónim|o anonymous
anormal abnormal
anot|ação *f* annotation; **~ar** *v/t* annotate
ânsia *f* anxiety
ansi|ar *v/t*, *v/i* yearn for, crave; **~edade** *f* anguish; **~oso** anxious; **estar ~oso por** be eager for
antagonista *m* antagonist
ante *prp* before
antebraço *m* forearm
antecâmara *f* antechamber, anteroom
anteced|ente *m*, *adj* antecedent; **~er** *v/t*, *v/i* precede
antecessor *m* predecessor
antecipar *v/t*, *v/r* anticipate
antemão: **de ~** beforehand
antena *f* antenna; aerial; **~ parabólica** satellite dish
anteontem the day before yesterday
antepassado *m* ancestor, forefather
anterior previous
antes before; rather; **~ de** before; **~ de mais nada** first of all; **~ que** before
antever *v/t* foresee
anti|aéreo anti-aircraft; **~ciclone** *m* anticyclone
antídoto *m* antidote
antigamente formerly
antig|o *adj* ancient, old; antique; **~uidade** *f* antiquity
antílope *m* antelope
anti|patia *f* antipathy; **~pático** antipathetic; disagreeable
antiquado antiquated, outmoded
antítese *f* antithesis
antro *m* cave, den
anual yearly, annual
anuir *v/i* assent, accede
anular *v/t* annul, cancel
anunciar *v/t* advertise; announce
anúncio *m* advertisement; **pôr um ~** advertise
anzol *m* fish-hook
ao to the; in the; at the; by the; **~ pé** near by; **~ pé de** close to
aonde where ... to, where; **~ vais?** where are you going?
apagar *v/t* extinguish; put out; switch off; *fam delete* zap
apaixon|ado passionate; **~ar** *v/t*, *v/r* fall in love; impassion
apalpa|dela *f* grope; **às ~delas** groping(ly); **~r** *v/t* feel, fumble; grope; **~r (o) terreno** spy out the land

apanhar *v/t, v/i* pick; be beaten; grasp; catch; seize; gather; get
aparador *m* sideboard
aparar *v/t* pare, clip; parry
aparato *m* pomp
aparec|er *v/i* appear; **~imento** *m* appearance
aparelhar *v/t* prepare; rig
aparelho *m* set; apparatus; MAR rigging; **~ auditivo** hearing aid; **~ de som** stereo (system)
aparência *f* appearance, aspect
aparent|ar *v/t* feign, pretend; **~e** apparent
aparição *f* apparition
aparo *m* nib
aparta|do *m* post-box; *adj* separated, secluded; **~mento** *m* apartment; **~r** *v/t, v/r* part, separate
aparte *m* aside
à parte apart
apatia *f* apathy
apático apathetic
apátrida *adj* stateless
apavorar *v/t* terrify
apaziguar *v/t* pacify
apear-se *v/r* get off; alight; dismount
apegar-se a *v/r* cling to; be attached to
apego *m* attachment to
apel|ação *f* appeal; **~ar** *v/i* appeal
apelido *m* surname
apenas *adv* hardly, scarcely; only
apêndice *m* appendix
apendicite *f* appendicitis
apenso *m* appendage; *adj* joined, added
aperceber *v/t, v/r* become aware of; perceive; distinguish
aperfeiçoamento *m* improvement
aperfeiçoar *v/t* perfect; improve
aperitivo *m* aperitif
apert|ão *m* squeeze; **~ar** *v/t, v/i* press; pinch; tie; tighten; squeeze; **~ar a mão** shake hands; **~o** *m* pressure; distress, scrape
apesar de in spite of; **~ ~ tudo** for all that
apetecer *v/t* feel like
apetite *m* appetite
apetitoso appetizing
apimentado peppery, spicy
apinhar *v/t* heap up; crowd
apit|ar *v/i* whistle; **~o** *m* whistle
aplacar *v/t, v/i* appease
aplanar *v/t* level
aplaudir *v/t, v/i* clap, applaud
aplauso *m* applause
aplica|ção *f* application; **~do** industrious; **~r** *v/t, v/i* apply
apoderar-se *v/r* seize, take hold of
apodo *m* scoff; taunt
apodrecer *v/i* rot
apogeu *m* apogee
apoiado *adj* supported; *int* hear! hear!
apoi|ar *v/t* support, prop up; **~o** *m* support, prop
apólice *f* policy; **~ de seguro** insurance policy
apologia *f* apology, defence

apont|amento *m* note, annotation; **~ar** *v/t* note down; take aim at; point at
apoplexia *f* apoplexy
apoquent|ado upset; **~ar** *v/t* worry, bother
aportar *v/i* call at a port
após *prp* after; behind; **~-guerra** *m* post-war time
aposent|ação *f* retirement; **~ar** *v/t* lodge; retire, pension off; **~o** *m* apartment; room
apost|a *f* bet, wager; **~ar** *v/t* bet, wager
aprazar *v/t* appoint, fix
aprazível pleasant, agreeable
apre! by jingo!
apreci|ação *f* appreciation; **~ar** *v/t* appreciate; **~ável** appreciable
apreço *m* estimate; esteem
apreensivo apprehensive
aprend|er *v/t*, *v/i* learn; **~iz** *m* apprentice; **~izagem** *f* apprenticeship
apresent|ação *f* introduction; **~ar** *v/t*, *v/r* present; introduce
apressado hasty, hurried
apressar *v/t*, *v/r* hasten; make haste, hurry up
apresto *m* preparation
aprisionar *v/t* imprison
aprofundar *v/t* deepen
aprontar *v/t* prepare, get ready
a-propósito *adv* to the purpose; by the way
apropria|ção *f* appropriation; **~do** appropriate; **~r** *v/t*, *v/i* appropriate
aprovação *f* approval; approbation
aprovar *v/t* approve; pass
aproveitar *v/t*, *v/i*, *v/r* avail of; profit by
aprovisionar *v/t* equip; victual
aproxima|ção *f* approximation; approach; **~damente** approximately; **~do** approximate; **~r** *v/t*, *v/r* approximate; come near to; approach
aptidão *f* aptitude
apto apt, fit
apunhalar *v/t* stab
apupar *v/t* hiss at; hoot at
apurar *v/t* purify; verify
apuro *m* refinement; hardship; **estar em ~s** be hard up; **ver-se em ~s** be in a tight corner
aquário *m* aquarium
aquec|edor *m* heater; **~er** *v/t*, *v/i* warm, heat; **~imento** *m* **central** central heating; **~imento** *m* **global** global warming
aquel|e, **~a** that
àquele to that (one)
aquém *adv* below; on this side; **estar ~ de** not to come up to; **~ e além** here and there
aqui *adv* here
aquietar *v/t* quiet(en)
aquilo that
ar *m* air; look; **ao ~ livre** in the open air, outdoors; **dar-se ~es de** put on airs, give oneself airs
árabe *m* Arab; Arabic; *adj* Arabian; Arabic
arado *m* plough
arame *m* wire; **~ farpado**

barbed wire; **ir aos ~s** see red
aranha *f* spider; **andar às ~s** be irresolute; **tirar as teias de ~** blow away the cobwebs
arar *v/t* plough
arbitrar *v/t* arbitrate; referee
arbitrário arbitrary
arbítrio *m* will, judg(e)ment
árbitro *m* referee, umpire
arbusto *m* bush
arca *f* chest, coffer; ark
arcebispo *m* archbishop
archote *m* torch
arco *m* bow; arc; arch
ardente ardent
arder *v/i* burn
ardil *m* stratagem, trick; **~oso** subtle, crafty
ardina *m* news-boy, *US* paper--boy
ardor *m* ardo(u)r
ardósia *f* slate
árduo arduous; steep; hard
área *f* area
areal *m* sands
areia *f* sand
arejado airy
arejar *v/t, v/i* take the air, get some fresh air; air, ventilate
arenoso sandy
arenque *m* herring
aresta *f* edge
arfar *v/i* pant
argila *f* clay
argola *f* ring
argúcia *f* subtlety
arguir *v/t, v/i* reprove; argue
argument|ar *v/i* argue; **~o** *m* argument; summary
arguto shrewd
ária *f* aria
aridez *f* aridity, dryness
árido arid, dry
arisco *adj* sandy; surly; coy
aritmética *f* arithmetic
arma *f* weapon
armada *f* fleet
armadilha *f* snare, trap
armador *m* shipowner
arm|amento *m* armament; **~ar** *v/t, v/i, v/r* plot; lay; arm
armário *m* cupboard
armazém *m* store; warehouse
armistício *m* armistice
aro *m* ring, hoop
aroma *m* aroma, scent
aromático aromatic
arquear *v/t, v/r* arch, curve
arquejar *v/i* pant; gasp
arquite(c)t|o *m* architect; **~ura** *f* architecture
arquivo *m* archives; COMP file
arrabalde *m* suburb, environs
arraia *f* ZOO skate
arraial *m* encampment; festival; *Braz* hamlet
arrais *m* skipper; coxswain
arranc|ar *v/t* start; pull, tug; draw out; **~o** *m* tug; jolt; jerk
arranha-céu *m* skyscraper
arranhar *v/t* scratch; scrape
arranjar *v/t, v/r* manage; get; tidy; arrange; fix; **ele que se arranje** let that be his problem
arranque *m* AUTO starter
arrasar *v/t* raze, level, demolish; overflow
arrastar *v/t, v/r* drag, haul; crawl, creep; **~ a asa** court
arre! gee up!

arrebatar *v/t* snatch
arredar *v/t* remove, set aside; **não ~ pé** stay put
arredondar *v/t* round (off)
arredores *m/pl* surroundings, environs; outskirts
arrefec|er *v/i* cool; **~imento** *m* cooling
arreig|ado deep-seated; **~ar** *v/i* take root
arreliar *v/t, v/r* tease, vex; worry
arrematar *v/t* auction
arremessar *v/t* throw, dump
arremeter *v/i* attack
arrend|amento *m* hire; lease; **~ar** *v/t* hire; let; lease; rent
arrepend|er-se *v/r* repent; **~imento** *m* repentance
arrepi|ar *v/t, v/r* shudder; **~ar caminho** retrace one's steps; **~o** *m* shudder
arribação *f* arrival; **de ~** of passage
arriscar *v/t, v/r* risk, hazard
arrogância *f* arrogance
arrogante arrogant
arroj|ado bold, daring; **~ar** *v/t* cast; **~o** *m* boldness; effrontery
arrombar *v/t* stave in; force open
arrot|ar *v/i* belch; **~o** *m* belch
arroz *m* rice
arruinar *v/t* ruin
arrum|ação *f* arrangement; stowage; **~ar** *v/t* stow; tidy; arrange
arte *f* art
artéria *f* artery
artesanato *m* workmanship
articula|ção *f* articulation; **~do** articulate; articulated
artífice *m* artisan
artificial artificial
artifício *m* artifice; trick
artigo *m* article
artista *m, f* artist
árvore *f* tree; mast
as *pl of* **a**
ás *m* ace
asa *f* wing
ascen|der *v/i* ascend; **~sor** *m* lift, elevator
asfixiar *v/t* asphyxiate, suffocate
asiático-americano Asian-American
asilo *m* asylum
asma *f* asthma
asneira *f* nonsense
asno *m* ass
aspe(c)to *m* aspect; appearance
aspereza *f* harshness; bleakness
áspero harsh; bleak
aspirador *m* vacuum cleaner, hoover
aspirar *v/t, v/i* aspirate; draw in; **~ a** aspire to
assado *m* roast, roasted meat
assalt|ar *v/t* assault; **~o** *m* assault
assar *v/t* roast
assassin|ar *v/t* murder; assassinate; **~o** *m* murderer; assassin
assassínio *m* murder; assassination
asseado neat, tidy; clean

assegurar *v/t, v/r* ensure; make sure of; assure
asseio *m* neatness, tidiness; cleanliness
assembleia *f* assembly
assemelhar *v/r* resemble
assent|ar *v/t* place, settle; write down; **~o** *m* seat
asseverar *v/t* maintain, asseverate
assiduidade *f* assiduity
assíduo assiduous
assim so, thus; **~ que** as soon as
assimilar *v/t* assimilate
assin|ar *v/t, v/i* subscriber; sign; **~ante** *m, f* subscriber; **~atura** *f* signature; subscription
assist|ência *f* assistance, presence; **~ente** *m, f* assistant; bystander; **~ir** *v/t, v/i* be present at; attend
assoar *v/t, v/r* blow one's nose
assobi|ar *v/t, v/i* whistle; **~o** *m* whistle, hiss
associ|ação *f* association; **~ar** *v/t, v/r* associate
assombr|ar *v/t, v/i, v/r* shadow; astonish; **~o** *m* astonishment, awe
assumir *v/t* assume, take upon oneself
assunto *m* subject, topic, matter, case
assustar *v/t, v/r* frighten
astro *m* star
astúcia *f* astuteness, cunning
atacador *m* shoe-lace
atacar *v/t* attack
atado *adj* timid
atalh|ar *v/t, v/i* intercept; cut across; interrupt; **~o** *m* short cut
ataque *m* attack
atar *v/t* tie, fasten
até *prp* till; until; up to; *adv* even; **~ a próxima**, *Braz* **~ logo** cu (see you); see you later; **~ onde?** how far?; **~ que** until
atemorizar *v/t, v/r* frighten, horrify
aten|ção *f* attention; regard; **~cioso** kind, polite; **~der** *v/t* attend, pay attention
atentado *m* attempt, assault
atento attentive
atenu|ante attenuating; **~ar** *v/t* attenuate
aterra|gem *f* AVIA landing; **~r** *v/t, v/i* terrify; AVIA land
atest|ado *m* certificate; **~ar** *v/t* attest, certify
ateu *m* atheist
atilho *m* band, tie, string
atingir *v/t* attain; **~ a maioridade** come of age
atirar *v/t, v/r* cast, throw; **~-se a alguém** throw oneself at someone
atitude *f* attitude
atleta *m, f* athlete
átomo *m* atom
atónito astounded, astonished
atormentar *v/t* torment
atracar *v/i* moor
atra(c)ção *f* attraction
atraente attractive
atraiçoar *v/t* betray
atrair *v/t* attract
atrapalhar *v/t, v/r* muddle; confuse

atrás behind, back; ~ **de** after; behind
atras|ado backward; late, delayed; slow; **~ar** *v/t*, *v/r* put back; delay, retard; get in arrears; **~o** *m* delay
através de across; through
atravessar *v/t* cross; pass through
atrev|er-se *v/r* dare; **~ido** bold, daring
atribuir *v/t* attribute to, ascribe to
atrito *m* attrition; friction; **~s** *m/pl* difficulties
atrocidade *f* atrocity
atropelar *v/t* run over
atroz atrocious
atum *m* tunny, tuna
audácia *f* audacity
audaz audacious
audi|ção *f* audition; **~ência** *f* audience; **~tório** *m* auditorium; audience
audível audible
auge *m* height, climax
aula *f* class-room; lesson
aument|ar *v/t*, *v/i* increase; grow; **~o** *m* increase
aurora *f* dawn
auscultador *m* receiver
ausência *f* absence
ausent|ar-se *v/r* absent oneself; **~e** *adj* absent
auster|idade *f* austerity; **~o** austere
australiano *adj*, *s* Australian
austríaco *adj*, *s* Austrian
autenticidade *f* authenticity
autêntico authentic
autocarro *m* bus
auto-escola *f* driving school
auto-estrada *f* motorway, *US* highway
autógrafo *m* autograph
automático automatic
autómato *m* automaton
autom|obilismo *m* motoring; **~obilista** *m* motorist; **~óvel** *m* car; **~óvel de praça** taxi
autor *m* author
autor|idade *f* authority; **ser uma ~ em** be an expert in; **~ização** *f* authorization; **~izar** *v/t* authorize
auxiliar *v/t* help
auxílio *m* help
avalancha *f* avalanche
avaliar *v/t* appraise, evaluate
avançar *v/t*, *v/i* advance
avante *adv* forward(s); onward(s)
avar|ento avaricious, miserly; **~eza** *f* avarice
avaria *f* damage; breakdown
ave *f* bird; ~ **de arribação** bird of passage; **~s de capoeira** poultry
aveia *f* oats
avelã *f* hazel-nut, filbert
avença *f* agreement
avenida *f* avenue
avental *m* apron
aventura *f* adventure; love affair
averigu|ação *f* inquiry, investigation; **~ar** *v/t* ascertain, find out
avermelhado reddish
avessas *f/pl* opposite; **às ~** in-

side out; upside down
avesso *m* reverse, back
avestruz *m* ostrich
avia|ção *f* aviation; **~dor** *m* flier
avião *m* (aero)plane, *US* airplane
aviar-se *v/r* hasten, hurry up
avidez *f* avidity, eagerness
ávido avid; greedy; eager
aviltar *v/t* vilify; degrade
avis|ado sensible, circumspect; **~ar** *v/t* inform; advise; warn; **~o** *m* warning; notice
avistar *v/t* catch sight of, glimpse
avô *m* grandfather
avó *f* grandmother
à vontade *adv* at ease
avós *m/pl* grandparents; forefathers
avulso single
avultar *v/t* augment, enlarge
azáfama *f* hurry, bustle
azar *m* bad luck; **jogo** *m* **de ~** game of chance
azedo *adj* sour, tart
azeit|e *m* olive oil; **~ona** *f* olive
azia *f* heartburn
aziago unlucky, ill-fated
azo *m* occasion, motive, pretext
azul blue
azulejo *m* tile

B

bacalhau *m* cod(-fish)
bacana *Braz* splendid, posh
baci|a *f* basin; **~o** *m* chamber-pot
baço *adj* tarnished; dull, dim; *m* spleen
badal|ada *f* clang of a bell; **~ar** *v/t*, *v/i* clang; gossip, chatter; **~o** *m* clapper
badejo *m* haddock
bafo *m* breath; protection
baga *f* berry
bagaceira *f* brandy
bagaço *m* husk; money
bagageiro *m* porter
bagagem *f* luggage, *US* baggage
bagatela *f* bagatelle, trifle
bago *m* grape; berry; cash, dough
baía *f* bay
bail|ar *v/t*, *v/i* dance; **~arina** *f* ballerina; **~arino** *m* male ballet-dancer; **~e** *m* dance, ball
bainha *f* hem
bairro *m* district, ward, quarter; **~ da lata** slum; **~ económico** housing estate
baixa *f* decrease, fall
baixa-mar *f* low tide, ebb
baixar *v/t*, *v/i* lower, bring down; let down
baixela *f* table-ware
baixeza *f* vileness
baixio *m* sandbank, shoal
baixo *adj* low; vile; short; *adv* in a low voice; **~** *adj* **em gorduras** low fat
bala *f* bullet
balanç|a *f* scales, balance; **~ar**

v/t, *v/i* balance; swing; rock; **~o** *m* COM balance
balão *m* balloon
balaustrada *f* balustrade
balbuciar *v/t*, *v/i* stammer, stutter
balbúrdia *f* confusion, disorder; tumult
balcão *m* counter
baldado void, frustrated, ineffectual
balde *m* bucket
baldear *v/t* transfuse, decant; transship
baleia *f* whale
balela *f* false report, lie, fib
baliza *f* seamark; landmark; buoy; beacon; goal post
balouç|ar *v/t* swing, rock; **~o** *m* swing
baluarte *m* bulwark
bambo slack, loose
bambolear *v/i*, *v/r* swagger
banana *f* banana
banc|a *f* stake, pool; stand, stall; **~ada** *f* row of benches or seats
bancarrota *f* bankruptcy
banco *m* bench, form; COM bank
banda *f* side; MUS band
bandeira *f* flag, banner
bandeja *f* tray
bandido *m* bandit
bando *m* band, flock; gang; faction
bandolim *m* mandolin
banha *f* lard, fat
banh|ar *v/t*, *v/r* bath; bathe; **~eira** *f* bath(-tub); **~eiro** *m* beach attendant; **~ista** *m*, *f* bather; **~o** *m* bath; **~os** *m/pl* banns of marriage
banir *v/t* banish; outlaw
banqueiro *m* banker
banquete *m* banquet
banzé *m* row, brawl
ba(p)t|ismo *m* baptism; **~izar** *v/t* baptize
baque *m* fall; thud; throb; *Braz* instant
barafunda *f* tumult, confusion, bustle
baralh|ar *v/t* shuffle; **~o** *m* pack of cards
barão *m* baron
barata *f* cockroach
barato cheap
barba *f* beard; **nas ~s de alguém** to someone's face; **fazer a ~** shave
barbaridade *f* barbarity
bárbaro *m* barbarian; *adj* barbarous, barbaric
barbatana *f* fin
barbear *v/t*, *v/r* shave
barbearia *f* barber's shop
barbeiro *m* barber
barbo *m* ZOO barbel
barc|a *f* bark; ferry-boat; **~aça** *f* barge
barco *m* boat; ship; **~ de arrasto** trawler; **~ a motor** motor-boat; **~ a remos** rowing-boat; **~ à vela** sailing-boat
barda *f* hedge; fence; **em ~** in plenty, a lot of
barómetro *m* barometer
baronesa *f* baroness
barqueiro *m* boatman, ferryman

barra *f* bar; crow-bar; ~ **de espaço** COMP spacebar
barraca *f* hut; tent; stall
barragem *f* dam
barranco *m* ravine
barrar *v/t* bar, impede; spread
barreira *f* barrier; toll-gate; clay pit
barrento clayey
barrete *m* cap, beret
barrica *f* cask
barrig|a *f* belly; **~a da perna** calf of the leg; **~udo** pot-bellied
barril *m* barrel
barro *m* clay
barulhento noisy
barulho *m* noise, din
base *f* base; **~ar (em)** *v/t, v/r* base, found (on, upon)
básico basic
basta! *int* enough!
bastante *adj* enough, sufficient; *adv* quite
bastão *m* staff, stick
bastar *v/i* be enough
basto *adj* thick; numerous
bata *f* gown
batalh|a *f* battle; **~ar** *v/i* fight, struggle
batata *f* potato; **~s** *f/pl* **fritas** chips, *US* French fries
bate|deira *f* **(elé(c)trica)** mixer; **~dor** *m* whisk
batel *m* skiff
bate-papo *m* chat
bater *v/t, v/i* beat, strike; knock; ~ **palmas** clap one's hands
bateria *f* battery; ~ **de cozinha** kitchen utensils
batida *f* tracking, drive; reprimand; *Braz* shake
batido *m* **(de leite)** (milk) shake
batom *m* lipstick
batota *f* fraud, cheating
batuta *f* conductor's baton
baú *m* trunk, chest
baunilha *f* vanilla
bávaro *m, adj* Bavarian
bazófia *f* boast; swagger
bazofiar *v/i* boast; swagger
beat|ificar *v/t* beatify; **~o** *adj* blessed; bigoted
bebedeira *f* drunkenness
bêbedo *adj* drunk(en); *s* drunk(ard)
bebedouro *m* water-trough
beb|er *v/t, v/i* drink; **~ida** *f* drink, beverage
beco *m* alley; ~ **sem saída** *fig* deadlock
beiço *m* lip
beij|ar *v/t* kiss; **~o** *m* kiss
beira *f* edge, brink
beira-mar *f* seaside, sea-shore; **à** ~ by the sea
belas-artes *f/pl* fine arts
beldade *f* beauty
beleza *f* beauty
belga *m, f, adj* Belgian
beliche *m* berth; bunk
bélico warlike
beligerante belligerent
beliscar *v/t* pinch, nip
belo *adj* fine, fair, beautiful
bem *s* good; darling; *adv* right, very, well; *int* well; **se ~ que** although; **levar a ~** take in good part
bem-estar *m* well-being, wel-

fare
bem-querer *m* affection
bem-vindo welcome
bem-visto beloved
bênção *f* blessing
bendizer *v/t* bless; praise
benefic|ência *f* beneficence; **~iar** *v/t* benefit
benefício *m* benefit
benéfico beneficial
benevolência *f* benevolence
benévolo benevolent
benfeitor *m* benefactor
bengal|a *f* walking-stick; **~eiro** *m* hat and umbrella stand
benigno benign
benquisto beloved
bens *m/pl* estate, property; **~ de consumo** consumer goods
benzer *v/t* bless, hallow
berbigão *m* cockle
berço *m* cradle
beringela *f* aubergine, egg-plant
berma *f* roadside
berrante glaring
berr|ar *v/t, v/i* bellow; cry, shout; bawl; **~eiro** *m* bawling; **~o** *m* bellow; scream
besta *f* beast; blockhead
bestial bestial; swell
besuntar *v/t* besmear, daub
beterraba *f* beetroot
bétula *f* birch
betume *m* bitumen
bexig|a *f* bladder; **~as** *f/pl* smallpox; **~as doidas** chicken-pox
bezerro *m* calf
biberão *m* feeding bottle
Bíblia *f* Bible
bibliotec|a *f* library; **~ário** *m* librarian
bicha *f* leech; queue; **~ solitária** tapeworm
bichano *m* pussy-cat
bicho *m* worm; animal; *fig* ugly person; **ter ~s carpinteiros** be fidgety
bicicleta *f* bicycle, bike
bico *m* beak, bill; nib; **~-de-obra** *m* knotty problem
bicudo *adj* difficult; beaked; pointed
bidé *m* bidet
bienal biennial
bife *m* (beef)steak; *fig* Englishman
bifurc|ação *f* bifurcation; **~ar** *v/t, v/r* bifurcate
bigamia *f* bigamy
bigode *m* moustache
bigorna *f* anvil
bilhar *m* billiards
bilhet|e *m* ticket; **~e de ida** single ticket; **~e de ida e volta** return ticket; **~eira** *f* booking-office; box-office
bilião *m* billion
bilingue bilingual
bílis *f* bile
bilro *m* bobbin
binóculo *m* binoculars; opera-glasses; field-glasses
biografia *f* biography
biógrafo *m* biographer
biologia *f* biology
biólogo *m* biologist
biombo *m* screen
biqueira *f* toecap; gutter, spout

birr|a *f* whim; peevishness; **~ento** obstinate; peevish
bis *adv* twice; *int* encore!
bisavô *m* great-grandfather
bisbilhotar *v/i* tittle-tattle
biscoito *m* biscuit; bun; cookie
bisnaga *f* tube
bispo *m* bishop; **ter ~** be burnt
bitola *f* gauge, standard; pattern; model
bizarr|ia *f* elegance; ostentation; **~o** elegant; ostentatious
blasfemar *v/t, v/i* blaspheme
blasfémia *f* blasphemy
blindado armo(u)red
bloco *m* block; bloc; writing-pad
bloqu|ear *v/t* blockade, block; **~eio** *m* blockade
blusa *f* blouse
boa *adj* good; **é ~!** amazing! really!; **metido em ~s** in a tight spot, in a real fix
Boas-festas *f/pl* Christmas wishes
boas-vindas *f/pl* welcome
boate *m* discotheque; night club; *US* nightspot
boato *m* rumo(u)r, hearsay
bobagem *f* nonsense
bobina *f* coil
bobo *m* buffoon; jester
boca *f* mouth; **à ~ cheia** frankly, openly
bocado *m* bit, piece; short while; **há ~** recently, a short time ago
bocej|ar *v/i* yawn; **~o** *m* yawn
bochecha *f* cheek
boda *f* wedding breakfast; **~s** *f/pl* **de prata** silver wedding
bode *m* (billy-)goat; **~ expiatório** scapegoat
bofetada *f* slap, cuff
boi *m* ox
bóia *f* buoy; **~ de salvação** life buoy
boiar *v/i* float
boina *f* beret
bola *f* ball
bolacha *f* biscuit; slap
bolbo *m* BOT bulb
boleia *f* lift
boletim *m* bulletin; **~ meteorológico** weather-forecast
bolha *f* bubble; blister; **ter ~** be dotty/cracked
bolo *m* cake; slate
bolor *m* mo(u)ld; **~ento** mo(u)ldy
bolota *f* acorn
bolsa *f* purse; COM stock exchange; scholarship, grant
bolseiro *m* scholar
bolso *m* pocket
bom *adj* good; kind
bomb|a *f* bomb; pump; **~a de gasolina** petrol pump; filling/gas station; **~ardear** *v/t* bomb(ard); **~ardeio** *m* bombardment; **~eiro** *m* fireman
bombom *m* sweet, bonbon
bombordo *m* port
bonança *f* calm; prosperity
bondade *f* goodness, kindness, bounty
bonde *m* *Braz* tram
bondoso kind-hearted
boné *m* cap
boneca *f* doll

bonito *adj* pretty, fine
boquiaberto gaping
boquilha *f* cigarette holder
borboleta *f* butterfly
borborinho *m* murmur, rumble
borbulh|a *f* pimple; bud; bubble; **~ar** *v/i* gush; bubble
borda *f* bank; brink; brim; border
bordado *m* embroidery
bordão *m* staff
bordo *m* tack; **a ~** on board
borla *f* tassel; doctoral cap; **de ~** gratis, free
borracha *f* india-rubber; eraser, rubber
borr|ão *m* blot; rough draft; **~ar** *v/t* blot, stain
borrasca *f* storm, squall
borrifar *v/t* sprinkle; damp
bosque *m* wood, forest
bota *f* boot
botânica *f* botany
botão *m* button; bud; knob
botar *v/t* put, cast, throw; pour out
bote *m* boat
botequim *m* coffee-house; bar
botija *f* flagon
boxe *m* boxing
bracelete *m* bracelet
braço *m* arm; worker, hand; **de ~ dado** arm in arm
brad|ar *v/t, v/i* bawl; **~o** *m* bawl, roar
bram|ido *m* bellow; **~ir** *v/i* bellow; bluster
branc|o *adj* white; blank; *m* COMP blank, space; **~ de memória** lapse of memory; **~ura** *f* whiteness
brandir *v/t* brandish
brand|o soft, gentle; bland; **~ura** *f* softness, gentleness
branquear *v/t, v/i* whiten
bras|a *f* live coal; ember; **estar em ~a** be on tenterhooks; **~eiro** *m* brazier
brasileiro *m, adj* Brazilian
brav|io *adj* wild; savage; **~o** *int* bravo; *adj* brave; wild; rugged; **~ura** *f* bravery
breca *f* cramp; **com a ~!** damn it!
brecar *v/t Braz* brake
brecha *f* breach
breque *m Braz* brake
breu *m* pitch; tar
brev|e *adj* short, brief; *adv* soon; **em ~** soon, shortly; **~idade** *f* brevity
bricolage *f* do-it-yourself, DIY
brida *f* bridle; **a toda a ~** at full gallop; at full speed
briga *f* strife
brigad|a *f* brigade; **~eiro** *m* brigadier
brigar *v/i* fight; quarrel
brilh|ante *s* brilliant; bright, shining; **~ar** *v/i* shine; **~o** *m* shine, brilliance
brinca|deira *f* fun, joke; **~lhão** *m* wag, joker
brincar *v/i* play; joke
brinco *m* ear-ring
brind|ar *v/t, v/i* offer, present; drink a toast; **~e** *m* present; toast
brinquedo *m* toy; plaything

brio *m* hono(u)r; mettle; **~so** proud
brisa *f* breeze
britânico British
broa *f* maize bread; **~ de mel** gingerbread
broca *f* drill
broche *m* brooch
bronco coarse; stupid; dull
bronquite *f* bronchitis
bronz|e *m* bronze; **~ear** *v/t, v/r* tan; bronze
brotar *v/t, v/i* spring, well; produce; bud; sprout
broxa *f* paint-brush
brum|a *f* fog; **~oso** foggy
brusco rough; brusque
brut|al brutal; **~alidade** *f* brutality; **~o** *adj* raw, coarse; *m* brute, beast
brux|a *f* witch; **~aria** *f* witchcraft
bucha *f* wad; bung; mouthful
buço *m* down
búfalo *m* buffalo
bufar *v/i* puff, blow
bufete *m* buffet
bugigangas *f/pl* knick-knack
bula *f* MED package insert, instruction leaflet
bule *m* teapot
bulh|a *f* noise, din; disorder; **~ar** *v/i* squabble
bulício *m* bustle
bulir *v/t, v/i* move, stir
buraco *m* hole; **~ (na camada) de ozônio** ozone hole
burg|uês *m* bourgeois; **~uesia** *f* bourgeoisie
burl|a *f* fraud, trick; **~ar** *v/t* dupe, trick; **~esco** *adj* burlesque
burr|ice *f* stupidity, blunder; **~o** *m* ass, donkey; blockhead; *adj* stupid, obstinate
busc|a *f* search; **~ar** *v/t* look for
bússola *f* compass
busto *m* bust
buxo *m* box(-tree)
buzina *f* AUTO horn
buzinar *v/i* hoot
búzio *m* ZOO whelk, conch

C

cá *adv* here
cabaça *f* gourd
cabal just, complete, exact
cabana *f* hut
cabeça *f* head; **quebrar a ~** rack one's brains
cabeçal
cabeceira *f* upper end; head of a bed
cabeço *m* top, summit; hillock
cabeçudo headstrong
cabedal *m* leather; capital; means; stock
cabel|eira *f* head of hair; wig; **~eireiro** *m* hairdresser; **~o** *m* hair
caber *v/i* fit; have room for; concern; **não ~ em si de contente** be overjoyed
cabide *m* coat-hanger

cabidela *f* stewed giblets
cabimento *m* reason
cabisbaixo downcast, dejected
cabo *m* end; cape, headland; handle; cable; MIL corporal
caboclo *Braz m* mestizo, half-breed; *adj* copper-coloured; sunburnt
cabular: aula play truant, *US* play hook(e)y (from school)
cabra *f* goat; nannygoat
caç|a *f* chase; hunting; hunt; game; **~ador** *m* huntsman; **~ar** *v/t*, hunt; chase
cacarejar *v/i* cluck, cackle
caçarola *f* saucepan, casserole
cacatua *f* cockatoo
cacau *m* cacao; cocoa
cachaça *f* rum
cachecol *m* scarf
cachimbo *m* pipe
cacho *m* bunch, cluster
cachopa *f* lass, girl
cachopo *m* lad, urchin
cachorro *m* pup; whelp; cub; **~ quente** hot dog
caco *m* potsherd
caçoila *f* stew-pan
cacto *m* cactus
cada each; every; **~ vez que** whenever
cadafalso *m* scaffold
cadastr|ado *m* known criminal; **~o** *m* cadastre; census; criminal record
cadáver *m* corpse, cadaver
cadeado *m* padlock
cadeia *f* chain; prison; **~ de montanhas** mountain chain
cadeira *f* chair; **~ de braços** arm-chair; **~ de rodas** wheel-chair; **~s** *f/pl* ANAT hip
cadela *f* bitch
cadência *f* cadence, rhythm
cadern|eta *f* notebook; register; passbook, bank-book; **~o** *m* exercise-book
caduc|ar *v/i* become decrepit; lapse, become invalid; **~o** decrepit
caf|é *m* coffee; café; **~ com leite** white coffee; **~eteira** *f* coffee-pot
cágado *m* tortoise
caiar *v/t* whitewash
cãibra *f* cramp
caipira *adj Braz* rural; **música ~** *Braz* folk music
cair *v/i* fall, tumble, drop; **~ duro** *fam* be completely stunned
cais *m* (*pl* **cais**) quay
caix|a *f* box; **~a económica** savings bank; **~ão** *m* chest; coffin
caixote *m* case; **~do lixo** dustbin, *US* garbage can
cal *f* lime; whitewash
calafrio *m* shiver, chill
calamidade *f* calamity
calar *v/t*, *v/r* silence; hush up; omit; be silent; **~ a boca**, **~ o bico** shut up, shut one's mouth
calça|ada *f* roadway, street; causeway; **~adeira** *f* shoe-horn; **~ado** *m* footwear
calcanhar *m* heel
calcar *v/t* tread, trample
calçar *v/t* put on
calças *f/pl* trousers
calcetar *v/t* pave

calcular *v/t* calculate
cálculo *m* calculation; calculus
calda *f* syrup
caldas *f/pl* spa
caldeira *f* kettle; boiler
caldeirada *f* fish stew
caldo *m* broth; **~ verde** cabbage soup
calendário *m* calendar
calhar *v/i* happen; suit; **se ~** probably
calibre *m* caliber
cálice *m* wine-glass
cálido hot; sanguine
caligrafia *f* calligraphy
calm|a *f* calm; heat; **~a!** take it easy!; **~o** calm
calo *m* callus; corn
calor *m* heat, warmth; **~ífero** *m* heater; **~oso** hot, warm
caloteiro *m* swindler
caluda! silence!, quiet!
calúnia *f* calumny, slander
caluniar *v/t* calumniate, slander
calv|a *f* baldness; **~o** *adj* bald; bare
cama *f* bed; **~ de casal** double bed
camada *f* layer; stratum; **~ de ozônio** ozone layer
câmara *f* chamber; **~ (fotográfica)** camera; **~ digital** digicam; **~ municipal** town/city hall
camarada *m* comrade
camarão *m* prawn
camarote *m* THEAT box; cabin
cambalear *v/i* totter, stagger
cambiar *v/t* exchange
câmbio *m* exchange; rate of exchange
camelo *m* camel
camião, caminhão *m* lorry
caminh|ar *v/t, v/i* walk, go; **~o** *m* path, road, way; **~o de ferro** railway, *US* railroad
camioneta *f* bus, coach
camisa *f* shirt; **~ de dormir** night-dress, *US* night-gown
camisola *f* pullover; **~ interior** vest, *US* undershirt
camomila *f* camomile
campa *f* grave(stone)
campainha *f* bell
campanário *m* steeple, belfry
campanha *f* campaign
campe|ão *m* champion; **~onato** *m* championship
campin|a *f* plain; **~o** *m* countryman; herdsman
campo *m* field; country; court, ground
camponês *m* peasant
camurça *f* chamois
cana *f* cane; reed
canal *m* canal; channel; **~izar** *v/t* canalize
canário *m* canary
canastra *f* basket
canção *f* song
cancela *f* gate; wicket
cancelar *v/t* cancel
canceroso cancerous
cancro *m* MED cancer
candeeiro *m* lamp
candelabro *m* chandelier
caneca *f* mug; tankard
canela *f* cinnamon; shin; shuttle

caneta *f* pen; **~ de tinta permanente** fountain-pen
cânhamo *m* hemp
canhão *m* cannon
canhoto *adj* left-handed
canil *m* kennel
canivete *m* penknife
canja *f* chicken broth; cinch
cano *m* pipe, tube
canoa *f* canoe
cansa|ço *m* weariness; **~do** weary, tired; **~r** *v/t, v/i, v/r* weary, tire; get tired
cantar *v/t, v/i* sing
cântaro *m* pitcher, jug
canteiro *m* flower-bed
cantiga *f* song
cantina *f* canteen
canto *m* singing; corner
cantor *m* singer
canudo *m* pipe, tube
cão *m* dog; **~ de água** poodle
capa *f* cloak, cape; cover, wrapper
capacete *m* helmet
capacho *m* mat
capacidade *f* capacity; capability
capar *v/t* geld, castrate
capaz capable, able; fit
capel|a *f* chapel; **~ão** *m* chaplain
capim *m* grass
capital *m, f, adj* capital
capitalista *adj, m, f* capitalist
capitão *m* captain
capitular *v/i* capitulate
capítulo *m* chapter
capoeira *f* hen-coop
capota *f* bonnet, *US* hood
capotar *v/i* capsize
capote *m* cloak
caprichar em *v/i* take pride in
capricho *m* whim, caprice; **~so** painstaking; capricious
cápsula *f* capsule
capt|ar *v/t* captivate; **~ura** *f* capture; **~urar** *v/t* capture
cara *f* face; look, appearance
carabina *f* rifle; carbine
caracol *m* snail
cará(c)ter *m* character
cara(c)terísti|ca *f* characteristic; **~co** *adj* characteristic
cara(c)terizar *v/t* characterize
caramelo *m* caramel, toffee
caranguejo *m* crab
carapau *m* horse-mackerel
carbúnculo *m* carbuncle
carburador *m* carburet(t)or
cárcere *m* prison
carcunda *f* hump
cardápio *Braz m* menu
cardeal *m, adj* cardinal
cardo *m* thistle
cardume *m* shoal
careca *f* baldness; *adj* bald
carecer *v/i* want, need; lack
carestia *f* dearness; scarcity
careta *f* grimace
carga *f* load, burden; cargo
cargo *m* post, position
cargueiro *m* freighter
carícia *f* caress
carid|ade *f* charity; **~oso** charitable
carimb|ar *v/t* stamp; **~o** *m* rubber stamp
carinh|o *m* affection; **~oso** affectionate

carioca *m* weak coffee; *Braz m, f* native of Rio de Janeiro
carnal carnal
carnaval *m* carnival
carne *f* flesh; meat; **~ assada** roasted meat; **~ de carneiro** mutton; **~ de porco** pork; **~ de vaca** beef; **~ de vitela** veal
carneiro *m* sheep, ram
carn|iceiro *m* butcher; **~ívoro** carnivorous; **~udo** fleshy; meaty
caro *adj* dear; expensive
caroço *m* stone
carona *f Braz* lift, ride
carpa *f* carp
carpete *f* carpet
carpinteiro *m* carpenter
carranc|a *f* frown; grimace; **~udo** sullen, surly
carrasco *m* hangman; executioner
carreg|ador *m* porter; **~ar** *v/t, v/i* weigh, rest on; load; charge
carreira *f* race; career
carriça *f* wren
carril *m* rail
carro *m* (motor-car); **~ elé(c)trico** tram, *US* streetcar
carroça *f* cart
carrocel *m* roundabout, merry-go-round, *US* carousel
carruagem *f* carriage; **~-cama** *f* sleeping-car; **~-restaurante** *f* dining/restaurant car
carta *f* letter; map; (playing) card; **~ de condução**, *Braz* **~ de motorista** driving licence, *US* driver's license
cartão *m* card, cardboard; **~ de débito** debit card; **~ de visita** visiting-card; **~-presente** gift card; **~ telefónico** phone-card
cartaz *m* bill, poster, placard
carteira *f* wallet; desk; brief-case
carteirista *m* pickpocket
carteiro *m* postman
cartório *m* notary's office; file, archive
carvalho *m* oak
carvão *m* coal
casa *f* house; home; button-hole; room; firm; square; **~ de câmbio** money-changer's
casac|a *f* dress-coat; **~o** *m* coat, jacket
cas|ado married; **~al** *m* married couple; farm-house; **~amento** *m* wedding, marriage; **~ar** *v/t, v/i, v/r* marry, get married
casca *f* bark; shell; peel; skin; husk; pod, rind
cascata *f* waterfall; cascade
casco *m* skull; hoof; cask; hull
caserna *f* barracks
caso *m* case; accident; event; matter
caspa *f* dandruff, scurf
casta *f* lineage; breed; caste
castanh|a *f* chestnut; **~eiro** *m* chestnut-tree
castanho *adj* brown
castelo *m* castle; **fazer ~s no ar** build castles in the air/in Spain
castiçal *m* candlestick
castiço pure, genuine; pure-bred
castidade *f* chastity

castig|ar *v/t* punish; **~o** *m* punishment
casto chaste
castor *m* beaver
castrar *v/t* castrate
casual casual, accidental; **~idade** *f* chance
catálogo *m* catalogue
catarata *f* waterfall; MED cataract
catástrofe *f* catastrophe
cata-vento *m* weather vane
cátedra *f* university chair
catedral *f* cathedral
catedrático *m* professor
categoria *f* category
categórico categorical
cativ|ante captivating; **~ar** *v/t* captivate; **~eiro** *m* captivity; **~o** *m* captive
católico Catholic
catorze fourteen
caução *f* bail; guarantee; surety
caucho, **cauchu** *m* caoutchouc, rubber
cauda *f* tail
caudal *m* torrent; **~oso** torrential
caudilho *m* leader
caule *m* stem, stalk
caus|a *f* cause; origin; JUR case; **por ~ de** because of; **~ar** *v/t* cause
cáustico caustic
cautel|a *f* care, caution; **~oso** cautious
cava *f* armhole
cavaco *m* chat; **dar o ~ por** be very fond of; **não dar ~** say nothing
cavala *f* mackerel
caval|ariça *f* stable; **~eiro** *m* horseman; knight; **~ete** *m* easel; trestle; **~gar** *v/t*, *v/i* ride
cavalheiro *m* gentleman
cavalo *m* horse
cavar *v/t*, *v/i* dig
caverna *f* cave, cavern
cavidade *f* cavity
caxumba *f Braz* MED mumps
cear *v/t*, *v/i* dine; have supper
cebo|la *f* onion; **~linha** *f* chives
ceder *v/i* yield, give in; cede
cedo *adv* early, soon; **mais ~ ou mais tarde** sooner or later
cedro *m* cedar
cédula *f* certificate; note
ceg|ar *v/t*, *v/i* blind; **~o** blind; **~ueira** *f* blindness
ceia *f* supper
celebr|ação *f* celebration; **~ar** *v/t* celebrate
célebre famous
celebridade *f* celebrity
celeiro *m* granary, barn
celest|e, **~ial** heavenly, celestial
celibat|ário *m* bachelor; **~o** *m* celibacy
célula *f* cell; **~ solar** solar cell
celular *m* mobile (phone); *US* cell(ular) phone
cem hundred
cemitério *m* cemetery
cen|a *f* scene; **~ário** *m* scenery
cenoura *f* carrot
censo *m* census
cens|or *m* censor; **~ura** *f* censorship; **~urar** *v/t* censor; censure

centeio *m* rye
centelha *f* spark
centen|a *f* hundred; **~ário** *m* centenary
centésimo hundredth
centímetro *m* centimeter
cento *m* hundred
centr|al *adj* central; *f* station; **~al eló(c)trica** power station/ plant; **~al telefónica** telephone exchange; **~o** *m* centre, *US* center
cepa *f* vine
cepo *m* stump; block; log
cé(p)tico sceptical
cera *f* wax
cerâmica *f* ceramics
cerca *f* fence; hedge; *adv* near; about; *prep* **~ de** near; nearly
cerc|adura *f* border; **~anias** *f/pl* surroundings, environs; **~ar** *v/t*, *v/r* enclose; surround; besiege
cerco *m* siege; circle
cereal *m* cereal
cerebral cerebral
cérebro *m* brain
cerej|a *f* cherry; **~eira** *f* cherry--tree
cerimónia *f* ceremony; **~ civil** civil ceremony
ceroulas *f/pl* underpants
cerrar *v/t*, *v/r* close in; shut, close; lock
cert|eiro sure; well-aimed; **~eza** *f* certainty; **você tem ~eza?** are you sure?
certidão *f* certificate
certific|ado *m* certificate; **~ar** *v/t*, *v/r* assure; certify; make sure of
certo *adj* certain; exact
cervej|a *f* beer; **~aria** *f* pub; brewery; **~eiro** *m* brewer
cervo *m* stag
cessar *v/t*, *v/i* cease; **sem ~** incessantly
cesta *f* wicker basket
cesto *m* basket; **~ de papéis** waste-paper basket
céu *m* sky; heaven; **~ da boca** *fig* roof of the mouth, palate
cevada *f* barley
chá *m* tea; tea party
chácara *f Braz* farm; country house
chacota *f* scorn; derision
chafariz *m* public fountain
chaga *f* wound; sore
chaleira *f* kettle
chama *f* flame
cham|ada *f* call; roll-call; **~ar** *v/t*, *v/i*, *v/r* call; name; **como se ~a?** what is your name?
chaminé *f* chimney; funnel
champanhe *m* champagne
chamuscar *v/t* singe
chantag|em *f* blackmail; **fazer ~em** blackmail; **~ista** *m*, *f* blackmailer
chão *m* ground; floor; *adj* smooth; level; plain
chapa *f* plate, sheet
chapéu *m* hat
charada *f* charade
charco *m* puddle, pool
charcutaria *f* delicatessen shop
charlatão *m* charlatan
charneca *f* heath
charrua *f* plough

charuto *m* cigar
chatear *v/t* annoy, bore
chato *adj* dull; annoying; flat
chave *f* key; **~ de fenda** screwdriver; **~ geral** main switch; **~ inglesa** screw wrench
chávena *f* cup
chef|e *m* chief; leader; **~iar** *v/t* lead
cheg|ada *f* arrival; **~ar** *v/i*, *v/r* approach; arrive
chei|a *f* high water; flood; **~o** *adj* full; **em ~o** completely
cheir|ar *v/t*, *v/i* smell; **~o** *m* smell
cheque *m* cheque, *US* check; **~ cruzado** COM crossed cheque; **~ frio** uncovered cheque; **~ de viagem** traveller's cheque
cherne *m* turbot
chiar *v/i* creak; squeak; chirp
chibata *f* switch, rod
chicana *f* chicanery
chiclete *m* chewing gum
chicória *f* chicory
chicot|ada *f* lash; **~e** *m* whip; **~ear** *v/t* whip
chifre *m* horn; antler
chilr|(e)ar *v/i* twitter; **~(ei)o** *m* twittering
chinel|a *f*, **~o** *m* slipper
chinês *adj*, *m* Chinese
chiqueiro *m* pigsty, *US* pigpen
chispa *f* spark; **~r** *v/i* spark
chocalh|ar *v/i* jingle; **~o** *m* cowbell
chocar *v/t*, *v/i* shock; incubate; brood; collide
choco *m* cuttle-fish; *adj* broody; addled
chocolate *m* chocolate
chofre *m* blow; **de ~** suddenly; unexpectedly
choque *m* shock; collision
chorão *m* BOT weeping willow; cry-baby
chorar *v/i* weep, cry
choro *m* weeping, tears
choupana *f* hut
choupo *m* poplar
chouriço *m* pork sausage
chover *v/i* rain; **~ a cântaros** rain cats and dogs
chuchar *v/t* suck
chulo *adj* coarse; vulgar
chumb|ar *v/t* plug with lead; fail; **~o** *m* lead
chupar *v/t* suck
churrasco *m* barbecue
chuv|a *f* rain; **~iscar** *v/i* drizzle; **~isco** *m* drizzle; **~oso** rainy
ciber- *prp* *Internet* cyber…; **~espaço** *m* cyberspace; **~nauta** *m* cybernaut
cicatriz *f* scar; **~ar** *v/t*, *v/i* scar
ciclista *m* cyclist
ciclo *m* cycle
ciclone *m* cyclone
cidad|ão *m* citizen; **~e** *f* city; town
cidra *f* cider
ciência *f* science
cient|ífico scientific; **~ista** *m*, *f* scientist
cifr|a *f* cypher; **~ão** *m* sign for dollar or escudo ($)
cigano *m* gipsy, *US* gypsy
cigarr|eira *f* cigarette-case; **~o** *m* cigarette
cilada *f* ambush; trap

cilindro *m* cylinder
cima *f* top; **em ~** on; over; above; **para ~** upward(s); **por ~** above, over
ciment|ar *v/t* cement; *fig* strengthen; **~o** *m* cement, concrete
cimo *m* summit
cinco five
cinema *m* cinema, pictures, *US* movies
cingir *v/t*, *v/r* restrict oneself; surround
cínico cynical
cinquenta fifty
cint|a *f* sash; **~o** *m* belt; **~ de segurança** seat belt; **~ura** *f* waist
cinz|a *f* ash; **~eiro** *m* ash tray
cinzel *m* chisel; **~ar** *v/t* carve, chisel
cinzento grey
cioso jealous; envious
cipreste *m* cypress
circo *m* circus
circuito *m* circuit
circul|ação *f* circulation; **~ar** *v/t*, *v/i* circulate; *adj* circular; *f* circular
círculo *m* circle
circundar *v/t* surround
circunferência *f* circumference
circunscrição *f* circumscription
circunstância *f* circumstance
cirurgi|a *f* surgery; **~ão** *m* surgeon
cismar *v/t*, *v/i* rack one's brains, brood over
cisne *m* swan
cit|ação *f* citation, quotation; **~ar** *v/t* cite, quote
cítara *f* zither
ciúme *m* jealousy; envy
ciumento jealous; envious
cívico civic
civil *adj* civil; **~idade** *f* civility; **~ização** *f* civilization; **~izar** *v/t* civilize
clam|ar *v/t*, *v/i* shout; clamo(u)r; **~or** *m* clamo(u)r
clandestino clandestine
clara *f* (**de ovo**) white (of egg)
clarabóia *f* skylight
clarão *m* gleam; flash
clar|ear *v/t*, *v/i* clear (up); **~eira** *f* clearing; glade; **~idade** *f* brightness; clarity; **~o** *adj* clear; evident
class|e *f* class; **~ificação** *f* classification; **~ificar** *v/t* classify
claustro *m* cloister
cláusula *f* clause
clavícula *f* clavicle
clem|ência *f* clemency; **~ente** merciful
clerical clerical
clérigo *m* clergyman
clero *m* clergy
client|e *m*, *f* patient; customer; client; **~ela** *f* clientele
clima *m* climate
clínica *f* clinic; practice
clínico *adj* clinical
clonar *v/t* clone; *m* clone
clonagem *f* cloning
coabitar *v/t*, *v/i* cohabit, live together
coa(c)ção *f* coercion
coagir *v/t* coerce, force

coar *v/t* strain, filter
cobard|e *m, f* coward; *adj* cowardly; **~ia** *f* cowardice
cobert|a *f* cover; quilt; NAUT deck; **~o** *adj* covered; **~or** *m* blanket; **~ura** *f* covering
cobiç|a *f* covetousness; **~ar** *v/t* desire
cobra *f* snake
cobr|ador *m* collector; **~ar** *v/t* collect; regain
cobre *m* copper
cobrir *v/t* cover
coçar *v/t* scratch
cócegas *f/pl* tickles
coche *m* coach
cochichar *v/t, v/i* whisper
coco *m* coco-nut
côdea *f* crust
código *m* code
codorniz *f* quail
coeducação *f* co-education
coeficiente *m* coefficient
coelh|eira *f* burrow, warren; **~o** *m* rabbit
coerente coherent
coexistir *v/i* coexist
cofre *m* coffer, chest, safe
cogitar *v/t, v/i* think, cogitate
cognome *m* cognomen
cogumelo *m* mushroom
coibir *v/t* curb, repress
coincid|ência *f* coincidence; **~ir** *v/i* coincide
coisa *f* thing; matter
coitado *int* poor fellow/thing; *adj* poor, unfortunate
coito *m* coitus, intercourse
cola *f* gum, glue; crib
colabor|ação *f* collaboration; **~ador** *m* collaborator; **~ar** *v/i* collaborate
colar *m* necklace; *v/t* glue, stick; **~inho** *m* collar
colcha *f* quilt, counterpane
colchão *m* mattress
colear *v/i* meander
cole(c)|ção *f* collection; **~cionador** *m* collector; **~cionar** *v/t* collect
cole(c)tividade *f* collectivity
colega *m, f* colleague
colégio *m* college, school
cólera *f* anger; cholera
colérico choleric
colete *m* waistcoat, *US* vest
colheita *f* harvest, crop
colher *v/t* pick, gather
colher *f* spoon
colidir *v/i* collide
coligação *f* coalition
coligir *v/t* collect, gather
colina *f* hill
colisão *f* collision
colmeia *f* beehive
colmo *m* thatch
colo *m* neck; lap; **ao ~** in one's arms; on one's lap
coloc|ação *f* job; placing; **~ar** *v/t, v/r* get a job; put, place, set
colónia *f* colony; **~ de férias** summer camp
coloni|al colonial; **~zação** *f* colonization; **~zar** *v/t* colonize
colono *m* settler; colonist
colóquio *m* colloquy
color|ido *m* colo(u)ring; **~ir** *v/t* colo(u)r
coluna *f* column
com with

comand|ante *m* commandant; commander; **~ar** *v/t* command; **~o** *m* command
comarca *f* district, region
combat|e *m* combat; **~er** *v/t, v/i* combat, fight
combin|ação *f* combination; slip, petticoat; **~ar** *v/t, v/i, v/r* settle, fix; match; combine; agree
comboio *m* train; convoy; **~ dire(c)to** through train; **~ expresso** express (train)
combust|ão *f* combustion; **~ível** *m* fuel; *adj* combustible
começ|ar *v/t, v/i* begin, start; **~o** *m* start, beginning
comédia *f* comedy; play
comemor|ação *f* commemoration; **~ar** *v/t* commemorate
coment|ar *v/t* comment (on); **~ário** *m* commentary
comer *v/t, v/i* eat
comerci|al commercial; **~ante** *m, f* merchant; **~ar** *v/i* trade, do business
comércio *m* trade, commerce
comestív|eis *m/pl* eatables; **~el** eatable
cometer *v/t* commit
comichão *m* itch
comício *m* meeting, assembly
cómico comic(al), funny
comida *f* food; meal; **~ de plástico** junk food
comigo with me
cominho *m* cumin
comiss|ão *f* commission; committee; **~ária** *f Braz* stewardess; **~ário** *m* commissioner; **~ário de polícia** chief constable
como *conj* as; like; *int* what!, why!; *adv* how
comoção *f* commotion; emotion
cómoda *f* chest of drawers
comodidade *f* convenience; comfort
cómodo *adj* comfortable
como|vente moving, touching; **~ver** *v/t, v/i* move, touch
compactar *v/t* pack; COMP compress
compadecer-se de *v/r* sympathize with
compaixão *f* pity, compassion
companheiro *m* companion
companhia *f* company
compar|ação *f* comparison; **~ar** *v/t* compare; **~ativo** *adj, m* comparative; **~ável** comparable
comparecer *v/i* appear
comparti|lhar *v/t* share (in); **~mento** *m* compartment
compasso *m* beat; rhythm; compasses
compat|ibilidade *f* compatibility; **~ível** compatible
compatriota *m, f* compatriot, countryman, countrywoman
compêndio *m* compendium
compens|ação *f* compensation; **~ar** *v/t* compensate
compet|ência *f* competence; competition; **~ente** competent; suitable; **~ição** *f* competition
competidor *m* competitor

competir *v/i* compete, vie; be incumbent on
compil|ação *f* compilation: **~ar** *v/t* compile
compleição *f* physical constitution
complement|ar *adj* complementary; **~o** *m* complement
complet|ar *v/t* complete, finish; **~o** *adj* complete
complic|ação *f* complication; **~ado** complicated; **~ar** *v/t* complicate
componente *m* component
compor *v/t, v/r* compose (oneself)
comportamento *m* behavio(u)r
comportar *v/r* behave
composi|ção *f* arrangement; composition; **~tor** *m* composer; compositor
compostura *f* composure
compota *f* jam; **~ de laranja** marmalade
compr|a *f* purchase; **(fazer) ~as em linha** (go) on-line shopping; **ir às ~as** go shopping
compr|ador *m* buyer, purchaser; **~ar** *v/t* buy, purchase
compreen|der *v/t* understand, realize; **~são** *f* understanding, comprehension; **~sível** understandable, comprehensible; **~sivo** comprehensive, comprehending
compri|do *adj* long; **~mento** *m* length
comprim|ido *m* tablet, pill; **~ir** *v/t* (com)press
comprometer *v/t, v/r* compromise; commit oneself
compromisso *m* compromise
comprovação *f* confirmation
comprovar *v/t* confirm; verify; prove
compungido contrite
computador *m* computer; **~ portátil** laptop
computar *v/t* compute
comum *adj* common; general, ordinary
comuna *f* community
comunhão *f* communion
comunic|ação *f* communication; **~ado** *m* communiqué; **~ar** *v/t* communicate; **~ativo** communicative
comunidade *f* community
comun|ismo *m* communism; **~ista** *m, f, adj* communist
comut|ador *m* switch; **~ar** *v/t* commute
côncavo *adj* concave
conceber *v/t, v/i* conceive (of)
conceder *v/t* allow, grant, concede
conceito *m* concept; opinion
concelho *m* municipality
concentrar *v/t, v/r* concentrate
concepção *f* conception
concertar *v/t, v/i* settle; adjust
concertina *f* concertina
concerto *m* concert
concessão *f* concession
concha *f* shell, conch
conciliar *v/t* conciliate; reconcile; win
conciso concise
conclu|ir *v/t, v/i, v/r* conclude;

infer; ~são *f* conclusion; inference
concordar *v/t, v/i* agree
concórdia *f* concord, harmony
concorr|ência *f* throng; competition; **~ente** *m, f* competitor, **~er** *v/i* gather; compete
concretizar *v/t* make concrete
concreto *adj* concrete
concurso *m* competition
cond|ão *m* prerogative, privilege; **~e** *m* count; earl
condecor|ação *f* decoration, medal; **~ar** *v/t* decorate, invest
conden|ação *f* condemnation; **~ar** *v/t* condemn
condens|ação *f* condensation; **~ar** *v/t* condense
condescend|ência *f* compliance; **~ente** condescending, **~er** *v/i* condescend, comply
condessa *f* countess
condição *f* condition
condicional *adj* conditional
condicionar *v/t* condition
condigno condign, merited
condimento *m* spice
condiscípulo *m* schoolfellow
condizer *v/i* tally, match; suit
condolência *f* condolence
condução *f* conduction; transport
conduta *f* conduct; conduit
condutor *m* driver; conductor
conduzir *v/t, v/i, v/r* conduct; lead; drive
confeccionar *v/t* make
confederação *f* confederation
confeitaria *f* confectioner's
confer|ência *f* lecture; conference; **~enciar** *v/i* confer, consult together; **~encista** *m, f* lecturer; **~ir** *v/t* check; confer, bestow
confessar *v/t* confess
confi|ança *f* confidence; **~ar** *v/t, v/i* trust, confide; entrust
confidente *m, f* confidant(e)
confinar *v/t, v/i* confine; border
confins *m/pl* confines
confirm|ação *f* comfirmation; **~ar** *v/t* confirm
confisc|ação *f* confiscation; **~ar** *v/t* confiscate
confissão *f* confession
conflito *m* conflict
confluir *v/i* join, flow
conform|ar *v/t, v/i, v/r* conform; harmonize; resign oneself to; **~e** *conj* as, according to; *adv* in agreement; **(é) ~!** it depends; **~idade** *f* conformity
confortar *v/t* comfort
confortável comfortable
conforto *m* comfort
confrontar *v/t* confront
confundir *v/t* confuse
confus|ão *f* confusion; **~o** confused; embarrassed
congelar *v/t* freeze; congeal
congénere identical
congénito congenital
congestão *f* congestion
congestionar *v/t, v/r* congest
congratular *v/t, v/r* congratulate
congress|ista *m, f* Congresswoman, Congressman; **~o** *m* congress
conhec|edor *m* connoisseur,

expert; **~er** *v/t, v/i, v/r* know; get to know; be acquainted with; **~ido** *adj* known; *m* acquaintance; **~imento** *m* acquaintance; knowledge; **~imentos** *m/pl* knowledge
conje(c)tur|a *f* conjecture; **~ar** *v/t, v/i* conjecture
conjugar *v/t* conjugate
cônjuge *m* spouse
conjunção *f* conjunction
conjunto *m* assemblage; whole; entirety
conjur|ação *f* conspiracy; **~ado** *m* conspirator; **~ar** *v/i* conspire
con(n)osco with us
conquanto although
conquist|a *f* conquest; **~ar** *v/t* conquer
consagr|ação *f* consecration; **~ar** *v/t* consecrate
consci|ência *f* conscience; consciousness; **~encioso** conscientious
consciente conscious
consecutivo consecutive
conseguinte consequent; **por ~** in consequence
conseguir *v/t* get, obtain; succeed in, manage
conselheiro *m* counsel(l)or, adviser
conselho *m* counsel, advice
consent|imento *m* consent; **~ir** *v/t, v/i* consent (to)
consequência *f* consequence
conserva *f* preserves; mixed pickles; **~ção** *f* preservation; **~dor** *adj, m* conservative; **~r** *v/t, v/r* conserve; preserve; keep
consider|ação *f* consideration; **~ar** *v/t, v/r* consider; **~ável** considerable
consigo *pron* with him(self)/her(self)/itself; with themselves; with you
consist|ência *f* consistency; **~ente** consistent
consistir em *v/i* consist in, of
consoada *f* Christmas eve dinner
consoante *f, adj* consonant; *prp* according to
consol|ação *f* consolation; **~ar** *v/t, v/r* solace, console
consolid|ação *f* consolidation; **~ar** *v/t* consolidate
consolo *m* consolation
consórcio *m* partnership
consorte *m, f* consort
conspir|ação *f* conspiracy; **~ador** *m* conspirator; **~ar** *v/i* conspire, plot
constância *f* constancy
constante constant
constar *v/i* be known, be reported; **~ de** consist of
constern|ação *f* consternation; **~ar** *v/t, v/i* dismay
constip|ação *f* cold; **~ado** having a cold; **~ar-se** *v/r* catch cold
constitucional *adj* constitutional
constituição *f* constitution
constituinte *adj* constituent
constituir *v/t* constitute
constru|ção *f* construction; **~ir**

v/t construct; **~tor** *m* constructor
cônsul *m* consul
consulado *m* consulate
consult|a *f* consultation; COMP query; **~ar** *v/t* consult; **~ório** *m* consulting room
consum|idor *m* consumer; **~ir** *v/t* consume
consumo *m* consumption
conta *f* account; bill; **~ do usuário** COMP user account
contabil|idade *f* book-keeping; **~ista** *m*, *f* book-keeper; accountant
contactar *v/t*, *v/i* contact
conta(c)to *m* contact
contado counted; told, narrated
cont|agiar *v/t* infect, **~ágio** *m* contagion; **~agioso** contagious
contanto que provided that
conta-quilómetros *m* speedometer
contar *v/t*, *v/i* tell; count; relate; **~ com** rely on
contempl|ação *f* contemplation; **~ar** *v/t* contemplate
contemporâneo *m*, *adj* contemporary
contenda *f* strife, quarrel
content|amento *m* contentment; **~ar** *v/t*, *v/r* satisfy, content; **~e** content(ed), happy
conter *v/t*, *v/r* contain
contest|ar *v/t*, *v/i* dispute; contest; **~ável** contestable
conteúdo *m* contents
contigo with you
continência *f* continence
continente *m* continent
continu|ação *f* continuation; **~ar** *v/t*, *v/i* go on, continue; **~idade** *f* continuity
contínuo *adj* continuous, continual; *m* care-taker, *US* janitor
conto *m* tale
contornar *v/t* outline; go round
contorno *m* outline; contour
contra *prp* against
contraband|ista *m*, *f* smuggler; **~o** *m* contraband
contra(c)ção *f* contraction
contraceptivo *m* contraceptive
contradição *f* contradiction
contradizer *v/t*, *v/i*, *v/r* contradict
contrair *v/t* contract
contramestre *m* foreman
contrapartida *f* counterpart
contrapeso *m* counterpoise
contrapor *v/t* oppose
contrari|ar *v/t*, *v/r* thwart; annoy; **~edade** *f* contrariety; worry
contrário *adj* contrary, opposite
contraste *m* contrast
contrat|ar *v/t* contract; **~o** *m* contract
contraveneno *m* antidote
contribu|ição *f* contribution; **~inte** *m*, *f* taxpayer; **~ir** *v/i* contribute
contrição *f* contrition
contristar *v/t* sadden
contrito contrite

controle *m* control
controvérsia *f* controversy
contudo *conj* nevertheless
contusão *f* bruise, contusion
convalesc|ença *f* convalescence; **~er** *v/i* convalesce
convenção *f* convention; agreement
convencer *v/t, v/r* convince
convencion|al *adj* conventional; **~ar** *v/t* stipulate
conveni|ência *f* convenience; propriety; **~ente** convenient; proper
convénio *m* pact, covenant
convento *m* convent
converg|ência *f* convergence; **~ir** *v/i* converge
convers|a *f* talk, chat; **~ação** *f* conversation; **~ar** *v/t* converse
conversão *f* conversion
converter *v/t* convert
convés *m* deck
convic|ção *f* conviction; **~to** *adj* convinced
convid|ado *m* guest; **~ar** *v/t* invite
convincente convincing
convir *v/i* suit, be proper; befit
convite *m* invitation
conviver *v/i* be on familiar terms
convívio *m* banquet; conviviality
convoc|ação *f* convocation; **~ar** *v/t* convoke
convulsão *f* convulsion
cooper|ação *f* co-operation; **~ar** *v/i* co-operate; **~ativa** *f* co-operative society; **~ativo** co-operative
coorden|ação *f* co-ordination; **~ar** *v/t* co-ordinate
copa *f* treetop; crown; pantry; **~s** *f/pl* hearts
cópia *f* copy
copiar *v/t* copy
copioso copious
copista *m* copyist
copo *m* glass
coqueiro *m* coconut tree
cor *f* colo(u)r
cor: de ~ by heart
coração *m* heart
corado red, ruddy
coragem *f* courage
corajoso courageous
coral *m* coral
corante *m* colo(u)ring
corar *v/i* blush
corça *f* doe, hind
corcovar *v/t* stoop; curve
corcunda *m, f* hunchback
cord|a *f* rope; string; **~ão** *m* cord; twine; cordon
cordeiro *m* lamb
cordel *m* string
cordial *adj* hearty, cordial
cordoeiro *m* rope-maker
córneo horny, corneous
cornet|a *f* cornet; bugle; **~eiro** *m* bugler
corno *m* horn
coro *m* chorus; choir
coro|a *f* crown; **~ação** *f* coronation; **~ar** *v/t* crown
coronel *m* colonel
coronha *f* butt end
corpo *m* body; MIL corps
corporação *f* corporation

corpóreo corporeal
corpulento corpulent
corre(c)ção *f* correction
corredor *m* passage, corridor
correia *f* strap; belt
correio *m* post, *US* mail; post office; **~ aéreo** airmail; **~ eletrônico** COMP e-mail; **~ de voz** TEL voice mail; **na volta do ~** by return of post
correlação *f* Correlation
corrente *adj*, *f* current; **~ alterna** alternating current; **~ contínua** direct current
correr *v/t*, *v/i* run; flow; draw; examine
correspond|ência *f* correspondence; **~ente** *m*, *f*, *adj* correspondent; **~er** *v/i* correspond
corretor *m* broker
corrida *f* race, run; **~ de touros** bullfight
corrigir *v/t* correct
corrimão *m* handrail
corroer *v/t* corrode
corromper *v/t* corrupt
corrosão *f* corrosion
corru(p)ção *f* corruption
cort|ar *v/t*, *v/i*, *v/r* cut; **~e** *m* cut, gash
corte *f* court; **~jar** *v/t* court;
cortejo *m* procession; cortège; retinue
cortês polite, courteous
cortesia *f* courtesy
cortiça *f* cork
cortina *f* curtain
cortinado *m* curtain
coruja *f* owl
coruscar *v/i* flash, glitter
corvo *m* raven
coser *v/t*, *v/i* sew
cosmético *adj*, *m* cosmetic
costa *f* coast; shore; **~s** *f/pl* back
costela *f* rib
costeleta *f* cutlet, chop
costumar *v/t*, *v/i* use (to)
costume *m* custom; **como de ~** as usual
costur|a *f* sewing; seam; **~eira** *f* seamstress
cota *f* quota
coto *m* stump
cotovelo *m* elbow
cotovia *f* lark
couro *m* leather
couve *f* cabbage; **~-de-Bruxelas** Brussels (sprout); **~-flor** *f* cauliflower; **~ galega** kale; **~ lombarda** white cabbage
cova *f* cave
covil *m* den
coxa *f* thigh
coxear *v/i* limp
coxo *adj* lame
cozer *v/t* cook; boil; bake
cozido *m* (**à portuguesa**) Portuguese stew
cozinh|a *f* kitchen; cooking; **~ar** *v/t*, *v/i* cook; **~eiro** *m* cook
cravar *v/t* nail; stare
cravinho *m* clove
cravo *m* nail; BOT carnation; **~-da-índia**, **~-de-cabecinha** clove
creditar *v/t* credit
crédito *m* credit
credor *m* creditor

creme *m* cream; custard
cren|ça *f* belief; **~te** *m, f* believer
crepúsculo *m* twilight, dusk
crer *v/t, v/i* suppose; believe
crescer *v/i* grow
criação *f* creation
criada *f* maid, servant
criado *m* waiter; servant
criança *f* child
criar *v/t* create; rear
criatura *f* creature
crim|e *m* crime; **~inoso** *m, adj* criminal
crise *f* crisis
cristandade *f* Christendom
crist|ão *m, adj* Christian; **~ianismo** *m* Christianity
crítica *f* cirticism
criticar *v/t* criticize
crítico *m* critic; *adj* critical
crivar *v/t* riddle; sift
crivo *m* sieve; riddle
crocodilo *m* crocodile
croquete *m* croquette
cru raw; rough; coarse
cruel cruel; **~dade** *f* cruelty
cruz *f* cross
cruzado *m former Brazilian currency*
cruzar *v/t* cross
cruzeiro *m former Brazilian currency*
cubo *m* cube
cuco *m* cuckoo
cuecas *f/pl* (under)pants, briefs, panties
cuidado *m* care; **~so** careful
cuidar (de) *v/t* care for, tend
cujo whose; of which
culp|a *f* blame; guilt; fault; **~ado** *adj* guilty; **~ar** *v/t* blame
cultivar *v/t* cultivate, till
cultivo *m* cultivation, tillage
culto *adj* cultivated, cultured; *m* cult
cultura *f* culture; cultivation
cume *m* summit
cumpriment|ar *v/t* greet; compliment; **~o** *m* greeting; fulfil(l)ment; **~os** *m/pl* kind regards, greetings; best wishes
cumprir *v/t, v/i, v/r* accomplish, fulfil(l), carry out; **~ a palavra** keep one's word
cúmulo *m* height, acme
cunha *f* wedge
cunha|da *f* sister-in-law; **~do** *m* brother-in-law
cunho *m* stamp, impress
cúpula *f* dome
cura *m* parish priest; *f* cure, healing
curandeiro *m* quack
curar *v/t, v/i, v/r* cure, heal
curios|idade *f* curiosity; **~o** curious
curral *m* corral, pen
curso *m* course
curtir *v/t* tan; soak
curt|o short; **~o-circuito** *m* short circuit
curv|a *f* bend, curve; **~ar** *v/t, v/i* curve, bend; **~o** curved, bent
cusp|ir *v/i* spit; **~o** *m* spittle
cust|ar *v/t, v/i* cost; be difficult; **~ear** *v/t* defray; **~o** *m* cost(s), expense; **a ~o** with difficulty
custódia *f* custody
custoso costly, expensive

cutelaria *f* cutlery
cutel|eiro *m* cutler; **~o** *m* chopper; cutlass
cútis *f* skin

D

da *contr of* **de** *and* **a**
da(c)til|ógrafa *f* typist; **~ografar** *v/t*, *v/i* type
dado *m* dice **~s** *m/pl* data
daí from there, thence; therefore; **~ em diante** from then on; **e ~?** and what then?
dama *f* lady; queen; **~s** *f/pl* draughts
damasco *m* apricot; damask
danar *v/t*, *v/r* irritate, get angry
danç|a *f* dance; **~ar** *v/t*, *v/i* dance
danificar *v/t* damage, spoil
dano *m* hurt, injury; damage
dantes before, formerly
dar *v/t*, *v/i*, *v/r* give; beat; **~ com** meet, come across; **~-se bem com** get on well with; **~ às de vila-diogo** take to one's heels; **~ um passeio** take a walk
dardo *m* dart
dat|a *f* date; **~ar (de)** *v/t*, *v/i* date (from)
de of; from; by; on; in
debaixo underneath; **~ de** under
debalde in vain
debandl|ada *f* dispersing; stampede; **~ar** *v/t*, *v/i* disband
debat|e *m* debate; **~er** *v/t* debate
débil weak
debilidade *f* debility, weakness
debitar *v/t*, *v/r* debit
débito *m* debit
debruar *v/t* hem, border
debruçar-se *v/r* lean out
debulh|a *f* threshing; **~adora** *f* threshing-machine; **~ar** *v/t* thresh; **~ar-se em lágrimas** dissolve into tears
década *f* decade
decadência *f* decadence
decair *v/i* fall, decay
decapitar *v/t* behead
dec|ência *f* decency; **~ente** decent
decepar *v/t* mutilate, mangle
decepção *f* disappointment
decepcionar *v/t* disappoint
decidido resolute
decidir *v/t*, *v/i*, *v/r* decide
decifrar *v/t* decipher
décimo *m*, *adj* tenth
decis|ão *f* decision; **~ivo** decisive
declam|ação *f* declamation; **~ar** *v/t*, *v/i* declaim
declar|ação *f* declaration; **~ar** *v/t*, *v/r* declare
declin|ação *f* declination; declension; **~ar** *v/t*, *v/i* decline
declínio *m* decline
decompo|r *v/t*, *v/r* decompose; **~sição** *f* decomposition
decor|ação *f* decoration; **~ar**

v/t, decorate; learn by heart
decor|o *m* decorum; **~oso** decorous
decorrer *v/i* pass away, elapse; occur
decote *m* low neckline
decrépito decrepit
decrescer *v/i* decrease
decret|ar *v/t* decree; **~o** *m* decree
decurso *m* lapse, course
ded|ada *f* finger-print; **~al** *m* thimble
dedic|ação *f* dedication, devotion; **~ar** *v/t*, *v/r* dedicate, devote
dedo *m* finger; **~ do pé** toe
dedu|ção *f* deduction; **~zir** *v/t* deduct; deduce
defectivo defective
defeit|o *m* defect; **~uoso** defective, faulty
defen|der *v/t*, *v/r* defend; **~sável** defensible; **~siva** *f* defensive; **~sor** *m* defender
deferência *f* deference
defer|imento *m* granting; compliance; **~ir** *v/t*, *v/i* yield, concede, grant; defer
defes|a *f* defence; **~as** *f/pl* tusks; **~o** *m* closed season; *adj* prohibited
defici|ência *f* deficiency; **~ente** deficient
definhar *v/t*, *v/i*, *v/r* wilt; pine; languish
defin|ição *f* definition; **~ido** *adj* defined, definite; **~ir** *v/t* define; **~itivo** definitive
deflagr|ação *f* deflagration; **~ar** *v/i* deflagrate
deform|ação *f* deformation; **~ar** *v/t* deform
deformidade *f* deformity
defraud|ação *f* defrauding; **~ar** *v/t* defraud, cheat
defrontar *v/t* face
defronte opposite, facing; **~ de** in front of
defumar *v/t* smoke
defunto *adj* defunct, deceased
degelar *v/t*, *v/i* thaw
degelo *m* thaw
degener|ação *f* degeneration; **~ar** *v/i* degenerate
degrad|ação *f* degradation; **~ar** *v/t* degrade
degrau *m* step, stair; rung
degredar *v/t* deport, exile
degredo *m* deportation
deitado in bed; lying down
deitar *v/t*, *v/i*, *v/r* lay; cast; throw; pour; go to bed, lie down
deixar *v/t*, *v/i*, *v/r* quit; let; leave; **~ de** give up; **~ cair** drop; **não poder ~ de** can't help it
dele *contr of* **de + ele** his
deleg|ação *f* delegation; **~ado** *m* delegate; **~ar** *v/t* delegate
deleit|ar *v/t*, *v/r* delight; **~e** *m* delight; **~oso** delightful
delgado *adj* thin, slender
deliberar *v/t*, *v/i* deliberate
delicad|eza *f* delicacy, gentleness; **~o** delicate
delícia *f* delight
delici|ar *v/t*, *v/r* delight; **~oso** delicious; delightful

delinear *v/t* delineate
delinquente *m* delinquent
delir|ante delirious, raving; **~ar** *v/i* be delirious, rave
delírio *m* delirium
delito *m* crime, offense
demais *adv* besides; *adj* too much, too; **o ~** *m* the rest; **~ a mais** furthermore
demanda *f* lawsuit; plea; quest; **em ~ de** in search of
demasi|a *f* excess; **~ado** *adv* too; *adj* excessive
demência *f* madness, insanity
demente *adj* mad, insane
demissão *f* dismissal; resignation
demitir *v/t*, *v/r* dismiss; resign
democra|cia *f* democracy; **~ta** *m*, *f* democrat
demolir *v/t* demolish
demónio *m* demon, devil
demonstr|ação *f* demonstration; **~ar** *v/t* demonstrate; **~ativo** demonstrative; **~ável** demonstrable
demor|a *f* delay; **~ar** *v/t*, *v/r* be long; delay
demover *v/t* dissuade
denodado bold
denodo *m* boldness
denomin|ação *f* denomination; **~ar** *v/t*, *v/r* denominate, name
denotar *v/t* denote
dens|idade *f* density; **~o** dense
dent|ada *f* bite; **~ado** indented, jagged; **~adura** *f* set of teeth; **~adura postiça** false teeth; **~al** *adj* dental; **~e** *m* tooth; **~ifrício** *m* dentifrice; **~ista** *m*, *f* dentist
dentro inside, within; **~ de** in, within; **~ em breve** soon, shortly
denúncia *f* denunciation; publication of banns
denunci|ante *m*, *f* denunciator; **~ar** *v/t* denounce
deparar *v/t*, *v/r* reveal; come across; present
departamento *m* department
depenar *v/t* deplume, pluck
depend|ência *f* dependence; outbuilding; **~ente** dependent; **~er de** *v/i* depend on
depilar *v/t* depilate
deplorar *v/t* deplore
deplorável deplorable
depoimento *m* deposition, evidence
depois afterwards; then; **~ de** after; **~ de amanhã** the day after tomorrow; **e ~?** what of it?; **~ que** after; since
depor *v/t*, *v/i* put aside; depose
deportar *v/t* deport
deposição *f* deposition
depositar *v/t* deposite
depósito *m* deposit
depravar *v/t* deprave
depreci|ação *f* depreciation; **~ar** *v/t* depreciate
depreender *v/t* perceive
depressa quickly, fast
depressão *f* depression
deprimir *v/t* depress
depurar *v/t* purify
deputado *m* deputy; member of parliament

deriv|ação *f* derivation; **~ar** *v/t, v/i, v/r* derive from
derradeiro last
derramar *v/t* scatter, spread; spill; shed
derrapar *v/i* skid, sideslip
derreter *v/t, v/r* melt
derroc|ada *f* collapse; **~ar** *v/t* knock down; demolish
derrot|a *f* rout, defeat; **~ar** *v/t* rout, defeat
desabafar *v/t, v/i* uncover, relieve; open one's heart
desab|amento *m* crumbling; **~ar** *v/i* crumble
desabitado uninhabited
desabituar *v/t* wean from, cure of a habit
desabotoar *v/t, v/r* unbutton
desabrido sharp; rough; peevish
desabrigado unsheltered; exposed, open
desabrochar *v/i* bloom, blossom
desaf|iar *v/t* defy, challenge; **~io** *m* challenge; contest; match
desafog|ar *v/t, v/i* unburden; ease; **~o** m ease, comfort
desagrad|ar *v/t* displease; **~ável** disagreeable; **~o** *m* displeasure
desaguar *v/i* flow
desaire *m* setback; awkwardness
desajeitado clumsy, awkward
desalent|ar *v/t, v/i, v/r* discourage; **~o** *m* dejection, dismay
desalinho *m* slovenliness; disorder
desalojar *v/t* dislodge
desampar|ado abandoned, forsaken; **~ar** *v/t* forsake, abandon; **~o** *m* abandonment
desanim|ado discouraged; **~ar** *v/t, v/i* discourage
desânimo *m* discouragement
desaparec|er *v/i* disappear; **~ido** *adj* missing; **~imento** *m* disappearance
desapertar *v/t* loosen, slacken
desaprovar *v/t* disapprove
desarmar *v/t* disarm
desarmonia *f* disharmony
desarranj|ar *v/t* disarrange; **~o** *m* disorder
desarrumar *v/t* disarrange
desassosseg|ar *v/t* disquiet, disturb; **~o** *m* uneasiness
desastr|ado unlucky; awkward; **~e** *m* disaster
desastroso disastrous
desatar *v/t, v/i* untie, unfasten; **~ a chorar** burst out crying; **~ a rir** burst out laughing
desatento heedless
desavergonhado shameless
desavindo at variance
desbarat|ar *v/t* destroy; defeat; **~o** *m* havoc; defeat; **ao ~o** at a sacrifice, dirt-cheap
desbotar *v/t, v/i* fade
descabido improper
descair *v/i* decay; droop
descalçar *v/t, v/r* take off
descalço barefoot
descans|ado rested; tranquil, easy; **~ar** *v/t, v/i* rest; **~o** *m* rest; repose

descar|ado cheeky, impudent; **~amento** *m* effrontery
descarg|a *f* unloading; discharge; volley; **~o** *m* acquittal
descarregar *v/t, v/i* relieve; unload; discharge
descarril|amento *m* derailment; **~ar** *v/t, v/i* derail
descascar *v/t* peel, shell
descend|ência *f* progeny, offspring; **~ente** *m, f* descendant; *adj* descending
descender *v/i* descend from
descer *v/t, v/i* descend; get/go down
desclassificar *v/t* disqualify
descob|erta *f* discovery; **~rimento** *m* discovery; **~rir** *v/t, v/i, v/r* uncover; discover
descol|agem *f* AVIA take-off; **~ar** *v/i* take off
descompactar *v/t* COMP unzip
descomp|or *v/t* disarrange; **~ostura** *f* rebuke
desconcertado disconcerted, upset
desconfi|ado distrustful; **~ança** *f* distrust; **~ar** *v/t, v/i* distrust; suspect
descongelar *v/t* thaw
desconhecido *adj* unknown
descont|ar *v/t* discount; **~o** *m* discount
descorado colo(u)rless; pale
descoser *v/t* unsew, unstitch
descrédito *m* discredit
descren|ça *f* disbelief; **~te** *m, f* unbeliever
descrever *v/t* describe
descrição *f* description
descritivo descriptive
descuid|ado careless; negligent; **~ar** *v/t, v/r* disregard, neglect; **~o** *m* oversight, neglect
desculp|a *f* excuse; **~ar** *v/t, v/r* apologize, excuse; **~e!** sorry!, excuse me
descurar *v/t* neglect
desde since; from; **~ que** since; as soon as, provided
desdém *m* disdain
desdenh|ar *v/t, v/i* disdain; **~oso** disdainful
desdita *f* misfortune
desdizer *v/t* contradict
desdobr|amento *m* unfolding; **~ar** *v/t* unfold; duplicate
desej|ar *v/t* desire, wish; **~ável** desirable; **~o** *m* desire; wish; **~oso** desirous
desembaraç|ar *v/t, v/r* rid; disentangle; disembarrass; **~o** *m* ease
desembarcar *v/t, v/i* disembark, land
desembarque *m* disembarking, landing
desemboc|adura *f* mouth; **~ar** *v/i* flow out
desembols|ar *v/t* disburse, spend; **~o** *m* disbursement, outlay
desembrulhar *v/t* unwrap; unravel
desempacotar *v/t* unpack
desempat|ar *v/t* decide, resolve; **~e** *m* decision
desempenh|ar *v/t* redeem from pawn; perform; **~ar um papel** play a part; **~o** *m* dis-

charge; performance
desempregado unemployed
desemprego *m* unemployment
desencadear *v/t, v/r* break, burst; unchain
desencalhar *v/t* refloat
desencaminhar *v/t* lead astray; mislead
desencontr|ado disagreeing, opposite; **~ar** *v/t, v/r* fail to meet; disagree
desencorajar *v/t* discourage
desencostar *v/t* straighten up, not to lean
desenferrujar, *v/t* clean the rust off; **~ a língua** find one's tongue
desenfre|ado unbridled; **~ar** *v/t, v/r* unbridle
desengan|ar *v/t, v/r* undeceive; **~o** *m* undeceiving
desengatar *v/t* unhook
desengonç|ado unhinged; ungainly; **~ar** *v/t, v/r* totter; unhinge
desenh|ador *m* draughtsman; designer; **~ar** *v/t, v/i* draw; design; **~o** *m* drawing; design
desenlace *m* dénouement
desenredar *v/t* unravel
desenrolar *v/t, v/r* unfold; spread; unroll
desenterrar *v/t* dig up
desentupir *v/t* unstop
desenvolt|o nimble; **~ura** *f* nimbleness
desenvolv|er *v/t, v/r* develop; **~imento** *m* development
desenxabido insipid; silly
desequilibrar *v/t, v/r* unbalance; throw off balance
desequilíbrio *m* imbalance
deser|ção *f* desertion; **~tar** *v/t, v/i* desert; **~to** *m* desert; *adj* deserted
desesperado *adj* desperate
desesperar *v/i* despair
desespero *m* despair
desfalcar *v/t* embezzle
desfalec|er *v/t* faint; **~imento** *m* faintness
desfalque *m* embezzlement
desfavorável unfavo(u)rable
desfazer *v/t* undo, unmake; annul; **~-se em lágrimas** burst into tears
desfech|ar *v/t, v/i* fire; end; burst; hurl; **~o** *m* outcome, upshot
desfeita *f* insult
desfigurar *v/t* disfigure
desfiladeiro *m* gorge, defile
desfil|ar *v/i* file past; **~e** *m* march-past
desforr|a *f* revenge; **~ar-se** *v/r* be/get even with, revenge
desfrutar *v/t* enjoy
desgarr|ado astray; **~ar** *v/i, v/r* go astray
desgastar *v/t* wear away
desgost|ar *v/t, v/i* dislike; displease; **~o** *m* sorrow, trouble
desgovernado wasteful
desgraç|a *f* mishap, misfortune; **~ado** unfortunate
desgrenhado dishevelled
design|ação *f* designation; **~ar** *v/t* designate, appoint
desígnio *m* design, purpose

desigual unequal; **~dade** *f* inequality
desilu|dir *v/t* disillusion; **~são** *f* disillusion(ment)
desimpedir *v/t* disencumber; clear away
desinfe(c)tar *v/t* disinfect
desinteligência *f* misunderstanding
desinteress|ado disinterested; uninterested; **~ar-se** *v/r* lose interest
desinteresse *m* disinterestedness
desist|ência *f* desistance; **~ir** *v/i* desist, give up
desleal disloyal
desleix|ado slovenly, negligent; **~ar** *v/t*, *v/i* neglect; become negligent; **~o** *m* slovenliness, negligence
desligar *v/t* untie, unfasten; switch off; ring off
desliz|ar *v/i* slip, slide; **~e** *m* faux pas
desloc|ação *f* dislocation; **~ar** *v/t* dislocate
deslumbrar *v/t* dazzle
desmai|ado fainted; pale; **~ar** *v/i* faint
desmanchar *v/t*, *v/r* disarrange; undo
desmascarar *v/t*, *v/r* unmask
desmazelado slovenly
desmazelo *m* slovenliness
desmedido excessive
desment|ido *m* denial; **~ir** *v/t* belie; deny
desmesurado excessive, enormous
desmont|ar *v/t*, *v/i*, *v/r* dismantle, take to pieces; dismount; **~ável** collapsible
desmoraliz|ação *f* demoralization; **~ar** *v/t* demoralize
desmoron|amento *m* collapse, cave-in; **~ar** *v/i*, *v/r* demolish; cave in
desnatado skimmed
desnaturado unnatural
desnecessário unnecessary
desnivelado uneven
desnorte|ado bewildered; **~ar** *v/t* put off course; bewilder
desnudar *v/t* strip, denude
desobed|ecer *v/t*, *v/i* disobey; **~iência** *f* disobedience; **~iente** disobedient
desobstruir *v/t* disencumber; clear of obstructions
desocup|ação *f* leisure; **~ado** idle; vacant, unoccupied; **~ar** *v/t* vacate; evacuate
desol|ação *f* desolation; **~ado** desolate; **~ar** *v/t* desolate; lay waste
desonestidade *f* dishonesty
desonesto dishonest
desonrar *v/t* dishono(u)r
desord|eiro *adj*, *s* rowdy; **~em** *f* rowdiness; disorder; **~enado** disordered; disorderly
desorganiz|ação *f* disorganization; **~ar** *v/t* disorganize
desorient|ação *f* disorientation; bewilderment; **~ar** *v/t*, *v/r* mislead; lead astray; bewilder
despach|ar *v/t*, *v/i*, *v/r* make haste; expedite; dispatch;

fam kill zap; **~o** *m* dispatch
despedaçar *v/t* smash to pieces, shatter
desped|ida *f* leave taking, good-bye; **~ir** *v/t, v/r* say good-bye, take leave; dismiss
despegar *v/t* detach
despeito *m* spite; **a ~ de** in spite of
despejar *v/t* empty; pour out
despenh|adeiro *m* precipice; **~ar** *v/r* crash
despensa *f* pantry, larder
despercebido unnoticed
desperd|içar *v/t* waste, squander; **~ício** *m* waste; **~ícios** *m/pl* refuse, waste products
despert|ador *m* alarm-clock; **~ar** *v/t, v/i* wake (up), awake(n); **~o** awake
despesa *f* expense
desp|ido naked; bare; **~ir** *v/t, v/r* take off; undress
despistar *v/t* mislead; throw off the track
despojo *m* loot, spoils, booty
despontar *v/i* break
desport|ista *f, m* sportswoman, sportsman; **~ivo** sports, sporting; **~o** *m* sport
despovoar *v/t* depopulate
despregar *v/t* draw out; unfurl; **~ os olhos de** take one's eyes off
desprend|er *v/t, v/r* loose, unfasten; **~imento** *m* loosening; indifference
despreocupação *f* carelessness
despreocupado care-free, unconcerned
desprevenido unwary; unprovided
desprez|ar *v/t* despise; disregard; **~ível** despicable
desprezo *m* scorn, contempt
desproporcionado disproportionate
despropositado ill-timed; absurd
despropósito *m* nonsense, absurdity
desregr|ado unruly; **~amento** *m* unruliness
desrespeito *m* disrespect
destacar *v/t, v/r* detach; project, surpass
destapar *v/t* uncover; take the top off …
destemido fearless, bold
destemperado uncontrolled
desterrar *v/t* banish, exile
desterro *m* banishment, exile
destilar *v/t* distil
destin|ar *v/t, v/r* determine; destine; **~atário** *m* addressee
destino *m* destiny; destination
destitu|ição *f* dismissal; **~ir** *v/t* deprive of; dismiss, discharge
desto|ante discordant; out-of-key; **~ar** *v/i* jar
destreza *f* skill, dexterity
destrinçar *v/t* specify, particularize
destro dext(e)rous, skil(l)ful
destroçar *v/t* destroy; ruin; shatter
destroço *m* destruction, havoc; **~s** *m/pl* wreck(age)
destru|ição *f* destruction; **~ir**

v/t destroy
desumano inhuman
desun|ião *f* disunion; **~ir** *v/t* disunite, separate
desuso *m* disuse
desvair|ado *adj* bewildered; **~ar** *v/t, v/i, v/r* distract, mislead, bewilder
desvalorização *f* devaluation
desvalorizar *v/t* devalue
desvanec|er *v/t, v/r* fade, vanish; dissipate; **~imento** *m* disappearance
desvant|agem *f* disadvantage; **~ajoso** disadvantageous
desvão *m* loft, attic
desvario *m* extravagance
desvelar *v/t, v/r* unveil, reveal; be zealous; keep awake
desvendar *v/t* unveil, disclose
desventur|a *f* misfortune; **~ado** unfortunate
desvi|ar *v/t, v/r* divert; deviate; embezzle; go astray; **~o** *m* deviation; diversion; detour
detalh|ar *v/t* describe minutely; **~e** *m* detail
detenção *f* detention
deter *v/t, v/r* detain; stop
detergente *m* detergent
deterior|ação *f* deterioration; **~ar** *v/t* deteriorate
determin|ação *f* determination; **~ar** *v/t, v/r* decide, determine
detest|ar *v/t* detest; **~ável** detestable
detido hindered, detained
detonação *f* detonation
detrás behind
deturpar *v/t* alter, disfigure
Deus *m* God; **♀a** *f* goddess
devagar *adv* slowly
devan|ear *v/t, v/i* muse, daydream; **~eio** *m* fancy, daydream
devass|idão *f* debauchery; **~o** *adj* debauched
devast|ação *f* devastation; **~ar** *v/t* lay waste, devastate
devedor *m* debtor
dever *v/t* owe; ought; must; *m* duty
deveras truly, indeed
devido *adj* due; proper; **~ a** owing to
devoção *f* devotion
devolução *f* devolution
devolver *v/t* give back, return
devorar *v/t* devour
devotar *v/t* devote to
dez ten
dezanove nineteen
dezasseis sixteen
dezassete seventeen
Dezembro *m* December
dezoito eighteen
dia *m* day; **~ a ~** day by day; **~ de anos** birthday; **~ feriado** holiday; **~ útil** working day, workday; **~ sim, ~ não** every other day
diabo m devil
diáfano diaphanous
diale(c)to *m* dialect
diálogo *m* dialog(ue)
diamante *m* diamond
diâmetro m diameter
diante in front; **~ de** in front of, before; **em ~** henceforth, here-

after
dianteira *f* front, vanguard
diapositivo *m* slide
diária *f* daily expense; daily charge
diário *adj* daily; *m* daily newspaper; diary
di(c)ção *f* diction
dicionário *m* dictionary
dieta *f* diet
difam|ação *f* defamation; **~ante** defamatory; **~ar** *v/t* defame
diferenç|a *f* difference; **~ar** *v/t* distinguish, differentiate
diferente different
diferir *v/t*, *v/i* differ; defer
difícil difficult
dificuldade *f* difficulty
dificultar *v/t* make difficult
difundir *v/t*, *v/r* diffuse
difusão *f* diffusion
digerir *v/t*, *v/i* digest
digestão *f* digestion
digi|tação *f* COMP input; **~tal** digital; **impressões** *f/pl* **~tais** fingerprints; **~tar** *v/t* key in
dignar-se *v/r* deign
dignidade *f* dignity
digno worthy
digressão *f* digression
dilacerar *v/t* dilacerate
dilat|ação *f* dilation; **~ar** *v/t*, *v/r* dilate
diligência *f* diligence
diligenciar *v/i* exert oneself, do one's best
diligente diligent
diluir *v/t* dilute
dilúvio *m* deluge
dimensão *f* dimension
diminu|ição *f* diminution; **~ir** *v/t*, *v/i* diminish
diminutivo *m* diminutive
diminuto tiny, minute
dinamarquês *m* Dane; *adj* Danish
dinamite *f* dynamite
dinheirão *m* large sum of money
dinheiro *m* money
diploma *m* diploma
diplom|acia *f* diplomacy; **~ata** *m*, *f* diplomat; **~ático** diplomatic
dique *m* dike
dire(c)|ção *f* direction; administration; steering; **~tivo** directive; **~to** direct; **~tor** *m* director; **~tório** COMP directory
direita *f* right hand; **à ~** on/to the right; **às ~s** as it should be, upright
direito *m* law; right duty, tax; *adj* straight; right
dirig|ente *m* manager, director; **~ir** *v/t*, *v/r* address; run, manage; conduct; make for; direct
dis
car *v/t*, *v/i* dial
discern|imento *m* discernment; **~ir** *v/t* discern
disciplin|a *f* discipline; subject; **~ar** *v/t* discipline; *adj* disciplinary
discípulo *m* disciple
disco *m* disc; record; **~ compacto** compact disc, CD; **~ rígido** COMP hard disk
discord|ância *f* discord(ance), disagreement; **~ar** *v/i* discord,

dissent

discórdia *f* discord

discorrer *v/i* ponder; talk

discrepância *f* discrepancy

discreto discreet

discrição *f* discretion; **à ~ at** will, at one's discretion

discurs|ar (**sobre**) *v/i* discourse (up)on; **~o** *m* discourse

discussão *f* discussion

discutir *v/t*, *v/i* discuss

disfarç|ado disguised, in disguise; **~ar** *v/t* disguise

disfarce *m* disguise

disforme deformed

disparar *v/t* shoot, fire

disparatado foolish, silly

disparat|ar *v/i* blunder; talk nonsense; **~e** *m* nonsense, rubbish

dispendioso expensive, costly, dear

dispens|a *f* exemption; **~ar** *v/t* exempt, excuse

dispensário *m* dispensary

dispensável dispensable

dispersar *v/t*, *v/i* disperse

disponibilidade *f* availability

disponível available

dispor *v/t*, *v/i*, *v/r* count on; settle, decide; dispose; arrange; prepare; *m* disposal; **ao seu ~** at your disposal

disposi|ção *f* disposition; **~tivo** *m* contrivance, device, gear

disposto *adj* disposed, inclined; **bem ~** feeling fine, in good fettle; **mal ~** indisposed; in a mood

disput|a *f* dispute; **~ar** *v/t* dispute; **~ável** disputable

dissabor *m* annoyance, nuisance

dissecar *v/t* dissect

disseminar *v/t* disseminate

dissert|ação *f* dissertation; **~ar sobre** *v/i* discourse on

dissid|ência *f* dissidence; **~ente** *adj*, *m*, *f* dissident

dissimul|ação *f* dissimulation; **~ar** *v/t*, *v/i* disguise, dissemble

dissipar *v/t* dissipate

dissolu|ção *f* dissolution; **~to** dissolute

dissol|úvel dissoluble; **~vente** *m*, *f* dissolvent; **~ver** *v/t*, *v/r* dissolve

dissonância *f* dissonance

dissuadir *v/t* dissuade

distância *f* distance

distanciar *v/t*, *v/r* move away; (out)distance

distante distant, far-off

distar *v/i* be distant

distensão *f* distension

distinção *f* distinction

distinguir *v/t*, *v/r* distinguish

distintivo *m* badge; *adj* distinctive

distinto distinct

distra(c)ção *f* distraction

distraído distracted, absent-minded

distrair *v/t*, *v/r* amuse, entertain; distract

distribu|ição *f* distribution; **~ir** *v/t* distribute; **~tivo** distributive

distrito *m* district

distúrbio *m* disorder, row, riot,

disturbance
dita *f* good luck
ditado *m* dictation; proverb, saying
ditad|or *m* dictator; **~ura** *f* dictatorship
ditame *m* dictate
ditar *v/t* dictate
ditoso fortunate
diurno *adj* daily
divã *m* divan
divag|ação *f* divagation, digression; **~ar** *v/i* digress
diversão *f* diversion; pastime
diverso diverse; **~s** various, several
divert|ido amusing; **~imento** *m* amusement; entertainment; **~ir** *v/t*, *v/r* divert; amuse; enjoy oneself
dívida *f* debt
dividir *v/t* divide
divin|dade *f* divinity; **~o** *adj* divine
divisa *f* emblem, motto, device; exchange rate
divisão *f* division; room
divisar *v/t* discern, descry
divórcio *m* divorce
divulg|ação *f* divulgence; **~ar** *v/t* divulge; spread
dizer *v/t*, *v/i*, *v/r* say, tell, speak; **~ respeito a** concern; **a bem ~** properly speaking; **por assim ~** so to speak
do *contr of* **de** *and* **o**
dó *m* pity, compassion
doação *f* donation
doar *v/t* donate
dobra *f* fold, tuck
dobradiça *f* hinge
dobra *v/t*, *v/i* fold; double; bend, yield
dobre *adj* double; *m* knell
dobro *m* double
doca *f* dock
doçaria *f* confectioner's (shop); sweets
doce *m* sweet; *adj* sweet; mild, gentle
dócil docile
documento *m* document
doçura *f* sweetness
doen|ça *f* disease, sickness, illness; **~te** *m*, *f* patient; *adj* sick, ill; **~tio** sickly
doer *v/i* ache, hurt
doid|ice *f* foolishness, madness; **~o** *adj* silly, mad
dois *m* two
doloroso painful; sorrowful; grievous
dom *m* gift; endowment
dom|ador *m* tamer; **~ar** *v/t* tame
doméstico domestic
dom-fafe *m* zoo bullfinch
domicílio *m* domicile
domin|ação *f* domination; **~ante** *adj* dominant; **~ar** *v/t*, *v/i* control; overlook; dominate
domingo *m* Sunday
domínio *m* dominion; domain; control
dona *f* Mrs; owner; **~ de casa** housewife
donaire *m* grace, charm
donativo *m* donation, gift
donde from where

dono *m* master, owner, proprietor; ~ **de casa** master of the house; ~ **da taverna** innkeeper
dor *f* pain; grief
dormente *adj* asleep, numb
dorm|ida *f* night's lodging; **~ir** *v/t, v/i* sleep; **~itório** *m* dormitory; *Braz* bedroom
dorso *m* back
dos|ar *v/t* dose; **~e** *f* dose
dot|ação *f* endowment, foundation; **~ar** *v/t* endow; **~e** *m* dowry
dourar *v/t* gild
dout|o learned; **~or** *m* doctor
doutrin|a *f* doctrine; **~ação** *f* indoctrination; **~ar** *v/t* indoctrinate
download *m* COMP download
doze twelve
dragão *m* dragon; MIL dragoon
dragar *v/t* dredge
dram|a *m* drama, play; **~ático** dramatic; **~atizar** *v/t* dramatize; **~aturgo** *m* dramatist, playwright
drive *f* **de disquetes** COMP disk drive
drog|a *f* drug; **~aria** *f* chemist's, drugstore; **~uista** *m, f* druggist
dualismo *m* dualism
duas *f of* **dois**
dúbio doubtful, dubious
ducha *f*, **duche** *m* douche, shower
dúctil ductile
duelo *m* duel
duende *m* goblin
dueto *m* duet
duna *f* dune
duplic|ação *f* duplication; **~ar** *v/t* duplicate
duplo *adj* double; **fazer ~ clique** COMP double click
duque *m* duke; **~sa** *f* duchess
duração *f* duration
durante during
dur|ar *v/i* last; **~ável** durable
dur|eza *f* hardness, toughness; **~o** hard
dúvida *f* doubt
duvid|ar *v/t, v/i* doubt; **~oso** dubious; doubtful
duzentos two hundred
dúzia *f* dozen
DVD *m* DVD; **~-ROM** *m* DVD-ROM

E

e and
ébano *m* ebony
ébrio *adj* drunk
ebulição *f* ebullition
eclesiástico *adj* ecclesiastical; *m* ecclesiastic
eclipse *m* eclipse
eco *m* echo; **~ar** *v/t, v/i* echo
economia *f* economy; economics; **~s** *f/pl* savings
económico economic(al)
economizar *v/t, v/i* save, econ-

omize
edição *f* edition
edific|ação *f* edification; **~ar** *v/t* edify; build
edifício *m* building
edital *m* notice, order
editar *v/t* edit; publish
édito *m* notice, edict
editor *m* publisher
edredão *m* eider-down
educação *f* education; **~ ambiental** environmental education
educa|dor *m* educator; **~r** *v/t* educate; **~tivo** educative
efe(c)ti|vamente in fact, really; effectively; **~vidade** *f* effectiveness; **~vo** *adj* effective
efe(c)tuar *v/t* effect(uate)
efeito *m* effect; **com ~** indeed
efémero ephemeral
efeminado effeminate
efervescência *f* effervescence
efic|ácia *f* efficacy; **~az** effective, efficient
efusão *f* effusion
egoísmo *m* egoism
egoísta *m*, *f* egoist; *adj* egoistical, selfish
égua *f* mare
eira *f* threshing-floor
eis here is, here are
eixo *m* axle; axis
ela she; it; her
elabor|ação *f* elaboration; **~ar** *v/t* elaborate
elasticidade *f* elasticity
elástico *adj*, *m* elastic
ele he; it; him
ele(c)tricidade *f* electricity
elé(c)trico *adj* electric; *m* tram
ele(c)trifi|cação *f* electrification; **~car** *v/t* electrify
elefante *m* elephant
eleg|ância *f* elegance; **~ante** *adj* elegant
eleger *v/t* elect, choose
elei|ção *f* election; **~to** *adj* elected, chosen; **~tor** *m* elector; **~torado** *m* electorate; **~toral** electoral
elementar elementary
elemento *m* element
elev|ação *f* elevation; **~ador** *m* lift, US elevator; **~ar** *v/t* elevate; raise
elimin|ação *f* elimination; **~ar** *v/t* eliminate
elo *m* link; BOT tendril
elog|iar *v/t* praise; **~io** *m* praise; eulogy
eloqu|ência *f* eloquence; **~ente** eloquent
elucidar *v/t* elucidate
em *prp* in; into; at; on; **~ casa** at home
emagrec|er *v/t*, *v/i* lose weight, get thin; **~imento** *m* emaciation
e-mail *m* e-mail; **enviar um ~** e-mail
emanar *v/i* emanate from
emancip|ação *f* emancipation; **~ar** *v/t*, *v/r* emancipate
emaranhar *v/t* entangle
embaciar *v/t*, *v/i* steam up; dull, dim, tarnish
embaixad|a *f* embassy; **~or** *m* ambassador
embal|agem *f* crating, packing;

~ar *v/t* lull, rock; wrap, pack
embandeirar *v/t* flag
embaraçado embarrassed, ill at ease
embaraç|ar *v/t* embarrass; disturb; **~o** *m* embarrassment; **~oso** embarrassing; perplexing
embarca|ção *f* boat, ship; **~douro** *m* landing-stage; **~r** *v/t*, *v/i* embark
embargo *m* embargo; seizure, distraint; **sem ~** nevertheless
embarque *m* embarcation
embasbacado gaping, aghast
embat|e *m* collision; impact; **~er** *v/i* collide
embebedar *v/t*, *v/r* intoxicate
embebido drenched, soaked; *fig* enraptured
embelezer *v/t* embellish, beautify
embirrar *v/i* be obstinate, be stubborn; **~ com** dislike
emblema *m* emblem
embocadura *f* mouth; mouthpiece
êmbolo *m* piston
embolsar *v/t* pocket
embora *conj* (al)though
emborrachar *v/t* intoxicate
emboscada *f* ambush
embranquecer *v/t*, *v/i* whiten; bleach; grow white
embravecer-se *v/r* get rough
embriag|ar *v/t*, *v/r* intoxicate; enrapture; **~uez** *f* intoxication, drunkenness
embriagem *f* MEC clutch
embrião *m* embryo
embroma *m* *Braz* humbug, cheating
embrulh|ada *f* imbroglio; mess; **~ar** *v/t*, *v/r* confuse; wrap up, pack; **~o** *m* parcel, packet
embuçar *v/t* disguise
embuste *m* artifice, trick
emend|a *f* emendation, amendment; **~ar** *v/t*, *v/r* amend, emend; improve
ementa *f* menu
emerg|ência *f* emergence; emergency; **~ir** *v/i* emerge
emigr|ação *f* emigration; **~ado** *m* émigré; **~ante** *m*, *f* emigrant; **~ar** *v/i* emigrate
eminente eminent
emiss|ão *f* emission; broadcast; **~or** *m* transmitter; **~ora** *f* broadcasting station
emitir *v/t* emit; broadcast
emoção *f* emotion, excitement
emocion|ante thrilling, moving, exciting; **~ar** *v/t*, *v/r* excite
emoldurar *v/t* frame, encase
empacotar *v/t* pack up, bale
empada *f* pie
empadão *m* pie
empalidecer *v/i* grow pale
emparelhar *v/t*, *v/i* couple, pair, match
empatado drawn
empat|ar *v/t*, *v/i* tie, draw; **~e** *m* tie, draw, dead heat
empe|cer *v/t*, *v/i* impede, hinder; **~cilho** *m* hindrance, snag
empeçonhar *v/t* poison
empedernir *v/t*, *v/i* petrify
empedr|ado *m* stone-pavement; **~ar** *v/t* pave

empenh|ar *v/t, v/r* exert oneself; pawn, pledge; mortgage; **~o** *m* pawn, pledge; mortgage; desire; diligence
empilhar *v/t* head up; pile up
empinar *v/t, v/r* tip up, rear
emplast(r)o *m* plaster
empobrec|er *v/t, v/i* impoverish; grow poor; **~imento** *m* impoverishment
empola *f* blister
empolgar *v/t* grip; grasp, seize
empório *m* emporium; *Braz* grocer's (shop)
empossar *v/t, v/r* take possession (of)
empreend|er *v/t* undertake; **~imento** *m* undertaking, enterprise
empregada *f* (**doméstica**) maid, servant
empreg|ado *m* employee; clerk; **~ar** *v/t* employ; use; **~o** *m* use; employment; job
empreit|ada *f* piece-work; **~eiro** *m* contractor
empresa *f* undertaking, enterprise; firm, company
emprestar *v/t* lend, US loan
empréstimo *m* loan; borrowing
empunhar *v/t* grasp, grip
empurr|ão *m* push, shove; **~ar** *v/t* push, shove
emudecer *v/t, v/i* silence; become silent
enaltecer *v/t* extol, exalt
enamorar-se de *v/r* fall in love with
encade|amento *m* connection; chaining; concatenation; **~ar** *v/t* chain, link together
encaderna|ção *f* binding, bookbinding; **~dor** *m* bookbinder; **~r** *v/t* bind
encaixar *v/t, v/i* fit (in); pack; encase; enchase
encaixilhar *v/t* frame
encaixotar *v/t* pack; encase
encalhar *v/t, v/i* strand; run aground
encaminhar *v/t, v/r* make for; set on the right road; guide
encanar *v/t* canalize
encandear *v/t* dazzle
encantado delighted; enchanted
encant|ador *m* sorcerer; *adj* charming; **~amento** *m* enchantment; **~ar** *v/t* delight; enchant; charm; **~o** *m* enchantment; charm; spell
encapelado rough
encapotar *v/t* cloak; disguise; muffle
encarar *v/t* face; face up to
encarcerar *v/t* imprison, incarcerate
encardido soil
encarec|er *v/t, v/i* raise the price; enhance; exaggerate; **~imento** *m* enhancement
encargo *m* charge, office; order, commission
encarnado *adj, m* red
encarniçado bloodthirsty, fierce, relentless
encarregar *v/t, v/r* undertake; charge, entrust; order
encen|ação *f* staging; **~ar** *v/t*

stage
encer|ado *m* oilcloth, linoleum; **~ar** *v/t* wax
encerr|amento *m* close; **~ar** *v/t* enclose; close
encetar *v/t* begin, start
encharcar *v/t* soak, drench
ench|ente *f* flood; highwater; THEAT full house; **~er** *v/t*, *v/i*, *v/r* fill
enciclopédia *f* encyclop(a)edia
enclausurar *v/t* enclose
encoberto *adj* overcast, dull; concealed, hidden
encobrir *v/t* hide, conceal
encolher *v/t*, *v/i* shrink; **~ os ombros** shrug one's shoulders
encolhido *adj* shrunk
encomend|a *f* order, commission; **~ar** *v/t*, *v/r* order, commission; entrust
encontr|ão *m* jostle; **~ar** *v/t*, *v/i*, *v/r* find; encounter, meet; **~o** *m* encounter, meeting
encorajar *v/t* encourage
encorpado substantial; bulky
encost|a *f* declivity, slope; **~ar** *v/t*, *v/r* prop (up); lean on; **~o** *m* prop; back
encrespado choppy
encrespar *v/t*, *v/r* ripple, get choppy; curl, crisp, frizzle
encruzilhada *f* crossroads
encurtar *v/t* shorten, curtail
encurvar *v/t* bend, arch
endereçar *v/t* address;
endereço *m* address; **~ de e--mail** e-mail address
endiabrado devillish; mischievous
endinheirado well-off, rich
endireitar *v/t*, *v/i*, *v/r* straighten (up)
endividado in debt
endividar *v/t*, *v/r* run into debt
endoidecer *v/t*, *v/i* go mad
endoss|ado *m* endorsee; **~ante** *m* endorser; **~ar** *v/t* endorse; **~o** *m* endorsement
endurec|er *v/t*, *v/i*, *v/r* harden; **~imento** *m* hardness
enegrecer *v/t*, *v/i*, *v/r* blacken
energia *f* energy
enérgico energetic
enevoado cloudy; foggy; misty
enevoar *v/t* dim, blur, cloud
enfad|ar *v/t*, *v/r* weary, annoy; **~o** *m* annoyance; drudgery; **~onho** troublesome, tiresome
ênfase *f* emphasis
enfastiar *v/t*, *v/i*, *v/r* weary, disgust
enfático emphatic
enfeitar *v/t* embellish, adorn
enfeite *m* adornment, ornament
enferm|ar *v/i* fall ill; **~aria** *f* ward, sickbay; **~eira** *f* nurse; **~eiro** *m* male nurse; **~idade** *f* infirmity, sickness, illness; **~o** *adj* infirm
enferrujado rusty
enferrujar *v/t*, *v/i* rust
enfezado lean, rickety
enfiar *v/t* thread; slip on
enfim finally, at last
enforcar *v/t* hang
enfraquecer *v/t*, *v/i* weaken;

enfeeble
enfrentar *v/t* confront, face
enfurecer *v/t, v/i, v/r* infuriate, enrage; rage
engan|ar *v/t, v/r* deceive; be mistaken; **~o** *m* deceit; mistake; trick; delusion
engarrafamento *m* congestion, traffic jam
engarrafar *v/t* bottle
engasgar *v/t, v/r* choke; gag
engatar *v/t* cramp, couple
engelhar *v/t, v/i, v/r* wrinkle, shrivel
engenharia *f* engineering; **engenheiro** *m* engineer
engenh|o *m* talent, wit, skill; mill; **~oso** ingenious, witty
engodo *m* allurement; decoy; snare
engolir *v/t* swallow
engordar *v/t, v/i* fatten; grow fat
engraçado pleasant; funny
engrandec|er *v/t, v/i* aggrandize; enlarge; **~imento** *m* aggrandizement
engraxar *v/t* black, polish
engrenagem *f* gear, gearing
engripado down with flu
engrossar *v/t, v/i* swell, thicken
enguia *f* eel
enguiç|ar *v/t* bewitch; **~o** *m* bad omen, ill-luck
enigma *m* enigma, puzzle
enjeitar *v/t* reject; repudiate
enjoado seasick
enjoar *v/t, v/i, v/r* sicken, nauseate; be seasick
enjoo *m* seasickness
enla|çar *v/t* bind, entwine, entangle; **~ce** *m* union, joining; marriage
enlamear *v/t* splash, spatter with mud
enlatar *v/t* can
enle|ado perplexed; **~ar** *v/t* fasten, attach; perplex
enleio *m* perplexity
enlevar *v/t, v/r* charm; enrapture
enlevo *m* ecstasy, rapture
enlouquecer *v/t, v/i* madden; go mad
enobrecer *v/t, v/r* ennoble
enoj|ar *v/t* disgust; **~o** *m* disgust, nausea
enorme enormous
enquanto while; **por ~** for the time being
enraizar *v/t, v/i, v/r* root, take root
enrasc|adela *f* scrape, fix; **~ar** *v/t* ensnare
enredar *v/t, v/i, v/r* entangle, ensnare, embroil
enredo *m* intrigue; plot
enregelar *v/t, v/i* freeze
enrijecer *v/t, v/i* harden, stiffen
enriquecer *v/t, v/i* enrich; get rich
enrodilhar *v/t* twist
enrolar *v/t* roll up, wrap
enroscar *v/t, v/r* twist; coil up
enrouquecer *v/t, v/i* get hoarse
enrugar *v/t, v/i, v/r* crease; wrinkle
ensaboar *v/t* soap; *fig* scold
ensai|ar *v/t* rehearse; test; **~o** *m* essay; rehearsal; test; attempt

ensanguentado blood--stained
ensejo *m* opportunity
ensin|ar *v/t* teach, instruct; **~o** *m* instruction, teaching
ensopado *adj* drenched
ensopar *v/t, v/r* sop; drench
ensurdecer *v/t, v/i* deafen; grow deaf
entabular *v/t* start, open
entalar *v/t* stick, pinch
entalhar *v/t, v/i* carve, engrave
entanto meanwhile; **no ~** nevertheless
então *int* what!; well then; now then!; *adj* then
entardecer *v/i* grow dark
ente *m* being; creature
entead|a *f* stepdaughter; **~o** *m* stepson
entend|er *v/t* understand; mean; *m* opinion; **~ido** experienced, skilful; understood; **~imento** *m* understanding
enternec|er *v/t, v/r* move, touch; **~imento** *m* tenderness
enterr|ar *v/t, v/r* sink; bury, inter; **~o** *m* burial, interment
entesar *v/t* stretch, stiffen
entidade *f* entity
entoação *f* intonation
entoar *v/t* intone
entontecer *v/t, v/i* stun
entornar *v/t, v/i, v/r* spill; upset
entorpec|er *v/t* numb; **~imento** *m* torpor
entortar *v/t, v/i, v/r* twist; crook; **~ os olhos** (have a) squint
entrada *f* entry; entrance; entrance fee; beginning; first course
entranh|ar *v/t, v/r* penetrate; drive into; **~as** *f/pl* entrails, bowels
entrar (em) *v/i* enter, go in
entrave *m* encumbrance; trammels
entre among; between
entreab|erto ajar; **~rir** *v/t* open half-way; leave ajar
entrecosto *m* rib
entreg|a *f* delivery; **~ar** *v/t, v/r* deliver; give over/up to; hand over; **~ue a** delivered; given over to
entrelaçar *v/t* interlace
entrem|ear *v/t* intermingle, intermix; **~eio** *m* interstice; interim
entrementes *adv* meanwhile
entretanto *adv* meanwhile
entret|enimento *m* amusement, entertainment; **~er** *v/t, v/r* amuse, entertain
entrevado *adj, m* paralytic
entrever *v/t* glimpse
entrevist|a *f* interview; **~ar** *v/t* interview
entristecer *v/t, v/i* sadden
entroncamento *m* junction
entronização *f* enthronement
entrudo *m* Shrovetide
entulho *m* rubbish
entup|imento *m* blockage; **~ir** *v/t* block, stop up
entusiasm|ar *v/t, v/r* fill with enthusiasm; **~o** *m* enthusiasm
entusi|asta *m, f* enthusiast; *adj* enthusiastic; **~ástico** enthusiastic

enumer|ação *f* enumeration; **~ar** *v/t* enumerate
enunciar *v/t* enunciate
envelhecer *v/t, v/i* age, grow old
envenen|amento *m* poisoning; **~ar** *v/t* poison
envergadura *f* spread, span; scope
envergonh|ado ashamed; **~ar** *v/t, v/r* shame; be ashamed of
envernizar *v/t* varnish
enviar *v/t* send
envidraçar *v/t* glaze
envio *m* remittance, sending
enviuvar *v/t, v/i* become a widow(er)
envolver *v/t* wrap; involve
enxame *m* swarm; **~ar** *v/i* swarm
enxada *f* hoe
enxaguar *v/t* rinse
enxaqueca *f* migraine
enxergar *v/t* discern
enxerto *m* graft
enxofre *m* sulphur
enxotar *v/t* scare away, drive
enxovalhar *v/t* crumple, rumple
enxu|gar *v/t, v/i* dry; **~to** *adj* dry
épico *adj* epic
epidemia *f* epidemic
epidémico epidemic
epílogo *m* epilogue
episcopal episcopal
episódio *m* episode
epitáfio *m* epitaph
época *f* epoch
epopeia *f* epic
equador *m* equator
equil|ibrar *v/t* balance; **~íbrio** *m* balance, equilibrium
equipa *f* team
equipagem *f* crew; supplies
equipamento *m* equipment
equipar *v/t* equip
equiparar *v/t* compare
equitação *f* horsemanship, riding
equitativo equitable
equival|ência *f* equivalence; **~ente** *adj*; *m* equivalent; **~er a** *v/i* be equivalent to
equivocar *v/t, v/r* equivocate; be mistaken, make a mistake
equívoco *adj* equivocal; *m* ambiguity, equivocation
era *f* era
ere(c)ção *f* erection
erguer *v/t, v/r* rise; raise, lift; erect
eriçar *v/t* bristle, stand on end
erigir *v/t* erect
ermo *adj* retired, secluded, waste; *m* desert
eros|ão *f* erosion; **~ivo** erosive
erótico erotic
err|ante erring; wandering, errant; **~ar** *v/t, v/i* miss; err; wander; **~o** *m* error, mistake; fault; **~óneo** erroneous
erudi|ção *f* erudition; **~to** *adj* erudite
erupção *f* eruption
erva *f* grass
ervilha *f* pea
esbaforido panting, gasping
esbanja|dor *adj* extravagant; *m* spendthrift; **~mento** *m* squandering; **~r** *v/t* waste, squander

esbarrar contra *v/i* run into, dash against
esbelto slender, svelte
esboçar *v/t* sketch; draft
esboço *m* sketch; rough draft
esborrachar *v/t* crush, squash
escabeche *m* marinade; uproar
escabroso rough, rugged, craggy; coarse; difficult, ticklish
escada *f* staircase, stairs; **~ de caracol** spiral staircase; **~ rolante** escalator, moving staircase; **~ria** *f* staircase
escala *f* scale; port of call; gamut; **em grande ~** on a large scale; **por ~** in rotation; **fazer ~ em** call at
escalar *v/t* scale, climb up
escaldar *v/t*, *v/i* burn, scald
escalfar *v/i* poach
escalope *m* cutlet
escama *f* scale
escancarar *v/t* throw wide open
escandalizar *v/t*, *v/i*, *v/r* shock, scandalize
escândalo *m* scandal; uproar
escandaloso scandalous
escandinavo *adj* Scandinavian
escangalhar *v/t* make a mess of; break up
escanhoar *v/t* shave
escapar *v/i*, *v/r* escape
escapatória *f* evasion, excuse, loop-hole
escape *m* escape, outlet; **~ de gases** exhaust (pipe)
escaravelho *m* beetle
escarlat|e scarlet; **~ina** *f* scarlatina; scarlet fever
escar|necer *v/t*, *v/i* scoff at; jeer; **~ninho** *adj* scoffing, jeering
escárnio *m* scorn
escarpa *f* slope; scarp
escarr|ar *v/t*, *v/i* spit; **~o** *m* spittle, phlegm
escass|ez *f* scarcity; **~o** scarce, rare; scanty
escavação *f* excavation
escavar *v/t* excavate
esclarec|er *v/t* clear up; enlighten; **~imento** *m* enlightenment
esco|amento *m* drainage; **~ar-se** *v/r* drain off/away
escocês *adj* Scottish, Scotch; *m* Scot, Scotsman
escol *m* élite, pick, cream
escola *f* school
escolh|a *f* choice; selection; **~er** *v/t*, *v/i* choose; select
escolho *m* reef
escolt|a *f* escort; **~ar** *v/t* escort
escombros *m/pl* rubbish, debris; havoc
esconder *v/t*, *v/r* hide; **~ijo** *m* hiding-place
escondidas *f/pl* hide-and-seek; **às ~** in secret, by stealth
esconjur|ar *v/t* exorcize; **~o** *m* exorcism
escopo *m* aim, object
escopro *m* chisel
escora *f* prop, support
escória *f* dross
escorregadi(ç)o slippery
escorregar *v/i* slip, slide

escorrer *v/t, v/i* drain, drip
escov|a *f* brush; **~ar** *v/t* brush
escrav|idão *f* slavery; **~izar** *v/t* enslave; **~o** *m* slave
escrev|er *v/t, v/i* write; **~inhar** *v/t, v/i* scribble
escrit|a *f* writing; **~o** *m* note, bill; **~or** *m* writer; **~ório** *m* office; study; **~ura** *f* deed, indenture; **~uração** *f* book-keeping; **~urar** *v/t* keep the books
escrivaninha *f* desk
escrivão *m* clerk; scribe
escrúpulo *m* scruple
escrutinar *v/t, v/i* count (votes)
escrutínio *m* scrutiny, ballot
escudo *m* shield; escutcheon; escudo (*former Portuguese currency*)
escul|tor *m* sculptor; **~tura** *f* sculpture; **~tural** sculptural
escum|a *f* froth, foam, scum; **~adeira** *f* skimmer; **~oso** frothy, foamy
escuna *f* schooner
escuras: **às ~** in the dark
escur|ecer *v/t, v/i* darken; become dark; **~idão** *f* darkness; obscurity; **~o** dark; obscure
escusado needless
escusar *v/t, v/i* have no need of, needn's; exempt
escutar *v/t, v/i* listen (to)
esfalfar *v/t, v/r* tire out, overwork
esfaquear *v/t* knife, stab
esfarrapado ragged, tattered
esfera *f* sphere
esferográfica *f* ball(-point) pen, biro
esfolar *v/t* flay, skin; strip; fleece
esfomeado hungry, famished
esforç|ado valiant; strong; **~ar-se** *v/r* try hard, strive
esforço *m* effort
esfregar *v/t* scour, scrub, rub
esfri|amento *m* cooling; **~ar** *v/t, v/i* grow cold, cool, chill
esganar *v/t* strangle
esganiçar *v/t, v/r* yelp, screech
esgar *m* grimace
esgaravatar *v/t* scratch, scrape
esgot|ado out of print; exhausted, worn out; **~ar** *v/t, v/r* exhaust; use up
esgoto *m* drain, sewer
esgrim|a *f* fencing; **~ador** *m* fencer; **~ir** *v/i* fence
esguelha *f* slant; **de ~** askance
esguich|ar *v/t, v/i* spurt, squirt; **~o** *m* jet, squirt
esguio thin, slender, lean
eslavo *adj* Slavonic; *m* Slav
esmagador *adj* smashing, crushing
esmagar *v/t* crush, squash
esmalte *m* enamel
esmeralda *f* emerald
esmerar *v/t, v/r* finish to perfection; take pains with
esmero *m* care, pains
esmiuçar *v/t* investigate minutely
esmo: **a ~** at random
esmola *f* alms
esmorecer *v/t, v/i* discourage; lose heart
espaç|ar *v/t* extend, space out; **~o** *m* space, room; COMP space

character, blank; **~oso** spacious
espada *f* sword
espádua *f* shoulder-blade
espairecer *v/t, v/i* amuse
espaldar *m* chair back
espalhafato *m* fuss, bustle
espalhar *v/t, v/r* scatter, spread
espalmar *v/t* flatten
espanador *m* duster
espancar *v/t* spank, thrash
espanhol *adj* Spanish; *m* Spanish; Spaniard; **~ada** *f* swaggering, blustering
espantalho *m* scarecrow
espant|ar *v/t, v/r* frighten; scare away; astonish; **~o** *m* fright; astonishment; **~oso** astonishing
espargo *m* asparagus
esparso sparse, scattered
espatifar *v/t* smash, shatter; squander
espaventoso ostentatious
espavorir *v/t, v/r* frighten
especial special; **em ~** specially; **~idade** *f* speciality; **~ista** *m, f* specialist; **~ização** *f* specialization; **~izar** *v/t, v/r* particularize; specialize
especiaria *f* spice
espécie *f* kind, sort; species
especific|ação *f* specification; **~ar** *v/t* specify
espe(c)t|áculo *m* spectacle; show, performance; **~aculoso** spectacular
espectador *m* spectator, onlooker
espe(c)tro *m* spectre
especul|ação *f* speculation; **~ar** *v/i* speculate
espelhar *v/t, v/r* mirror, reflect
espelho *m* mirror
esper|a *f* wait; delay; expectation; **à ~ de** waiting for; **~ança** *f* hope; **~ar** *v/t, v/i* wait; hope; expect
espert|eza *f* astuteness; sharpness; **~o** astute, sharp
espess|o thick; **~ura** *f* thickness
espetar *v/t* impale, spit
espeto *m* spit
espia *m, f* spy
espi|ão *m* spy; **~ar** *v/t* spy (on)
espicaçar *v/t* peck; prick
espichar *v/t* pierce
espiga *f* ear of corn; pin, bolt; drawback, snag
espinafre *m* spinach
espingarda *f* gun, rifle
espinh|a *f* fish-bone; backbone, spine; **~o** *m* thorn; prickle; trouble; **~oso** thorny; difficult, troublesome
espiolhar *v/t* examine closely
espionagem *f* espionage
espionar *v/t, v/i* spy
espiral *f* spiral
espírito *m* mind; spirit
espiritual spiritual
espirituoso witty; generous, full-bodied; spirituous
espirr|ar *v/i* sneeze; **~o** *m* sneeze
esplêndido splendid
esplendor *m* splendo(u)r
espoli|ação *f* spoliation; **~ar** *v/t* spoliate, despoil

espólio *m* spoils
esponja *f* sponge
esponsais *m/pl* betrothal
espon|taneidade *f* spontaneity; **~tâneo** spontaneous
espor|a *f* spur; **~ear** *v/t* spur (on)
espos|a *f* wife; **~ar** *v/t* marry; **~o** *m* husband
espraiar *v/r* expand, spread
espreguiçar-se *v/r* stretch, sprawl
espreitar *v/t* spy out; peep
espremer *v/t* squeeze (out)
espum|a *f* froth, foam; spray; **~ante** *m* sparkling wine; **~oso** frothy, foamy
esquadr|a *f* fleet; police-station; **~ilha** *f* flotilla; squadron; **~o** *m* set square, *US* triangle
esquartejar *v/t* quarter
esquec|er *v/t, v/r* forget; **~imento** *m* forgetfulness; oblivion
esquel|ético lean; **~eto** *m* skeleton
esquem|a *m* scheme, plan; **~ático** schematic
esquentador *m* boiler, geyser
esquerd|a *f* left; **à ~** to/on the left; **~o** left
esqui *m* ski; **~ aquático** water skiing
esquiador *m* skier
esquife *m* bier; skiff
esquilo *m* squirrel
esquina *f* corner
esquisit|ice *f* eccentricity, oddity; **~o** exquisite; strange, odd
esquiv|ar *v/t, v/r* avoid, shun, disdain; **~o** coy; disdainful; intractable
essa *pron* that; **~ é boa!** that's a good one!
esse *pron* that
essência *f* essence
essencial essential
estabelec|er *v/t, v/r* establish; **~imento** *m* establishment
estabilidade *f* stability
estábulo *m* stable
estac|a *f* stake, prop, pole; **~ada** *f* stockade
estação *f* station; season; **~ de caminho de ferro** railway station; **~ dos correios** post office; **~ emissora** wireless station
estacar *v/t, v/i* stake; prop; stop
estacionamento *m* parking
estacionar *v/i* stop; park
estad(i)a *f* stay
estádio *m* stadium; **~ de futebol** football, *US* soccer stadium
estad|ista *m, f* statesman; **~o** *m* state; condition; **~o-maior** *m* general staff
estaf|a *f* fatigue; **~ar** *v/t, v/i* tire, weary
estágio *m* training, probation
estagn|ação *f* stagnation; **~ante** stagnant; **~ar** *v/i* stagnate
estala|gem *f* inn; **~jadeiro** *m* innkeeper
estalar *v/t, v/i* crack, split; crackle; break out
estaleiro *m* shipyard
estalido *m* crack(le)
estamp|a *f* picture, print; **~ar**

v/t, v/r print, stamp
estampido *m* crash, crack; bang, report
estampilha *f* stamp; slap
estancar *v/t* staunch
estância *f* LIT stanza; spa, resort
estanho *m* tin
estante *f* bookcase; bookshelf
estar *v/i, v/aux* be; ~ **em/de pé** stand
estático static
estatística *f* statistics
estátua *f* statue
estatuir *v/t* establish, decree
estatura *f* height, stature
estatuto *m* statute
estável stable
este *m* east
este *pron* this (one)
esteio *m* prop, stay
esteira *f* mat; wake
estender *v/t, v/i, v/r* extend, stretch
estenograf|ar *v/t* take down in shorthand; **~ia** *f* stenography, shorthand
estenógrafo *m* shorthand typist, *US* stenographer
estepe *f* steppe
esterco *m* dung, manure
estéril sterile
esteril|idade *f* sterility; **~ização** *f* sterilization; **~izar** *v/t* sterilize
estétic|a *f* (a)esthetics; **~o** (a)esthetic
estibordo *m* starboard
esticar *v/t* stretch (out); ~ **a canela/o pernil** kick the bucket
estilhaç|ar *v/t* splinter; **~o** *m* splinter
estilo *m* style
estima *f* esteem
estim|ação *f* estimation; estimate; esteem; **~ar** *v/t* estimate; esteem; **~ável** estimable
estimul|ação *f* stimulation; **~ante** *m* stimulant; **~ar** *v/t* stimulate
estímulo *m* stimulus
estio *m* summer
estiolar *v/t* wither
estipular *v/t* stipulate
estirar *v/t* stretch (out)
estirpe *f* stock, race
estofar *v/t* stuff; upholster
estofo *m* padding; **~s** *m/pl* upholstery
estoirar *v/t, v/i* explode
estojo *m* case, set
estômago *m* stomach, tummy
estontear *v/t* stun, astound
estopa *f* tow; oakum
estopada *f* drudgery
estorninho *m* starling
estorvar *v/t* hinder, encumber
estorvo *m* hindrance, encumbrance, trammels
estouvado heedless, rash, hot-headed
estrábico *adj* cross-eyed
estrabismo *m* squint
estrada *f* road, highway
estrado *m* dais, platform
estrag|ar *v/t* spoil, damage; waste; **~o** *m* damage, havoc
estrangeiro *m* foreigner; *adj* foreign; **no** ~ abroad
estrangular *v/t* strangle
estranh|ar *v/t* wonder at; **~eza** *f*

strangeness; **~o** *adj* strange
estrear *v/t*, *v/r* try on; make one's debut
estreia *f* first night; debut
estreit|ar *v/t*, *v/i*, *v/r* narrow, contract; **~eza** *f* narrowness; **~o** *adj* narrow
estrela *f* star
estrelado starry; fried
estrelar *v/t* star, stud with stars; **~ovos** fry eggs
estremec|er *v/t*, *v/i* shake; frighten; shudder; love tenderly; **~imento** *m* shudder
estrépito *m* noise, din
estribo *m* stirrup
estridente strident
estrito strict
estrofe *f* strophe
estroin|a *adj* wild; hare-brained; **~ice** *f* folly, spree
estrond|o *m* din; **~oso** noisy, clamorous
estropiar *v/t* maim, cripple; mutilate; *fig* spoil
estrume *f* manure
estrutura *f* structure
estud|ante *m*, *f* student; **~ar** *v/t*, *v/i* study; **~ioso** studious
estúdio *m* studio
estudo *m* study
estufa *f* stove; hothouse, greenhouse
estufado *m* stew
estufar *v/t* stew
estupefacto stupefied
estupendo stupendous
estupidez *f* stupidity
estúpido stupid
estupor *m* stupor
esturrado scorched
esvaecer *v/i*, *v/r* vanish, disappear
esvaziar *v/t* empty
esvoaçar *v/i* flutter
etapa *f* stage
etern|idade *f* eternity; **~izar** *v/t* etern(al)ize; **~o** eternal
ética *f* ethics
etiqueta *f* etiquette; label
étnico ethnic
etnografia *f* ethnography
eu *pron* I
eucaristia *f* Eucharist
euro *m* euro (*currency*)
europeu *m*, *adj* European
evacu|ação *f* evacuation; **~ado** *m* evacuee; **~ar** *v/t* evacuate
evadir *v/t*, *v/r* evade; escape
evapor|ação *f* evaporation; **~ar** *v/t*, *v/r* evaporate
evasão *f* evasion; escape
eventual contingent; **~idade** *f* contingency, eventuality
evidência *f* evidence
eviden|ciar *v/t*, *v/r* show, make evident; **~te** evident
evit|ar *v/t* avoid; **~ável** avoidable
evocar *v/t* evoke
evolução *f* evolution
exacerbar *v/t* exacerbate
exa(c)t|idão *f* exactitude; **~o** exact
exager|ar *v/t*, *v/i* exaggerate; **~o** *m* exaggeration
exaltação *f* exaltation
exaltado *adj* exalted
exaltar *v/t*, *v/r* lose one's temper; exalt

exame *m* exam(ination)
examinar *v/t* examine
exarar *v/t* engrave; set down in writing
exasper|ação *f* exasperation; **~ar** *v/t*, *v/r* exasperate
exaurir *v/t* exhaust
exausto exhausted
exced|ente *adj* exceeding; *m* surplus; **~er** *v/t*, *v/r* exceed, surpass, excel
excel|ência *f* excellence; excellency; **~ente** excellent
excentricidade *f* eccentricity
excêntrico eccentric
exce(p)|ção *f* exception; **~cionalmente** exceptionally; **~to** except(ing), save; **~tuar** *v/t* except, exclude
excess|ivo excessive; **~o** *m* excess
excit|ação *f* excitation; **~ado** excited; **~ante** *m* stimulant; *adj* stimulating; exciting; **~ar** *v/t* excite, stimulate
exclam|ação *f* exclamation; **~ar** *v/t*, *v/i* exclaim
exclu|ir *v/t* exclude; **~são** *f* exclusion; **~sivo** exclusive
excremento *m* excrement
excret|ar *v/t* excrete; **~o** *m* excretions
excursão *f* excursion; outing
execu|ção *f* execution; **~tar** *v/t* execute; **~tivo** *adj*, *m* executive; **~tor** *m* executor
exempl|ar *m* model, copy; specimen; *adj* exemplary; **~ificar** *v/t* exemplify; **~o** *m* example
exéquias *f/pl* obsequies, funeral rites
exercer *v/t* exercise; practise
exerc|ício *m* exercise; **~itar** *v/t* exercise
exército *m* army
exib|ição *f* exhibition; **~ir** *v/t* exhibit
exig|ência *f* exigence; **~ente** exigent; **~ir** *v/t* exact, demand
exíguo exiguous
exilar *v/t* exile
exílio *m* exile, banishment
exímio eminent
exist|ência *f* existence; **~ente** *adj* existent; **~ir** *v/i* exist
êxito *m* success
êxodo *m* exodus
exorbit|ância *f* exorbitance; **~ante** exorbitant
exort|ação *f* exhortation; **~ar** *v/t* exhort
exótico exotic
expan|dir *v/t*, *v/r* expand; **~são** *f* expansion; **~sivo** expansive
expatriar *v/t* expatriate
expe(c)tativa *f* expectation
expedição *f* expedition; enterprise; dispatch
expediente *m* expedient; office hours; office papers
expedir *v/t* dispatch, forward; expedite
expensas *f/pl* expenses, costs; **a ~ de** at the expense of
experi|ência *f* experience; experiment; **~ente** *adj* experienced
expi|ação *f* expiation, atonement; **~ar** *v/t* expiate, atone

for
expira|ção *f* expiration, expiry; **~r** *v/i* expire
explic|ação *f* explanation; **~ar** *v/t*, *v/r* explain
explícito explicit
explodir *v/i* explode
explora|ção *f* exploration; exploitation; **~dor** *m* explorer; exploiter; **~r** *v/t* explore; exploit
explo|são *f* explosion; **~sivo** *adj*, *m* explosive
expor *v/t*, *v/r* state; express; expose (to); expound
exporta|ção *f* export(ation); **~dor** *m* exporter; **~r** *v/t* export
exposi|ção *f* exhibition; exposition; exposure; **~tor** *m* expositor, exhibitor
express|ão *f* expression; **~ar** *v/t*, *v/r* express; **~ivo** expressive, significant
expresso *adj* express; *m* express (train)
exprimir *v/t*, *v/r* express
expropri|ação *f* expropriation; **~ar** *v/t* expropriate
expuls|ão *f* expulsion; **~ar** *v/t* expel
expurgar *v/t*, *v/r* expurgate
êxtase *m* ecstasy
extasiar *v/t*, *v/r* enrapture
extens|ão *f* extension; extent; **~ivo** extensive
extenso long; extensive; **por ~** in full
extenuar *v/t* extenuate
exterior *adj* exterior, outer; *m* exteror, outside; **~izar** *v/t* exteriorize, express
extermin|ação *f* extermination; **~ar** *v/t* exterminate
externo *adj* external; *m* day-boy
extinção *f* extinction
extinguir *v/t*, *v/r* extinguish
extirpar *v/i* extirpate
extorquir *v/t* extort
extra(c)ção *f* extraction
extra(c)to *m* extract
extradi|ção *f* extradition; **~tar** *v/t* extradite
extrair *v/t* extract
extraordinário *adj* extraordinary
extravag|ância *f* extravagance; **~ante** extravagant
extraviar *v/t*, *v/r* lead astray; embezzle; mislay
extrem|idade *f* extremity, end; **~ista** *m*, *f* extremist; **~o** *adj* last, extreme; *m* extreme
extrínseco extrinsic
exuber|ância *f* exuberance; **~ante** exuberant
exult|ação *f* exultation; **~ante** exultant; **~ar** *v/i* exult

F

fábrica *f* factory
fabric|ação *f* manufacture; **~ante** *m, f* manufacturer; **~ar** *v/t* manufacture; **~o** *m* manufacture
fábula *f* fable
fabuloso fabulous
faca *f* knife
façanha *f* deed, feat
fa(c)ção *f* faction
face *f* face; cheek; front; **à/em ~ de** in view of; **fazer ~ a** face, meet
fachada *f* façade
facho *m* torch
fácil easy
facili|dade *f* facility; **~tar** *v/t* facilitate
fa(c)to *m* fact; deed; event; **de ~** in fact; **ao ~** aware
fa(c)tur|a *f* invoice; account; **~ar** *v/t* invoice
facul|dade *f* faculty; **~tar** *v/t* facilitate; **~tativo** *adj* optional; *m* physician, doctor
fad|a *f* fairy; **~ar** *v/t* destine; **~ário** *m* fate, lot
fadiga *f* fatigue
fado *m* fate; popular song
fagulha *f* spark
faia *f* BOT beech
faiança *f* faience
faina *f* task, work
faisão *m* pheasant
faísca *f* spark
faiscar *v/t, v/i* spark
faixa *f* band, belt; zone; **~ de rodagem** roadway
fala *f* speech; **~dor** *m* chatterer; *adj* talkative; **~r** *v/t, v/i, v/r* speak, talk; **~r de papo** talk big; **~r pelos cotovelos** talk/speak nineteen to the dozen, talk one's head off
falec|er *v/i* die, pass away; **~ido** *adj, m* deceased; **~imento** *m* decease
falência *f* bankruptcy
falésia *f* cliff
falh|a *f* crack, flaw, blemish; **~ar** *v/t, v/i* crack; split; fail; miss
falir *v/i* go bankrupt
fals|ário *m* forger, counterfeiter; **~ear** *v/t* distort, misrepresent; **~idade** *f* falsehood; falsity; **~ificação** *f* falsification, forgery, counterfeit; **~ificar** *v/t* falsify, forge, counterfeit; **~o** *adj* false
falta *f* lack, want, shortage; fault, defect; **por ~ de** for lack of; **sem ~** without fail; **~ de energia** power failure
faltar *v/i* be lacking; fail; miss; lack, need
fama *f* fame, reputation
família *f* family
familiar *adj, m, f* familiar; **~idade** *f* familiarity; **~izar** *v/t, v/r* familiarize (come with)
faminto hungry, starving
famoso famous

fanfarr|ão *m* boaster, braggart, bully; **~onar** *v/i* swagger, brag, boast
fanico *m* small piece; faint
fantasia *f* fancy; fantasy
fantasma *m* phantom; **~goria** *f* phantasmagory
fantástico fantastic
fantoche *m* puppet
fanzine *f* fanzine
faqueiro *m* knife-case
fard|a *f* uniform; livery; **~ar** *v/t* uniform
fardo *m* burden; bale
farejar *v/t*, *v/i* sniff, scent
farelo *m* bran; trifle
farináceo farinaceous
faringe *f* pharynx
farinha *f* flour, meal
farmacêutico *m* chemist, pharmacist
farmácia *f* pharmacy; chemist's (shop)
farol *m* lighthouse; headlight, headlamp; **~im** *m* beacon
farpa *f* banderilla; barb; splinter
farpado barbed
farrapo *m* rag, tatter
farrusco sooty
farsa *f* farce
fart|ar *v/t*, *v/r* satiate, sate; **~o** *adj* sated; full; fed up; **~ura** *f* plenty, abundance
fascin|ação *f* fascination; **~ar** *v/t* fascinate
fase *f* phase
fastio *m* loathing
fatal fatal
fatalidade *f* fatality
fatia *f* slice
fatig|ante tiring; **~ar** *v/t* fatigue, tire
fato *m* suit; *Braz* fact
faust|o *m* pageantry, pomp; *adj* lucky, happy; **~oso** luxurious, gaudy
fava *f* broad bean
favela *f* *Braz* slum
favo *m* honeycomb
favor *m* favo(u)r; **por ~ se faz ~ faça ~** please; **a/em ~ de** on/in behalf of; **~ável** favo(u)rable; **~ecer** *v/t* favo(u)r
fazend|a *f* estate; farm; ranch cloth, material; **~eiro** *m* farmer
fazer *v/t*, *v/i*, *v/r* do; make; be become; **~ anos** celebrate one's birthday; **~ (as vezes) de** take the place of; **~ download** COMP download; **~ duplo clique** COMP double click; **~ por** try to; **~ login** *v/i* COMP login; **~ logon** *v/i* COMP logon; **~ logout** *v/i* COMP log out; **não faz mal** never mind; it doesn't matter
fé *f* faith
fealdade *f* ugliness
febra *f* fibre; lean
febr|e *f* fever; **~il** feverish
fechadura *f* lock
fech|ar *v/t*, *v/i* shut, close; **~ar à chave** lock; **~o** *m* bolt; end; **~o de correr** zip(per)
fecund|ar *v/t*, fecundate; **~o** fecund
feder *v/i* stink
feder|ação *f* federation; **~al** *adj*

federal; **~ar** *v/t* federate
fedor *m* stink, stench
feiç|ão *f* form, aspect; **~ões** *f/pl* features
feijão *m* kidney bean; harico bean; **~ verde** French bean
feijoada *f* beans dish
feio ugly
feira *f* fair, market
feiti|çaria *f* sorcery, witchcraft; **~ceiro** *m* sorcerer; *adj* bewitching; **~ço** *m* sorcery; fetish
feitio *m* temper, manner; shape, form; make
feito *m* feat, deed; *adj* done, made; **é bem ~** it serves you right
feixe *m* bundle, truss, sheaf
fel *m* gall; bitterness
feli|cidade *f* happiness; good luck; **~citações** *f/pl* congratulations; **~citar** *v/t*, *v/r* congratulate; **~z** *adj* happy; lucky, fortunate; **~zardo** *m fam* lucky devil *m*
felpudo shaggy
feltro *m* felt
fêmea *f* female
feminino feminine
fend|a *f* split, crack, rift; **~er** *v/t*, *v/r* split, crack
feno *m* hay
fenómeno *m* phenomenon
fera *f* wild animal
féria *f* weekly wage; **~s** *f/pl* holidays, *US* vacation
feriado *m* holiday
ferida *f* wound; sore
fer|imento *m* wound; **~ir** *v/t*, *v/r* wound; hurt
ferment|ação *f* fermentation; ferment; **~ar** *v/t*, *v/i* ferment; **~o** *m* ferment, yeast, leaven
fer|o wild; **~ocidade** *f* ferocity; **~oz** ferocious
ferradela *f* bite
ferra|dura *f* horseshoe; **~gem** *f* ironwork; hardware
ferramenta *f* tool
ferrão *m* sting
ferreiro *m* (black)smith
ferro *m* iron
ferrolho *m* bolt; latch
ferrovia *f* railway, *US* railroad
ferroviário *m* railwayman
ferrugem *f* rust
ferrugento rusty
fértil fertile
fertil|idade *f* fertility; **~izar** *v/t* fertilize
ferv|ente fervent; seething; **~er** *v/t*, *v/i* boil; seethe
fervor *m* fervo(u)r
fest|a *f* festival; feast; party; **~ança** *f* merrymaking, spree; **~as** *f/pl* caress; **boas-~as** Merry Christmas; Happy New Year; **~ejar** *v/t* celebrate; **~ival** *m* festival; **~ividade** *f* festivity; **~ivo** festive
feto *m* fern; ANAT f(o)etus
Fevereiro *m* February
fiador *m* bailsman; surety
fiambre *m* boiled ham
fiança *f* surety; bail, security
fiar *v/t*, *v/i*, *v/r* spin; trust
fibr|a *f* fibre; nerve; **~oso** fibrous
ficar *v/i* stay, remain; be; **~ com**

keep; ~ **bem** suit (well)
ficção *f* fiction
fich|a *f* counter; plug; card index; **~eiro** *m* filing cabinet
fictício fictitious
fidalg|o *m* nobleman, lord; *adj* noble; **~uia** *f* nobility
fidedigno trustworthy
fidelidade *f* fidelity
fiel *adj* faithful
fígado *m* liver
fig|o *m* fig; **~ueira** *f* fig tree
figura *f* figure
figurar *v/t, v/i* figure; depict
figurino *m* fashion plate
fila *f* file, rank, row
filatelia *f* philately
filete *m* fillet
filh|a *f* daughter; **~o** *m* son
fili|ação *f* filiation; **~al** *adj* filial; *f* branch
filiar *v/t, v/r* affiliate
film|agem *f* filming; **~ar** *v/t* film; **~e** *m* film
filtrar *v/t* filter, strain
filtro *m* filter
fim *m* end; aim; **a ~ de** in order to; **por ~** at last
finado *m* deceased; **dia** *m* **de ~s** All Souls' Day
final *adj, m* final
finalidade *f* purpose; finality
finanças *f/pl* finances
financeiro *m* financier
financi|amento *m* financing; **~ar** *v/t* finance
fincar *v/t* fix, drive
findar *v/t, v/i* end, finish
fineza *f* fineness; kindness
fingido *adj* feigned
fing|imento *m* feigning; pretence; **~ir** *v/t, v/i* feign, pretend
finito finite
finlandês *m* Finn; *adj* Finnish
fin|o fine; thin; shrewd; courteous; **~ura** *f* cunning; finesse; nicety; courtesy
fio *m* thread, yarn; wire
firma *f* firm; signature
firm|e firm; **~eza** *f* firmness
fiscal *adj* fiscal; **~izar** *v/t* supervise, control
físic|a *f* physics; **~o** *m* physicist; physique; *adj* physical
fisionomia *f* physiognomy
fístula *f* fistula
fita *f* ribbon; film; tape; scene
fitar *v/t* stare at
fito *m* aim, purpose; *adj* fixed
fivela *f* buckle
fix|ar *v/t* fix; affix; **~e** reliable; **~o** fixed
flagrante flagrant
flamante flaming; flamboyant
flanela *f* flannel
flauta *f* flute
flecha *f* arrow
flexibilidade *f* flexibility
flexível flexible
floco *m* flake
flor *f* flower; blossom; bloom; **~ação** *f* flowering, blossoming; **~eira** *f* flower-vase; **~escer** *v/t, v/i* flourish
floresta *f* forest
florir *v/i* flower, blossom
flu|ência *f* fluency; **~ente** fluent, flowing; **~ir** *v/i* flow; ooze
flutu|ação *f* fluctuation; **~ar** *v/i* fluctuate; float

fluvial fluvial
fluxo *m* flux; flow
foca *f* seal
focar *v/t* focus
focinho *m* snout, muzzle
foco *m* focus
fofo *adj* soft, puffy, spongy
fogão *m* stove
fogareiro *m* primus (stove)
fogo *m* fire; **~-de-artifício** fireworks
fogoso fiery; hot-tempered
fogueira *f* bonfire
foguete *m* rocket
foice *f* scythe
foicinha *f* sickle
fole *m* bellows
fôlego *m* breath; wind
folga *f* rest, repose; recreation
folgado slack, loose
folgar *v/t*, *v/i* rest; rejoice; widen
folha *f* leaf; sheet; blade; **~ de cálculo** COMP spreadsheet; **~ serviço** personal file, dossier; **novo em ~** brand-new
folhado *m* puff pastry
folhagem *f* foliage
folhear *v/t* thumb through
folhetim *m* feuilleton, serial
folheto *m* booklet, leaflet
fome *f* hunger; famine
foment|ar *v/t* foment; **~o** *m* fomentation
fonte *f* fountain; spring; source, origin; ANAT temple
fora *prp* except; *int* out! off!; *adv* abroad; outside; out; **lá ~** outside; abroad; **~ de si** beside oneself
foragido fugitive
forasteiro *m* stranger
forca *f* gallows
forç|a *f* force, strength; **~ar** *v/t* force, compel; **~oso** inevitable; necessary
forj|a *f* forge, smithy; **~ar** *v/t* forge
forma *f* shape, form; **de ~ que** so that
forma *f* mo(u)ld, last; cake tin
form|ação *f* formation; **~ado** *adj*, *m* graduate; **~al** *adj* formal; **~alidade** *f* formality; **~ar** *v/t*, *v/i*, *v/r* graduate, take one's degree; shape, form; **~ativo** formative; **~ato** *m* format, size, shape; **~atura** *f* formation; degree, graduation
formidável formidable, tremendous
formig|a *f* ant; **~ueiro** *m* ant-hill; tingle, itch; swarm
formos|o beautiful; **~ura** *f* beauty
fórmula *f* formula; form
formular *v/t* formulate
fornalha *f* furnace
fornec|er *v/t*, *v/r* supply, provide; **~imento** *m* supply
forno *m* oven
forrar *v/t* line; cover
forro *m* lining
fort|alecer *v/t* strengthen; fortify; **~aleza** *f* strength; fortress; **~e** *m* fort; *adj* strong; robust
fortific|ação *f* fortification; **~ar** *v/t* fortify
fortuito fortuitous
fortuna *f* fortune; chance

fosco dim
fósforo *m* match
fosso *m* ditch
foto *f* photo; **~cópia** *f* photocopy; **~grafar** *v/t* photograph; **~grafia** *f* photography; photograph, picture; **~grafia** *f* **digital** digital photo; **~gráfico** photographic
fotógrafo *m* photographer
fotómetro *m* exposure meter
foz *f* river mouth
fracass|ar *v/i* fail, collapse; **~o** *m* failure
fra(c)|ção *f* fraction; **~cionar** *v/t* fractionate; **~cionário** fractional
fraco *adj* weak, feeble, frail
fra(c)tura *f* fracture
frade *m* friar
fragata *f* frigate
frágil fragile
fragilidade *f* fragility
fragment|ar *v/t* fragment; **~o** *m* fragment
fragor *m* noise, crash
fralda *f* nappy, *US* diaper; shirt-tail; foot of a hill
framboesa *f* raspberry
francês *m* French(man); *adj* French
franco *adj* frank
franga *f* pullet
frangalho *m* rag, tatter
frango *m* cockerel; chicken
franja *f* fringe; tassel
franqu|ear *v/t* frank; stamp; **~eza** *f* frankness, sincerity
franquia *f* postage
franzir *v/t* pucker, wrinkle; fold; **~ as sobrancelhas** frown
fraqueza *f* weakness, frailty
frasco *f* flask
frase *f* sentence; phrase
fratern|al fraternal; **~idade** *f* fraternity
fraud|e *f* fraud, trick, guile; **~ulento** fraudulent
fregu|ês *m* customer; parishioner; **~esia** *f* parish; customers
freio *m* horse-bit; brake
freira *f* nun
freixo *m* ash(-tree)
frem|ente trembling, quivering; roaring; **~ir** *v/i* quiver; roar
frémito *m* trembling, quivering; roaring
fren|esi(m) *m* frenzy; **~ético** frantic; phrenetic
frente *f* front; face; **à ~ de** at the head of; **em ~ de** opposite
frequ|ência *f* frequency; **~entador** *m* frequenter; **~entar** *v/t* frequent; **~ente** frequent
fresco *adj* fresh; cool
frescura *f* freshness; coolness
fresta *f* cleft; slit
fret|ar *v/t* charter, hire out; **~e** *m* freight; annoyance, trouble
fricassé *m* fricassee
fricção *f* friction
friccionar *v/t* rub
fri|eira *f* chilblain; **~eza** *f* coldness; indifference
frigideira *f* frying-pan, *US* skillet
frígido frigid
frigorífico *m* refrigerator, fridge, *US* ice-box

frincha *f* chink
frio *adj*, *m* cold; **está/faz ~** it's cold; **tenho ~** I'm cold
frisar *v/t* frizzle, curl; emphasize, stress
fritar *v/t* fry
frívolo *adj* frivolous
frondoso leafy
fronha *f* pillow-case/-slip
front|al *adj* frontal; **~e** *f* forehead; front; **~eira** *f* frontier, border; **~eiriço** bordering, adjacent; **~ispício** *m* frontispiece; façade
frota *f* fleet
frouxo *adj* slack, lax, weak
frugal frugal
fruir *v/t* enjoy
frustrar *v/t*, *v/r* frustrate, thwart
frut|a *f* fruit; **~eira** *f* fruit bowl; **~ífero** fruit-bearing; fruitful; **~ificar** *v/i* fructify; **~o** *m* profit, advantage; fruit, fruits; **~uoso** fruitful, profitable
fug|a *f* flight; leak; **~az** fleeting; **~ir** *v/i* flee; **~itivo** *m*, *adj* fugitive
fulano *m* (Mr) so-and-so
fulgor *m* splendo(u)r, gleam
fulgurar *v/i* shine, flash, gleam
fuligem *f* soot
fulminar *v/t* fulminate
fum|aça *f* puff of smoke; smoke; **~ador** *m* smoker; **~ar** *v/t*, *v/i* smoke; **~e(g)ar** *v/i* fume, smoke; **~o** *m* smoke; **~o passivo** passive smoking; **~oso** smoky
fun|ção *f* function; **em ~ção** in working order; **~cionamento** *m* functioning, performance; working; **~cionar** *v/i* function; work; **~cionário** *m* official, civil servant
funda|ção *f* foundation, establishment; **~dor** *m* founder
fundament|al fundamental; **~ar** *v/t*, *v/r* base on; establish; **~o** *m* basis; groundwork; *fig* kernel; foundation
fundar *v/t* found, establish
funeadoiro *m* anchorage
fundear *v/i* cast anchor
fund|ição *f* smelting; foundry; **~ir** *v/t*, *v/r* fuse; cast; smelt
fundo *adj* deep; *m* bottom; **a ~** thoroughly; **no ~** at bottom, in essence; **~s** *m/pl* funds
fúnebre funeral; mournful
funeral *m* funeral
funesto baleful; fatal
fungar *v/t*, *v/i* sniff, snuffle
fungo *m* fungus; mushroom; toadstool
funil *m* funnel
furacão *m* hurricane
fur|ador *m* awl, punch; **~ar** *v/t* bore, pierce, punch
furg|ão *m* luggage-van; **~oneta** *f* delivery van
fúria *f* fury; rage
furioso furious; fierce
furna *f* cavern, cave, den
furo *m* hole, puncture; loop-hole, way out
furor *m* rage, fury
furt|ar *v/t*, *v/r* escape, evade; steal, rob; **~ivo** furtive; **~o** *m* theft, robbery, larceny
fusão *f* fusion; union

fusco *adj* tawny; dusky
fusionar *v/t* amalgamate, fuse with
fusível *m* fuse
fuso *m* spindle
fuste *m* shaft
futebol *m* football, soccer; **~ista** *m, f* footballer
fútil futile
futilidade *f* futility
futura *f* fiancée
futurar *v/t* foretell; *v/i* conjecture
futur|idade *f* futurity; **~ismo** *m* futurism; **~o** *m* future; fiancé
fuzil *m* rifle; **~ar** *v/t* shoot dead; **~aria** *f* volley; fusillade; **~eiro** *m* fusilier

G

gabar *v/t, v/r* boast, brag; praise
gabardina *f* raincoat
gabarola *m, f* boaster
gabinete *m* cabinet; study; office
gado *m* cattle; livestock
gafanhoto *m* grasshopper
gag|o *adj* stammering; *m* stammerer; **~uejar** *v/i* stammer; stutter
gaiato *m* urchin; *adj* romping, boisterous
gaio *m* jay
gaiola *f* cage; jail
gaita *f* mouth-organ, harmonica; **~ de foles** (bag)pipes
gaiteiro *adj* smart, spruce; gay
gaivota *f* sea-gull
gajo *m* guy, type
galant|aria *f* courtliness, gallantry; **~e** *adj* gallant
galão *m* galloon; spring; glass of milky coffee
galego *m, adj* Galician; *Braz* Portuguese
galeria *f* gallery
galgar *v/t, v/i* leap over
galgo *m* greyhound
galheta *f* cruet
galheteiro *m* cruet stand
galho *m* twig, branch; antler
galhofa *f* fun; derision; **fazer ~ de** make fun of, laugh at
galinha *f* hen
galinheiro *m* hen-house
galo *m* cock
galocha *f* galosh, overshoe
galop|ar *v/t, v/i* gallop; **~e** *m* gallop
gama *f* gamut; doe
gamela *f* trough
gamo *m* deer, fallow deer
gana *f* desire, craving
ganância *f* covetousness
ganancioso covetous
gancho *m* hook; hairpin, hair grip
gangrena *f* gangrene
ganh|ar *v/t, v/i* earn; gain; win; **~o** *m* gain, profit
ganir *v/i* yelp
ganso *m* goose, gander
garagem *f* garage
garant|ia *f* guarantee, warran-

ty; **~ir** *v/t* guarantee
garb|o *m* elegance, grace; **~oso** elegant, graceful
garça *f zoo* heron
garção *m Braz* waiter
garço greenish-blue
gare *f* platform
gargo *m* fork
gargalhada *f* laughter; guffaw; chuckle
garganta *f* throat; gorge
gargarejar *v/t, v/i* gargle
garoa *f Braz* drizzle
garoto *m* urchin; lad; white coffee
garra *f* claw
garraf|a *f* bottle; **~ão** *m* demijohn
garrido stylish; bright, gay
gárrulo *adj* garrulous
gás *m* gas
gaseificar *v/t* gasify
gasolina *f* petrol, *US* gas(oline); *m* motor boat
gas|ómetro *m* gasometer, gasholder; **~osa** *f* (fizzy) lemonade, *US* lemon soda
gast|ar *v/t, v/r* spend; wear; waste; use; **~o** *m* expense, charge
gata *f* she-cat
gatilho *m* trigger
gato *m* cat; tom-cat
gatuno *m* pickpocket; pilferer
gaveta *f* drawer
gavião *m* sparrow-hawk
gazela *f* gazelle
gazeta *f* gazette, newspaper; **fazer ~** play truant/hook(e)y
gazua *f* picklock
geada *f* frost
gear *v/t, v/i* freeze; frost
gelado *adj* frozen; icy; *m* ice-cream
gelar *v/t, v/i, v/r* congeal, freeze (up)
gelatin|a *f* gelatin(e); **~oso** gelatinous
geleia *f* jelly
geleira *f* glacier; ice-box
gélido gelid, frozen
gelo *m* ice
gelosia *f* Venetian blind
gema *f* gem; bud; yolk
gémeo *m* twin
gemer *v/t, v/i* groan, moan; wail
gemido *m* groan, moan
general *m* general
generalidade *f* generality
generalizar *v/t, v/i* generalize
género *m* kind, type; gender; **~s** *m/pl* goods, products; **~s alimentícios** groceries
generos|idade *f* generosity; **~o** *adj* generous
genética *f* genetics
geneticamente *adj* genetically; **~mente manipulado** genetically engineered
genético *adj* genetic
gengibre *m* ginger
gengiva *f* gum
génio *m* genius; temper
genital genital
genro *m* son-in-law
gente *f* people; **a ~** we, you, one
gentil *adj* kind; polite; **~eza** *f* kindness; politeness
gentio *m, adj* gentile; heathen
genuino genuine

geografia *f* geography
geologia *f* geology
geração *f* generation
gerador *m* generator
geral *adj* general
gerar *v/t* generate
gerência *f* management
gerente *m*, *f* manager
gerir *v/t* manage, direct
germe *m* germ
germinar *v/i* germinate
gesso *m* plaster of Paris
gestão *f* management, administration
gesto *m* gesture
giesta *f* BOT broom
gigant|e *m* giant; **~esco** gigantic
ginásio *m* gymnasium
ginástica *f* gymnastics
ginja *f* morello (cherry)
ginjinha *f* morello brandy
gira-discos *m* record player, *US* phonograph
girafa *f* giraffe
girar *v/i* gyrate, rotate, spin
girassol *m* sun-flower
giratório gyratory
gíria *f* jargon; argot
giro *m* rotation; turn; stroll, walk; *adj* funny, nice
giz *m* chalk
glacial glacial, icy
glande *f* acorn
glândula *f* gland
glicerina *f* glycerin(e)
global *adj* global **~ização** *f* globalization
globo *m* globe
glória *f* glory
glorific|ação *f* glorification; **~ar** *v/t*, *v/r* glorify
glorioso glorious
glos|a *f* gloss, interpretation; **~ar** *v/t* gloss, interpret
glutão *m* glutton; *adj* gluttonous
goela *f* throat, gullet
goiaba *f* guava
gola *f* collar, neckband
gole *m* gulp, swallow
golfar *v/t*, *v/i* spout, gush
golfe *m* golf
golfinho *m* dolphin
golfo *m* gulf
golo *m* goal
golp|e *m* blow, knock, slash; **~ear** *v/t* strike, slash
goma *f* gum; *Braz* tapioca; **~ de mascar** chewing gum
gôndola *f* gondola
gorar *v/t*, *v/i*, *v/r* frustrate; addle; miscarry
gordo fat
gordura *f* fat; grease; **sem ~** fat free
gorduroso greasy
gorila *m* gorilla
gorjear *v/i* warble
gorjeta *f* tip, gratuity
gorro *m* bonnet, cap
gostar de *v/i* be fond of, like
gosto *m* taste; flavo(u)r, savo(u)r; relish; pleasure; **com muito ~** with great pleasure; **~so** tasty; pleasing
gota *f* drop; MED gout
goteira *f* gutter
gotejar *v/t*, *v/i* drip, drop, trickle

gótico *adj* Gothic
governador *m* governor
governamental governmental
governante *adj* governing
governar *v/t*, *v/i*, *v/r* manage; govern
governo *m* government
gozar *v/t*, *v/i* enjoy
gozo *m* enjoyment
graça *f* grace; wit; **de ~** free, gratis; **~s a** thanks to; **~s a Deus** thank God
gracejar *v/i* joke, jest
gracios|idade *f* gracefulness; **~o** *adj* graceful; witty
grade *f* grating; harrow; railing; crate
grado *m* goodwill
gradu|ação *f* graduation; MIL rank; **~al** *adj* gradual; **~ar** *v/t*, *v/r* graduate
gralha *f* rook; jackdaw; misprint
grama *f* gram(me)
gramado *m Braz* football field; lawn
gramática *f* grammar
grampo *m* cramp; clamp
granada *f* grenade
grand|e *adj* large; big; great; **~eza** *f* greatness; grandeur; size; **~iosidade** *f* greatness, grandeur; **~ioso** grand
granel *m* barn, cornloft; **a ~** by heaps, in bulk
granito *m* granite
granizo *m* hail
granjear *v/t* win, get
grão *m* grain
grassar *v/i* spread
gratidão *f* gratitude
gratific|ação *f* gratuity, tip; **~ar** *v/t* tip; reward
grátis free, gratis
grato grateful; pleasing
gratuito gratuitous; free
grau *m* degree; rank, grade
grav|ação *f* engraving; recording; **~ador** *m* engraver; (tape) recorder; **~ador de CD/DVD** CD/DVD writer; **~ar** *v/t* engrave; record
gravata *f* tie
grave *adj* serious; grave; earnest
grávida *adj* pregnant
gravidade *f* gravity
gravidez *f* pregnancy
gravura *f* engraving
graxa *f* shoe-polish
grego *adj*, *m* Greek; **isso para mim é ~** it's all Greek to me
grelar *v/i* sprout
grelha *f* grill
grelhar *v/t* grill
grelo *m* sprout
grémio *m* guild; society
greta *f* crack, chink
gretar *v/t*, *v/i*, *v/r* crack, split; chap
greve *f* strike; **fazer ~** strike
grevista *m*, *f* striker
grilo *m* cricket
grinalda *f* garland; wreath
gripe *f* influenza, flu
grit|ar *v/t*, *v/i* shout; cry; yell; scream; **~aria** *f* shouting; **~o** *m* shout, cry
grosseiro coarse, rude
gross|o *adj* thick, dense; **~ura** *f*

thickness
grou *m* zoo crane
grua *f* crane, derrick
grude *m* glue
grunhir *v/i* grunt
grupo *m* group
gruta *f* grotto
guarda *f* guard, watch; *m* guard, keeper, warden
guarda|-chuva *m* umbrella; **~-fato** *m* wardrobe; **~-lama** *m* AUTO mudguard, *US* fender; **~-livros** *m* book-keeper; **~napo** *m* napkin, serviette; **~-no(c)turno** *m* night-watchman
guardar *v/t* guard; keep; watch over
guarda|-redes *m* goalkeeper, goalie; **~-roupa** *m* wardrobe; **~-sol** *m* sunshade; **~-vestidos** *m* wardrobe
guarida *f* den, cave; shelter, refuge
guarn|ecer *v/t* furnish, provide; garnish; **~ição** *f* garrison
guelra *f* gill
guerr|a *f* war; **~ear** *v/t, v/i* wage war; **~eiro** *adj* warlike; *m* warrior; **~ilha** *f* guerrilla war
guia *f* guide(-book); *m* guide
guiador *m* handle-bars; steering-wheel
guiar *v/t, v/i, v/r* steer; guide
guiché *m* counter; booking-office
guinada *f* swerve; sudden pain
guincho *m* shriek, squeal
guindaste *m* crane
guis|ado *m* stew; **~ar** *v/t* stew, cook
guita *f* string, twine
guitarra *f* guitar
gula *f* gluttony
gulodice *f* titbit
guloso *adj* greedy; **ser ~** have a sweet tooth
gume *m* edge
guri *m Braz* child
gusano *m* (wood)worm
gustativo gustatory

H

hábil able, skilful, capable, clever
habilid|ade *f* ability, skill; **~oso** *adj* accomplished, dext(e)rous
habili|tação *f* qualification; **~tar** *v/t* qualify; enable
habit|ação *f* dwelling, residence; **~ante** *m, f* inhabitant; **~ar** *v/t, v/i* inhabit; **~ável** inhabitable
hábito *m* habit
habitu|al habitual; **~ar** *v/t, v/r* accustom, inure to
hálito *m* breath
harmonia *f* harmony
harmoni|oso harmonious; **~zar** *v/t, v/i, v/r* harmonize
harpa *f* harp
haste *f* staff; stem; **~ar** *v/t* hoist
haver *v/i, v/aux* there + be, ex-

ist; **há** there is, there are; ago; **~ de** have to; will, shall; **~es** *m/pl* possessions
hebraico *adj* Hebraic; Hebrew
hectare *m* hectare
hediondo hideous, loathsome
hélice *f* propeller, screw
helicóptero *m* helicopter
hemorragia *f* hemorrhage
hemorróidas *f/pl* hemorrhoids
hepatite *f* hepatitis
hera *f* ivy
herança inheritance; heritage
herdade *f* farm, estate
herd|ar *v/t, v/i* inherit; **~eira** *f* heiress; **~eiro** *m* heir
hereditariedade *f* heredity
hereditário hereditary
here|ge *m, f* heretic; **~sia** *f* heresy
her|ói *m* hero; **~óico** heroic; **~oína** *f* heroine; **~oísmo** *m* heroism
hesit|ação *f* hesitation; **~ante** hesitant; **~ar** *v/i* hesitate
heterogéneo heterogeneous
hibern|ação *f* hibernation; **~ar** *v/i* hibernate
hidráulico hydraulic
hidroavião *m* seaplane
hidrogénio *m* hydrogen
hiena *f* hyena
hierarquia *f* hierarchy
higi|ene *f* hygiene; **~énico** hygienic
hilari|ante hilarious; **~dade** *f* hilarity
hino *m* hymn; **~ nacional** national anthem
hipismo *m* horse-racing
hipocrisia *f* hypocrisy
hipócrita *m, f* hypocrite
hipódromo *m* hippodrome; racecourse
hipopótamo *m* hippopotamus
hipotec|a *f* mortgage; **~ar** *v/t* mortgage
hipótese *f* hypothesis
hipotético hypothetical
história *f* history; story
historiador *m* historian
histórico historic(al)
hodierno present-day
hoje *adv* today; **~ em dia** nowadays; **de ~ em diante** from this day on
holandês *adj* Dutch; *m* Dutch; Dutchman
homem *m* man
homenagem *f* homage
homicídio *m* homicide, murder
homogéneo homogeneous
honest|idade *f* honesty; **~o** honest
honorário *adj* honorary; **~s** *m/pl* fees
honra *f* hono(u)r; **~dez** *f* honesty; **~do** honest; hono(u)rable; **~r** *v/t* hono(u)r; **~ria** *f* distinction, rank
honroso hono(u)rable, decorous
hóquei *m* hockey
hor|a *f* hour; time; **à última ~** at the eleventh hour; **a toda a ~** at all hours; **~s extraordinárias** overtime; **que ~s são?** what time is it?; **~ário** *m* time-table

horda *f* horde
horizont|al horizontal; **~e** *m* horizon
horrendo horrid
horripilante horrifying
horrível horrible
horror *m* horror
horroroso horrible, dreadful, awful
hort|a *f* kitchen garden; **~aliça** *f* greens, vegetable(s)
hortelã *f* mint; **~ pimenta** peppermint
horticul|tor *m* horticulturist; **~tura** *f* horticulture
hosped|agem *f* lodging, accommodation; **~ar** *v/t, v/r* lodge, put up
hóspede *m, f* guest; host
hospital *m* hospital; **~eiro** hospitable; **~idade** *f* hospitality
hospitalizar *v/t* hospitalize
hostil hostile; **~idade** *f* hostility; **~izar** *v/t* bear ill will to
hotel *m* hotel
hulh|a *f* coal; **~eira** *f* coal-mine, pit
human|idade *f* humanity; mankind; **~o** *adj* human; humane
(h)umedecer *v/t, v/i, v/r* humidify; moisten
(h)umidade *f* humidity; dampness, moistness
(h)úmido damp, moist; humid
humil|dade *f* humility; **~de** humble
humilh|ação *f* humiliation; **~ar** *v/t, v/r* humiliate
humor *m* humo(u)r; temper
humorista *m, f* humorist
húngaro *adj* Hungarian

I

iate *m* yacht
ibérico *adj* Iberian
içar *v/t* raise, hoist
i(c)terícia *f* jaundice
ida *f* departure, going; **~s e vindas** comings and goings
idade *f* age
ideia *f* idea; **fazer ~** imagine, realize; **não fazer ~** have no idea
idêntico identical
identi|dade *f* identity; **bilhete** *m* **de ~dade** identity card/certificate; **~ficação** *f* identification; **~ficar** *v/t, v/r* identify
idílico idyllic
idílio *m* idyl(l)
idioma *m* language, idiom
idiota *m, f* idiot; *adj* idiotic
ídolo *m* idol
idoneidade *f* suitability
idóneo suitable
ignição *f* ignition
ignóbil ignoble
ignomínia *f* ignominy
ignominioso ignominious
ignor|ância *f* ignorance; **~ante** *adj* ignorant; **~ar** *v/t* to be ignorant of; ignore
ignoto unknown
igreja *f* church

igual *adj, m, f* equal; **~ar** *v/t, v/r* equalize; equal; **~dade** *f* equality
iguaria *f* delicacy, titbit
ilegal illegal
ilegítimo illegitimate
ilegível illegible
ileso unhurt, safe
ilha *f* island; isle
ilharga *f* flank; slope
ilhéu *m* islander
ilícito illicit
ilimitado unlimited, illimitable
ilógico illogical
iludir *v/t, v/r* delude, trick, deceive
ilumin|ação *f* illumination; **~ar** *v/t, v/r* illuminate
ilusão *f* illusion
ilustr|ação *f* illustration; **~ado** illustrated; **~ar** *v/t* illustrate; **~e** illustrious
imã *m* magnet
imagem *f* image
imagin|ação *f* imagination; **~ar** *v/t, v/i, v/r* imagine; **~ário** imaginary; **~ativo** imaginative
imbecil imbecile
imbuir *v/t, v/r* imbue (**de** with)
imediato *adj* immediate; next, following
imens|idade *f* immensity; **~o** immense
imerecido undeserved
imergir *v/t* immerse
imersão *f* immersion
imigr|ação *f* immigration; **~ante** *m, f* immigrant; **~ar** *v/i* immigrate
iminente imminent
imit|ação *f* imitation; **~ar** *v/t* imitate
imobilidade *f* immobility
imoderado immoderate
imodesto immodest
imolar *v/t* immolate
imoral immoral; **~idade** *f* immorality
imortal immortal; **~idade** *f* immortality; **~izar** *v/t* immortalize
imóvel *adj* immovable; immobile; unmovable; motionless
impaci|ência *f* impatience; **~entar** *v/t, v/r* make/get impatient; **~ente** impatient
impagável unpayable; *fig* humorous, comic
ímpar odd; unmatched
imparcial impartial; **~idade** *f* impartiality
impasse *m* impasse
impassível impassive
impávido fearless, intrepid
impecável impeccable
impedimento *m* obstruction, impediment
impedir *v/t* prevent, obstruct, hinder, impede
impelir *v/t* impel
impenetrável impenetrable
impensado thoughtless; unexpected, unforeseen
imper|ador *m* emperor; **~atriz** *f* empress
imperceptível imperceptible
imperdoável unforgivable, inexcusable
imperecível imperishable
imperfei|ção *f* imperfection;

~to *adj* imperfect, faulty
império *m* empire; dominion
imperioso imperious
impermeável *adj* impermeable; waterproof; *m* raincoat, mackintosh
impertin|ência *f* impertinence; **~ente** *adj* impertinent
imperturbável imperturbable
impessoal impersonal
ímpeto *m* impetus; violence
impetuoso impetuous
impiedoso pitiless
ímpio impious
implacável implacable
implantar *v/t* implant
implicar *v/t*, *v/i* pick a quarrel; implicate; imply
implícito implicit
implorar *v/t* implore
imponderado rash, thoughtless
imponente imposing
impor *v/t*, *v/r* impose
importação *f* importation; import
importador *m* importer
import|ância *f* importance; **~ante** *adj* important; **~ar** *v/t*, *v/i*, *v/r* concern oneself; import; matter; **não ~a** never mind; **que ~a?** what does it matter?
importun|ar *v/t* importune; **~o** *adj* importunate, irksome
imposs|ibilidade *f* impossibility; **~ível** impossible
imposto *m* tax, duty
impost|or *m* impostor; **~ura** *f* imposture
impot|ência *f* impotence; powerlessness; **~ente** *adj* impotent; powerless
impraticável impracticable
imprecação *f* imprecation
impregnar *v/t* impregnate
imprensa *f* printing press; press
impres|são *f* impression; imprint; **~sões** *f/pl* **digitais** fingerprints
impress|ionar *v/t* impress; **~ionante** touching, moving; impressive; **~o** *adj* printed; *m* printed matter; **~ora** *f* printer; **~ora (a) jato de tinta** ink-jet printer
impreterível indispensable
imprevidente improvident
imprevisto unforeseen; unforeseeable
imprimir *v/t* print
improbabilidade *f* improbability
improdutivo unproductive
impróprio improper; unsuitable
improvável improbable
improvis|ação *f* improvisation; **~ar** *v/t* improvise
imprud|ência *f* imprudence; rashness; **~ente** *adj* imprudent, rash
impudente impudent
impudor *m* impudence
impugnar *v/t* impugn
impulsionar *v/t* impel
impuls|ivo impulsive; **~o** *m* impulse
impune unpunished, with impunity

impur|eza *f* impurity; **~o** impure
imput|ar *v/t* impute to; **~ável** imputable
imund|ície *f* dirt, filth; **~o** dirty, filthy
imune immune
imutável immutable, changeless
inabalável unshak(e)able; inexorable
inábil unable; unskilful
inabordável unapproachable
ina(c)ção *f* inaction; sluggishness
inaceitável unacceptable
inacessível inaccessible
inacreditável incredible
ina(c)tividade *f* inactivity
ina(c)tivo inactive
inadequado inadequate
inadiável not postponable; unavoidable
inadmissível inadmissible
inadvertência *f* oversight
inalienável unalienable
inalter|ado unaltered; **~ável** unalterable
inapto inapt, unfit
inato innate
inaudito unheard-of
inaudível inaudible
inauguração inauguration
inaugur|al inaugural; **~ar** *v/t* inaugurate
incalculável incalculable
incansável tireless
incapaz incapable; unable
incauto unwary, careless
incendi|ar *v/t* set fire to; **~ário** *adj* incendiary
incêndio *m* fire, blaze, conflagration
incenso *m* incense
incentivo *m* incentive
incert|eza *f* uncertainty; **~o** uncertain
incessante incessant
incesto *m* incest
inchar *v/t, v/i, v/r* swell
incidência *f* incidence
incidente *m* incident
incinerar *v/t* incinerate
incipiente incipient
incisão *f* incision
incit|ação *f* incitement; **~ar** *v/t* incite
inclem|ência *f* inclemency; **~ente** inclement
inclin|ação *f* inclination; **~ar** *v/t, v/i, v/r* incline; bend down
inclu|ir *v/t* include; **~são** *f* inclusion; **~sive** inclusive(ly); **~so** included
incoerente incoherent
incógnito *adj* unknown, incognito
incolor colo(u)rless
incólume safe and sound
incombustível incombustible
incomensurável immeasurable
incomodar *v/t, v/r* put oneself out; bother; disturb; trouble
incómodo *adj* uncomfortable; *m* inconvenience
incomparável incomparable
incompat|ibilidade *f* incompatibility; **~ível** incompatible
incompet|ência *f* incompe-

tence; **~ente** incompetent
incompleto incomplete
incompreen|são *f* incomprehension; **~sível** incomprehensible
incomunicável incommunicable; incommunicado
inconcebível inconceivable
incondicional unconditional
inconsci|ência *f* unconsciousness; **~ente** *adj* unconscious
inconsequ|ência *f* inconsequence; **~ente** inconsequent; contradictory
inconsiderado inconsiderate
inconsistente inconsistent
inconsolável inconsolable
incontestável incontestable
inconveni|ência *f* inconvenience; **~ente** *adj* inconvenient; improper, rude; *m* snag, handicap, nuisance
incorre(c)|ção *f* incorrectness; innacuracy; impoliteness; **~to** wrong, incorrect
incorrer *v/i*: **~ em** incur
incorrigível incorrigible
incorru(p)tível incorruptible
incrédulo incredulous
incremento *m* increment
incriminar *v/t* incriminate
incrível incredible
incrust|ação *f* incrustation; **~ar** *v/t* incrust
inculcar *v/t* inculcate
inculpar *v/t* accuse
inculto uncultivated; uncultured, uneducated
incumbir *v/t*, *v/i* charge, entrust
incurável incurable
incursão *f* incursion
incutir *v/t* inculcate, infuse
indag|ação *f* investigation; research; **~ar** *v/t*, *v/i* inquire into, investigate
indec|ência *f* indecency; **~ente** indecent
indecifrável indecipherable
indeciso undecided, indecisive
indecoroso indecorous
indefensável indefensible
indeferir *v/t* reject
indefeso undefended
indefin|ido indefinite; undefined; **~ível** undefinable
indelével indelible
indelicad|eza *f* indelicacy; **~o** indelicate
inde(m)niz|ação *f* indemnity, indemnification; **~ar** *v/t* indemnify
independ|ência *f* independence; **~ente** independent
indescritível indescribable
indesculpável inexcusable
indesejável undesirable
indeterminado indeterminate
indiano *adj*, *m* Indian
indic|ação *f* indication; **~ar** *v/t* indicate, point out
índice *m* index
indício *m* sign, token, hint
indiferen|ça *f* indifference; **~te** *adj* indifferent
indígena *adj* indigenous, native
indig|ência *f* indigence; **~ente** *adj* indigent
indigerível indigestible
indigest|ão *f* indigestion; **~o**

undigested; indigestible
indign|ação *f* indignation; **~ado** indignant; **~ar** *v/t*, *v/r* shock, incense; **~idade** *f* indignity; **~o** *adj* unworthy
índio *adj*, *m* Indian, Native American
indire(c)to indirect
indisciplinado indisciplined
indiscrecão *f* indiscretion
indiscreto indiscreet
indispensável indispensable
indisponível unavailable
indispor *v/t* indispose
indisp|osição *f* indisposition; **~osto** indisposed, ill
indissolúvel indissoluble
indistinto indistinct
individual individual
indivíduo *m* individual; person
indivisível indivisible
índole *f* character, temper, disposition
indol|ência *f* indolence; **~ente** indolent
indomável indomitable; untamable
indómito untamed
indubitável indubitable
indulgência *f* indulgence
indul|tar *v/t* pardon, forgive; **~to** *m* indult
indústria *f* industry
industrial *adj* industrial
industrializar *v/t*, *v/r* industrialize
induzir *v/t* induce
inebriar *v/t*, *v/r* inebriate
inédito *adj* inedited, unpublished
inefável ineffable
ineficácia *f* inefficacy
ineficaz ineffective
inegável undeniable
inepto inept
inércia *f* inertia
inerente inherent
inerte inert
inesgotável inexhaustible
inesperado unexpected
inesquecível unforgettable
inesvitável inevitable, unavoidable
inexa(c)t|idão *f* inexactitude, inexactness; **~o** inexact
inexorável inexorable
inexperiente inexperienced
inexplicável inexplicable
inexpressivo inexpressive
infalibilidade *f* infallibility
infalível infallible
infame *adj* infamous
infâmia *f* infamy
infância *f* infancy, childhood
infantil infantile, childish
infatigável indefatigable
infe(c)|ção *f* infection; **~cioso** infectious; **~tar** *v/t*, *v/r* infect
infel|icidade *f* unhappiness; **~iz** unhappy
inferior *adj* inferior; lower
inferir *v/t* infer
infern|al infernal; hellish; **~o** *m* hell
infi|delidade *f* infidelity; **~el** *adj* unfaithful, disloyal
infiltr|ação *f* infiltration; **~ar** *v/t*, *v/r* infiltrate
ínfimo lowest, meanest
infinidade *f* infinity

infinito *adj* infinite
inflação *f* inflation
inflam|ação *f* inflammation; **~ar** *v/t* inflame
inflexível inflexible
infligir *v/t* inflict, impose
influ|ência *f* influence; **~enciar** *v/t* influence; **~ente** *adj* influential; **~ir (em)** *v/i* influence
inform|ação *f* information; **~ante** *m*, *f* informant; **~ador** *m* informer; **~ar** *v/t*, *v/r* inform; inquire after
infortúnio *m* misfortune
infra(c)ção *f* infringement
infringir *v/t* infringe
infrutífero fruitless
infundado unfounded, groundless
ingenuidade *f* ingenuousness; naivety
ingénuo ingenuous; naive
ingerir *v/t*, *v/r* interfere, meddle
inglês *adj* English; *m* English; Englishman
ingrat|idão *f* ingratitude; **~o** ungrateful
íngreme steep
ingressar *v/i* enter, join
ingresso *m* ingress, entry
inibir *v/t* inhibit
inici|ação *f* initiation; **~al** *adj*, *f* initial; **~ar** *v/t* begin, initiate; **~ativa** *f* initiative
início *m* outset, beginning
inimigo *m* enemy
inimizade *f* enmity
ininterrupto uninterrupted
inje(c)|ção *f* injection; **~tar** *v/t* inject
injúria *f* insult; harm
injuriar *v/t* insult; harm
injust|iça *f* injustice; **~o** *adj* unjust
inoc|ência *f* innocence; **~ente** *adj* innocent
inodoro odo(u)rless
inofensivo inoffensive
inolvidável unforgettable
inoportuno inopportune
inov|ação *f* innovation; **~ar** *v/t* innovate
inquérito *m* investigation; inquiry; inquest
inquiet|ação *f* uneasiness; unrest; **~ar** *v/t*, *v/r* worry; disquiet; disturb; **~o** uneasy; restless
inquilino *m* tenant
inquirir *v/t*, *v/i* inquire; interrogate
insaciável insatiable
insalubre insalubrious
insatisfeito displeased, dissatisfied
inscr|ever *v/t*, *v/r* register; inscribe; **~ição** *f* inscription; registration
inse(c)ticida *f* insecticide
inse(c)to *m* insect
inseguro insecure
insensat|ez *f* folly, stupidity; **~o** senseless, foolish
insens|ibilidade *f* insensibility; **~ível** insensible
inseparável inseparable
inserção *f* insertion
insigne eminent
insignific|ância *f* insignificance; **~ante** *adj* insignificant
insinu|ação *f* insinuation; **~ar**

v/t, v/r insinuate (into)
insípido insipid
insist|ência *f* insistence; **~ente** insistent; **~ir (em)** *v/i* insist (on)
insolação *f* sunstroke
insolente *adj* insolent
insólito unwonted, unusual
insolúvel insoluble
insónia *f* insomnia, sleeplessness
inspe(c)|ção *f* inspection; **~cionar** *v/t* inspect; **~tor** *m* inspector
inspiração *f* inspiration
inspirar *v/t* inspire
instabilidade *f* instability
instal|ação *f* installation; **~ar** *v/t, v/r* install
instant|âneo *m* snapshot; *adj* instantaneous; **~e** *m* instant; *adj* urgent
instar *v/i* urge
instável unstable
instigar *v/t* instigate
instin|tivo instinctive; **~to** *m* instinct
institu|ição *f* institution; **~ir** *v/t* institute
instituto *m* institute
instru|ção *f* instruction; **~ído** learned; **~ir** *v/t* instruct; teach
instrumento *m* instrument
insubordinado insubordinate
insuficiente insufficient
insult|ar *v/t* insult; **~o** *m* insult
insuportável intolerable
insurgir-se *v/r* revolt
insurreição *f* insurrection
insuspeito unsuspected
insustentável untenable
inta(c)to intact
inté cu (see you)
integral *adj* integral
integrar *v/t* integrate
integridade *f* integrity
íntegro entire; upright
inteir|ar *v/t, v/r* find out; complete; **~eza** *f* entirety; **~o** *adj* entire, whole
intelect|o *m* intellect; **~ual** intellectual
intelig|ência *f* intelligence; **~ente** *adj* intelligent
intempérie *f* inclemency
intempestivo unseasonable, untimely
inten|ção *f* intention; **~cional** intentional
intendente *m* manager; superintendent
intens|idade *f* intensity; **~o** intense
intent|ar *v/t* try, attempt; **~o** *m* intention
intercalar *v/t* intercalate
intercâmbio *m* interchange
interceptar *v/t* intercept
interdi|ção *f* prohibition; **~zer** *v/t* prohibit
interess|ado *adj* interested; **~ante** interesting; **~ar** *v/t, v/i, v/r* interest; concern
interesse *m* interest; concern
interesseiro *adj* self-seeking
interferência *f* interference
interferir *v/i* interfere
interino *adj* interim; provisional
interior *adj* interior; inner; in-

land; *m* interior
intermediário *m* intermediary; go-between
intermédio *adj* intermediate; *m* mediator; **por ~** through, by means of
interminável interminable
interno *adj* internal
interpor *v/t, v/r* interpose
interpretar *v/t* interpret
intérprete *m* interpreter
interrog|ação *f* interrogation; **~ar** *v/t* interrogate; **~atório** *m* cross-examination
interromper *v/t* interrupt
interrup|ção *f* interruption; **~tor** *m* ELECT switch
interurbano *adj* interurban; *m Braz* trunk-call, *US* long-distance call
intervalo *m* interval; pause
intervenção *f* intervention
intervir *v/i* intervene
intestino *m* intestine
intimidade *f* intimacy
intimidar *v/t* intimidate
íntimo *adj* intimate; *m* intimate
intolerável intolerable
intoxicação *f* intoxication
intraduzível untranslatable
intransitável impassable
intransmissível non-transferable
intratável intractable; coy; unsociable
intrepidez *f* intrepidity
intrépido intrepid
intriga *f* intrigue
intrínseco intrinsic
introdu|ção *f* introduction; **~zir** *v/t, v/r* introduce, bring in; insert
intrometer *v/r* interfere, meddle in
intrujão *m* impostor, swindler
intruso *m* intruder
intui|ção *f* intuition; **~tivo** intuitive
intuito *m* aim, purpose
inúmero innumerable, countless
inund|ação *f* inundation, flood; **~ar** *v/t* inundate, flood
inútil useless
inutilidade *f* uselessness
invadir *v/t* invade
inválido *adj* invalid; *m* disabled, invalid
invariável invariable
invas|ão *f* invasion; **~or** *m* invader, aggressor
invej|a *f* envy; **~ar** *v/t* envy; **~oso** envious
invenção *f* invention
invencível invincible
inven|tar *v/t* invent; **~to** *m* invention; **~tor** *m* inventor
inverno *m* winter
inverosímil improbable; unlikely
invers|ão *f* inversion; **~o** *adj, m* inverse
inverter *v/t* invert; reverse
investig|ação *f* investigation; **~ar** *v/t* investigate
invicto unconquered
invisível invisible
invoc|ação *f* invocation; **~ar** *v/t* invoke, call on
invólucro *m* covering, case

involuntário involuntary
iodo *m* iodine
iogurte *m* yogh(o)urt
ir *v/i, v/r* go; **~ a pé** walk; **~ a cavalo** ride; **~ buscar** fetch; **~ de carro** go by car; **~-se embora** go away
ira *f* anger
irlandês *adj* Irish; *m* Irishman
irmã *f* sister
irmão *m* brother
ironia *f* irony
irónico ironic
irra! damn!
irradiar *v/t, v/i, v/r* irradiate
irreal unreal
irrealizável impracticable, unfeasible
irreconciliável irreconcilable
irregular irregular; uneven
irremediável irremediable
irresoluto irresolute
irresponsável irresponsible
irrequieto restless; fidgety
irrevogável irrevocable
irrigar *v/t* irrigate
irrisório laughable
irrit|ação *f* irritation; **~ar** *v/t* irritate; **~ável** irritable
irromper *v/t* burst into, break into
isca *f* bait; fried liver
isen|ção *f* exemption; **~tar** *v/t* exempt; **~to** exempt
isol|ador *m* insulator; isolator; **~amento** *m* isolation; insulation; **~ar** *v/t, v/r* insulate; isolate
isquoiro *m* (cigarette-)lighter
isso that; **por ~** therefore
isto this
italiano *adj, m* Italian
itinerário *m* itinerary

J

já now; already; **até ~** cheerio, see you later; **~ agora** even now; **~ não** no longer, no more; **~ que** since
jacaré *m* alligator
jacinto *m* hyacinth
ja(c)to *m* jet
jamais never, at no time
Janeiro *m* January
janela *f* window
jangada *f* raft
janota *adj* chic, slick
jantar *v/t, v/i* dine; *m* dinner
japonês *adj, m* Japanese
jaqueta *f* jacket
jardi|m *m* garden; **~nagem** *f* gardening; **~neiro** *m* gardener
jarr|a *f* vase; **~o** *m* jug, *US* pitcher
jaula *f* cage
javali *m* wild boar
jaz|er *v/i* lie; **~ida** *f* restingplace; GEOL mineral deposit; **~igo** *m* tomb, grave; GEOL mineral deposit
jeit|o *m* manner; knack; **~oso** skilful, handy
jejum *m* fast

joalheiro *m* jewe(l)ler
jocoso jocose
joelho *m* knee
jog|ador *m* player; gambler; **~ar** *v/i* play; gambling
jogo *m* game; match; **~ internacional** international (match); **~ de móveis** suite; **estar en ~** be at stake
joguete *m* plaything
jóia *f* jewel
jóquei *m* jockey
jornada *f* trip, journey; day's work
jornal *m* newspaper; daily wage; **~eiro** *m* day-labo(u)rer; **~ista** *m*, *f* journalist
jorrar *v/i* spout, gush out
jorro *m* gush
jovem *adv* young; *m*, *f* young lady; youth, young man
jovial jovial; **~idade** *f* joviality
juba *f* mane
jubileu *m* jubilee
júbilo *m* joy, jubilation
jud|aico Jewish; **~aísmo** *m* Judaism; **~eu** *m* Jew; *adj* Jewish; **~ia** *f* Jewess
judiciário judicial
jugo *m* yoke
juiz *m* (*pl* **juízes**) judge
juízo *m* judg(e)ment; opinion; common sense
julgar *v/t*, *v/i* judge; think
Julho *m* July
jumento *m* ass, donkey
junção *f* junction, joining
junco *m* rush, reed
Junho *m* June
junt|a *f* junta; ANAT joint; **~ar** *v/t* join, connect; **~o** *adj* joined, united; *adv* near; together; **juntura** *f juncture*
jur|a *f* oath; curse; **~ado** *m* juror; **~amento** *m* oath; **~ar** *v/t*, *v/i* swear
júri *m* jury
jur|ídico juridical; **~isconsulto** *m* jurisconsult; **~isdição** *f* jurisdiction; **~isprudência** *f* jurisprudence; **~ista** *m*, *f* jurist
juro *m* interest
jusante *f* ebb, low tide
justamente exactly, just
justapor *v/t*, *v/r* juxtapose, place side by side
justeza *f* accuracy
justi|ça *f* justice; **~ceiro** impartial, severe; **~ficação** *f* justification; **~ficar** *v/t* justify
justo *adj* fair, just; exact; accurate
juven|il juvenile; youthful; **~tude** *f* youth, youthfulness

L

lá *adv* in that place, there
lã *f* wool
labareda *f* flame, blaze
lábio *m* lip
labut|a *f* hard work, drudgery; **~ar** *v/i* work hard
laca *f* lacquer
laç|ada *f* slipknot; **~o** *m* noose; snare; lasso, *US* lariat; bow, knot
lacónico laconic
lacrar *v/t* seal
lacrau *m* scorpion
lacre *m* sealing-wax
lacuna *f* gap, lacuna
ladeira *f* slope; hillside
ladino *adj* cunning, sly
lado *m* side; **ao ~ de** beside, next to
ladr|a *f* woman thief; **~ão** *m* thief, robber
ladrar *v/i* bark
lagart|a *f* caterpillar; **~o** *m* lizard
lago *m* lake
lagosta *f* lobster
lagostim *m* crayfish
lágrima *f* tear
lama *f* mud; **~çal** *m* slough; **~cento** muddy; slushy
lamb|areiro *adj* greedy; sweet-toothed; **~arice** *f* greediness, gluttony
lamber *v/t* lick
lambreta *f* motor scooter
lament|ação *f* lamentation; **~ar** *v/t*, *v/r* regret; lament; **~ável** lamentable; **~o** *m* lament
lâmina *f* blade
lâmpada *f* lamp; **~ elé(c)trica** light bulb
lampejar *v/i* flash, glitter
lampião *m* lantern; street-lamp
lanç|a *f* lance; spear; **~amento** *m* throwing; launching; dropping; COM entry; **~ar** *v/t*, *v/r* throw, cast; launch
lance *m* event; **~ de olhos** glance
lancha *f* launch
lanche *m* afternoon tea; snack
lanço *m* bid; **~ de oscadas** flight of stairs
lânguido languid
lanterna *f* lantern
lápide *f* tablet; tombstone
lápis *m* pencil
lapiseira *f* propelling pencil
lapso *m* lapse
lar *m* home; fireside
laranj|a *f* orange; **~ada** *f* orangeade; **~eira** *f* orange tree
larápio *m* pilferer
lareira *f* hearth; fireplace
largar *v/t*, *v/i*, *v/r* let out; let go, release; sail, put to sea
larg|o *adj* broad, wide; *m* square; **ao ~** aloof; **~ura** *f* breadth, width
laringe *f* larynx
larva *f* larva
lasc|a *f* splinter; **~ar** *v/t*, *v/i*

splinter
lascivo lascivious
lass|idão *f* lassitude; **~o** weary; loose, slack
lástima *f* pity; pitiful thing
lastim|ar *v/t, v/r* deplore; regret; **~ável** regrettable
lastro *m* ballast
lata *f* tin-plate; tin, can; cheek, impudence
latão *m* brass
latejar *v/i* throb
latente latent
lateral lateral
latifúndio *m* large estate
latim *m* Latin
latino *adj* Latin
latir *v/i* bark, yelp
latitude *f* latitude
lato extensive, vast
lavagem *f* wash
lava-louça *m* sink
lavandaria *f* laundry
lava|r *v/t, v/r* wash; **~tório** *m* wash-basin; *US* sink
lavável washable
lavor *m* needlework
lavoura *f* ploughing, farming
lavrad|eira *f* farmer's wife; **~or** *m* farmer
lavrar *v/t* plough, till; carve; plane
laxante *m, adj* laxative
leal loyal; **~dade** *f* loyalty
leão *m* lion
lebre *f* hare
le(c)cionar *v/t, v/i* teach
legação *f* legation
legado *m* legate; legacy
legal legal; *Braz* right, correct, o.k; **~idade** *f* legality; **~izar** *v/t* legalize
legar *v/t* bequeath
legenda *f* caption; key
legisl|ação *f* legislation; **~ar** *v/t, v/i* legislate
legitimar *v/t* legitimize
legítimo legitimate
legível legible
legume *m* vegetable
lei *f* law
leilão *m* auction
leitaria *f* dairy
leit|e *m* milk; **~eiro** *m* milkman
leito *m* bed; bedstead
leit|or *m* reader; lecturer; **~ de CDs** CD player; **~orado** *m* lectureship; **~ura** *f* reading
lebr|ança *f* remembrance, memory; keepsake; souvenir; **~ar** *v/t, v/i, v/r* recall; remind; remember
leme *m* tiller; rudder
lenço *m* handkerchief
lençol *m* sheet
lend|a *f* legend; **~ário** legendary
lenh|a *f* (fire)wood; **~ador** *m* woodcutter; **~o** *m* block, log
lente *m* lecturer; *f* lens
lentidão *f* slowness
lentilha *f* lentil
lento *adj* slow
leopardo *m* leopard
lepra *f* leprosy
leque *m* fan
ler *v/t, v/i* read
lesão *f* lesion, wound
lesar *v/t* hurt, damage
leste *m* east

lesto brisk, nimble
letra *f* letter; handwriting; **à/ao pé da ~** literally; **~ de câmbio** bill of exchange; **~s** *f/pl* letters, learning
letreiro *m* inscription, caption
leva *f* weighing anchor; levy
levant|amento *m* survey; insurrection; **~ar** *v/t, v/i, v/r* lift, raise; rise, get up; **~ar a mesa** clear the table; **~ar voo** take off
levar *v/t* carry, bear, convey, take; **~ a cabo** carry through; **~ a mal** take amiss; **~ em conta** take into account
leve light; slight
levedura *f* yeast
leveza *f* lightness
levian|dade *f* frivolity; **~o** frivolous, inconsiderate
lezíria *f* marsh
lhan|eza *f* plainness; sincerity; **~o** plain; sincere
lhe to it; to him; to her; to you
liberal *adj, m, f* liberal; **~idade** *f* liberality
liber|dade *f* freedom, liberty; **~tação** *f* liberation; JUR discharge; **~tar** *v/t, v/r* liberate, set free; **~tino** *m* libertine
libidinoso libidinous
libra *f* pound; **~ esterlina** pound sterling
lição *f* lesson
licença *f* licence; permission; leave, furlough
licenci|ado *m* licenciate, graduate; **~ar** *v/t, v/r* graduate; licence; **~atura** *f* degree of licentiate
liceu *m* grammar-school, *US* high school
licitar *v/t, v/i* bid; auction
lícito lawful
licor *m* liquor; liqueur
lid|a *f* work, job, chore; **~ar** *v/i* work; **~ar com** deal with; **~e** *f* fight, struggle; controversy
lido *adj* well-read
lig|a *f* league; alloy; **~ação** *f* connection, COMP link; **~adura** *f* bandage; ligature; **~ar** *v/t* bind; switch on
ligeir|eza *f* lightness; swiftness; **~o** light; swift
lilás *m* lilac
lima *f* file; lime
limão *m* lemon
limar *v/t* file
limiar *m* threshold
limit|ação *f* limitation; **~ar** *v/t* limit; **~e** *m* limit; boundary
limítrofe bordering
limonada *f* lemonade, lemon squash
limpa-pára-brisas *m* windscreen wiper; **~-chaminés** *m* chimney-sweep(er)
limp|adela *f* cleaning; **~ar** *v/t, v/r* clean; **~eza** *f* clean(li)ness
límpido limpid, clear
limpo *adj* clean
lince *m* lynx
lindo pretty; fine; neat
língua *f* tongue; language
linguado *m* ZOO sole
linguagem *f* language, speech
linguiça *f* thin sausage
ling|uista *m, f* linguist; **~uísti-**

co linguistic
linha *f* line; ~ **de chat** chatline
linhagem *f* lineage
linho *m* linen; BOT flax
lipoaspiração *f* liposuction
liquid|ação *f* liquidation; **~ar** *v/t, v/i* liquidate
líquido *m adj* liquid
lírico *adj* lyric(al)
lírio *m* lily
lisboeta *m, f* native of Lisbon
liso smooth; lank
lisonj|a *f* flattery; **~eador** *m* flatterer; **~ear** *v/t, v/r* flatter; **~eiro** flattering
lista *f* list; menu; ~ **telefónica** telephone directory
literal literal
liter|ário literary; **~atura** *f* literature
litig|ante *m, f* litigant; **~ar** *v/i* litigate, defend in court
litígio *m* litigation, lawsuit; contention
litro *m* litre
lívido livid
livrar *v/t, v/r* get rid of; free, release
livraria *f* bookshop, *US* bookstore
livre *adj* free; **~-câmbio** *m* free trade
livreiro *m* bookseller
livrete *m* booklet
livro *m* book; ~ **electrónico** e-book
lix|a *f* sandpaper; **~ar** *v/t* sandpaper
lixívia *f* lye
lixo *m* filth, dirt; garbage, litter
lobo *m* wolf
lobo *m* lobe
lôbrego dark, dismal, gloomy
local *adj* local; **~idade** *f* locality; **~izar** *v/t* localize
loção *f* lotion
locatário *m* lessee, tenant
locomo|ção *f* locomotion; **~tiva** *f* locomotive
locução *f* locution, idiom
locutor *m* announcer
lodaçal *m* puddle
lodo *m* mud, mire; **~so** muddy
lógic|a *f* logic; **~o** *adj* logical; *m* logician
logo *adv* presently; soon; immediately; *conj* therefore, so, then; ~ **que** as soon as; **até** ~ cheerio, see you later
lograr *v/t* get; succeed in
logro *m* fraud, hoax
loj|a *f* shop; **~ista** *m, f* shopkeeper
lomba *f* ridge, brow
lombo *m* loin; back
lona *f* canvas
longa-metragem *f* feature film
long|e *adv*, far; *adj* distant, far off; **ao ~e** in the distance; **~ínquo** distant; **~itude** *f* longitude; **~o** long; **ao ~o de** along
loquaz loquacious
lot|ação *f* capacity; **~ação esgotada** full house; **~ar** *v/t* allot
lotaria *f* lottery
lote *m* lot
louça *f* crockery, china
louc|o mad; **~ura** *f* madness
loureiro *m* bay; laurel
louro *m* laurel; *adj* fair, blond

lousa *f* slate; tombstone
louv|ar *v/t* praise; **~ável** praiseworthy; **~or** *m* praise
lua *f* moon; **~ de mel** honeymoon
luar *m* moonlight
lubrific|ação *f* lubrication; **~ar** *v/t* lubricate
lúcido lucid
lúcio *m* pike
lucr|ar *v/t, v/i* gain; profit by; **~ativo** lucrative; **~o** *m* gain; profit
ludibriar *v/t* ridicule, mock
ludíbrio *m* mockery
lufada *f* squall, gust; **às ~s** by fits and starts
lufa-lufa *f* hurly-burly; **à ~** in a hurry
lugar *m* place; seat; spot, village; **em ~ de** instead of; **~ejo** *m* hamlet
lúgubre lugubrious; dismal
lume *m* fire; glow; light
luminoso luminous
lunar *adj* lunar
luneta *f* eye-glass
lupa *f* magnifying glass
lúpulo *m* hops
lusco-fusco *m* dusk, nightfall; **ao ~** at twilight
lusitano, **luso** *m, adj* Lusitanian, Portuguese
lustrar *v/t, v/i* glaze, polish
lustre *m* gloss, lustre; chandelier, sconce
luta *f* struggle; strife; wrestling
lutar *v/i* struggle; strive; wrestle
luto *m* mourning
luv|a *f* glove; **~as** *f/pl* gratuity, tip; **~eiro** *m* glover
lux|o *m* luxury; **~uoso** luxurious; **~úria** *f* lust; **~uriante** luxuriant, rank; **~urioso** luxurious
luz *f* light
luzidio glistening
luzir *v/i* shine, glow

M

má *adj, f, of* **mau** bad, evil
maca *f* stretcher; litter
maça *f* club; mace
maçã *f* apple
macacão *m Braz* overalls
macaco *m* monkey
maça|da *f* bore, nuisance; **~dor** *adj* boring
maçar *v/t* bore; beat, pound
macarrão *m* mac(c)aroni
macela *f* camomile
machado *m* ax(e)
macho *m* mule; male
maciço *adj* massive; *m* massif
macioira *f* apple-tree
macio soft, smooth; mild
maço *m* mallet; packet, bundle
má-criação *f* ill-breeding; bad manners
mácula *f* stain
madeir|a *f* wood, timber; **~o** *m* trunk; beam; plank
madeixa *f* tuft, lock
madrasta *f* stepmother

madre *f* nun
madrepérola *f* mother-of--pearl
madressilva *f* honeysuckle
madrinha *f* godmother
madrug|ada *f* dawn; **~ador** *m* early riser; **~ar** *v/i* rise early
madur|ar *v/t*, *v/i* mature; ripen; **~o** *adj* ripe
mãe *f* mother
magia *f* magic
mágico *adj* magic(al)
magis|tério *m* teaching profession; **~trado** *m* magistrate; **~tral** *adj* masterly; **~tratura** *f* magistracy
magnânimo magnanimous
magnate *m* magnate
magnific|ência *f* magnificence; **~ente** generous
magnífico magnificent
mágoa *f* grief
magoar *v/t* hurt
magote *m* band, group
magr|eza *f* thinness, leanness; **~o** thin, lean
Maio *m* May
maiô *m* bathing suit
maionese *f* mayonnaise
maior *adj* of age; bigger, greater; larger; **a ~ parte** most; **~es** *m/pl* ancestors; **~ia** *f* majority; **~idade** *f* majority, coming-of--age
mais *adv* more; any more; *adj* more; **a ~** in excess, over; **de ~** too much; **de ~ a ~** besides; **por ~ que** however much
maiúscula *f* capital letter
majest|ade *f* majesty; **~oso** majestic
major *m* major
mal *adv* badly; hardly; *m* evil; harm; illness
mala *f* suitcase; trunk
mal-agradecido ungrateful
malandro *m* scoundrel
malária *f* malaria
malcriado ill-bred; ill-mannered
maldade *f* wickedness
maldisposto ill-humo(u)red, cross; indisposed
maldito *adj* damned
maldizer *v/t*, *v/i* slander; curse
maleável malleable
maledicência *f* slander
mal|efício *m* evil; **~éfico** harmful
mal|-educado ill-bred, impolite; **~-entendido** *m* misunderstanding; **~-estar** *m* indisposition
maleta *f* small suitcase
malevo|lência *f* malevolence, ill-will; **~lente** malevolent
malfadado ill-fated
malfeitor *m* malefactor
malga *f* bowl
malh|a *f* mesh; speckle; ladder; **~ado** *adj* speckled; **~ar** *v/t*, *v/i* thresh; beat
mal-humorado ill-tempered
mal|ícia *f* malice; **~icioso** malicious
maligno *adj* malignant
malmequer *m* daisy
malograr *v/t*, *v/r* frustrate; fail; upset
malogro *m* failure

malta *f* gang; mob; band
maltrapilho *m* ragamuffin
maltratar *v/t* maltreat; ill-treat
malu|co *adj* barmy; mad, crazy; **~quice** *f* madness, folly
malvad|ez *f* wickedness; **~o** *adj* wicked
mama *f* breast
mamã *f*, *Braz* **mamãe** mum, mummy, *US* mom(my)
mamão *m* papaya, pawpaw
mamar *v/t*, *v/i* suckle
mamífero *m* mammal
mana *f* sister
manada *f* herd, drove
manancial *m* spring, fountain; source
manar *v/t*, *v/i* flow; issue
mancar *v/i* limp
mancebo *m* youth
manch|a *f* spot, stain; **~ar** *v/t* stain, soil, sully
manco *m* cripple
mand|ado *m* order; errand; writ; **~amento** *m* commandment; **~ar** *v/t*, *v/i* command; send; **~ar buscar** send for; **~atário** *m* attorney, proxy; **~ato** *m* mandate
mandíbula *f* mandible, jaw-bone
mandioca *f* bot cassava
mando *m* command, power; authority
mandrião *m* sluggard, idler
mandriar *v/i* lounge, idle
manducar *v/t*, *v/i* chew, eat
maneira *f* manner, way; **de ~ nenhuma** not at all; in no way; **de ~ que** so that
manej|ar *v/t*, *v/i* handle; manage; **~o** *m* handling
manequim *m* model; dummy
maneta *adj* one-armed
manga *f* sleeve; BOT mango
mangar *v/t* mock, joke
mangueira *f* hose; mango-tree
manha *f* craft, trick, cunning; bad habit
manhã *f* morning; **de ~** in the morning
manhoso crafty, artful
man|ia *f* mania; craze; **~íaco** *m* maniac; **~icómio** *m* mental hospital/home
manifest|ação *f* manifestation; demonstration; **~ar** *v/t*, *v/r* manifest; demonstrate; **~o** *adj* manifest; *m* manifesto
manipul|ação *f* manipulation; **geneticamente ~ado** genetically engineered; **~ar** *v/t* manipulate
manivela *f* handle, crank
manjar *m* food; titbit, delicacy
manjedoura *f* crib, manger
mano *m* brother
manobr|a *f* manœuvre, *US* maneuver; **~ar** *v/t*, *v/i* manœuvre, *US* maneuver
manquejar *v/i* limp
mansarda *f* garret
man|sidão *f* meekness, gentleness; **~so** meek, gentle; tame
manta *f* blanket; rug
manteig|a *f* butter; **~ueira** *f* butter-dish
manter *v/t*, *v/r* maintain; keep
manual *m*, *adj* manual
manufa(c)tur|a *f* manufacture;

~ar *v/t* manufacture
manuscrito *m* manuscript
manutenção *f* maintenance
mão *f* hand; **à ~** at hand; **~-de-obra** *f* handwork; **~s** *f/pl* **livres** free-hand
mapa *m* map; **~-mundi** world map
maquilhagem *f* make-up
máquina *f* machine; **~ de barbear** electric razor; **~ de costura** sewing-machine; **~ de escrever** typewriter; **~ de lavar (roupa)** washing-machine; **~ de lavar louça** dish-washer; **~ fotográfica** camera
maquin|ação *f* machination; **~al** mechanical; **~aria** *f* machinery; **~ismo** *m* machinery; **~ista** *m, f* machinist; engine-driver
mar *m* sea
maracujá *m* passion fruit
maravilh|a *f* marvel; **~ar** *v/t, v/r* marvel
maravilhoso *adj* marve(l)lous, wonderful
marca *f* mark; brand, make
marcação *f* demarcation; booking, reservation
marcar *v/t* mark; dial; fix; book, reserve
marceneiro *m* joiner
marcha *f* march
marchar *v/i* march
marco *m* landmark; mark; **~ postal** pillar box
Março *m* March
maré *f* tide; **~ alta** high tide; **~ baixa** low tide; **~ enchente** flood tide; **~ vazante** ebb tide
marechal *m* marshal
marfim *m* ivory
marg|em *f* bank; margin; **~inal** marginal
marido *m* husband
marinha *f* navy
marinheiro *m* sailor, seaman
marisco *m* shellfish
marítimo *adj* maritime
marmel|ada *f* quince jam; **~o** *m* quince
mármore *m* marble
maroto *m* rascal
marqu|ês *m* marquis; **~esa** *f* marchioness; couch
marr|ada *f* butt; **~ar** *v/i* butt, push with the head
martel|ada *f* blow with a hammer; **~ar** *v/t, v/i* hammer; **~o** *m* hammer
mártir *m* martyr
martírio *m* martyrdom
marujo *m* sailor, seaman
mas *conj* but
mascar *v/t* chew
máscara *f* mask
mascote *m, f* mascot
masculino *adj, m* masculine
másculo virile
massa *f* dough; mass; *slang* money
massacr|ar *v/t* massacre; **~e** *m* massacre
massag|em *f* massage; **~ista** *m* masseur; *f* masseuse
massudo massive
mastigar *v/t* chew, masticate
mastro *m* mast
mata *f* thicket, wood

mata-borrão *m* blotting-paper
mat|adouro *m* slaughterhouse; **~ança** *f* slaughter, killing, butchery; **~ar** *v/t, v/r* quench; kill; slaughter
matemátic|a *f* mathematics; **~o** *m* mathematician
matéria *f* material; matter; **~ prima** raw material
material *m, adj* material
matern|al maternal; motherly; **~idade** *f* maternity
matilha *f* pack
matinal morning, early
matiné *f* matinée
matiz *m* hue, nuance, tone
mato *m* undergrowth; jungle
matrícula *f* matriculation (fee); roll; list
matrim|onial matrimonial; **~ónio** *m* matrimony
matriz *f* matrix; womb; origin
maturação *f* maturation
maturidade *f* maturity
matutino *adj* morning
mau *adj* bad, evil; naughty
mavioso tender, sweet; melodious
maxila *f* jaw
máxima *f* maxim
máximo *m* maximum; *adj* greatest
mazela *f* wound, sore; illness
me me; to me
meado *m* middle
mealheiro *m* money-box
mecânic|a *f* mechanics; **~o** *m* mechanic; *adj* mechanical
mecanismo *m* mechanism
mecha *f* wick; haste; speed
medalha *f* medal
média *f* average
medi|aneiro *m* mediator; **~ano** middling, medium
mediante *prp* by means of
medicamento *m* medicine
medição *f* measurement
med|icar *v/t* treat, doctor; **~icina** *f* medicine
medicinal medicinal
médico *m* doctor, physician
medida *f* measure, size
medieval medi(a)eval
médio *adj* middle; middling, average; intermediary
medíocre *adj* mediocre
medir *v/t* measure
medit|ação *f* meditation; **~ar** *v/t, v/i* meditate
mediterrâneo *adj* Mediterranean
medo *m* fear
medonho frightful
medrar *v/i* thrive
medroso timid, fearful
medula *f* marrow, pith
meia *f* stocking
meia|-lua *f* half-moon; **~-luz** *f* half-light; **~-noite** *f* midnight
meig|o mild, meek, gentle; **~uice** *f* mildness, gentleness; **~uices** *f/pl* caress
meio *m* middle, centre; *adj* half; **~-a-~** *fam* fifty-fifty; **~-ambiente** *m* environment; **~-dia** *m* noon, midday; south
mel *m* honey
melancia *f* water-melon
melão *m* melon
melhor *adj* better; best; **~a** *f* im-

provement; **~amento** *m* improvement; **~ar** *v/t, v/i* get better; improve; **~ia** *f* improvement
melindr|ar *v/t, v/r* hurt, offend; **~e** *m* touchiness, sensitiveness; **~oso** touchy, sensitive
melodia *f* melody
melro *m* blackbird
membro *m* member; limb
mem|orável memorable
memória *f* memory; record, report; **de ~** by heart; **~s** *f/pl* memoirs
men|ção *f* mention; **~cionar** *v/t* mention
mendicidade *f* begging
mendig|ar *v/t, v/i* beg; **~o** *m* beggar
men|ear *v/t* shake; wag; **~eio** *m* shaking; wagging
menin|a *f* girl; miss, young lady; **~o** *m* boy; lad
menor *adj* less(er); smaller; younger; minor; *m* minor
menos *prp* but, except; *adj, adv* less, least; **~ mal** so so, not too bad; **ao/pelo ~** at least; **a ~ que** unless, except
mensag|eiro *m* messenger
mensagem *f* message; **~ SMS** TEL text message
mensal monthly
menstruação *f* menses, menstruation
ment|al mental; **~alidade** *f* mentality; **~e** *f* mind
mentir *v/i* lie; **~a** *f* lie
mercado *m* market; **~ria** *f* goods, merchandise
mercante *adj* mercantile, merchant
mercê *f* reward; mercy
merce|aria *f* grocery; grocer's shop; **~eiro** *m* grocer
mercúrio *m* mercury
merda *f* shit
merec|edor deserving; **~er** *v/t* deserve, merit; **~ido** merited, deserved, just, due; **~imento** *m* merit, worth
merend|a *f* snack, picnic meal, light meal; **~ar** *v/i* eat a snack
mergulh|ador *m* diver; **~ar** *v/t, v/i* plunge, dip, dive
meridional *adj* southern
mérito *m* merit
mero *adj* mere
mês *m* (*pl* **meses**) month
mesa *f* table; **~ de cabeceira** bedside table
mesada *f* monthly allowance
mescla *f* mixture, medley
mesmo *adj* same; self; *adv* even
mesquinho stingy, mean
mestr|a *f* mistress, teacher; **~e** *m* master, teacher; **~ia** *f* mastery
meta *f* limit, end; goal
metade *f* half
metal *m* metal; **~urgia** *f* metallurgy
metamorfose *f* metamorphosis
meter *v/t, v/r* put, place, set **~ o nariz em** poke one's nose into something; **~-se com alguém** provoke someone
meticuloso meticulous

método *m* method
metralhadora *f* machine-gun
metro *m* metre; tube
metrópole *f* metropolis
metro(politano) *m* underground, *US* subway
meu *adj* mine; *pron* (o) ~ my
mexer *v/t, v/i, v/r* touch; stir, move, shake
mexerico *m* gossip
mexilhão *m* mussel
miar *v/i* miaow, *US* meow
micro|chip *m* COMP microchip; **~fone** *m* microphone
migalha *f* crumb, scrap
migração *f* migration
mil thousand
milagr|e *m* miracle; **~oso** miraculous
milha *f* mile
milhão *m* million
milhar *m* thousand
milho *m* maize
milícia *f* militia
milionário *m* millionaire
militar *adj* military; *m* regurlar, professional soldier
mim me
mimo *m* caress, pat; **~so** *adj* tender; soft; delicate
min|a *f* mine; **~ar** *v/t* mine; undermine; **~eiro** *m* miner, collier; **~eral** *adj, m* mineral
míngua *f* lack, shortage
minha *f of* **meu** my, mine
minhoca *f* earth-worm
mínimo *adj* least; slightest; *m* minimum
ministério *m* ministry
ministr|ar *v/t* administer to; **~o** *m* minister
minoria *f* minority
min|úcia *f* minutia; **~uciosidade** *f* accuracy; **~ucloso** meticulous, detailed; **~úscula** *f* small letter; **~úsculo** minute, tiny
minuta *f* minutes
minuto *m* minute
miolos *m/pl* brains
míope *adj* short-sighted, *US* near-sighted; myopic
mira *f* sight; aim, end, goal
mir|ante *m* belvedere; **~ar** *v/t, v/i, v/r* aim (at); look (at)
mirim *adj Braz* small
mirrar *v/t, v/i* dry, wither
mirto *m* myrtle
miscelânea *f* miscellany
miser|ando pitiable, wretched; **~ável** *adj* miserable, wretched; niggardly
miséria *f* misery, wretchedness
misericórdia *f* mercy; compassion
mísero *adj* scarce; miserable, wretched
missa *f* mass
missão *f* mission
mister *m* need; duty function; **ser** ~ be necessary
mist|ério *m* mystery; **~erioso** mysterious
místico *adj, m* mystic
mistificar *v/t* mystify
mist|o *adj* mixed; **~ura** *f* mixture; **~urar** *v/t* mix
mitigar *v/t* mitigate
mito *m* myth
miudeza *f* minuteness; **~s** *f/pl*

giblets; odds and ends/sods, gewgaws, trifles
miúdo *m* boy, youngster; *adj* small, minute; petty; **~s** *m/pl* small change
mobília *f* furniture
mobilidade *f* mobility
mobilizar *v/t* mobilize
moça *f* young woman, girl; girl friend
moção *f* motion
mochila *f* rucksack
mocho *m* owl
mocidade *f* youth
moço *m* boy, young man; boy friend; servant
moda *f* fashion
modalidade *f* modality
modelar *v/t* model
modelo *m* model
moder|ação *f* moderation; **~ar** *v/t* moderate
moderno *adj* modern
mod|éstia *f* modesty; **~esto** modest
módico moderate
modific|ação *f* modification; **~ado** *adj* modified; **geneticamente ~ado** genetically modified; **~ar** *v/t* modify
modo *m* way, manner, mode; **de ~ nenhum** not at all; **de ~ que** so that; **~ de usar** instruction for use
moeda *f* coin
moela *f* gizzard
moer *v/t, v/r* wear out; grind
mof|a *f* mockery, banter; **~ar** *v/t* scoff at, mock at
mofo *m* mo(u)ld, mustiness
mogno *m* mahogany
moinho *m* mill
mola *f* spring; **~ real** mainspring
mold|ar *v/t* mo(u)ld; **~e** *m* mo(u)ld; model; **~ura** *f* mo(u)lding; picture frame
mole *adj* soft; indolent, inert
moleiro *m* miller
molestar *v/t* annoy, disturb; molest
moléstia *f* trouble
moleque *m* little Negro; *Braz* urchin
moleza *f* softness; slackness
molhar *v/t, v/r* (get) wet
molhe *m* mole, pier
molho *m* bundle
molho *m* sauce, gravy
moment|âneo momentary; **~o** *m* moment
monar|ca *m* monarch; **~quia** *f* monarchy
monástico monastic
mondar *v/t* weed, hoe
monetário *adj* monetary
monge *m* monk
monja *f* nun
mono *m* ape
monopólio *m* monopoly
monotonia *f* monotony
monótono monotonous
monstr|o *m* monster; **~uoso** monstrous
monta *f* amount; worth
montagem *f* erection; montage; fitting
montanh|a *f* mountain; **~oso** mountainous
montante *m* amount, total
montar *v/t, v/i* ride; mount; put

up, set up; come to
montaria *f* hunting
monte *m* hill; heap
montra *f* shop-window, show-case
monumento *m* monument
mor|ada *f* address, residence; **~adia** *f* villa, house; **~ador** *m* resident, inhabitant
moral *f, adj* moral; **~idade** *f* morality
morango *m* strawberry
morar *v/i* live, dwell
mórbido morbid
morcego *m* bat
morcela *f* black pudding
mordaça *f* gag
mord|az mordant; biting; **~edura** *f* bite; **~er** *v/t, v/i, v/r* bite
moreno *adj* dark-skinned
moribundo *adj* moribund
morno lukewarm
moroso sluggish
morrer *v/i* die
morro *m* mound, hillock
mortal *adj* mortal; deadly; **~idade** *f* mortality; death-rate
mortandade *f* slaughter
morte *f* death
mortiço dull, lifeless
mortific|ação *f* mortification; **~ar** *v/t, v/r* mortify
morto *adj* dead; killed; **estar ~ por** be dying for/to; **~ de cansaço** fagged
mosca *f* fly
mosqui|teiro *m* mosquito net; **~to** *m* mosquito
mostarda *f* mustard
mosteiro *m* monastery
mostra *f* sample, specimen
mostrador *m* face, dial
mostrar *v/t* show; display
motej|ar *v/t, v/i* mock at, deride; **~o** *m* jeer, banter
motim *m* mutiny; riot
motivar *v/t* motivate
motivo *m* reason; motive
motocicl|eta *f* motor-cycle; **~ista** *m, f* motor-cyclist
motor *m* motor; engine; **~ exterior móvel** outboard motor; **~ista** *m, f* motorist
motriz *adj* motive, driving
mouco deaf
móveis *m/pl* movables; furniture
móvel *adj* movable, mobile; *m* motive; piece of furniture
mov|er *v/t, v/i, v/r* move; **~imento** *m* movement
mucos|a *f* mucous membrane; **~o** mucous
mud|a *f* change; moulting; **~ança** *f* change; removal; **~ar** *v/t, v/i, v/r* change; remove; moult **~ável** mutable; changeable
mud|ez *f* dumbness; **~o** *adj* dumb, mute
mugir *v/i* bellow, low, moo
muito *adj* a lot of, much, *pl* many; *adv* very; much; too; too much
mula *f* she-mule
mulher *f* woman; wife
multa *f* fine
multicolor multicolo(u)red
multicultural *adj* multicultural
multidão *f* crowd; multitude

multiplex *m* (*cinema*) multiplex
multiplic|ação *f* multiplication; **~ar** *v/t*, *v/i* multiply
múltiplo *adj*, *m* multiple
mundano worldly, mundane
mund|ial world-wide; **~ de futebol** football, *US* soccer World Cup; **~o** *m* world
mungir *v/t* milk
munição (am)munition
municipal *adj* municipal; **~idade** *f* municipality; town ship
município *m* borough
munir *v/t*, *v/r* provide
muralha *f* wall, rampart
murch|ar *v/t*, *v/i* wither, fade; **~o** withered, faded
murmurar *v/t*, *v/i* murmur whisper
murmúrio *m* murmur
muro *m* wall
murro *m* blow, punch
músculo *m* muscle
musculoso muscular, brawny
museu *m* museum
musgo *m* moss
música *f* music; **~ pop** pop (music); **~ rap** rap (music); **~ rock** rock (music)
music|al *m* musical; **~ar** *v/t* make music; **~ata** *f* bras band; piece of music
músico *adj* musical; *m* musician
mut|abilidade *f* mutability; **~ação** *f* mutation
mutil|ação *f* mutilation; **~ado** *adj* mutilated, disabled; **~ar** *v/t* mutilate
mutismo *m* dumbness; muteness
mutuar *v/t* exchange
mútuo mutual

N

na *contr of* **em** *and* **a**
nabo *m* turnip
nácar *m* mother-of-pearl
nacional *adj* national; **~idade** *f* nationality; **~ismo** *m* nationalism; **~ização** *f* nationalization; **~izar** *v/t* nationalize
nada *adv*, *m* nothing; **de ~** not at all
nad|ador *m* swimmer; **~ar** *v/i* swim
nádega *f* buttock
nado *m* swim; **a ~** by swimming
namor|ada *f* girl friend; **~ado** *m* boy friend; **~ar** *v/t* court; **~i(s)car** *v/t*, *v/i* flirt; **~o** *m* courtship
não *adv* no; not
narciso *m* narcissus
narcótico *m* narcotic
nariz *m* nose
narr|ação *f* narration; **~ar** *v/t* narrate, relate; **~ativa** *f* narrative
nascente *f* source, spring
nasc|er *v/i* be born; arise; **~imento** *m* birht; origin
nata *f* cream

natação *f* swimming
natal *adj* natal, native; **♀** *m* Christmas
matalício natal
natalidade *f* birth-rate
natividade *f* nativity
nativo native, natural
natural *adj* natural; **~idade** *f* naturalness; nationality
naturalizar *v/t*, *v/r* naturalize
natureza *f* nature; **~ morta** still life
naufragar *v/i* shipwreck
naufrágio *m* shipwreck
náufrago *adj* shipwrecked
náusea *f* nausea
naval naval
navalha *f* razor
nave *f* nave
nave|gação *f* navigation; **~gar** *v/t*, *v/i* navigate; **~ na Net** COMP surf the net; **~gável** navigable
navio *m* ship, boat
neblina *f* fog, mist
nebuloso nebulous, cloudy
necessário *adj* necessary
necess|idade *f* necessity; **itar** *v/t* need
necrologia *f* necrology
nédio sleek, fat, plump
neg|ação *f* negation, denial; **~ar** *v/t*, *v/i*, *v/r* refuse; deny; **~ativa** *f* negative; **~ativo** *m*, *adj* negative
neglig|ência *f* negligence; **~ente** negligent
negoci|ação *f* negotiation; **~ante** *m*, *f* trader; businessman; **~ar** *v/i*, *v/t* negotiate; **~ável** negotiable
negócio *m* business; trade
negro *adj* dark; black
nela, nele *contr of* **em** *and* **ela, ele**
nem *conj* neither; nor; *adv* not **~ … ~** neither … nor; **~ sequer** not even
nené *m* baby
nervo *m* nerve; **~so** nervous
néscio *adj* ignorant, foolish
nesse, neste *contr of* **em** *and* **esse, este**
Net *f* COMP Internet, net
net|a *f* granddaughter; **~o** *m* grandson
neutral neutral
neutro *adj*, *m* neuter
nev|ada *f* snow-fall; **~ão** *m* snow-storm; **~ar** *v/i* snow; **~e** *f* snow
névoa *f* fog, mist
nevo|eiro *m* thick fog; **~ento** foggy, misty
nicho *m* niche
ninguém nobody, no one
ninho *m* nest
nisso, nisto *contr of* **em** *and* **isso, isto**
nitidez *f* clearness; sharpness
nítido clear; shining; sharp
nível *m* level; **~ de vida** standard of living, living standard
no *contr of* **em** *and* **o**
nó *m* knot; knuckle
nobre *adj*, *m* noble; **~za** *f* nobility
noção *f* notion
nocico harmful
no(c)turno *adj* nocturnal
nódoa *f* stain

nogueira *f* walnut-tree
noite *f* night; **à/de ~** at/by night
noiv|a *f* bride; fiancée **~o** *m* bridegroom; fiancé
noj|ento nauseous, disgusting; **~o** *m* nausea; disgust
nom|e *m* name; **~eação** *f* nomination; **~eada** *f* renown; **~ear** *v/t* nominate, appoint; name
nono *adj* ninth
nora *f* daughter-in-law
nordeste *m* north-east
nórdico *adj* Nordic
norma *f* norm, standard
noroeste *m* north-west
nort|ada *f* north-wind; **~e** *m* north
norueguês *adj*, *m* Norwegian
nos *pers pron* (to) us; (to) ourselves
nós we; us
nosso *pron*, *adj* our; ours
not|a *f* note; mark; **~ar** *v/t* note; observe; notice; **~ário** *m* notary; **~ável** remarkable, notable
not|ícia *f* news; **~iciador** *m* reporter
noticiário *m* newscast
not|oriedade *f* notoriety; **~ório** notorious, well-known
noutro *contr of* **em** *and* **outro**
nova *f* news
nove nine
novela *f* novel, story
novelo *m* ball, clew
Novembro *m* November
noventa ninety
novidade *f* novelty
novilho *m* young steer; bullock
novo *adj* new; young; **de ~** again, anew
noz *f* walnut
nu *adj* naked, nude, bare
nublado *adj* cloudy
nuca *f* nape, scruff
núcleo *m* nucleus, kernel
nuclear nuclear
nulidade *f* nullity; invalidity; nonentity
nulo null, void
num, numa *contr of* **em** *and* **um, uma**
numer|ação *f* numeration; **~al** *adj*, *m* numeral; **~ar** *v/t* number
número *m* number; **~ de código PIN** PIN number
numeroso numerous
nunca never; **~ mais** never again
núpcias *f/pl* nuptials, marriage, wedding
nutr|ição *f* nutrition; **~ir** *v/t*, *v/r* nourish; **~itivo** nutritive
nuvem *f* cloud

O

o *art* the; *pron* it, him, he; the one; **~ que** what; he who, the one that
oásis *m* oasis
obcec|ação *f* obstinacy; **~ar** *v/t* blind, bewilder
obedecer *v/i* obey
obedi|ência *f* obedience; **~ente** obedient
obeso obese
óbito *m* decease
obje(c)|ção *f* objection; **~tar** *v/t* object
obje(c)tivo *adj*, *m* objective
obje(c)to *m* object
oblíquo oblique
obr|a *f* work; **~a-prima** *f* masterpiece; **~ar** *v/t*, *v/i* act; work; **~eiro** *m* workman, worker
obrig|ação *f* obligation; **~ado** *adj* obliged; *int* thank you; **~ar** *v/t* oblige; compel; **~atório** obligatory
obscen|idade *f* obscenity; **~o** obscene
obscur|ecer *v/t*, *v/i*, *v/r* darken; **~idade** *f* obscurity; **~o** obscure; dark
obséquio *m* favo(u)r, kindness
observ|ação *f* observation; remark; **~ador** *m* observer; **~ância** *f* observance; **~ar** *v/t*, *v/r* observe; remark; **~atório** *m* observatory
obsessão *f* obsession
obsoleto obsolete
obstáculo *m* obstacle
obstante hindering; **não ~** in spite of, notwithstanding
obstar *v/i* hinder, obstruct
obstin|ação *f* obstinacy; **~ado** obstinate; **~ar** *v/t*, *v/r* persist (**em** in)
obstru|ção *f* obstruction; **~ir** *v/t* obstruct
obtenção *f* obtainment
obter *v/t* obtain, get
obtur|ador *m* obturator, shutter; **~ar** *v/t* fill; plug, stop up
obtuso obtuse
óbvio obvious
ocasião *f* occasion; opportunity
ocasion|al occasional; **~ar** *v/t* occasion, cause
ocaso *m* setting; west; *fig* decadence, end
oceano *m* ocean
ocident|al western, occidental; **~e** *m* west, occident
ócio *m* idleness, leisure
ocios|idade *f* idleness; **~o** *adj* idle
oco hollow
ocorr|ência *f* occurrence; **~er** *v/i* occur
oculista *m*, *f* optician; oculist
óculos *m/pl* specs, spectacles, glasses
ocultar *v/t*, *v/r* hide
ocupa|ção *f* occupation; **~do** busy; occupied, taken; **~r** *v/t*,

v/r occupy
odiar *v/t* hate
ódio *m* hate, hatred
odor *m* odo(u)r; scent
odre *m* wineskin
oeste *m* west
ofegante panting, breathless
ofegar *v/i* pant, puff
ofender *v/t*, *v/r* offend; insult
ofensa *f* offence; insult
ofensiva *f* offensive, attack
oferec|er *v/t* offer; **~imento** *m* offering
oferta *f* offer; tender
oficial *adj* official; *m* officer; official
oficina *f* workshop
ofício *m* trade, craft duty, office
ofuscar *v/t* obfuscate; bewilder
oitavo *adj* eighth
oitenta eighty
oito eight
oitocentos eight hundred
olaria *f* pottery
oleado *m* oilcloth, linoleum
olear *v/t* oil
oleiro *m* potter
óleo *m* oil; **~ de fígado de bacalhau** cod-liver oil
olfa(c)to *m* sense of smell
olha(de)la *f* glance, look
olhar *v/t*, *v/i*, *v/r* look (at); *m* look, glance
olheiras *f/pl* shadows under the eyes
olho *m* eye; **a ~ vistos** visibly; **até aos ~s** to the teeth
olimpíada *f* Olympiad
olival *m* olive grove
oliveira *f* olive-tree
olmo *m* elm
ombro *m* shoulder
omeleta *f* omelette
omissão *f* omission
omitir *v/t* omit
o(m)nipot|ência *f* omnipotence; **~ente** *adj* omnipotent
onça *f* ounce; zoo lynx
onda *f* wave
onde *adv* where; **~ quer que** wherever
ondulação *f* undulation
oneroso onerous, burdensome
ónibus *m* bus
ontem yesterday; **~ à noite** last night
onze eleven
opaco opaque
opção *f* option
ópera *f* opera
operação *f* operation
operador *m* poerator
operar *v/t*, *v/i* operate
operário *m* workman
opinião *f* opinion
opor *v/t*, *v/r* oppose
oportunidade *f* opportunity
oportuno opportune
oposição *f* opposition
oposto *m adj* opposite
opressão *f* oppression
oprimir *v/t* oppress
ó(p)tico *m* optician
o(p)timista *m*, *f* optimist
ó(p)timo excellent
opulento opulent
ora *conj* but; *int* well! oh!; *adv* now; **~ bem** well now; **~ essa**; why!, the very idea!
oração *f* oration; prayer;

clause, sentence
orador *m* orator
oral *adj* oral
orar *v/i* pray
orbe *m* orb, sphere, globe
órbita *f* orbit
orç|amento *m* estimate; budget; **~ar** *v/t* estimate
ordem *f* order; command
ordenação *f* ordination; ordinance; arrangement
ordenado *m* salary
ordenar *v/t, v/i* order, command; put in order, arrange
ordinário *adj* ordinary
orelha *f* ear
orfanato *m* orphanage
órfão *m* (*f* **órfã**) orphan
orgânico organic
organismo *m* organism
organização *f* organization
organizar *v/t* organize
órgão *m* organ
orgulhar-se *v/r* pride oneself
orgulho *m* pride; **~so** *adj* proud
oriental *adj* oriental, eastern
orientar *v/t, v/r* orient(ate); find one's bearings
oriente *m* orient, east
orifício *m* orifice, hole
origem *f* origin
original *adj, m* original; **~idade** *f* originality
originar *v/t, v/r* originate
originário de native of
orla *f* fringe, edge
ornament|ar *v/t* ornament; decorate; **~o** *m* ornament
ornar *v/t* adorn
orquestra *f* orchestra
orquídia *f* orchid, orchis
ortografia *f* orthography, spelling
orvalho *m* dew
oscil|ação *m* oscillation; **~ar** *v/i* oscillate
ósculo *m* kiss
osso *m* bone
ostensível ostensible
ostentação *f* ostentation
ostentar *v/t, v/i* show off
ostra *f* oyster
ou either; or
ouriço(-cacheiro) *m* hedgehog; **~-do-mar** sea urchin
ourives *m* goldsmith
ourivesaria *f* goldsmith's shop, jewellery
ouro *m* gold
ousad|ia *f* boldness; daring; **~o** daring, bold
ousar *v/t* dare
outono *m* autumn, *US* fall
outorgar *v/t* grant
outrem other people
outro *adj, pron* other; another
outrora formerly
outrossim likewise, also
Outubro *m* October
ouvido *m* ear; hearing
ouvinte *m, f* listener, hearer
ouvir *v/t, v/i* listen to; hear; **~ dizer que** be told that; **~ falar de** hear of
ova *f* roe
ovação *f* ovation
ovelha *f* sheep; ewe
ovo *m* egg; **~ escalfado** poached egg; **~ estrelado**

fried egg; **~ mexido** scrambled egg; **~ moles** sweet eggs
oxalá! let's hope!, would that!
oxigénio *m* oxygen

P

pá *f* shovel, spade
pacato *adj* peaceful, placid
pachorrento sluggish
paciência *f* patience
paciente *m*, *adj* patient
pacific|ação *f* pacification; **~ar** *v/t*, *v/r* pacify
pacífico *adj* pacific, calm
pacote *m* packet, parcel
pacto *m* pact
padaria *f* bakery
padec|er *v/t*, *v/i* suffer; **~imento** *m* suffering
padeiro *m* baker
padrão *m* stone monument; pattern, sample; standard
padrasto *m* stepfather
padre *m* priest; Father
padrinho *m* godfather
padroeiro *m* patron saint
paga *f* pay; **~mento** *m* payment; **~mento anticipado** COM cash in advance
pagão *m* pagan, heathen
pagar *v/t*, *v/i*, *v/r* pay (for)
página *f* page; **virar a ~** turn over the page; *fig* change the subject
paginar *v/t*, *v/i* leaf; COMP scroll
pai *m* father
painel *m* panel; painting
paio *m* thick sausage
pais *m/pl* parents
país *m* country
paisagem *f* landscape, countryside
paisano *m* civilian
paixão *f* passion
palácio *m* palace
paladar *m* taste
palato *m* palate
palavra *f* word
palavrão *f* swear-word
palco *m* THEAT stage
palerma *m*, *f* simpleton, dolt
palestra *f* talk, chat
palha *f* straw
palhaço *m* clown
palhinha *f* straw
palhota *f* straw hut
paliativo *m* palliative
paliçada *f* palisade
pálido pale, pallid
palito *m* toothpick
palma *f* palm; **~s** *f/pl* clappin
palmada *f* clap, slap
palmeira *f* palm-tree
palmo *m* span; **~ a ~** inch by inch; step by step
pálpebra *f* eyelid
palpit|ação *f* palpitation; **~ante** thrilling, exciting; **~ar** *v/i* palpitate; **~e** *m* presentiment inkling
palrador *m* chatterbox
palrar *v/i* chatter
pancada *f* blow, knock
pançudo pot-bellied

pândega *f* spree, frolic, revelry
panela *f* pot
panfleto *m* pamphlet
pânico *m* panic
pano *m* cloth; ~ **de fundo** backdrop, backcloth; ~ **de boca** THEAT curtain
pântano *m* swamp, marsh
pantera *f* panther
pantufa *f* slipper
pão *m* bread; loaf; ~**zinho** *m* roll
papa *m* Pope; *f* pap
papá *m* dad(dy), *US* papa, poppa
papagaio *m* parrot; kite
paparazzi *m/pl* paparazzi
papai *m Braz* dad, papa
papeira *f* mumps
papel *m* paper; THEAT role, part; ~ **higiénico** toilet paper; ~**ão** *m* cardboard; ~**aria** *f* stationer's (shop); ~**inhos** *m/pl* confetti; ~**-moeda** *m* paper money
papoila *f* poppy
par *m* pair; *adj* even; equal
para for; to; towards; in order to; ~ **que** so that; ~ **quê?** what for?; **estar** ~ be about to
parabéns *m/pl* congratulations
pára|-brisas *m* wind-screen; ~**-choques** *m* bumper, buffer
parada *f* parade; *Braz* bus stop
parafuso *m* screw
paragem *f* bus stop
paraíso *m* paradise
paralisar *v/t*, *v/i*, *v/r* paralyse
paralisia *f* paralysis
paralítico *adj*, *m* paralytic
parapeito *m* window-sill
pára-quedas *m* parachute
parar *v/t*, *v/i* stop, halt
pára-raios *m* lightning-conductor
parceiro *m* partner
parcial *adj* partial; ~**idade** *f* partiality; ~**mente** partly; partially
parco frugal, thrifty
pardal *m* sparrow
pardo *adj* grey
parecer *v/i*, *v/r* resemble, look like; seem, appear; *m* opinion; appearance
parecido similar, like, resembling
parede *f* wall
parelha *f* pair, couple
parente *m* relative
parentela *f* kindred
pargo *m* sea bream
paridade *f* parity
parir *v/t* give birth to, bear
parlamento *m* parliament
parlapatão *m* braggart
pároco *m* parish priest
parque *m* park
parte *f* part
parteira *f* midwife
particip|ação *f* participation; ~**ante** *m*, *f* participant; ~**ar** *v/t*, *v/i* participate; announce
particular *adj* particular, peculiar, private
partida *f* departure; match, game; trick
partidário *m* partisan
partido *m* (political) party; *adj* divided; broken

partilh|a *f* share; **~ar** *v/t* share
partir *v/t, v/i, v/r* break; divide; depart, leave; **a ~ de** from … on
parto *m* child-birth
parvo *adj* stupid
Páscoa *f* Easter
pasm|ar *v/t, v/i, v/r* astonish; **~o** *m* astonishment
passa *f* raisin
passadeira *f* zebra crossing; runner, stair-carpet
passado *m* past; *adj* passed; past, last
passador *m* strainer, colander
passageiro *m* passenger; *adj* transitory; passing
passagem *f* passage; passing; way through; fare
passaporte *m* passport
passar *v/t, v/i, v/r* happen; cross; pass; spend; **~ a ferro** iron, press; **~ por alto** overlook; **não ~ de** be no more than, be only; **~ sem** do without; **passou bem?** how are you?
pássaro *m* bird
passatempo *m* pastime, hobby
passe *m* pass, free pass
passear *v/t, v/i* walk, stroll
passeio *m* walk; pavement, *US* sidewalk; promenade
passivo *adj* passive
passo *m* pace, step, stride; passage; **ao ~ que** while
pasta *f* paste; brief-case; portfolio
past|agem *f* pasturage; **~ar** *v/t, v/i* graze
pastel *m* pie, pastry; pastel
pastelaria *f* confectioner's shop; confectionery
pasto *m* pasture; food
pastor *m* shepherd
pata *f* paw, foot; duck; **à ~** on foot
patamar *m* landing
patear *v/i* kick, stamp
patente *adj, f* patent
patentear *v/t* manifest
paternidade *f* paternity
patife *m* rogue, scoundrel
patim *m* skate; **~ de rodas** roller-skate
patinar *v/i* skate
pátio *m* yard, courtyard
pato *m* drake, duck
patrão *m* master, boss
pátria *f* mother country, fatherland
património *m* patrimony
patrocinar *v/t* sponsor, support
patrocínio *m* patronage
patrulha *f* patrol
patusco *adj* boisterous
pau *m* stick, pole; wood
pausa *f* pause
pauta *f* ruled paper; list
pavão *m* peacock
pavilhão *m* pavilion
pavimento *m* paving; floor, sto-r(e)y
pavor *m* dread; **~oso** dreadful
paz *f* peace; quiet
pé *m* foot; leg; **~ de vento** gust of wind; **a ~** on foot; **ao ~ de** near, close to; **de/em ~** standing

peão *m* pedestrian; pawn
peça *f* piece; play
peca|do *m* sin; **~dor** *m* sinner; **~r** *v/i* sin
pechincha *f* bargain
peçonh|a *f* poison; **~ento** poisonous
peculiar peculiar, exclusive
pecúlio *m* savings, hoard
pedaço *m* bit, piece, fragment
pedido *m* request; COM order
pedir *v/t* ask (for), request; **~ desculpa** apologize; **~ emprestado** borrow
pedr|a *f* stone; **~eira** *f* quarry; **~eiro** *m* stone-mason
pega *f* magpie
pega *f* handle; quarrel
pegada *f* footprint, trace
pegado stuck; near to
pegar *v/t*, *v/i*, *v/r* start; catch; grasp, seize; take root; glue, stick; **~ fogo a** set fire to; **~ no sono** get to sleep
peito *m* chest; breast; *fig* heart
peitoril *m* sill; parapet
peix|e *m* fish; **~eiro** *m* fishmonger
pejo *m* shyness, coyness
pela *contr of* **por** *and* **a**
pelar *v/t*, *v/r* skin; peal; **~-se por** be very fond of
pele *f* skin; fur
peleja *f* fight; **~r** *v/i* fight
pelica *f* kid (leather)
pelo *contr of* **por** *and* **o**
pêlo *m* hair
peludo *adj* hairy
pena *f* feather; quill; punishment; grief, sorrow; pity; **é (uma) ~!** it's a pity; **ter ~ de** be sorry for
penal penal; **~idade** *f* penalty
penar *v/i* pain, grieve
pendente *adj* pendent; *m* pendant
pender *v/i* hang
pendor *m* slope; propensity
pêndulo *m* pendulum
pendurar *v/t* hang up
penedo *m* rock, boulder
peneira *f* sieve; **~r** *v/t* sieve
penetr|ação *f* penetration; sagacity; **~ante** piercing, penetrating; **~ar** *v/t* penetrate, pierce; **~ável** penetrable
penha *f* rock, crag, cliff
penhasco *m* cliff
penhor *m* pledge; security; token
penhora *f* seizure, distraint; **~r** *v/t* seize, impound, confiscate
península *f* peninsula
penitência *f* penance; penitence
penitenciária *f* penitentiary
penitente *m*, *adj* penitent
penoso irksome, laborious
pensamento *m* thought
pensão *f* pension; boarding-house
pensar *v/t*, *v/i* think; intend to
pensativo thoughtful, pensive
penso *m* bandage, dressing
pente *m* comb; **~ado** *m* coiffure; **~ar** *v/t* comb
penugem *f* down, fluff
penúltimo penultimate
penumbra *f* penumbra
penúria *f* penury

pepino *m* cucumber
pequeno *adj* small, little
pêra *f* (*pl* **peras**) pear
perante before, in the presence of
perceber *v/t* understand; perceive
percentagem *f* percentage
percepção *f* perception
perceptível perceptible
percevejo *m* bedbug; drawing-pin, *US* thumb-tack
percorrer *v/t* go through, travel all over
percurso *m* course; route
percussão *f* percussion
perda *f* loss
perdão *m* pardon; **~!** I'm sorry!
perder *v/t*, *v/i*, *v/r* get lost; lose; miss; waste; **~ de vista** lose sight of
perdido *adj* lost; **~ de riso** beside oneself with laughter
perdiz *f* partridge
perdo|ar *v/t* pardon, forgive; **~ável** pardonable, forgivable
perdulário *adj* wasteful; *m* spendthrift
perecer *v/i* perish
peregrin|ação *f* pilgrimage; **~ar** *v/i* go on a pilgrimage; **~o** *m* pilgrim
pereira *f* pear-tree
peremptório peremptory
perene perennial
perfazer *v/t* complete
perfeição *f* perfection
perfeito perfect
pérfido perfidious, treacherous
perfil *m* profile
perfilhar *v/t* adopt
perfum|aria *f* perfumery, perfumier's; **~e** *m* perfume
perfurar *v/t* perforate, bore, drill
pergaminho *m* parchment
pergunta *f* question; **~r** *v/t*, *v/i* ask, question
perícia *f* skill
perigo *m* danger, peril; **~so** dangerous, perilous
periódico *adj* periodical; *m* newspaper
período *m* period
periquito *m* parakeet
perito *adj* skiful, able; *m* expert, connoisseur
perjúrio *m* perjury
perjuro *m* perjurer
permanecer *v/i* remain, stay
perman|ência *f* permanence stay; **~ente** *f* perm, *US* permanent; *adj* permanent
permissão *f* permission
permitir *v/t* permit
permut|a *f* permutation; **~ar** *v/t* permute; exchange
perna *f* leg
pernicioso pernicious
pernoitar *v/i* spend the night
pérola *f* pearl
perpendicular *adj*, *f* perpendicular
perpetuar *v/t*, *v/r* perpetuate
perpétuo perpetual
perplexo perplexed
persa *adj* Persian
perscrutar *v/t* peruse, scan
persegu|ição *f* persecution; **~ir** *v/t* pursue; persecute

persever|ança *f* perseverance; **~ante** persevering; **~ar** *v/t* persevere
persiana *f* Venetian blind
persist|ência *f* persistance; **~ente** persistent; **~ir** *v/i* persist
personagem *m, f* character, personage
personificar *v/t* personify
perspe(c)tiva *f* prospect; perspective
perspic|ácia *f* perspicacity; **~az** perspicacious
persuadir *v/t, v/i, v/r* persuade; convince
persuasão *f* persuasion
persuasivo persuasive
perten|cente belonging, appertaining; **~cer** *v/i* belong; appertain to
pertin|ácia *f* pertinacity; **~az** pertinacious, stubborn
perto *adv* close, near; **~ de** nearly; nearby; **de ~** intimately; closely
perturb|ação *f* perturbation; **~ar** *v/t, v/r* disturb, perturb
peru *m* turkey
pesadelo *m* nightmare
pesado heavy
pêsames *m/pl* condolences
pesar *v/t, v/i, v/r* weight; *m* sorrow, grief; regret
pesaroso sorry, sorrowful
pesca *f* fishing
pescada *f* ZOO hake, whiting
pescador *m* fisherman; **~ à linha** angler
pescar *v/t, v/i* fish; **~ à linha** angle
pescoço *m* neck
peso *m* weight
pesquis|a *f* search, inquiry; investigation; **~a textual** COMP full-text search; **~ar** *v/t* search; investigate, prospect for
pêssego *m* peach
pessimista *m, f* pessimist
péssimo very bad
pessoa *f* person
pessoal *adj* personal; *m* staff, personnel
pestana *f* eyelash
peste *f* plague
petição *f* petition
petisco *m* titbit
petiz *m* child, nipper
petroleiro *m* oil tanker
petróleo *m* petroleum, paraffin
petulância *f* petulance
peúga *f* sock
pia *f* sink
piada *f* joke, wisecrack
piano *m* piano; **~ de cauda** grand piano
piar *v/i* chirp, cheep
picada *f* prick; sting
picadeiro *m* riding-school
picante *adj* hot, piquant
picar *v/t* prick; sting
picareta *f* pickax(e)
pico *m* peak; **e ~** odd, and a bit
piedade *f* piety; pity
piedoso pious; pitiful
piegas *adj* soppy, faint-hearted
pijama *m* pyjamas, *US* pajamas
pilar *m* pillar
pilha *f* pile; battery
pilhar *v/t* pillage; steal
piloto *m* pilot

pílula *f* pill
pimenta *f* pepper
pimento *m* paprika
pinça *f* tweezers
pincel *m* brush; ~ **da barba** shaving-brush
pinga *f* drop; wine
pingar *v/i* drip; trickle
pingo *m* drop
pingue-pongue *m* ping-pong
pinguin *m* penguin
pinh|a *f* pine-cone; crowd; **~al** *m* pinewood; **~eiro** *m* pine--tree; **~o** *m* pine
pino *m* top; handstand; **a ~** perpendicular, upright; **no ~ do inverno** in the depth of winter; **no ~ do verão** at the height of summer
pinta *f* spot, mark
pintar *v/t*, *v/i* paint
pintarroxo *m* robin (redbreast)
pinto *m* chicken
pint|or *m* painter; **~ura** *f* painting, picture
piolho *m* louse
pior *adj*, *adv* worse; **~ar** *v/i* get worse
pipa *f* cask, barrel
pires *m* saucer; *adj* silly
pisar *v/t* tread, trample; bruise
pisca-pisca *m* indicator light
piscar *v/t* wink, blink
piscina *f* swimming-pool
piso *m* floor; ground; stor(e)y
pista *f* track; runway
pito *m Braz* pipe
placa *f* plaque; sheet; **~ de som** COMP sound card
plácido placid
planalto *m* plateau
plane(j)ar *v/t* plan (out)
planície *f* plain
plano *m* plan; *adj* flat, level
planta *f* plant; sole; **~ção** *f* plantation; **~r** *v/t* plant
plataforma *f* platform
plátano *m* plane(-tree)
plateia *f* THEAT pit, stalls
plausível plausible
pleito *m* lawsuit
plenipotenciário *adj*, *m* plenipotentiary
pleno full; absolute
pluma *f* plume
pneu *m* tyre, *US* tire
pneumonia *f* pneumonia
pó *m* powder; dust
pobre *adj* poor; **~za** *f* poverty
poça *f* puddle
poço *m* well
poder *v/t*, *v/i* be able, can; may; *m* power; **~oso** powerful
podr|e *adj* rotten; **~e de rico** money-bags; **~idão** *f* rottenness
poeir|a *f* dust; **~ento** dusty
poente *m* west
poesia *f* poetry; poem
poeta *m* poet
pois *conj* for; then; as, since; **~ bem** well then; **~ é** that's it; **~ não** of course, certainly; **~ sim** oh sure; yes, that's right; **~ quê?** why so?
polaco *adj* Polish; *m* Pole
polegar *m* thumb
polémica *f* polemic
polícia *f* police; *m* policeman
policial *m Braz* policeman

polid|ez *f* politeness; **~o** polite; polished
polir *v/t* polish
política *f* politics; policy
político *adj* political; *m* politician
pólo *m* pole; polo
poltrona *f* armchair
poluição *f* pollution
polvilhar *v/t* powder
polvo *m* octopus
pólvora *f* gunpowder
pomada *f* ointment
pomar *m* orchard
pomba *f*, **pombo** *m* dove; pigeon
pomp|a *f* pomp; **~oso** pompous
ponderar *v/t*, *v/i* ponder
ponta *f* point; tip; edge; stub; **nas ~s dos pés** on tiptoe
pontada *f* stitch, pain
pontapé *m* kick
ponte *f* bridge
ponteiro *m* hand; pointer
ponto *m* stitch; point, dot, spot
pontual punctual; **~idade** *f* punctuality
popa *f* stern, poop
população *f* population
popular *adj* popular; **~idade** *f* popularity
populoso populous
por for; by; through
pôr *v/t*, *v/r* put, set; lay; **~-se de pé** stand up
porão *m* hold
porção *f* portion
porcaria *f* filth, rubbish
porcelana *f* porcelain
porco *m* pig
porém but, however
pormenor *m* detail
porquanto considering that, seeing that
porque because; why
porquê why
porta *f* door
porta|-aviões *m* aircraft carrier; **~-bagagens** *m* boot, *US* trunk
portador *m* bearer, holder
portagem *f* toll; tollgate
porta-moedas *m* purse
portanto therefore
portão *m* gate(way)
portaria *f* main gate; entrance-hall; decree, order
portar-se *v/r* behave, conduct
porte *m* postage; bearing
porteiro *m* porter, doorkeeper
portento *m* wonder; **~so** portentous
porto *m* port, harbo(u)r; **~ franco** *m* free port
português *m*, *adj* Portuguese
porventura by chance, perhaps
posição *f* position
possante powerful
posse *f* possession
possibilidade *f* possibility
possível *adj* possible
possuidor *m* possessor
possuir *v/t* possess
posta *f* slice; **~-restante** poste restante, *US* general delivery
postal *m* postcard; *adj* postal
poste *m* post
posteridade *f* posterity
posterior *adj*, *m* posterior
postiço false, artificial

postigo *m* peep-hole
posto *m* job, post; military rank; ~ **que** although
póstumo posthumous
potável drinkable
pote *m* pot
potência *f* power; authority; potency
potente powerful; potent
pouco *adj*, *adv* little; ~**s** few
poupar *v/t*, *v/i*, *v/r* save; spare
pousada *f*, inn, hotel
pousar *v/t*, *v/i* perch; put, set down
povo *m* people; ~**ação** *f* population; township
povoar *v/t*, *v/r* people
praça *f* square; market-place; ~ **de touros** bullring
prado *m* meadow
praga *f* curse; plague
praguejar *v/t*, *v/i* curse
praia *f* beach; shore; seaside
pranto *m* weeping, lamentation
prata *f* silver
prateado silvery
prática *f* practice
praticar *v/t* practise
prático *adj* practical
prato *m* plate; dish; course
praxe *f* practice, custom
prazer *m* pleasure; **muito** ~! how do you do?
prazo *m* period, term; **a longo/ /curto** ~ in the long/short term
pré *m* military pay
precário precarious
precaução *f* precaution
precaver *v/t*, *v/r* guard against
prece *f* prayer
precedência *f* precedence
preceder *v/t*, *v/i* precede
preceito *m* precept
precios|idade *f* preciousness; ~**o** precious
precipício *m* precipice
precipit|ação *f* precipitation; rashness; ~**ado** *adj* rash; *m* CHEM precipitate; ~**ar** *v/t*, *v/i*, *v/r* precipitate
precis|ão *f* precision, accuracy; ~**ar** *v/t*, *v/i* need; ~**o** necessary; precise
preço *m* price; ~ **de liquidação** ridiculously low price
precoce precocious
preconceito *m* prejudice, preconception
precursor *m* precursor
predestinação *f* predestination
predição *f* prediction
predile(c)ção *f* predilection
prédio *m* building
predizer *v/t* predict
predominar *v/i* predominate
predomínio *m* predominance
preencher *v/t* fill in/up
prefácio *m* preface
prefeito *m* prefect
prefer|ência *f* preference; ~**ir** *v/t* prefer; ~**ível** preferable
prega *f* fold, pleat
pregar *v/t*, *v/i* preach
pregar *v/t* nail; fix; ~ **os olhos em** fix one's eyes on; ~ **uma partida** play a trick; **não** ~ **olho** not to sleep a wink
prego *m* nail
preguiç|a *f* laziness; ~**oso** lazy,

idle
prejudicar *v/t* damage, harm
prejuízo *m* prejudice; damage
preliminar *m, adj* preliminary
prelúdio *m* prelude
prematuro premature
premedit|ação *f* premeditation, **~ar** *v/t* premeditate
premiar *v/t* reward
prémio *m* prize; premium
prenda *f* gift
prender *v/t, v/i, v/r* fasten; seize, grasp; arrest, capture
prenhe pregnant
prensa *f* press
prenúncio *m* presage
preocupação *f* worry; preoccupation
preocupar *v/t, v/i* worry; preoccupy
prepar|ação *f* preparation; **~ar** *v/t, v/r* prepare; **~ativo** *m* preparation; **~atório** preparatory
preponderante preponderant
prerrogativa *f* prerogative
presa *f* prey; talon; claw
prescrever *v/t* prescribe
prescrição *f* prescription
presença *f* presence
presenciar *v/t* witness, be present at
presente *m, adj* present
presentear *v/t* present
presépio *m* crib
preservar *v/t, v/i* preserve
presidente *m, f* president
presidir *v/t, v/i* preside (over)
preso *m* prisoner; *adj* captured, held
pressa *f* haste, hurry
pressão *f* pressure
pressentimento *m* presentiment
pressentir *v/t* surmise, have a presentiment of
prestação *f* instalment
prestar *v/t, v/r* give, render; be good; be suitable for; **~ atenção** pay attention; **~ juramento** take an oath; **não ~ para nada** be of no use
prestes *adj* ready
prestígio *m* prestige
préstimo *m* merit; utility
presumir *v/t* presume
presunção *f* presumption
presunto *m* ham, gammon
pretender *v/t* claim
pretens|ão *f* pretence; pretention; **~ioso** pretentious
pretexto *m* pretext
preto *adj* black
prevalecer *v/i* prevail
prevenção *f* prevention
prevenir *v/t, v/r* warn; prevent; provide against
prever *v/t* foresee
previdente farseeing
previsão *f* foresight; forecast
prezar *v/t* prize
prima *f* cousin
primário primary
primavera *f* spring; BOT primrose
primazia *f* primacy
primeiro *adj* first
primitivo *adj* primitive
primo *m* cousin
principal *adj* main, principal
príncipe *m* prince

principi|ante *m* beginner; **~ar** *v/t*, *v/i* begin
princípio *m* beginning; principle
prioridade *f* priority
prisão *f* imprisonment; prison; **~ de ventre** constipation
prisioneiro *m* prisoner
privada *f* toilet, lavatory
privado *adj* private
privar de *v/t*, *v/r* deprive of
privilégio *m* privilege
proa *f* bow, prow
probabilidade *f* probability
probidade *f* probity
problema *m* problem
probo honest, upright
proceder *v/i* proceed from; act, behave
procedimento *m* behavio(u)r; procedure
process|ador *m* **~ de textos** COMP word processor; **~amento** *m* **de dados** COMP data processing
processo process; lawsuit
procissão *f* procession
proclamar *v/t* proclaim
procura *f* search; demand
procuração *f* proxy
procurador *m* proxy
procurar *v/t* look for; try to
prodígio *m* prodigy
pródigo prodigal
produção *f* production
produtivo productive
produto *m* product; produce
produzir *v/t* produce
proeminente prominent
profan|ar *v/t* profane; **~o** *adj* profane
profecia *f* prophecy
proferir *v/t* utter, pronounce
professor *m* teacher; professor
profissão *f* profession
profund|idade *f* profundity; depth; **~o** *adj* profound; deep
profus|ão *f* profusion; **~o** profuse
prognóstico *m* prognostic
progredir *v/i* progress
progresso *m* progress
proib|ição *f* prohibition; **~ir** *v/t* prohibit, forbid
proje(c)tar *v/t* plan; project
projé(c)til *m* projectile
proje(c)to *m* plan, project
proje(c)tor *m* projector
prol: **em ~ de** in favo(u)r of
prole *f* offspring
prolongar *v/t*, *v/r* prolong
promessa *f* promise
prometer *v/t*, *v/i* promise
promoção *f* promotion
promover *v/t* promote
pronto *adj* prompt; ready
pronúncia *f* pronunciation
pronunciar *v/t* pronounce; utter
propaganda *f* propaganda
propor *v/t*, *v/i* propose
proporção *f* proportion
proporcionar *v/t* give, afford
propósito *m* purpose; **a ~** by the way; **de ~** on purpose
proposta *f* proposal
propriedade *f* property
proprietário *m* proprietor, owner
próprio *adj* own; proper; self

propulsão *f* propulsion
propulsor *adj* propellant
próspero *adj* prosperous
prosseguir *v/t*, *v/i* pursue
protagonista *m*, *f* protagonist
prote(c)|ção *f* protection; **~tor** *m* protector
proteger *v/t* protect
protelar *v/t* delay, put off
protest|ar *v/t*, *v/i* protest; **~o** *m* protest
prova *f* proof; trial, try-out; test; **à ~ de água** waterproof
provar *v/t* prove; try; test; try on; taste
provável probable, likely
proveito *m* profit; **~so** profitable
prover *v/t* provide, supply
provérbio *m* proverb
providência *f* providence
província *f* province
provir *v/i* proceed (**de** from)
provisão *f* provision
provisório *adj* provisional
provoc|ação *f* provocation; **~ar** *v/t*, *v/i* provoke
proximidade *f* proximity
próximo *adj* near, next; *m* fellow-creature
prudência *f* prudence
prudente prudent
pseudónimo *m* pseudonym
psíquico psychic
publicar *v/t* publish
publicidade *f* publicity; advertising
público *m*, *adj* public
pudim *m* pudding
pudor *m* bashfulness, shame
pugilis|mo *m* boxing; pugilism; **~ta** *m*, *f* boxer, pugilist
pujança *f* might; vigo(u)r
pular *v/i* spring, jump, leap
pulga *f* flea
pulmão *m* lung
pulo *m* spring, jerk
pulsação *f* pulsation
pulseira *f* bracelet
pulso *m* pulse; wrist
pulveriz|ador *m* sprayer; **~ar** *v/t* spray; pulverize
punhado *m* handful
punhal *m* dagger
punho *m* fist
pun|ição *f* punishment; **~ir** *v/t* punish; **~itivo** punitive; **~ível** punishable
pupila *f* ward; pupil
pupilo *m* ward
puré *m* puree; **~ de batata** mashed potatoes
pureza *f* purity
purg|ante *m* purgative; **~ar** *v/t* purge
purific|ação *f* purification; **~ar** *v/t* purify
puro pure; mere, sheer
pus *m* pus
pústula *f* pustule
puta *f* whore
putrefa(c)|ção *f* putrefaction; **~to** putrefied
puxa *int* why! now!
puxador *m* handle, knob
puxão *m* tug, pull, jerk
puxar *v/t*, *v/i* draw, drag, tug, pull

Q

quadra *f* square room; time, period; *Braz* block
quadrado *adj*, *m* square
quadril *m* hip
quadrilha *f* gang, band
quadro *m* picture, painting; table, list; black-board; tableau; staff
quádruplo *m* quadruple
qual *pron* which, that; *int* what; *adj* which
quali|dade *f* quality; **~ficação** *f* qualification; **~ficar** *v/t* qualify
qualquer *adj*, *pron* either; any
quando *adv*, *conj* when; **~ menos** at least; **de ~ em ~** from time to time
quantia *f* sum, amount
quantidade *f* quantity
quanto *adv* how; *adj*, *pron* how many; how much; all that; **~ a** as for/to; **~ antes** as soon as possible; **~ mais cedo, melhor** the sooner the better; **~ tempo?** how long?
quarenta forty
quaresma *f* Lent
quarta-feira *f* Wednesday
quarteirão *m* block
quartel *m* barracks
quarto *adj* fourth; *m* quarter; room; **~ de casal** double room
quase almost, nearly
quatro four
quatrocentos four hundred
que *pron* who(m), which, that; *conj* that; than; as; *int* what a; how; **o ~** what; he who; **os ~** those who
quê *m* something; complication; *pron* what?; **não tem de ~** not at all
quebra *f* rupture, breach; breakage; COM bankruptcy
quebra|-gelo *m* ice-breaker; **~-luz** *m* lamp-shade; **~-mar** *m* breakwater; **~-nozes** *m* nutcracker
quebrant|ar *v/t* break; weary; **~o** *m* prostration; weariness; evil eye
quebrar *v/t*, *v/i* break, shatter, smash
queda *f* fall; downfall; **~ de água** waterfall
quedar *v/i*, *v/r* remain
quedo quiet, still
queijada *f* cheese-cake
queijo *m* cheese
queima *f* burning; **~dura** *f* burn; scorch; **~r** *v/t*, *v/i*, *v/r* tan; burn; **à ~-roupa** point-blank
queix|a *f* complaint; **~ar-se** *v/r* grumble; complain; **~o** *m* jaw, chin; **~oso** *adj* plaintive
quem who; **de ~** whose; **~ me dera** I wish I could; **~ quer que** whoever
quente *adj* warm, hot
queque *m* small cake
quer *conj* either, or; wheth-

er
querela *f* plaint, suit; **~do** *m* defendant; **~nte** *m* plaintiff; **~r** *v/i* sue
querer *v/t* wish, want; desire; **~ dizer** mean
querido *adj* dear, beloved
quest|ão *f* question; **~ionar** *v/t* dispute; question; **~ionário** *m* questionnaire
quiçá perhaps
quiet|ação *f* quietness; **~o** quiet; **~ude** *f* quiet(ude)
quilate *m* carat; *fig* excellence, quality
quilha *f* keel
quilo(grama) *m* kilo(gram)
quilómetro *m* kilometre
quimera *f* chimera
químic|a *f* chemistry; **~o** *adj* chemical; *m* chemist
quinhão *m* share, portion
quinhentos five hundred
quinquilharia *f* hardware
quinta *f* farm; estate
quinta-feira *f* Thursday
quintal *m* yard; quintal
quinto *adj* fifth
quíntuplo *adj* quintuple
quinze fifteen
quinzena *f* fortnight
quiosque *m* kiosk
quisto *m* cyst
quite *adj* free; quits
quota *f* share; quota
quotidiano daily

R

rã *f* frog
rabanada *f* French toast
rabanete *m* radish
rabicho *m* pigtail
rabiscar *v/t, v/i* scrawl, scribble
rabo *m* tail; buttocks
rabugento morose, peevish
rabujar *v/i* be sullen; sulk
raça *f* race, breed
ração *f* ration, portion
rach|a *f* splinter; cleft, chink, slit; **~ar** *v/t, v/i, v/r* cleave, split
racioc|inar *v/i* reason, ratiocinate; **~ínio** *m* reasoning
racional *adj* rational
racionalizar *v/t* rationalize
racionar *v/t* ration
radar *m* radar
radi|ação *f* radiation; **~ador** *m* radiator; **~ante** *adj* radiant; beaming
radic|al *adj, m* radical; **~ar** *v/t, v/r* root
rádio *m* radius; radium; radio set; *f* radio
radio|a(c)tividade *f* radioactivity; **~a(c)tivo** radioactive; **~grafia** *f* radiography; **~logia** *f* radiology; **~terapia** *f* radiotherapy; **~uvinte** *m, f* radio listener
ráfia *f* raffia
raia *f zoo* ray, skate; line, stroke, streak
raiar *v/t, v/i* border on; streak, stripe; radiate

rainha *f* queen
raio *m* beam, ray; spoke
raiv|a *f* rage; **~oso** angry, furious
raiz *f* (*pl* **raízes**) root
rajada *f* squall, gust, blast
ral|ação *f* worry; **~ador** *m* grater; **~ar** *v/t* grate; vex
ralhar *v/i* scold, rebuke
ram|agem *f* foliage, branches; **~al** *m* branch railway, branch road; **~alhete** *m* bouquet, bunch; **~ificação** *f* ramification; **~ificar** *v/t*, *v/r* ramify, branch (out); **~o** *m* branch; bunch
rancho *m* mess; band, party; *Braz* shack
rancor *m* ranco(u)r
rançoso rancid
ranger *v/t*, *v/i* creak; gnash
ranho *m* mucus, snot
ranhura *f* groove, slot
rapar *v/t* scrape
rapariga *f* girl
rapaz *m* boy
rapidez *f* rapidity
rápido *adj* quick, rapid; *m* express train; rapid
rapina *f* plunder
raposa *f* fox
rapt|ar *v/t* abduct, kidnap; **~o** *m* abduction, kidnapping; rapture
raqueta *f* racket
raridade *f* rarity
raro *adj* scarce; rare
rascunho *m* sketch, draft
rasg|ar *v/t*, *v/r* tear, rip; **~o** *m* burst; flight, flash; dash, stroke; **de um ~o** at/with one blow
raso *adj* level, even, flat
raspar *v/t*, *v/r* clear off; scrape, rasp, erase
rastejar *v/i* creep, crawl
rasto *m* track, trace, trail
rata *f* disgrace
ratazana *f* rat
ratific|ação *f* ratification; **~ar** *v/t* ratify
rat|o *m* mouse; **~oeira** *f* mouse-trap
ratoneiro *m* pilferer
razão *f* reason; sense; rate; **ter ~** be right
razoável reasonable
ré *f* culprit; NAUT stern
reabastecer *v/t* replenish
reabilit|ação *f* rehabilitation; **~ar** *v/t*, *v/r* rehabilitate
rea(c)ção *f* reaction
reagir *v/i* react
real *adj* real; royal, regal, kingly; *m* real (*Brazilian currency*)
real|çar *v/t*, *v/i* set off; enhance; **~ce** *m*, **~ço** *m* lustre, distinction
realejo *m* barrel organ, hurdy-gurdy
realidade *f* reality
realiz|ação *f* realization, fulfilment; staging; **~ar** *v/t*, *v/r* realize, achieve, fulfil; take place; **~ável** realizable, feasible
reanimar *v/t* cheer up; revive
rearmamento *m* rearmament
reatar *v/t* tie again; reestablish; renew, resume
reaver *v/t* recover, get back

rebaixar *v/t, v/r* lower; demean, debase
rebanho *m* flock, herd
rebat|e *m* alarm; rebate; **~er** *v/t* repel; confute; discount
rebel|de *adj* rebellious; *m* rebel; **~ião** *f* rebellion
rebent|ar *v/t, v/i* burst, explode; break out; **~o** *m* sprout, shoot
reboc|ador *m* tugboat; **~ar** *v/t* tow
rebolar *v/i, v/r* tumble, roll
reboque *m* tow
rebuçado *m* sweet
recado *m* message, errand; **mandar ~** send word
recaí|da *f* relapse; **~ir** *v/i* relapse
recalcitrante *adj, m, f* recalcitrant
recambiar *v/t* return, send back
recapitul|ação *f* recapitulation; **~ar** *v/t* recapitulate
recat|ado retiring; **~ar** *v/t, v/r* safeguard; hide; **~o** *m* prudence, circumspection
recear *v/t, v/i, v/r* fear
receb|er *v/t* receive; **~imento** *m* receiving, reception
recelo *m* fear
receit|a *f* recipe; prescription; **~ar** *v/t* prescribe
recém-|casado *m, adj* newlywed, **~nascido** *m, adj* newly born
recense|amento *m* census; **~ar** *v/t* take a census of
recente recent
receoso fearful, timid
recepção *f* reception
receptor *m* receiver
reche|ar *v/t* stuff, cram; **~io** *m* force-meat, stuffing
recibo *m* receipt
recife *m* reef
recinto *m* precinct
recipiente *m* receptacle
reciprocidade *f* reciprocity
recíproco reciprocal
récita *f* performance, recital
recit|ação *f* recitation; **~al** *m* recital; **~ar** *v/t* recite
reclam|ação *f* claim, demand; **~ar** *v/t, v/i* reclaim, claim; demand
reclame *m* advertisement; catchword
reclinar *v/t, v/r* recline
reclus|ão *f* reclusion; **~o** *m* recluse
recobrar *v/t* recover, regain
recolher *v/t, v/i, v/r* retire, gather, collect, assemble
recomend|ação *f* recommendation; **~ar** *v/t* recommend; **~ável** recommendable
recompens|a *f* recompense; reward; **~ar** *v/t* recompense; reward
reconcili|ação *f* reconciliation; **~ar** *v/t, v/r* reconcile
reconfortar *v/t* strengthen, soothe, relieve
reconhec|er *v/t* acknowledge; recognize; **~ido** acknowledged; grateful
reconhecimento *m* recognition; acknowledg(e)ment; gratitude; reconnaissance
reconquistar *v/t* reconquer
reconstituir *v/t* reconstitute

reconstru|ção *f* reconstruction; **~ir** *v/t* reconstruct
record|ação *f* remembrance, recollection; souvenir; **~ar** *v/t, v/r* recall; remind
recorrer *v/i* have recourse; JUR appeal
recortar *v/t, v/r* outline; cut out
recorte *m* outline; cut-out
recostar *v/t* lean, rest
recreio *m* recreation; playground
recruta *m* recruit
re(c)tidão *f* rectitude
re(c)tific|ação *f* rectification; **~ar** *v/t* rectify
re(c)to *adj* straight; right; *m* rectum
recu|ar *v/t, v/i* recoil; back; **~o** *m* recoil; retreat
recuper|ação *f* recuperation; **~ar** *v/t* recover; recuperate
recurso *m* recourse; JUR appeal; **~s** *m/pl* resources
recus|a *f* refusal; **~ar** *v/t, v/r* refuse
reda(c)ção *f* editing; wording; editorial staff; composition
reda(c)tor *m* editor
rede *f* net; COMP network; **a Rede** Internet
rédea *f* rein
redenção *f* redemption
redigir *v/t* draw up; edit
redobrar *v/t, v/i* redouble
redondeza *f* roundness; surroundings
redondo *adj* round
redor *m* circuit; **ao ~ de** around …
redução *f* reduction
reduzir *v/t* reduce
reedição *f* new edition
reedificar *v/t* rebuild
reeducar *v/t* re-educate
reembols|ar *v/t* reimburse; **~o** *m* reimbursement
refazer *v/t, v/r* remake; do again; restore, rally
refeição *f* meal
refeitório *m* refectory
refém *m* hostage
refer|ência *f* reference; **~ente** referring to; **~ir** *v/t, v/r* refer; relate
refinar *v/t* refine
refinaria *f* refinery
refle|(c)tir *v/t, v/i, v/r* reflect; meditate; **~xão** *f* reflection; **~xivo** reflexive; **~xo** *m, adj* reflex
reflorestamento *m* reforestation, tree replanting
reforçar *v/t* reinforce
reforço *m* reinforcement
reforma *f* reform; **~ção** *f* reformation; **~r** *v/t* reform
refrescar *v/t, v/i, v/r* refresh; cool
refresco *m* refreshment
refrig|erante *m* cool drink; **~ério** *m* comfort, relief
refugi|ado *m* refugee; **~ar-se** *v/r* take refuge
refúgio *m* refuge
refut|ação *f* refutation; **~ar** *v/t* refute
rega *f* irrigation; **~dor** *m* watering can
regalar *v/t, v/r* regale (o.s.) on;

delight
regal|ia *f* royal prerogative; privilege; **~o** *m* treat, feast
regar *v/t* irrigate, water
regatear *v/t, v/i* haggle; wrangle
regato *m* brook
regelar *v/t* congeal, freeze
regener|ação *f* regeneration; **~ar** *v/t* regenerate
rege|nte *m* MUS conductor; **~r** *v/t, v/r* rule, govern; MUS lead
região *f* region
regime *m* regime; diet; regimen
regis|t(r)ar *v/t* register; **~t(r)o** *m* registry; register
rego *m* furrow; rut
regozij|ar *v/t, v/r* delight, gladden; **~o** *m* rejoicing
regra *f* rule
regravável *adj* COMP rewritable
regress|ar *v/i* return; **~o** *m* return
régua *f* ruler
regulamento *m* regulation, rule
regular *v/t, v/i* adjust; regulate; *adj* regular; normal; **~idade** *f* regularity
regularizar *v/t* regularize
rei *m* king
reimpressão *f* reprint
reinado *m* reign
reinar *v/i* reign, rule
reinicializar *v/i, v/t* COMP reboot
reino *m* kingdom
reintegrar *v/t* reinstate
reitor *m* rector; headmaster
reivindic|ação *f* claim; **~ar** *v/t* claim
rejeitar *v/t* reject; refuse
relação *f* relation
relacionar *v/t, v/r* connect; become acquainted with
relâmpago *m* lightning
relampaguear *v/i* lighten
relat|ar *v/t* relate; **~o** *m* account; **~ório** *m* report
relaxar *v/t, v/r* relax, slacken
relevo *m* relief
religi|ão *f* religion; **~osa** *f* nun; **~oso** *adj, m* religious
relinchar *v/i* whinny, neigh
relógio *m* clock; watch
relojoeiro *m* watch-maker
relut|ância *f* reluctance; **~ante** reluctant
reluzir *v/i* gleam
relva *f* lawn; grass
relvado *m* lawn
remar *v/t, v/i* row
remat|ar *v/t* end, conclude; **~e** *m* end, conclusion
remediar *v/t* remedy
remédio *m* remedy
remend|ar *v/t* mend; patch; **~o** *m* patch
reme|ssa *f* remittance; shipment; **~tente** *m* sender, remitter; **~ter** *v/t* send, remit
remexer *v/t* stir again; rummage
reminiscência *f* reminiscence
remir *v/t* redeem; ransom
remo *m* oar
remoinho *m* whirl(pool)
remontar *v/i* go back to
remorso *m* remorse
remoto remote
remover *v/t* remove

remuner|ação *f* remuneration; **~ar** *v/t* remunerate
renascença *f* renascence; renaissance
renascer *v/i* be born again
renda *f* rent; income; lace
rend|er *v/t, v/i, v/r* subdue; produce; surrender; **~ição** *f* surrender; **~ido** conquered; ruptured; **~imento** *m* income; profit; **~oso** profitable
renhido fierce
renit|ência *f* resistance; reluctance; **~ente** recalcitrant
renome *m* renown
renov|ação *f* renovation; renewal; **~ar** *v/t* renovate; renew
renúncia *f* renunciation
renunciar a *v/t* renounce
reorganiz|ação *f* reorganization; **~ar** *v/t* reorganize
repar|ação *f* reparation; repair; **~ar** *v/t, v/i* repair, mend; notice
reparo *m* attention, notice
repart|ição *f* distribution; department; **~ir** *v/t* distribute, share out
repatriar *v/t, v/r* repatriate
repel|ão *m* pull; push, shove; **~ir** *v/t* repel
repentino sudden
repercussão *f* repercussion
repertório *m* repertoire
repet|ição *f* repetition; **~ir** *v/t, v/i, v/r* repeat
repleto replete, full
réplica *f* retort, reply
replicar *v/t, v/i* retort, reply
repolho *m* savoy (cabbage)
repor *v/t* replace, restore
report|agem *f* report, reportage; **~ar** *v/r* refer to
repórter *m* reporter
reposição *f* restitution
reposteiro *m* hangings, *US* drapery
repous|ar *v/i* rest, repose; **~o** *m* rest, repose
repreen|der *v/t* rebuke, scold; **~são** *f* rebuke
represa *f* dam
represent|ação *f* representation; performance; **~ante** *m, f; adj* representative; **~ar** *v/t, v/i* represent; perform
repressão *f* repression
reprimir *v/t* repress
reprodu|ção *f* reproduction; **~zir** *v/t, v/r* reproduce
reprov|ação *f* reproof; failure; **~ar** *v/t* fail; reprove; disapprove; **~ável** blameworthy
república *f* republic
rep|udiar *v/t* repudiate; **~údio** *m* repudiation
repugn|ância *f* repugnance; **~ar** *v/i* be repugnant
repulsa *f* repulsion; repulse
reputação *f* reputation
repuxo *m* jet, fountain
requeijão *m* curd
requentar *v/t* warm up/over
requer|er *v/t* require; **~imento** *m* request, application
requinte *m* refinement; acme
requisi|ção *f* requisition; **~tar** *v/t* requisition; **~to** *m* requisite
rés-do-chão *m* ground floor
reserv|a *f* reserve; reservation; **~ado** *adj* booked; reserved;

~ar *v/t* reserve; book; **~atório** *m* reservoir
resfri|ado *adj* cooled; *m* cold; **~amento** *m* chill, cold; **~ar** *v/t*, *v/i*, *v/r* cool; catch (a) cold
resgat|ar *v/t* ransom; **~e** *m* ransom
resguard|ar *v/t* preserve; defend; protect; **~o** *m* protection; defence
resid|ência *f* residence; **~ente** *adj* resident; **~ir** *v/i* reside
resíduo *m* residue
resign|ação *f* resignation; **~ar** *v/t*, *v/r* resign
resina *f* resin
resist|ência *f* resistance; **~ente** resistant; **~ir (a)** *v/i* resist
resmungar *v/t*, *v/i* mumble, grumble
resolução *f* resolution
resolver *v/t*, *v/r* solve; resolve; decide
respe(c)tivo respective
respeit|ar *v/t*, *v/i* respect; concern; **~ável** respectable; **~o** *m* respect; **a ~o de, com ~o a** with respect to
respir|ação *f* respiration, breathing; **~ar** *v/t*, *v/i* breathe
resplandecer *v/i* shine, glow
resplendor *m* brightness; splendo(u)r
responder *v/i* answer, reply, respond
responsabili|dade *f* responsibility; **~zar** *v/t*, *v/r* be responsible for
responsável responsible; **~** *m* **financeiro** COM CFO
resposta *f* answer, reply, response
ressaltar *v/t*, *v/i* emphasize; jut out; rebound
ressentido resentful
ressentir *v/t*, *v/r* resent
ressequido parched, withered
ressurgir *v/i* reappear
ressurreição *f* resurrection
restabelecer *v/t*, *v/r* re-establish; recover
restar *v/i* be left over, remain
restaur|ação *f* restoration; **~ante** *m* restaurant; **~ar** *v/t* restore
restitu|ição *f* restitution; **~ir** *v/t* give back
resto *m* rest, remainder; **de ~** besides
restrição *f* restriction
restringir *v/t* restrict
result|ado *m* result; **~ar** *v/i* result from/in; turn out
resum|ir *v/t* abridge, sum up, summarize; **~o** *m* summary
resvalar *v/i* slip, glide, slide
retalh|ar *v/t* shred; **~o** *m* shred, scrap; **a ~o** by retail
retardar *v/t* delay, retard
ret|enção *f* retention; **~er** *v/t* retain; withhold
retesar *v/t* stretch, tighten
retir|ada *f* retreat; withdrawal; **~ar** *v/t*, *v/r* withdraw; retreat
retocar *v/t* retouch, touch up
retomar *v/t* resume
retorcer *v/t*, *v/r* twist, wind; writhe, wriggle
retornar *v/i* return
retorquir *v/t*, *v/i* retort

retra|imento *m* reserve; retirement; **~ir** *v/t*, *v/r* retract, draw back, withdraw
retrato *m* portrait
retrete *f* lavatory, toilet
retribu|ição *f* retribution; **~ir** *v/t* reciprocate
retroceder *v/i* recede
retrógrado *adj* retrograde
retrospe(c)tivo retrospective
retumbar *v/i* resound
réu *m* accused, culprit
reun|ião *f* meeting; gathering; reunion; **~ir** *v/t*, *v/r* reunite, join, gather, meet
revel|ação *f* revelation; development; **~ar** *v/t*, *v/r* develop; reveal
rever *v/t*, *v/r* review, revise
rever|ência *f* reverence; **~ente** reverent
revés *m* setback, reverse; **ao ~** wrong way round; upside-down
revezar *v/t*, *v/i*, *v/r* alternate
reviravolta *f* turn, veering
revis|ão *f* revision; **~or** *m* ticket collector
revista *f* review; magazine; revue
revistar *v/t* search; examine
reviver *v/i* revive
revogar *v/t* revoke
revolta *f* revolt
revoltar *v/t*, *v/r* revolt
revolução *f* revolution
revolver *v/t* stir; spin, revolve; roll
revólver *m* revolver
rezar *v/t*, *v/i* pray
riacho *m* brook, stream
riba *f* cliff, high bank
ribalta *f* footlights
ribeir|a *f* riverside; riverbank; small river; **~o** *m* brook, stream
ribombar *v/i* thunder
rico rich
ridículo ridiculous
rifa *f* raffle
rifão *m* proverb, adage
rifar *v/t* raffle
rigidez *f* rigidity
rígido rigid
rigor *m* rigo(u)r, severity
rijo sturdy; hard
rim *m* kidney
rima *f* rhyme
rio *m* river
riqueza *f* wealth; riches
rir *v/i*, *v/r* laugh
risada *f* laughter
risca *f* parting, *US* part; stripe; **à ~** exactly
riscar *v/t* cross out/off, delete
risco *m* risk; stroke; streak
riso *m* laugh(ter)
risonho smiling, cheerful
ríspido harsh, severe
rival *m* rival; **~idade** *f* rivalry; **~izar** *v/i* vie
rixa *f* brawl, row
robalo *m* snook
robe *m* dressing-gown
robust|ecer *v/t*, *v/i*, *v/r* fortify; grow robust; **~o** robust
roçar *v/t*, *v/i* graze, skim
roch|a *f* rock; **~edo** *m* crag, cliff; **~oso** rocky
roda *f* wheel

rodagem *f* set of wheels; **em ~** AUTO running in
rodar *v/t, v/i* roll; *m* rumbling, rattling, rolling
rodear *v/t* surround
rodopi|ar *v/i* spin; **~o** *m* spin
rodovia *f* high road, *US* highway
roer *v/t, v/i* gnaw, nibble
rogo *m* request, entreaty
rojar *v/i, v/r* trail
rol *m* list; **~ de roupa** laundry list
rola *f* turtle-dove
rolar *v/t, v/i, v/r* roll
roldana *f* pulley
roleta *f* roulette
rolha *f* cork
rolo *m* roll
romã *f* pomegranate
romanc|e *m* novel; romance; **~ista** *m, f* novelist
românico *adj* Romance
romano *adj, m* Roman
romântico *adj, m* romantic
romantismo *m* romanticism
romaria *f* pilgrimage; popular festival
romeno *m, adj* Rumanian
romper *v/t* break; burst
roncar *v/i* snore
rond|a *f* watch, patrol; **~ar** *v/t, v/i* pratrol; haunt; prowl, lurk
ros|a *f* rose; **~ário** *m* rosary
rosbife *m* roast beef
rosca *f* worm; coil
roseira *f* rose
rosnar *v/i* growl, snarl
rosto *m* face
rota *f* route, course
rotação *f* rotation
roteador *m* router
roteiro *m* guide-book
roto torn; broken
rotular *v/t* label
rótulo *m* label
rotura *f* breach; rupture
roub|ar *v/t, v/i* rob, steal; **~o** *m* theft, robbery
rouco hoarse
roupa *f* clothes; laundry, wash
roupão *m* dressing-gown
rouquidão *f* hoarseness
rouxinol *m* nightingale
roxo *adj* purple, violet
rua *f* street
rubor *m* blush; shame
rubrica *f* rubric; caption; initials
rubricar *v/t* caption; initial
rude rude, primitive, rough
rudimento *m* rudiment
ruga *f* wrinkle; crease
rugir *v/i* roar
ruído *m* noise; din
ruim bad, evil, wicked
ruína *f* ruin
ruir *v/i* collapse, crumble, fall in
ruivo *adj* red-haired
ruminar *v/i* ruminate
rumo *m* direction, course
rumor *m* rumo(u)r; noise; **~ejar** *v/i* rustle; babble; murmur
rural rural
rusga *f* scuffle; roundup, mass arrest
russo *m, adj* Russian
rústico rustic
rutilar *v/i* shimmer

S

sábado *m* Saturday
sabão *m* soap
sab|edoria *f* wisdom; **~er** *v/t, v/i* know; know how, can; taste; *m* knowledge, learning; **a ~** namely
sábio *adj* wise, learned
sabonete *m* toilet soap
sabor *m* flavo(u)r, taste; **~ear** *v/t, v/i* taste; savo(u)r; relish; **~oso** tasty, savo(u)ry
sabotagem *f* sabotage
sabotar *v/t* sabotage
saca *f* sack, large bag
sacada *f* balcony
sacar *v/t* draw, take out
saca-rolhas *m* cork-screw
sacerdote *m* priest
saci|ar *v/t, v/i* sate, satiate; **~edade** *f* satiety
saco *m* bag
sacrificar *v/t, v/i* sacrifice
sacrifício *m* sacrifice
sacrilégio *m* sacrilege
sacrílego sacrilegious
sacro holy, sacred
sacudir *v/t, v/r* jolt; shake
sadio healthy, wholesome
safanão *m* shove, jerk
safar-se *v/r* clear off
sagaz wise, sagacious
sagrado *adj* sacred
saia *f* skirt
saibro *m* gravel
saída *f* way out; exit; departure; sally, quip
sair *v/t, v/r* come out; take after; turn out; go out; leave; depart
sal *m* salt
sala *f* room; **~ de chat** chat room
salada *f* salad
salão *m* saloon; salon
salário *m* salary, pay
saldar *v/t* balance, settle
saldo *m* sale; balance, surplus
salgar *v/t* salt
salgueiro *m* willow-tree
salient|ar *v/t, v/r* set off, enhance; stand out; **~e** salient
salitre *m* saltpetre
saliva *f* saliva
salmão *m* salmon
salmoura *f* pickle, brine
salpicar *v/t* spatter, splash; sprinkle
salsa *f* parsley
salsicha *f* sausage
saltar *v/i* jump, leap
saltitar *v/i* hop, skip
salto *m* jump, leap
salubre *adj* healthy, wholesome, salubrious
salutar salutary
salva *f* sage; salvo; salver
salvação *f* salvation
salva|dor *m* savio(u)r; rescuer; **~guarda** *f* safeguard; **~mento** *m* salvage; rescue; safety
salvar *v/t, v/r* save; rescue; salvage
salva-vidas *m* lifeboat; lifebelt

salvo *prp* except, save; *adj* safe; **a ~** in safety; **~ erro** if I'm not mistaken; **~-conduto** *m* safe conduct
sanção *f* sanction
sancionar *v/t* sanction
sandália *f* sandal
sanduíche *m* sandwich
saneamento *m* sanitation
sanear *v/t* cleanse; make sanitary
sangr|ar *v/t, v/i* bleed; **~ento** bleeding, bloody
sangue *m* blood; **~-frio** in sang-froid; **a ~-frio** in cold blood
sanguíneo *adj* sanguine
sanha *f* wrath
sanitário sanitary
sant|idade *f* sanctity, holiness; **~ificar** *v/t* sanctify; **~o** *m* saint; *adj* holy; **~uário** *m* sanctuary
são *adj* sane; sound, healthy, wholesome; *abbr of* **santo**; **~ e salvo** safe and sound
sapador *m* sapper
sapat|aria *f* shoe-shop; **~eiro** *m* shoemaker; **~o** *m* shoe
sapiência *f* wisdom
sapo *m* toad
saque *m* sack, pillage; COM draft; **~ar** *v/t* sack, pillage
saraiva *f* hail; **~r** *v/i* hail
sarampo *m* measles
sarar *v/t, v/i* heal; cure
sarau *m* soirée, party
sarda *f* mackerel; freckle
sardinha *f* sardine
sargaço *m* seaweed
sargento *m* sergeant
sarilho *m* hubbub, mess
sarna *f* itch
satélite *m* satellite
sátira *f* satire
satisfa|ção *f* satisfaction; **~tório** satisfactory; **~zer** *v/t, v/i, v/r* satisfy
satisfeito satisfied
saturar *v/t* saturate
saud|ação *f* salutation, greeting; **~ade** *f* longing, yearning, nostalgia; **~ar** *v/t* greet; salute
saudável healthy
saúde *f* health
saudoso longing, yearning
sazonado ripe; experienced
se *conj* if; *pron* oneself; one; himself; herself; itself; themselves; yourself, yourselves
sé *f* cathedral; see
seara *f* corn field
sebe *f* hedge
sebento dirty, greasy
sebo *m* tallow
seca *f* drought
secador *m* hair-drier/dryer
secar *v/t, v/i, v/r* dry
se(c)ção *f* section
sécia *f* BOT aster
seco dry
secreção *f* secretion
secretaria *f* office; secretariat
secretária *f* desk; secretary
secretário *m* secretary
secreto *adj* secret
se(c)tor *m* sector
secular *adj* age-old; secular
século *m* century
secundar *v/t* second
secundário secondary
secura *f* dryness

seda *f* silk
sedativo *m, adj* sedative
sede *f* thirst
sede *f* see; seat
sedentário *adj* sedentary
sedento thirsty
sedimento *m* sediment
sedoso silky
sedu|ção *f* seduction; allure; **~tor** *adj* seductive; **~zir** *v/t* seduce; entice
seg|a *f* reaping; harvest; **~ar** *v/t* mow, reap
segredar *v/t, v/i* whisper
segredo *m* secret; secrecy
segreg|ação *f* segregation; **~ar** *v/t* segregate
seguida *f* following; **em ~** afterwards, thereupon, next
seguinte *adj, m* following
seguir *v/t, v/i* follow; carry on, continue
segunda-feira *f* Monday
segundo *m, adj* second; *prp* according to
segur|ança *f* safety; security; assurance; **~ar** *v/t, v/r* insure; grasp, seize; secure; **~o** *adj* safe, secure; *m* insurance
seio *m* breast; bosom
seis six
seiscentos six hundred
seita *f* sect
seiva *f* sap
seixo *m* pebble
sela *f* saddle
selar *v/t* saddle; seal
sele(c)|ção *f* selection; **~cionar** *v/t* select; **~ta** *f* anthology; **~to** *adj* select
selim *m* (bicycle-)saddle
selo *m* seal; stamp
selva *f* jungle
selvagem *adj, m, f* savage
sem without
semáforo *m* semaphore; traffic light/signal
semana *f* week; **~l** *adj* weekly
semanário *m* weekly
semblante *m* countenance
semear *v/t* sow
semelhan|ça *f* resemblance; **~te** *adj* alike, similar, like; such a
sement|e *f* seed; **~eira** *f* seed--time; sowing
semestr|al half-yearly; **~e** *m* half-year
seminário *m* seminary; seminar
sêmola *f* semolina
sem-par matchless
sempiterno everlasting
sempre always; still; ever; **~ que** whenever
senado *m* senate; **~r** *m* senator
senão *conj* otherwise, or else; *prp* but; except; **~ quando** all of a sudden
senda *f* (foot-)path
senha *f* password; voucher
senhor *m* master; lord; sir; mister, Mr.; **o ~** you; **~a** *f* lady; mistress; madam; Mrs.; **~ia** *f* landlady; **~il** ladylike; lordly; **~inha** *f* miss; **~io** *m* landlord; **~ita** *f Braz* miss
senil senile; **~idade** *f* senility
sensa|ção *f* sensation; **~cional** sensational

sensat|ez *f* good sense; **~o** sensible
sensibilidade *f* sensibility
sensibilizar *v/t, v/r* move, touch; sensitize
sensível sensitive; perceptible
senso *m* sense
sensual sensual
sentado sitting, seated
sentar-se *v/r* sit down
senten|ça *f* sentence, judg(e)ment; maxim; **~ciar** *v/t, v/i* sentence
sentido *m* sense; meaning; direction; *adj* hurt, sensitive; sorrowful, grieved
sentiment|al sentimental; **~o** *m* feeling; sentiment
sentinela *f* sentry
sentir *v/t, v/i, v/r* feel; sense; regret
separ|ação *f* separation; **~adamente** separately; **~ar** *v/t, v/r* part with; separate
sepulcro *m* sepulchre, tomb
sepult|ar *v/t* bury; **~ura** *f* grave
sequência *f* sequence
sequestr|ação *f* sequestration; kidnapping; **~ar** *v/t* sequestrate; kidnap
séquito *m* retinue
ser *v/i* exist, be; *m* being; **~ de** belong to; come from, *US* hail from; be made of; **a não ~ que** unless
serão *m* soirée, party; overtime, night-work
sereia *f* mermaid; siren
serenar *v/t, v/i* calm
serenidade *f* serenity
sereno *adj* serene
série *f* series
seriedade *f* seriousness
seringa *f* syringe
sério *adj* earnest; serious
sermão *m* sermon
serpente *f* serpent
serpentear *v/i* meander, wind
serpentina *f* paper-streamer
serra *f* saw; mountain range
serralheiro *m* locksmith
serran|ia *f* ridge of mountains; **~o** *m* mountain-dweller
serrar *v/t* saw
serrote *m* handsaw
sertã *f* frying-pan, *US* skillet
sertanejo *m* backwoodsman
sertão *m* backwoods; hinterland
servente *m, f* servant
serviçal *adj* obliging; *m* servant
serviço *m* service; **de ~** on duty
servidor *m* servant
servir *v/t, v/i, v/r* help oneself; use; suit; serve; avail o.s. of
servo *m* serf
sessão *f* session; sitting
sessenta sixty
sesta *f* siesta
seta *f* arrow
sete seven; **~centos** seven hundred
Setembro *m* September
setenta seventy
setentrional *adj* northern
sétimo *adj* seventh
seu, sua *adj, pron* his; her(s); its; your(s); their(s)
sever|idade *f* severity; **~o** severe

sexo *m* sex
sexta-feira *f* Friday
sexto *adj* sixth
sezão *f* intermittent fever
si *pron* himself; herself; itself; oneself; yourself; themselves; yourselves; you
sibilante sibilant; hissing
sibilar *v/i* hiss, whistle
siderurgia *f* iron and steel industry
sidra *f* cider
sifão *m* siphon
sigilo *m* secret; secrecy
signatário *m* signatory
signific|ação *f* significance; meaning; **~ado** *m* meaning; **~ar** *v/t* signify; mean
signo *m* sign
sílaba *f* syllable
silêncio *m* silence
silencioso silent
silhueta *f* silhouette
silvar *v/i* whistle; hiss
silvestre wild
silvicultura *f* forestry
sim *adv* yes
símbolo *m* symbol
similar *adj* similar
simpatia *f* sympathy
simpático *adj* nice, friendly
simpatizar *v/i* like, take to
simples *adj* simple
simplicidade *f* simplicity
simplificar *v/t* simplify
simulacro *m* sham, pretence
simular *v/t* simulate
simultâneo simultaneous
sina *f* fate, lot, destiny
sinal *m* sign; signal; **~ de alarme** alarm-signal; communication cord; **~ horário** time-signal; **~eiro** *m* signal-man; traffic warden
sinalização *f* traffic signals
sincer|idade *f* sincerity; **~o** sincere
síncope *f* syncope; faint
sindicalismo *m* syndicalism
sindicato *m* syndicate; trade/labour union
singel|eza *f* simplicity; **~o** single; simple, plain
singular *adj* singular; odd, strange; **~idade** *f* singularity
sinistro *adj* sinister; *m* disaster, accident; damage
sino *m* bell
síntese *f* synthesis
sintético synthetic
sintetizador *m* synthesizer
sintoma *m* symptom
sintonizar *v/t* tune in
sinuos|idade *f* sinuosity; **~o** sinuous
sismo *m* earthquake
siso *m* sense; judg(e)ment
sistema *m* system
sisudo *adj* sensible, judicious
site *m*: **~ da Web** Website
sítio *m* place, spot; site; siege
sito *adj* situated
situ|ação *f* situation; **~ar** *v/t* situate
SMS *m* TEL SMS; **enviar um ~** text
só *adj* alone; *adv* only; merely
soalho *m* floor
soar *v/t*, *v/i* sound
sob under, beneath

sobej|ar *v/i* be left over; **~o** *adj* excessive; **~os** *m/pl* left-overs
soberan|ia *f* sovereignty; **~o** *adj m* sovereign
soberb|a *f* pride; **~o** *adj* proud
sobra *f* excess, surplus
sobrado *m* floor
sobranceiro *adj* overlooking, overhanging; *fig* haughty
sobrancelha *f* eyebrow
sobrar *v/i* be left over
sobras *f/pl* left-overs, remains
sobre *prp* on, over, above
sobrecarga *f* overload
sobrecarregar *v/t* overload
sobreiro *m* cork-oak
sobremaneira *adv* excessively
sobremesa *f* dessert
sobrenome *m* surname
sobrepesca *f* overfishing
sobrepor *v/t* superimpose
sobrescrito *m* envelope
sobressair *v/i* stand out; overtop
sobressalt|ar *v/t, v/r* startle, frighten; **~o** *m* sudden fear, start
sobresselente *adj* spare
sobretaxa *f* surtax, surcharge
sobretudo *adv* above all, especially; *m* overcoat
sobrevir *v/i* occur
sobreviv|ente *m, f* survivor; **~er** *v/i* survive; outlive
sobriedade *f* sobriety
sobrinha *f* niece
sobrinho *m* nephew
sóbrio sober; frugal
social social
socialista *adj, m, f* socialist
socializar *v/t* socialize
sociável sociable
sociedade *f* society; **~ anónima** joint-stock company
sócio *m* associate, partner
sociologia *f* sociology
soco *m* blow, cuff, sock
soçobrar *v/t, v/i* overturn, capsize
socorr|er *v/t, v/r* rescue; resort to; help, aid; **~o** *m* aid, help, assistance
sôfrego greedy
sofr|er *v/t, v/i* suffer; **~imento** *m* suffering
sogra *f* mother-in-law
sogro *m* father-in-law
sol *m* sun; sunshine
sola *f* sole
solar *m* manor-house
solavanco *m* jolt, jerk, bump
soldado *m* soldier
soldar *v/t* solder
soldo *m* military pay
soleira *f* threshold
solen|e solemn; **~idade** *f* solemnity
soletrar *v/t, v/i* spell out
solh|a *f* flounder; **~o** *m* plaice
solicit|ação *f* solicitation; **~ar** *v/t, v/i* solicit
solícito solicitous
solidão *f* solitude, loneliness
solidariedade *f* solidarity
solidário joint, common
solid|ez *f* solidity; **~ificar** *v/t* solidify
sólido *adj, m* solid
solitária *f* tapeworm
solitário *adj* solitary, alone,

lonely
solo *m* soil
sol|-pôr *m*, **-posto** *m* sunset
solstício *m* solstice
soltar *v/t*, *v/r* let out; release; untie, loosen, set loose
solteir|ão *m* bachelor; **~o** *adj* single, unmarried; **~ona** *f* spinster
solto loose, free
soltura *f* freeing; looseness
solução *f* solution
soluçar *v/i* sob
solucionar *v/t* solve
soluço *m* sob
solúvel soluble
solv|ência *f* solvency; **~ente** solvent
solver *v/t* repay
som *m* sound
soma *f* sum
somar *v/t*, *v/i* add up, tot up
sombr|a *f* shadow; shade; tinge; **à ~ de** in the shade; under; **nem por ~s** not in the least; **~ear** *v/t*, *v/i* shade; **~inha** *f* sunshade; **~io** *adj* dark, shady; sombre
somenos of little worth
somente only
sonante sounding, sonorous
sond|a *f* probe; plummet; **~ar** *v/t* sound, probe, plumb
soneca *f* nap, snooze
sonegar *v/t* conceal
soneto *m* sonnet
sonh|ador *m* dreamer; **~ar** *v/t*, *v/i* dream
sonho *m* dream; fritter
sono *m* sleep; **com ~** sleepy
sonoro sonorous
sopa *f* soup
sopé *m* foot, base
sopeira *f* soup tureen; maid
soprar *v/t*, *v/i* blow
sopro *m* puff, blow
sórdido sordid
soro *m* serum, whey
sorr|idente smiling; **~ir** *v/i* smile; **~iso** *m* smile
sort|e *f* fate, lot; luck; **~ear** *v/t* raffle; draw lots; **~eio** *m* draw, raffle
sortido *m* assortment
sorver *v/t* sip
sorvete *m* ice-cream
sorvo *m* sip
sósia *m*, *f* double
sossegado quiet, calm
sossegar *v/t*, *v/i*, *v/r* quiet(en), calm (down)
sossego *m* quiet, calm, peace
sótão *m* garret, loft, attic
sotaque *m* accent
soterrar *v/t* bury
soturno *adj* sullen, morose
sova *f* beating, hiding
sovaco *m* arm-pit
sovar *v/t* knead; trash
soviético Soviet
sovin|a *adj* miserly; **~ice** *f* avarice, stinginess
sozinho alone
suar *v/i* sweat, perspire
suav|e suave; smooth, soft; gentle; mild; **~idade** *f* gentleness; mildness
suavizar *v/t* soften, soothe
subalterno *m* subaltern
subconsciente *m* subcon-

scious
subcontratar *v/t* outsource
subdiretório *m* COMP subdirectory
sú(b)dito *m* subject
subdivi|dir *v/t* subdivide; **~são** *f* subdivision
subentender *v/t* assume, understand
subida *f* ascent, way up; rise
subir *v/i* go up, climb up, mount, ascend; rise; raise
súbito *adj* sudden; **de ~** suddenly
subjugar *v/t* subjugate
sublev|ação *f* insurrection; **~ar** *v/t*, *v/r* raise, revolt
sublime *adj* sublime
sublinhar *v/t* underline
sublocar *v/t* sublease, sublet
submarino *m*, *adj* submarine
submergir *v/t* submerge
submeter *v/t*, *v/r* subject; submit
submissão *f* submission
submisso submissive
subordin|ação *f* subordination; **~ado** *adj*, *m* subordinate; **~ar** *v/t* subordinate
suborn|ar *v/t* bribe, suborn; **~o** *m* bribery; bribe
subscrever *v/t*, *v/i* subscribe
subscrição *f* subscription
subsequente subsequent
subsidiar *v/t* subsidize
subsídio *m* subsidy; allowance
subsistência *f* subsistence
subsistir *v/i* subsist
subsolo *m* subsoil
substância *f* substance
substancial *adj* substantial
substitu|ição *f* substitution; **~ir** *v/t* substitute
substituto *m* substitute
subterfúgio *m* subterfuge
subterrâneo *adj* underground, subterranean
subtil *adj* subtle
subtra(c)ção *f* subtraction
subtrair *v/t* subtract
subúrbio *m* suburb
subven|ção *f* grant, allowance; **~cionar** *v/t* subsidize
subversivo subversive
subverter *v/t* subvert
sucata *f* scrap iron
suceder *v/i*, *v/r* succeed; happen
sucessão *f* succession
sucesso *m* success; event, happening
sucinto succinct
suco *m* juice
suculento succulent
sucumbir *v/i* succumb
sucursal *f* COM branch
su(d)este *m* south-east
sudoeste *m* south-west
sueco *m* Swede; *adj* Swedish
suficiente *adj* sufficient
sufoc|ação *f* suffocation; **~ar** *v/t*, *v/i* suffocate
sufrágio *m* suffrage
sugar *v/t* suck
sugerir *v/t* suggest
sugestão *f* suggestion
sugestivo suggestive
suicidar-se *v/r* commit suicide
suicídio *m* suicide
suíço *m*, *adj* Swiss

sujar *v/t, v/r* dirty, soil
sujeição *f* subjection
sujeitar *v/t, v/r* subject
sujeito *m* GRAM subject; chap, fellow, bloke
sujidade *f* dirt, filth
sujo dirty, filthy
sul *m* South, south
sulc|ar *v/t* plough, furrow; **~o** *m* furrow
suma *f* sum; **em ~** in short
sumarento juicy, succulent
sumário *m, adj* summary
sumir *v/t, v/r* vanish, disappear; sink; hide
sumo *m* juice
sumptuoso, *Braz* **suntuoso** sumptuous
suor *m* sweat, perspiration
superabundar *v/i* be superabundant
superar *v/t* surmount; surpass; overcome
superficial superficial
superfície *f* surface
supérfluo *adj* superfluous
superior *adj* superior; upper; **~idade** *f* superiority
superstição *f* superstition
supersticioso *adj* superstitious
supervisão *f* supervision
suplantar *v/t* supplant
suplement|ar supplementary; **~o** *m* supplement
suplente *m, f* substitute
súplica *f* supplication
suplicar *v/t* beg, implore, entreat
suplício *m* torment; torture
supor *v/t* suppose
suport|ar *v/t* support; put up with; **~ável** tolerable, endurable
suporte *m* support; **~ de vida** life support
suposição *f* supposition
suposto *adj* supposed; **~ que** supposing that
supremacia *f* supremacy
supremo *adj* supreme
supressão *f* suppression
suprimir *v/t* suppress
suprir *v/t, v/i* supply; make up for, do duty for
surdez *f* deafness
surdo *adj* deaf
surdo-mudo *adj* deaf and dumb; *m* deaf-mute
surgir *v/i* surge, arise; emerge, appear
surpreend|ente surprising; **~er** *v/t* surprise
surpresa *f* surprise
surra *f* thrashing
surtir *v/t, v/i* occasion; turn out, result; **~ efeito** take effect
susce(p)tibilidade *f* susceptibility
susce(p)tível susceptible, tender
suscitar *v/t* stir up, raise
suspeit|a *f* suspicion; **~ar** *v/t, v/i* suspect; **~o** *adj, m* suspect; **~oso** suspicious
suspender *v/t* suspend
suspensão *f* suspension
suspensórios *m/pl* braces, *US* suspenders
suspir|ar *v/t, v/i* sigh; **~o** *m* sigh;

meringue
sussurrar *v/i* rustle; babble
sussurro *m* murmur, whisper
sustentáculo *m* prop, stay, support
sustent|ar *v/t, v/r* support, prop up; maintain; live on; **~o** *m* maintenance; sustenance
suster *v/t* sustain; support; hold up
susto *m* fright
sutiã *m* bra

T

tabac|aria *f* tobacconist's (shop); **~o** *m* tobacco
tabela *f* list, table, schedule
tabelião *m* notary (public)
taberna *f* inn; bar
tábua *f* board; list, table
tabuleiro *m* tray; garden bed; landing
tabuleta *f* signboard
taça *f* wine-glass; cup
tacão *m* heel
tacha *f* tack, stud; blemish
tacho *m* pan
tácito tacit
taciturno taciturn
ta(c)tear *v/i* grope, fumble
tá(c)tica *f* tactics
ta(c)to *m* touch; tact
tagarel|ar *v/i* prattle; **~ice** *f* prattle, chatter
tal *adj, pron* such (a); like
talão *m* heel; counterfoil, stub
talento *m* talent; **~so** talented
talha *f* carving
talhada *f* slice
talhar *v/t, v/i* cut, carve, slice; curdle
talher *m* cover; place
talho *m* butcher's (shop)
talo *m* stem, stalk; shaft
taluda *f* top lottery prize
talvez perhaps, maybe
tamanco *m* wooden clog
tamanho *m* size
tâmara *f* date
também *int* really; *adv* as well, also, too; **~ eu** so do/did I; so am/have I
tambor *m* drum; eardrum
tampa *f* lid, cover
tampão *m* tampon
tanga *f* loin-cloth; **estar de ~** be broke
tangerina *f* tangerine, mandarin(e) (orange)
tanque *m* tank; pond
tanto *adj* as much, so much
tão so, as
tapar *v/t* cover, stop up, block up
tapeçaria *f* tapestry; upholstery
tapete *m* carpet
tapume *m* fence; hedge
taquigrafia *f* shorthand
tara *f* tare; derangement
tard|ar *v/t, v/i* linger, be tardy, be late; **sem mais ~ar** without delay; **~e** *adv* late; *f* afternoon; **~inha** *f* evening

tarefa *f* task
tareia *f* thrashing, flogging
tarifa *f* tariff
tarimba *f* bunk
tarraxa *f* screw
tartaruga *f* tortoise; turtle
tasca *f* pub, dive
tatuagem *f* tattoo
tauromaquia *f* bullfighting
taxa *f* rate; duty; **~r** *v/t* rate
táxi *m* taxi
te you, to you
tear *m* loom
teatro *m* theatre
tece|lagem *f* weaving; **~lão** *m* weaver; **~r** *v/t* weave
tecido *m* material, cloth; tissue
tecla *f* key; **~do** *m* keyboard
técnic|a *f* technique; **~o** *m* technician; *adj* technical
te(c)to *m* ceiling
tédio *m* tedium
teia *f* weft; web; plot; **~ de aranha** cobweb
teim|a *f* obstinacy; **~ar** *v/t, v/i* be obstinate, persist; **~oso** *adj* stubborn, obstinate
tela *f* linen; canvas
teleférico *m* funicular (railway)
telefon|ar *v/t, v/i* (tele)phone, ring up; **~e** *m* telephone; **~e sem fios** wireless phone; **~ema** *m* call; **~ia** *f* telephony
telegrafar *v/t, v/i* telegraph, wire, cable
telegrama *m* telegram
telemóvel *m* mobile (phone); *US* cell phone
telenovela *m* daily soap
telescritor *m* teleprinter
televisão *f* television
telha *f* tile; **~do** *m* roof
tema *m* theme; exercise
temer *v/t* fear
temer|ário rash, foolhardy; **~idade** *f* temerity, rashness
temor *m* fear
têmpera *f* temper; tempera; distemper
temper|ado temperate; **~amento** *m* temperament; **~ança** *f* temperance; **~ar** *v/t* temper; season; **~atura** *f* temperature
tempero *m* seasoning
tempest|ade *f* tempest, storm; **~ivo** seasonable, opportune; **~uoso** tempestuous, stormy
templo *m* temple
tempo *m* time; weather; GRAM tense; **há muito ~** long ago; **a ~** on/in time; **~ de exposição** *foto* exposure time; **mal ~** (thunder)storm; **meio ~** *sport* half-time
tempo|rada *f* period, while; THEAT season; **~ral** *m* storm; **~rário** temporary; **~rizar** *v/t, v/i* temporize
ten|acidade *f* tenacity; **~az** *adj* tenacious; *f* tongs, pincers
tenção *f* intention
tencionar *v/t* intend
tenda *f* tent; stall, booth
tendão *m* tendon; sinew
tend|ência *f* tendency; **~er** *v/t, v/i* tend
tenebroso dark, gloomy
tenente *m* lieutenant; **~coronel** *m* lieutenant-colonel

ténia *f* tapeworm
ténis *m* tennis
tenro tender
tens|ão *f* tension; ~ **arterial** blood pressure; **~o** tense, tight, taut
tent|ação *f* temptation; allurement; **~ador** *m* tempter; *adj* tempting; **~ar** *v/t* tempt; attempt, try; **~ativa** *f* attempt, trial, try-out
tento *m* care, circumspection; *Braz* goal; **sem** ~ careless
ténue tenuous, thin
teor *m* course, tenor
teoria *f* theory
teórico *adj* theoretic(al)
tépido tepid
ter *v/t*, *v/i*, *v/r* have (got), possess; hold; get; ~ **de/que** have to; **ir ~ com** meet; ~ **cuidado** be careful, take care
terça-feira *f* Tuesday
ter|ceirização *f* outsourcing; **~ceiro** *adj* third; **~ço** *m* third (part)
terebentina *f* turpentine
termas *f/pl* spa, hot springs
termin|ação *f* termination, end; **~ar** *v/t*, *v/i* terminate, end
término *m* terminus; termination, end
termo *m* limit, boundary; period; term, expression
termómetro *m* thermometer
tern|o *adj* tender; *m Braz* suit; **~ura** *f* tenderness, affection
terra *f* earth, land
terraço *m* terrace
terremoto *m* earthquake
terreno *m* ground, terrain
terrestre terrestrial, earthly
terrina *f* tureen
território *m* territory
terrível terrible
terror *m* terror; **~ismo** terrorism; **~ista** *m*, *f* terrorist; **~izar** *v/t* terrorize
tese *f* thesis
teso *adj* broke; stiff; inflexible
tesoura *f* scissors
tesour|aria *f* treasury; **~eiro** *m* treasurer; **~o** *m* treasure
testa *f* forehead
testament|eiro *m* executor; **~o** *m* will, testament
teste *m* test
testemunh|a *f* witness; **~ar** *v/t*, *v/i* bear witness to; testify; **~o** *m* testimony, evidence
testículo *m* testicle
teta *f* nipple, teat
teu *adj* your; *pron* **o ~** yours
text|o *m* text; **~ual** textual
texugo *m* badger
tez *f* complexion
ti *pron* you
tia *f* aunt
tibieza *f* lukewarmness; *fig* indifference
tíbio lukewarm; *fig* indifferent
tifo *m* typhus
tigela *f* bowl, basin
tigre *m* tiger
tijolo *m* brick
tília *f* linden, lime-tree
timbr|ar *v/t* stamp; **~e** *m* crest; emblem; tone
time *m Braz* team
timidez *f* timidity; shyness

tímido *adj* timid; shy, bashful
tina *f* tub
tingir *v/t* tinge; dye
tinir *v/i* tinkle
tino *m* judg(e)ment, sense
tint|a *f* ink; paint; **~eiro** *m* inkpot
tintim por tintim in minute detail
tinto dyed; red
tintur|a *f* dye; tincture; **~aria** *f* dyer's
tio *m* uncle
típico typical
tipo *m* type; features; fellow
tipografia *f* typography
tique *m* tic, twitch
tira *f* strip
tiragem *f* drawing; printing
tirano *m* tyrant
tira-nódoas *m* stain remover
tirar *v/t, v/r* take off; remove; extract; draw, pull; print; deduce, infer; deduct; **~ uma fotografia** take a photograph
tiro *m* shot
tiroteio *m* volley, shooting
titubear *v/i* waver, stagger, hesitate
título *m* title
toa *f* tow-line; **à ~** at random
toada *f* tune, air, melody
toalha *f* towel; **~ de mesa** tablecloth
toar *v/i* (re)sound; fit
toca *f* burrow; lair
toca-discos *m Braz* record player
tocar *v/t, v/i, v/r* touch; play
tocha *f* torch
todavia *adv, conj* however, yet, nevertheless
todo *m* whole; *adj* whole; all, every; **em ~ o caso** in any case; **~s** everybody; all
toldo *m* awning; sun-blind
toler|ância *f* tolerance; **~ante** tolerant; **~ar** *v/t* tolerate; **~ável** tolerable
tol|ice *f* folly, stupidity; **~o** *adj* foolish, stupid
tom *m* tone
tom|ada *f* taking; seizure; socket; **~ar** *v/t, v/i* have; take; seize; capture
tomate *m* tomato
tomb|ar *v/t, v/i* throw down, knock down; fall down; **~o** *m* tumble, fall
tomilho *m* thyme
tomo *m* volume; tome
tonel *m* cask; vat
tonela|da *f* ton; **~gem** *f* tonnage
tonificar *v/t* invigorate, refresh
tont|o stupid; giddy, dizzy; **~ura** *f* giddiness, dizziness
topar *v/t, v/i* come across; find; **~ com** stumble across/on
tópico *m* topic
toque *m* touch
toranja *f* grape-fruit
torc|er *v/t, v/i, v/r* writhe; twist, wrench; distort; wring; turn; **~ida** *f* wick
tordo *m* thrush
torment|a *f* storm; **~o** *m* torment; **~oso** stormy, boisterous
tornar *v/t, v/i, v/r* come back, return; do again; become

tornear *v/t* turn; encompass
torneio *m* tournament
torneira *f* tap
torno *m* lathe; **em ~ de** *prp* around …
tornozelo *m* ankle
torpe shameful, vile; torpid
torpedeiro *m* torpedo-boat
torpeza *f* baseness
torpor *m* torpor
torrada *f* toast
torrão *m* clod
torrar *v/t* toast; roast
torre *f* tower
torren|cial torrential; **~te** *f* torrent
torresmo *m* rasher, crackling
tórrido torrid
torta *f* tart
torto *adj* twisted, crooked; deformed; **a ~ ou a direito** by hook or by crook
tortuoso tortuous
tortur|a *f* torture; **~ar** *v/t* torture
torvelinho *m* whirlwind; whirlpool; eddy
tosar *v/t* shear; drub
tosco coarse, rough
tosquiar *v/t* shear
toss|e *f* cough; **~ir** *v/i* cough
tostão *m* 10 centavos
tostar *v/t* parch, toast
total *m, adj* total; **~idade** *f* totality
toucador *m* dressing-table
toucinho *m* bacon
toupeira *f* zoo mole
tour|ada *f* bullfight; **~eiro** *m* bullfighter, toreador; **~o** *m* bull
tóxico *m* poison; *adj* toxic
trabalh|ador *m* labo(u)rer, workman; *adj* hard-working; **~ar** *v/i* work; **~o** *m* work
traça *f* moth
traç|ado *m* outline, sketch, plan; **~ar** *v/t* trace, outline; sketch, draw
tra(c)ção *f* traction
traço *m* line; dash; stroke; trace; **~ de união** hyphen
tra(c)tor *m* tractor
tradição *f* tradition
tradu|ção *f* translation; **~ção autorizada** certified translation; **~tor** *m* translator; **~zir** *v/t* translate
tráfego *m* traffic
trafic|ante *m, f* trafficker; **~ar** *v/t, v/i* traffic in, trade
tráfico *m* trade, traffic
tragar *v/t* swallow
tragédia *f* tragedy
trai|ção *f* treason; betrayal; treachery; **~çoeiro** treacherous; **~r** *v/t, v/r* betray
traje *m* dress, garb
traje(c)to *m* way, route; tract
traje(c)tória *f* trajectory
tramar *v/t* plot
trâmite *m* path
trampolim *m* spring-board
trança *f* plait, *US* braid
trancar *v/t* bar, bolt
tranquil|idade *f* tranquil(l)ity; **~izar** *v/t, v/r* tranquil(l)ize; **~o** tranquil
transa(c)ção *f* transaction; **~to** past, bygone; former
transfer|ência *f* transference;

~ir *v/t* transfer
transform|ação *f* transformation; **~ar** *v/t*, *v/r* transform
transgre|dir *v/t* transgress; **~ssão** *f* transgression
transi|ção *f* transition; **~gente** *adj* condescending, compliant; **~tar** *v/i* travel, journey, pass along
trânsito *m* transit; traffic; **em ~** in transit
transitório transitory
transmi|ssão *f* transmission; **~tir** *v/t* broadcast; transmit
transpar|ência *f* transparency; **~ente** *adj* transparent
transpir|ação *f* transpiration; **~ar** *v/i* transpire
transplantar *v/t* transplant
transpor *v/t* transpose
transport|ar *v/t* transport; **~e** *m* transport
transtorn|ar *v/t* upset; **~o** *m* upset; inconvenience
transversal *adj* transversal, transverse
trapalhada *f* jumble, mess
trapo *m* rag
traquina(s) *adj* impish, naughty
trasbordar *v/t* tranship; transfer
trasbordo *m* transhipment; **fazer ~** change trains
traseira *f* back part, rear
traseiro *m* buttocks, behind; *adj* back, rear
trasladar *v/t* transcribe; remove, convey
traste *m* piece of furniture; scamp, rogue
trat|ado *m* treaty; treatise; **~amento** *m* treatment; **~ante** *m*, *f* swindler; **~ar** *v/t*, *v/i*, *v/r* treat; deal with; **~ar de** try to; **~ar-se de** be a question of
trato *m* treatment; manners
trav|ão *m* brake; **~ar** *v/t*, *v/i* engage in; brake; **~ar conhecimento com** become acquainted with
trave *f* beam
travessa *f* lane, alley; railway-sleeper; dish, *US* platter
travessão *m* dash
travesseiro *m* bolster
travessia *f* voyage, crossing
travess|o naughty; **~ura** *f* naughtiness; trick, prank
travo(r) *m* tartness; aftertaste
trazer *v/t* bring; wear; carry
trecho *m* period, interval; passage, extract
trégua *f* truce
treinar *v/t*, *v/r* train
treino *m* training
trem *m* carriage; *Braz* train
tremelicar *v/i* tremble
trem|endo tremendous; awful; **~er** *v/i* tremble, quiver; **~oço** *m* lupin; **~or** *m* tremor, tremble, shudder; **~or de terra** earthquake
tremular *v/i* wave; waver
trémulo tremulous
trenó *m* sleigh, sledge
trep|adeira *f* BOT creeper; **~ar** *v/t*, *v/i* climb
trepidação *f* trepidation
três three

tresandar *v/i* reek of
tresloucar *v/i* become mad
trevas *f/pl* darkness
trevo *m* clover
treze thirteen
trezentos three hundred
triangular *adj* triangular
triângulo *m* triangle
tribunal *m* tribunal, court
tribut|ar *v/t* tax; pay tribute to; **~ário** *adj, m* tributary; **~o** *m* tribute
trig|o *m* wheat; **~ueiro** *adj* swarthy
trilh|ar *v/t* thresh; tread; **~o** *m* harrow
trimestre *m* term; quarter
trinado *m* warbling
trincar *v/t* crunch, munch
trincheira *f* trench
trinco *m* latch
trinta thirty
tripa *f* gut; tripe; entrails
triplo *adj* triple
tripulação *f* crew
triste *adj* sad; **~za** *f* sadness
triturar *v/t* grind, triturate
triunf|ar *v/i* triumph; **~o** *m* triumph
trivial *adj* trivial
triz *m* moment; **por um ~** by the skin of one's teeth
troar *v/i* thunder
troca *f* barter
troça *f* mockery, scorn, ridicule
trocar *v/t* barter, swap; exchange; change
troçar *v/t, v/i* mock, scorn, ridicule
troco *m* change; **a ~ de** in exchange for
troço *m* section; fragment
tromba *f* trunk; snout; **~ de água** waterspout
trombeta *f* trumpet; *m* trumpeter
trombone *m* trombone
tronco *m* trunk; stem
trono *m* throne
tropa *f* troop
tropeçar *v/i* stumble
trôpego hobbling, tottery
tropical tropical
trópico *m* tropic
trot|ar *v/i* trot; **~e** *m* trot
trovão *m* thunder
trovejar *v/i* thunder
trufa *f* truffle
trunfo *m* trump
truque *m* trick, dodge
truta *f* trout
tu *pron* you
tubarão *m* shark
tubo *m* tube
tudo everything, all
tudo-nada *m* iota, jot
tufão *m* typhoon
tufo *m* tuft
tulipa *f* tulip
túmido tumid; haughty
tumor *m* tumo(u)r
túmulo *m* tomb; tumulus
tumulto *m* tumult
túnel *m* tunnel
turbilhão *m* whirl; swirl
turbina *f* turbine
turbulento *adj* turbulent
turco *m* Turk; *adj* Turkish
turis|mo *m* tourism, travel; **~ta** *m,f* tourist

turma *f* class, group; *Braz* people
turno *m* turn; shift **por ~s** by turns
turv|ar *v/t* disturb, muddle, confuse; **~o** *adj* muddy, dim, troubled
tutela *f* guardianship, tutelage
tutor *m* guardian; tutor
tutoria *f* guardianship; tutorship

U

úbere *adj* fertile, abundant
ufan|ar-se *v/r* pride on; **~o(so)** proud, vain
uiv|ar *v/i* howl; **~o** *m* howl
úlcera *f* ulcer
ulmo *m* elm
ulterior ulterior; further
ultimamente recently
ultimato *m* ultimatum
último *adj* last; **por ~** at last
ultraj|ar *v/t* outrage; **~e** *m* outrage; insult
ultramar *m* overseas; **~ino** overseas
ultrapassar *v/t* surpass; overtake, outstrip
ulular *v/i* howl; wail
um, uma *art* a, an; one
umbigo *m* navel
unânime unanimous
unanimidade *f* unanimity
ungir *v/t* anoint
unguento *m* ointment, salve
unha *f* nail; claw
união *f* union
único single, sole, only; unique
unidade *f* unity; **~ de disco** COMP disk drive
unific|ação *f* unification; **~ar** *v/t* unify
uniform|e *adj*, *m* uniform; **~idade** *f* uniformity
unir *v/t* unite
uníssono *m* unison
universal *adj* universal
universidade *f* university
universitário *adj* of a university; *m* university teacher
universo *m* universe
untar *v/t* grease; smear
unto *m* lard; fat; grease
urânio *m* uranium
urbaniz|ação *f* urbanization; **~ar** *v/t* urbanize
urbano *adj* urban; urbane
urbe *f* city
urdir *v/t* warp, weave; plot, contrive
urgência *f* urgency; emergency
urgente urgent
urgir *v/i* urge
urina *f* urine
urna *f* urn; ballot-box
urr|ar *v/i* roar, bellow; **~o** *m* roar, bellow
urso *m* bear
urtiga *f* nettle
urze *f* heather
usado used; worn out
usar *v/t*, *v/r* use; wear (out)

usina *f Braz* factory
uso *m* use; custom, usage; wear
usu|al usual, customary; **~ário** *m* user
usufru|ir *v/t* enjoy use of; **~to** *m* usufruct; **~tuário** *m* usufructuary
usura *f* usury
usurpar *v/t* usurp
utensílio *m* utensil, tool
útero *m* uterus, womb
útil *adj* useful
utilidade *f* usefulness; utility
utilizar *v/t* utilize, use
utópico utopian
uva *f* grape

V

vaca *f* cow
vacil|ação *f* vacilation; indecision; **~ar** *v/i* vacilate
vacina *f* vaccine
vacin|ação *f* vaccination; **~ar** *v/t* vaccinate
vácuo *adj* void, empty; *m* vacuum
vadi|agem *f* vagrancy; **~ar** *v/i* wander, roam
vadio *m* vagrant; vagabond
vaga *f* wave; vacancy
vagão *m* railway carriage; **~-cama, ~-leito** *m* sleeping-car; **~-restaurante** *m* dining/restaurant-car
vagar *v/i* be vacant; be idle; *m* leisure; **~oso** slow, leisurely
vagem *f* husk, pod
vagido *m* wail
vagina *f* vagina
vago vague; vacant
vaguear *v/i* rove, roam, ramble
vaia *f* hissing, hooting
vaidade *f* vanity
vaidoso *adj* vain
vaivém *m* fluctuation, coming and going
vala *f* ditch
vale *m* valley, vale; **~ postal** postal order, *US* money order
valent|e *adj* brave, valiant; **~ia** *f* valo(u)r
valer *v/t, v/i, v/r* be worth; **~ a pena** be worth-while; **a ~** in earnest, really; **~-se de** make use of; profit by
valeta *f* gutter
valia *f* value, merit
validade *f* validity
válido valid; robust
valioso valuable
valor *m* value, worth; stock, bond; **~izar** *v/t* increase the value of; **~oso** brave
valsa *f* waltz
válvula *f* valve
vampiro *m* vampire
vangloriar-se *v/r* boast
vanguarda *f* vanguard
vantagem *f* advantage
vantajoso advantageous
vão *adj* vain, futile
vapor *m* vapo(u)r, steam; steamboat
vara *f* rod, pole, stick

varanda *f* balcony; veranda(h)
varapau *m* cudgel
varar *v/t, v/i* strike, beat; pierce; run aground
vari|ação *f* variation; **~ar** *v/t, v/i* vary; **~ável** *adj* variable, changeable; **~edade** *f* variety
vários *pl* various, several
varonil virile; manly
varrer *v/t, v/i* sweep
vasilha *f* vessel; keg; barrel
vaso *m* flowerpot; vase
vassoura *f* broom
vast|idão *f* vastness, immensity; **~o** *adj* vast
vaticinar *v/t* prophesy, foretell
vau *m* ford
vaz|ante *f* ebb; **~ar** *v/t, v/i, v/r* ebb; empty; pour out
vazio *adj* empty
veado *m* deer, hart, stag
ved|ação *f* barrier, fence, enclosure; **~ar** *v/t* forbid; fence off
vedeta *f* THEAT star
veem|ência *f* vehemence; **~ente** vehement
veget|ação *f* vegetation; **~al** *adj, m* vegetable
veia *f* vein
veículo *m* vehicle
vela *f* candle; sail
velar *v/t, v/i* watch over; stay awake
veleiro *m* sailing ship
velejar *v/i* sail
velhac|aria *f* deceit; **~o** *m* rogue
velhice *f* old age
velho *adj* old; *m* old man
velocidade *f* velocity, speed; AUTO gear; **~ de cruzeiro** AUTO cruising speed
veloz swift
veludo *m* velvet
vencedor *m* winner
vencer *v/t, v/i* conquer, defeat; win
vencimento *m*, COM maturity, due date; salary
venda *f* sale; shop; blindfold; **estar à ~** be for sale; **~ sob prescriçao médica** available only on prescription
vend|er *v/t* sell; **~ível** sal(e)able
veneno *m* poison; **~so** poisonous
vener|ação *f* veneration; **~ar** *v/t* venerate, revere
vénia *f* permission; bow
venta *f* nostril; **~s** *f/pl* nose
ventilação *f* ventilation
ventilador *m* ventilator
ventilar *v/t* ventilate
vento *m* wind; **~so** windy
ventoinha *f* fan
ventre *m* belly
ventur|a *f* luck; fate; **~oso** lucky
ver *v/t* see
veracidade *f* veracity, truthfulness
verão *m* summer
verba *f* item, clause; sum
verbal verbal
verbo *m* verb
verdade *f* truth
verdadeiro *adj* true; real
verde *adj* green
verdejar *v/i* grow green

verdura *f* greens; verdure
vereda *f* foot-path
verga *f* switch, shoot; yardarm
vergar *v/t*, *v/i* bend, curve
vergonh|a *f* shame; **~oso** shameful
vergôntea *f* shoot, sprout; offspring
verídico truthful
verific|ação *f* verification; **~ar** *v/t* verify; ascertain
verme *m* worm
vermelho *adj* red
vernáculo vernacular
verniz *m* varnish
verosímil probable, likely
verosimilhança *f* probability, likelihood
verruga *f* wart
verruma *f* gimlet
versado (em) conversant (with), versed (in)
versão *f* translation; version
verso *m* verse
vertente *f* slope
verter *v/t*, *v/i* leak; turn (**para** into); spill, pour
vertical *adj*, *f* vertical
vertig|em *f* dizziness, vertigo; **~inoso** dizzy
vesgo *adj* squint-eyed, squinting
vespa *f* wasp
véspera *f* eve; day before
vestiário *m* cloak-room, *US* check-room
vestíbulo *m* vestibule, hall; foyer
vestido *m* dress
vestígio *m* vestige, trace
vestir *v/t*, *v/i*, *v/r* put on; dress
vestuário *m* wardrobe, clothes, clothing
veterinária *f* veterinary medicine
vetusto ancient
véu *m* veil
vex|ame *m* vexation; **~ar** *v/t* vex, harass, annoy
vez *f* time; occasion; turn; **cada ~ mais** more and more; **de ~ em quando** now and then; **em ~ de** instead of; **uma ~** once; **às ~es** sometimes; **muitas ~es** often
via *f* way; road; **~ férrea** railway; **por ~ aérea** by air mail
viagem *f* journey, travel; **estar em ~** be away; be travelling
viajante *m*, *f* travel(l)er
viajar *v/i* travel
viatura *f* vehicle
víbora *f* viper, adder
vicejar *v/i* thrive
viciado *m* addict
viciar *v/t*, *v/r* addict; vitiate
vicioso vicious; corrupt
viçoso luxuriant, rank
vida *f* life
videira *f* vine
vidraça *f* pane
vidraceiro *m* glazier
vidro *m* glass; pane
viga *f* beam
vigarista *m*, *f* swindler
vigi|a *f* watch; vigil; porthole; *m* look-out; **~ar** *v/t*, *v/i* watch over; guard
vigilante *adj* vigilant
vigor *m* vigo(u)r; **entrar en ~**

come into effect; **~ar** *v/t*, *v/i* invigorate; be in force; **~oso** vigorous
vil *adj* vile, mean
vila *f* small town; villa
vinagre *m* vinegar
vinco *m* crease
vínculo *m* tie, bond
vinda *f* coming, arrival
vindicar *v/t* claim, vindicate
vindima *f* grape harvest, vintage; **~dor** *m* grape-picker
vindouro *adj* future, yet to come
ving|ança *f* vengeance; **~ar** *v/t*, *v/r* avenge; take vengeance on; revenge
vinha *f* vineyard
vinho *m* wine; **~ branco** white wine; **~ tinto** red wine
viol|ação *f* violation; **~ar** *v/t* violate
violência *f* violence
violent|ar *v/t* do violence to; **~o** violent
vir *v/i* come; **vem cá!** come here!; **~ a ser** become
virar *v/t*, *v/i* turn; veer
virgem *f* virgin
viril virile, manly
virtude *f* virtue
virtuoso virtuous
vírus *m* MED, COMP virus
visão *f* vision
visar *v/t* aim at
viscoso viscous
visibilidade *f* visibility
visita *f* visit; visitor; **~nte** *m*, *f* visitor; **~r** *v/t* visit
visível visible
vista *f* view; vista
visto *m* visa
vistoria inspection, survey
vistoso showy, flashy
vital *adj* vital; **~ício** lifelong, for life; **~idade** *f* vitality
vitela *f* heifer; veal
vítima *f* victim
vitória *f* victory
vitrina *f* shop-window; show--window; show-case
viúva *f* widow
viúvo *m* widower
vivacidade *f* vivacity
vivaz vivacious
vivenda *f* dwelling, home
viver *v/i* live
víveres *m/pl* provisions
vívido vivid
vivo lively; alive, living
vizinh|ança *f* neighbo(u)rhood; vicinity; **~o** *m* neighbo(u)r; *adj* neighbo(u)ring
voar *v/i* fly
vocação *f* vocation
você, *pl* **~s** you
vogar *v/i* row; sail
volante *m* steering-wheel; shuttlecock
voleibol *m* volley-ball
volta *f* turn; return; circuit; bend, curve; walk, stroll; **por ~ de** about
voltagem *f* voltage
voltar *v/t*, *v/i*, *v/r* come back, return; turn round
volume *m* volume; piece of luggage
volumoso voluminous
voluntário *adj* voluntary

voluntarioso headstrong
volver *v/t, v/i* turn, revolve
vomitar *v/t* vomit, throw up
vontade *f* will; wish, desire
voo *m* flight
vos *pron* you, to you
vós *pron* you
vosso *adj* your; *pron* yours
vot|ação *f* poll, voting; **~ar** *v/i* vote; **~o** *m* vote; vow; wish
vovó *f* granny, grannie
vovô *m* grandpa
voz *f* voice; **~earia** *f* hullabaloo, clamo(u)r
vulcão *m* volcano
vulgar *adj* common, ordinary; **~izar** *v/t, v/r* popularize
vulgo *m* populace, rabble
vulnerar *v/t* wound
vulto *m* countenance, mien; bulk; figure, form

xadrez *m* chess; *Braz* jail
xa(i)le *m* shawl
xairel *m* saddle-cloth
xarope *m* syrup
xeque *m* check; **~-mate** checkmate
xícara *f* cup
xingar *v/t Braz* scold, rail

Z

zanga *f* anger; quarrel; **~do** angry
zangar *v/t, v/r* annoy; get angry
zapping *m* **fazer ~** zap
zelar *v/t* watch over
zelo *m* zeal; **~so** zealous; eager
zé-povinho *m* (the) Portuguese
zé-povo *m* (the) Brazilian
zerinho *m fam* brand-new
zero *m* zero; nil; nought
zomb|ador *m* scoffer; **~ar** *v/i* jeer, scoff (**de** at)
zona *f* area, district; **~ para pedestres** pedestrian precinct
zoológico *m* zoo, zoological garden
zorro *m* fox
zumb|ido *m* buzzing, humming; **~ir** *v/i* hum, buzz
zunir *v/i* hum, buzz; whir(r); whistle
zurrapa *f* rough wine
zurzir *v/t* thrash; cudgel; flog

A

a [ei; ə], **an** [æn, ən] um *m*, uma *f*
aback [ə'bæk]: **taken ~** desconcertado, surpreso
abandon [ə'bændən] *v/t* abandonar; entregar, -se; **~ment** abandono *m*
abase [ə'beis] *v/t* humilhar, rebaixar
abate [ə'beit] *v/t*, *v/i* abater; JUR anular; diminuir; **~ment** diminuição *f*
abb|ess ['æbis] abadessa *f*; **~ey** ['-i] abadia *f*; **~ot** ['-ət] abade *m*
abbreviat|e [ə'bri:vieit] *v/t* abreviar; **~ion** [-'eiʃən] abreviatura *f*
abdicate ['æbdikeit] *v/t*, *v/i* abdicar, renunciar a
abdomen ['æbdəmen] abdome, abdómen *m*
abduct [æb'dʌkt] *v/t* sequestrar, raptar
abet [ə'bet] *v/t* incitar, instigar; **~tor** cúmplice *m*, *f*
abeyance [ə'beiəns] suspensão *f*; **in ~** (em) suspenso
abhor [əb'hɔ:] *v/t* aborrecer, detestar; **~rence** aversão *f*; **~rent** repugnante
abide [ə'baid] *v/t* aguentar, suportar; *v/i* morar
ability [ə'biliti] habilidade *f*; capacidade *f*; aptidão *f*
abject ['æbdʒekt] abje(c)to
abjure [əb'dʒuə] *v/t* abjurar; renunciar a
able ['eibl] apto; hábil, capaz; **be ~ to** poder, ser capaz de
abnegate ['æbnigeit] *v/t* abnegar
abnormal [æb'nɔ:məl] anormal
aboard [ə'bɔ:d] *adv* a bordo
abolish [ə'bɔliʃ] *v/t* abolir
abominable [ə'bɔminəbl] abominável
abominate [ə'bɔmineit] *v/t* abominar, detestar
abortion [ə'bɔ:ʃən] aborto *m*
abound [ə'baund] *v/i* abundar; **~ in**, **~ with** ser rico em, estar cheio de
about [ə'baut] *prp* em volta de; sobre, acerca de; *adv* pouco mais ou menos; quase; **be ~ to** estar a ponto de
above [ə'bʌv] *prp* sobre, por cima de, acima de; *adv* acima, em cima; **~ all** sobretudo
abreast [ə'brest] de frente; lado a lado
abridge [ə'bridʒ] *v/t* abreviar, resumir

abroad [ə'brɔːd] no (ao) estrangeiro
abrupt [ə'brʌpt] abrupto; brusco
abscess ['æbsis] abcesso *m*
absence ['æbsəns] ausência *f*; falta *f*
absent ['æbsənt] *adj* ausente; *v/r* [æb'sent] ausentar-se; **~-minded** distraído
absolve [əb'zɔlv] *v/t* absolver
absorb [əb'sɔːb] *v/t* absorver
abstain [əb'stein] **(from)** *v/i* abster-se (de)
abstemious [æb'stiːmjəs] abstémio, sóbrio
abstract [æb'strækt] *v/t* abstrair; resumir; ['æbstrækt] *adj* abstra(c)to; *s* resumo *m*; extra(c)to *m*
absurd [əb'səːd] absurdo
abundan|ce [ə'bʌndəns] abundância *f*; **~t** abundante
abus|e [ə'bjuːs] *s* abuso *m*; *v/t* [ə'bjuːz] abusar; insultar; **~ive** abusivo; insultante
abyss [ə'bis] abismo *m*
academic [ˌækə'demik] *adj*, *s* académico *m*
academy [ə'kædəmi] academia *f*
accede [æk'siːd] *v/i* aceder
accelerat|e [ək'seləreit] *v/t*, *v/i* acelerar; **~or** acelerador *m*
accent ['æksənt] *s* sotaque *m*; acento *m*
accentuate [æk'sentjueit] *v/t* acentuar
accept [ək'sept] *v/t* aceitar; **~able** aceitável; **~ance** aceitação *f*; COM aceite *m*
access ['ækses] acesso *m*; admissão *f*; **~ible** [ək'sesəbl] acessível; **~ory** *adj* acessório; *s* JUR (*pl* **-ries**) cúmplice *m*; *pl* acessórios *m*/*pl*
accident ['æksidənt] acidente *m*, desastre *m*; **by ~** por acaso; **~al** [ˌ-'dentl] *adj* acidental
acclaim [ə'kleim] *v/t* aplaudir, aclamar
acclimatize [ə'klaimətaiz] *v/t*, *v/i* aclimatar (-se)
accommodat|e [ə'kɔmədeit] *v/t* acomodar; **~ion** [əˌkɔmə'deiʃən] acomodação *f*; alojamento *m*
accompan|iment [ə'kʌmpənimənt] acompanhamento *m*; **~ist** MUS acompanhante *m*; **~y** *v/t* acompanhar
accomplice [ə'kɔmplis] cúmplice *m*, *f*
accomplish [ə'kɔmpliʃ] *v/t* efe(c)tuar, realizar; completar; **~ed** acabado, perfeito; consumado; **~ment** conclusão *f*; realização *f*
accord [ə'kɔːd] *v/t*, *v/i* concordar; conceder; *s* acordo *m*; **of one's own ~** de moto próprio; **with one ~** de comum acordo; **~ing to** segundo, conforme, de acordo com; **~ingly** em consequência; conforme(mente)
accost [ə'kɔst] *v/t* abordar
account [ə'kaunt] *v/t* considerar; *s* conta *f*; **~ for** dar conta de; justificar, explicar; **on ~**

of por causa de; **on no ~** de modo algum; **take into ~** levar em conta; **turn to ~** tirar lucro; **~able** responsável; **~ancy** contabilidade *f*; **~ant** contabilista *m, f*

accredit [ə'kredit] *v/t* acreditar

accrue [ə'kru:] *v/i* acrescer; provir

accumulat|e [ə'kju:mjuleit] *v/t, v/i* acumular(-se); **~or** acumulador *m*

accura|cy ['ækjurəsi] exa(c)tidão *f*, precisão *f*; **~te** exa(c)to, preciso

accusation [ˌækju(:)'zeiʃən] acusação *f*

accuse [ə'kju:z] *v/t* acusar; **~d** *s* réu *m*; ré *f*

accustom [ə'kʌstəm] *v/t* acostumar

ace [eis] ás *m*

ache [eik] *s* dor *f*; *v/i* doer

achieve [ə'tʃi:v] *v/t* executar, realizar, conseguir; **~ment** realização *f*; proeza *f*

acid ['æsid] *adj, s* ácido *m*

acidity [ə'siditi] acidez *f*

acknowledge [ək'nɔlidʒ] *v/t* reconhecer; confirmar; admitir; **~ment** reconhecimento *m*; confirmação *f*; aviso *m* de recepção

acorn ['eikɔ:n] bolota *f*

acoustics [ə'ku:stiks] acústica *f*

acquaint [ə'kweint] *v/t* familiarizar; informar; **be ~ed with** conhecer pessoalmente; **~ance** conhecimento *m*

acquiesce [ˌækwi'es] *v/i* aquiescer; **~nce** [ˌækwi'esəns] aquiescência *f*

acqui|re [ə'kwaiə] *v/t* adquirir; **~sition** [ˌækwi'ziʃən] aquisição *f*

acquit [ə'kwit] *v/t* absolver; ilibar; liquidar; **~tal** absolvição *f*

acre ['eikə] acre *m*

acrid ['ækrid] acre, picante

acrimony ['ækriməni] acrimónia *f*

acrobat ['ækrəbæt] acrobata *m, f*; **~ics** acrobacia *f*

across [ə'krɔs] *prp* do outro lado de; através de

act [ækt] *s* lei *f*, decreto *m*; a(c)ção *f*, a(c)to *m*; *v/t, v/i* representar; agir, a(c)tuar; funcionar; **~ion** a(c)ção *f*

active ['æktiv] a(c)tivo

activity [æk'tiviti] (*pl* **-ties**) a(c)tividade *f*

actor ['æktə] a(c)tor *m*

actress ['æktris] a(c)triz *f*

actual ['æktʃuəl] verdadeiro, real; a(c)tual; **~ly** na realidade; presentemente

acute [ə'kju:t] agudo; penetrante; **~ness** agudeza *f*; acuidade *f*

adage ['ædidʒ] adágio *m*

adapt [ə'dæpt] *v/t* adaptar; **~ation** [ˌædæp'teiʃən] adaptação *f*

add [æd] *v/t, v/i* acrescentar, juntar; somar, adicionar

adder ['ædə] víbora *f*

addict ['ædikt] *s* viciado *m*; **~ed** [ə'diktid] (**to**) adi(c)to (a); ape-

gado (a)
addition [əˈdiʃən] adição *f*; soma *f*; **in ~ to** em aditamento a, além de; **~al** adicional
address [əˈdres] *s* endereço *m*; alocução *f*; *v/t* dirigir-se a; endereçar; **~ee** [ˌædreˈsiː] destinatário *m*
adduce [əˈdjuːs] *v/t* aduzir
adept [ˈædept] *adj, s* perito *m*
adequate [ˈædikwit] adequado
adhe|re [ədˈhiə] *v/i* aderir; **~sion** [ædˈhiːʃən] adesão *f*
adhesive [ədˈhiːsiv] *adj* adesivo; **~ tape** adesivo *m*
adjacent [əˈdʒeisənt] adjacente, contíguo
adjective [ˈædʒiktiv] adje(c)tivo *m*
adjoin [əˈdʒɔin] *v/t, v/i* confinar (com)
adjourn [əˈdʒəːn] *v/t* adiar, diferir
adjudicate [əˈdʒuːdikeit] *v/t, v/i* adjudicar
adjunct [ˈædʒʌŋkt] adjunto *m*, auxiliar *m*
adjust [əˈdʒʌst] *v/t* ajustar; consertar
administ|er [ədˈministə] *v/t* administrar; **~ration** [-ˈtreiʃən] administração *f*; **~rative** [-trətiv] administrativo
admirable [ˈædmərəbl] admirável
admiral [ˈædmərəl] almirante *m*
admiration [ˌædməˈreiʃən] admiração *f*
admire [ədˈmaiə] *v/t* admirar
admirer [ədˈmaiərə] admirador *m*
admiss|ible [ədˈmisəbl] admissível; **~ion** admissão *f*; entrada *f*
admit [ədˈmit] *v/t* admitir; **~tance** admissão *f*; entrada *f*
admoni|sh [ədˈmɔniʃ] *v/t* admoestar; **~tion** [ˌædməˈniʃən] admoestação *f*
ado [əˈduː] tumulto *m*, alarido *m*, barulho *m*; **much ~ about nothing** muito alarido por nada
adopt [əˈdɔpt] *v/t* ado(p)tar; **~ion** ado(p)ção *f*
ador|able [əˈdɔːrəbl] adorável; **~ation** [ˌædɔːˈreiʃən] adoração *f*; **~e** *v/t* adorar
adorn [əˈdɔːn] *v/t* adornar
adrift [əˈdrift] *adv* à deriva
adroit [əˈdrɔit] destro
adult [ˈædʌlt] *adj, s* adulto *m*
adulter|ate [əˈdʌltəreit] *v/t* adulterar; **~er** adúltero *m*; **~ess** adúltera *f*; **~y** (*pl* **-ries**) adultério *m*
advance [ədˈvɑːns] *s* avanço *m*; adiantamento *m*; *v/t, v/i* avançar; adiantar; progredir; **~d** avançado, adiantado
advantage [ədˈvɑːntidʒ] vantagem *f*; **take ~ of** tirar vantagem de; **~ous** [ˌædvənˈteidʒəs] vantajoso
adventur|e [ədˈventʃə] aventura *f*; **~er** aventureiro *m*; **~ous** aventuroso
advers|ary [ˈædvəsəri] adversário *m*; **~e** adverso; **~ity**

adversidade *f*

ad(vert) ['ædvə:t] *s GB abbr* of **advertisement**

advertise ['ædvətaiz] *v/t* anunciar; *v/i* pôr anúncios; **~ment** [əd'və:tismənt] anúncio *m*; **~r** anunciante *m*

advertising ['ædvətaiziŋ] publicidade *f*

advice [əd'vais] aviso *m*; conselho *m*

advisable [əd'vaizəbl] aconselhável

advise [əd'vaiz] *v/t* aconselhar; prevenir, avisar; **~r** conselheiro *m*

advisory [əd'vaizəri] consultivo

advocate ['ædvəkit] *s* advogado *m*; defensor *m*; ['ædvəkeit] *v/t* advogar

aerial ['ɛəriəl] *adj* aéreo; *s* antena *f*

aero|drome ['ɛərədrəum] aeródromo *m*; **~dynamic** ['ɛərəudai'næmik] aerodinâmico; **~dynamics** aerodinâmica *f*; **~nautical** [-'nɔ:tikəl] aeronáutico; **~nautics** aeronáutica *f*; **~plane** ['-plein] *GB* aeroplano *m*

aesthetic [i:s'θetik] estético

affable ['æfəbl] afável

affair [ə'fɛə] questão *f*, assunto *m*; aventura *f* amorosa; **that's my ~** isso é comigo

affect [ə'fəkt] *v/t* afe(c)tar; aparentar; **~ation** afe(c)tação *f*; **~ed** afe(c)tado; **~ing** comovente; **~ion** afeição *f*; **~ionate** [-ʃnit] afe(c)tuoso

affiliate [ə'filieit] *v/t*, *v/i* (a)filiar

affinity [ə'finiti] afinidade *f*

affirm [ə'fə:m] *v/t* afirmar; **~ation** [ˌæfə:'meiʃən] afirmação *f*; **~ative** [-mətiv] *s* afirmativa *f*; *adj* afirmativo

afflict [ə'flikt] *v/t* afligir; **~ion** aflição *f*

affluence ['æfluəns] afluência *f*

affluent ['æfluənt] *adj*, *s* afluente *m*

afford [ə'fɔ:d] *v/t* ter recursos para; dar-se ao luxo de, permitir-se

afforestation [æˌfɔris'teiʃən] florestação *f*, reflorestamento *m*

affront [ə'frʌnt] *v/t* afrontar; *s* afronta *f*

afloat [ə'fləut] *adv* à tona

afoot [ə'fut] *adv* em progresso, em a(c)ção

afore|said [ə'fɔ:sed] sobredito; **~thought** premeditado

afraid [ə'freid] amedrontado, assustado; **be ~ of** ter medo de; recear

afresh [ə'freʃ] de novo, outra vez

African ['æfrikən] *adj*, *s* africano *m*; **~-American** [-ə'merican] *adj*, *s* afro-americano *m*

after ['ɑ:ftə] *adv* depois, em seguida; *conj* depois que; *prp* depois de, após; **~ all** afinal, no fim de contas; **~noon** tarde *f*; **~wards** [-wədz] depois

again [ə'gen] outra vez, de novo; **~ and ~** repetidamente;

muitas vezes; **now and ~** de vez em quando
against [ə'genst] contra
age [eidʒ] *s* idade *f*; era *f*; **of ~** de maioridade; *v/t, v/i* envelhecer; **~d** *adj* idoso
agency ['eidʒənsi] (*pl* **-cies**) agência *f*
agent ['eidʒənt] agente *m*
aggravate ['ægrəveit] *v/t* agravar; incomodar
aggression [ə'greʃən] agressão *f*
aggressive [ə'gresiv] agressivo
aghast [ə'gɑːst] aterrado; embasbacado
agil|e ['ædʒail] ágil; **~ity** [ə'dʒiliti] agilidade *f*
agitat|e ['ædʒiteit] *v/t* agitar; **~ion** agitação *f*; **~or** agitador *m*
ago [ə'gəu] *adv* há, faz; antes; **long ~** há muito tempo
agoniz|e ['ægənaiz] *v/t, v/i* torturar; agonizar; **~ing** angustioso, atroz
agony ['ægəni] agonia *f*; angústia *f*
agrarian [ə'grεəriən] *adj, s* agrário *m*
agree [ə'griː] *v/t, v/i* concordar; convir; combinar; entender-se; **~ to** consentir em; **~able** de acordo; aprazível, agradável; **~d** combinado; **~ment** acordo *m*, ajuste *m*
agricultur|al [ˌægri'kʌltʃərəl] agrícola, agrário; **~e** agricultura *f*
ague ['eigjuː] sezão *f*
ahead [ə'hed] à frente, avante, adiante; **straight ~** sempre em frente
aid [eid] *s* ajuda *f*, auxílio *m*; *v/t* ajudar, auxiliar
ail [eil] *v/t* afligir, doer; **~ing** doente; **~ment** mal *m*, doença *f*
aim [eim] *s* obje(c)tivo *m*; mira *f*, alvo *m*; *v/t, v/i* (**at**) almejar; apontar (para); visar (a); **~less** sem obje(c)tivo
air [εə] *s* ar *m*; aspecto *m*; **in the open ~** ao ar livre; *v/t* arejar, ventilar; **~-base** base *f* aérea; **~-brake** freio *m* pneumático; **~-conditioned** com ar *m* condicionado; **~craft** avião *m*; **~craft carrier** porta-aviões *m*; **~ force** força *f* aérea; **~ hostess** hospedeira *f* de bordo, *Braz* aeromoça *f*; **~ing** ventilação *f*; **~line** linha *f* aérea; **~liner** avião *m* de carreira; **~-mail** correio *m* aéreo; **~-plane** *US* = **aeroplane**; **~port** aeroporto *m*; **~ raid** ataque *m* aéreo; **~-sick** enjoado; **~tight** hermético
aisle [ail] nave *f* lateral; coxia *f*
ajar [ə'dʒɑː] *adj* entreaberto
akin [ə'kin] aparentado; análogo
alarm [ə'lɑːm] *s* alarme *m*; rebate *m*; *v/t* alarmar; **~-clock** despertador *m*; **~ing** alarmante
alas! [ə'lɑːs] ai!
albatross ['ælbətrɔs] albatroz *m*
alcohol ['ælkəhɔl] álcool *m*; **~ic**

alcoólico
ale [eil] cerveja *f* inglesa
alert [ə'lə:t] *adj*, *s* alerta *m*
alibi ['ælibai] álibi *m*
alien ['eiljən] *adj* estranho; alheio; *s* estrangeiro *m*
alienate ['eiljəneit] *v/t* alienar
alight [ə'lait] *v/i* apear-se; *adj* aceso, em fogo
alike [ə'laik] *adj* parecido, semelhante; *adv* do mesmo modo
alimony ['æliməni] pensão *f* alimentícia
alive [ə'laiv] vivo, com vida
all [ɔ:l] *adj*, *pron* todo(s), toda(s); tudo; *adv* inteiramente; **~ at once** de repente; **~ right!** está bem! muito bem!; **~ the better** tanto melhor; **not at ~** de modo nenhum; não tem de quê
allege [ə'ledʒ] *v/t* alegar
allegiance [ə'li:dʒəns] fidelidade *f*
allegory ['æligəri] alegoria *f*
alleviate [ə'li:vieit] *v/t* aliviar
alley ['æli] álea *f*; viela *f*
All Fools' Day ['ɔ:l'fu:lzdei] (1º de Abril) dia *m* dos enganos, *Braz* dia *m* dos bobos
allot [ə'lɔt] *v/t* destinar; repartir, distribuir; **~ment** lote *m*, quinhão *m*
allow [ə'lau] *v/t* permitir; conceder; admitir; **~ for** levar em conta; **~ance** subsídio *m*; subvenção *f*; autorização *f*; desconto *m*
alloy ['ælɔi] *s* liga *f* (de metais)
allude [ə'lu:d] *v/i* **~ to** aludir
allure [ə'ljuə] *v/t* engodar; **~ment** engodo *m*
ally [ə'lai] *v/t*, *v/i* aliar(-se), unir(-se); ['ælai] (*pl* **-lies**) *s* aliado *m*
almanac ['ɔ:lmənæk] almanaque *m*
almighty [ɔ:l'maiti] *adj* todopoderoso
almond ['ɑ:mənd] amêndoa *f*; amendoeira *f*
almost ['ɔ:lməust] quase
alms [ɑ:mz] *s* (*sing*, *pl*) esmola *f*
alone [ə'ləun] *adj* só, sozinho; *adv* só, apenas; **leave ~** deixar em paz
along [ə'lɔŋ] *prp* por; ao longo de; *adv* para diante; **~side** *adv*, *prp* ao lado (de)
aloof [ə'lu:f] *adj* afastado, à parte
aloud [ə'laud] em voz alta
alphabet ['ælfəbit] alfabeto *m*; **~ical** [ˌ-'betikəl] alfabético
Alps [ælps] *s/pl* Alpes *m/pl*
already [ɔ:l'redi] já
alright ['ɔ:l'redi] já
alright ['ɔ:l'rait] = **all right**
also ['ɔ:lsəu] também
altar ['ɔ:ltə] altar *m*
alter ['ɔ:ltə] *v/t*, *v/i* alterar(-se)
alternat|e [ɔ:l'tə:nit] *v/t*, *v/i* alternar(-se); **~ive** [-nətiv] *s* alternativa *f*; *adj* alternativo
although [ɔ:l'ðəu] posto que, embora, se bem que
altogether [ˌɔ:ltə'geðə] *adv* completamente
always ['ɔ:lwəz] sempre

am [æm; əm] 1st *sg pres of* **be**
a.m. ['ei'em] *abbr of* **ante meridiem** antes do meio-dia, de manhã
amass [ə'mæs] *v/t* acumular, juntar
amateur ['æmətə] *adj, s* amador *m*
amaz|e [ə'meiz] *v/t* espantar, assombrar; **~ement** espanto *m*; assombro *m*; **~ing** espantoso, estupendo
ambassador [æm'bæsədə] embaixador *m*
ambigu|ity [ˌæmbi'gju(:)iti] ambiguidade *f*; **~ous** [-'bigjuəs] ambíguo
ambit ['æmbit] âmbito *m*; **~ion** [-'biʃən] ambição *f*; **~ious** [-'biʃəs] ambicioso
ambulance ['æmbuləns] ambulância *f*
ambush ['æmbuʃ] *s* emboscada *f*; *v/t, v/i* emboscar(-se)
amen ['ɑː'men] *int, s* amém (*m*), ámen (*m*)
amend [ə'mend] *v/t, v/i* emendar(-se); **~ment** emenda *f*; **~s** *s/pl* inde(m)nização *f*
amenity [ə'miːniti] (*pl* **-ties**) amenidade *f*
American [ə'merikən] *adj, s* americano *m*
amiable ['eimjəbl] amável, afável
amicable ['æmikəbl] amigável, amistoso
amiss [ə'mis] *adj* impróprio; *adv* mal; **take ~** levar a mal
ammonia [ə'məunjə] amónia *f*
ammunition [ˌæmju'niʃən] munições *s/pl*
amnesty ['æmnisti] *s* a(m)nistia *f*
amok [ə'mɔk] = **amuck**
among (st) [ə'mʌŋ(st)] entre, no meio de
amorous ['æmərəs] enamorado; amoroso; carinhoso
amount [ə'maunt] *s* montante *m*; quantia; **~ to** *v/i* importar em, montar a
amphitheatre ['æmfiˌθiətə]; *US* **-ter** anfiteatro *m*
ampl|e ['æmpl] amplo, extenso; **~ifier** [-ifaiə] amplificador *m*; **~ify** [-ifai] *v/t* ampliar, amplificar
amputate ['æmpjuteit] *v/t* amputar
amuck [ə'mʌk]: **run ~** correr em frenesi
amuse [ə'mjuːz] *v/t* divertir; entreter; **~ment** divertimento *m*
amusing [ə'mjuːziŋ] divertido
an [æn, ən] *art* um, uma
an(a)emia [ə'niːmjə] anemia *f*
an(a)esthesia [ænis'θiːzjə] anestesia *f*
an(a)esthetic [ˌænis'θetik] anestésico *m*
analog|ous [ə'næləgəs] análogo; **~y** [-dʒi] analogia *f*
analyse ['ænəlaiz] *v/t* analisar
analysis [ə'næləsis] (*pl* **-ses**) análise *f*
anarch|ist ['ænəkist] anarquista *m, f*; **~y** anarquia *f*
anatomy [ə'nætəmi] anatomia

f

ancest|or ['ænsistə] antepassado *m*; **~ral** [æn'sestrəl] ancestral; **~ry** (*pl* **-ries**) linhagem *f*

anchor ['æŋkə] *s* âncora *f*; *v/t, v/i* ancorar

ancient ['einʃənt] *adj* antigo

and [ænd, ən(d)] e

anew [ə'njuː] de novo

angel ['eindʒəl] anjo *m*

anger ['æŋgə] *s* ira *f*, cólera *f*

angle ['æŋgl] *s* ângulo *m*; *v/i* pescar à linha

Anglican ['æŋglikən] *adj, s* anglicano *m*

Anglo-Saxon ['æŋgləu'sæksən] *adj, s* anglo-saxão *m*

angry ['æŋgri] zangado

anguish ['æŋgwiʃ] angústia *f*

angular ['æŋgjulə] angular

animal ['æniməl] *adj, s* animal *m*

animat|e ['ænimeit] *v/t* animar; **~ion** [ˌ-'meiʃən] animação *f*

animosity [ˌæni'mɔsiti] (*pl* **-ties**) animosidade *f*

ankle ['æŋkl] tornozelo *m*

annex ['æneks] *s* anexo *m*; dependência *f*; [ə'neks] *v/t* anexar

annihilate [ə'naiəleit] *v/t* aniquilar

anniversary [ˌæni'vəːsəri] (*pl* **-ries**) aniversário *m*

annotate ['ænəuteit] *v/t* anotar

announce [ə'nauns] *v/t* anunciar; **~ment** anúncio *m*; aviso *m*; **~r** locutor *m*

annoy [ə'nɔi] *v/t* aborrecer, incomodar; **~ance** aborrecimento *m*; **~ing** aborrecido

annual ['ænjuəl] *adj* annual

annuity [ə'nju(:)iti] (*pl* **-ties**) anuidade *f*

annual [ə'nʌl] *v/t* anular

anomal|ous [ə'nɔmələs] anómalo; **~y** anomalia *f*

anonymous [ə'nɔniməs] anónimo

another [ə'nʌðə] *adj, pron* outro; um outro; mais um

answer ['ɑːnsə] *v/t, v/i* contestar, responder; *s* resposta *f*

ant [ænt] formiga *f*

antagoni|sm [æn'tægənizəm] antagonismo *m*; **~st** antagonista *m*

antarctic [ænt'ɑːktik] *adj* antár(c)tico

antechamber ['æntiˌtʃeimbə] antecâmara *f*

antelope ['æntiləup] antílope *m*

anthem ['ænθəm] hino *m*

anti-aircraft ['ænti'eəkrɑːft] *adj* antiaéreo

antibiotic ['æntibai'ɔtik] *adj, s* antibiótico *m*

anticipat|e [æn'tisipeit] *v/t* prever; antecipar; **~ion** [ænˌtisi'peiʃən] expectção *f*; previsão *f*; antecipação *f*

antidote ['æntidəut] antídoto *m*

antipathy [æn'tipəθi] antipatia *f*

antiquated ['æntikweitid] antiquado

antique [æn'tiːk] *adj* antigo; *s* antigualha *f*

antiquity [æn'tikwiti] antiguidade *f*
antiseptic [ˌænti'septik] *adj*, *s* anti-séptico *m*
anvil ['ænvil] bigorna *f*
anxiety [æŋ'zaiəti] ansiedade *f*
anxious ['æŋkʃəs] ansioso
any ['eni] *adj*, *pron* todo, toda; qualquer; algum, alguma, alguns, algumas; *adv* de qualquer modo; **is he ~ better?** ele está melhor?; **~body** qualquer pessoa; alguém; **~how** de qualquer modo; **~one** qualquer um, alguém; **~thing** qualquer (alguma) coisa; **~thing but** tudo menos; **~way** de qualquer maneira; em todo o caso; **~where** em qualquer parte; em parte alguma
apart [ə'pɑːt] *adv* à parte
apartment [ə'pɑːtmənt] aposento *m*; apartamento *m*
apath|etic [ˌæpə'θetik] apático; **~y** ['æpəθi] apatia *f*
ape [eip] *s* macaco *m*; *v/t* imitar, macaquear
apéritif [ə'peritif] aperitivo *m*
aperture ['æpətjuə] abertura *f*; diafragma *m*
apiary ['eipjəri] (*pl* **-ries**) colmeal *m*
apiece [ə'piːs] por peça; por cabeça; cada (um)
apolog|ist [ə'pɔlədʒist] apologista *m*, *f*; **~ize** *v/i* pedir desculpa; **~y** (*pl* **-gies**) desculpa *f*; satisfação *f*; apologia *f*
apoplexy ['æpəupleksi] apoplexia *f*
apostle [ə'pɔsl] apóstolo *m*
appal|(l) [ə'pɔːl] *v/t* espantar, aterrar; **~ling** horroroso, apavorante
apparatus [ˌæpə'reitəs] aparelho *m*; aparato *m*
apparent [ə'pærənt] evidente; aparente
appeal [ə'piːl] *s* JUR apelação *f*; apelo *m*; petição *f*; atra(c)ção *f*; *v/i* apelar; atrair
appear [ə'piə] *v/i* parecer; aparecer; JUR comparecer; **~ance** ar *m*, aspecto *m*; aparência *f*; aparição *f*; JUR comparência *f*
appease [ə'piːz] apaziguar; *v/t* aplacar
append [ə'pend] *v/t* apensar; **~icitis** [əˌpendi'saitis] apendicite *f*; **~ix** [-iks] apêndice *m*
appertain [ˌæpə'tein] *v/i*: **~ to** pertencer
appetite ['æpitait] apetite *m*
applaud [ə'plɔːd] *v/t*, *v/i* aplaudir
applause [ə'plɔːz] aplauso *m*
apple ['æpl] maçã *f*; **the ~ of one's eye** a menina *f* dos olhos; **~-pie** torta *f* de maçã; **~-tree** macieira *f*
appliance [ə'plaiəns] utensílio *m*, ferramenta *f*, instrumento *m*
applicant ['æplikənt] candidato *m*
application [ˌæpli'keiʃən] aplicação *f*; candidatura *f*
apply [ə'plai] *v/t*, *v/i* (to) referir-se a; requerer, concorrer; dirigir-se a; aplicar(-se a)

appoint [ə'pɔint] (**to, for**) *v/t* designar; nomear; marcar; **~ment** nomeação *f*; encontro *m* marcado
apportion [ə'pɔ:ʃən] *v/t* repartir; partilhar; **~ment** partilha *f*
appraise [ə'preiz] *v/t* avaliar
appreciate [ə'pri:ʃieit] *v/t* estimar, avaliar; prezar
apprehen|d [,æpri'hend] *v/t* prender; apreender; temer; **~sion** apreensão *f*; receio *m*; **~sive** receoso, apreensivo; perspicaz
apprentice [ə'prentis] *s* aprendiz *m*; *v/t* pôr de aprendiz; **~ship** aprendizagem *f*
approach [ə'prəutʃ] *v/t, v/i* aproximar(-se); abordar; *s* aproximação *f*; acesso *m*; **~able** acessível
appropriat|e [ə'prəupriit] *adj* apropriado; [ə'prəuprieit] *v/t* apropriar-se de; **~ion** [ə,prəupri'eiʃən] apropriação *f*
approv|al [ə'pru:vəl] aprovação *f*; **~e** *v/t, v/i* aprovar
approximat|e [ə'prɔksimit] *adj* aproximado; [ə'prɔksimeit] *v/t, v/i* aproximar(-se); **~ely** aproximadamente; **~ion** [ə,prɔksi'meiʃən] aproximação *f*
apricot ['eiprikɔt] damasco *m*
April ['eiprəl] Abril *m*
apron ['eiprən] avental *m*
apt [æpt] apto
aptitude ['æptitju:d] aptidão *f*
aquarium [ə'kwεəriəm] aquário *m*
aquatic [ə'kwætik] *adj* aquático
aquiline ['ækwilain] aquilino
Arab ['ærəb] *adj, s* árabe *m, f*; **~ian** [ə'reibjən] *adj* árabe; **~ic** *adj, s* arábico *m*
arbitrary ['ɑ:bitrəri] arbitrário
arbitrat|e ['ɑ:bitreit] *v/t, v/i* arbitrar; **~ion** [ɑ:bi'treiʃən] arbitragem *f*
arbo(u)r ['ɑ:bə] caramanchão *m*
arcade [ɑ:'keid] arcada *f*
arch [ɑ:tʃ] ARCH, *s* arco *m*; abóbada *f*; *v/t* arquear
archaeologist [,ɑ:ki'ɔlədʒist] arqueólogo *m*
archaic [ɑ:'keiik] arcaico
arch|bishop ['ɑ:tʃ'biʃəp] arcebispo *m*; **~deacon** ['-'di:kən] arcediago *m*; **~duke** ['-dju:k] arquiduque *m*
archer ['ɑ:tʃə] arqueiro *m*; **~y** tiro *m* de arco
architect ['ɑ:kitekt] arquitecto *m*; **~ure** [-tʃə] arquitectura *f*
archives ['ɑ:kaivz] *s/pl* arquivo *m*
arctic ['ɑ:ktik] *adj* ár(c)tico
ard|ent ['ɑ:dənt] ardente, fogoso; **~o(u)r** veemência *f*; ardor *m*; **~uous** [-djuəs] árduo, difícil
are [ɑ:] *pres pl u.* 2nd *sg of* **be**
area ['εəriə] área *f*, zona *f*
arena [ə'ri:nə] arena *f*
Argentine ['ɑ:dʒəntain] *adj, s* argentino *m*
argu|e ['ɑ:gju:] *v/t, v/i* arguir, argumentar; discutir; **~ment** ar-

gumento *m*; discussão *f*
aria ['ɑːriə] ária *f*
arid ['ærid] árido
arise [ə'raiz] *v/i* levantar-se, erguer-se, surgir
aristocra|cy [ˌæris'tɔkrəsi] aristocracia *f*; **~t** ['æristəkræt] aristocrata *m, f*; **~tic** [ˌæristə'krætik] aristocrático
arithmetic [ə'riθmətik] *s* aritmética *f*; **~al** [ˌæriθ'metikəl] aritmético
ark [ɑːk] arca *f*; **Noah's ♀** Arca *f* de Noé
arm [ɑːm] *s* braço *m*; arma *f*; *v/t, v/i* armar(-se); **~ in ~** de braço dado; **child in ~s** criança *f* de colo
armament ['ɑːməmənt] armamento *m*
arm-chair ['ɑːm'tʃɛə] poltrona *f*; cadeira *f* de braços
armful ['ɑːmful] braçada *f*
armistice ['ɑːmistis] armistício *m*
armo(u)r ['ɑːmə] armadura *f*; **~y** arsenal *m*
arm-pit ['ɑːmpit] sovaco *m*
arms [ɑːmz] *s/pl* armas *f/pl*
army ['ɑːmi] exército *m*
aroma [ə'rəumə] aroma *m*; **~tic** [ˌærəu'mætik] aromático
around [ə'raund] *adv* em volta, em redor; *prp* em volta de, em redor de, ao redor de, à roda de
arouse [ə'rauz] *v/t* despertar; excitar; provocar
arrange [ə'reindʒ] *v/t, v/i* planear; chegar a acordo; arranjar; **~ment** arranjo *m*; disposição *f*; combinação *f*; *pl* preparativos *m/pl*
arrears [ə'riəz] *s/pl* débitos *m/pl*; **in ~** atrasado
arrest [ə'rest] *s* prisão *f*, captura *f*, detenção; *v/t* deter, capturar, prender
arriv|al [ə'raivəl] chegada *f*; **~e** *v/i* chegar
arrogan|ce ['ærəgəns] arrogância *f*; **~t** arrogante
arrow ['ærəu] flecha *f*, seta *f*
arson ['ɑːsn] JUR fogo *m* posto
art [ɑːt] *s* arte *f*; jeito *m*; destreza *f*
artery ['ɑːtəri] (*pl* **-ries**) artéria *f*
artful ['ɑːtful] manhoso, ardiloso
artichoke ['ɑːtitʃəuk] alcachofra *f*
article ['ɑːtikl] *s* artigo *m*
articulate [ɑː'tikjuleit] *v/t, v/i* articular(-se); [-lit] *adj* articulado
artifice ['ɑːtifis] artifício *m*; **~r** [ɑː'tifisə] artífice *m*
artificial [ˌɑːti'fiʃəl] artificial
artillery [ɑː'tiləri] artilharia *f*
artist ['ɑːtist] artista *m, f*; **~e** [ɑː'tiːst] artista *m, f*; **~ic** [ɑː'tistik] artístico
artless ['ɑːtlis] natural; simples
as [æz, əz] *adv* como; **~ ... ~** tão ... como; *conj* como; porque; enquanto; quando; **~ if** como se; *prp* como; **~ soon ~** assim que, logo que; **~ such** como tal; em si; **~ well** também; **~**

well ~ tanto como, assim como
asbestos [æz'bestɔs] amianto *m*
ascend [ə'send] *v/t, v/i* ascender, subir
ascension [ə'senʃən] ascensão *f*
ascent [ə'sent] subida *f*, ascensão *f*
ascertain [ˌæsə'tein] *v/t* averiguar, verificar
ascetic [ə'setik] *adj* ascético
ascribe [əs'kraib] *v/t* ~ **to** atribuir, imputar
ash [æʃ] cinza *f*
ashamed [ə'ʃeimd] envergonhado; **be** ~ **of** ter vergonha de
ashen ['æʃn] acinzentado
ashore [ə'ʃɔ:] *adv* em terra; **go** ~ desembarcar
ash-tray ['æʃtrei] cinzeiro *m*
Asia ['eiʃə] Ásia *f*; ~**n** *adj, s* asiático *m*; ~**-American** [ə'merikən] *adj, s* asiático-americano *m*
aside [ə'said] *adv* de lado; à parte; *s* aparte *m*
ask [ɑ:sk] *v/t, v/i* interrogar, perguntar; pedir; convidar; ~ **after** perguntar por; ~ **for** pedir
ask|ance [əs'kæns] de soslaio; ~**ew** [-'kju:] *adv* de través
aslant [ə'slɑ:nt] *adv* obliquamente
asleep [ə'sli:p] adormecido; **fall** ~ adormecer
asparagus [əs'pærəgəs] espargo *m*
aspect ['æspekt] aspecto *m*
asphalt ['æsfælt] *s* asfalto *m*
aspire [əs'paiə] *v/i* aspirar
ass [æs] asno *m*, jumento *m*
assail [ə'seil] *v/t* assaltar; ~**ant** assaltante *m*
assassinate [ə'sæsineit] *v/t* assassinar
assault [ə'sɔ:lt] *v/t* assaltar; *s* assalto *m*
assembl|e [ə'sembl] *v/t, v/i* ajuntar; MEC montar; reunir (-se); ~**y** (*pl* **-lies**) assembleia *f*, reunião *f*; MEC montagem *f*
assent [ə'sent] *s* consentimento *m*, assentimento *m*; *v/i* consentir, assentir
assert [ə'sə:t] *v/t* asseverar; ~ **oneself** impor-se; ~**ion** asseveração *f*
assess [ə'ses] *v/t* avaliar; fixar; taxar; ~**ment** avaliação *f*; cota *f*
assets ['æsets] *s/pl* COM a(c)tivo *m*; ~**s and liabilities** a(c)tivo *m* e passivo *m*
assidu|ity [ˌæsi'dju(:)iti] assiduidade *f*; ~**ous** [ə'sidjuəs] assíduo
assign [ə'sain] *v/t* atribuir; designar; ~**ment** atribuição *f*; cessão *f*
assimilate [ə'simileit] *v/t, v/i* assimilar(-se)
assist [ə'sist] *v/t, v/i* assistir, ajudar; ~**ance** ajuda *f*; ~**ant** auxiliar *m*, ajudante *m, f*
assizes [ə'saiziz] *s/pl GB* sessão *f* periódica de tribunal
associat|e [ə'səuʃieit] *v/t, v/i* associar(-se); [... ʃiit] *s* associado *m*; ~**ion** associação *f*, so-

ciedade *f*; **~ion football** futebol *m*
assort|ed [ə'sɔ:tid] sortido; **~ment** sortimento *m*
assum|e [ə'sju:m] *v/t* assumir; presumir; **~ed** suposto; **~ption** [ə'sʌmpʃən] assunção *f*; suposição *f*
assurance [ə'ʃuərəns] segurança *f*; seguro *m*
assure [ə'ʃuə] *v/t* assegurar; **~d** [-d] *adj* seguro, certo; *s* segurado *m*
astir [ə'stə:] *adj* agitado, em movimento
astonish [əs'tɔniʃ] *v/t* espantar, pasmar; **~ing** surpreendente, espantoso; **~ment** espanto *m*, assombro *m*
astound [əs'taund] *v/t* pasmar, aturdir
astray [əs'trei] *adj*, *adv* extraviado; **go ~** extraviar-se
astride [əs'traid] *adj*, *adv* escarranchado
astringent [əs'trindʒənt] MED *adj*, *s* adstringente *m*
astro|loger [əs'trɔlədʒə] astrólogo *m*; **~logy** astrologia *f*; **~naut** ['æstrənɔ:t] astronauta *m*, *f*; **~nomer** [æs'trɔnəmə] astrónomo *m*; **~nomy** astronomia *f*
astute [əs'tju:t] astuto, astucioso
asunder [ə'sʌndə] à parte; em pedaços
asylum [ə'sailəm] asilo *m*
at [æt, ət] de; por; em; a; **~ all** absolutamente; **~ hand** à mão; **~ home** em casa; **~ last** enfim, por fim; **~ least** pelo menos
atheist ['eiθiist] ateu *m*
athlet|e ['æθli:t] atleta *m*, *f*; **~ic** [-'letik] atlético; **~ics** [-'letiks] atletismo *m*
atlas ['ætləs] atlas *m*
ATM [eiti:'em] ATM *f*
atmosphere ['ætməsfiə] atmosfera *f*
atom ['ætəm] átomo *m*; **~ic** [ə'tɔmik] atómico; **~izer** ['ætəmaizə] atomizador *m*
atone [ə'təun] *v/i* (for) expiar
atroc|ious [ə'trəuʃəs] atroz; **~ity** [ə'trɔsiti] (*pl* **-ties**) atrocidade *f*
atrophy ['ætrəfi] MED *s* atrofia *f*; *v/t*, *v/i* atrofiar
at-seat TV [ət 'si:t ti:ˌvi:] *s* ecrã *m* de televisão individual
attach [ə'tætʃ] *v/t*, *v/i* ligar; unir; **~ment** afe(c)to *m*, apego *m*
attack [ə'tæk] *v/t* atacar; *s* ataque *m*; **~er** atacante *m*
attain [ə'tein] *v/t*, *v/i* conseguir; atingir; **~ment** obtenção *f*
attempt [ə'tempt] *s* esforço *m*, tentativa *f*; *v/t* tentar, intentar
attend [ə'tend] *v/t*, *v/i* assistir, frequentar; prestar atenção, atender; cuidar; **~ance** assistência *f*; **~ant** *s* contínuo *m*, servidor *m*; *adj* subordinado; assistente
attention [ə'tenʃən] atenção *f*
attentive [ə'tentiv] atento
attest [ə'test] *v/t*, *v/i* atestar, cer-

tificar
attic ['ætik] *s* sótão *m*
attitude ['ætitju:d] atitude *f*; postura *f*
attorney [ə'tə:ni] procurador *m*; *US* advogado *m*
attract [ə'trækt] *v/t* atrair; **~ion** atra(c)ção *f*; **~ive** atraente, atra(c)tivo
attribute [ə'tribju(:)t] *v/t* atribuir; ['ætribju(:)t] *s* característica *f*; atributo *m*
auburn ['ɔ:bən] *adj* ruivo
auction ['ɔ:kʃən] *s* leilão *m*; *v/t* leiloar; **~eer** [ˌ-'niə] leiloeiro *m*
audaci|ous [ɔ:'deiʃəs] audaz; **~ty** [ɔ:'dæsiti] audácia *f*
audible ['ɔ:dəbl] audível
audience ['ɔ:djəns] assistência *f*; auditório *m*; audiência *f*
audit ['ɔ:dit] COM *s* exame *m* oficial de contas; **~or** revisor *m* de contas
auditorium [ˌɔ:di'tɔ:riəm] auditório *m*
augment [ɔ:g'ment] *v/t*, *v/i* aumentar
August ['ɔ:gəst] *s* Agosto *m*; ♀ *adj* augusto
aunt [ɑ:nt] tia *f*
auspic|es ['ɔ:spisiz] *s/pl* auspícios *m/pl*; **~ious** [ɔ:s'piʃəs] auspicioso, favorável
auster|e [ɔs'tiə] austero; **~ity** [-'teriti] austeridade *f*
Australian [ɔs'treiljən] *adj*, *s* australiano *m*
Austrian ['ɔstriən] *adj*, *s* austríaco *m*
authentic [ɔ:'θentik] autêntico
author ['ɔ:θə] autor *m*; **~itarian** [ɔ:θɔri'tɛəriən] *adj* autoritário; **~itative** [ɔ:'θɔritətiv] autorizado; autoritário; **~ity** [ɔ:'θɔriti] (*pl* **-ties**) autoridade *f*; **~ize** ['ɔ:θəraiz] *v/t* autorizar; **~ship** autoria *f*
autobiography [ˌɔ:təubai'ɔgrəfi] (*pl* **-phies**) autobiografia *f*
autocracy [ɔ:'tɔkrəsi] (*pl* **-cies**) autocracia *f*
automatic [ˌɔ:tə'mætik] *adj* automático
automation [ˌɔ:tə'meiʃən] automatização *f*
automobile ['ɔ:təməbi:l] *US* automóvel *m*
autonom|ous [ɔ:'tɔnəməs] autónomo; **~y** autonomia *f*
autumn ['ɔ:təm] outono *m*; **~al** [ɔ'tʌmnəl] outonal
auxiliary [ɔ:g'ziljəri] *adj* auxiliar
avail [ə'veil] *s* proveito; *v/t*, *v/i* prestar; **~ oneself of** valer-se de; **of no ~** inútil
available [ə'veiləbl] disponível; válido
avalanche ['ævəlɑ:nʃ] avalancha *f*
avaricious [ˌævə'riʃəs] avarento, avaro
avenge [ə'vendʒ] *v/t* vingar; **~ oneself on** vingar-se de; **~r** vingador *m*
avenue ['ævinju:] avenida *f*
average ['ævəridʒ] *s* média *f*; *adj* mediano; médio; **on an**

(**the**) ~ em média
avers|e [əˈvəːs] oposto, relutante; **~ion** aversão *f*
avert [əˈvəːt] *v/t* desviar; impedir
aviary [ˈeivjəri] (*pl* **-ries**) aviário *m*
aviation [ˌeiviˈeiʃən] aviação *f*
aviator [ˈeivieitə] aviador *m*
avoid [əˈvɔid] *v/t* evitar
avow [əˈvau] *v/t* declarar, confessar; **~al** declaração *f*, confissão *f*
await [əˈweit] *v/t* esperar, aguardar
awake [əˈweik] *v/t, v/i* acordar, despertar; *adj* desperto, acordado
award [əˈwɔːd] *v/t* adjudicar; premiar; *s* prémio *m*
aware [əˈwɛə] sabedor, ciente; **be ~ of** ter conhecimento de, saber
away [əˈwei] *adj* ausente; *adv* embora, (para) longe; **run ~** *v/i* fugir
awe [ɔː] *s* pavor *m*; respeito *m*; **~struck** aterrado
awful [ˈɔːful] terrível; horrível, péssimo; **~ly** extremamente, muito
awhile [əˈwail] por um momento, algum tempo
awkward [ˈɔːkwəd] embaraçoso, incómodo; desajeitado, desastrado
awl [ɔːl] sovela *f*
awning [ˈɔːniŋ] toldo *m*
awry [əˈrai] *adj, adv* de través, torto
ax(e) [æks] machado *m*
axis [ˈæksis] (*pl* **axes**) eixo *m*
axle [ˈæksl] eixo *m* (de roda)
ay(e) [ai] *adv* sim; *s* voto *m* a favor
azure [ˈæʒə] *adj, s* azul-celeste *m*

B

babble [ˈbæbl] *v/t, v/i* palrar; tagarelar; balbuciar; *s* parolagem *f*
baby [ˈbeibi] *s* (*pl* **-bies**) bebé *m, f*; **~hood** primeira infância *f*; **~ish** infantil
bachelor [ˈbætʃələ] solteiro *m*, solteirão *m*; bacharel *m*
back [bæk] *s* costas *f/pl*; dorso *m*; *adv* atrás, para trás; *v/t, v/i* (fazer) recuar; fazer marcha atrás; apoiar; apostar (em); *adj* traseiro; remoto; passado; **~bone** espinha *f* dorsal; **~gammon** gamão *m*; **~ground** fundo *m*, segundo plano *m*; **~stairs** escada *f* de serviço; **~stroke** braçada *f* de costas; **~ward(s)** *adj* atrasado; retrógrado; acanhado; *adv* para trás; de regresso
bacon [ˈbeikən] toucinho *m*
bacterium [bækˈtiəriəm] (*pl* **-ria**) bactéria *f*

bad [bæd] *adj* mau, ruim; nocivo; **from ~ to worse** de mal a pior
badge [bædʒ] *s* emblema *m*, insígnia *f*
badger ['bædʒə] *s* texugo *m*; *v/t* atormentar, ralar
badminton ['bædmintən] badminton *m*, jogo *m* do volante / *Braz* da peteca
badness ['bædnis] maldade *f*
bad-tempered ['bæd'tempəd] mal-humorado
baffle ['bæfl] *v/t* confundir
bag [bæg] *s* saco *m*, bolsa *f*; maleta *f*; *v/t* ensacar
baggage ['bægidʒ] *us* bagagem *f*
bagpipe ['bægpəip] gaita *f* de foles
bail [beil] *s* caução *f* fiança *f*
bailiff ['beilif] bailio *m*, meirinho *m*
bait [beit] *s* isca *f*, engodo *m*; *v/t* iscar, engodar
bake [beik] *v/t v/i* assar, cozer no forno; **~r** padeiro *m*; **~ry** ['-əri] (*pl* **-ries**) padaria *f*
balance ['bæləns] *s* balança *f*; equilíbrio *m*; COM balanço *m*; *v/t* pesar; COM saldar; equilibrar
balcony ['bælkəni] (*pl* **-nies**) varanda *f*; THEAT balcão *m*
bald [bɔːld] calvo; **~ness** calvície *f*; careca *f*
bale [beil] *s* fardo *m*; *v/t* enfardar, empacotar
balk [bɔːk] *s* obstáculo *m*; viga *f*; *v/t*, *v/i* impedir, frustrar
ball [bɔːl] bola *f*; bala *f*; baile *m*; novelo *m*
ballad ['bæləd] balada *f*
ballast ['bæləst] lastro *m*
balloon [bə'luːn] balão *m*
ballot ['bælət] *s* votação *f* secreta; (boletim *m* de) voto *m*; **~ box** urna *f* eleitoral; **~ paper** boletim *m* de voto, *Braz* cédula *f*
ball-point (pen) ['bɔːl (pɔint) pen] esferográfica *f*
balm [baːm] bálsamo *m*
Baltic ['bɔːltik] *adj*, *s* Báltico *m*
balustrade [ˌbæləs'treid] balaustrada *f*
ban [bæn] *v/t* proibir, proscrever; *s* interdito *m*
banana [bə'nɑːnə] banana *f*
band [bænd] *s* faixa *f*; bando *m*; MUS banda *f*
bandage ['bændidʒ] *s* ligadura *f*
bandit ['bændit] bandido *m*
bang [bæŋ] *v/t* bater; *s* pancada *f*, golpe *m*; estoiro *m*, estrondo *m*
banish ['bæniʃ] *v/t* desterrar; banir; **~ment** desterro *m*
bank [bæŋk] *s* margem *f*; baixio *m*; COM banco *m*; **~er** banqueiro *m*; **~ing** *s* negócio *m* bancário; **~-note** nota *f* de banco; **~-rate** taxa *f* de desconto; **~rupt** *adj*, *s* falido (*m*)
bankruptcy ['bæŋkrəptsi] (*pl* **-cies**) falência *f*; bancarrota *f*
banns [bænz] *s/pl* banhos *m/pl*, proclama *m*
banquet ['bæŋkwit] *s* banquete

m

banter ['bæntə] *s* gracejo *m*

bapti|sm ['bæptizəm] ba(p)tismo *m*; **~st** ba(p)tista *m*; **~ze** [bæp'taiz] *v/t* ba(p)tizar

bar [bɑː] *s* barra *f*; faixa *f*; bar *m*; teia *f*, barreira *f*; *v/t* trancar; impedir; excluir

barbarian [bɑː'bɛəriən] *adj*, *s* bárbaro *m*

barbed [bɑːbd] *adj* mordaz; **~ wire** arame *m* farpado

barber ['bɑːbə] barbeiro *m*

bare [bɛə] *adj* despido, nu; descoberto; mero, simples; **~faced** descarado; **~foot(ed)** descalço; **~-headed** de cabeça descoberta; **~ly** mal, apenas

bargain ['bɑːgin] *s* ajuste *m*, contrato *m*; pechincha *f*; *v/t*, *v/i* regatear

barge [bɑːdʒ] *s* barcaça *f*

baritone ['bæritəun] barítono *m*

bark [bɑːk] *s* casca *f*, cortiça *f*; latido *m*; *v/i* latir, ladrar

barkeeper ['bɑːkiːpə] botequineiro *m*

barley ['bɑːli] cevada *f*

bar|maid ['bɑːmeid] empregada *f* de bar, *Braz* garçonete *f*; **~man** (*pl* **-men**) empregado *m* de bar

barn [bɑːn] celeiro *m*

barracks ['bærəks] *s/pl* quartel *m*, caserna *f*

barrel ['bærəl] *s* barril *m*; barrica *f*; cano *m* de espingarda

barren ['bærən] *adj* árido; estéril

barrier ['bæriə] barreira *f*

barrister ['bæristə] advogado *m*

barrow ['bærəu] carrinho *m* de mão; túmulo *m*

barter ['bɑːtə] *s* troca *f*; *v/t*, *v/i* permutar, trocar

base [beis] *s* base *f*; fundamento *m*; *adj* baixo, vil, *v/t* basear, fundar; **~less** sem base, infundado

basement ['beismənt] cave *f*

bashful ['bæʃful] acanhado

basin ['beisn] bacia *f*

basket ['bɑːskit] cesta *f*, cesto *m*; **~-ball** basquetebol *m*, básquete *m*

bass [beis] *s*, MUS baixo *m*

bastard ['bæstəd] *adj*, *s* ilegítimo *m*, bastardo *m*

baste [beist] *v/t* alinhavar

bat [bæt] *s*, ZOO morcego *m*

bath [bɑːθ] *s* banho *m*; banheira *f*; *v/t*, *v/i* dar banho a; tomar banho; **~e** [beið] *v/t*, *v/i* banhar(-se); **~room** casa *f* de banho, *Braz* banheiro *m*; **~tub** banheira *f*

baton ['bætən] MUS batuta *f*

battalion [bə'tæljən] batalhão *m*

batter ['bætə] *v/t*, *v/i* bater; (des)gastar, demolir; *s* pasta *f* culinária

battery ['bætəri] (*pl* **-ries**) bateria *f*

battle ['bætl] *s* batalha *f*; *v/i* batalhar, combater

Bavarian [bə'vɛəriən] *adj*, *s* bávaro *m*

bawl [bɔːl] *v/t*, *v/i* bradar
bay [bei] *s* baía *f*; vão *m* de janela; BOT louro *m*; *adj* baio; *v/i* ladrar
bayonet ['beiənit] *s* baioneta *f*
bay window [bei 'windəu] janela *f* de sacada
be [biː,bi] *v/i*, *v/aux* ser; estar; ficar; existir; haver; **~ in** estar em casa; **~ out** não estar em casa; **~ to** haver de, dever
beach [biːtʃ] praia *f*
beacon ['biːkən] baliza *f*, farol *m*
bead [biːd] conta *f*; gota *f*; **~s** rosário *m*
beak [biːk] bico *m*
beam [biːm] viga *f*, trave *f*; raio *m*; *v/t*, *v/i* irradiar, emitir
bean [biːn] feijão *m*; grão *m*
bear [bɛə] *v/t* aguentar, suportar; dar à luz, gerar; *s* ZOO urso *m*; COM baixista *m*, *f*; **~ out** confirmar
beard [biəd] barba *f*
bear|er ['bɛərə] portador *m*; **~ing** porte *m*; **~ings** orientação *f*, rumo *m*
beast [biːst] animal *m*, besta *f*; **~ly** brutal, bestial
beat [biːt] *v/t* bater; derrotar; *s* MUS compasso *m*; ronda *f* (*polícia*); toque *m* (*tambor*); pulsação *f*
beauti|ful ['bjuːtəful] belo, formoso; **~fy** ['-tifai] *v/t* embelezar
beauty ['bjuːti] beleza *f*; **~parlo(u)r/saloon** salão *m* de beleza
beaver ['biːvə] castor *m*
because [bi'kɔz] *conj* porque; **~ of** *prp* por causa de
beckon ['bekən] *v/t*, *v/i* acenar
becom|e [bi'kʌm] *v/i* fazer-se, tornar-se; *v/t* convir, assentar bem; ser próprio a; **~ing** conveniente; apropriado
bed [bed] *s* cama *f*, leito *m*; canteiro *m*; **go to ~** (ir) deitar-se; **~ding** roupa *f* de cama; **~room** quarto *m* (de dormir), *Braz* dormitório *m*; **~spread** colcha *f*; **~time** hora *f* de (ir) dormir
bee [biː] abelha *f*
beech [biːtʃ] faia *f*
beef [biːf] *s* carne *f* de vaca; **~steak** bife *m*, *Braz* bifesteque *m*
bee|hive ['biːhaiv] colmeia *f*, cortiço *m*; **~-line** linha *f* re(c)ta
beer [biə] cerveja, *f*
beet [biːt] beterraba *f*
beetle ['biːtl] escaravelho *m*
beetroot ['biːtruːt] raiz *f* de beterraba
befall [bi'fɔːl] *v/t*, *v/i* acontecer, suceder
befit [bi'fit] *v/t* convir
before [bi'fɔː] *prp* antes de; diante de; *adv* antes; *conj* antes que; **~hand** de antemão, antecipadamente
beg [beg] *v/t*, *v/i* pedir, suplicar; mendigar
beggar ['begə] mendigo *m*
begin [bi'gin] *v/t*, *v/i* começar; principiar; **~ner** principiante *m*, *f*; **~ning** começo *m*; princípio *m*

beguile [bi'gail] *v/t* enganar; seduzir; divertir
behalf [bi'hɑːf] **on ~ of** em nome de, por, da parte de
behav|e [bi'heiv] *v/i* comportar-se, conduzir-se; **~io(u)r** conduta *f*, comportamento *m*
behead [bi'hed] *v/t* degolar, decapitar
behind [bi'haind] *prp* atrás de, detrás de; *adv* atrás, detrás; *s* *3m, Braz* bunda *f*
being ['biːiŋ] *s* ser *m*, ente *m*; existência *f*; **for the time ~** por agora
belated [bi'leitid] atrasado, tardio
belch [beltʃ] *v/t, v/i* arrotar; vomitar
belfry ['belfri] campanário *m*
Belgi|an ['beldʒən] *adj, s* belga *m, f*; **~um** Bélgica *f*
belie [bi'lai] *v/t* desmentir
belie|f [bi'liːf] crença *f*; convicção *f*; **~vable** crível, verosímil; **~ve** *v/t, v/i* acreditar, crer; **~ver** crente *m, f*
belittle [bi'litl] *v/t* minimizar, depreciar
bell [bel] sino *m*; campainha *f*; **~boy** mandarete *m*, paquete *m*
belligerent [bi'lidʒərənt] *adj, s* beligerante *m, f*
bellow ['beləu] *v/i* mugir; berrar; **~s** *s/pl* fole *m*
belly ['beli] (*pl* **-lies**) ventre *m*, barriga *f*
belong [bi'lɔŋ] *v/i* pertencer; **~ings** *s/pl* pertences *m/pl*
beloved [bi'lʌvd] *adj, s* querido *m*, amado *m*
below [bi'ləu] *prp* debaixo de; inferior; *adv* abaixo, por baixo
belt [belt] cinto *m*; faixa *f*; MEC correia *f*
bench [bentʃ] banco *m*; tribunal *m*
bend [bend] *s* curva *f*; volta *f*; *v/t, v/i* curvar(-se), dobrar; inclinar(-se); **on ~ed knees** de joelhos
beneath [bi'niːθ] *prp* debaixo de, sob; *adv* abaixo
benediction [,beni'dikʃən] bênção *f*
benefactor ['benifæktə] benfeitor *m*
beneficial [beni'fiʃəl] benéfico, proveitoso, útil
benefit ['benifit] *s* benefício *m*; vantagem *f*
benevolent [bi'nevələnt] benévolo
benign [bi'nain] benigno
bent [bent] *s* propensão *f*, tendência *f*
benz|ene ['benziːn] benzeno *m*; **~ine** benzina *f*
bequ|eath ['bikwiːð] *v/t* legar; **~est** [-'kwest] legado *m*
bereave [bi'riːv] *v/t* despojar, privar; **~ment** luto *m*; privação *f*
beret ['berei] boina *f*
berry ['beri] (*pl* **-ries**) bago *m*; baga *f*
berth [bəːθ] *s* beliche *m*; MAR ancoradouro *m*; *v/t* atracar
beset [bi'set] *v/t* assediar, assal-

tar

beside [bi'said] *prp* ao lado de; **~s** *prp fig* além de; *adv* além disso

besiege [bi'siːdʒ] *v/t* sitiar, cercar

best [best] *adj, adv* o melhor; **at ~** quando muito; **do one's ~** fazer o melhor possível; **make the ~ of** tirar o melhor partido de; **~ man** padrinho *m* de casamento de; **~ seller** êxito *m* de livraria

bestow [bi'stəu] *v/t* conferir, outorgar

bet [bet] *s* aposta *f*; *v/t, v/i* apostar

betray [bi'trei] *v/t* trair, atraiçoar; **~al** traição *f*; **~er** traidor *m*

betrothed [bi'trəuðd] *s* prometido *m*, noivo *m*

better ['betə] *adj, adv* melhor; *v/t* melhorar; **we** (*etc.*) **had ~** era melhor; **so much the ~** tanto melhor; **get the ~ of** levar a melhor de

between [bi'twiːn] *prp, adv* entre

bevel ['bevəl] *s* bisel *m*

beverage ['bevəridʒ] bebida *f*

beware [bi'wɛə] *v/t, v/i* acautelar-se; **~ of ...!** cuidado com ...!

bewilder [bi'wildə] *v/t* confundir, desnortear; **~ment** desnorteamento *m*

bewitch [bi'witʃ] *v/t* enfeitiçar, enguiçar

beyond [bi'yɔnd] *adv* além; *prp* além de

bias ['baiəs] *s* viés *m*; tendência *f*; preconceito *m*; *v/t* predispor

bib [bib] babador *m*, babete *m*

Bible ['baibl] Bíblia *f*

bibliography [ˌbibli'ɔgrəfi] bibliografia *f*

bicarbonate [bai'kaːbənit] bicarbonato *m*

bicycle ['baisikl] bicicleta *f*

bid [bid] *v/t, v/i* licitar, lançar; oferecer; mandar; *s* lanço *m*

bier [biə] ataúde *m*; essa *f*

big [big] grande; importante; **to talk ~** vangloriar-se, falar do papo; **~ game** caça *f* grossa

bigamy ['bigəmi] bigamia *f*

bigwig ['bigwig] magnate *m, f*, *Braz* mandachuva *m*

bike [baik] *abbr of* **bicycle**

bile [bail] bílis *f*, fel *m*

bill [bil] *s* conta *f*; cartaz *m*; proje(c)to *m* de lei; **~ of exchange** letra *f* de câmbio; **~ of fare** ementa *f*, lista *f*, *Braz* cardápio *m*; **~ of lading** MAR conhecimento *m* de carga

billet ['bilit] *s* MIL boleto *m*; *v/t* aboletar

billiard|-cue ['biljədkjuː] taco *m*; **~s** ['-z] bilhar *m*

billion ['biljən] bilhão *m*, bilião *m*

billow ['biləu] *v/i* ondular; *s* os carcéu *m*

bind ['baind] *v/t, v/i* atar; ligar; encadernar; obrigar(-se); **~ing** *s* encadernação *f*; *adj* obrigatório

biography [bai'ɔgrəfi] biogra-

fia *f*
biology [bai'ɔlədʒi] biologia *f*
birch [bəːtʃ] vidoeiro *m*, bétula *f*
bird [bəːd] pássaro *m*, ave *f*; **~ of passage** ave *f* de arribação; **~ of prey** ave *f* de rapina; **~'seye view** vista *f* geral
birth [bəːθ] nascimento *m*; **give ~ to** dar à luz; **~ control** controle *m* de natalidade; **~day** aniversário *m*, dia *m* de anos; **~-place** terra *f* natal; **~-rate** natalidade *f*
biscuit ['biskit] bolacha *f*
bishop ['biʃəp] bispo *m*
bison ['baisn] bisão, bisonte *m*
bit [bit] *s* bocado *m*; **~ by ~** bouco a pouco, aos poucos
bitch [bitʃ] *s* cadela *f*
bite [bait] *v/t*, *v/i* morder; *s* mordedura *f*, dentada *f*
bitter ['bitə] *adj* penetrante; amargo; **~ness** amargura *f*, amargor *m*
bitters ['bitəz] licor *m* amargo
black [blæk] *adj*, *s* preto *m*, negro *m*; **~berry** amora *f* silvestre; **~bird** melro *m*; **~-board** lousa *f*, quadro *m* negro; **~en** *v/t*, *v/i* escurecer(-se); **~ eye** olho *m* pisado; **~mail** *s* chantagem *f*; **~ market** mercado *m* negro; **~-out** obscurecimento *m*, extinção *f* de luzes; **~smith** ferreiro *m*
bladder ['blædə] bexiga *f*
blade [bleid] lâmina *f*; folha *f* lanceolada; pá *f*
blame [bleim] *s* culpa *f*, censura *f*; *v/t* culpar, censurar; **~less** sem culpa
bland [blænd] brando, suave
blank [blæŋk] *adj* em branco; vago; vazio; **~ verse** verso *m* branco
blanket ['blæŋkit] *s* cobertor *m*; manta *f*
blasphemy ['blæsfimi] blasfémia *f*
blast [blɑːst] *s* rajada *f* de vento; sopro *m*; carga *f* de explosivos; explosão *f*; *v/t* (fazer) explodir; **~ furnace** alto-forno *m*; **~ it!** maldito seja!; **~-off** *s* lançamento *m* (de foguetão)
blaze [bleiz] *s* chama *f*, labareda *f*; *v/t*, *v/i* chamejar; resplandecer
bleach [bliːtʃ] *v/t*, *v/i* branquear, corar, *Braz* coarar
bleak [bliːk] gelado; desabrigado; sombrio
bleat [bliːt] *v/i*, *v/t* balir; lamuriar; *s* balido *m*; lamúria *f*
bleed [bliːd] *v/t*, *v/i* sangrar, perder sangue
blemish ['blemiʃ] *v/t* danificar; manchar; *s* mancha *f*, defeito *m*
blend [blend] *v/t*, *v/i* lotar; misturar(-se), combinar(-se); *s* mistura *f*
bless [bles] *v/t* abençoar; consagrar; **~ me!** valha-me Deus!; **~ed** bendito, abençoado; **~ing** bênção *f*; graça *f* divina
blind [blaind] *s* toldo *m*, estore *m*; *fig* pretexto *m*; *adj* cego; *v/t* cegar; **~ alley** beco *m* sem saí-

da; **~ness** cegueira *f*

blink [bliŋk] *v/t, v/i* piscar, pestanejar; *s* piscadela *f*

bliss [blis] bem-aventurança *f*

blister ['blistə] *s* bolha *f*, empola *f*

blizzard ['blizəd] nevasca *f*

bloat|ed [bləutid] inchado, cheio de si; **~er** arenque *m* defumado

block [blɔk] *s* cepo *m*; bloco *m*; quarteirão *m*; *v/t* obstruir; bloquear; **~ade** *s* bloqueio *m*; **~head** cepo *m*; **~ letters** letra *f* de imprensa

blond(e) [blɔnd] *adj, s* loiro (-a *f*) *m*

blood [blʌd] *s* sangue *m*; **in cold ~** a sangue frio; **~shed** matança *f*; **~shot** inje(c)tado de sangue; **~thirsty** sanguinário; **~-vessel** vaso *m* sanguíneo; **~y** ensanguentado, sangrento; maldito

bloom [blu:m] *s* flor *f*; florescimento *m*; *v/i* florescer, florir

blossom ['blɔsəm] *s* flor *f*; *v/i* florescer, enflorar

blot [blɔt] *s* borrão *m*; **~ out** encobrir; exterminar; (es-) borratar **~ting-paper** mataborrão *m*

blouse [blauz] blusa *f*

blow [bləu] *s* sopro *m*; golpe *m*; revés *m*; *v/t, v/i* soprar; **~ one's nose** assoar-se; **~ up** *v/t, v/i* explodir; ampliar; inflar; **~pipe** maçarico *m*

blue [blu:] *adj, s* azul *m*; melancólico; **~bell** BOT campainha *f*; **~bottle** varejeira *f*; **~ print** calco *m* heliográfico; proje(c)to *m*

bluff [blʌf] *s* logro *m*, engano *m*, *Braz* blefe *m*; *adj* franco, abrupto; *v/t, v/i* lograr, enganar, *Braz* blefar

blunder ['blʌndə] *s* erro *m* crasso, deslize *m*; *Braz* gafe *f*; *v/t, v/i* cometer um lapso; tropeçar

blunt [blʌnt] *adj* embotado; *v/t* embotar

blur [blə:] *s* mancha *f*; *v/t, v/i* ofuscar, embaciar

blush [blʌʃ] *s* rubor *m*; *v/i* corar, ruborizar(-se)

bluster ['blʌstə] *v/t, v/i* esbravejar

boar [bɔ:] varrão *m*, cerdo *m*

board [bɔ:d] *s* tábua *f*, prancha *f*; junta *f*; *v/t, v/i* embarcar; assoalhar; hospedar; **on ~** a bordo; **~ and lodging** cama *f* e mesa *f*; **♀ of Trade** Ministério *m* (*Braz* Câmara) do Comércio; **~er** hóspede *m*; aluno *m* interno; **~ing-card** cartão *m* de embarque; **~ing-house** pensão *f*; **~-school** internato *m*

boast [bəust] *v/t, v/i* jactar-se; gabar(-se); *s* gabarolice *f*, jactância *f*

boat [bəut] barco *m*, bote *m*; **go ~ing** andar de barco, barque(j)ar; **~man** barqueiro *m*; **~-race** regata *f*

bob [bɔb] *s fam* xelim *m*; *v/i* bambolear-se

bobby ['bɔbi] *fam* polícia *m*

bodice ['bɔdis] corpete *m*
body ['bɔdi] (*pl* **-dies**) corpo *m*; substância *f*; grupo *m*; junta *f*; **~guard** guarda-costas *m*
bog ['bɔg] brejo *m*, paul *m*
boil [bɔil] *v/t*, *v/i* ferver; cozer; *s* furúnculo *m*; **~ over** deitar por fora; ferver em pouca água; **~ed egg** ovo *m* cozido; **~er** caldeira *f*
boisterous ['bɔistərəs] barulhento, turbulento
bold [bəuld] afoito
bolster ['bəulstə] *s* travesseiro *m*
bolt [bəult] *s* ferrolho *m*; parafuso *m*; raio *m*; *v/t*, *v/i* abalar, escapulir-se; aferrolhar; **~upright** direito como um fuso
bomb [bɔm] *s* bomba *f*; *v/t* bombardear; **~ard** [-'bɑ:d] *v/t* bombardear
bombastic [bɔm'bæstik] bombástico
bomber ['bɔmə] AVIA bombardeiro *m*
bond [bɔnd] *s* laço *m*, vínculo *m*; JUR obrigação *f*; COM caução *f*; *v/t* caucionar; **~age** escravidão *f*, servidão *f*; **~ed warehouse** entreposto *m* alfandegário
bone [bəun] *s* osso *m*; espinha *f*
bonfire ['bɔn͵faiə] fogueira *f*
bonnet ['bɔnit] touca *f*; boné *m*
bonus ['bəunəs] bónus *m*
bony ['bəuni] ossudo
book [buk] *s* livro *m*; MUS libreto *m*; *v/t* reservar, marcar; regist(r)ar; **~binder** encadernador *m*; **~case** estante *f*; **~ing clerk** bilheteiro *m*; **~ing office** bilheteira *f*, *Braz* bilheteria *f*; **~-keeper** guarda-livros *m*; **~-keeping** contabilidade *f*; **~let** folheto *m*; **~seller** livreiro *m*; **~shop**, **~store** livraria *f*
boom [bu:m] *s* prosperidade *f*
boor [buə] alarve *m*
boost [bu:st] *s* incremento; *v/t* levantar; fomentar
boot [bu:t] *s* bota *f*; AUTO porta-bagagens *m*, *Braz* porta-mala *m*; **to ~** além disso; **~black** engraxador *m*, *Braz* engraxate *m*; **~ee** botina *f*; botinha *f*
booth [bu:ð] tenda *f*, barraca *f*
border ['bɔ:də] *s* borda *f*; fronteira *f*; *v/t*, *v/i* debruar; confinar
bor|e [bɔ:] *v/t*, *v/i* perfurar; maçar, aborrecer; *s* maçador *m*; maçada *f*; **~edom** aborrecimento *m*; **~ing** maçador
borough ['bʌrə] município *m*
borrow ['bɔrəu] *v/t*, *v/i* pedir emprestado
bosom ['buzəm] peito *m*; seio *m*
boss [bɔs] *s* bossa *f*; chefe *m*, patrão *m*; *v/t* chefiar; **~y** mandão
botch [bɔtʃ] *v/t* remendar, atamancar
both [bəuθ] *adj*, *pron* os dois, as duas; ambos, ambas; **~ ... and** ... não só ... mas também
bother ['bɔðə] *v/t*, *v/i* molestar;

s moléstia *f*
bottle ['bɔtl] *v/t* engarrafar; *s* garrafa *f*
bottom ['bɔtəm] *s* fundo *m*; **at the ~** no fundo
bough [bau] ramo *m*, galho *m*
bounce [bauns] *s* salto *m*, ressalto *m*; *v/t*, *v/i* pular; ressaltar
bound [baund] *s* limite *m*; salto *m*; *v/t* limitar; *v/i* saltar; *adj* sujeito, obrigado; encadernado; com destino a; **~ary** ['-əri] (*pl* **-ries**) limite *m*; fronteira *f*; **~less** ilimitado
bounty ['baunti] (*pl* **-ties**) generosidade *f*; prémio *m*
bouquet ['bukei] ramalhete *m*, *Braz* buquê *m*; aroma *m*
bourgeois ['buəʒwa:] *adj*, *s* burguês *m*
bovine ['bəuvain] bovino
bow [bau] *s* vénia *f*, inclinação *f*, reverência *f*; proa *f*; *v/t*, *v/i* fazer uma reverência, inclinar-se, curvar-se; submeter-se; [bəu] *s* arco *m*; laço *m*
bowels ['bauəlz] *s/pl* intestinos *f/pl*; entranhas *f/pl*
bowl [bəul] *s* tigela *f*; bola *f* de madeira; *v/t*, *v/i* rolar
box [bɔks] *s* caixa *f*; bofetada *f*; THEAT camarote *m*; BOT buxo *m*; *v/t*, *v/i* encaixotar, esbofetear; boxear; **~er** pugilista *m*, *Braz* boxador *m*; **~ing** pugilismo *m*, boxe *m*; **~-office** bilheteira *f*, *Braz* bilheteria *f*
boy [bɔi] rapaz *m*, moço *m*, garoto *m*, menino *m*
boycott ['bɔikət] *v/t* boicotar
boy|friend ['bɔifrend] namorado *m*; **~hood** meninice *f*; **~ish** pueril
bra [bra:] *abbr of* **brassière**
brace [breis] *s* par *m*, parelha *f*; gancho *m*; *v/t*, *v/i* atar; entesar; revigorar; **~let** bracelete *m*; **~s** *s/pl* suspensórios *m/pl*
bracket ['brækit] *s* suporte *m*; grampo *m*; parêntesis *m*; colchete *m*; *v/t* emparelhar
brackish ['brækiʃ] salobre
brag [bræg] *v/i* jactar-se
braid [breid] *s* galão *m*; trança *f*
brain [brein] *s* cérebro *m*,
brains [breinz] *s/pl* miolos *m/pl*
brake [breik] *s* travão *m*, *Braz* breque *m*; *v/t*, *v/i* travar, *Braz* brecar
bramble ['bræmbl] sarça *f*
bran [bræn] farelo *m*
branch [bra:ntʃ] *s* ramo *m*, galho *m*; COM filial *f*, sucursal *f*; *v/i* ramificar-se; **~ line** ramal *m*
brand [brænd] *s* tição *m*; marca *f*; *v/t* marcar; estigmatizar; **~-new** ['-d'nju:] novo em folha
brass [bra:s] latão *m*
brassière ['bræsiεə] sutiã *m*
brat [bræt] rapazelho *m*, fedelho *m*
brave [breiv] *adj* valente, bravo; **~ry** valentia *f*
bravo ['bra:vəu] *int* bravo!
brawl [brɔ:l] *s* rixa *f*, refrega *f*
bray [brei] *v/i* zurrar
brazen ['breizn] *adj* brônzeo; *fig* descarado
Brazilian [brə'ziljən] *adj*, *s* brasileiro *m*

breach [bri:tʃ] brecha *f*; infra(c)ção *f*
bread [bred] pão *m*; **~ and butter** *fig* ganha-pão *m*
breadth [bredθ] largura *f*
break [breik] *s* intervalo *m*, pausa *f*, recreio *m*; fra(c)tura *f*, rotura *f*; romper *m*; *v/t*, *v/i* quebrar(-se), partir(-se); interromper; **~ away** escapar(-se); **~ down** sucumbir; falhar; demolir; **~ in** assaltar, arrombar; interromper; **~ up** dissolver, dispersar(-se); **breakfast** ['brekfəst] *s* pequeno-almoço *m*, *Braz* café *m* da manhã; *v/i* tomar o pequeno almoço
breast [brest] *s* peito *m*; seio *m*
breath [breθ] fôlego *m*; hálito *m*; **hold one's ~** reter o fôlego; **~e** [bri:ð] *v/t*, *v/i* respirar; **~ing** ['bri:ðiŋ] respiração *f*; **~less** ['breθlis] esbaforido
breeches ['britʃiz] *s/pl* calções *m/pl*
breed [bri:d] *v/t*, *v/i* educar, instruir; produzir; criar; *s* raça *f*; espéçie *f*; **~ing** criação *f*; educação *f*
breez|e [bri:z] *s* brisa *f*, aragem *f*; **~y** jovial, alegre
brevity ['breviti] brevidade *f*
brew [bru:] *v/t*, *v/i* infundir; tramar; fermentar, fazer cerveja; *s* infusão *f*; **~er** cervejeiro *m*; **~ery** (*pl* **-ries**) fábrica *f* de cerveja
bribe [braib] *s* suborno *m*; *v/t* subornar; **~ry** suborno *m*
brick [brik] tijolo *m*; **~layer** pedreiro *m*, alvenéu *m*; **~work** alvenaria *f*
bridal ['braidl] nupcial
bride [braid] noiva *f*; **~groom** noivo *m*; **~smaid** dama *f* de honor
bridge [bridʒ] *s* ponte *f*; MUS cavalete *m*; brídege *m*
bridle ['braidl] *s* freio *m*; *v/t*, *v/i* refrear, conter
brief [bri:f] *adj* breve; *s* breve *m* pontifício; resumo *m*; JUR causa *f*; *v/t* instruir, dar instruções a; **~-case** pasta *f*
brigade [bri'geid] brigada *f*
bright [brait] vivo; esperto; claro, brilhante; luminoso; **~en** *v/t*, *v/i* iluminar; animar; **~ness** brilho *m*, claridade *f*; vivacidade *f*
brillian|ce, **~cy** ['briljəns] brilho *m*, esplendor *m*; **~t** *adj*, *s* brilhante *m*
brim [brim] *s* borda *f*; aba *f*; **~ful** cheio até à borda
brine [brain] salmoira *f*
bring [briŋ] *v/t* trazer; levar; apresentar; **~ about** causar, provocar; **~ forth** produzir; gerar; **~ forward** apresentar; COM transportar; **~ up** educar, criar
brink [briŋk] borda *f*, beira *f*
brisk [brisk] vivo, animado
bristle ['brisl] *s* cerda *f*, pêlo *m*; *v/i* eriçar-se
British ['britiʃ] britânico
brittle ['britl] frágil, quebradiço
broach [brəutʃ] *v/t* espichar; encetar, abordar
broad [brɔ:d] *adj* largo; exten-

so; indecente; ~ **bean** fava *f*; **~cast** *v/t*, *v/i* radiodifundir; difundir; *s* emissão *f*, difusão *f*; **~casting** radiodifusão *f* **~en** *v/t*, *v/i* alargar; **~minded** tolerante

broil [brɔil] *v/t*, *v/i* grelhar

broke [brəuk] *adj* teso, *Braz* pronto

broker ['brəukə] corretor *m*

bronze [brɔnz] *s* bronze *m*

brooch [brəutʃ] broche *m*

brood [bru:d] *s* ninhada *f*; *fig* prole *f*; *v/i* chocar; cismar

brook [bruk] *s* regato *m*, riacho *m*

broom [bru:m] BOT giesta *f*; [brum] vassoura *f*

broth [brɔθ] caldo *m*

brothel ['brɔθl] bordel *m*

brother ['brʌðə] irmão *m*; **~hood** irmandade *f*; fraternidade *f*; **~-in-law** cunhado *m*; **~ly** fraternal

brow [brau] testa *f*; cume *m*; sobrancelha *f*

brown [braun] *adj* moreno; castanho; *s* castanho *m*; *v/t*, *v/i* bronzear(-se)

bruise [bru:z] *v/t* magoar, machucar; *s* contusão *f*, amolgadela *f*

brush [brʌʃ] *s* escova *f*; pincel *m*; *v/t*, *v/i* escovar

brussels(sprouts) ['brʌsl 'sprauts] couve-de-Bruxelas *f*

brutal ['bru:tl] brutal; **~ity** [-'tæliti] brutalidade *f*

bubble ['bʌbl] *s* bolha *f*; *v/i* borbulhar

buck [bʌk] *s* gamo *m*; bode *m*; macho; *US* dólar *m*

bucket ['bʌkit] balde *m*

buckle ['bʌkl] *s* fivela *f*; *v/t*, *v/i* afivelar

bud [bʌd] *s* BOT rebento *m*, botão *m*; *v/i* brotar, criar botões

budget ['bʌdʒit] *s* orçamento *m*, verba *f*

buffalo ['bʌfələu] búfalo *m*

buffet ['bufei] *s* bufete *m*; ['bʌfit] *s* bofetada *f*; aparador *m*; *v/t* esbofetear

bug [bʌg] percevejo *m*

bugle ['bju:gl] clarim *m*

build [bild] *v/t*, *v/i* edificar, construir; **~er** construtor *m*; **~ing** *s* construção *f*; edifício *m*, prédio *m*

bulb [bʌlb] BOT bolbo *m*; lâmpada *f* elé(c)trica

bulge [bʌldʒ] *s* bojo *m*; *v/t*, *v/i* fazer bojo

bulk [bʌlk] *s* volume *m*, tamanho *m*; massa *f*; carga *f*; a maior parte; **in ~** a granel; **~y** avultado

bull [bul] *s* ZOO touro *m*; COM altista *m*; **~dog** cão *m* de fila, buldogue *m*

bullet ['bulit] bala *f*; **~in** boletim *m*

bull|fight ['bulfait] tourada *f*; **~fighter** toureiro *m*; **~fighting** tauromaquia *f*; **~finch** pisco; **~headed** cabeçudo

bullion ['buljən] ouro *m* ou prata *f* em barra

bully ['buli] (*pl* **-lies**) *s* valentão *m*, fanfarrão *m*; *v/t* intimidar,

tiranizar
bumble-bee ['bʌmblbiː] abelhão *m*, zângão *m*
bump [bʌmp] *s* pancada *f*, colisão *f*; baque *m*; inchaço *m*; *v/t*, *v/i* bater contra; colidir, chocar
bun [bʌn] bolo *m* de passas
bunch [bʌntʃ] *s* molho *m*, feixe *m*; cacho *m*; ramo *m*, ramalhete *m*
bundle ['bʌndl] *s* feixe *m*, trouxa *f*; *v/t* entrouxar
bungalow ['bʌŋgələu] bangaló *m*
bungle ['bʌŋgl] *v/t*, *v/i* atamancar
bunk [buŋk] *s* tarimba *f*
bunker ['bʌŋkə] paiol *m*, carvoeira *f*
bunny ['bʌni] (*pl* **-nies**) coelhinho *m*
buoy [bɔi] *s* bóia *f*; **~ant** flutuante; alegre
burden ['bəːdn] *s* carga *f*, peso *m*; fardo *m*; *v/t* carregar; sobrecarregar; **~some** oneroso
bureau [bjuə'rəu] (*pl* **-reaux**) escrevaninha *f*; escritório *m*; **~cracy** [bjuə'rɔkrəsi] burocracia *f*; **~cratic** [ˌ-'krætik] burocrático
burgl|ar ['bəːglə] assaltante *m*, ladrão *m*; **~ary** (*pl* **-ries**) assalto *m* no(c)turno, arrombamento *m*
burial ['beriəl] enterro *m*
burn [bəːn] *v/t*, *v/i* queimar; arder; *s* queimadura; **~ing** ardente
burnish ['bəːniʃ] *v/t*, *v/i* brunir
burst [bəːst] *v/t*, *v/i* rebentar; irromper; quebrar; *s* explosão *f*, estoiro *m*; **~ into tears** desfazer-se em lágrimas; **~ out crying** desatar a chorar
bury ['beri] *v/t* enterrar
bus [bʌs] *s* autocarro *m*, *Braz* ónibus *m*
bush [buʃ] arbusto *m*; mato *m*; **~y** basto
business ['biznis] assunto *m*; ocupação *f*; dever *m*; negócio *m*, comércio *m*; **no ~ of yours** não è da tua (sua) conta; **~ hours** horas *f/pl* de expediente; **~ letter** carta *f* comercial; **~-like** prático, metódico; **~ man** (*pl* **-men**) homem *m* de negócios
bust [bʌsl] *s* busto *m*
bustle ['bʌstl] *s* azáfama *f*; alvoroço *m*; *v/i* mexer-se, alvoroçar-se
busy ['bizi] *adj* ocupado, atarefado
but [bʌt, bət] *adv* apenas; *prp* exce(p)to, sem; *conj* mas, porém; senão; **the last ~ one** o penúltimo
butcher ['butʃə] *s* carniceiro *m*; açougueiro *m*; **~'s shop** carniçaria *f*, talho *m*
butler ['bʌtlə] mordomo *m*
butt [bʌt] *v/t*, *v/i* marrar; *s* coronha *f*; alvo *m*
butter ['bʌtə] manteiga *f*; **~cup** ranúnculo *m*; **~fly** borboleta *f*
buttock ['bʌtək] nádega *f*; **~s** traseiro *m*

button ['bʌtn] *s* botão *m*; *v/t*, *v/i* abotoar; **~hole** casa *f* de botão
buy [bai] *v/t* comprar; **~er** comprador *m*
buzz [bʌz] *v/i* zumbir; *s* zumbido *m*
by [bai] *adv* perto, próximo; *prp* durante; por, de; perto de; **~ oneself** sozinho; **~ the way** a propósito
bye-bye ['bai'bai] *fam* **good-bye**
by-election ['baii,lekʃən] eleição *f* suplementar; **~gone** passado, antigo; **~pass** desvio *m*; **~-product** subproduto *m*; **~stander** circunstante *m*, *f*; **~-way** atalho *m*; **~word** adágio *m*, rifão *m*

C

cab [kæb] cabriolé *m*; táxi *m*; cabine *f* de maquinista
cabbage ['kæbidʒ] couve *f*; **white ~** repolho *m*
cabin ['kæbin] cabina *f*; MAR camarote *m*; cabana *f*
cabinet ['kæbinit] armário *m*; gabinete *m*
cable ['keibl] *v/t*, *v/i* telegrafar; *s* cabo *m*; amarra *f*; telegrama *m*; cabograma *m*
cab-rank ['kæbræŋk] praça *f* (*Braz* ponto *m*) de táxis
cackle ['kækl] *v/i* cacarejar; *s* cacarejo *m*
cactus ['kæktəs] (*pl* **cacti** ['kæktai]) cacto *m*
cadaver [kə'deivə] cadáver *m*
café ['kæfei] café *m*, café-restaurante *m*
cage [keidʒ] *v/t* engaiolar; *s* gaiola *f*; jaula *f*
cake [keik] *s* bolo *m*; pastel *m*; queque *m*
calamity [kə'læmiti] calamidade *f*
calcula|te ['kælkjuleit] *v/t* calcular; **~tion** [,-'leiʃən] cálculo *m*
calendar ['kælində] calendário *m*
calf [kɑ:f] (*pl* **-calves**) ZOO vitela *f*, bezerro *m*; ANAT barriga *f* da perna
call [kɔ:l] *s* chamada *f*, grito *m*; visita *f*; *v/t*, *v/i* chamar(-se); nomear; gritar; **~ at** visitar; fazer escala; **~ back** voltar a telefonar; **~ for** exigir, pedir; **~ on** visitar; apelar; **~ up** telefonar; recrutar; **~-box** cabina *f* telefónica; **~er** visita *f*, visitante *m*, *f*
calling ['kɔ:liŋ] chamada *f*; vocação *f*
callous ['kæləs] caloso; insensível
calm [kɑ:m] *s* calma *f*, tranquilidade *f*; *adj* calmo, sereno; *v/t*, *v/i* acalmar(-se), serenar
calumn|iate [kə'lʌmnieit] *v/t* caluniar; **~y** ['kæləmni] calúnia *f*

cambric ['keimbrik] cambraia *f*
camel ['kæməl] camelo *m*
camera ['kæmərə] máquina *f* fotográfica; **digital** ~ câmara *f* digital; **~man** operador *m* cinematográfico
camomile ['kæməmail] camomila *f*, macela *f*
camp [kæmp] *v/i* acampar; *s* acampamento *m*
campaign [kæm'pein] *s* campanha *f*
camp-bed ['kæmp'bed] cama *f* de campanha
camphor ['kæmfə] cânfora *f*
camp-stool ['kæmpstu:l] assento *m* dobradiço
can [kæn, kən] *v/aux* ser capaz de, poder; saber
can [kæn] *s* lata; *v/t* enlatar
Canadian [kə'neidjən] *adj*, *s* canadiano *m*
canal [kə'næl] canal *m*
cancel ['kænsəl] *v/t*, *v/i* cancelar; **~lation** [ˌ-'leiʃən] cancelamento *m*
cancer ['kænsə] MED cancro *m*; Câncer *m* (*zodiac*)
candid ['kændid] cândido, franco
candidate ['kændidit] candidato *m*
candied ['kændid] cristalizado, confeitado
candle ['kændl] vela *f*; candeia *f*; **~stick** castiçal *m*
cando(u)r ['kændə] candura *f*, franqueza *f*
candy ['kændi] *s* cândi *m*; (*pl* **-dies**) *US* rebuçado *m*
cane [kein] *s* cana *f*; bengala *f*
canister ['kænistə] lata *f*, caixa *f*
cannon ['kænən] *s* canhão *m*; carambola *f* (*billiards*)
cannot ['kænɔt] *contr of* **can** *and* **not**
canny ['kæni] fino, astuto
canoe [kə'nu:] *s* canoa *f*
canon ['kænən] cânon(e) *m*
canopy ['kænəpi] (*pl* **-pies**) dossel *m*
cant [kænt] *s* hipocrisia *f*
canteen [kæn'ti:n] cantina *f*
canter ['kæntə] *s* meio galope *m*
canvas ['kænvəs] tela *f*; lona *f*
canvass ['kænvəs] *v/t*, *v/i* angariar
canyon ['kænjən] canhão *m*, ravina *f*
cap [kæp] *s* gorro *m*, barrete *m*, boné *m*
capab|ility [ˌkeipə'biliti] (*pl* **-ties**) capacidade *f*; **~le** capaz; hábil
capacity [kə'pæsiti] (*pl* **-ties**) capacidade *f*; qualidade *f*
cape [keip] GEOL cabo *m*; capa *f*
caper ['keipə] *s* cabriola *f*; BOT alcaparra *f*; *v/i* cabriolar; **cut a ~** fazer das suas
capital ['kæpitl] *adj* capital; maiúsculo; *s* COM capital *m*; capital *f*; ARCH capitel *m*; **~ (letter)** (letra *f*) maiúscula *f*; *int* ó(p)timo; **~ism** capitalismo *m*
capitulate [kə'pitjuleit] *v/i* capitular
capric|e [kə'pri:s] capricho *m*;

~ious [-iʃəs] caprichoso
capsize [kæp'saiz] *v/t, v/i* capotar
captain ['kæptin] capitão *m*
caption ['kæpʃən] legenda *f*; cabeçalho *m*
captious ['kæpʃəs] capcioso
captivate ['kæptiveit] *v/t* cativar
captiv|e ['kæptiv] *adj, s* cativo *m*, prisioneiro *m*; **~ity** [-'tiviti] cativeiro *m*
capture ['kæptʃə] *s* captura *f*; *v/t* capturar
car [kɑ:] carro *m*; automóvel *m*
caramel ['kærəmel] caramelo *m*
carat ['kærət] quilate *m*
caravan ['kærəvæn] *GB* reboque *m*, rulóte *f*; caravana *f*
carbon ['kɑ:bən] carbono *m*; **~-paper** papel *m* químico
carbuncle ['kɑ:bʌŋkl] carbúnculo *m*
carburettor ['kɑ:bjuretə] carburador *m*
card [kɑ:d] *v/t* cardar; *s* carda *f*; cartão *m*; carta *f* de jogar; **~-board** cartão *m*, papelão *m*
cardigan ['kɑ:digən] casaco *m* de lã, jaqueta *f*
cardinal ['kɑ:dinl] *s* cardeal *m*; *adj* principal, cardeal
care [kεə] *s* cuidado *m*, cautela *f*, atenção *f*; inquietação *f*; *v/i* importar-se; **~ about** fazer caso de; **~ for** cuidar de, olhar por; importar-se com, fazer caso de, gostar de; **take ~!** tenha cuidado; **take ~ of** tomar conta de, tratar; **what do I ~?** que me importa?
career [kə'riə] *s* carreira *f*
care|-free ['kεəfri:] despreocupado; **~ful** cuidadoso; **~less** descuidado, negligente; **~lessness** descuido *m*, negligência *f*
caress [kə'res] *s* carícia *f*; *v/t* acariciar
care-|taker ['kεə,teikə] porteiro *m*; guarda *m*; **~worn** consumido
cargo ['kɑ:gəu] (*pl* **-go(e)s**) carga *f*, frete *m*
caricature [,kærikə'tjuə] *s* caricatura *f*
carnal ['kɑ:nl] carnal
carnation [kɑ:'neiʃən] *s* BOT cravo *m*
carnival ['kɑ:nivəl] carnaval *m*
carol ['kærəl] *s* cântico *m* de Natal
carp [kɑ:p] *s* carpa *f*; *v/i* **~ (at)** censurar, criticar
carpenter ['kɑ:pintə] carpinteiro *m*
carpet ['kɑ:pit] *s* carpete *f*; alcatifa *f*; tapete *m*
carpool ['kɑ:(r)pu:l] *v/t, v/i* partilha *f* de viaturas
carriage ['kæridʒ] carruagem *f*; frete *m*, transporte *m*
carrier ['kæriə] MED transmissor *m*, portador *m*; carregador *m*
carrot ['kærət] cenoura *f*
carry ['kæri] *v/t, v/i* carregar, transportar, levar; alcançar; transmitir; trazer; **~ away** ar-

rebatar; **~ on** continuar; **~ out** levar a cabo; **~ the day** vencer, levar a melhor

cart [kɑːt] *v/t* acarretar; *s* carroça *f*, carreta *f*; **~er** carreteiro *m*; **~-horse** cavalo *m* de tiro

cartoon [kɑː'tuːn] *s* caricatura *f*; desenhos *m/pl* animados

cartridge ['kɑːtridʒ] cartucho *m*; **~-belt** cartucheira *f*

carv|e [kɑːv] *v/t, v/i* esculpir, gravar, entalhar; trinchar (*meat*); **~er** entalhador *m*, gravador; **~ing** gravura *f*; arte *f* de gravar; **~ing knife** trinchante *m*

cascade [kæs'keid] *s* cascata *f*

case [keis] *s* caso *m*; JUR causa *f*; estojo *m*; **in ~** no caso de; **in any ~** em todo o caso

casement ['keismənt] janela *f* de batentes

cash [kæʃ] *s* dinheiro *m* de contado; *v/t* descontar, cobrar; **~ down** pronto pagamento *m*, pagamento *m* à vista; **~ in advance** COM pagamento *m* antecipado; **~ on delivery** envio *m* à cobrança, entrega *f* contra reembolso; **~ desk** caixa *f*; **~ier** [-'ʃiə] caixa *m, f*; **~ register** caixa *f* registadora

cask [kɑːsk] pipa *f*, barrica *f*; **~et** guarda-jóias *m*

cassette [kə'set] cassete *f*

cast [kɑːst] *v/t, v/i* moldar, fundir; THEAT distribuir os papéis; atirar, lançar, arremessar; *s* lanço *m*; tom *m*, matiz *m*; THEAT elenco *m*; molde *m*

caste [kɑːst] casta *f*, classe *f*

cast iron ['kɑːst'aiən] ferro *m* fundido

castle ['kɑːsl] torre *f* (xadrez); castelo *m*

castor ['kɑːstə] pimenteiro *m*; saleiro *m*

castor oil ['kaːstə ɔil] óleo *m* de rícino; **~ sugar** açúcar *m* refinado

casual ['kæʒjuəl] *adj* casual, fortuito; despreocupado; **~ty** (*pl* **-ties**) sinistro *m*; sinistrado *m*; MIL baixas *f/pl*; perdas *f/pl*, mortos e feridos *m/pl*

cat [kæt] gato *m*, gata *f*

cataract ['kætərækt] catarata *f*

catarrh [kə'tɑː] catarro *m*

catastrophe [kə'tæstrəfi] catástrofe *f*

catch [kætʃ] *v/t, v/i* agarrar, apanhar; pegar; perceber; **~ (a) cold** apanhar ama constipação; **~ fire** pegar fogo; **~ up** alcançar; **~ing** contagioso; **~word** THEAT deixa *f*; lema *m*; **~y** atra(c)tivo

category ['kætigəri] (*pl* **-ries**) categoria *f*

cater ['keitə] *v/i* fornecer

caterpillar ['kætəpilə] lagarta *f*

cathedral [kə'θiːdrəl] *sé f*, catedral *f*

Catholic ['kæθəlik] *adj*, *s* católico *m*

cattle ['kætl] *s/pl* gado *m* vacum

cauliflower ['kɔliflauə] couve-flor *f*

cause [kɔːz] causa *f*; *v/t* causar, ocasionar, motivar; **~less** in-

fundado
causeway ['kɔːzwei] calçada *f*
cauti|on ['kɔːʃən] *s* admoestação *f*; cautela *f*; *v/t* advertir; admoestar; **~ous** cauto, cauteloso
cavalry ['kævəlri] cavalaria *f*
cave [keiv] *s* caverna *f*, antro *m*; **~ in** *v/t*, *v/i* aluir, ruir
cavern ['kævən] caverna *f*
cavity ['kæviti] (*pl* **-ties**) cavidade *f*
caw [kɔː] *v/i* grasnar, crocitar
CD [siː'diː] CD *m*; **~ player** ['pleiə] leitor *m* de CDs; **~ ROM** ['rɔm] CD-Rom *m*
cease [siːs] *v/t*, *v/i* cessar
cedar ['siːdə] BOT cedro *m*
cede [siːd] *v/t* ceder
ceiling ['siːliŋ] te(c)to *m*; máximo *m*
celebrat|e ['selibreit] *v/t* celebrar; festejar; **~ed** célebre; **~ion** [ˌ-'breiʃən] celebração *f*
celebrity [si'lebriti] (*pl* **-ties**) celebridade *f*
celerity [si'leriti] celeridade *f*
celery ['seləri] aipo *m*
celestial [si'lestjəl] celeste, celestial
celibacy ['selibəsi] celibato *m*, *Braz* solteirismo *m*
cell [sel] cela *f*; BOT célula *f*; ELECT elemento *m*; **~ (phone)** [fəun] *US* telemóvel *m*
cellar ['selə] cave *f*; adega *f*
cellular phone ['seluləfəun] telemóvel *m*, celular *m*
Celt [kelt] celta *m*, *f*; **~ic** *s* celta *m*, língua *f* céltica; *adj* céltico
cement [si'ment] *s* cimento *m*; *v/t* cimentar (*a fig*)
cemetery ['semitri] (*pl* **-ries**) cemitério *m*
censor ['sensə] *s* censor *m*; *v/t* censurar; **~ship** censura *f*
censure ['senʃə] *s* censura *f*, repreensão *f*; *v/t* censurar, repreender
census ['sensəs] (*pl* **-suses**) censo *m*, recenseamento *m*
cent [sent] cêntimo *m*; **per ~** por cento; **~enary** *adj*, *s* (*pl* **-ries**), *US* **~ennial** centenário
centi|grade ['sentigreid] centígrado *m*; **~metre**, *US* **-ter** centímetro *m*; **~pede** centopeia *f*
central ['sentrəl] central; **~ize** *v/t*, *v/i* centralizar
centre, *US* **-ter** ['sentə] *s* centro *m*; **~ forward** avançadocentro *m*, *Braz* centro-avante *m*; **~ half** médio-centro *m*, *Braz* centro-médio *m*
century ['senʃuri] (*pl* **-ries**) século *m*
CEO [siː iː 'əu] COM administrador *m* executivo
cereal ['siəriəl] cereal *m*
cerebral ['seribrəl] *adj* cerebral
ceremon|ial [ˌseri'məunjəl] *s*, *adj* cerimonial *m*; **~ious** cerimonioso, **~y** ['-məni] (*pl* **-nies**) cerimónia *f*
certain ['səːtn] certo; **~ty** (*pl* **-ties**) certeza *f*
certificate [sə'tifikit] *s* certificado *m*, certidão *f*
certify ['səːtifai] *v/t* certificar, atestar

CFO [siː ef 'əu] responsável *m* financeiro
chafe [tʃeif] *v/t*, *v/i* irritar(-se)
chaff [tʃaːf] *s* debulho *m*; zombaria *f*; *v/t* zombar-se de
chaffinch ['tʃæfintʃ] tentilhão *m*
chain [tʃein] *s* cadeia *f*; série *f*; *v/t* encadear
chair [tʃɛə] *s* cadeira *f*; **~man** presidente *m*, *f*
chalk [tʃɔːk] *s* giz *m*
challenge ['tʃælindʒ] *s* desafio *m*, repto *m*; *v/t* desafiar
chamber ['tʃeimbə] câmara *f*; **~-maid** criada *f* de quarto, *Braz* arrumadeira *f*; **~ pot** bacio *m*
chameleon [kə'miːljən] camaleão *m*
champagne [ʃæm'pein] champanhe *m*
champion ['tʃæmpjən] *s* campeão *m*; **~ship** campeonato *m*
chance [tʃaːns] *s* chance *f*; oportunidade *f*; probabilidade *f*; sorte *f*, acaso *m*; *v/t*, *v/i* acontecer, calhar; arriscar; *adj* casual, acidental; **by ~** por acaso
chancellor ['tʃaːnsələ] chanceler *m*; **℃ of the Exchequer** Ministro *m* das Finanças
chandelier [ˌʃændi'liə] candelabro *m*, lustre *m*
change [tʃeindʒ] *s* mudança *f*; troco *m*; câmbio *m*; *v/t*, *v/i* mudar; trocar; cambiar; **for a ~** para variar; **~able** variável, instável; **~less** imutável
channel ['tʃænl] canal *m*
chant [tʃaːnt] *s* cântico *m*; salmodia *f*; *v/t*, *v/i* cantar; salmodiar
chap [tʃæp] *v/t*, *v/i* gretar; *s* tipo *m*, sujeito *m*, moço *m*
chapel ['tʃæpəl] capela *f*
chaplain ['tʃæplin] capelão *m*
chapter ['tʃæptə] capítulo *m*
character ['kæriktə] *s* cará(c)ter *m*; personagem *f*; **~istic** [-'ristik] *adj* característico; *s* característica *f*
charcoal ['tʃaːkəul] carvão *m* de lenha; (desenho *m* a) carvão *m*
charge [tʃaːdʒ] *v/t*, *v/i* cobrar, levar; carregar; encarregar, confiar; acusar; atacar; investir; *s* carga *f*; encargo *m*; acusação *f*; investida *f*; preço *m*; **free of ~** grátis; **in ~ of** encarregado de; **in my ~** a meu cargo
charit|able ['tʃæritəbl] caridoso; **~y** caridade *f*
charm [tʃaːm] *s* encanto *m*; feitiço *m*; amuleto *m*; *v/t* encantar; enfeitiçar; **~ing** encantador
chart [tʃaːt] *s* carta *f* náutica; gráfico *m*, tabela *f*; *v/t* traçar
charter ['tʃaːtə] *s* carta *f* de privilégio; estatuto *m*; fretamento *m*; *v/t* fretar
charwoman ['tʃaːwumən] (*pl* **-women**) mulher *f* a dias, *Braz* arrumadeira *f*
chase [tʃeis] *s* caça *f*; perseguição *f*; *v/t* caçar, perseguir; afugentar
chasm ['kæzəm] abismo *m*

chassis ['ʃæsi] chassi *m*
chast|e [tʃeist] casto, puro; **~ity** ['tʃæstiti] castidade *f*
chat [tʃæt] *s* cavaco *m*, cavaqueira *f*, *Braz* bate-papo *m*; *v/i* cavaquear; **~ter** *s* tagarelice *f*; chilro *m*; *v/i* tagarelar; chilrear; **~terbox** tagarela *m*, *f*, fala-barato *m*, *f*
cheap [tʃi:p] *adj* barato; reles; **~en** *v/t*, *v/i* baratear; depreciar
cheat [tʃi:t] *s* engano *m*, fraude *f*; vigarice *f*; vigarista *m*, *f*, embusteiro *m*; *v/t*, *v/i* enganar, defraudar
check [tʃek] *v/t*, *v/i* verificar; conferir; refrear; pôr em xeque; *s* verificação *f*; obstáculo *m*; xeque *m*; quadrado *m*; **~ in** dar entrada ao hotel; **~ out** sair do hotel, deixar o hotel; **~ed** axadrezado
cheek [tʃi:k] *s* face *f*, bochecha *f*; descaro *m*; **~y** descarado, impertinente
cheer [tʃiə] *v/t*, *v/i* aplaudir, dar vivas; animar; *s* viva *m*; alegria *f*; ânimo *m*; **~ful** jovial, animado, alegre; **~ing** vivas *m/pl*; **~ up!** ânimo, coragem!
cheerio [tʃiəri'əu] *GB* adeus
cheese [tʃi:z] queijo *m*
chemical ['kemikəl] *adj* químico; *s* produto *m* químico
chemist ['kemist] farmacêutico *m*; **~ry** química *f*; **~'s (shop)** farmácia *f*
cheque [tʃek] cheque *m*
cherish ['tʃeriʃ] *v/t* apreciar, estimar
cherry ['tʃeri] (*pl* **-ries**) cereja *f*
chess [tʃes] xadrez *m*; **~-board** tabuleiro *m* dexadrez
chest [tʃest] peito *m*, tórax *m*; arca *f*, baú *m*; **~ of drawers** cómoda *f*
chestnut ['tʃesnʌt] *s* castanha *f*; *adj* castanho; **~-tree** castanheira *f*
chew [tʃu:] *v/t*, *v/i* mascar, mastigar; **~ing gum** pastilha *f* elástica, goma *f* de mascar
chicken ['tʃikin] *s* frango *m*; galinha *f*; medrica(s) *m*, *f*; **~ pox** ['-pɔks] varicela *f*
chicory ['tʃikəri] chicória *f*
chief [tʃi:f] *s* chefe *m*; comandante *m*; *adj* principal
chilblain ['tʃilblein] frieira *f*
child [tʃaild] (*pl* **children** ['tʃildrən]) criança *f*; filho (a) *m* (*f*); **~-birth** parto *m*; **~hood** infância *f*; **~ish** acriançado; infantil, pueril; **~like** infantil, inocente
chill [tʃil] *s* calafrio *m*; resfriado *m*; frieza *f*; *adj* frio, gelado; indiferente; *v/t*, *v/i* gelar, esfriar, arrefecer
chime [tʃaim] *s* carrilhão *m*; *v/t*, *v/i* tocar carrilhão; repicar; bater as horas
chimney ['tʃimni] chaminé *f*; **~-sweep(er)** limpa-chaminés *m*
chin [tʃin] queixo *m*
china ['tʃainə] louça *f*, porcelana *f*
Chinese ['tʃai'ni:z] *adj*, *s* chinês *m*
chink [tʃiŋk] frincha *f*, greta *f*,

racha *f*
chip [tʃip] *s* cavaco *m*, lasca *f*; ficha *f*; *v/t*, *v/i* lascar(-se); escavacar; **~s** *GB* batatas *f/pl* fritas
chirp [tʃəːp] *v/t* palrar; *v/i* gorjear, chilrear; *s* gorjeio *m*, chilro *m*
chisel ['tʃizl] *s* cinzel *m*; *v/t* cinzelar
chit [tʃit] fedelho *m*; pivete *m*;
chivalr|ous ['ʃivəlrəs] cavalheiresco; **~y** cavalheirismo *m*; cavalaria *f*
chives ['tʃaivz] *s/pl* cebolinha *f*
choice [tʃɔis] *s* escolha *f*; *adj* sele(c)to, escolhido
choir ['kwaiə] coro *m*
choke [tʃəuk] *v/t*, *v/i* abafar, sufocar(-se), engasgar(-se); *s* AUTO borboleta *f* de ar
cholera ['kɔlərə] MED cólera *f*
choose [tʃuːz] *v/t*, *v/i* optar; resolver; escolher
chop [tʃɔp] *s* costeleta *f*; *v/t*, *v/i* picar; cortar; **~py** MAR agitado, encapelado
chord [kɔːd] MUS acorde *m*; corda *f*
Christ [kraist] Cristo *m*
christen ['krisn] *v/t* ba(p)tizar
Christ|ian [ˌ-tjən] *s adj* cristão (*m*); **~ian name** nome *m* de ba(p)tismo; **♀ianity** [ˌ-ti'æniti] cristianismo *m*; **♀ mas** ['-məs] Natal *m*
chron|ic ['krɔnik] crónico; **~icle** *s* crónica *f*; **~ological** [ˌ-nə'lɔdʒikəl] cronológico; **~ology** [krə'nɔlədʒi] cronologia *f*
chuck [tʃʌk] *v/t* *fam* botar
chuckle ['tʃʌkl] *s* riso *m* abafado; *v/i* rir-se à socapa
chum [tʃʌm] *s* *fam* amigo *m*, camarada *m*
church [tʃəːtʃ] *s* igreja *f*; **♀ of England** Igreja Anglicana; **~yard** adro *m*
churn [tʃəːn] *s* desnatadeira *f*, batedeira *f*; *v/t*, *v/i* fazer manteiga; bater
cider ['saidə] cidra *f*
cigar [si'gaː] charuto *m*; **~et(te)** [ˌsigə'ret] cigarro *m*; **~et(te)-case** cigarreira *f*; **~et(te)-holder** boquilha *f*, *Braz* piteira *f*
cinder ['sində] escória *f*; brasa *f*; **~s** cinza *f*
cinema ['sinəmə] cinema *m*
cinnamon ['sinəmən] *s* canela *f*
cipher ['saifə] cifra *f*, zero *m*
circle ['səːkl] *v/t*, *v/i* circundar; *s* círculo *m*
circuit ['səːkit] circuito *m*; **~-breaker** ELECT interruptor *m*
circular ['səːkjulə] *s*, *adj* circular *f*
circulat|e ['səːkjuleit] *v/t*, *v/i* (fazer) circular; **~ion** [ˌ-'leiʃən] circulação *f*
circum|ference [sə'kʌmfərəns] circumferência *f*; **~scribe** ['səːkəmskraib] circunscrever;
circum|stance ['səːkəmstəns] circunstância *f*; **~stantial** [ˌ-'stænʃəl] circunstancial; **~vent** [ˌ-'vent] *v/t* lograr; rodear
circus ['səːkəs] circo *m*
cistern ['sistən] cisterna *f*

cite [sait] *v/t* citar
citizen ['sitizn] cidadão *m*; **~ship** cidadania *f*
city ['siti] (*pl* **-ties**) cidade *f*; **~ hall** *US* câmara *f* municipal, *Braz* prefeitura *f*
civic ['sivik] cívico; **~s** educação *f* cívica
civil ['sivl] civil; cortês; **~ian** [-'viljən] *adj*, *s* civil *m*; **~ization** [ˌ-lai'zeiʃən] civilização *f*; **~ize** *v/t* civilizar; **~ rights** direitos *m/pl* civis; **~ servant** funcionário *m* público
claim [kleim] *v/t*, *v/i* exigir, reclamar, reivindicar; *s* reclamação *f*, reivindicação *f*
clairvoyance [klɛə'vɔiəns] clarividência *f*
clamber ['klæmbə] *v/i* escalar
clammy ['klæmi] pegajoso
clamorous ['klæmərəs] clamoroso
clamo(u)r ['klæmə] *s* clamor *m*, vozearia *f*; *v/i* clamar, gritar
clamp [klæmp] *s* gancho *m*, torno *m*; *v/t* grampar
clan [klæn] clã *m*, tribo *f*
clandestine [klæn'destin] clandestino
clang [klæŋ] *s* tinido *m*; *v/t*, *v/i* tinir; ressoar
clap [klæp] *v/t*, *v/i* aplaudir; bater palmas
claret ['klærət] clarete *m*
clarify ['klærifai] *v/t*, *v/i* esclarecer(-se); clarificar
clarinet [ˌklæri'net] clarinete *m*
clarity ['klæriti] claridade *f*, clareza *f*
clash [klæʃ] *s* choque *m*; *fig* conflito *m*; *v/t*, *v/i* colidir, chocar (-se); opor-se
clasp [klɑːsp] *s* colchete *m*, fivela *f*; abraço *m*; *v/t*, *v/i* apertar; afivelar; abraçar
class [klɑːs] *s* classe *f*; aula *f*; *v/t* classificar
classic ['klæsik] *adj*, *s* clássico *m*; **~al** clássico
classification [ˌklæsifi'keiʃən] classificação *f*
classify ['klæsifai] *v/t* classificar
class-mate ['klɑːsmeit] condiscípulo *m*, colega *m*, *f*, companheiro *m*
class-room ['klɑːsrum] classe *f*, (sala *f* de) aula *f*
clause [klɔːz] cláusula *f*
claw [klɔː] *s* garra *f*; pinça; *v/t* arranhar
clay [klei] argila *f*, barro *m*
clean [kliːn] *adj* limpo; puro; *v/t*, *v/i* limpar(-se); **~ out** limpar (*a fig*); **~er's** tinturaria *f*, lavandaria *f* **~liness** asseio *m*, limpeza *f*; **~ly** ['klenli] *adj* limpo, asseado; **~ up** fazer as limpezas
cleanse [klenz] *v/t* limpar, purificar
clear [kliə] *adj* claro; distinto; evidente; livre; vazio; *v/t*, *v/i* aclarar; esclarecer; desobstruir; saldar, liquidar; levantar (a mesa); **~ out** safar-se; **~ing** clareira *f*; **~ up** tirar a limpo; aclarar, desanuviar-se
clear-sighted ['kliə'saitid] cla-

rividente
cleave [kli:v] *v/t* fender, rachar
clef [klef] MUS clave *f*
cleft [kleft] racha *f*, fenda *f*
clemency ['klemənsi] clemência *f*
clench [klentʃ] *v/t* agarrar, segurar; cerrar
clergy ['klə:dʒi]: **the ~** clero *m*; **~man** clérigo *m*
clerical ['klerikəl] clerical; de escritório
clerk [klɑ:k] *s* empregado *m*; caixeiro *m*; amanuense *m*, *f*
clever ['klevə] esperto; destro, hábil; inteligente
click [klik] *s* estalido *m*; clique *m*; *v/t*, *v/i* dar estalidos; ter sucesso; COMP clicar
client ['klaiənt] cliente *m*, *f*; **~èle** [kli:ã:n'teil] clientela *f*
cliff [klif] penhasco *m*
cliff-hanging ['klifhæŋiŋ] *adj* de tirar o fôlego, eletrizante
climate ['klaimit] clima *m*
climb [klaim] *v/t*, *v/i* trepar, subir, escalar; *s* subida *f*; **~er** trepador *m*; alpinista *m*, *f*; ZOO trepadora *f*; BOT trepadeira *f*
cling [kliŋ] *v/i* agarrar-se
clinic ['klinik] clínica *f*; **~al** clínico
clink [kliŋk] *s* tinido *m*; *v/t*, *v/i* tinir, tilintar
clip [klip] *v/t* (re)cortar; tosquiar; furar (bilhetes); *s* clipe *m*, grampo *m*
cloak [kləuk] *s* capa *f*, manto *m*; *v/t* esconder; encapotar; **~-room** vestiário *m*
clock [klɔk] *s* relógio *m*; **~work** mecanismo *m* de corda
clod [klɔd] torrão *m*
clog [klɔg] *s* tamanco *m*, soco *m*
clone [kləun] *s* clone *m*; *v/t* clonar
cloning [kləuniŋ] *s* clonagem *f*
close [kləuz] *v/t*, *v/i* encerrar; fechar; cerrar; *s* conclusão *f*, fim *m*; [kləus] *adj*, *adv* próximo, perto; fechado; estreito; íntimo, caro; abafado; de perto; **~ to** perto de; **from ~ by** de perto
closet ['klɔzit] *s* US armário *m* de parede
cloth [klɔθ] *s* pano *m*, tecido *m*
clothe [kləuð] *v/t* vestir; **~s** *s/pl* roupa *f*, vestuário *m*; **~s-hanger** cabide *m*; **~ing** roupa *f*
cloud [klaud] *s* nuvem *f*; *v/t*, *v/i* nublar(-se); turvar(-se); **~less** desanuviado; **~y** nublado
clove [kləuv] *s* cravo-da-índia *m*
clover ['kləuvə] trevo *m*
clown [klaun] *s* palhaço *m*
club [klʌb] *s* clava *f*, cacete *m*; paus *m/pl*; clube *m*; **~-house** clube *m* desportivo
clue [klu:] *s* vestígio *m*, indício *m*; **~d up** bem informado
clump [klʌmp] *s* moita *f*, maciço *m*
clumsy ['klʌmzi] deselegante; desajeitado
cluster ['klʌstə] *s* cacho *m*; grupo *m*; *v/i* agrupar-se, apinhar-se
clutch [klʌtʃ] *s* ninhada *f*; aper-

to *m*; AUTO embraiagem *f*; *v/t*, *v/i* agarrar(-se); **~ at** fazer por agarrar

Co. [kəu] *abbr for* **Company**

c/o [si:'əu] a/c *abbr for* **(in) care of** ao cuidado de

coach [kəutʃ] *s* coche *m*; treinador *m*, *GB* camioneta *f*, *Braz* ónibus *m*; carruagem *f*; *v/t* preparar; treinar

coagulate [kəu'ægjuleit] *v/t*, *v/i* coagular(-se)

coal [kəul] *s* carvão *m*

coalition [ˌkəuə'liʃən] coalizão *f*

coal|-mine ['kəulmain], **~-pit** hulheira *f*, mina *f* de carvão

coarse [kɔ:s] rude, grosseiro; áspero; ordinário;

coast [kəust] *s* costa *f*; **~line** litoral *m*

coat [kəut] *v/t* cobrir; *s* casaco *m*; camada *f*; pele *f*; **~-hanger** cabide *m*, cruzeta *f*; **~ing** camada *f*, demão *f*; cobertura *f*; **~ of arms** brasão *m*

coax [kəuks] *v/t* aliciar; adular; seduzir

cobble ['kɔbl] *v/t* pavimentar com gobos; **~r** sapateiro *m*

cobweb ['kɔbweb] teia *f* de aranha

cock [kɔk] *s* galo *m*; macho *m* (de ave); válvula *f*, torneira *f*; *v/t* levantar; erguer(-se)

cockle ['kɔkl] amêijoa *f*

cockney ['kɔkni] *adj*, *s* londrino *m*

cock|pit ['kɔkpit] AVIA carlinga *f*, cabina *f*; **~roach** ['-rəutʃ] barata *f*; **~tail** coquete(i)l *m*

cocoa ['kəukəu] cacau *m*

coco-nut ['kəukənʌt] coco *m*

cocoon [kə'ku:n] casulo *m*

cod [kɔd] ZOO bacalhau *m*

code [kəud] *v/t* codificar; *s* código *m*

coerc|e [kəu'ə:s] *v/t* coagir; reprimir; **~ion** coerção *f*

coffee ['kɔfi] café *m*; **~-bean** grão *m* de café; **~-pot** cafeteira *f*

coffin ['kɔfin] ataúde *m*, caixão *m*

cog-wheel ['kɔgwi:l] roda *f* dentada

cohe|rence [kəu'hiərəns] coerência *f*; **~rent** coerente; **~sion** [-'hi:ʒən] coesão *f*

coil [kɔil] *s* rolo *m*; bobina *f*; serpentina *f*; *v/t*, *v/i* enrolar; enroscar

coin [kɔin] *s* moeda *f*; *v/t* cunhar (*a fig*); **~age** cunhagem *f*

cold [kəuld] *adj* frio; *s* frio *m*; resfriamento *m*, constipação *f*; **be ~** ter frio; fazer frio; **~ness** frieza *f*, indiferença *f*, **~-shoulder** *v/t* desdenhar

collaborat|e [kə'læbəreit] *v/i* colaborar; **~ion** [-'reiʃən] colaboração *f*; **~or** colaborador *m*

collapse [kə'læps] *v/t*, *v/i* sucumbir; ter um colapso; desmoronar(-se); *s* colapso *m*; desmoronamento *m*

collapsible [kə'læpsəbl] dobradiço, desmontável

collar ['kɔlə] *s* colarinho *m*; gola *f*; coleira *f*; **~-bone** clavícula *f*

collate [kɔ'leit] *v/t* cotejar, comparar
colleague ['kɔliːg] colega *m, f*
collect [kə'lekt] *v/t, v/i* cole(c)cionar, coligir; reunir(-se); *s* cole(c)ta *f*; **~ion** cole(c)ção *f*; **~ive** *adj* cole(c)tivo; **~or** cole(c)cionador *m*; cobrador *m*; ELECT cole(c)tor *m*
college ['kɔlidʒ] colégio *m*; escola *f* superior
collide [kə'laid] *v/i* colidir
collie ['kɔli] cão *m* de pastor
collier ['kɔliə] *GB* mineiro *m*
collision [kə'liʒən] colisão *f*
colloquial [kə'ləukwiəl] familiar, coloquial
colonel ['kəːnl] coronel *m*
colonial [kə'ləunjəl] *adj* colonial; **~ism** colonialismo *m*
colon|ist ['kɔlənist] colono *m*; **~ize** *v/t* colonizar; **~y** (*pl* **-nies**) colónia *f*
colo(u)r ['kʌlə] *s* cor *f*; colorido *m*; matiz *m*; *v/t, v/i* pintar; colorir; corar, ruborizar-se; **~-blind** daltónico; **~ful** colorido; **~ing** *s* corante *m*; coloração *f*; cor *f*; **~less** incolor; descorado, semcor; **~ line** *US* barreira *f* racial; **~s** *s/pl* bandeira *f*
colt [kəult] potro *m*, poldro *m*
column ['kɔləm] coluna *f*
comb [kəum] *s* pente *m*; *v/t* pentear(-se)
combat ['kɔmbət] *s* combate *m*; *v/t, v/i* combater
combination [kɔmbi'neiʃən] combinação *f*
combine [kəm'bain] *v/t, v/i* ligar(-se), coligar-se; combinar; ['kɔmbain] *s* debulhadora *f* segadoira
come [kʌm] *v/i* vir; acontecer; vir a ser; chegar; **~ about** suceder; **~ across** deparar com; **~ along** ir; **~ back** voltar; **~ down** descer; **~ for** vir buscar; **~ in** entrar; **~ on!** vamos!; vá lá! **~ out** sair; **~ up** subir; **~-back** *s* regresso *m*
comed|ian [kə'miːdjən] comediante *m*; **~y** ['kɔmidi] (*pl* **-dies**) comédia *f*
comfort ['kʌmfət] *s* conforto *m*; *v/t* confortar; **~able** confortável, cómodo
comic ['kɔmik] *adj, s* cómico *m*; **~s** *US*, **~ strip** história *f* aos quadradinhos
comma ['kɔmə] vírgula *f*
command [kə'maːnd] *v/t, v/i* comandar; *s* comando *m*; ordem *f*; **~er** comandante *m*; **~ment** mandamento *m*
commemorat|e [kə'meməreit] *v/t* comemorar; **~ion** [-'reiʃən] comemoração *f*
commence [kə'mens] *v/t, v/i* começar; **~ment** começo *m*
commend [kə'mend] *v/t* recomendar; encomiar
comment ['kɔment] *v/t, v/i* fazer comentários; comentar; *s*, **~ary** (*pl* **-ries**) comentário *m*; **~ator** ['-eitə] comentador *m*; comentarista *m, f*
commerce ['kɔmə(ː)s] comércio *m*
commercial [kə'məːʃəl] co-

mercial; **~ize** *v/t* comercializar
commission [kə'miʃən] *s* comissão *f*; *v/t* comissionar; **~er** comissário *m*
commit [kə'mit] *v/t* cometer; comprometer(-se); condenar; **~ment** compromisso *m*; **~tee** comissão *f*, comité *m*
commodity [kə'mɔditi] (*pl* **-ties**) mercadoria *f*, produto *m*
common ['kɔmən] *adj* comum; **2 Market** Mercado *m* Comum; **~place** *adj* trivial, banal; *s* lugar-comum *m*; **2 s** *s/pl* **the ~** a Câmara *f* dos Comuns; **~ sense** senso *m* comum, bom senso *m*
Commonwealth ['kɔmənwelθ] **~ of Nations** Comunidade *f* das Nações Britânicas
commotion [kə'məuʃən] comoção *f*
communicat|e [kə'mju:nikeit] *v/t*, *v/i* comunicar, comungar; **~ion** comunicação *f*; **~ive** comunicativo
communion [kə'mju:njən] comunhão *f*
communis|m ['kɔmjunizəm] comunismo; **~t** *adj*, *s* comunista *m*, *f*
community [kə'mju:niti] (*pl* **-ties**) comunidade *f*
commutation [ˌkɔmju'teiʃən] comutação *f*
commute [kə'mju:t] *v/t* comutar
compact ['kɔmpækt] *adj* compacto; **~ disc** disco *m* compacto
companion [kəm'pænjən] companheiro *m*
company ['kʌmpəni] (*pl* **-nies**) companhia *f*
comparable ['kɔmpərəbl] comparável
compar|ative [kəm'pærətiv] *adj*, *s* comparativo *m*; **~e** [-'pɛə] *v/t* comparar(-se); **~ison** [-'pærisn] comparação *f*
compartment [kəm'pɑ:tmənt] compartimento *m*
compass ['kʌmpəs] *s* bússola *f*; **~es** *pl* compasso *m*
compassion [kəm'pæʃən] compaixão *f*; **~ate** [-ʃənit] compassivo
compatible [kəm'pætəbl] compatível
compatriot [kəm'pætriət] compatriota *m*, *f*
compel [kəm'pel] *v/t* compelir
compensat|e ['kɔmpenseit] *v/t* compensar; inde(m)nizar; **~ion** [ˌ-'seiʃən] compensação *f*; inde(m)nização *f*
compete [kəm'pi:t] *v/i* competir, concorrer
competen|ce ['kɔmpitəns] competência *f*; **~t** competente
competit|ion [ˌkɔmpi'tiʃən] competição *f*; **~or** [kəm'petitə] competidor *m*, concorrente *m*, *f*
compile [kəm'pail] *v/t* compilar
complacent [kəm'pleisnt] complacente
complain [kəm'plein] *v/i* queixar-se; **~t** queixa *f*
complement ['kɔmplimənt]

complemento *m*; **~ary** complementar
complet|e [kəm'pli:t] *adj* completo; *v/t* completar; **~ion** acabamento *m*
complex ['kɔmpleks] *adj, s* complexo *m*; **~ion** tez *f*; compleição *f*; **~ity** complexidade *f*
compliance [kəm'plaiəns] conformidade *f*; condescendência *f*
complicat|e ['kɔmplikeit] *v/t* complicar(-se); **~ed** complicado; **~ion** [ˌ-'keiʃən] complicação *f*
compliment ['kɔmplimənt] *s* cumprimento *m*; *v/t* cumprimentar; **~ary** obsequioso; lisonjeiro
comply [kəm'plai] *v/i*: **~ with** conformar-se com; acatar
component [kəm'pəunənt] *adj s* componente *m, f*
compos|e [kəm'pəuz] *v/t, v/i* compor; **~er** MUS compositor *m*
composit|e ['kɔmpəzit] *adj, s* composto *m*; **~ion** [ˌ-'ziʃən] composição *f*
compos|itor [kəm'pɔzitə] tipógrafo *m*; **~ure** [-'pəuʒə] compostura *f*
compote ['kɔmpəut] compota *f*, doce *m*
compound ['kɔmpaund] *adj, s* composto *m*
comprehen|d [ˌkɔmpri'hend] *v/t* compreender; **~sible** compreensível; **~sion** compreensão *f*; **~sive** compreensivo
compress ['kɔmpres] *s* compressa *f*; [kəm'pres] *v/t* comprimir; COMP compactar, comprimir; **~ion** [kɔm'preʃən] compressão *f*
comprise [kəm'praiz] *v/t* incluir, abranger
compromise ['kɔmprəmaiz] *s* compromisso *m*; *v/t, v/i* comprometer(-se)
compuls|ion [kəm'pʌlʃən] compulsão *f*; **~ory** compulsório
compunction [kəm'pʌŋkʃən] compunção *f*
comput|e [kəm'pju:t] *v/t, v/i* computar; **~er** computador *m*
comrade ['kɔmrid] camarada *m, f*; **~ship** camaradagem *f*
conceal [kən'si:l] *v/t* esconder, ocultar, encobrir
concede [kən'si:d] *v/t* conceder
conceit [kən'si:t] presunção *f*, vaidade *f*; **~ed** presumido, vaidoso
conceiv|able [kən'si:vəbl] concebível; **~e** *v/t, v/i* conceber
concentrat|e ['kɔnsəntreit] *v/t, v/i* concentrar(-se); **~ion** [ˌ-'treiʃən] concentração *f*
conception [kən'sepʃən] concepção *f*
concern [kən'sə:n] *s* inquietação *f*; interesse *m*; empresa *f*; *v/t* inquietar; interessar; tocar, concernir; **~ed** preocupado; **~ing** concernente, relativo a
concert ['kɔnsət] *s* concerto *m*;

[kən'sɜːt] *v/t* concertar; **~ed** combinado

concession [kən'seʃən] concessão *f*

conciliat|e [kən'silieit] *v/t* conciliar; **~ion** conciliação *f*

concise [kən'sais] conciso; **~ness** concisão *f*

conclu|de [kən'kluːd] *v/t, v/i* concluir; **~sion** [-ʒən] conclusão *f*; **~sive** conclusivo

concord ['kɔŋkɔːd] *s* concórdia *f*; GRAM concordância *f*; acordo *m*

concourse ['kɔŋkɔːs] afluência *f*; confluência *f*

concrete ['kɔnkriːt] *adj* concreto; *s* betão *m*, concreto *m*

concur [kən'kɜː] *v/i* coincidir; concorrer

concussion [kən'kʌʃən] concussão *f*

condemn [kən'dem] *v/t* condenar; **~ation** [ˌkɔndem'neiʃən] condenação *f*

condense [kən'dens] *v/t, v/i* condensar(-se); **~er** condensador *m*

condescend [ˌkɔndi'send] *v/i* condescender, dignar-se

condition [kən'diʃən] *v/t* condicionar; *s* condição *f*; **~al** condicional

condole [kən'dəul] *v/i*: **~ with** condoer-se de

condolences [kən'dəulənsiz] *s/pl* condolências *f/pl*

conduct ['kɔndʌkt] *s* conduta *f*; [kən'dʌkt] *v/t, v/i* conduzir (-se); **~or** condutor *m*; MUS colaborador *m*; maestro *m*

cone [kəun] cone *m*

confectioner [kən'fekʃənə] confeiteiro *m*; **~'s (shop)** confeitaria *f*

confedera|cy [kən'fedərəsi] (*pl* **-cies**), **~tion** [kənfedə'reiʃən] confederação *f*; **~te** *adj*, *s* confederado *m*; *v/t, v/i* confederar(-se)

confer [kən'fɜː] *v/t, v/i* conferenciar; conferir; **~ence** ['kɔnfərens] conferência *f*

confess [kən'fes] *v/t, v/i* confessar(-se); **~ion** confissão *f*; **~or** confessor *m*

confid|ant [ˌkɔnfi'dænt] confidente *m*; **~e** [kən'faid] *v/t, v/i* confiar; **~ence** ['kɔnfidəns] confiança *f*; confidência *f*; **~ent** confiado; confiante; **~ential** [ˌ-'denʃəl] confidencial

confine [kən'fain] *v/t* confinar, limitar; MED estar de parto; **~ment** MED puerpério *m*; reclusão *f*

confirm [kən'fɜːm] *v/t* confirmar; **~ation** [ˌkɔnfə'meiʃən] confirmação *f*; **~ed** *adj* inveterado

confiscate ['kɔnfiskeit] *v/t* confiscar

conflict ['kɔnflikt] *s* conflito *m*, luta *f*; [kən'flikt] *v/i* estar em conflito

conform [kən'fɔːm] *v/t, v/i* conformar(-se); **~ity** conformidade *f*

confound [kən'faund] *v/t* confundir; **~ you!** vai (vá) para o diabo!; **~ed** maldito

confront [kən'frʌnt] *v/t* confrontar

confus|e [kən'fju:z] *v/t* confundir; **~ed** confuso; **~ion** [-ʒən] confusão *f*

confute [kən'fju:t] *v/t* refutar

congestion [kən'dʒestʃən] MED congestão *f*; congestionamento *m*

conglomerate [kən'glɔmərit] *s*, *adj* conglomerado *m*

congratulat|e [kən'grætjuleit] *v/t* felicitar, congratular(-se); **~ions** [-'leiʃənz] *s/pl* parabéns *m/pl*

congregat|e ['kɔŋgrigeit] *v/t*, *v/i* congregar(-se); **~ion** [ˌ-'geiʃən] fléis *m/pl*; congregação *f*

congress ['kɔŋgres] congresso *m*

conjecture [kən'dʒektʃə] *s* conje(c)tura *f*; *v/t*, *v/i* conje(c)turar

conjugat|e ['kɔndʒugeit] *v/t*, *v/i* conjugar(-se); **~ion** [kəndʒu'geiʃən] conjugação *f*

conjunction [kən'dʒʌŋkʃən] conjunção *f*

conjunctive [kən'dʒʌŋktiv] *adj*, *s* conjuntivo *m*, *Braz* subjuntivo *m*

conjure ['kʌndʒə] *v/t*, *v/i* prestidigitar

conjurer ['kʌndʒərə] prestidigitador *m*

connect [kə'nekt] *v/t*, *v/i* ligar (-se); relacionar; fazer (um)a ligação; **~ed** ligado; relacionado; **~ing rod** biela *f*; **~ion** conexão *f*; ligação *f*; relação *f*

connive [kə'naiv] *v/i* ser conivente

conquer ['kɔŋkə] *v/t* conquistar; **~or** conquistador *m*

conquest ['kɔnkwest] conquista *f*

conscien|ce ['kɔnʃəns] consciência *f*; **~tious** [ˌ-ʃi'enʃəs] consciencioso

conscious ['kɔnʃəs] cônscio, consciente; **~ly** conscientemente; **~ness** consciência *f*; conhecimento *m*

consecrate ['kɔnsikreit] *v/t* consagrar; dedicar

consecutive [kən'sekjutiv] consecutivo, sucessivo

consent [kən'sent] *v/i* consentir; *s* consentimento *m*, permissão *f*

consequen|ce ['kɔnsikwəns] consequência *f*; importância *f*; **in ~ce** por conseguinte; **~t** consequente

conservation [ˌkɔnsə'veiʃən] conservação *f*

conserva|tism [kən'sə:vətizəm] conservantismo *m*; **~tive** *adj*, *s* conservador *m*; **~tory** [-tri] (*pl* **-ries**) MUS conservatório *m*; estufa *f*

conserve [kən'sə:v] *v/t* conservar

consider [kən'sidə] *v/t* considerar; **~able** considerável; **~ate** [-dərit] atencioso; **~ation** consideração *f*; **~ing** considerando que; em vista de

consign [kən'sain] *v/t* consignar; confiar; **~ment** consignação *f*
consist [kən'sist] *v/i* consistir; **~ence**, **~ency** consistência *f*; **~ent** consistente
consolation [ˌkɔnsə'leiʃən] consolação *f*
consol|e [kən'səul] *v/t* consolar; **~ing** consolador
consolidat|e [kən'sɔlideit] *v/t*, *v/i* consolidar(-se); **~ion** consolidação *f*
consonant ['kɔnsənənt] consoante *f*
consort ['kɔnsɔːt] consorte *m, f*
conspicuous [kən'spikjuəs] conspícuo, notável; **be ~ by one's absence** brilhar pela ausência
conspir|acy [kən'spirəsi] (*pl* **-cies**) conspiração *f*; **~ator** [-tə] conspirador *m*; **~e** [-'spaiə] *v/t*, *v/i* conspirar
constable ['kʌnstəbl] oficial *m* de polícia; condestável *m*
constancy ['kɔnstənsi] constância *f*
constant ['kɔnstənt] constante
constipation [ˌkɔnsti'peiʃən] prisão *f* de ventre
constituency [kən'stitjuənsi] (*pl* **-cies**) eleitorado *m*, círculo *m* eleitoral
constitut|e ['kɔnstitjuːt] *v/t* constituir; **~ion** [kɔnsti'tjuːʃən] constituição *f*; **~ional** *adj* constitucional
constrain [kən'strein] *v/t* forçar, constranger; **~t** constrangimento *m*
construct [kən'strʌkt] *v/t* construir; **~ion** construção *f*; **~ive** construtivo; **~or** construtor *m*
consul ['kɔnsəl] cônsul *m*; **~ar** ['-sjulə] consular; **~ate** ['-sjulit] consulado *m*
consult [kən'sʌlt] *v/t* consultar; **~ation** [ˌkɔnsəl'teiʃən] consulta *f*; **~ative** [kən'sʌltətiv] consultivo; **~ing** consultor; de consulta
consum|e [kən'sjuːm] *v/t* consumir; **~er** consumidor *m*; **~er goods** *s/pl* bens *m/pl* de consumo
consummat|e [kən'sʌmit] *adj* consumado; ['kɔnsʌmeit] *v/t* consumar
consumption [kəns'ʌmpʃən] consumo *m*, gasto *m*
contact ['kɔntækt] *s* conta(c)to *m*; [kən'tækt] *v/t* conta(c)tar
contagious [kən'teidʒəs] contagioso, contagiante
contain [kən'tein] *v/t* conter (-se)
contaminat|e [kən'tæmineit] *v/t* contaminar; **~ion** [-'neiʃən] contaminação *f*
contemplat|e ['kɔntempleit] *v/t* contemplar; **~ion** [kɔntem'pleiʃən] contemplação *f*; **~ive** contemplativo
contemporary [kən'tempərəri] *adj*, *s* (*pl* **-ries**) contemporâneo *m*
contempt [kən'tempt] desprezo *m*

contend [kən'tend] *v/i, v/t* contender; afirmar
content [kən'tent] *adj* contente; *v/t* contentar; ['kɔntent] *s* conteúdo *m*; assunto *m*; **~ed** contente, satisfeito; **~ion** [-'tenʃən] contenda *f*
contest ['kɔntest] *s* competição *f*, concurso *m*, prova *f*; [kən't-est] *v/t, v/i* disputar; contestar
context ['kɔntekst] contexto *m*
continent ['kɔntinənt] *s* continente *m*; **~al** [ˌ-'nent] *adj* continental
contingent [kən'tindʒənt] *adj, s* contingente *m*
continu|al [kən'tinjuəl] contínuo; **~ance**, **~ation** continuação *f*; **~e** [-juː] *v/t, v/i* continuar; **~ity** [-'ju(ː)iti] continuidade *f*; **~ous** seguido, contínuo
contort [kən'tɔːt] *v/t* contorcer; **~ion** contorção *f*
contraband ['kɔntrəbænd] *s* contrabando *m*
contraceptive [ˌkɔntrə'septiv] *adj, s* anticonceptivo *m*
contract [kən'trækt] *v/t, v/i* contratar; contrair(-se); ['kɔn-trækt] *s* contrato *m*; **~ion** [-'trækʃən] contra(c)ção *f*; **~or** empreiteiro *m*
contradict [ˌkɔntrə'dikt] *v/t* contradizer(-se); **~ion** contradição *f*; **~ory** contraditório
contrary ['kɔntrəri] *adj, s* (*pl* **-ries**) contrário *m*; **on the ~** pelo contrário
contrast ['kɔntræst] *s* contraste *m*; [kən'træst] *v/t, v/i* contrastar
contribut|e [kən'tribju(ː)t] *v/t, v/i* contribuir; **~ion** [ˌkɔntri'b-juːʃən] contribuição *f*; **~or** [kən'tribjutə] contribuinte *m*
contrite ['kɔntrait] contrito
contriv|ance [kən'traivəns] ideia *f*, invenção *f*; aparelho *m*, engenhoca *f*; **~e** *v/t* conseguir, arranjar
control [kən'trəul] *v/t* controlar, dominar; *s* controle *m*; comando *m*
controver|sial [ˌkɔntrə'vəːʃəl] controverso; **~sy** ['-vəːsi] (*pl* **-sies**) controvérsia *f*
contuse [kən'tjuːz] *v/t* contundir
convales|ce [ˌkɔnvə'les] *v/i* convalescer; **~cence** convalescência *f*; **~cent** *adj, s* convalescente *m, f*
convenien|ce [kən'viːnjəns] comodidade *f*, conveniência *f*; **~t** conveniente, cómodo
convent ['kɔnvənt] convento *m*
convention [kən'venʃən] convenção *f*; **~al** convencional
converge [kən'vəːdʒ] *v/i* convergir
convers|ant [kən'vəːsənt] versado; **~ation** [ˌkɔnvə'seiʃən] conversação *f*, conversa *f*; **~e** *v/i* conversar; **~ion** conversão *f*
convert ['kɔnvəːt] *s* convertido *m*; [kən'vəːt] *v/t* converter; **~ible** *adj* conversível; *s* descapotável *m*
convey [kən'vei] *v/t* transpor-

tar, conduzir, levar; exprimir; **~ance** JUR cedência *f*; **~er belt** correia *f* transportadora
convict ['kɔnvikt] *s* convicto *m* condenado *m*; [kən'vikt] *v/t* condenar, sentenciar
convince [kən'vins] *v/t* convencer
convoy ['kɔnvɔi] *s* comboio *m*; escolta *f*
cook [kuk] *s* cozinheiro *m*; *v/t*, *v/i* cozinhar, cozer; **~ery** culinária *f*; **~ie**, **~y** biscoito *m*
cool [ku:l] *adj* fresco; frio, distante; *v/t*, *v/i* arrefecer, refrescar; *s* frescura *f*; calma; **~ down**, **~ off** acalmar(-se)
cooper ['ku:pə] tanoeiro *m*
cooperat|e [kəu'ɔpəreit] *v/i* cooperar; **~ion** cooperação *f*; **~ive** [-rətiv] *s* cooperativa *f*; *adj* cooperativo
coordinate [kəu'ɔ:dnit] *adj* coordenado; *s* coordenada *f*
cope [kəup] *v/t*; **~(with)** fazer frente (*a*), enfrentar
copious ['kəupjəs] copioso
copper ['kɔpə] cobre *m*
copy ['kɔpi] *v/t*, *v/i* copiar; *s* (*pl* **-pies**) cópia *f*; **~ist** copista *m*; **~right** direitos *m*/*pl* de autor, propriedade *f* literária
coral ['kɔrəl] *s* coral *m*
cord [kɔ:d] *s* cordel *m*, cordão *m*
cordial ['kɔ:djəl] cordial
corduroy ['kɔ:dərɔi] bombazina *f*; **~s** *pl* calças *f*/*pl* de bombazina
core [kɔ:] caroço *m*; âmago *m*
cork [kɔ:k] *s* cortiça *f*; rolha *f*; *v/t* (ar)rolhar; **~-screw** saca-rolhas *m*
corn [kɔ:n] *s* calo *m*; cereal *m*; milho *m*; trigo *m*
corner ['kɔ:nə] *v/t*, *v/i* monopolizar; virar, fazer uma curva; *s* canto *m*, esquina *f*; **~ (kick)** (pontapé *m* de) canto *m*; *Braz* escanteio *m*
Cornish ['kɔ:niʃ] *adj* da Cornualha; *s* córnico *m*
coronation [ˌkɔrə'neiʃən] coroação *f*
corpor|al ['kɔ:pərəl] *s* MIL cabo *m*; *adj* corporal, corpóreo; **~ate** [-rit] associado, cole(c)tivo; **~ation** corporação *f*
corpse [kɔ:ps] cadáver *m*
corpulent ['kɔ:pjulənt] corpulento
correct [kə'rekt] *adj* corre(c)to; *v/t* corrigir; **~ion** corre(c)ção *f*
correspond [ˌkɔris'pɔnd] *v/i* corresponder(-se); **~ence** correspondência *f*; **~ent** *s* correspondente *m*, *f*; **~ing** correspondente
corridor ['kɔridɔ:] corredor *m*
corro|de [kə'rəud] *v/t*, *v/i* corroer(-se); **~sion** [-ʒən] corrosão *f*
corrupt [kə'rʌpt] *adj* corru(p)to; *v/t*, *v/i* corromper(-se); **~ion** corru(p)ção *f*
corset ['kɔ:sit] espartilho *m*
cosmetic(s) [kɔz'metik(s)] *adj*, *s* cosmético *m*
cosmonaut ['kɔzmənɔ:t] cosmonauta *m*, *f*

cost [kɔst] *v/i* custar; *s* custo *m*, preço *m*; **~ly** dispendioso; **~s** JUR custas *f/pl*
costume ['kɔstjuːm] *s* traje *m*
cosy ['kəuzi] *adj* confortavel, cómodo
cot [kɔt] *GB* cama *f* de grades
cottage ['kɔtidʒ] casa *f* de campo
cotton ['kɔtn] algodão *m*; **~ wool** algodão *m* em rama
couch [kautʃ] *s* divã *m*, canapé *m*; **~ potato** adepto *m* de sofá
cough [kɔf] *v/i* tossir; *s* tosse *f*
council ['kaunsl] *s* conselho *m*; concílio *m*
counsel ['kaunsəl] conselho *m*
count [kaunt] *v/t*, *v/i* contar; *s* conde *m*; conta *f*
countenance ['kauntinəns] *s* semblante *m*
counter ['kauntə] *s* balcão *m*; ficha *f*; **~act** [ˌ-'rækt] *v/t* contrariar, neutralizar; **~feit** ['-fɪt] *adj* falsificado; *v/t* falsificar; **~foil** talão *m*; **~mand** [ˌ-'maːnd] *v/t* revogar; **~march** contramarcha *f*; *v/i* contramarchar; **~pane** colcha *f*, coberta *f*
countess ['kauntis] condessa *f*
countless ['kauntlis] inumerável
country ['kʌntri] (*pl* **-ries**) país *m*; nação *f*; campo *m*; **~man** camponês *m*; compatriota *m*, *f*; **~side** campo *m*, zona *f* rural
county ['kaunti] (*pl* **-ties**) condado *m*, comarca *f*
couple ['kʌpl] *s* par *m*; casal *m*; **a ~ of** *fam* alguns, uns; *v/t*, *v/i* copular; emparelhar
courage ['kʌridʒ] coragem *f*; **~ous** [kə'reidʒəs] corajoso
courier ['kuriə] correio *m*, mensageiro *m*
course [kɔːs] *s* curso *m*; pista *f*, campo *m*; rumo *m*; prato *m*; **a matter of ~** uma coisa natural; **in due ~** na devida altura; **of ~** claro, com certeza; evidentemente
court [kɔːt] *s* pátio *m*; campo *m* de ténis; JUR tribunal *m*; corte *f*; *v/t* cortejar; solicitar; **~eous** ['kəːtjəs] cortês; **~esy** ['kəːtisi] (*pl* **-sies**) cortesia *f*; **~yard** pátio *m*
cousin ['kʌzn] primo *m*, prima *f*
cove [kəuv] enseada *f*
cover ['kʌvə] *v/t* cobrir; *s* cobertura *f*; abrigo *m*; talher *m*; **~age** reportagem *m*; riscos *m/pl* cobertos por seguro
covert ['kʌvət] *adj* encoberto, oculto
covet ['kʌvit] *v/t* cobiçar; **~ous** cobiçoso
cow [kau] *s* vaca *f*
coward ['kauəd] cobarde *m*; **~ice** ['-is] cobardia *f*
cowboy ['kaubɔi] vaqueiro *m*, *Braz* boiadeiro *m*
cower ['kauə] *v/i* agachar-se
cowslip ['kauslip] BOT primavera *f*
coxcomb ['kɔkskəum] peralvilho *m*

cox(swain) ['kɔkswein] arrais *m*

coy [kɔi] acanhado, modesto

crab [kræb] *s* caranguejo *m*

crack [kræk] *s* fenda *f*, racha *f*; estalido *m*; (*drug*) crack *m*; *v/t*, *v/i* fender(-se); estalar; **~er** bolacha *f* de água e sal; estalinho *m*, estalo-da-china *m*

crackle ['krækl] *v/i* crepitar

cradle ['kreidl] *s* berço *m*

craft [krɑːft] *s* habilidade *f*, arte *f*; embarcação *f*; artimanha *f*; **~sman** artífice *m*, artesão; **~y** astucioso

crag [kræg] fraga *f*

cram [kræm] *v/t*, *v/i* abarrotar; empinar, estudar

cramp [kræmp] *s* caimbra *f*; grampo *m*; *v/t* grampar

cranberry ['krænbəri] (*pl* **-ries**) arando *m*, uva-do-monte *f*

crane [krein] *s* ZOO grou *m*; MEC grua *f*, guindaste *m*

crank [kræŋk] MEC manivela *f*; excêntrico *m*

crash [kræʃ] *s* estrondo *m*; choque *m*, colisão *f*, queda *f*; *v/t*, *v/i* estalelar-se, espatifar-se; colidir; estrondear

crass [kræs] crasso

crater ['kreitə] cratera *f*

crav|e [kreiv] (**for**) *v/t* suspirar (por); **~ing** *s* ânsia *f*, desejo *m* ardente

crawl [krɔːl] *v/i* rastejar; gatinhar

crayfish ['kreifiʃ] **crawfish** ['krɔ-] lagostim *m*

crazy ['kreizi] doido, louco

creak [kriːk] *v/i* chiar, ranger

cream [kriːm] *s* nata *f* (*a fig*); creme *m*; *v/t* bater até fazer creme; desnatar; **~y** cremoso

crease [kriːs] *s* ruga *f*, vinco *m*; *v/t*, *v/i* enrugar(-se); vincar

creat|e [kri'eit] *v/t* criar; **~ion** criação *f*; **~ive** criativo, criador; **~or** criador *m*; **~ure** ['kriːtʃə] criatura *f*

credentials [kri'denʃəlz] *s/pl* credenciais *m/pl*

credible ['kredəbl] crível

credit ['kredit] *s* crédito *m*; honra *f*; *v/t* dar credito a; acreditar; on **~** a crédito; **~ card** cartão *m* de crédito; **~or** credor *m*

creed [kriːd] credo *m*, crença *f*

creek [kriːk] enseada *f*

creep [kriːp] *v/i* arrastar-se, rojar-se; **~er** BOT trepadeira *f*

cremate [kri'meit] *v/t* cremar, incinerar

crescent ['kresnt] *s* quarto crescente *m*; *adj* crescente

cress [kres] agrião *m*

crest [krest] *s* crista *f*; cimeira *f*; timbre *m*; **~fallen** abatido

crevice ['krevis] racha *f*, greta *f*

crew [kruː] *s* equipagem *f*, tripulação *f*

crib [krib] *s* presépio *m*; manjedoura *f*; *US* cama *f* de grades; *v/t*, *v/i* *fam* copiar, cabular, *Braz* colar

cricket ['krikit] críquete *m*; ZOO grilo *m*

crime [kraim] crime *m*

criminal ['kriminl] *s* criminoso *m*; *adj* criminal; criminoso

crimson ['krimzn] *adj, s* carmesim *m*
cripple ['kripl] *s* aleijado *m*, paralítico *m*, estropiado *m*; *v/t* estropiar
crisis ['kraisis] (*pl* **-ses**) crise *f*
crisp [krisp] *adj* tostado, estaladinho; crespo; fresco; rápido, decidido; *s* batata *f* frita
critic ['kritic] crítico *m*; **~al** crítico; **~ism** ['-sizəm] crítica *f*; **~ize** ['-saiz] *v/t, v/i* criticar
croak [krəuk] *v/i* grasnar
crockery ['krɔkəri] faiança *f*, louça *f* de barro
crook [kruk] *s* gancho *m*; cajado *m*; caloteiro *m*, escroque *m*; **~ed** *adj* desonesto; curvo
crop [krɔp] *s* colheita *f*; chicote *m*; papo *m*; *v/t* colher; ceifar, segar; cortar; tosquiar
cross [krɔs] *s* cruz *f*; *v/t, v/i* cruzar(-se); atravessar(-se); *adj* mal humorado, zangado; **~ing** cruzamento *m*; MAR travessia *f*; **~-road(s)** encruzilhada *f*; **~word (puzzle)** palavras *f/pl* cruzadas
crouch [krautʃ] *v/i* agachar-se, acocorar-se
crow [krəu] *s* corvo *m*; *v/i* cantar, cucuritar; **~-bar** alavanca *f*, pé-de-cabra *m*
crowd [kraud] *v/t, v/i* agrupar (-se), apinhar(-se); *s* multidão *f*, turba *f*; **~ed** apinhado
crown [kraun] *s* coroa *f*; *v/t* coroar
crucial ['kru:ʃəl] crucial
crucif|ix ['kru:sifiks] crucifixo *m*; **~ixion** [ˌ-'fikʃən] crucificação *f*; **~y** ['-fai] *v/t* crucificar
crude [kru:d] bruto; rude; grosseiro
cruel [kruəl] cruel; **~ty** (*pl* **-ties**) crueldade *f*
cruet ['kru(:)it] galheta *f*; **~-stand** galheteiro *m*
cruis|e [kru:z] *v/i* navegar; andar em cruzeiro; *s* cruzeiro *m*, travessia *f*; **~er** cruzador *m*
crumb [krʌm] migalha *f*; **~le** ['-bl] *v/t, v/i* esmigalhar(-se), esfarelar(-se)
crumple ['krʌmpl] *v/t, v/i* amarrotar(-se)
crusad|e [kru:'seid] *s* cruzada *f*; **~er** cruzado *m*
crush [krʌʃ] *v/t* esmagar; moer, triturar; *s* aperto *m*, compressão *f*; aglomeração *f*
crust [krʌst] *s* crosta *f*; côdea *f*; folhado *m*
crutch [krʌtʃ] muleta *f*
cry [krai] (*pl* **cries**) *s* grito *m*; choro *m*; *v/t, v/i* gritar; chorar
crypt [kript] cripta *f*
crystal ['kristl] cristal *m*
cu [si: 'ju:] (= **see you**) *fam* até mais tarde, *Braz* até logo
cub [kʌb] filhote *m*, cachorro *m*
cube [kju:b] cubo *m*
cubic ['kju:bik] cúbico
cuckoo ['kuku:] cuco *m*
cucumber ['kju:kʌmbə] pepino *m*, cogombro *m*
cuddle ['kʌdl] *v/t, v/i* abraçar (-se); *s* abraço *m*
cudgel ['kʌdʒəl] *s* clava *f*, bastão *m*; *v/t* esbordoar

cue [kjuː] THEAT deixa *f*; taco *m* (de bilhar); sinal *m*, indicação *f*
cuff [kʌf] *s* punho *m* (de camisa); palmada *f*; *v/t* dar palmadas
culp|able ['kʌlpəbl] culpável; **~rit** ['-rit] culpado *m*
cult [kʌlt] culto *m*; **~ivate** *v/t* ['-iveit] cultivar; **~ivated** culto; cultivado; **~ivation** cultivo *m*, cultura *f*
culture ['kʌltʃə] cultura *f*
cumbersome ['kʌmbəsəm] incómodo, enfadonho
cumulative ['kjuːmjulətiv] cumulativo
cunning ['kʌniŋ] *adj* astuto, manhoso; *s* astúcia *f*, manha *f*
cup [kʌp] *s* chávena *f*, xícara *f*; taça *f*; **~board** ['kʌbəd] guarda-louça *m*
cupidity [kju(ː)'piditi] cupidez *f*
curable ['kjuərəbl] curável
curat|e ['kjuərit] cura *m*, pároco *m*; **~or** [-'reitə] conservador *m*
curb [kəːb] *v/t* refrear
curd [kəːd] coalhada *f*, requeijão *m*; **~le** ['-dl] *v/t*, *v/i* coalhar (-se)
cure [kjuə] *s* cura *f*; *v/t*, *v/i* remediar; curar(-se)
curfew ['kəːfjuː] recolher *m* obrigatório
curiosity [ˌkjuəri'ɔsiti] curiosidade *f*
curious ['kjuəriəs] curioso
curl ['kəːl] *s* anel *m*, caracol *m*; *v/t*, *v/i* encaracolar(-se)
currant ['kʌrənt] corinto *m*; groselha *f*
curren|cy ['kʌrənsi] (*pl* **-cies**) moeda *f* corrente; circulação *f*; aceitação *f* geral; **~t** *adj*, *s* corrente *f*
curry ['kʌri] (*pl* **-ries**) *s* caril *m*
curse [kəːs] *v/t* amaldiçoar; *v/i* praguejar; *s* maldição *f*; praga *f*
curt [kəːt] abrupto, brusco
curtail [kəː'teil] *v/t* reduzir; encurtar
curtain ['kəːtn] *s* cortina *f*; THEAT pano *m* de boca
curve [kəːv] curva *f*; *v/t*, *v/i* curvar(-se), encurvar
cushion ['kuʃən] *s* almofada *f*, coxim *m*
custard ['kʌstəd] leite-creme *m*
custody ['kʌstədi] cuidado *m*; custódia *f*
custom ['kʌstəm] costume *m*; **~ary** consuetudinário, habitual; **~er** freguês *m*, cliente *m*, *f*; **~(s)house** alfândega *f*; **~s** alfândega *f*; direitos *m/pl* alfandegários; **~s duties** direitos *m/pl* aduaneiros
cut [kʌt] *v/t*, *v/i* cortar; talhar; *s* corte *m*, golpe *m*; **~away** *s* fraque *m*; **~ down** deitar abaixo, derrubar; reduzir; **~ in** interromper, intrometer(-se)
cutler ['kʌtlə] cuteleiro *m*; **~y** cutelaria *f*
cutlet ['kʌtlit] costeleta *f*
cutthroat ['kʌtθrəut] *s*, degola-

dor *m*, assassino *m*; *adj* cruel, sanguinário

cutting ['kʌtiŋ] *adj* cortante; mordaz; *s* recorte *m*; BOT estaca *f*; corte *m*

cyber... ['saibə] *prp Internet* ciber...; **~space** *s* ciberespaço *m*

cycl|e ['saikl] *v/i* andar de bicicleta; *s* ciclo *m*; bicicleta *f*; **~ic (-al)** cíclico; **~ist** ciclista *m*, *f*

cyclone ['saikləun] ciclone *m*

cylinder ['silində] cilindro *m*

cymbal ['simbəl] pratos *m/pl*, címbalo *m*

cynic ['sinik] *s* cínico *m*; **~al** cínico; **~ism** cinismo *m*

cypress ['saipris] cipreste *m*

czar [zaː] czar *m*

Czech [tʃek] *adj*, *s* checo *m*, *Braz* tcheco *m*

D

dad [dæb] *s* pancadinha *f*; *v/t* esfregar, esponjar

dad(dy) [dæd(i)] (*pl* **-dies**) papá *m*, *Braz* papai *m*; **~ longlegs** melga *f*, *Braz* pernilongo *m*

daffodil ['dæfədil] asfódelo *m*, narciso *m* amarelo

daft [dɑːft] palerma, tolo

dagger ['dægə] punhal *m*

daily ['deili] *adj* quotidiano, diário; *adv* diariamente; *s* diário *m*

dainty ['deinti] *s* (*pl* **-ties**) *s* guloseima *f*; *adj* delicado, refinado; elegante

dairy ['dɛəri] (*pl* **-ries**) leitaria *f*

daisy ['deizi] (*pl* **-sies**) BOT bonina *f*, margarida *f*

dam [dæm] *s* barragem *f*; dique *m*; *v/t* represar

damage ['dæmidʒ] *s* dano *m*, prejuizo *m*; estrago *m*, avaria *f*; *v/t* deteriorar, danificar; **~s** *pl* inde(m)nização *f* por perdas e danos

damask ['dæməsk] damasco *m*

damn [dæm] *v/t* condenar; amaldiçoar; *s* maldição *f*; **~ it!** maldito seja!; **I'll be damned if ...** diabos me levem se ...; **I don't care a ~** não faço caso; **~ation** [-'neiʃən] danação *f*, condenação *f*

damp [dæmp] *v/t*, *v/i* (h)umedecer; abafar; *s* (h)umidade; *adj* (h)úmido

danc|e ['dɑːns] *v/t*, *v/i* bailar, dançar; *s* baile *m*, dança *f*; **~er** dançarino *m*, bailarino *m*; **~ing** *adj* dançante; *s* dança *f*

dandelion ['dændilaiən] BOT dente-de-leão *m*

danger ['deindʒə] perigo *m*; **~ous** perigoso

dangle ['dæŋgl] *v/t*, *v/i* suspender; acenar (com)

Danish ['deiniʃ] *adj*, *s* dinamarquês *m*

dappled ['dæpld] malhado

dare [dɛə] *v/t, v/i* ousar, atrever-se a; desafiar; **I ~ say** creio bem; sem dúvida; suponho
daring ['dɛəriŋ] *s* ousadia *f*; *adj* ousado
dark [dɑːk] *adj* escuro, sombrio, obscuro; *s* escuridão *f*, trevas *f/pl*; escuro *m*; **~en** *v/t, v/i* escurecer(-se); **~ness** escuridão *f*, trevas *f/pl*
darling ['dɑːliŋ] *adj, s* querido *m*, amor *m*
darn [dɑːn] *v/t* cerzir; *s* cerzidura *f*
dart [dɑːt] *s* dardo *m*; flecha *f*; *v/t, v/i* lançar(-se), precipitar (-se)
dash [dæʃ] *s* travessão *m*; energia *f*; ímpeto *m*; arremetida *f*, arranco *m*; *v/t, v/i* arrojar; despedaçar; precipitar-se
dashboard ['dæʃbɔːd] AUTO painel *m*
dashing ['dæʃiŋ] *adj* impetuoso, arrojado; chibante
data ['deitə] *s/pl* dados *m/pl*
date [deit] *s* data *f*; encontro *m* marcado, entrevista *f*; BOT tâmara *f*; *v/t, v/i* datar; **out of ~** antiquado, fora de moda; **up to ~** moderno; em dia; **~ed** antiquado, obsoleto
daub [dɔːb] *v/t* (bes)untar
daughter ['dɔːtə] filha *f*; **~-in-law** nora *f*
daunt [dɔːnt] *v/t* intimidar; **~less** intrépido
dawn [dɔːn] *s* aurora *f*, alvorecer *m*, madrugada *f*, amanhecer *m*; *v/i* amanhecer; despontar
day [dei] dia *m*; jornada *f*; **~ after ~** dia após dia; **~ in ~ out** dia a dia; **~ by ~** dia por dia; **the ~ after tomorrow** depois de amanhã; **the ~ before yesterday** anteontem; **~break** romper *m* do dia; **~dream** *s* devaneio *m*; **~light** luz *m* do dia; **~-school** externato *m*; **~ spa** spa *m*
daze [deiz] *v/t* aturdir; *s* aturdimento *m*
dazzle ['dæzl] *v/t* ofuscar, encadear; deslumbar
deacon ['diːkən] diácono *m*
dead [ded] *adv* completamente; *s*: **in the ~ of** em pleno ...; *adj* profundo; sem corrente; morto, falecido, defunto; inerte; **~en** *v/t* amortecer; **~ end** beco *m* sem saída; **~line** prazo *m* marcado; **~lock** impasse *f*
deaf [def] surdo; **turn a ~ ear to** fazer ouvidos de mercador; **~-mute** *adj, s* surdo-mudo *m*; **~en** *v/t* ensurdecer; **~ness** surdez *f*
deal [diːl] *s* parte *f*, porção *f*, quantidade *f*; mão *f* em jogo de cartas; acordo *m*; **a great ~, a good ~** muito; uma grande quantidade; *v/t, v/i* distribuir, dar cartas; **~er** negociante *m*; **~ with** tratar de; lidar com; **~ings** *s/pl* negócios *m/pl*
dear [diə] *adj* caro, dispendioso; querido, caro; *int* **oh ~!** com a breca! **~ me!** valha-me Deus!
death [deθ] morte *f*, falecimen-

to *m*; **~bed** leito *m* de morte; **~-rate** taxa *f* de mortalidade
debase [di'beis] *v/t* aviltar
debate [di'beit] *s* debate *m*; *v/t*, *v/i* debater
debauch [di'bɔːtʃ] *v/t* corromper; perverter; **~ee** libertino *m*; **~ery** libertinagem *f*, devassidão *f*
debit ['debit] *s* débito *m*; *v/t* debitar; **~ card** cartão *m* de débito
debt [det] dívida *f*; **~or** devedor *m*
decade ['dekeid] década *f*
decaden|ce ['dekədəns] decadência *f*; **~t** *adj*, *s* decadente *m*
decapitate [di'kæpiteit] *v/t* decapitar
decay [di'kei] *s* declínio *m*, decadência *f*; cárie *f*; *v/t*, *v/i* decair, declinar; apodrecer, cariar
decease [di'siːs] falecimento *m*; **~d** *adj*, *s* falecido *m*
decei|t [di'siːt] engano *m*, fraude *f*, dolo *m*; **~tful** enganoso, falso; **~ve** [-v] *v/t* enganar; **~ver** enganador *m*
December [di'sembə] Dezembro *m*
decen|cy ['diːsnsi] decência *f*; **~t** decente
decept|ion [di'sepʃən] decepção *f*; engano *m*; **~ive** [-tiv] enganador, ilusório
decid|e [di'said] *v/t*, *v/i* decidir (-se); **~ed** decidido
decipher [di'saifə] *v/t* decifrar
decision [di'siʒən] decisão *f*
decisive [di'saisiv] decisivo; decidido
deck [dek] *s* convés *m*, coberta *f*; **~-chair** cadeira *f* de lona, *Braz* preguiçosa *f*
declaim [di'kleim] *v/t*, *v/i* declamar
declar|ation [ˌdeklə'reiʃən] declaração *f*; **~e** [di'klɛə] *v/t*, *v/i* declarar
decline [di'klain] *s* declínio *m*; *v/t*, *v/i* declinar; decair
decompose [ˌdiːkəm'pəuz] *v/t*, *v/i* decompor(-se)
decorat|e ['dekəreit] *v/t*, ornamentar, decorar; **~ion** decoração *f*, adorno *m*; **~ive** ['-rətiv] decorativo; **~or** decorador *m*
decor|ous ['dekərəs] decoroso; **~um** [di'kɔːrəm] decoro *m*, decência *f*
decoy [di'kɔi] *v/t* engodar
decrease ['diːkriːs] *s* decrescimento *m*, diminuição *f*; [diː'kriːs] *v/t*, *v/i* decrescer, diminuir
decree [di'kriː] *s* decreto *m*; *v/t*, *v/i* decretar
dedicat|e ['dedikeit] *v/t* dedicar, consagrar; **~ion** [dedi'keiʃən] dedicação *f*; dedicatória *f*
deduce [di'djuːs] *v/t* deduzir
deduct [di'dʌkt] *v/t* descontar, subtrair; **~ion** dedução *f*; desconto *m*
deed [diːd] façanha *f*, feito *m*, a(c)to *m*; JUR escritura *f*
deep [diːp] *adj* fundo; profundo; penetrante; grave; *s* pélago *m*; *adv* profundamente; ~

blue azul vivo; **~en** *v/t*, *v/i* aprofundar(-se); **~-freeze** *s* congelador *m*; *v/t* congelar
deer [diə] veado *m*, cervo *m*
deface [di'feis] *v/t* desfigurar
defame [di'feim] *v/t* difamar
defeat [di'fi:t] *s* derrota *f*; *v/t* derrotar
defect [di'fekt] *s* defeito *m*; **~ive** defeituoso; GRAM defectivo
defence [di'fens] defesa *f*
defend [di'fend] *v/t* defender; **~ant** JUR réu *m*; **~er** defensor *m*
defensive [di'fensiv] *s* defensiva *f*; *adj* defensivo
defer [di'fə:] *v/t* adiar, diferir; **~ to** ceder, deferir; **~ence** ['defərəns] deferência *f*; **~ential** [ˌdefə'renʃəl] deferente
defian|ce [di'faiəns] provocação *f*, desafio *m*; **~t** provocador, desafiante
deficien|cy [di'fiʃənsi] (*pl* **-cies**) deficiência *f*; **~t** deficiente
deficit ['defisit] défice *m*, deficit *m*
defile [di'fail] *v/t* aviltar; [di'fail] *s* desfiladeiro *m*
defin|e [di'fain] *v/t*, *v/i* definir; **~ite** ['definit] definido; **~ition** [ˌ-'niʃən] definição *f*; **~itive** [-'finitiv] definitivo
deflate [di'fleit] *v/t*, *v/i* esvaziar(-se)
deform [di'fɔ:m] *v/t* deformar; **~ed** disforme; **~ity** deformidade *f*
defrost [di:'frɔst] *v/t*, *v/i* descongelar, degelar
deft [deft] hábil, destro
defy [di'fai] *v/t* desafiar
degenerate [di'dʒenereit] *v/i* degenerar(-se)
degrade [di'greid] *v/t*, *v/i* degradar(-se)
degree [di'gri:] grau *m*
deign [dein] *v/i* dignar-se
deity ['di:iti] (*pl* **-ties**) divindade *f*
deject|ed [di'dʒektid] abatido, desanimado; **~ion** desalento *m*
delay [di'lei] *s* atraso *m*, demora *f*; *v/t*, *v/i* atrasar, (re)tardar; demorar(-se)
delegate ['deligit] *s* delegado *m*; ['deligeit] *v/t* delegar
deliberat|e [di'libərit] *adj* deliberado; [-'libəreit] *v/t*, *v/i* deliberar; **~ely** deliberadamente; **~ion** [-'reiʃən] deliberação *f*
delicacy ['delikəsi] (*pl* **-cies**) delicadeza *f*; acepipe *m*, pitéu *m*
delicious [di'liʃəs] delicioso; saboroso
delight [di'lait] *s* deleite *m*; *v/t*, *v/i* deleitar(-se)
delineate [di'linieit] *v/t* delinear
delinquent [di'liŋkwənt] *adj*, *s* delinquente *m*, *f*
deliver [di'livə] *v/t* entregar; distribuir; partejar, assistir ao parto; **~er** libertador *m*; **~y** (*pl* **-ries**) parto *m*; entrega *f*, distribuição *f*

delude [di'lu:d] *v/t* enganar
deluge ['delju:dʒ] *s* dilúvio *m*; *v/t* inundar, alagar
delus|ion [di'lu:ʒən] ilusão *f*; engano *m*; **~ive** [-siv] ilusório
demand [di'mɑ:nd] *s* demanda *f*; procura *f*; exigência *f*; *v/t*, *v/i* exigir, reclamar
demilitarize ['di:'militəraiz] *v/t* desmilitarizar
demise [di'maiz] falecimento *m*
democracy [di'mɔkrəsi] (*pl* **-cies**) democracia *f*
democrat ['deməkræt] democrata *m*, *f*; **~ic** democrático
demolish [di'mɔliʃ] *v/t* demolir
demolition [ˌdemə'liʃən] demolição *f*
demon ['di:mən] demónio *m*
demonstrat|e ['demənstreit] *v/t*, *v/i* demonstrar; manifestar; **~ion** [-'streiʃən] demonstração *f*; manifestação *f*; **~ive** demonstrativo
demure [di'mjuə] sério, modesto
den [den] covil *m*, antro *m*
denial [di'naiəl] desmentido *m*; negativa *f*; recusa *f*
denote [di'nəut] *v/t* denotar
denounce [di'nauns] *v/t* denunciar
dens|e [dens] compacto; obtuso; denso; espesso; **~ity** densidade *f*
dent [dent] *s* mossa *f*; *v/t*, *v/i* amolgar(-se)
dent|al ['dentl] dental; **~ist** dentista *m*; **~istry** medicina *f* dentária; **~ure** ['-tʃə] dentadura *f* postiça
denude [di'nju:d] *v/t* desnudar
deny [di'nai] *v/t* negar
deodorize [di:'əudəraiz] *v/t* desodorizar
depart [di'pɑ:t] *v/i* partir, sair; **~ed** ido, passado; falecido
department [di'pɑ:tmənt] repartição *f*; departmento *m*; se(c)ção; **~ment store** armazém; **departure** [di'pa:tʃə] partida *f*
depend [di'pend] *v/i* depender; **~able** de confiança; **~ence** dependência *f*; **~ent** dependente
deplor|able [di'plɔ:rəbl] deplorável; **~e** *v/t* deplorar
deport [di'pɔ:t] *v/t* deportar; **~ation** deportação *f*
depos|e [di'pəuz] *v/t* depor; destituir; **~it** [-'pɔzit] *s* depósito *m*; *v/t* depositar; **~ition** depoimento *m*; deposição *f*
depot ['depəu] armazém *m*, depósito *m*; *US* estação *f* de caminhos de ferro, *Braz* estação *f* ferroviária
depreciate [di'pri:ʃieit] *v/t*, *v/i* depreciar; desvalorizar(-se)
depress [di'pres] *v/t* deprimir; **~ing** deprimente; **~ion** depressão *f*
deprive [di'praiv] *v/t*: **~of** privar, despojar de
depth [depθ] profundeza *f*, profundidade *f*
deputy ['depjuti] (*pl* **-ties**) deputado *m*; delegado *m*; substituto *m*

derail [di'reil] *v/t, v/i* descarrilar; **~ment** descarrilamento *m*
derange [di'reindʒ] *v/t* transtornar; **~ment** loucura *f*
derision [di'riʒən] galhofa *f*, chacota *f*
derive [di'raiv] *v/t*: **~from** derivar de
descend [di'send] *v/t, v/i* descer; descender; **~ant** descendente *m, f*
descent [di'sent] descida *f*; linhagem *f*, descendência *f*
descri|be [dis'kraib] *v/t* descrever; **~ption** [-'kripʃən] descrição *f*; **~ptive** [-'kriptiv] descritivo
desegregate [di:'segrigeit] *v/t, v/i* abolir a segregação (de)
desert [di'zə:t] *v/t, v/i* desertar, abandonar; ['dezət] *s* deserto *m*; **~er** [di'zə:tə] desertor *m*
deserv|e [di'zə:v] *v/t* merecer; **~edly** merecidamente; **~ing** merecedor, digno
design [di'zain] *v/t, v/i* plane(j)ar; esboçar, desenhar; *s* desenho *m*; desígnio *m*
designat|e ['dezigneit] *v/t* designar; **~ion** designação *f*
designer [di'zainə] desenhista *m, f*
desir|e [di'zaiə] *s* desejo *m*; *v/t* desejar; **~ous** desejoso
desk [desk] escrivaninha *f*, secretária *f*
desolate ['desəlit] *adj* desolado; deserto, despovoado; ['-leit] *v/t* desolar; despovoar
despair [dis'pɛə] *s* desespero *m*; *v/i* desesperar
despatch [dis'pætʃ] *s, v/t* = **dispatch**
desperat|e ['despərit] desesperado; **~ion** desespero *m*, desesperação *f*
despi|cable ['despikəbl] desprezível; **~se** [dis'paiz] *v/t* desprezar, desdenhar
despite [dis'pait] *prp* a despeito de, apesar de
desponden|cy [dis'pɔndənsi] desânimo *m*, abatimento *m*; **~t** desanimado
despot ['despɔt] déspota *m, f*; **~ic** despótico; **~ism** despotismo *m*
dessert [di'zə:t] sobremesa *f*
destin|ation [,desti'neiʃən] destino *m*, destinação *f*; **~ed** ['-tind] *adj* destinado; **~y** destino *m*
destitut|e ['destitju:t] necessitado, desamparado; **~ion** [desti'tju:ʃən] indigência *f*
destroy [dis'trɔi] *v/t* destruir, destroçar
destruct|ion [dis'trʌkʃən] destruição *f*; **~ive** destrutivo
detach [di'tætʃ] *v/t* destacar; desligar; separar; **~able** separável, destacável; **~ed** *adj* separado; **~ment** separação *f*; destacamento *m*; desapego *m*
detail ['di:teil] *s* pormenor *m*, detalhe *m*; **in ~** com detalhes, pormenorizadamente
detain [di'tein] *v/t* deter, reter
detect [di'tekt] *v/t* descobrir,

detectar; **~ion** descoberta *f*; dete(c)ção *f*; **~ive** dete(c)tive *m*; **~ive story** conto *m* policial
detention [di'tenʃən] detenção *f*, retenção *f*
deter [di'tə:] *v/t* dissuadir
detergent [di'tə:dʒənt] *s* detergente *m*
deteriorate [di'tiəriəreit] *v/t*, *v/i* deteriorar(-se)
determin|ation [di,tə:mi'neiʃən] determinação *f*; **~e** [di'tə:min] *v/t* determinar; **ed** determinado
detest [di'test] *v/t* detestar; **~able** detestável
detour ['deituə] *s* desvio *m*
detract [di'trækt] *v/i*: **~ from** difamar; diminuir; **~or** detra(c)tor *m*
devastat|e ['devəsteit] *v/t* devastar; **~ing** *adj* devastador
develop [di'veləp] *v/t*, *v/i* revelar; desenvolver(-se); **~ment** desenvolvimento *m*; revelação *f*
deviate ['di:vieit] *v/i* desviar-se
device [di'vais] dispositivo *m*; emblema *m*; meio *m*, expediente *m*
devil ['devl] diabo *m*, demónio *m*
devise [di'vaiz] *v/t* idear, inventar
devoid [di'vɔid] falto, desprovido
devolve [di'vɔlv] (on) *v/i* transferir; recair (em)
devotion [di'vəuʃən] devoção *f*
devour [di'vauə] *v/t* devorar
devout [di'vaut] devoto; sincero, ardente
dew [dju:] orvalho *m*; **~y** orvalhoso, orvalhado
dexterity [deks'teriti] destreza *f*
diagnose ['daiəgnəuz] *v/t* diagnosticar
dial ['daiəl] *s* disco *m*; mostrador *m*; *v/t* marcar, ligar, *Braz* discar
dialect ['daiəlekt] diale(c)to *m*
dialog(ue) ['daiəlɔg] diálogo *m*
diamond ['daiəmənd] diamante *m*
diaper ['daiəpə] *US* fralda *f*, cueiro *m*
diaphragm ['daiəfræm] diafragma *m*
diary ['daiəri] (*pl* **-ries**) diário *m*
dice [dais] *v/i* jogar (os) dados; *s* dado *m*
dictat|e [dik'teit] *v/t*, *v/i* ditar; *s* ditame *m*; **~ion** ditado *m*; **~or** ditador *m*; **~orship** ditadura *f*
dictionary ['dikʃənri] (*pl* **-ries**) dicionário *m*
die [dai] *s* matriz *f*; *v/i* morrer; **~ away** des vanecer-se; **~ down** extinguir-se; **~-hard** intransigente *m*
diet ['daiət] *s* dieta *f*, regime *m*
differ ['difə] *v/i* diferir, divergir; **~ence** diferença *f*; **~ent** diferente, distinto
difficult ['difikəlt] difícil; **~y** (*pl* **-ties**) dificuldade *f*
diffident ['difidənt] tímido
diffus|e [di'fju:z] *v/t*, *v/i* difundir(-se); [-'fju:s] *adj* difuso; **~ion** [-ʒən] difusão *f*

dig [dig] *v/t, v/i* cavar
digest [di'dʒest] *v/t, v/i* digerir; **~ion** digestão *f*; **~ive** *adj* digestivo
digital ['didʒitl] digital; **~ camera** câmara *f* digital; **~ photo** fotografia *f* digital
digni|tary ['dignitəri] (*pl* **-ries**) dignitário *m*; **~ty** dignidade *f*
digress [dai'gres] *v/i* divagar, digressionar; **~ion** digressão *f*
dike [daik] dique *m*, açude *m*
dilapidated [di'læpideitid] estragado, dilapidado
dilat|e [dai'leit] *v/t, v/i* dilatar (-se); **~ion** dilatação *f*; **~ory** ['dilətəri] lento, dilatório
diligen|ce ['dilidʒəns] diligência *f*; **~t** diligente
dilute [dai'lju:t] *v/t* diluir
dim [dim] *adj* obscuro, escuro, sombrio; indistinto, *v/t, v/i* obscurecer, ofuscar
dimension [di'menʃən] dimensão *f*
diminish [di'miniʃ] *v/t, v/i* diminuir
diminution [ˌdimi'nju:ʃən] diminuição *f*
dimple ['dimpl] covinha *f*
din [din] *s* estrondo *m*
dine [dain] *v/t* jantar; **~ out** jantar fora
dingy ['dindʒi] manchado, sujo
dining|-car ['dainiŋ-ka:] vagão-restaurante *m*, carruagem-restaurante *f*; **~-room** sala *f* de jantar
dinner ['dinə] jantar *m*; almoço *m*
dip [dip] *s* mergulho *m*; declive *m*; *v/t, v/i* baixar; mergulhar
diploma [di'pləumə] diploma *m*; **~cy** diplomacia *f*; **~t** ['dipləmæt] diplomata *m, f*; **~tie** [ˌ-plə'mætik] diplomático
dire ['daiə] extremo; terrível
direct [dai'rekt] *adj* dire(c)to; *adv* dire(c)tamente; *v/t* dirigir endereçar; **~ion** dire(c)ção *f*; **~ions** intruções *f/pl*; **~or** dire(c)tor *m*; **~ory** (*pl* **-ries**) lista *f* telefónica
dirigible ['diridʒəbl] *adj, s* dirigível *m*
dirt [də:t] sujidade *f*, porcaria *f*; sujeira *f*; **~y** *adj* sujo, imundo, porco; *v/t, v/i* sujar(-se)
disab|ility [ˌdisə'biliti] (*pl* **-ties**) incapacidade *f*; **~le** [-'eibl] *v/t* incapacitar; mutilar; **~led** *s* mutilado *m*
disadvantage [ˌdisəd'va:ntidʒ] desvantagem *f*; **~ous** [ˌdisædva:n'teidʒəs] desvantajoso
disagree [ˌdisə'gri:] *v/i* discordar; **~ment** desacordo *m*
disappear [ˌdisə'piə] *v/i* desaparecer, sumir-se; **~ance** desaparecimento *m*
disappoint [ˌdisə'pɔint] *v/i* desapontar; **~ment** desapontamento *m*
disappro|val [ˌdisa'pru:vəl] desaprovação *f*; **~ve (of)** *v/i* desaprovar, reprovar
disarm [dis'ɑ:m] *v/t, v/i* desarmar(-se); **~ament** desarmamento *m*

disarrange ['disə'reindʒ] *v/t* desarranjar, transtornar
disast|er [di'zɑːstə] desastre *m*; **~rous** desastroso
disband [dis'bænd] *v/t, v/i* debandar; MIL licenciar
disbelie|f ['disbi'liːf] incredulidade *f*, descrença *f*; **~ve** ['-'liːv] *v/t* descrer, não acreditar
disburse [dis'bəːs] *v/t, v/i* desembolsar
disc [disk] disco *m*
discern [di'səːn] *v/t* discernir; **~ing** *adj* discernente; **~ment** discernimento *m*
discharge [dis'tʃɑːdʒ] *s* descarga *f*; despedimento *m*; desempenho *m*; *v/t, v/i* desempenhar(-se); descarregar; despedir
discipl|e [di'saipl] discípulo *m*; **~ine** ['disiplin] *s* disciplina *f*; *v/t* disciplinar
disclos|e [dis'kləuz] *v/t* revelar, descobrir, desvendar; **~ure** [-ʒə] revelação *f*
discolo(u)r [dis'kʌlə] *v/t, v/i* descolorar(-se), desbotar(-se)
discomfort [dis'kʌmfət] desconforto *m*, incómodo *m*
discompose [ˌdiskəm'pauz] *v/t* descompor
disconcert [ˌdiskən'səːt] *v/t* desconcertar; **~ing** desconcertante
disconnect ['diskə'nekt] *v/t* desligar; **~ed** *adj* desconexo
disconsolate [dis'kɔnsəlit] desconsolado
discontent ['diskən'tent] *s* descontentamento *m*; **~ed** *adj* descontente
discontinue [diskən'tinjuː] *v/t, v/i* descontinuar
discord ['diskɔːd] discórdia *f*, discordância *f*; MUS dissonância *f*; **~ant** discordante; dissonante
discount ['diskaunt] *v/t* descontar; *s* desconto *m*
discourage [dis'kʌridʒ] *v/t* desanimar, desencorajar; **~ment** desânimo *m*, desencorajamento *m*
discover [dis'kʌvə] *v/t* descobrir; **~er** descobridor *m*; **~y** (*pl* **-ries**) descoberta *f*, descobrimento *m*
discredit [dis'kredit] *s* descrédito *m*; *v/t* desacreditar; **~able** desonroso
discreet [dis'kriːt] discreto
discretion [-'kreʃən] discrição *f*
discriminat|e [dis'krimineit] *v/i* discriminar; **~ion** [-'neiʃən] discriminação *f*
discuss [dis'kʌs] *v/t* discutir; **~ion** [-'kʌʃən] discussão *f*
disdain [dis'dein] *s* desdém *m*; *v/t* desdenhar
disease [di'ziːz] doença *f*
disembark ['disim'bɑːk] *v/t, v/i* desembarcar
disengag|e ['disin'geidʒ] *v/t, v/i* desengatar; desembaraçar(-se); **~ed** livre
disentangle ['disin'tæŋgl] *v/t, v/i* desemaranhar(-se), desenredar(-se)

disfigure [dis'figə] *v/t* desfigurar

disgrace [dis'greis] *s* vergonha *f*; desgraça *f*; *v/t* desonrar; **~ful** vergonhoso, desonroso

disguise [dis'gaiz] *v/t* disfarçar; *s* disfarce *m*

disgust [dis'gʌst] *s* repugnância *f*, aversão *f*; *v/t* repugnar; **~ing** repugnante; desgostante

dish [diʃ] *s* prato *m*

dishearten [dis'hɑ:tn] *v/t* desanimar, desalentar

dishes [diʃiz] *s/pl* louça *f*

dishevel(l)ed [di'ʃevəld] desgrenhado

dishonest [dis'ɔnist] desonesto; **~y** desonestidade *f*

dishono(u)r [dis'ɔnə] *s* desonra *f*; *v/t* desonrar; **~able** desonroso

dish-washer ['diʃ,wɔʃə] máquina *f* de lavar louça

disillusion [,disi'lu:ʒən] *v/t* desiludir; *s* desilusão *f*

disinclin|ation [,disinkli'neiʃən] aversão *f*; **~ed** ['-'klaind] pouco disposto

disinfectant [,disin'fektənt] *s* desinfe(c)tante *m*

disinherit ['disin'herit] *v/t* deserdar

disintegrate [dis'intigreit] *v/t*, *v/i* desagregar(-se), desintegrar(-se)

disinterested [dis'intristid] desinteressado

disjointed [dis'dʒɔintid] incoerente

disk [disk] *US* disco *m*; **~ drive** COMP drive *f* de disquetes

dislike [dis'laik] *s* aversão *f*, antipatia *f*; *v/t* não gostar de, antipatizar com

dislocat|e ['disləkeit] *v/t* deslocar; **~ion** deslocamento *m*

dismal ['dizməl] lúgubre

dismay [dis'mei] *s* consternação *f*; *v/t* consternar

dismember [dis'membə] *v/t* desmembrar

dismiss [dis'mis] *v/t* demitir; **~al** demissão *f*

dismount [dis'maunt] *v/t*, *v/i* desmontar; apear(-se)

disobedien|ce [,disə'bi:djəns] desobediência *f*; **~t** desobediente

disobey ['disə'bei] *v/t*, *v/i* desobedecer (a)

disorder [dis'ɔ:də] *s* desarranjo *m*; desordem *f*; *v/t* desordenar; desarranjar; **~ly** desordenado; turbulento

disown [dis'əun] *v/t* (re)negar

disparage [dis'pæridʒ] *v/t* amesquinhar

dispar|ate ['dispərit] desigual, díspar; **~ity** [-'pæriti] disparidade *f*

dispatch [dis'pætʃ] *v/t* despachar expedir

dispel [dis'pel] *v/t* dissipar, dispersar

dispensable [dis'pensəbl] dispensável

dispense [dis'pens] *v/t* distribuir, repartir; dispensar

disperse [dis'pə:s] *v/t*, *v/i* dispersar(-se)

displace [dis'pleis] *v/t* deslocar; desalojar
display [dis'plei] *v/t* exibir, expor, ostentar; *s* exibição *f*, exposição *f*, ostentação *f*
displeas|e [dis'pli:z] *v/t* desagradar; **~ing** desagradável; **~ure** [-'pleʒə] descontentamento *m*, desagrado *m*
dispos|al [dis'pəuzəl] disposição *f*; **~e** *v/t* dispor; **~e of** desfazer-se de; dispor de
disposition [ˌdispə'ziʃən] disposição *f*; génio *m*, índole *f*
disproof ['dis'pru:f] refutação *f*
disproportionate [ˌdisprə'pɔ:ʃnit] desproporcionado
disprove ['dis'pru:v] *v/t* refutar
dispute [dis'pju:t] *s* disputa *f*; *v/t*, *v/i* disputar
disqualif|ication [disˌkwɔlifi'keiʃən] desqualificação *f*; **~y** [-'--fai] *v/t* desqualificar, desclassificar
disquiet [dis'kwaiət] *v/t* inquietar; *s* inquietude *f*
disregard ['disri'gɑ:d] *s* descuido *m*, negligência *f*; *v/t* desdenhar; desatender, ignorar
disreput|able [dis'repjutəbl] desonroso, desacreditado; **~e** ['-ri'pju:t] descrédito *m*, má reputação *f*
disrespectful [ˌdisris'pektful] desrespeitoso, irreverente
dissatisf|action ['disætis'fækʃən] descontentamento *m*; **~ied** ['-'sætisfaid] descontente
dissect [di'sekt] *v/t* dissecar; **~ion** dissecação *f*
dissension [di'senʃən] dissensão *f*
dissent [di'sent] *s* dissentimento *m*, dissidência *f*; *v/i* dissentir, divergir; **~ing** dissidente
dissimilar ['di'similə] dissimilar; dissemelhante
dissipat|e ['disipeit] *v/t*, *v/i* dissipar(-se); **~ion** dissipação *f*
dissociate [di'səuʃieit] *v/t* dissociar
dissolut|e ['disəlu:t] dissoluto; **~ion** dissolução *f*
dissolve [di'zɔlv] *v/t*, *v/i* dissolver(-se)
dissua|de [di'sweid] *v/t* dissuadir; **~sive** dissuasivo
distance ['distəns] *s* distância *f*; **at a ~** à distância, de longe; **in the ~** ao longe
distant ['distənt] distante
distaste ['dis'teist] aversão *f*, desgosto *m*
distend [dis'tend] *v/t*, *v/i* distender(-se)
distiller [dis'tilər] destilador *m*; **~y** (*pl* **-ries**) destilaria *f*
distinct [dis'tiŋkt] claro, distinto; **~ion** distinção *f*; **~ive** distintivo
distinguish [dis'tiŋgwiʃ] *v/t*, *v/i* distinguir(-se); discernir; **~ed** *adj* distinto, notável
distort [dis'tɔ:t] *v/t* deformar, deturpar; (dis)torcer; **~ion** deformação *f*, distorção *f*
distract [dis'trækt] *v/t* distrair; perturbar; **~ed** adj distraído; perturbado; **~ion** distra(c)ção

f; perturbação *f*
distress [dis'tres] *s* aflição *f*, pesar *m*; *v/t* afligir, desolar; **~ing** aflitivo
distribut|e [dis'tribju(:)t] *v/t* distribuir, repartir; **~ion** [-bju:ʃən] distribuição *f*; **~or** distribuidor *m*
district ['distrikt] distrito *m*; comarca *f*
distrust [dis'trʌst] *s* desconfiança *f*; *v/t* desconfiar; **~ful** desconfiado
disturb [dis'tə:b] *v/t* perturbar, incomodar, inquietar; **~ance** perturbação *f*, distúrbio *m*
disuni|on [dis'ju:njən] desunião *f*; **~te** ['-'nait] *v/t*, *v/i* desunir(-se)
disus|e ['dis'ju:s] *s* desuso *m*; **~ed** desusado
ditch [ditʃ] *s* fosso *m*, vala *f*, rego *m*
ditty ['diti] (*pl* **-ties**) cançoneta *f*
div|e [daiv] *v/i* mergulhar; *s* mergulho *m*; **~er** mergulhador *m*
diverse [dai'və:s] diverso
diversion [dai'və:ʃən] desvio *m*; diversão *f*, divertimento *m*
diversity [dai'və:siti] diversidade *f*
divert [dai'və:t] *v/t* desviar; divertir
divide [di'vaid] *v/t*, *v/i* dividir (-se)
dividend ['dividend] dividendo *m*
divin|e [di'vain] *adj* divino; *v/t*, *v/i* adivinhar; **~ity** [-'viniti] divindade *f*; teologia *f*
division [di'viʒən] divisão *f*
divorce [di'vɔ:s] *s* divórcio *m*; *v/t*, *v/i* divorciar(-se)
DIY [diai'wai] (= **do-it-yourself**) bricolage *f*, faça você mesmo
dizz|iness ['dizinis] vertigem *f*; **~y** *adj* tonto, vertiginoso
do [du:] *v/t*, *v/i* fazer; executar; cumprir; cozer, passar; bastar, ser suficiente; arranjar; **~ away with** abolir, pôr de parte; **how ~ you ~?** como está? **~ without** passar sem
docil|e ['dəusail] dócil; **~ity** [dou'siliti] docilidade *f*
dock [dɔk] *s* JUR teia *f*; doca *f*; *v/t* cortar, encurtar; *v/t*, *v/i* (**at**) entrar em doca; **~er** estivador *m*; **~yard** estaleiro *m*
doctor ['dɔktə] *s* médico *m*, doutor *m*; *v/t* medicar; **~ate** doutorado *m*
doctrine ['dɔktrin] doutrina *f*
document ['dɔkjumənt] *s* documento *m*; **~ary** *s* documentário *m*
dodge [dɔdʒ] *v/t*, *v/i* esquivar-se; *s* evasiva *f*, trapaça *f*
doe [dəu] corça *f*; gama *f*
dog [dɔg] *s* cão *m*, cachorro *m*; **~ days** canícula *f*; **~ged** pertinaz
doings ['du(:)iŋz] *s/pl* feitos *m/pl*, acontecimentos *m/pl*
dole [dəul] *s* donativo *m*, doação *f*; **go/be on the ~** receber subsídio de desemprego; **~ out** racionar, aquinhoar; **~ful** triste, sombrio

doll [dɔl] boneca *f*
dollar ['dɔlə] dólar *m*
dolphin ['dɔlfin] delfim *m*, golfinho *m*
dome [dəum] cúpula *f*
domestic [də'mestik] *adj* doméstico
domicile ['dɔmisail] *s* domicílio *m*
domin|ant ['dɔminənt] *adj* dominante; **~ate** *v/t, v/i* dominar; **~ation** [-'neiʃən] dominação *f*; **~eer** [-'niə] *v/i* tiranizar, dominar; **~eering** dominante, tirânico
donat|e [dəu'neit] *v/t, v/i* doar; **~ion** doação *f*
done [dʌn] acabado, feito; pronto, assado, cozido
donkey ['dɔŋki] burro *m*
donor ['dəunə] doador *m*
doom [du:m] *s* destino *m*; ruína *f*, morte *f*; *v/t* condenar; **♀-sday** dia *m* do Juízo Final
door [dɔ:] porta *f*; **out of ~s** fora de casa, ao ar livre
door|-keeper ['dɔ:ˌki:pə] porteiro *m*; **~way** vão *m*, soleira *f*
dope [dəup] *s fam* estupefaciente *m*; *v/t* dopar
dormant ['dɔ:mənt] latente, ina(c)tivo
dose [dəus] *s* dose *f*; *v/t* dosar
dot [dɔt] *s* ponto *m*; *v/t* pontuar, pôr pontos em; **on the ~** em ponto, pontual
dotage ['dəutidʒ] senilidade *f*, segunda infância *f*
dote [dəut] *v/t*: **~ (up)on** ser/estar doido por
double ['dʌbl] *adj* dobro, duplo; *s* sósia *m*; dobro *m*; *v/t, v/i* dobrar; duplicar; *adv* aos pares, duplicadamente; **~-click** *v/t, v/i* fazer duplo clique; **~-decker** autocarro *m* de dois pisos; **~(-bedded) room** quarto *m* de casal
doubt [daut] *v/t* duvidar; *s* dúvida *f*; **~ful** duvidoso; **~less** sem dúvida
douche [du:ʃ] chuveiro *m*, duche *m*
dough [dəu] massa *f*
dove [dʌv] *s* pombo *m*; **~cot(e)** pombal *m*; **~tail** *s* malhete *m*; *v/t, v/i* malhetar
down [daun] *adj* descendente; desanimado; baixo; *adv* em baixo, abaixo, para baixo; no chão, por terra; *prp* em baixo, por … abaixo; *s* penugem *f*, buço *m*; *v/t* abater; pousar; **~cast** cabisbaixo; baixo; **~fall** queda *f*, ruína *f*; **~-hearted** abatido, desanimado; **~hill** *adv* pela encosta abaixo; em declínio; **~load** *s* COMP download *m*; *v/t* COMP fazer download; **~pour** aguaceiro *m*, carga *f* de água; **~right** *adv* completamente; *adj* direito, dire(c)to; completo; **~stairs** *adv* lá em baixo; para baixo; *s* rés-do-chão *m*; *adj* de baixo; **~stream** rio abaixo; **~ward(s)** para baixo
dowry ['dauəri] (*pl* **-ries**) dote *m*
doze [dəuz] *s* soneca *f*; *v/i* dor-

mitar

dozen ['dʌzn] dúzia *f*

drab [dræb] *adj* monótono

draft [drɑːft] *s* esboço *m*, rascunho *m*; *v/t* esboçar, rascunhar; **~sman** desenhador *m*

drag [dræg] *s* draga *f*; *v/t*, *v/i* arrastar(-se); dragar

dragon ['drægən] dragão *m*; **~-fly** libelinha *f*, libélula *f*

drain [drein] *v/t*, *v/i* drenar; escoar(-se), escorrer; *s* escoadoiro *m*, dreno *m*; **~age** drenagem *f*, escoamento *m*

drama ['drɑːma] drama *m*; **~tic** [drə'mætik] dramático; **~tist** ['dræmətist] dramaturgo *m*

draper ['dreipə] negociante *m* de panos

draught [drɑːft] = *US* **draft** corrente *f* de ar; NAUT calado *m*; trago *m*, gole *m*; **~s** damas *f/pl*; **~sman** desenhador *m*; **~y** cheio de correntes de ar

draw [drɔː] *s* empate *m*; extra(c)ção *f*; tiragem *f*; atra(c)ção *f*; *v/t*, *v/i* atrair; empatar; levantar; puxar; tirar; extrair; estirar; traçar, desenhar; **~ the curtain** correr a cortina; **~ away** afastar(-se); **~back** *s* desvantagem *f*, inconveniente *m*; **~bridge** ponte *f* levadiça

drawer [drɔːə] gaveta *f*

drawing [drɔːiŋ] desenho *m*

dread [dred] *s* pavor *m*; *v/t* temer, recear; **~ful** pavoroso, horrível

dream [driːm] *v/t*, *v/i* sonhar; *s* sonho *m*; **~y** sonhador

dreary ['driəri] aborrecido; triste, monótono

dredge [dredʒ] *v/t*, *v/i* dragar

dregs [dregz] *s/pl* fezes *f/pl*, sedimento *m*; escória *f*, ralé *f*

drench [drentʃ] *v/t* encharcar, ensopar

dress [dres] *s* vestido *m*; roupa *f*, indumentária *f*, traje *m*; *v/t*, *v/i* vestir(-se); **~circle** primeiro balcão *m*

dressing ['dresiŋ] curativo *m*; tempero *m*, condimento *m*; **~-gown** robe *m*, roupão *m*; **~-table** toucador *m*, *Braz* penteadeira *f*

dressmaker ['dresmeikə] costureira *f*, modista *f*

dress rehearsal ['dres,ri'həːsəl] THEAT ensaio *m* geral

drift [drift] *s* dire(c)ção *f*, rumo *m*, tendência *f*; *v/i*, *v/i* ir à deriva; amontoar(-se); flutuar

drill [dril] *s* broca *f*; semeador *m*; exercício *m*, dril *m*; brim *m*; *v/t*, *v/i* brocar; perfurar; exercitar

drink [driŋk] *v/t*, *v/i* beber; *s* bebida *f*

drip [drip] *s* gotejamento *m*, gotejar *m*; goteira *f*; *v/i* gotejar, pingar; **~ping** gordura *f* de assado

drive [draiv] *s* passeio *m* de carro; *fig* iniciativa *f*; estrada *f*, caminho *m*; impulso *m*; *v/t*, *v/i* dirigir, guiar, conduzir; impelir; levar de carro; **~ at** insinuar; **~-thru** restaurante onde se compra a comida sentado no carro

driver ['draivə] motorista *m*, condutor *m*, chofer *m*; **~'s licence** carta *f* de condução, *Braz* carta *f* de motorista
driving condução *f*; **~ school** auto-escola *f*
drizzle ['drizl] *s* chuvisco *m*; *v/i* chuviscar
droll [drəul] cómico, engraçado, divertido
droop [dru:p] *v/i* inclinar-se, descair, pender
drop [drɔp] *v/t*, *v/i* baixar; pingar; (deixar) cair; *s* gota *f*, pingo *m*; queda *f*; baixa *f*; rebuçado *m*; **~ someone a line** escrever umas linhas a alguém
drought [draut] seca *f*
drown [draun] *v/t*, *v/i* afogar (-se)
drowsy ['drauzi] amodorrado, sonolento
drug [drʌg] *s* droga *f*; *v/t* drogar (-se); **~gist** *US* droguista *m*, *f*, farmacêutico *m*; **~store** *US* farmácia *f*, drograria *f*
drum [drʌm] *s* tambor *m*; MEC cilindro *m*; *v/t*, *v/i* tamborilar; tocar tambor
drunk [drʌŋk] *adj*, *s* bêbedo *m*; **~ard** bêbedo *m*, ébrio *m*; **~enness** bebedeira *f*, embriaguez *f*
dry [drai] *adj* seco; enxuto; *v/t*, *v/i* secar(-se), enxugar; **~-clean** *v/t* limpar a seco; **~-cleaning** limpeza *f* a seco; **~-dock** doca *f* seca; **~ness** secura *f*, aridez *f*
dubious ['dju:bjəs] dúbio
duchess ['dʌtʃis] duquesa *f*
duck [dʌk] *s* pato *m*, pata *f*; brim *m*; *v/t*, *v/i* desviar(-se); esquivar(-se); abaixar-(se); **~ling** patinho *m*
ductile ['dʌktail] dúctil
due [dju:] *adj* devido; próprio, conveniente; COM vencido; *s* devido *m*; **in ~ course/time** -na devida altura, a seu tempo; **~ to** devido a
duel ['dju(:)əl] *s* duelo *m*; *v/i* (:) bater-se em duelo
duke [dju:k] duque *m*
dull [dʌl] *v/t*, *v/i* entorpecer, embotar; *adj* sombrio, carregado; embotado; tapado, obtuso; triste; escuro; **~ness** estupidez *f*; monotonia *f*; marasmo *m*
dumb [dʌm] mudo; **~found** *v/t* emudecer, confundir; **~ness** mudez *f*
dummy ['dʌmi] *s* (*pl* **-mies**) manequim *m*; pateta *m*, *f*; testa *f* de ferro; chupeta *f*
dump [dʌmp] *s* entulheira *f*, lixeira *f*; paiol *m*; *v/t*, *v/i* despejar, descarregar
dumpling ['dʌmpliŋ] pudim *m*
dunce [dʌns] estúpido *m*, ignorante *m*
dung [dʌŋ] bosta *f*; estrume *m*, esterco *m*
dungeon ['dʌndʒən] calabouço *m*, enxovia *f*
dung-hill ['dʌŋhil] monturo *m*
dupe [dju:p] *v/t* lograr, burlar; *s* joguete *m*
duplicate ['dju:plikit] *v/t* duplicar; *s*, *adj* duplicado *m*

durab|ility [ˌdjuərə'biliti] durabilidade *f*; **~le** durável
duration [djuə'reiʃən] duração *f*
during ['djuəriŋ] durante
dusk [dʌsk] crepúsculo *m*, entardecer *m*, anoitecer *m*; **~y** moreno, trigueiro; escuro, sombrio
dust [dʌst] *s* poeira *f*, pó *m*; *v/t* limpar o pó de, espanar; **~bin** caixote *m* do lixo; **~er** espanador *m*, pano *m* do pó; **~y** empoeirado, poeirento
Dutch [dʌtʃ] *adj*, *s* holandês *m*, neerlandês *m*
dutiable ['dju:tjəbl] sujeito a direitos alfandegários
dutiful ['dju:tiful] obediente, respeitador
duty ['dju:ti] (*pl* **-ties**) dever *m*; imposto *m*; direitos *m/pl* alfandegários, **be on ~** estar de serviço; **be off ~** estar de folga; **do one's ~** cumprir o seu dever; **~-free** isento de direitos
DVD [di:vi'di:] *s* DVD *m*; **~-ROM** DVD-ROM *m*
dwarf [dwɔ:f] *v/t* enfezar; *s* anão *m*
dwell [dwel] *v/i* residir; **~er** habitante *m*, *f*, residente *m*, *f*; **~ing** habitação *f*, residência *f*, domicílio *m*
dwindle ['dwindl] *v/i* definhar, diminuir
dye [dai] *s* tintura *f*, tinta; *v/t*, *v/i* tingir(-se); **~ing** tinturaria *f*; **~r** tintureiro *m*
dynam|ic [dai'næmik] dinâmico; **~ics** dinâmica *f*
dynamite ['dainəmait] dinamite *f*
dynamo ['dainəməu] dínamo *m*
dynasty ['dinəsti] (*pl* **-ties**) dinastia *f*
dysentery ['disntri] disenteria *f*
dyspepsia [dis'pepsiə] dispepsia *f*

E

each [i:tʃ] *adj* cada; *pron* cada um; **~ one** cada um; **~ other** mutuamente, um ao outro
eager ['i:gə] ávido, ansioso; impaciente; **~ness** avidez *f*, ânsia *f*
eagle ['i:gl] águia *f*; **~t** filhote *m* de águia, aguieta *f*
ear [iə] orelha *f*; ouvido *m*; BOT espiga *f*; **~drum** tímpano *m*
earl [ə:l] conde *m*
early ['ə:li] *adv* cedo; *adj* antecipado, adiantado; temporão
earn [ə:n] *v/t* ganhar; merecer
earnest ['ə:nist] *s* seriedade *f*; *adj* sincero, sério
earnings ['ə:niŋz] *s/pl* salário *m*; lucro *m*
ear-ring ['iəriŋ] brinco *m*
earth [ə:θ] *s* terra *f*; mundo *m*; solo *m*; **~enware** *adj* de barro; *s* louça *f* de barro; **~ly** terrestre,

terreno; possível; **~quake** terremoto *m*; **~worm** minhoca *f*
ease [iːz] *s* sossego *m*; facilidade *f*; bem-estar *m*; *v/t, v/i* aliviar, afrouxar; facilitar; **at ~** à vontade; **stand at ~** MIL descansar
easel ['iːzl] cavalete *m*
east [iːst] *s* este *m*, oriente *m*; *adj* oriental, de leste; **~ward(s)** a leste, para o leste
Easter ['iːstə] Páscoa *f*
eastern ['iːstən] oriental
easy ['iːzi] *adj* fácil; agradável; tranquilo; **take it ~!** calma!, não se incomode!
easy chair ['iːzi'tʃɛə] poltrona *f*
eat [iːt] *v/t, v/i* comer; **~ away** corroer; **~ up** devorar; acabar de comer, comer tudo; **~able** *adj* comestível
eatables ['iːtəblz] *s/pl* comestíveis *m/pl*
eating-house ['iːtiŋhaus] casa *f* de pasto
eaves [iːvz] *s/pl* beiral *m*, goteira *f*
ebb [eb] *s* baixa-mar *f*, vazante *f*; refluxo *m*; *v/i* baixar, vazar; **~ and flow** fluxo *m* e refluxo *m*
ebony ['ebəni] *s* ébano *m*; *adj* de ébano
e-book ['iːbuk] *s* livro *m* electrónico
eccentric [ik'sentrik] excêntrico; **~ity** [-'trisiti] excentricidade *f*
ecclesiastical [iˌkliːzi'æstikəl] eclesiástico
echo ['ekəu] *s* eco *m*; *v/t, v/i* ecoar
eclipse [i'klips] *s* eclipse *m*; *v/t* eclipsar; **~ of the moon** eclipse *m* da lua
econom|ic [ˌiːkə'nɔmik] económico; **~ical** económico, poupado; **~ics** economia *f*
econom|ist [i'kɔnəmist] economista *m*; **~ize** *v/i* economizar; **~y** (*pl* **-mies**) economia *f*, frugalidade *f*
ecstasy ['ekstəsi] (*pl* **-sies**) êxtase *m*; arrebatamento *m*
eddy ['edi] (*pl* **-dies**) *s* re(de-)moinho *m*; *v/i* redemoinhar
edge [edʒ] *s* borda *f*, margem *f*; *v/t* aguçar; deslocar
edge|ways ['edʒweiz], **~wise** de lado
edifice ['edifis] edifício *m*, prédio *m*
edify ['edifai] *v/t* edificar
edit ['edit] *v/t* editar; **~ out** eliminar, suprimir; **~ion** [i'diʃən] edição *f*
editor ['editə] editor *m*; reda(c)tor *m*; **~ial** [ˌ-'tɔːriəl] *s* artigo *m* de fundo; *adj* editorial
educat|e ['edju(ː)keit] *v/t* educar, instruir; **~ion** [-'keiʃən] educação *f*, instrução *f*
eel [iːl] enguia *f*
efface [i'feis] *v/t* apagar
effect [i'fekt] *v/t* efe(c)tuar; *s* efeito *m*, resultado *m*; **come into ~** entrar en vigor; **in ~** com efeito; **~ive** efe(c)tivo
effeminate [i'femineit] efeminado
effervescent [ˌefə'vesnt] efer-

vescente

efficien|cy [i'fiʃənsi] eficiência *f*, eficácia *f*; **~t** eficiente, eficaz

effort ['efət] esforço *m*

effus|ion [i'fju:ʒen] efusão *f*; **~ive** efusivo

e.g. ['i:'dʒi:] = **exempli gratia** por exemplo

egg [eg] *s* ovo *m*; **fried ~** ovo estrelado; **hard-boiled ~** ovo cozido; **soft-boiled ~** ovo meio cozido; **~-plant** berinjela *f*; **~shell** casca *f* de ovo

egotism ['egəutizəm] egoísmo *m*

Egyptian [i'dʒipʃən] *adj*, *s* egípcio *m*

eider-down ['aidədaun] edredão *m*

eight [eit] oito; **~een** dezoito; **~h** [-θ] oitavo; **~ hundred** oitocentos; **~y** oitenta

either ['aiðə] *adj*, *pron* um ou outro; um dos dois; ambos; *conj* ou; também não, tão-pouco; **~ … or** ou … ou, quer … quer

ejaculate [i'dʒækjuleit] *v/t* ejacular

eject [i(:)'dʒekt] *v/t* lançar, expulsar, eje(c)tar

eke [i:k] **out** *v/t* remediar, suprir

elaborate [i'læbərit] *adj* elaborado; [-bəreit] *v/t* elaborar

elapse [i'læps] *v/i* passar, decorrer

elasti|c [i'læstik] *s*, *adj* elástico *m*; **~city** [-'tisiti] elasticidade *f*

elated [i'leitid] *adj* inchado, orgulhoso

elbow ['elbəu] *s* cotovelo *m*; *v/t* acotovelar; **give somebody the ~** *fig* mandar alguém passear

elder ['eldə] *adj* mais velho, mais idoso; *s* BOT sabugueiro *m*; ancião *m*; primogénito *m*

eldest ['eldist] *adj*, *s* o mais velho

elect [i'lekt] *adj* eleito, escolhido; *v/t* eleger; **~ion** eleição *f*; **~or** eleitor *m*; **~oral** eleitoral; **~orate** eleitorado *m*

electri|c [i'lektrik] elé(c)trico; **~cal** elé(c)trico; **~cian** [-'triʃən] ele(c)tricista *m*; **~city** [-'trisiti] ele(c)tricidade *f*; **~fy** [-fai] *v/t* ele(c)trificar

electrocut|e [i'lektrəkju:t] *v/t* ele(c)trocutar; **~ion** ele(c)trocução *f*

electron [i'lektrɔn] ele(c)trão *m*; **~ic** ele(c)trónico

elegan|ce ['eligəns] elegância *f*; **~t** elegante

element ['elimənt] elemento *m*; **~ary** [ˌ-'mentəri] elementar

elephant ['elifənt] elefante *m*

elevat|e ['eliveit] *v/t* elevar; exaltar; **~ion** elevação *f*; altura *f*; **~or** elevador *m*, ascensor *m*

eleven [i'levn] onze; **at the ~th hour** no último momento, à última hora

elf [elf] (*pl* **elves**) duende *m*

eligible ['elidʒəbl] elegível

eliminat|e [i'limineit] *v/t* eliminar; **~ion** [-'neiʃən] eliminação *f*

elk [elk] alce *m*

elm [elm] olmo *m*
elocution [ˌelə'kjuːʃən] elocução *f*
elongate ['iːlɔŋgeit] *v/t, v/i* alongar(-se)
elope [i'ləup] *v/i* fugir de casa com amante ou namorado
eloquen|ce ['eləkwəns] eloquência *f*; **~t** eloquente
else [els] *adv* mais; **anybody ~?** mais alguém?; **anything ~?** mais alguma coisa?; **nobody ~** mais ninguém; **nothing ~** nada mais; **or ~** ou então, quando não; **somebody ~** alguém mais; **what ~?** que mais? **who ~?** quem mais?
elsewhere ['els'wɛə] noutro lugar, noutro lado
elu|de [i'luːd] *v/t* eludir, evitar; escapar; **~sive** esquivo, elusivo
emaciate [i'meiʃieit] *v/t* emaciar
e-mail ['iːmeil] *s* e-mail *m*, correio *m* eletrônico; *v/i* enviar um e-mail a; **~ address** *s* endereço *m* de e-mail
emancipate [i'mænsipeit] *v/t* emancipar
embalm [im'bɑːm] *v/t* embalsamar
embankment [im'bæŋkmənt] represa *f*
embark [im'bɑːk] *v/t, v/i* embarcar(-se)
embarrass [im'bærəs] *v/t* embaraçar; **~ing** embaraçoso; **~ment** embaraço *m*
embassy ['embəsi] (*pl* **-sies**) embaixada *f*
embed [im'bed] *v/t* embutir
embellish [im'beliʃ] *v/t* embelecer, enfeitar
embers ['embəz] *s/pl* brasas *f/pl*
embezzle [im'bezl] *v/t* desfalcar; **~ment** desfalque *m*
embitter [im'bitə] *v/t* amargurar
emblem ['embləm] emblema *m*
embod|iment [im'bɔdimənt] incorporação *f*; **~y** *v/t* incorporar; encarnar
embolden [im'bəuldən] *v/t* encorajar, animar
embrace [im'breis] *v/t, v/i* abraçar(-se); abranger; *s* abraço *m*
embroider [im'brɔidə] *v/t* bordar; **~y** bordado *m*
emerald ['emərəld] *s* esmeralda *f*
emerg|e [i'məːdʒ] *v/i* emergir, aparecer; **~ency** [i'məːdʒənsi] (*pl* **-cies**) emergência *f*
emetic [i'metik] *adj* emético
emigra|nt ['emigrənt] emigrante; **~te** ['-greit] *v/i* emigrar; **~tion** emigração *f*
eminen|ce ['eminəns] eminência *f*; **~t** eminente
emissary ['emisəri] (*pl* **-ries**) emissário *m*
emit [i'mit] *v/t* emitir
emotion [i'məuʃən] emoção *f*; **~al** emocional
emperor ['empərə] imperador *m*
empha|sis ['emfəsis] ênfase *f*; **~size** *v/t* dar ênfase a, acentuar; **~tic** [im'fætik] enfático

empire ['empaiə] império *m*
employ [im'plɔi] *v/t* empregar; **~ee** [ˌemplɔi'iː] empregado *m*; **~er** patrão *m*, *Braz* empregador *m*; **~ment** emprego *m*
empress ['empris] imperatriz *f*
emp|tiness ['emptinis] vazio *m*, vácuo *m*; **~ty** *adj* vazio; *v/t*, *v/i* esvaziar(-se)
enable [i'neibl] *v/t* habilitar, capacitar
enact [i'nækt] *v/t* decretar, promulgar; desempenhar
enamel [i'næməl] *s* esmalte *m*; *v/t* esmaltar
enamo(u)red [i'næməd] *adj* enamorado
encase [in'keis] *v/t* encaixar
enchain [in'tʃein] *v/t* encadear, acorrentar
enchant [in'tʃɑːnt] *v/t* encantar; enfeitiçar; **~ing** encantador; **~ment** feitiço *m*, encanto *m*; **~ress** feiticeira *f*
encircle [in'səːkl] *v/t* cercar, rodear
enclos|e [in'kləuz] *v/t* cercar, murar; juntar, incluir; **~ure** [-ʒə] cerca *f*; anexo *m*; clausura *f*
encore [ɔŋ'kɔː] *int* bis!; *v/t* bisar; *s* bis *m*
encounter [in'kauntə] *v/t* encontrar; *s* encontro *m*, recontro *m*
encourage [in'kʌridʒ] *v/t* encorajar, animar; **~ment** encorajamento *m*
encroach [in'krəutʃ]: **~ on** *v/i* invadir, usurpar; avançar
encrust [in'krʌst] *v/t* incrustar
encumb|er [in'kʌmbə] *v/t* estorvar, embaraçar; **~rance** estorvo *m*, empecilho *m*
end [end] *s* fim *m*; cabo *m*, extremidade *f*; termo *m*; *v/t*, *v/i* acabar, terminar, concluir; **in the ~** afinal; no fim de contas; **no ~ of** muito; **on ~ sem** fim; **put an ~ to** pôr termo a
endanger [in'deindʒə] *v/t* pôr em perigo, arriscar
endear [in'diə] (**to**) *v/t* encarecer, fazer estimar; **~ment** meiguice *f*, ternura *f*
endeavo(u)r [in'devə] *s* esforço *m*, empenho *m*; *v/i* esforçar-se, tentar
ending ['endiŋ] *s* fim *m*, conclusão *f*
endless ['endlis] sem fim, infinito, interminável
endorse [in'dɔːs] *v/t* endossar; **~ment** endosso *m*
endow [in'dau] *v/t* dotar, doar; **~ment** doação *f*; dote *m*
endur|able [in'djuərəbl] suportável, tolerável; **~ance** resistência *f*; **~e** *v/t* aguentar, suportar, tolerar
enemy ['enimi] (*pl* **-mies**) inimigo *m*
energ|etic [ˌenə'dʒetik] enérgico; **~y** ['-dʒi] (*pl* **-gies**) energia *f*
enervate ['enəːveit] *v/t* debilitar, enfraquecer
enfeeble [in'fiːbl] *v/t* enfraquecer
enfold [in'fəuld] *v/t* envolver,

abraçar

enforce [in'fɔːs] *v/t* forçar, obrigar, compelir; fazer cumprir

enfranchise [in'fræntʃaiz] *v/t* franquear, dar o direito de votar

engage [in'geidʒ] *v/t, v/i* ocupar(se); engatar; contratar, empregar; **~d** ocupado; engatado; impedido; noivo; **~ment** noivado *m*;

engine ['endʒin] motor *m*; locomotiva *f*

engineer [ˌendʒi'niə] *s* engenheiro *m*; mecânico *m*; maquinista *m*; *v/t* engendrar; construir; **~ing** *s* engenharia *f*

English ['iŋgliʃ] *adj, s* inglês *m*; **~man** (*pl* **-men**) inglês *m*

engrav|e [in'greiv] *v/t* gravar; **~er** gravador *m*; **~ing** *s* gravação *f*; gravura *f*

engross [in'grəus] *v/t* absorver, ocupar; tirar pública-forma

enhance [in'hɑːns] *v/t* encarecer; realçar

enigma [i'nigmə] enigma *m*; **~tic** [ˌenig'mætik] enigmático

enjoy [in'dʒɔi] *v/t* gozar (de), desfrutar, apreciar, ter prazer em; **~ oneself** divertir-se; **~able** agradável, divertido; **~ment** gozo *m*, prazer *m*

enlarge [in'lɑːdʒ] *v/t, v/i* aumentar; alargar(-se); dilatar; ampliar; **~ment** aumento *m*; ampliação *f*

enlighten [in'laitn] *v/t* esclarecer

enlist [in'list] *v/t, v/i* alistar(-se)

enliven [in'laivn] *v/t* animar

enmity ['enmiti] inimizade *f*

enorm|ity [i'nɔːmiti] enormidade *f*; **~ous** enorme

enough [i'nʌf] *adj* bastante; *adv* suficientemente; bastante

enrage [in'reidʒ] *v/t* enraivecer

enrapture [in'ræptʃə] *v/t* encantar, arrebatar

enrich [in'ritʃ] *v/t* enriquecer

enrol(l) [in'rəul] *v/t, v/i* alistar-se; matricular(-se); inscrever (-se)

ensign ['ensain] pavilhão *m*, bandeira *f*

enslave [in'sleiv] *v/t* escravizar

ensue [in'sjuː] *v/i* seguir(-se)

ensure [in'ʃuə] *v/t* assegurar

entangle [in'tæŋgl] *v/t* emaranhar

enter ['entə] *v/t, v/i* entrar (em, para); dar entrada (em)

enterprise ['entəpraiz] empresa *f*; espírito *m* empreendedor; empreendimento *m*

entertain [ˌentə'tein] *v/t, v/i* receber, hospedar; divertir, entreter; **~ing** *adj* divertido; **~ment** entretenimento *m*, diversão *f*; hospedagem *f*

enthusias|m [in'θjuːziæzəm] entusiasmo *m*; **~t** [-æst] entusiasta *m, f*; **~tic** [-'æstik] entusiástico, entusiasmado

entic|e [in'tais] *v/t* atrair, seduzir, tentar; **~ing** *adj* sedutor, tentador

entire [in'taiə] completo, inteiro

entitle [in'taitl] *v/t* intitular; dar

direito a
entrails ['entreilz] *s/pl* entranhas *f/pl*, tripas *f/pl*
entrance [in'trɑːns] *v/t* extasiar, arrebatar; ['entrəns] *s* entrada *f*; admissão *f*, ingresso *m*; **~ fee** jóia *f*
entreat [in'triːt] *v/t*, *v/i* suplicar
entrust [in'trʌst] *v/t* confiar
entry ['entri] (*pl* **-ries**) entrada *f*; acesso *m*; lançamento *m*, registo *m*; inscrição *f*
enumerate [i'njuːməreit] *v/t* enumerar
envelop [in'veləp] *v/t* envolver; **~e** ['envələup] envelope *m*, sobrescrito *m*
envi|able ['enviəbl] invejável; **~ous** invejoso
environment [in'vaiərənmənt] meio *m*, ambiente *m*; **~ally friendly** *adj* amigo de ambiente
envoy ['envɔi] enviado *m*
envy ['envi] *v/t* invejar; *s* inveja *f*
epidemic [ˌepi'demik] *s* epidemia *f*; *adj* epidémico
epilepsy ['epilepsi] epilepsia *f*
episode ['episəud] episódio *m*
epitaph ['epitɑːf] epitáfio *m*
epoch ['iːpɔk] época *f*
equal ['iːkwəl] *adj* igual; *v/t* igualar; *s* igual *m*, *f*, par *m*; **~ to the occasion** à altura das circunstâncias; **~ity** [i(ː)'kwɔliti] igualdade *f*
equanimity [ˌekwə'nimiti] equanimidade *f*
equation [i'kweiʒən] equação *f*
equator [i'kweitə] equador *m*
equilibrium [ˌiːkwi'libriəm] equilíbrio *m*
equip [i'kwip] *v/t* equipar, aprestar; **~ment** equipamento *m*
equitable ['ekwitəbl] equitativo
equivalent [i'kwivələnt] *adj*, *s* equivalente *m*
equivoca|l [i'kwivəkəl] equívoco; **~te** [-keit] *v/i* equivocar-se
era ['iərə] era *f*
eras|e [i'reiz] *v/t* apagar, safar; **~er** *US* borracha *f*
erect [i'rekt] *adj* levantado, ere(c)to; *v/t* erigir
erection [i'rekʃən] ere(c)ção *f*; montagem *f*
ermine ['əːmin] arminho *m*
err [əː] *v/i* errar
errand ['erənd] recado *m*, mandado *m*
erratic [i'rætik] errático; irregular
error ['erə] erro *m*
eruption [i'rʌpʃən] erupção *f*
erysipelas [ˌeri'sipiləs] erisipela *f*
escalator ['eskəleitə] escada *f* rolante
escape [is'keip] *v/t*, *v/i* escapar (-se); *s* fuga *f*, evasão *f*; escape *m*
escort ['eskɔːt] *s* escolta *f*; [is'kɔːt] *v/t* escoltar
espionage [ˌespiə'nɑːʒ] espionagem *f*
Esquire (**Esq.**) [is'kwaiə] Exmo. Sr.
essay ['esei] *s* ensaio *m*; **~ist** en-

saísta *m*
essence ['esns] essência *f*
essential [i'senʃəl] essencial
establish [is'tæbliʃ] *v/t* estabelecer; instalar; **~ment** estabelecimento *m*; instalação *f*
estate [is'teit] bens *m/pl*, propriedade *f*; quinta *f*, fazenda *f*
esteem [is'ti:m] *s* estima *f*; *v/t* estimar
estima|ble ['estiməbl] estimável; **~te** ['-meit] *s* estimativa *f*, avaliação *f*; *v/t* avaliar; **~tion** avaliação *f*
estrange [is'treindʒ] *v/t* apartar, alienar
etch [etʃ] *v/t* gravar com água forte
etern|al [i'tə:nl] eterno; **~ity** (*pl* **-ties**) eternidade *f*
ether ['i:θə] éter *m*
ethics ['eθiks] ética *f*
European [ˌjuərə'piən] *adj*, *s* europeu *m*
evacuate [i'vækjueit] *v/t* evacuar
evade [i'veid] *v/t* evitar, evadir (-se)
evaporat|e [i'væpəreit] *v/t*, *v/i* evaporar(-se); **~ion** evaporação *f*
evasive [i'veisiv] evasivo
eve [i:v] vigília *f*, véspera *f*; **on the ~ of** na véspera de
even ['i:vən] *adj* plano; regular; uniforme, par; empatado; *adv* mesmo, até, ainda; **be/get ~ with** estar/ficar quite com; **~ if / ~ though** mesmo que, ainda que; **~ so/then** mesmo assim/então; **not ~** nem sequer
evening ['i:vniŋ] noitinha *f*, tarde *f*, tardinha *f*; **~ dress** traje *m* de cerimónia
event [i'vent] acontecimento *m*, evento *m*; **at all ~s** em todo o caso, seja como for
eventful [i'ventful] acidentado, cheio de acontecimentos, memorável
eventual|ity [iˌventju'æliti] (*pl* **-ties**) eventualidade *f*; **~ly** [i'ventjuəli] com o tempo, finalmente
ever ['evə] sempre; já, alguma vez; **~ since** desde então; **for ~** para sempre; **for ~ and ~** para todo o sempre; **hardly ~** quase nunca
every ['evri] todo, cada; **~ now and then** de quando em quando; **~ other day** dia sim, dia não; **~body**, **~one** toda a gente, *Braz* todo o mundo; todos; **~thing** tudo; **~where** por/em toda a parte
eviden|ce ['evidəns] *s* evidência *f*; prova *f*, testemunho *m*; **give ~ce** dar testemunho; **~t** evidente
evil ['i:vl] *adj* mau, malvado; *s* mal *m*, pecado *m*; **~-doer** malfeitor *m*
evince [i'vins] *v/t* evidenciar, demonstrar
evoke [i'vəuk] *v/t* evocar
evolution [ˌi:və'lu:ʃən] evolução *f*
ewe ['ju:] ovelha *f*
exact [ig'zækt] *v/t* exigir; extor-

quir; *adj* exa(c)to, preciso; **~itude**, **~ness** exa(c)tidão *f*
exaggerat|e [ig'zædʒəreit] *v/t*, *v/i* exagerar; **~ion** exagero *m*
exaltation [ˌegzɔːl'teiʃən] exaltação *f*
examin|ation [igˌzæmi'neiʃən] exame *m*; examinação *f*; **~e** [-'zæmin] v/t examinar; **~er** examinador *m*
example [ig'zɑːmpl] exemplo *m*; **for ~** por exemplo
exasperate [ig'zɑːspəreit] *v/t* exasperar
excavate ['ekskəveit] *v/t* escavar
excavation [ˌekskə'veiʃən] escavação *f*
exceed [ik'siːd] *v/t* exceder; **~ingly** excessivamente, extremamente
excel|lence ['eksələns] excelência *f*; **2lency** Excelência *f*; **~lent** excelente
except [ik'sept] *v/t* exce(p)tuar; *prp* exe(p)to, salvo; **~ for** se não fosse; exce(p)tuando; **~ing** *prp* exce(p)to; **~ion** exce(p)ção *f*; **~ional** excepcional
excess [ik'ses] *s* excesso *m*; **~ive** excessivo
exchange [iks'tʃeindʒ] *s* troca *f*; câmbio *m*; Bolsa *f*; central *f* telefónica; *v/t* trocar, cambiar
exchequer [iks'tʃekə] tesouro *m* público
excitable [ik'saitəbl] excitável
excite [ik'sait] *v/t* excitar; **~ment** excitação *f*
exciting [ik'saitiŋ] *adj* excitante
exclaim [iks'kleim] *v/t*, *v/i* exclamar
exclamation [ˌeksklə'meiʃən] exclamação *f*; **~ mark**, *US* **~ point** ponto *m* de exclamação
exclu|de [iks'kluːd] *v/t* excluir; **~sion** [-ʒen] exclusão *f*; **~sive** [-siv] exclusivo
excruciating [iks'kruːʃieitiŋ] (ex)cruciante
excursion [iks'kəːʃən] excursão *f*; **~ist** excursionista *m*, *f*
excusable [iks'kjuːzəbl] desculpável
excuse [iks'kjuːz] *v/t* desculpar; dispensar; [-'kjuːs] *s* desculpa *f*; dispensa *f*; escusa *f*
execut|e ['eksikjuːt] *v/t* executar; **~ion** [-'kjuːʃən] execução *f*; desempenho *m*; **~ioner** carrasco *m*, executor *m*; **~ive** [ig'zekjutiv] *adj*, *s* executivo *m*; **~or** testamenteiro *m*
exempl|ary [ig'zempləri] exemplar; **~ify** [-plifai] *v/t* exemplificar
exempt [ig'zempt] *v/t* isentar, dispensar; *adj* isento, livre; **~ion** isenção *f*, dispensa *f*
exercise ['eksəsaiz] *s* exercício *m*; *v/t*, *v/i* exercitar(-se)
exert [ig'zəːt] *v/t* exercer; **~ oneself** esforçar-se, empenhar-se; **~ion** esforço *m*
exhalation [ˌekshə'leiʃən] exalação *f*
exhaust [ig'zɔːst] *v/t* exaurir, esgotar; *s* escape *m*, descarga *f*; **~ion** [-tʃən] exaustão *f*, esgotamento *m*; **~ive** exaustivo,

completo
exhibit [ig'zibit] *s* exibição *f*; *v/t, v/i* exibir, expor; **~ion** [-'biʃən] exposição *f*
exhilarate [ig'zilәreit] *v/t* alegrar, hilarizar
exhumation [ˌekshju:'meiʃən] exumação *f*
exile ['eksail] *s* exílio *m*, desterro *m*; exilado *m*, desterrado *m*; *v/t* exilar, desterrar
exist [ig'zist] *v/i* existir; **~ence** existência *f*; **~ent, ~ing** existente; a(c)tual
exit ['eksit] *s* saída *f*
exorbit|ance [ig'zɔ:bitəns] exorbitância *f*; **~ant** exorbitante
exotic [ig'zɔtik] exótico
expan|d [iks'pænd] *v/t, v/i* expandir(-se), dilatar(-se); **~sion** expansão *f*; **~sive** expansivo
expect [iks'pekt] *v/t* esperar, aguardar; contar com; supor; **~ant** esperançoso; **~ation** [ˌekspek'teiʃən] expectativa *f*
expedi|ency [iks'pi:djənsi] expediente *m*; **~ent** *s* expediente *m*; *adj* conveniente, oportuno; **~tion** [ˌekspi'diʃən] expedição *f*
expel [iks'pel] v/t expelir, expulsar
expen|d [iks'pend] *v/t* despender, gastar; **~diture** [-ditʃə] gasto *m*, despesa *f*; **~se** [-s] despesa *f*; *custo m*; **~sive** dispendioso, caro
experienc|e [iks'piəriəns] *s* experiência *f*; *v/t* experimentar; **~ed** [-t] experimentado, experiente
experiment [iks'perimənt] *s* experimento *m*, experiência *f*; *v/t* experimentar, ensaiar
expert ['ekspə:t] *adj* conhecedor, perito, experto; *s* perito *m*, técnico *m*, especialista *m, f*
expiration [ˌekspaiə'reiʃən] expiração *f*
expire [iks'paiə] *v/i* expirar; COM vencer
explain [iks'plein] *v/t, v/i* explicar(-se)
explanat|ion [ˌeksplə'neiʃən] explicação *f*; **~ory** [iks'plænətəri] explicativo
explicable ['eksplikəbl] explicável
explicit [iks'plisit] explícito; **~ness** clareza *f*
explode [iks'pləud] *v/t, v/i* explodir
exploit [iks'plɔit] *v/t* explorar; ['eksplɔit] *s* façanha *f*, proeza *f*
explor|ation [ˌeksplə'reiʃən] exploração *f*; **~e** [iks'plɔ:] *v/t* explorar; **~er** explorador *m*
explosi|on [iks'pləuʒən] explosão *f*; **~ve** [-siv] *s, adj* explosivo *m*
export [eks'pɔ:t] *v/t* exportar; *s* ['ekspɔ:t] exportação *f*; **~ation** [-'teiʃən] exportação *f*
expose [iks'pəuz] *v/t* expor
exposition [ˌekspə'ziʃən] exposição *f*
exposure [iks'pəuʒə] exposição *f*, orientação *f*; revelação

f; escândalo *m*

expound [iks'paund] *v/t* expor, explicar

express [iks'pres] *v/t* exprimir, expressar; mandar por expresso; *adj* expresso; explícito; rápido; *s* expresso *m*; **~ion** [-ʃən] expressão *f*; **~ive** expressivo

expropriate [eks'prəuprieit] *v/t* expropriar

expulsion [iks'pʌlʃən] expulsão *f*

exquisite ['ekskwizit] requintado, delicado, esquisito

extant [eks'tænt] existente

extend [iks'tend] *v/t*, *v/i* estender(-se)

extens|ion [iks'tenʃən] extensão *f*; prorrogação *f*; **~ive** extenso; extensivo

extent [iks'tent] extensão *f*, tamanho *m*; **to a certain ~** até certo ponto; **to a great ~** em grande parte

extenuat|e [eks'tenjueit] *v/t* atenuar; **~ing** *adj* atenuante; **~ion** atenuação *f*

exterior [eks'tiəriə] *adj*, *s* exterior *m*

exterminate [ikз'tə:mineit] *v/t* exterminar

external [eks'tə:nl] externo; exterior

extinct [iks'tiŋkt] extinto

extinguish [iks'tiŋgwiʃ] *v/t* extinguir; destruir; **~er** extintor *m*

extirpate ['ekstə:peit] *v/t* extirpar

extort [iks'tɔ:t] *v/t* **~ from** extorquir; **~ion** [-ʃən] extorsão *f*

extra ['ekstrə] *adj* extra, suplementar; *adv* extra(ordinariamente); *s* extra *m*; figurante *m*, *f*

extract [iks'trækt] *v/t* extrair; ['ekstrækt] *s* extra(c)to *m*; essência *f*; **~ion** extra(c)ção *f*

extraneous [eks'treinjəs] extrínseco

extraordinary [iks'trɔ:dnri] extraordinário

extravagan|ce [iks'trævigəns] extravagância *f*; **~t** extravagante; pródigo; excessivo

extrem|e [iks'tri:m] *adj*, *s* extremo *m*; **~ist** extremista *m*, *f*; **~ity** [-'tremiti] (*pl* **-ties**) extremidade *f*; medida *f* extrema

extricate ['ekstrikeit] *v/t* desembaraçar, desenredar, livrar

exuberan|ce [ig'zju:bərəns] exuberância *f*; **~t** exuberante

exude [ig'zju:d] *v/t*, *v/i* transpirar; emanar

exult [ig'zʌlt] *v/i* exultar, triunfar; **~ation** [ˌegzʌl'teiʃən] exultação *f*

eye [ai] *s* olho *m*; *v/t* olhar, contemplar; **~ball** globo *m* ocular; **~brow** sobrancelha *f*; **~-glass** monóculo *m*; **~lash** pestana *f*; **~let** ilhó *m*; **~lid** pálpebra *f*; **~sight** vista *f*; visão *f*; **~witness** testemunha *f* ocular

F

fable ['feibl] fábula *f*

fabric ['fæbrik] tecido *m*; estrutura *f*; **~ate** ['-keit] *v/t* fabricar

fabulous ['fæbjuləs] fabuloso

face [feis] *s* face *f*, rosto *m*, cara *f*; *v/t* encarar; enfrentar; **~ to ~** cara a cara, frente a frente; **make/pull a ~** fazer caretas

facetious [fə'si:ʃəs] chistoso, faceto

facile ['fæsail] fácil; ágil

facili|tate [fə'siliteit] *v/t* facilitar

facili|ties [fə'silitiz] *s/pl* vantagens *f/pl*; **~ty** facilidade *f*

facing ['feisiŋ] *s* adorno *m*, revestimento *m*

fact [fækt] fa(c)to *m*; realidade *f*; **in ~** de fa(c)to

faction ['fækʃən] facção *f*

factious ['fækʃəs] faccioso

factitious [fæk'tiʃəs] factício

factor ['fæktə] fa(c)tor *m*

factory ['fæktəri] (*pl* **-ries**) fábrica *f*

faculty ['fækəlti] (*pl* **-ties**) faculdade *f*; aptidão *f*

fade [feid] *v/t*, *v/i* murchar; **~ away** desvanecer-se

fag [fæg] *v/i* esfalfar-se, mourejar; *s* maçada *f*; cigarro *m*

fa(g)got ['fægət] feixe *m*

fail [feil] *v/t*, *v/i* falhar; falir; faltar; fracassar; **~ an exam(ination)** reprovar num exame

failure ['feiljə] falência *f*; falha *f*; fracasso *m*

faint [feint] *adj* fraco; tímido; débil; indistinto; *s* desmaio *m*; *v/i* desmaiar

fair [fɛə] *adj* leal, honesto, justo; loiro; lindo; mediano; *s* feira *f*; *adv* em cheio; com lealdade

fairly ['fɛəli] bastante; justamente

fairness ['fɛənis] honradez *f*; probidade *f*

fairy ['fɛəri] (*pl* **-ries**) fada *f*

faith [feiθ] fé *f*; **in good ~** de boa fé; **~ful** leal; fiel, crente; **~fulness** lealdade *f*, fidelidade *f*

fake [feik] *s* fraude *f*, patranha *f*; imitação *f*; *v/t* falsificar

falcon ['fɔ:lkən] falcão *m*

fall [fɔ:l] *s* queda *f*; baixa *f*; *US* outono *m*; *v/i* cair; baixar; diminuir; **~ down** cair no chão; **~ in love** enamorar-se, apaixonar-se; **~ flat** falhar, malograr; **~ short** faltar, ser insuficiente; **~ through** fracassar

fallac|ious [fə'leiʃəs] falaz; **~y** ['fæləsi] (*pl* **-cies**) falácia *f*; sofisma *m*

fallible ['fæləbl] falível

fallow ['fæləu] *adj*, *s* (de) pousio *m*

false [fɔ:ls] *adj* falso, desleal; **~ teeth** dentes *m/pl* postiços; **~hood** falsidade *f*; mentira *f*

falsify ['fɔ:lsifai] *v/t* falsificar

falter ['fɔ:ltə] *v/t*, *v/i* vacilar; hesitar; balbuciar

fam|e [feim] fama *f*, nomeada *f*; **~ed** *adj* afamado, famoso
familiar [fə'miljə] *adj* familiar; íntimo; versado; **~ity** [-ˌmili'æriti] familiaridade *f*
family ['fæmili] (*pl* **-lies**) família *f*; linhagem *f*
famine ['fæmin] fome *f*, carestia *f*
famished ['fæmiʃt] esfaimado, esfomeado, faminto
famous ['feiməs] famoso, célebre
fan [fæn] *s* leque *m*; ventilador *m*, fã *m*; *v/t* ventilar; abanar
fanatic [fə'nætik] *s*, *adj* fanático *m*; **~ism** [-sizəm] fanatismo *m*
fanciful ['fænsiful] extravagante, caprichoso
fancy ['fænsi] (*pl* **-cies**) *s* fantasia *f*; capricho *m*; inclinação *f*, afeição *f*; *v/t* imaginar, supor; gostar de, desejar; *adj* ornado, de fantasia; imaginário; invulgar; **take/catch the ~ of** atrair, captar; **~-dress** vestido *m* de fantasia
fang [fæŋ] presa *f*
fantastic [fæn'tæstik] fantástico
fanzine [fæn'iːn] *s* fanzine *f*
far [fɑː] *adv* longe, distante; muito; *adj* distante, longínquo; **as/so ~ as** até; tanto quanto; **by ~** de longe, decididamente; **~ and wide** por toda a parte; **how ~?** até que ponto?; **so ~** até agora, até ao presente
farce [fɑːs] farsa *f*
fare [fɛə] *s* bilhete *m*, passagem *f*; comida *f*; **bill of ~** ementa *f*, *Braz* cardápio *m*
farewell ['fɛə'wel] *s* adeus *m*, despedida *f*; *int* adeus!
far-fetched ['fɑː'fetʃt] forçado; artificial; afe(c)tado
farm [fɑːm] *s* quinta *f*, herdade *f*, fazenda *f*; **~er** lavrador *m*, fazendeiro *m*; **~-house** casal *m*
far-off [ˌfɑː'ɔf] distante, longínquo
far-sighted ['fɑː'saitid] presbita; previdente
farther ['fɑːðə] *adj* mais distante; *adv* mais longe
farthest ['fɑːðist] *adj* o mais distante; *adv* o mais longe
fascinate ['fæsineit] *v/t* fascinar
fascinat|ing ['fæsineitiŋ] *adj* fascinante; **~ion** [-'neiʃən] fascinação *f*
fascism ['fæʃizəm] fascismo *m*
fascist ['fæʃist] fascista *m*, *f*
fashion ['fæʃən] *s* moda *f*; *v/t* moldar, adaptar; **out of ~** fora da moda; **in ~** na moda; **~able** à/na moda, elegante; **~ model** maneca *f*
fast [fɑːst] *v/i* jejuar; *s* jejum *m*; *adj* rápido; adiantado; firme, fixo; *adv* depressa; **~ asleep** profundamente adormecido
fasten ['fɑːsn] *v/t*, *v/i* apertar; fixar, firmar; atar, prender
fastidious [fəs'tidiəs] fastidioso
fastness ['fɑːstnis] baluarte *m*;

firmeza *f*

fat [fæt] *adj* gordo; gorduroso; *s* banha *f*, gordura *f*; **~ free** *adj* sem gordura

fatal ['feitl] fatal; **~ism** fatalismo *m*; **~ity** [fə'tæliti] (*pl* **-ties**) fatalidade *f*

fate [feit] fado *m*, sorte *f*, destino *m*; **~ful** fatídico

father ['fɑːðə] *s* pai *m*; ECCL padre *m*; antepassado *m*; **~hood** paternidade *f*; **~-in-law** sogro *m*; **~ly** paternal

fathom ['fæðəm] *s* braça *f*; *v/t* sondar; compreender

fatigue [fə'tiːg] *s* fadiga *f*

fat|ness ['fætnis] gordura *f*; **~ty** *s* gorducho *m*, gordo *m*; *adj* gordurento

fatu|ity [fə'tju(ː)iti] fatuidade *f*; **~ous** fátuo

fault [fɔːlt] *s* falta *f*, culpa *f*; defeito *m*; erro *m*; falha *f*; **~less** perfeito; **~y** defeituoso

faun [fɔːn] fauno *m*; **~a** ['fɔːnə] fauna *f*

favo(u)r ['feivə] *s* favor *m*; *v/t* favorecer; parecer-se com; **~able** favorável; **~ite** ['-vərit] predile(c)to, favorito; **~itism** favoritismo *m*

fawn [fɔːn] *s* enho *m*, corça *f*

fear [fiə] *s* receio *m*, temor *m*, medo *m*; *v/t*, *v/i* temer; **~ful** medonho; medroso; **~less** intrépido

feast [fiːst] *s* festa *f*; banquete *m*; *v/t*, *v/i* festejar, banquetear

feat [fiːt] feito *m*, proeza *f*

feather ['feðə] *s* pena *f*

feature ['fiːtʃə] *s* feição *f*, traço *m*; característica *f*; *v/t* fazer sobressair, destacar

February ['februəri] Fevereiro *m*

feder|al ['fedərəl] federal; **~ate** ['-reit] *v/t* federar; **~ation** [ˌ-'reiʃən] federação *f*

fee [fiː] salário *m*, honorários *m*/*pl*

feeble ['fiːbl] fraco, débil

feed [fiːd] *v/t*, *v/i* alimentar(-se), (dar de) comer; **~ing-bottle** biberão *m*, mamadeira *f*

feel [fiːl] *v/t*, *v/i* apalpar; sentir (-se); **~er** antena *f*; **~ing** *s* ta(c)to *m*; sensação *f*; sensibilidade *f*; sentimento *m*

feet [fiːt] *pl of* **foot**

feint [feint] *v/i* fintar

felicitations [fiˌlisi'teiʃənz] *s*/*pl* felicitações *f*/*pl*

fell [fel] *v/t* abater, derribar; *s* monte *m* baldio, colina *f* baldia

fellow ['feləu] *s* companheiro *m*; membro *m*; tipo *m*, sujeito *m*; **~-citizen** concidadão *m*; **~-feeling** simpatia *f*; **~ship** sociedade *f*, associação *f*; camaradagem *f*

felt [felt] *s* feltro *m*

female ['fiːmeil] *s* fêmea *f*; *adj* feminino

feminine ['feminin] feminino

fen [fen] pântano *m*

fenc|e [fens] *s* cerca *f*, sebe *f*; *v/t* cercar; *v/i* esgrimir; **~er** esgrimador *m*; **~ing** ['fensiŋ] *s* esgrima *f*

fend [fend]: **~ for oneself** tratar da sua vida
fender ['fendə] guarda-fogo *m*; *US* pára-choques *m*
fennel ['fenl] funcho *m*
ferment ['fə:ment] *s* fermento *m*; agitação *f*; fermentação *f*; [fə:'ment] *v/t*, *v/i* fermentar
fern [fə:n] feto *m*
ferocious [fə'rəuʃəs] feroz
ferret ['ferit] *s* furão *m*
ferry ['feri] *v/t* transportar de barco; *s* (*pl* **-ries**) travessia *f*; barco *m* de travessia
fertil|e ['fə:tail] fértil; **~ity** [-'tiliti] fertilidade *f*; **~ize** ['-tilaiz] *v/t* fertilizar; fecundar; **~izor** adubo *m*, fertilizador *m*
fervent ['fə:vənt] fervente, ardente
fervo(u)r ['fə:və] fervor *m*, ardor *m*
festiv|al ['festəvəl] festa *f*, festival *m*; **~e** festivo; **~ity** [-'tiviti] (*pl* **-ties**) festividade *f*
fetch [fetʃ] *v/t* ir buscar, trazer
fetter ['fetə] grilhão *m*; *v/t* agrilhoar
feud [fju:d] rixa *f*, contenda *f*
fever ['fi:və] febre *f*; **~ish** febril
few [fju:] *adj*, *s* poucos; **a ~** uns poucos, alguns
fiancé [fi'ɑ̃:nsei] noivo *m*; **~e** noiva *f*
fib [fib] *s* peta *f*
fibre ['faibə] fibra *f*
fickle ['fikl] inconstante; **~ness** inconstância *f*
fict|ion ['fikʃən] ficção *f*; **~itious** [-'tiʃəs] fictício
fiddle ['fidl] *s* violino *m*, rabeca *f*; *v/i* tocar violino; matar o tempo
fidelity [fi'deliti] (*pl* **-ties**) fidelidade *f*
fidgety ['fidʒiti] inquieto, nervoso
field [fi:ld] *s* campo *m*; *v/t*, *v/i* meter no campo; **~ event** prova *f* de atletismo de campo
fiend [fi:nd] demónio *m*; **~ish** diabólico
fierce [fiəs] feroz
fiery ['faiəri] fogoso
fif|teen ['fif'ti:n] quinze; **~th** [fifθ] quinto;
fifty ['fifti] cinquenta; **~-~** *adv fam* meio-a-meio
fig [fig] figo *m*
fight [fait] *s* luta *f*; peleja *f*; *v/t*, *v/i* lutar, combater; **~er** lutador *m*
figment ['figmənt] quimera *f*, ficção *f*
fig-tree ['figtri:] figueira *f*
figurative ['figjurətiv] figurativo
figure ['figə] *s* figura *f*; algarismo *m*; *v/t*, *v/i* figurar; imaginar
file [fail] *s* arquivo *m*; fila *f*; lima *f*; *v/t* arquivar; limar; *v/i* desfilar
filial ['filjəl] filial
filigree ['filigri:] filigrana *f*
fill [fil] *v/t*, *v/i* encher(-se); **~ in** preencher
fillet ['filit] *s* fileté *m*
filling ['filiŋ] *s* obturação *f*; **~ station** bomba *f* / posto *m* de gasolina

film [film] *s* película *f*; filme *m*, fita *f*; *v/t*, *v/i* filmar
filter ['filtə] *s* filtro *m*; *v/t*, *v/i* filtrar(-se)
filth [filθ] porcaria *f*, imundície *f*; **~y** imundo, sujo
fin [fin] barbatana *f*
final ['fainl] *adj*, *s* final *f*; **~ly** finalmente, por fim
financ|e [fai'næns] *s* finança *f*; *v/t* financiar; **~ial** [-ʃəl] financeiro; **~ier** [-siə] financeiro *m*
finch [fintʃ] tentilhão *m*
find [faind] *v/t* achar, encontrar; **~ out** descobrir; **~er** achador *m*; **~ing** decisão *f*, veredicto *m*; achado *m*
fine [fain] *adj* belo, lindo; fino; *v/t* multar; *s* multa *f*; **I am ~** estou bem; **that is ~** é ó(p)timo; **~ arts** *pl* belas-artes *f/pl*
finger ['fiŋgə] *s* dedo *m*; *v/t* dedilhar; **~-board** teclado *m*; **~ing** dedilhado *m*; **~-nail** unha *f*; **~-print** impressão *f* digital; **~-stall** dedeira *f*
finish ['finiʃ] *v/t*, *v/i* acabar, terminar; *s* fim *m*; acabamento *m*
Finnish ['finiʃ] *adj*, *s* finlandês *m*
fir [fəː] abeto *m*; pinho *m*
fire ['faiə] *s* fogo *m*; lume *m*; incêndio *m*; *v/t*, *v/i* disparar, fazer fogo; deitar fogo a; incendiar; **on ~** em chamas, em fogo; **~-arm** arma *f* de fogo; **~-engine** furgão *m* de incêndio; **~-fly** pirilampo *m*; **~man** bombeiro *m*; **~works** fogos *m/pl* de artifício
firm [fəːm] *adj* firme, sólido; *s* firma *f*, casa *f* comercial
first [fəːst] *adv* em primeiro lugar; *adj* primeiro; **at ~** a princípio; **~ aid** primeiros socorros *m/pl*; **~ of all** primeiro que tudo; **at ~ sight** à primeira vista; **~-born** primogénito *m*; **~-class** *adj* de primeira classe; **~-hand** *adj* de primeira mão; **~-night** estreia *f*; **~-rate** de primeira qualidade
firth [fəːθ] braço *m* de mar, estuário *m*
fir-tree ['fəːtriː] pinheiro *m*
fish [fiʃ] *s* peixe *m*; *v/t*, *v/i* pescar; **~erman** pescador *m*; **~-hook** anzol *m*
fishing ['fiʃiŋ] pesca *f*; **~-boat** barco *m* de pesca; **~-rod** cana *f* de pesca
fissure ['fiʃə] fissura *f*
fist [fist] punho *m*
fit [fit] *s* desmaio *m*, síncope *f*; acesso *m*, *ataque m*; *adj* apto; próprio, adequado; em boa forma; *v/t*, *v/i* adaptar(-se), ajustar; montar; ficar bem
fitness ['fitnis] aptidão *f*, idoneidade *f*; boa condição *f* física
fitter ['fitə] ajustador *m*; MEC montador *m*
fitting ['fitiŋ] *adj* adequado, conveniente; *s* encaixe *m*, montagem *f*; prova *f*; **~s** *s/pl* instalações *f/pl*
five [faiv] cinco; **~ hundred** quinhentos
fix [fiks] *v/t* fixar, assentar; ar-

ranjar; consertar
fixed [fikst] fixo
fizz [fiz] *s* champanhe *m*; efervescência *f*; *v/i* efervescer
fizzle ['fizl] *v/i* silvar; **~ out** fazer fiasco, fracassar
flabbergasted ['flæbəgɑːstid] varado, estupefa(c)to
flabby ['flæbi] flácido, mole
flag [flæg] *s* bandeira *f*; laje *f*, lousa *f*; *v/i* enfraquecer
flagon ['flægən] botija *f*
flake [fleik] *s* lasca *f*; floco *m*; *v/i* lascar(-se)
flamboyant [flæm'bɔiənt] brilhante, flamante; flamejante
flam|e [fleim] *s* chama *f*; ardor *m*, paixão *f*; *v/i* chamejar; **~ing** *adj* chamejante; ardente
flamingo [flə'miŋgəu] flamingo *m*, *Braz* guará *m*
flank [flæŋk] *s* ilharga *f*; flanco *m*; *v/t* flanquear
flannel ['flænl] *s* flanela *f*
flap [flæp] *s* aba *f*; tapa *f*, palmada *f*; *v/t*, *v/i* bater, esvoaçar
flare [flɛə] *s* fulgor *m*, brilho *m*; *v/i* flamejar, cintilar; **~ up** inflamar-se
flash [flæʃ] *s* lampejo *m*; luz *m* de magnésio; clarão *m*; *v/i* cintilar, lampejar; dardejar; **~-light** holofote *m*; lâmpada *f* para instantâneos; lâmpada *f* elé(c)trica; **~y** vistoso
flask [flɑːsk] frasco *m*
flat [flæt] *adv* completamente, francamente; *adj* chato, plano, liso; *s* andar *m*, apartamento *m*; baixio *m*; furo *m*; MUS bemol *m*; **the ~ of the hand** a palma da mão
flatten ['flætn] *v/t*, *v/i* achatar
flatter ['flætə] *v/t* lisonjear; **~er** lisonjeador *m*; **~ing** *adj* lisonjeiro; **~y** lisonja *f*
flavo(u)r ['fleivə] *s* sabor *m*; *v/t* condimentar
flaw [flɔː] *s* falha *f*, defeito *m*; **~less** perfeito, impecável
flax [flæks] linho *m*; **~en** de linho; loiro
flay [flei] *v/t* esfolar
flea [fliː] pulga *f*
flee [fliː] *v/t*, *v/i* fugir
fleec|e [fliːs] *s* velo *m*, tosão *m*; *v/t* tosquiar; depenar, despojar; **~y** lanoso, lãzudo
fleet [fliːt] *s* armada *f*, esquadra *f*, frota *f*
fleeting ['fliːtiŋ] fugaz
Flemish ['flemiʃ] *adj*, *s* flamengo *m*
flesh [fleʃ] carne *f*; **~y** carnudo
flexible ['fleksəbl] flexível
flick [flik] *s* piparote *m*; estalido *m*; *v/t* chicotear
flicker ['flikə] *v/i* vacilar, bruxulear, tremeluzir; *s* centelha *f*; luz *f* vacilante
flight [flait] voo *m*; fuga *f*; lanço *m* de escadas
flimsy ['flimzi] *adj* débil, frágil, inconsistente; *s* papel *m* de cópias
flinch [flintʃ] *v/i* vacilar, titubear
fling [fliŋ] *v/t* lançar, atirar, arremessar
flint [flint] pedra *f* de isqueiro;

pederneira *f*, sílex *m*
flip [flip] *v/t*, *v/i* sacudir; desvairar; *s* sacudidela *f*
flippant ['flipənt] irreverente
flipper ['flipə] barbatana *f*
flirt [flə:t] *v/i* namori(s)car, flertar; *s* namori(s)co *m*, flerte *m*
flit [flit] *v/i* esvoaçar; mudar de casa
flitch [flitʃ] manta *f* de toucinho
float [fləut] *v/t*, *v/i* flutuar; *s* flutuador *m*; bóia *f*; **~ing** *adj* flutuante
flock [flɔk] *s* bando *m*; manada *f*; rebanho *m*; *v/i* congregar-se
flog [flɔg] *v/t* açoutar, fustigar, chicotear
flood [flʌd] *s* inundação *f*; cheia *f*; enchente *f*; *v/t*, *v/i* inundar, alagar
floor [flɔ:] *s* soalho *m*, sobrado *m*; chão *m*; *v/t* derrubar, deitar por terra; assoalhar
florist ['flɔrist] florista *m*, *f*
flounder ['flaundə] *s* solha *f*; *v/i* espojar-se, patinhar
flour ['flauə] *s* farinha *f*
flourish ['flʌriʃ] *v/i* florescer; prosperar, medrar; *v/t* brandir
floury ['flauəri] enfarinhado; farinhento
flout [flaut] *v/t* escarnecer
flow [fləu] *v/i* fluir, correr; *s* fluxo *m*, torrente *f*
flower ['flauə] *s* flor *f*; **~bed** canteiro *m*; **~pot** vaso *m*
flu [flu:] = **influenza**
fluctuate ['flʌktjueit] *v/i* flutuar
fluen|cy ['flu(:)ənsi] fluência *f*; **~t** fluente
fluff [flʌf] *s* cotão *m*; penugem *f*, lanugem *f*; **~y** fofo, felpudo
fluid ['flu:id] *s*, *adj* fluido *m*
flurry ['flʌri] *s* (*pl* **-ries**) agitação *f*; rajada *f*, lufada *f*
flush [flʌʃ] *s* jacto *m*, jorro *m*; rubor *m*; *v/i* corar, enrubescer; jorrar; *adj* ao mesmo nível; **~ with money** cheio de dinheiro
fluster ['flʌstə] *v/t* confundir, embaraçar; *s* confusão *f*
flut|e [flu:t] *s* flauta *f*; **~ed** estriado
flutter ['flʌtə] *v/t*, *v/i* esvoaçar, adejar; bater as asas; palpitar; *s* agitação *f*, alvoroço *m*; palpitação *f*
fly [flai] (*pl* **flies**) *s* mosca *f*; *v/i* voar; fugir; *v/t* arvorar, hastear; lançar
flying ['flaiiŋ] *s* aviação *f*; *adj* voador, volante; **~ saucer** disco *m* voador; **~ squad** rádio-patrulha *f*
foal [fəul] potro *m*, poldro *m*
foam [fəum] *s* espuma *f*; *v/i* espumar
focus ['fəukəs] (*pl* **-cuses** or **-ci** [-sai]) *s* foco *m*; *v/t* focar
foe [fəu] inimigo *m*
fog [fɔg] *s* nevoeiro *m*, cerração *f*; *v/t*, *v/i* enevoar(-se); velar-se; **~gy** enevoado, nevoento
foible ['fɔibl] (ponto *m*) fraco *m*
foil [fɔil] *s* florete *m* embodado; folha *f*, chapa *f*; contraste *m*, realce *m*; *v/t* frustrar
fold [fəuld] *s* prega *f*, dobra *f*; curral *m*, aprisco *m*; *v/t*, *v/i* em-

brulhar; dobrar; encurralar; **~ one's arms** cruzar os braços

folding ['fəuldiŋ] dibradiço

foliage ['fəuliidʒ] folhagem *f*

folk [fəuk] *s* povo *m*, gente *f*; **~lore** ['-lɔː] folclore *m*; **~s** família *f*, gente *f*; malta *f*; **~song** canção *f* popular

follow ['fɔləu] *v/t*, *v/i* seguir (-se); perceber; **as ~s** como se segue; **~er** adepto *m*; **~ing** *adj* seguinte; *s* partidários *m/pl*; **the ~ing** os seguintes

folly ['fɔli] (*pl* **-lies**) tolice *f*, loucura *f*

foment [fəu'ment] *v/t* fomentar

fond [fɔnd] afe(c)tuoso, terno; afeiçoado; vão; **to be ~ of** gostar de; **~le** ['-l] *v/t* afagar, amimar

food [fuːd] alimento *m*, comida *f*; **~-stuff** géneros *m/pl* alimentícios

fool [fuːl] *v/t*, *v/i* disparatar, bob(e)ar; enganar; *s* tolo *m*, bobo *m*, pateta *m*, *f* imbecil *m*, *f*; **make a ~ of oneself** fazerse ridículo; **make a ~ of someone** fazer de alguém tolo; **play the ~** fazer de tolo, *Braz* fazer de bobo

foolish ['fuːliʃ] tolo, tonto

foot [fut] (*pl* **feet** [fiːt]) *s* pé *m*; pata *f*; base *f*; *v/t* [illegible]ar; **~ it** ir a pé, andar a pé; **my ~!** ([illegible]); **on ~** a pé; **~ball** futebol *m*; **~fall** som *m* de passos; **~hold** ponto *m* de apoio; posição *f*; **~ing** situação *f*, pé *m*; **~lights** ribalta *f*; **~note** *s* nota *f* ao fundo da página, **~path** atalho *m*; **~print** pegada *f*; **~step** pegada *f*; passo *m*

for [fɔː; fə] *prp* por; para; por causa de; durante; *conj* porque; pois

forbear [fɔː'bɛə] *v/i* abster-se; reprimir-se; **~ance** paciência *f*

forbid [fə'bid] *v/t* proibir, impedir; **~den** *adj* proibido; **~ding** *adj* proibitivo, severo, ameaçador

force [fɔːs] *v/t* forçar, obrigar; *s* força *f*, vigor *m*; violência *f*; **in ~** em vigor, vigente; **~ful** vigoroso, enérgico

forceps ['fɔːseps] fórceps *m*

forcible ['fɔːsəbl] convincente; violento, forçado

ford [fɔːd] *s* vau *m*; *v/t* vadear; passar a vau

foro [fɔː] *adj* anterior, dianteiro; MAR de proa; **~arm** antebraço *m*; **~bode** *v/t* pressagiar; **~boding** *s* presságio *m*, pressentimento *m*; **~cast** *s* previão *f*; prognóstico *m*; *v/t* prever, prognosticar; **~father** antepassado *m*; **~finger** dedo *m* indicador; **~ground** primeiro plano *m*; **~head** ['fɔrid] testa *f*, fronte *f*

foreign ['fɔrin] alheio; estranho; estrangeiro, **~er** estrangeiro *m*

fore|land ['fɔːlənd] cabo *m*, promontório *m*; **~lock** topete *m*; **~man** capataz *m*, mestre *m*; **~most** *adj* mais ilustre; primeiro, mais avançado; **~see**

v/t prever; **~sight** previsão *f*
forest ['fɔrist] floresta *f*, mata *f*
fore|taste [fɔ:teist] antegosto *m*; **~tell** [-'tel] predizer
forever [fə'revə] para sempre
forewarn [fə'wɔ:n] *v/t* prevenir, avisar
foreword ['fɔ:wə:d] prefácio *m*
forfeit ['fɔ:fit] *s* multa *f*, pana *f*; *v/t* perder o direito a; **paly ~s** jogar às prendas
forg|e [fɔ:dʒ] *s* forja *f*; *v/t* forjar; falsificar; **~er** falsário *m*; **~ery** falsificação *f*
forget [fə'get] *v/t*, *v/i* esquecer, esquecer-se de; **~ful** esquecido; **~-me-not** miosótis *f*, não--me-esqueças *m*
forgive [fə'giv] *v/t*, *v/i* perdoar; **~ness** perdão *m*
forgiving [fə'giviŋ] *adj* clemente, indulgente
fork [fɔ:k] *s* garfo *m*; forquilha *f*; bifurcação *f*; *v/t*, *v/i* forcar; bifurcar(-se)
forlorn [fə'lɔ:n] desamparado
form [fɔ:m] *s* forma *f*; formulário *m*; figura *f*; classe *f*, turma *f*; *v/t*, *v/i* formar(-se); formular; **~al** formal; cerimonioso; **~ative** formativo
former ['fɔ:mə] primeiro, precedente, anterior, antigo, passado; **~ly** outrora, antigamente
formidable ['fɔ:midəbl] formidável
formul|a ['fɔ:mjulə] *s* fórmula *f*; **~ate** ['-leit] *v/t* formular; **~ation** formulação *f*
forsake [fə'seik] *v/t* abandonar, desertar, desamparar
fort [fɔ:t] MIL forte *m*
forth [fɔ:θ] adiante, avante, para a frente; **and so ~** e assim por diante; **~coming** vindoiro, próximo; **~with** imediatamente
fortify ['fɔ:tifai] *v/t* fortificar
fortnight ['fɔ:tnait] quinzena *f*, quinze dias *m/pl*
fortress ['fɔ:tris] fortaleza *f*
fortuitous [fɔ:'tju(:)itəs] fortuito
fortunate ['fɔ:tʃnit] afortunado, venturoso, feliz; **~ly** afortunadamente, felizmente
fortune ['fɔ:tʃən] fortuna *f*; sorte *f*, sina *f*; **~-teller** adivinho *m*, cartomante *m*, *f*
forty ['fɔ:ti] quarenta
forward ['fɔ:wəd] *s* avançado *m*; *adj* avançado; dianteiro; precoce; audaz; *adv* adiante; mais adiante; *v/t* enviar, remeter, expedir
fossil ['fɔsl] *s* fóssil *m*
foster ['fɔstə] *v/t* fomentar, alentar; alimentar, criar, nutrir; **~-son** filho *m* ado(p)tivo
foul [faul] *adj* sujo, imundo, porco; fétido; infame, vil, detestável; *v/t*, *v/i* sujar(-se), emporcalhar; *s* violação *f*, falta *f*
found [faund] *v/t* fundar, estabelecer; fundir
foundation [faun'deiʃən] fundação *f*, estabelecimento *m*; dotação *f*; **~s** alicerces *m/pl*
founder ['faundə] *s* fundador *m*
foundry ['faundri] (*pl* **-ries**)

fundição *f*
fountain ['fauntin] fonte *f*, repuxo *m*; **~-pen** caneta *f* de tinta permanente
four [fɔː] quatro; **go on all ~s** andar de gatinhas, engatinhar; **~ hundred** quatrocentos; **~teen** catorze
fourth [fɔːθ] quarto
fowl [faul] ave *f* de capoeira
fox [fɔks] raposa *f*; **~y** ladino, astuto
foyer ['fɔiei] THEAT salão *m*, vestíbulo *m*
fraction ['frækʃən] fra(c)ção *f*
fracture ['fræktʃə] *s* fra(c)tura *f*; *v/t*, *v/i* fra(c)turar(-se)
fragile ['frædʒail] frágil
fragment ['frægmənt] fragmento *m*
fragrance ['freigrəns] fragrância *f*
fragrant ['freigrənt] fragrante
frail [freil] débil, frágil, delicado; **~ty** fraqueza *f*; fragilidade *f*
frame [freim] *s* moldura *f*; caixilho *m*; estrutura *f*; *v/t* emoldurar, encaixilhar
franc [fræŋk] franco *m*
franchise ['fræntʃaiz] direito *m* de votar, sufrágio *m*
frank [fræŋk] *adj* franco; **~ness** franqueza *f*
frantic ['fræntik] frenético
fratern|al [frə'təːnl] fraternal; **~ity** fraternidade *f*; **~ize** ['frætənaiz] *v/i* fraternizar
fraud [frɔːd] fraude *f*; **~ulent** fraudulento
fray [frei] *s* refrega *f*; *v/t*, *v/i* coçar(-se), desgastar(-se)
freak [friːk] *s* capricho *m*, veleidade *f*; fenómeno *m*
freckles ['freklz] *s/pl* sardas *f/pl*
free [friː] *adj* livre; vago; grátis; *v/t* livrar, libertar
freedom ['friːdəm] liberdade *f*
freemason ['friːˌmeisn] franco-mação *m*, pedreiro-livre *m*
free trade ['friː'treid] livre-câmbio *m*
freez|e [friːz] *v/t*, *v/i* gelar, congelar; **~er** congelador *m*
freezing-point ['friːziŋpɔint] ponto *m* de congelação
freight [freit] *s* MAR frete *m*, carga *f*; *v/t* fretar, carregar; **~er** cargueiro *m*
French [frentʃ] *adj*, *s* francês *m*; **~ bean** feijão *m* verde; **~ fry** (*pl* **~ fries**) *US* batata *f* frita
frenzy ['frenzi] frenesi *m*
frequen|cy ['friːkwensi] frequência *f*; **~t** *adj* frequente, amiudado
fresh [freʃ] fresco; novo; puro; **in the ~ air** ao ar livre; **~er** caloiro *m*; **~water** de água doce
fret [fret] *v/t*, *v/i* afligir(-se); **~ful** irritável, rabugento
friar ['fraiə] frade *m*
friction ['frikʃən] atrito *m*; fricção *f*
Friday ['fraidi] sexta-feira *f*
fridge [fridʒ] *GB* = **refrigerator**
friend [frend] amigo *m*; **make ~s with** tornar-se amigo de; **~ly** amigável, amigo, amável;

~ship amizade *f*
frigate ['frigit] fragata *f*
fright [frait] susto *m*, medo *m*; **~en** *v/t* assustar; **~ful** terrível, assustador
frigid ['fridʒid] frígido, gélido
frill [fril] folho *m*
fringe [frindʒ] *s* franja *f*, orla *f*; *v/t* orlar
frisky ['friski] vivo, brincalhão; fogoso
fritter ['fritə] *s* frito *m*; **~ away** desperdiçar
frivol|ity [fri'vɔliti] frivolidade *f*; **~ous** ['-vələs] frívolo
frizz|le ['frizl] *v/t* frisar; **~(l)y** frisado, encaracolado
frock-coat [frɔk'kəut] sobrecasaca *f*
frog [frɔg] rã *f*
frolic ['frɔlik] *s* brincadeira *f*, travessura *f*; **~some** brincalhão, travesso
from [frɔm, frəm] de; desde; da parte de; **~ memory** de memória; **~ ... to** de ... a
frond [frɔnd] fronde *f*
front [frʌnt] *s* frente *f*; fachada *f*; *adj* anterior, da frente, dianteiro
frontier ['frʌntjə] fronteira *f*
frontispiece ['frʌntispi:s] frontispício *m*
frost [frɔst] *s* geada *f*; *v/t*, *v/i* gelar, cobrir de geada; foscar; polvilhar; **~y** gelado, glacial
froth [frɔθ] *s* espuma *f*, escuma *f*
frown [fraun] *s* franzimento *m* de sobrancelhas; *v/i* franzir as sobrancelhas; **~ on** desaprovar
frugal ['fru:gəl] frugal; **~ity** [-'gæliti] frugalidade *f*
fruit [fru:t] *s* fruto *m*; fruta *f*; **~erer** fruteiro *m*; **~ful** frutífero; **~s** *pl* frutos *m/pl*
frustrat|e [frʌs'treit] *v/t* frustrar; **~ion** frustração *f*
fry [frai] *v/t* frigir, fritar; **~ing pan** frigideira *f*, sertã *f*
fuel ['fjuəl] *s* combustível *m*
fugitive ['fju:dʒitiv] *s* fugitivo *m*; *adj* passageiro
fulfil(l) [ful'fil] *v/t* cumprir; **~ment** cumprimento *m*, execução *f*
full [ful] *adj* cheio; repleto; completo; pleno; *adv* completamente; em cheio; *s* totalidade *f*; plenitude *f*; **~ well** muito bem; **in ~** por extenso; na totalidade, completamente; **~length** de corpo inteiro, tamanho natural; **~ moon** lua *f* cheia
ful(l)ness ['fulnis] abundância *f*, plenitude *f*
full|stop ['fulstɔp] ponto *m*, final; **~-time** tempo *m* integral/ /completo; **~y** completamente; na integra
fumble ['fʌmbl] *v/t*, *v/i* ta(c)tear, apalpar, remexer
fume [fju:m] *v/i* fumegar; encolerizar-se; **~s** *s/pl* vapores *m/pl*, gás *m*, fumo *m*
fun [fʌn] graça *f*, divertimento *m*, diversão *f*; **for ~** por brincadeira; **have ~** divertir-se; **make ~ of** fazer troça/pouco de

function ['fuŋkʃən] *s* função *f*; *v/i* funcionar; **~al** funcional
fund [fʌnd] *s* reserva *f*, fundo *m*; **~s** fundos *m/pl*
funeral ['fju:nənəl] *s* funeral *m*; *adj* fúnebre
funicular [fju'nikjulə] funicular *m*
funnel ['fʌnl] funil *m*; tubo *m*; NAUT chaminé *f*
funny ['fʌni] invulgar, estranho; divertido, engraçado, cómico
fur [fə:] *s* pele *f*; pêlo *m*
furious ['fjuəriəs] furioso
furl [fə:l] *v/t*, *v/i* dobrar(-se), enrolar-(se); desfraldar
furlough ['fə:ləu] licença *f*, baixa *f* militar
furnace ['fə:nis] fornalha *f*
furnish ['fə:niʃ] *v/t* mobilar; fornecer
furniture ['fə:nitʃə] movéis *m/pl*, mobília *f*, mobiliário *m*
furrier ['fʌriə] peleiro *m*
furrow ['fʌrəu] *s* sulco *m*, rego *m*; *v/t* sulcar
further ['fə:ðə] *adj* mais distante; suplementar, adicional; *adv* mais longe; além disso; mais; mais adiante; *v/t* promover, favorecer; **~more** [fə:ðə'mɔ:] demais, além disso; **~most** ['fə:ðəməust] o mais distante, o mais afastado
furthest ['fə:ðist] *adj* extremo; o mais distante
furtive ['fə:tiv] furtivo
fury ['fjuəri] (*pl* **-ries**) fúria *f*
fuse [fju:z] *s* fusível *m*; *v/t*, *v/i* fundir(-se)
fuselage ['fju:zilɑ:ʒ] fuselagem *f*
fusion ['fju:ʒən] fusão *f*
fuss [fʌs] *v/i* espalhafatar, atarantar-se; *s* espalhafato *m*, estardalhaço *m*, barulho *m*; **~y** niquento
fustian ['fʌstiən] fustão *m*
fusty ['fʌsti] bafiento, mofento
futile ['fju:tail] fútil
future ['fju:tʃə] *s* futuro *m*, porvir *m*; *adj* futuro; vindoiro

G

gab [gæb] tagarelice *f*; **have the gift of the ~** ter boa lábia
gable ['geibl] empena *f*
gag [gæg] *s* mordaça *f*; *v/t* amordaçar
gage [geidʒ] *s* penhor *m*
gaiety ['geiəti] alegria *f*
gaily ['geili] alegremente
gain [gein] *s* ganho *m*, lucro *m*; *v/t*, *v/i* ganhar; adiantar-se
gait [geit] andar *m*
gaiter ['geitə] polaina *f*
gale [geil] ventania *f*
gall [gɔ:l] *s* fel *m*; amargura *f*, amargor *m*; *v/t* ferir, vexar
gallant ['gælənt] *adj* galante; valente
gall-bladder ['gɔ:lblædə] vesícula *f* biliar
gallery ['gæləri] (*pl* **-ries**) gale-

ria *f*
galley ['gæli] galera *f*; galé *f*
gallon ['gælən] galão *m*
gallop ['gæləp] *s* galope *m*, *v/i* galopar
gallows ['gæləuz] forca *f*
galosh [gə'lɔʃ] galocha *f*
gambl|e ['gæmbl] *v/t*, *v/i* jogar a dinheiro; **~er** jogador *m* de azar
gambol ['gæmbəl] *v/i* cabriolar
game [geim] *s* jogo *m*; caça *f*; partida *f*; *adj* corajoso, valente
gander ['gændə] ganso *m*
gang [gæŋ] bando *m*; malta *f*; grupo *m*; quadrilha *f*; **~ster** ['-stə] gatuno *m*, pistoleiro *m*; **~way** passagem *f*; prancha *f*
gaol [dʒeil] *s GB* cadeia *f*, prisão *f*; **~er** carcereiro *m*
gap [gæp] abertura *f*, fenda *f*; vazio *m*, lacuna *f*; intervalo *m*
gape [geip] *v/i* embasbacar
garage ['gærɑːdʒ] *s* garagem *f*
garbage ['gɑːbidʒ] *US* lixo *m*
garden ['gɑːdn] *s* jardim *m*; horta *f*
gargle ['gɑːgl] *v/i* gargarejar
garland ['gɑːlənd] grinalda *f*
garlic ['gaːlik] alho *m*
garment ['gɑːmənt] artigo *m* de vestuário, peça *f* de roupa
garnet ['gɑːnit] MIN granate *m*, granada *f*
garnish ['gɑːniʃ] *v/t* guarnecer
garret ['gærət] sótão *m*
garrison ['gærisn] guarnição *f*
garter ['gɑːtə] liga *f*; jarreteira *f*
gas [gæs] *s* gás *m*; cavaco *m*, conversa *f* fiada, *US* gasolina *f*; *v/t*, *v/i* gasear; tagarelar
gash [gæʃ] *s* incisão *f*; *v/t* acutilar
gas|light ['gæslait] lâmpada *f* a gás; **~-mask** máscara *f* antigás
gasoline ['gæsəliːn] *US* gasolina *f*
gasp [gɑːsp] *v/i* arfar, arquejar; *s* arfada *f*
gas|-stove ['gæsstəuv] fogão *m* a gás; **~-works** fábrica *f* de gás
gate [geit] portão *m*, entrada *f*; cancela *f*, porta *f*
gather ['gæðə] *v/t*, *v/i* juntar (-se), reunir(-se); **~ing** reunião *f*, assembleia *f*
gaudy ['gɔːdi] *adj* berrante, garrido
ga(u)ge [geidʒ] *v/t* medir, calibrar, aferir; *s* medida *f*, padrão *m*
gaunt [gɔːnt] magro, descarnado; desolado
gauze [gɔːz] gaze *f*
gay [gei] alegre
gaze [geiz] *s* olhar *m* fixo; *v/i*: **~ at** contemplar, fitar
gear [giə] *v/t*, *v/i* engrenar; *s* AUTO engrenagem *f*; equipamento *m*; **~-box** caixa *f* de velocidades, *Braz* caixa *f* de câmbio; **~ lever**, *US* **~ shift** alavanca *f* de velocidades, *Braz* alavanca *f* de câmbio
geld [geld] *v/t* capar, castrar
gem [dʒem] gema *f*, jóia *f*
gender ['dʒendə] GRAM género *m*

general ['dʒenərəl] *adj* geral; *s* general *m*; **in ~** em geral; **~ity** generalidade *f*; **~ize** *v/t*, *v/i* generalizar; **~ly** geralmente, em geral
generation [ˌdʒenə'reiʃən] geração *f*
generosity [ˌdʒenə'rɔsiti] generosidade *f*
generous ['dʒenərəs] generoso
genial ['dʒiːnjəl] ameno; afável
genius ['dʒiːnjəs] (*pl* **-ses**) génio *m*
gentian ['dʒenʃiən] genciana *f*
gentle ['dʒentl] suave, brando, dócil; ligeiro; **~folk** gente *f* da alta; **~man** (*pl* **-men**) cavalheiro *m*; **~ sex** sexo *m* fraco
gentry ['dʒentri] pequena nobreza *f*
genuine ['dʒenjuin] genuíno
geography [dʒi'ɔgrəfi] geografia *f*
geology [dʒi'ɔlədʒi] geologia *f*
geometry [dʒi'ɔmitri] geometria *f*
germ ['dʒəːm] germe *m*
German ['dʒəːmən] *adj*, *s* alemão *m*
germinate ['dʒəːmineit] *v/t*, *v/i* germinar
gerund ['dʒerənd] gerúndio *m*
gesticulate [dʒes'tikjuleit] *v/i* gesticular
gesture ['dʒestʃə] gesto *m*
get [get] *v/t*, *v/i* obter, ganhar, adquirir, conseguir; tornar-se, fazer-se; **~about** viajar; andar; espalhar-se; **~ along** ir-se embora; avançar, progredir; **~ along with** dar-se com; **~ away** escapar(-se), fugir; **~ back** regressar, voltar; **~ down** descer; engolir; apontar; ir-se abaixo; **~ in** chegar; entrar; **~ off** descer, sair; partir; **~ on** entrar, subir; continuar; montar; progredir; **~ out** sair, ir-se embora; publicar; **~ over** restabelecer-se; dominar, superar; **~ up** levantar-se
get-up ['getʌp] *s* arranjo *m*, traje *m*
ghastly ['gɑːstli] lívido; horrível
gherkin ['gəːkin] pepino *m* pequeno
ghost [gəust] *s* fantasma *m*, espe(c)tro *m*; **~ly** espe(c)tral
giant ['dʒaiənt] gigante *m*
giblets ['dʒiblits] *s/pl* miudezas *f/pl*, miúdos *m/pl*
giddy ['gidi] tonto, estonteado
gift [gift] dom *m*; oferta *f*, dádiva *f*; **~ card** cartão-presente *m*
gifted ['giftid] dotado
gigantic [dʒai'gæntik] gigantesco
giggle ['gigl] *s* risadinha *f*; *v/i* dar risadinhas
gild [gild] *v/t* dourar
gimlet ['gimlit] verruma *f*
gin [dʒin] gim *m*; genebra *f*
ginger ['dʒindʒə] *adj* ruivo; *s* gengibre *m*; **~bread** pão *m* de gengibre
gipsy ['dʒipsi] (*pl* **-sies**) cigano *m*
giraffe [dʒi'rɑːf] girafa *f*
gird [gəːd] *v/t* cingir; **~le** ['-dl] *s*

cinta *f*
girl [gəːl] rapariga *f*, moça *f*, menina *f*; **~ish** de rapariga, de moça, de menina
girth [gəːθ] volume *m*, espessura *f*; cilha *f*
give [giv] *s* elasticidade *f*; *v/t*, *v/i* dar; entregar; fornecer; ceder; **~ away** distribuir; revelar; **~ back** devolver, restituir; **~ in** ceder; entregar; **~ up** abandonar; desistir de; **~ oneself up** entregar-se, render-se
given ['givn] *adj* dado; fixado
glaci|al ['gleisjəl] glacial; **~er** ['glæsjə] geleira *f*, glaciar *m*
glad [glæd] satisfeito, contente, alegre; **~ly** de boa vontade; **~ness** alegria *f*, prazer *m*
glamo(u)r ['glæmə] encanto *m*, fascinação *f*
glance [glɑːns] *s* relance *m*, vista *f* de olhos; *v/t* **~ at** dar uma vista de olhos a; **at a ~** à primeira vista
gland [glænd] glândula *f*
glar|e [glɛə] *s* clarão *m*; olhar *m* furioso; *v/t*, *v/i* deslumbrar, ofuscar; lançar olhares furiosos; **~ing** deslumbrante, brilhante; evidente; penetrante
glass [glɑːs] vidro *m*; cipo *m*; espelho *m*; **~es** *pl* óculos *m/pl*; **~y** vidrado, vítreo
glaz|e [gleiz] *s* verniz *m*; *v/t* envidraçar; envernizar; **~ier** ['-zjə] vidraceiro *m*
gleam [gliːm] *s* raio *m*, vislumbre *m*; fulgor *m*, clarão *m*, *v/i* fulgurar, brilhar, cintilar
glean [gliːn] *v/t*, *v/i* respigar
glee [gliː] júbilo *m*; **~ful** jubiloso
glen [glen] vale *m* estreito
glide [glaid] *v/i* deslizar; planar
glider ['glaidə] planador *m*
glimmer ['glimə] *s* vislumbre *m*; *s* luz *f* fraca, *v/i* bruxulear, tremeluzir
glimpse [glimps] *s* vislumbre *m*; *v/t* vislumbrar, entrever
glint [glint] *v/i* reluzir
glisten ['glisn] *v/i* brilhar
glitter ['glitə] *v/i* luzir, resplandecer, cintilar; *s* brilho *m*, resplendor *m*; **~ing** resplandecente
globalization [gləubəlai'zeiʃən] *s* globalização *f*
globe [gləub] globo *m*
gloom [gluːm] escuridão *f*, trevas *f/pl*; *fig* melancolia *f*. **~y** escuro, sombrio; melancólico
glorious ['glɔːriəs] glorioso; esplêndido
glory ['glɔːri] *s* glória *f*; resplendor *m*
gloss [glɔs] *s* brilho *m*, lustre *m*; glosa *f*, comentário *m*; **~ary** ['-əri] glossário *m*; **~y** lustroso
glove [glʌv] luva *f*
glow [gləu] *v/i* arder, reluzir; *s* clarão *m*; ardor *m*; **~-worm** pirilampo *m*
glue [gluː] *s* grude *m*, cola *f*; *v/t* grudar, colar
glut [glʌt] *s* excesso *m*, superabundância *f*; **~ton** glutão *m*
gnarled [nɑːld] nodoso
gnash [næʃ] *v/t* ranger; **~ one's teeth** ranger os dentes

gnat [næt] mosquito *m*
gnaw [nɔː] *v/t, v/i* (co)roer
go [gəu] *v/i* ir; andar, marchar; funcionar; ir dar, ir ter; **~ ahead** avançar; começar; **~ away** ir-se embora; **~ by** passar; seguir, guiar-se; **~ by the name of** dar pelo nome de, ser conhecido pelo nome de; **~ in** entrar; **~ in for** dedicar-se; participar; **~ off** sair-se; explodir; **~ on** continuar; acontecer; **~ up** subir; **~ with** condizer com; **~ without** passar sem
goad [gəud] *s* aguilhão *m*; *v/t* aguilhoar
goal [gəul] obje(c)tivo *m*, meta *f*, fim *m*; ponto *m*, golo *m*; **~keeper** guarda-redes *m*, *Braz* goleiro *m*
goat [gəut] cabra *f*
go-between ['gəubiˌtwiːn] *s* intermediário *m*
goblet ['gɔblit] taça *f*, cálice *m*
goblin ['gɔblin] duende *m*
God [gɔd] Deus *m*; **thank ~** graças a Deus
god|child ['gɔdtʃaild] afilhado *m*; afilhada *f*; **~dess** deusa *f*; **~father** padrinho *m*; **~less** ímpio; ateu; **~mother** madrinha *f*
goggle ['gɔgl] *v/i* arregalar os olhos; **~s** ['-lz] *s/pl* óculos *m/pl* de prote(c)ção
going ['gəuiŋ] *s* ida *f*; **~s-on** ocorrências *f/pl*
goitre ['gɔitə] papeira *f*
gold [gəuld] ouro *m*; **~-dust** ouro *m* em pó; **~en** de ouro, dourado; **~smith** ourives *m*
golf [gɔlf] *s* golfe *m*; **~-course, ~-links** campo *m* de golfe
good [gud] *s* bem *m*; *adj* bom; **a ~ deal** muito; **~ afternoon!** boa tarde; **~bye** *int* adeus; **~-for-nothing** inútil; **♀ Friday** Sexta-Feira *f* Santa; **~-looking** bonito, formoso; **~-natured** de bom génio; **~ness** bondade *f*; **my ~ness!** meu Deus!
goods [gudz] *s/pl* bens *m/pl*, mercadorias *f/pl*; **~ train** comboio *m* de mercadorias
goodwill ['gud'wil] boa vontade *f*
goose [guːs] (*pl* **geese** [giːs]) gansa *f*; **~berry** ['guzbəri] groselha *f* verde
gorge [gɔːdʒ] *s* barranco *m*; *v/t* **~ on** empanturrar-se
gorgeous ['gɔːdʒəs] magnífico, esplêndido
gosh! [gɔʃ] caramba!
Gospel ['gɔspəl] Evangelho *m*
gossip ['gɔsip] *s* mexerico *m*, tagarelice *f*; tagarela *m, f*; *v/i* tagarelar
gourd [guəd] cabaça *f*
gout [gaut] gota *f*; **~y** gotoso
govern ['gʌvən] *v/t, v/i* GRAM reger; governar; **~ing** *adj* dire(c)tivo, administrativo; **~ment** governo *m*; **~or** governador *m*
gown [gaun] toga *f*; bata *f*; vestido *m* comprido; batina *f*
grab [græb] *v/t* apanhar, agarrar
grace [greis] graça *f*; favor *m*; **~ful** gracioso
gracious ['greiʃəs] cortês, amá-

vel; benévolo, benigno

grad|e [greid] *s* grau *m*; *v/t* graduar, classificar; **~ient** ['-jənt] declive *m*, rampa *f*; **~ual** ['grædʒuəl] gradual; **~uate** ['grædʒueit] *v/i* graduar-se, formar-se; ['grædʒuət] *s* graduado *m*

graft [grɑ:ft] *s* enxerto *m*; negociata *f*; *v/t* enxertar

grain [grein] grão *m*; fibra *f*; veio *m*; cereais *m/pl*

grammar ['græmə] gramática *f*; **~-school** liceu *m*; escola *f* secundária

gram(me) [græm] grama *m*

grand [grænd] *adj* grandioso, sublime; **~daughter** ['græn,dɔ:tə] neta *f*; **~eur** ['-dʒə] grandeza *f*; **~father** avô *m*; **~mother** avó *f*; **~son** neto *m*

grange [greindʒ] granja *f*

granite ['grænit] granito *m*

granny ['græni] (*pl* **-nies**) vovó

grant [grɑ:nt] *s* concessão *f*, doação *f*; subvenção *f*; bolsa *f*, subsídio *m*; *v/t* conceder, outorgar; **take for ~ed** tomar por certo

granul|ar ['grænjulə] granular; **~e** grânulo *m*

grape [greip] uva *f*; **~-fruit** toronja *f*

graphic ['græfik] gráfico

grapple ['græpl] *v/i*: **~ with** lutar com; agarrar(-se) a

grasp [grɑ:sp] *v/t* agarrar, empunhar; compreender; *s* aperto *m*; compreensão *f*

grass [grɑ:s] *s* relva *f*; erva *f*, grama *f*; **~hopper** gafanhoto *m*

grate [greit] *v/t* raspar; ralar; *s* grade *f*, grelha *f*

grateful ['greitful] grato, agradecido

grater ['greitə] ralador *m*

gratify ['grætifai] *v/t* gratificar

gratitude ['grætitju:d] gratidão *f*, reconhecimento *m*

gratuit|ous [grə'tju(:)itəs] gratuito; **~y** (*pl* **-ties**) gorjeta *f*

grave [greiv] *s* sepultura *f*, tumba *f*; *adj* grave, sério

gravel ['grævəl] *s* saibro *m*, cascalho *m*

gravestone ['greivstəun] campa *f*, lápide *f*

graveyard ['greivjɑ:d] cemitério *m*

gravitation [,grævi'teiʃən] gravitação *f*

gravity ['græviti] gravidade *f*

gravy ['greivi] molho *m*; **~-boat** molheira *f*

graze [greiz] *v/t*, *v/i* roçar; pastar

greas|e [gri:s] *s* gordura *f*; [-:z] *v/t* untar; **~y** ['-zi] gorduroso

great [greit] *adj* grande; célebre; ó(p)timo, excelente; **a ~ deal (of)** muito; **a ~ while** muito tempo; **a ~ many** muitos; **~-grandfather** bisavô *m*; **~-grandson** bisneto *m*; **~ness** grandeza *f*

greed [gri:d] avidez *f*; glutonaria *f*; **~y** ávido, voraz

Greek [gri:k] *adj*, *s* grego *m*

green [gri:n] *adj* verde; **~ery**

verdura *f*, verdor *m*; **~grocer** fruteiro *m*, hortaliceiro *m*, *Braz* quitandeiro *m*; **~house** estufa *f*; **~ish** esverdeado; **~s** *s/pl* verduras *f/pl*, hortaliça *f*

greet [gri:t] *v/t* cumprimentar, saudar; **~ing** saudação *f*, cumprimento *m*

grey [grei] *adj* cinzento; **~hound** galgo *m*

gridiron ['grid,aiən] grelha *f*

grief [gri:f] dor *f*, pesar *m*

grievance ['gri:vəns] agravo *m*, queixa *f*

grieve [gri:v] *v/t*, *v/i* afligir(-se); lamentar(-se)

grievous ['gri:vəs] penoso; grave, severo

grill [gril] *s* grelha *f*; *v/t*, *v/i* grelhar, assar na grelha

grim [grim] torvo, sinistro

grimace [gri'meis] *s* careta *f*

grin [grin] *s* sorriso *m* largo, arreganho *m*; *v/i* sorrir

grind [graind] *v/t* moer; esmagar; triturar; **~er** mó *m*; moleiro *m*; dente *m* molar

grip [grip] *s* aperto *m*; *v/t*, *v/i* agarrar, prender; apertar

grisly ['grizli] macabro, horrível

groan [grəun] *v/i* gemer; *s* gemido *m*

grocer ['grəusə] merceeiro *m*; **~y** mercearia *f*

grog [grɔg] grogue *m*

groggy ['grɔgi] cambaleante

groin [grɔin] virilha *f*

groom [grum] *s* moço *m* de estrebaria; noivo *m*; *v/t*: **~ horses** tratar de cavalos

groove [gru:v] *s* ranhura *f*

grope [grəup] *v/t*, *v/i* ta(c)tear; procurar às apalpadelas

gross [grəus] *s* grosa *f*; *adj* grosseiro; COM bruto

grotto ['grɔtəu] gruta *f*

ground [graund] *s* chão *m*; solo *m*, terreno *m*; terra *f*; motivo *m*, base *f*; fundo *m*; *v/t*, *v/i* encalhar; fundar, estabelecer; **~-floor** rés-do-chão *m*; **~s** *s/pl* borra *f*; razão *f*, motivo *m*

group [gru:p] *s* grupo *m*; *v/t*, *v/i* agrupar(-se)

grouse [graus] *v/i* queixar-se, resmungar

grove [grəuv] arvoredo *m*

grow [grəu] *v/t*, *v/i* crescer; aumentar; tornar-se, ficar; criar, cultivar

growl [graul] *v/i* rosnar; *s* rosnadela *f*

grown-up ['grəunʌp] *adj*, *s* adulto *m*

growth [grəuθ] crescimento *m*, aumento *m*

grudge [grʌdʒ] *s* rancor *m*; *v/t* dar de má vontade; invejar

gruel [gruəl] papa *f*

gruff [grʌf] rude, brusco

grumble ['grʌmbl] *v/i* resmungar; roncar; *s* resmungadela *f*

grunt [grʌnt] *v/i* grunhir; *s* grunhido *m*

guarantee [,gærən'ti:] *s* garantia *f*; caução *f*; *v/t* garantir; caucionar

guard [gɑ:d] *v/t* guardar; *s* guarda *f*; sentinela *f*; condutor *m*,

Braz guarda-trem *m*; **~ed** *adj* cauto, cauteloso
guardian ['gɑːdjən] tutor *m*; guardião *m*
guess [ges] *s* suposição *f*, conje(c)tura *f*; *v/t*, *v/i* adivinhar; supor
guest [gest] *s* hóspede *m*, convidado *m*
guidance ['gaidəns] orientação *f*; governo *m*, dire(c)ção *f*
guide [gaid] *v/t* guiar; *s* guia *m*; **~-book** guia *f*, roteiro *m*
guild [gild] corporação *f*, grémio *m*
guileless ['gaillis] inocente, ingénuo
guilt [gilt] culpa *f*; **~less** inocente; **~y** culpável; culpado
guinea pig ['ginipig] porquinho-da-India *m*
guise [gaiz] aparência *f*
guitar [gi'taː] guitarra *f*; viola *f*, violão *m*
gulf [gʌlf] MAR golfo *m*; abismo *m*
gull [gʌl] *s* gaivota *f*
gulp [gʌlp] *s* gole *m*, trago *m*; *v/t* tragar, engolir
gum [gʌm] *s* goma *f*; gengiva *f*; *v/t* engomar, colar
gumption ['gʌmpʃən] bom senso *m*; iniciativa *f*
gun [gʌn] espingarda *f*; canhão *m*; **~man** salteador *m* armado; **~ner** artilheiro *m*; **~powder** pólvora *f*; **~-smith** espingardeiro *m*
gurgle ['gəːgl] *v/i* gorgolejar, gorgolhar
gush [gʌʃ] *v/i* jorrar, brotar; *s* jorro *m*, borbotão *m*; **~ing** *adj* efusivo
gust [gʌst] pé *m* de vento, rajada *f*
gut [gʌt] *s* intestino *m*, tripa *f*; *v/t* desventrar, estripar; **~s** *s/pl fig* coragem *f*, valentia *f*
gutter ['gʌtə] *s* goteira *f*; sarjeta *f*
guy [gai] *s* sujeito *m*, gajo *m*; espantalho *m*
gymnas|ium [dʒim'neizjəm] ginásio *m*; **~t** ['-næst] ginasta *m*, *f*; **~tics** [-'næstiks] ginástica *f*
gynaecologist [ˌgaini'kɔlədʒist] ginecologista *m*, *f*
gyrate [ˌdʒaiə'reit] *v/i* girar

H

haberdasher ['hæbədæʃə] capelista *m*, *Braz* armarinheiro *m*
habit ['hæbit] hábito *m*, costume *m*
habit|able ['hæbitəbl] habitável; **~at** ['-æt] habitat *m*
habit|ual [hə'bitjuəl] habitual; **~ué** [hə'bitjuei] frequentador *m*
hack [hæk] *v/t*, *v/i* cortar, despedaçar; *s* cavalo *m* de aluguel;

sendeiro *m*, pileca *f*; mercenário *m*; escritor *m* mau

hackneyed ['hæknid] *adj* corriqueiro, banal

haddock ['hædək] eglefim *m*

haggard ['hægəd] macilento, pálido

hail [heil] *s* saraiva *f*; *v/i* saraivar; *v/t* aclamar, saudar; chamar

hair [hɛə] cabelo *m*; pêlo *m*; **~-cut** corte *m* de cabelo; **~do** penteado *m*; **~dresser** cabeleireiro *m*; **~pin** gancho *m*; **~-raising** arrepiante; **~y** peludo, cabeludo

half [hɑːf] (*pl* **halves** [hɑːvz]) *s* metade *f*, meio *m*; parte *f*, tempo *m*; *adj* meio; semi ...; *adv* meio; **~-breed** *adj*, *s* mestiço *m*; **~-time** meio tempo *m*; **~-way** *adj*, *adv* a meio caminho, a meia distância; **~-wit** parvo *m*, idiota *m*, *f*

halibut ['hælibət] hipoglosso *m*

hall [hɔːl] residência *f*; salão *m*; entrada *f*, vestíbulo *m*; refeitório *m*

hallo [hə'ləu] *int* olá; alô

hallow ['hæləu] *v/t* santificar, consagrar

halo ['heiləu] halo *m*; auréola *f*

halt [hɔːlt] *s* parada *f*, paragem *f*; *v/t*, *v/i* fazar alto, parar, deter (-se)

halve [hɑːv] *v/t* dividir ao meio

ham [hæm] *s* presunto *m*

hamlet ['hæmlit] lugarejo *m*, aldeola *f*

hammer ['hæmə] *s* martelo *m*; *v/t*, *v/i* martelar

hammock ['hæmək] rede *f*, maca *f*

hamper ['hæmpə] *s* canastra *f*; *v/t* embaraçar, estorvar

hand [hænd] *v/t* passar, dar, entregar; *s* mão *f*; ponteiro *m*; **at ~** à mão, perto; **at second ~** em segunda mão; **get the upper ~** levar vantagem; **give/lend a ~ to** dar uma ajuda; **~ in glove** unha e carne; **~ in ~** de mãos dadas; **on the other ~** por outro lado

hand|bag ['hændbæg] carteira *f*, bolsa *f*, mala *f*; **~ball** (h)andebol *m*; **~cuffs** *s/pl* algemas *f/pl*; **~ful** punhado *m*, mão-cheia *f*

handicap ['hændikæp] *s* desvantagem *f*

handicraft ['hændikrɑːft] habilidade *f* manual, mão-de-obra *f*

handkerchief ['hæŋkətʃif] lenço *m*

handle ['hændl] *s* cabo *m*, punho *m*; *v/t* tratar; manejar, manusear; **~-bars** *s/pl* guiador *m*, guidão *m*

hand|made ['hænd'meid] *adj* feito à mão, manufa(c)turado

handrail ['hændreil] corrimão *m*

hands-free ['hænsfriː] *adj* TEL mãos livres

handsome ['hænsəm] belo, formoso

handwriting ['hænd,raitiŋ] caligrafia *f*, letra *f*

handy ['hændi] hábil; jeitoso; à mão
hang [hæŋ] *v/t* pendurar, suspender; pender
hang [hæŋ] *v/t* enforcar
hangar ['hæŋə] hangar *m*
hangman ['hæŋmən] (*pl*-**men**) carrasco *m*, algoz *m*
hangover ['hæŋ,əuvə] *s* ressaca *f*, resto *m*
hanky ['hæŋki] = **handkerchief**
haphazard ['hæp'hæzəd] *adj* casual, acidental
happen ['hæpən] *v/i* acontecer, suceder, ocorrer; **~ing** *s* acontecimento *m*, sucesso *m*
happ|ily ['hæpili] felizmente; **~iness** felicidade *f*; **~y** feliz
harangue [hə'ræŋ] *s* arenga *f*; *v/t* arengar
harass ['hærəs] *v/t* acossar
harbo(u)r ['hɑːbə] *s* porto *m*; *fig* asilo *m*; *v/t* abrigar, acolher; acalentar
hard [hɑːd] *adv* demasiado, muito; *adj* duro; rude; difícil; **~en** *v/t*, *v/i* endurecer; **~-hearted** austero, inflexível; **~iness** robustez *f*; intrepidez *f*; **~ labour** trabalhos *m/pl* forçados; **~ly** mal, apenas; **~ness** dureza *f*; rigor *m*; **~ship** miséria *f*, privação; **~ware** quinquilharia *f*; ferragens *f/pl*; **~y** robusto; intrépido
hare [hɛə] *s* lebre *f*; **~-brained** insensato, cabeça-no-ar; **~lip** lábio *m* leporino
harm [hɑːm] *s* mal *m*, dano *m*, prejuízo *m*; *v/t* danificar; fazer mal a; **~ful** nocivo; **~less** inofensivo, inocente
harmony ['hɑːməni] harmonia *f*
harness ['hɑːnis] *s* arnês *m*, arreios *m/pl*; *v/t* ajaezar, arrear
harp [hɑːp] harpa *f*; **~ist** harpista *m*, *f*
harpoon [hɑː'puːn] *s* arpão *m*; *v/t* arpoar
harrow ['hærəu] *s* grade *f*, trilho *m*; *v/t* gradar; atormentar
harsh [hɑːʃ] áspero, severo
hart [hɑːt] veado *m*
harvest ['hɑːvist] *v/t* colher, ceifar; *s* ceifa *f*, colheita *f*; **~er** ceifeiro *m*; segadora *f*
hash [hæʃ] *s* picado *m*; *v/t* picar
hash(ish) ['hæʃ(iːʃ)] haxixe *m*
hast|e [heist] pressa *f*; **~en** ['-sn] *v/t*, *v/i* apressar(-se), aviar-se; **~y** apressado, precipitado
hat [hæt] chapéu *m*
hatch [hætʃ] *s* ninhada *f*; *v/t*, *v/i* incubar, chocar; tramar
hatchet ['hætʃit] machadinha *f*
hate [heit] *v/t* odiar, detestar; *s* ódio *m*; **~ful** odioso, detestável
hatred ['heitrid] ódio *m*
haught|iness ['hɔːtinis] altivez *f*; **~y** altivo, altaneiro
haunch [hɔːntʃ] anca *f*; quadril *m*
haunt [hɔːnt] *s* refúgio *m*, retiro *m*; *v/t* frequentar, visitar; assombrar, infestar; obcecar; **~ing** *adj* obsidiante, fixo
have [hæv, həv] *v/t* ter; receber, obter; tomar, comer; **~ to** ter

de, ter que; I *etc.* **had better** era melhor que; ~ **(something) done** mandar fazer (alguma coisa); ~ **it** insistir; ~ **on** trazer

haven ['heivn] abrigo *m*, refúgio *m*

havoc ['hævək] estrago *m*, destruição *f*; **play ~ with/among** causar grandes estragos em

hawk [hɔːk] *s* falcão *m*

hawthorn ['hɔːθɔːn] espinheiro alvar *m*

hay [hei] feno *m*; ~ **fever** febre *f* dos fenos; **~stack** meda *f* de feno

hazard ['hæzəd] *s* risco *m*, perigo *m*; *v/t* aventurar, arriscar; **~ous** arriscado, perigoso

haze [heiz] *s* cerração *f*

hazel ['heizl] *s* avelaneira *f*; **~-nut** avelã *f*

hazy ['heizi] enevoado; confuso, vago

he [hiː, hi] *pron* ele; *s* macho *m*; ~ **who** aquele que

head [hed] *s* cabeça *f*; cabeceira *f*; cabeçalho; dire(c)tor *m*, chefe *m*; *v/t* encabeçar, dirigir; cabecear; **~s or tails?** cara ou coroa?

head|ache ['hedeik] dor *f* de cabeça; **~ing** *s* cabeçalho *m*; **~-lamp**, **~-light** AUTO farol *m*; **~line** *s* título *m*; **~long** *adv* precipitadamente; *adj* impetuoso, precipitado; **~master** dire(c)tor *m*, reitor *m*; **~quarters** quartel-general *m*; **~strong** cabeçudo; **~way** progresso *m*

heal [hiːl] *v/t*, *v/i* curar, sarar, cicatrizar; **~ing** *s* cura *f*

health [helθ] saúde *f*; **~y** saudável, sadio, são

heap [hiːp] *s* montão *m*; *v/t* amontoar

hear [hiə] *v/t*, *v/i* ouvir; ouvir dizer; ~ **of** ouvir falar de; **~er** ouvinte, *m*, *f*; **~ing** *s* audição *f*; audiência *f*; interrogatório *m*

hearsay ['hiəsei] boato *m*

hearse [həːs] carro *m* fúnebre

heart [hɑːt] coração *m*; âmago *m*; coragem *f*; copas *f*; **at ~** no fundo, no íntimo; **by ~** de cor; **~-breaking** dilacerante; **~en** *v/t* animar, encorajar

hearth [hɑːθ] lar *m*; lareira *f*

heart|less ['hɑːtlis] cruel, desapiedado; **~-to-~** *adj* franco, sincero; **~y** cordial

heat [hiːt] *s* calor *m*; ardor *m*; *v/t*, *v/i* aquecer(-se); **~er** aquecedor *m*

heath [hiːθ] charneca *f*

heathen ['hiːðən] pagão *m*

heather ['heðə] urze *f*

heating ['hiːtiŋ] *s* aquecimento *m*

heave [hiːv] *v/t*, *v/i* elevar(-se), levantar; alçar, içar; lançar, arremessar; *s* lançamento *m*, arremesso *m*

heaven ['hevn] céu *m*; **good ~s!** céus!; **~ly** celeste, celestial

heav|iness ['hevinis] pesadume *f*; entorpecimento *m*; abatimento *m*; **~y** *adj* pesado; forte

Hebrew ['hiːbruː] *adj*, *s* hebreu *m*

hectic ['hektik] agitado, turbulento; héctico
hedge [hedʒ] *s* sebe *f*, cerca *f*; *v/t, v/i* vedar, cercar de sebes; ladear, fugir à pergunta
hedgehog ['hedʒhɔg] ouriço(-cacheiro) *m*
heed [hiːd] *s* atenção *f*, tento *m*; *v/t* prestar atenção a; **~less** imprudente
heel [hiːl] *s* calcanhar *m*, talão *m*; tacão *m*, salto *m*
heifer ['hefə] vitela *f*
height [hait] altura *f*; altitude *f*; cúmulo *m*, auge *m*; **~en** *v/t, v/i* aumentar, intensificar
heir [ɛə] herdeiro *m*; **~ess** herdeira *f*
helicopter ['helikɔptə] helicóptero *m*
helium ['hiːljəm] hélio *m*
hell [hel] *s* inferno *m*; **~ish** infernal
hello ['hə'ləu] = **hallo**
helm [helm] MAR temão *m*, barra *f* do leme
helmet ['helmit] elmo *m*, capacete *m*
help [help] *s* ajuda *f*, auxílio *m*; *v/t, v/i* ajudar; socorrer; servir; *int* socorro! **I can't ~** não posso deixar de, não posso evitar; **it can't be ~ed** não há remédio; **~er** ajudante *m*, auxiliar *m*; **~ful** serviçal; útil, proveitoso; **~ing** *s* porção *f*, dose *f*; **~less** desamparado
hem [hem] *s* bainha *f*
hemisphere ['hemisfiə] hemisfério *m*
hemlock ['hemlɔk] cicuta *f*
hemp [hemp] cânhamo *m*
hen [hen] galinha *f*
hence [hens] porr isso, portanto; **~forth**, **~forward** daqui em diante
hen-house ['henhaus] galinheiro *m*
her [həː, hə] *obj pron* a; ela; lhe; *poss* seu, dela
herald ['herəld] *s* arauto *m*, heraldo *m*; **~ic** [he'rældik] heráldico; **~ry** ['herəldri] heráldica *f*
herb [həːb] erva *f*; **~aceous** [-'beiʃəs] herbáceo; **~al** herbóreo; **~ivorous** [-'bivərəs] herbívoro
herd [həːd] *s* rebanho *m*, manada *f*
here [hiə] *adv* aqui, cá; **~ and there** cá e lá, aqui e acolá; **~'s to …!** à saúde de …!
heredit|ary [hi'reditəri] hereditário; **~y** hereditariedade *f*
here|sy ['herəsi] (*pl* **-sies**) heresia *f*; **~tic** herege *m, f*; **~tical** [hi'retikəl] herético
hermit ['həːmit] ermitão *m*, eremita *m, f*
hero ['hiərəu] herói *m*; **~ic** [hi'rəuik] heróico; **~ine** ['herəuin] heroína *f*; **~ism** ['herəuizəm] heroísmo *m*
heron ['herən] garça *f*
herring ['heriŋ] arenque *m*
hers [həːz] o seu, a sua, os seus, as suas; dela
herself [həː'self] se; ela mesma; si; si mesma; si própria
hesitat|e ['heziteit] *v/i* hesitar;

~ion [-'teiʃən] hesitação *f*

hew [hjuː] *v/t*, *v/i* abater, cortar; talhar

hey [hei] eh!; eia! ena!

heyday ['heidei] auge *m*, apogeu *m*

hi [hai] olá!

hibernate ['haibəneit] *v/i* hibernar

hiccup ['hikʌp] *s* soluço *m*; *v/i* estar com soluços

hide [haid] *v/t*, *v/i* esconder (-se), *s* pele *f*, couro *m*

hideous ['hidiəs] horrível, hediondo

hiding ['haidiŋ] *s* sova *f*, surra *f*

hi-fi ['hai'fai] *adj*, *s* (de) alta fidelidade *f*

high [hai] *adj* alto; elevado; eminente; superior; **~brow** intelectual *m*, *f*, sabichão *m*; **~-class** de primeira qualidade; de alta categoria; **~-fidelity** = **hi-fi** de alta qualidade; **~-handed** despótico, arbitrário; **~ life** via *f* da alta sociedade; **~ly** altamente; sumamente; **~-minded** magnânimo, de ideias largas; **~ness** altura *f*, elevação *f*; **♀ ness** Alteza *f*; **~ road** estrada *f* nacional; **~ school** *US* escola *f* secundária; **~ season** plena estação *f*; **~way** *US* estrada *f* nacional, *Braz* rodovia *f*

hijack ['haidʒæk] *v/t* assaltar; sequestrar

hike [haik] *v/i* andar a pé, caminhar

hilari|ous [hi'lɛəriəs] alegre; **~ty** [-'læriti] hilaridade *f*

hill [hil] colina *f*, outeiro *m*; **~side** encosta *f*, ladeira *f*; **~y** montanhoso

hilt [hilt] cabo *m*; copos *m/pl*, punho *m*

him [him, im] o; ele, a ele; lhe

himself [him'self] se; ele mesmo; si; si próprio

hind [haind] *s* corça *f*; *adj* posterior, traseiro

hinder ['hində] *v/t* impedir, embaraçar, estorvar

hindrance ['hindrəns] impedimento *m*, empecilho *m*, estorvo *m*

hinge [hindʒ] *s* gonzo *m*, charneira *f*

hint [hint] *s* sugestão *f*, indício *m*, lamiré *m*; *v/t*, *v/i* insinuar, sugerir

hip [hip] *s* anca *f*, quadril *m*; BOT fruto *m* da rosa brava

hire ['haiə] *s* aluguer *m*, aluguel *m*; salário *m*; *v/t* alugar; **~-purchase** compra *f* a prestações

his [hiz, iz] (o) seu, (a) sua, (os) seus, (as) suas; dele

hiss [his] *s* assobio *m*, silvo *m*; *v/i* assobiar; **~ at** apupar

histor|ian [his'tɔːriən] historiador *m*; **~ic(al)** [-'tɔrik(əl)] histórico; **~y** ['-təri] (*pl* **-ries**) história *f*

hit [hit] *s* golpe *m*, pancada *f*; acerto *m*; sucesso *m*, êxito *m*; sensação *f*; *v/t* golpear, bater; acertar; **~ the mark** acertar no alvo; **~ the nail on the head** acertar em cheio, dar no vinte

hitch [hitʃ] *s* puxão *m*; nó *m*, volta *f* de cabo; dificuldade *f*, encrenca *f*; *v/t* prender, amarrar; **~-hike** *v/i* andar à boleia, *Braz* viajar de carona

hive [haiv] *s* colmeia *f*, cortiço *m*

hoard [hɔːd] *s* tesouro *m*; reserva *f*; *v/t* amealhar, armazenar

hoarfrost ['hɔː'frɔst] geada *f*

hoarse [hɔːs] rouco; **~ness** rouquidão *f*

hoax [həuks] *s* engano *m*, logro *m*; *v/t* enganar, lograr

hobble ['hɔbl] *v/i* coxear, manquejar

hobby ['hɔbi] (*pl* **-bies**) passatempo *m*

hock [hɔk] *s* vinho *m* do Reno

hockey ['hɔki] hóquei *m*

hog [hɔg] *s* porco *m*

hoist [hɔist] *v/t* içar; guindar

hold [həuld] *v/t*, *v/i* possuir; conter, levar; manter; julgar, considerar; pegar, agarrar, segurar; *s* pega *f*; apoio *m*; domínio *m*, influência *f*; porão *m*; **~ on** aguentar; continuar, persistir; **~ up** exibir, mostrar; manter-se; fazer parar; demorar; **catch/lay ~ of** agarrar, deitar a mão a; **~er** possuidor *m*, detentor *m*; **~ing** *s* propriedade *f*; arrendamento *m*

hole [həul] *s* buraco *m*

holiday ['hɔlədi] *s* (dia *m*) feriado *m*; férias *f/pl*; **~-maker** veraneante *m*, *f*, *Braz* veranista *m*, *f*

hollow ['hɔləu] *adj* oco, côncavo; *s* vale *m*; cavidade *f*; recôncavo *m*; *v/t* cavar, escavar

holly ['hɔli] azevinho *m*, *Braz* azevim *m*

holy ['həuli] *adj* santo, sagrado; **≈ Ghost** Espírito *m* Santo; **≈ Land** Terra *f* Santa; **~ water** água *f* benta

homage ['hɔmidʒ] homenagem *f*, respeito *m*; **do ~**, **pay ~** prestar homenagem

home [həum] *s* lar *m*, casa *f* paterna; residência *f*, domicílio *m*; asilo *m*, albergue *m*; terra *f* natal; *adv* para casa; *adj* doméstico; nativo, nacional; **at ~** em casa; **~land** pátria *f*; **~ly** simples, caseiro; **≈ Office** Ministério *m* do Interior; **~ rule** autonomia *f*; **~sick** nostálgico, saudoso do lar ou da pátria; **~sickness** nostalgia *f*, saudade *f*; **~ truth** verdade *f* nua e crua; **~work** trabalhos *m/pl* de/para casa, deveres *m/pl* da escola

honest ['ɔnist] honesto, probo; **~y** honestidade *f*, probidade *f*

honey ['hʌni] mel *m*; *US* querido, amor; **~comb** favo *m* de mel; **~moon** *s* lua *f* de mel; **~suckle** madressilva *f*

honorary ['ɔnərəri] honorário

hono(u)r ['ɔnə] *s* honradez *f*, honra *f*; *v/t* honrar; **~able** honroso, honrado

hood [hud] capuz *m*, touca *f*; capelo *m*; AUTO capota *f*

hoodwink ['hudwiŋk] *v/t* lograr, enganar

hoof [huːf] casco *m*

hook [huk] *s* gancho *m*, colchete *m*; anzol *m*; *v/t* enganchar

hoop [huːp] *s* aro *m*, argola *f*

hoover ['huːvə] *s* = **vacuum cleaner**

hop [hɔp] *s* salto *m*, pulo *m*; baile *m*; BOT lúpulo *m*; *v/i* saltar ao pé coxinho, saltitar, pular

hope [həup] *v/i* esperar, ter esperança; *s* esperança *f*; **~ful** *adj* esperançoso; **~less** desesperado, desesperançado

horde [hɔːd] horda *f*

horizon [hə'raizn] horizonte *m*; **~tal** [ˌhɔri'zɔntl] horizontal

horn [hɔːn] chifre *m*, corno *m*; MUS corneta *f*; buzina *f*; **~et** ['-it] vespão *m*; **~y** caloso

horrible ['hɔrəbl] horrível

horrid ['hɔrid] hórrido, horrendo

horrify ['hɔrifai] *v/t* horrorizar

horror ['hɔrə] horror *m*

horse [hɔːs] cavalo *m*; cavalete *m*; **on ~back** a cavalo; **~hair** crina *f*; **~man** (*pl* **-men**) cavaleiro *m*; **~manship** equitação *f*; **~power** cavalo-vapor *m*; **~-racing** corrida *f* de cavalos; **~shoe** ferradura *f*

hose [həuz] *s* meias *f/pl*; peúgas *f/pl*; mangueira *f*; *v/t* regar com mangueira

hosier ['həuʒə] camiseiro *m*, negociante *m* de meias e roupa interior de homem

hospitable ['hɔspitəbl] hospitaleiro

hospital ['hɔspitl] hospital *m*

hospitality [ˌhɔspi'tæliti] hospitalidade *f*

host [həust] *s* anfitrião *m*, hospedeiro *m*; ECCL hóstia *f*; multidão *f*

hostage ['hɔstidʒ] refém *m*

hostel ['hɔstel] albergue *m*, lar *m*

hostess ['həustis] anfitriã *f*, hospedeira *f*, dona *f* de casa

hostil|e ['hɔstail] hostil; **~ity** [hɔs'tiliti] hostilidade *f*

hot [hɔt] quente; caloroso; cálido; picante; **~ dog** cachorro-quente *m*

hotel [həu'tel] hotel *m*

hound [haund] *s* podengo *m*, cão *m* de caça

hour ['auə] hora *f*; **~-glass** ampulheta *f*; **~ly** de hora em hora

house [haus] *s* casa *f*; câmara *f*; ≗ Câmara *f dos Comuns*, ≗ **of Commons** Câmara *f* dos Comuns; ≗ **of Lords** Câmara *f* dos Lordes; ≗**s of Parliament** Casas *f/pl* do Parlamento; **~hold** família *f*; governo *m* da casa, *Braz* negócios *m/pl* domésticos; **~keeper** governanta *f*; **~maid** criada *f*; **~wife** (*pl* **-wives**) dona *f* de casa; **~work** trabalho *m* doméstico

housing ['hauziŋ] *s* alojamento *m*, habitação *f*

hovel ['hɔvəl] cabana *f*, choupana *f*

hover ['hɔvə] *v/i* pairar

how [hau] *adv* quanto; como; quão; que; **~ are you?** como está?, como vai?; **~ come?** co-

mo se explica?; **~ do you do?** muito prazer; **~ far?** até onde?; **~ long?** quanto tempo?; **~ many?** quantos?; **~ever** *adv* de qualquer modo, seja como for; *conj* todavia, porém, contudo; **~ever much** por muito que
howl [haul] *v/i* uivar; *s* uivo *m*
hubbub ['hʌbʌb] alarido *m*
huddle ['hʌdl] *v/t*, *v/i* juntar (-se), amontoar(-se)
hue [hjuː] matiz *m*, tonalidade *f*
hug [hʌg] *v/t* abraçar; *s* abraço *m*
huge [hjuːdʒ] imenso, enorme, colossal
hull [hʌl] *s* casco *m*
hullo ['hʌ'ləu] = **hello**
hum [hʌm] *v/t*, *v/i* zumbir; trautear, cantarolar; *s* zumbido *m*
human ['hjuːmən] humano; **~e** [-'mein] humano, humanitário; **~itarian** [-ˌmæni'tɛəriən] *adj*, *s* humanitário *m*; **~ity** [-'mæniti] humanidade *f*
humble ['hʌmbl] *adj* humilde
humbug ['hʌmbʌg] *s* mistificação *f*, embuste *m*
humdrum ['hʌmdrʌm] monótono, banal
humid ['hjuːmid] (h)úmido
humidity [hjuː'miditi] (h)umidade *f*
humili|ate [hjuː'milieit] *v*[illegible]umilhar; **~ation** [-'eiʃ[illegible]] humilhação *f*; **~ty** [[illegible]iti] humildade *f*
humor[illegible] [[illegible]'hjuːmərist] humori[illegible] *m*, *f*
humorous ['hjuːmərəs] divertido, engraçado
humo(u)r ['hjuːmə] *s* humor *m*; *v/t* comprazer
hump [hʌmp] *s* corcova *f*, giba *f*, corcunda *f*, bossa *f*
hunch [hʌntʃ] *s* palpite *m*, pressentimento
hunchback ['hʌntʃbæk] corcunda *m*, *f*, corcovado *m*
hundred ['hʌndrəd] cento; cem; centena *f*
Hungarian [hʌŋ'gɛəriən] *s*, *adj* húngaro *m*
hunger ['hʌŋgə] *s* fome *f*
hungry ['hʌŋgri] esfomeado, esfaimado, faminto
hunt [hʌnt] *v/t*, *v/i* caçar; *s* caça *f*; caçada *f*; **~er** caçador *m*; **~ing** *s* caça *f*
hurdle ['həːdl] barreira *f*
hurl [həːl] *v/t* arremessar, arrojar, lançar
hurray! [hu'rei] hurra! viva!
hurricane ['hʌrikən] furacão *m*
hurry ['hʌri] *v/t*, *v/i* aviar-se, apressar(-se), despachar-se; pressa *f*; **in a ~** com pr[illegible]sa; **~ up** aviar-se, acele[illegible]
hurt [həːt] *v/t*, [illegible]doer, magoar; ferir
hush[illegible] ['hʌzbənd] *s* marido [illegible], esposo *m*
hush [hʌʃ] *s* silêncio *m*, quietude *f*; *v/t*, *v/i* aquietar, fazer calar; *int* silêncio!; **~ up** abafar, encobrir; **~-money** suborno *m*, peita *f*
husk [hʌsk] *s* casca *f*, folhelho *m*

husky ['hʌski] *adj* rouco, áspero

hustle ['hʌsl] *s* a(c)tividade *f*; *v/t*, *v/i* despachar, empurrar

hut [hʌt] cabana *f*; barraca *f*

hydro|carbon ['haidrə'kɑːbən] hidrocarboneto *m*; **~gen** ['-dʒən] hidrogénio *m*; **~phobia** hidrofobia *f*; **~plane** hidroplano *m*, hidrodeslizador *m*

hyena [hai'iːnə] hiena *f*

hygien|e ['haidʒiːn] higiene *f*; **~ic** [-'dʒiːnik] higiénico

hymn [him] hino *m*

hyphen ['haifən] hífen *m*, traço *m* de união

hypno|sis [hip'nəusis] hipnose *f*; **~tic** [hip'nɔtik] hipnótico; **~tism** ['hipnətizəm] hipnotismo *m*; **~tist** hipnotista *m*, *f*; **~-tize** ['hipnətaiz] *v/t* hipnotizar

hypo|chondria [ˌhaipə'kɔndriə] hipocondria *f*; **~chondriac** [ˌ-riæk] *s*, *adj* hipocondríaco *m*; **~crisy** [hi'pɔkrəsi] hipocrisia *f*; **~crite** ['hipəkrit] *s* hipócrita *m*, *f*

hypothetical [ˌhaipə'θetikəl] hipotético

hyster|ia [his'tiəriə] histeria *f*; **~ical** [-'terikəl] histérico; **~ics** [-'teriks] ataques *m/pl* histéricos

I

I [ai] eu

Iberian [ai'biəriən] *adj* ibérico

ice [ais] *s* gelo *m*; **~berg** icebergue *m*; **~-cream** sorvete *m*, gelado *m*

Icelandic [ais'lændik] *adj* islandês

icicle ['aisikl] sincelo *m*

icy ['aisi] gelado, álgido

idea [[illegible]'diə] ideia *f*

ideal [ai[illegible]] *adj*, *s* ideal *m*; **~ism** idealism[illegible] **~ist** idealista *m*, *f*

identi|cal [ai'dentikəl] idên[illegible] **~fication** [-ˌ-fi'keiʃən] identificação *f*; **~fy** [-fai] *v/t* identificar; **~ty** [-ti] (*pl* **-ties**) identidade *f*; **~ty card** bilhete *m* de identidade

idiom ['idiəm] idiotismo *m*, idioma *m*

idiot ['idiət] idiota *m*, *f*; **~ic** [ˌ-'ɔtik] idiota

idle ['aidl] *adj* preguiçoso; ocioso, desocupado; vão; **~ness** preguiça *f*; ócio *m*

idol ['aidl] ídolo *m*; **~atry** [-'dɔlətri] idolatria *f*; **~ize** ['-dəlaiz] *v/t* idolatrar

idyl(l) ['idil] idílio *m*; **~ic** idílico

i.e. ['ai'iː] = **that is (to say)** isto é

if [if] *conj* se

ignit|e [ig'nait] *v/t*, *v/i* inflamar(-se), acender; **~ion** [-'niʃən] [illegible]nição *f*

ignoble [ig'nəubəl] ignóbil

ignor|ance ['ignərəns] ignorância *f*; **~ant** ignorante; **~e** [-'nɔː]

v/t não fazer caso de, ignorar
ill [il] *s* mal *m*; *adj* doente; mau; *adv* mal; **~-advised** imprudente; **~-bred** malcriado, mal-educado
illegal [i'li:gəl] ilegal
illegible [i'ledʒəbl] ilegível
illegitimate [ˌili'dʒitimit] ilegítimo
ill-fated ['il'feitid] malaventurado
illicit [i'lisit] ilícito
illiterate [i'litərət] *adj*, *s* iletrado *m*, analfabeto *m*
ill|-natured ['il'neitʃəd] maldoso, malvado; **~ness** doença *f*; **~-timed** inoportuno; **~-treat** *v/t* maltratar
illuminat|e [i'lju:mineit] *v/t* iluminar; **~ion** [-'neiʃən] iluminação *f*
illus|ion [i'lu:ʒən] ilusão *f*; **~ive** [-siv] ilusório
illustrat|e ['iləstreit] *v/t* ilustrar; **~ion** [--'--] ilustração *f*
illustrious [i'lʌstriəs] ilustre
image ['imidʒ] imagem *f*
imagin|able [i'mædʒinəbl] imaginável; **~ary** imaginário; **~ation** imaginação *f*; **~e** [-in] *v/t* imaginar
imita|te ['imiteit] *v/t* imitar; **~tion** [-'teiʃən] imitação *f*; **~tor** imitador *m*
immature [ˌimə'tjuə] imaturo
immeasurable [i'meʒərəbl] imensurável
immediate [i'mi:djət] imediato
immerse [i'mə:s] *v/t* imergir
immigrat|e ['imigreit] *v/i* imigrar; **~ion** [-'greiʃən] imigração *f*
immoderate [i'mɔdərit] imoderado, desmedido
immodest [i'mɔdist] imodesto
immoral [i'mɔrəl] imoral
immortal [i'mɔ:tl] imortal
immovable [i'mu:vəbl] imóvel
immune [i'mju:n] imune, imunizado, isento
imp [imp] diabrete *m*
impact ['impækt] impacto *m*
impair [im'pɛə] *v/t* enfraquecer, prejudicar
impalpable [im'pælpəbl] impalpável
impart [im'pa:t] v/t participar, comunicar
impartial [im'pɑ:ʃəl] imparcial
impass|able [im'pɑ:səbl] intransitável; **~ive** [-'pæsiv] impassivo
impatien|ce [im'peiʃəns] impaciência *f*; **~t** impaciente
impediment [im'pedimənt] impedimento *m*, obstáculo *m*
impel [im'pel] *v/t* impelir
impending [im'pendiŋ] ameaçador, iminente
impenetrable [im'penitrəbl] impenetrável
imperative [im'perətiv] *s*, *adj* imperativo *m*
imperceptible [ˌimpə'septəbl] imperceptível
imperfect [im'pə:fikt] *s*, *adj* imperfeito *m*
imperial [im'piəriəl] imperial
imperil [im'peril] *v/t* pôr em perigo

imperishable [im'periʃəbl] imperecível
impersonal [im'pəːsnl] impessoal
impersonate [im'pəːsəneit] *v/t* personificar; representar
impertinen|ce [im'pəːtinəns] impertinência *f*; **~t** impertinente
impervious [im'pəːvjəs] impermeável
impetu|ous [im'petjuəs] impetuoso; **~s** ['-pitəs] ímpeto *m*
impish ['impiʃ] traquinas, travesso
implacable [im'plækəbl] implacável
implant [im'plɑːnt] *v/t* implantar
implement ['implimənt] *s* implemento *m*, apetrecho *m*
implicat|e ['implikeit] (**in**) *v/t* implicar (em); **~ion** [-'keiʃən] implicação *f*
implicit [im'plisit] implícito
implore [im'plɔː] *v/t* implorar
imply [im'plai] *v/t* implicar
impolite [impə'lait] descortês; **~ness** descortesia *f*
import ['impɔːt] *s* importância *f*; COM importação *f*; [im'pɔːt] *v/t* importar
importan|ce [im'pɔːtəns] importância *f*; **~t** importante
importation [ˌimpɔː'teiʃən] importação *f*
importunate [im'pɔːtjunit] importuno
impos|e [im'pəuz] *v/t* impor; **~e (up)on** incomodar, molestar; **~ing** imponente
impossib|ility [imˌpɔsə'biliti] impossibilidade *f*; **~le** [-'pɔsəbl] impossível
impostor [im'pɔstə] impostor *m*
impotent ['impətənt] impotente
impoverish [im'pɔvəriʃ] *v/t* empobrecer
impracticable [im'præktikəbl] impraticável
impress [im'pres] *v/t* imprimir; impressionar; **~ion** impressão *f*; **~ionable** impressionável; **~ive** impressionante, impressivo
imprint [im'print] *v/t* imprimir; ['imprint] *s* impressão *f*
imprison [im'prizn] *v/t* aprisionar; **~ment** aprisionamento *m*, prisão *f*
improbab|ility [imˌprɔbə'biliti] (*pl* **-ties**) improbabilidade *f*; **~le** [-'prɔbəbl] improvável
improper [im'prɔpə] impróprio; inconveniente
improve [im'pruːv] *v/t*, *v/i* melhorar, aperfeiçoar(-se); progredir; **~ment** melhoramento *m*, aperfeiçoamento *m*, progresso *m*
improvise ['imprəvaiz] *v/t*, *v/i* improvisar
impruden|ce [im'pruːdəns] imprudência *f*; **~t** imprudente
impud|ence ['impjudəns] impudência *f*; **~ent** impudente
impulse ['impʌls] impulso *m*
impulsive ['impʌlsiv] impulsi-

vo

impure [im'pjuə] impuro

imput|ation [ˌimpju'teiʃən] imputação *f*; **~e** [-'pju:t]: **~ to** imputar a

in [in] *prp* em; dentro de; *adv* dentro, em casa; **~ the afternoon** à tarde; **day ~ day out** dia após dia

inability [ˌinə'biliti] incapacidade *f*

inaccurate [in'ækjurit] inexa(c)to, incorre(c)to, erróneo

inaction [in'ækʃən] ina(c)ção *f*

inadequate [in'ædikwit] inadequado

inadmissible [ˌinəd'misəbl] inadmissível

inadvertent [ˌinəd'və:tənt] inadvertido

inanimate [in'ænimit] inanimado

inapplicable [in'æplikəbl] inaplicável

inapt [in'æpt] inapto

inarticulate [ˌinɑ:'tikjulit] inarticulado

inasmuch as [inəz'mʌtʃ əz] visto que, porquanto

inattentive [ˌinə'tentiv] desatento

inaudible [in'ɔ:dəbl] inaudível

inaugurate [i'nɔ:gjureit] *v/t* inaugurar

inborn ['in'bɔ:n] inato

incalculable [in'kælkjuləbl] incalculável

incandescent ['inkæn'desnt] incandescente

incapable [in'keipəbəl] incapaz

incapaci|tate [ˌinkə'pæsiteit] *v/t* incapacitar; **~ty** incapacidade *f*

incautious [inkɔ:ʃəs] incauto

incense ['insens] *s* incenso *m*; [in'sens] *v/t* irritar

incentive [in'sentiv] incentivo *m*

incessant [in'sesnt] incessante

inch [intʃ] *s* polegada *f*; **~ by ~** palmo a palmo

incident ['insidənt] *s* incidente *m*; **~al** [ˌ-'dentel] *adj* incidental, casual; **~ally** a propósito

incineration [inˌsinə'reiʃən] incineração *f*

incis|e [in'saiz] *v/t* incisar; **~ion** [in'siʒən] incisão *f*; **~ive** incisivo; **~or** incisivo *m*

incite [in'sait] *v/t* incitar

inclination [ˌinkli'neiʃən] inclinação *f*

incline [in'klain] *s* declive *m*, vertente *f*; *v/t*, *v/i* inclinar(-se)

include [in'klu:d] *v/t* incluir

inclusive [in'klu:siv] inclusivo

incoherent [ˌinkəu'hiərənt] incoerente

incombustible [ˌinkəm'bʌstəbl] incombusível

income ['inkʌm] rendimento *m*, renda *f*; **~-tax** imposto *m* de rendimento

incomparable [in'kɔmpərəbl] incomparável

incompatible [ˌinkəm'pætəbl] incompatível

incompetent [in'kɔmpitənt] incompetente

incomplete [ˌinkəm'pliːt] incompleto
incomprehensible [inkɔmpri'hensəbl] incompreensível
inconceivable [ˌinkən'siːvəbl] inconcebível
incongruous [in'kɔŋgruəs] incongruente
inconsidera|ble [ˌinkən'sidərəbl] insignificante; **~te** [ˌ-rit] inconsiderado
inconsistent [ˌinkən'sistent] inconsistente; incompatível
inconsolable [ˌinkən'səuləbl] inconsolável
inconstant [in'kɔnstənt] inconstante
inconvenien|ce [ˌinkən'viːnjəns] *s* inconveniência *f*; inconveniente *m*; **~t** incómodo, inconveniente
incorporat|e [in'kɔːpəreit] *v/t, v/i* incorporar(-se); **~ed** incorporado, associado
incorrect [ˌinkə'rekt] incorre(c)to
incorrigible [in'kɔridʒəbl] incorrigível
incorruptible [ˌinkə'rʌptəbl] incorru(p)tível
increase ['inkriːs] *s* aumento *m*; [in'kriːs] *v/t, v/i* aumentar
increasingly [in'kriːsiŋli] cada vez mais
incredible [in'kredəbl] incrível
incredulous [in'kredjuləs] incrédulo
incriminate [in'krimineit] *v/t* incriminar
incur [in'kəː] *v/t* incorrer em
incurable [in'kjuərəbl] incurável
indebted [in'detid] individado; obrigado, grato
indecen|cy [in'diːsnsi] (*pl* **-cies**) indecência *f*; **~t** indecente
indecision [ˌindi'siʒən] indecisão *f*
indeed [in'diːd] com efeito, deveras, de fa(c)to, na verdade
indefatigable [ˌindi'fætigəbl] infatigável
indefensible [ˌindi'fensəbl] indefensável
indefinite [in'definit] indefinido
indelicate [in'delikit] indelicado
indemni|fy [in'demnifai] *v/t* inde(m)nizar; **~ty** (*pl* **-ties**) inde(m)nização *f*; inde(m)nidade *f*
indent [in'dent] *v/t* recortar, dentear; **~ure** [-'dentʃə] *s* contrato *m*
independen|ce [ˌindi'pendəns] independência *f*; **~t** *adj* independente
indescribable [ˌindis'kraibəbl] indescritível
indestructible [ˌindis'trʌktəbl] indestrutível
indeterminate [ˌindi'təːminit] indeterminado
index ['indeks] (*pl* **-dexes**, **-dices**) ['indisiːz] índex *m*, índice *m*; **~ finger** dedo *m* indicador
Indian ['indiən] *adj, s* índio *m*; indiano *m*; **~ corn** milho *m*;

~ **summer** verão *m* de S. Martinho
india-rubber ['indjə'rʌbə] borracha *f*; cauchu *m*
indicat|e ['indikeit] *v/t* indicar; **~ion** indicação *f*; **~ive** [-'dikətiv] *adj*, *s* indicativo *m*
indict [in'dait] *v/t* acusar; **~ment** acusação *f*
indifferen|ce [in'difrəns] indiferença *f*; **~t** indiferente; medíocre
indigest|ible [ˌindi'dʒestəbl] indigesto; **~ion** [-tʃən] indigestão *f*
indign|ant [in'dignənt] indignado; **~ation** [-'neiʃən] indignação *f*; **~ity** indignidade *f*
indirect [ˌindi'rekt] indire(c)to
indiscreet [ˌindis'kriːt] indiscreto
indiscretion [ˌindis'kreʃən] indiscreção *f*
indiscriminate [ˌindis'kriminit] indiscriminado
indispensable [ˌindis'pensəbl] indispensável
indispos|ed [ˌindis'pəuzd] indisposto; **~ition** indisposição *f*
indisputable ['indis'pjuːtəbl] indisputável
indistinct [ˌindis'tiŋkt] indistinto
indistinguishable [ˌindis'tiŋgwiʃəbl] indistinguível
individual [ˌindi'vidjuəl] *s* indivíduo *m*; *adj* individual
indolen|ce ['indələns] indolência *f*; **~t** indolente
indoor ['indɔː] interior; caseiro; **~s** dentro, em casa
induce [in'djuːs] *v/t* induzir
induction [in'dʌkʃən] indução *f*
indulg|e [in'dʌldʒ] *v/t*, *v/i* saciar, satisfazer; ~ **in** entregarse a; **~nce** [-dʒəns] indulgência *f*; **~nt** [-dʒənt] indulgente
industri|al [in'dʌstriəl] industrial; **~alist** industrial *m*, *f*; **~alize** *v/t*, *v/i* industrializar; **~ous** industrioso
industry ['indəstri] (*pl* **-tries**) indústria *f*
ineffective [ˌini'fektiv] ineficaz
inept [i'nept] inepto
inequality [ˌini'kwɔliti] (*pl* **-ties**) desigualdade *f*
inequitable [in'ekwitəbl] injusto
inert [i'nəːt] inerte; **~ia** [-ʃjə] inércia *f*
inestimable [in'estiməbl] inestimável
inevitable [in'evitəbl] inevitável
inexcusable [ˌiniks'kjuːzəbl] indesculpável, imperdoável
inexhaustible [ˌinig'zɔːstəbl] inexaurível, inesgotável
inexorable [in'eksərəbl] inexorável
inexpensive [ˌiniks'pensiv] barato
inexperienced [ˌiniks'piəriənst] inexperiente
inexplicable [in'eksplikəbl] inexplicável
inexpressible [ˌiniks'presəbl] inexprimível

inextinguishable [ˌiniks'tiŋgwiʃəbl] inextinguível
infallible ['infæləbl] infalível
infam|ous ['infəməs] infame; **~y** infamia *f*
infancy ['infənsi] infância *f*
infant ['infənt] infante *m*, criança *f*; **~ile** [-tail] infantil
infantry ['infəntri] infantaria *f*
infatuated [in'fætjueitid] *adj* apaixonado
infect [in'fekt] *v/t* infe(c)tar; **~ion** [-kʃən] infecção *f*; **~ious** infeccioso
infer [in'fəː] *v/t* deduzir, inferir; **~ence** ['infərəns] inferência *f*, dedução *f*
inferior [in'fiəriə] inferior; **~ity** [infiəri'ɔriti] inferioridade *f*
infernal [in'fəːnl] infernal
infest [in'fest] *v/t* infestar
infidelity [ˌinfi'deliti] (*pl* **-ties**) infidelidade *f*
infinit|e ['infinit] infinito; **~ive** [-'finitiv] *adj*, *s* infinitivo *m*; **~y** infinidade *f*; infinito *m*
infirm [in'fəːm] enfermo; débil, fraco; **~ary** (*pl* **-ries**) enfermaria *f*; **~ity** (*pl* **-ties**) enfermidade *f*
inflame [in'fleim] *v/t* inflamar
inflamm|able [in'flæməbl] inflamável; **~ation** [ˌinflə'meiʃən] inflamação *f*
inflat|e [in'fleit] *v/t* inflar; **~ion** inflação *f*
inflexibility [inˌfleksə'biliti] inflexibilidade *f*
inflict [in'flikt] *v/t* infligir
influen|ce ['influəns] *s* influência *f*; *v/t* influir em, influenciar; **~tial** [ˌ-'enʃəl] influente
influenza [ˌinflu'enzə] gripe *f*, influenza *f*
inform [in'fɔːm] *v/t* informar; **~ against** denunciar
informal [in'fɔːml] sem cerimónia
inform|ation [infə'meiʃən] informação *f*, informações *f/pl*; **~ed** *adj* informado, inteirado; **~er** delator *m*, informante *m*, *f*
infringe [in'frindʒ] *v/t* infringir
infuriate [in'fjuərieit] *v/t* enfurecer
infus|e [in'fjuːz] *v/t*, *v/i* infundir; **~ion** [-ʒən] infusão *f*
ingen|ious [in'dʒiːnjəs] engenhoso; **~uity** [ˌ-'njuːiti] engenho *m*, habilidade *f*; **~uous** [-'dʒenjuəs] ingénuo
ingratitude [in'grætitjuːd] ingratidão *f*
ingredient [in'griːdjənt] ingrediente *m*
inhabit [in'hæbit] *v/t* habitar; **~able** habitável; **~ant** habitante *m*
inhale [in'heil] *v/t*, *v/i* inalar
inherent [in'hiərənt] inerente
inherit [in'herit] *v/t*, *v/i* herdar; **~ance** herança *f*
inhibit [in'hibit] *v/t* inibir; **~ion** [-'biʃən] inibição *f*
inhospitable [in'hɔspitəbl] inóspito; inospitaleiro
inhuman [in'hjuːmən] inumano, desumano
initial [i'niʃəl] *adj*, *s* inicial *f*
initiate [i'niʃieit] *v/t* iniciar

initiative [i'niʃiətiv] iniciativa *f*
inject [in'dʒekt] *v/t* inje(c)tar; **~ion** inje(c)ção *f*
injur|e ['indʒə] *v/t* prejudicar; injuriar; ferir, lesar; **~ious** [-'dʒuəriəs] prejudicial, nocivo; **~y** (*pl* **-ries**) injúria *f*; lesão *f*; dano *m*, prejuízo *m*
injustice [in'dʒʌstis] injustiça *f*
ink [iŋk] tinta *f*
inkling ['iŋkliŋ] menor ideia *f*
inland ['inlənd] *adj* (do) interior; interno, nacional
inlay ['in'lei] *v/t* embutir
inlet ['inlet] enseada *f*, angra *f*
inmate ['inmeit] ocupante *m, f*, residente *m, f*
inmost ['inməust] íntimo, recôndito
inn [in] estalagem *f*
innate ['i'neit] inato
inner ['inə] interior; oculto
innkeeper ['inˌki:pə] estalajadeiro *m*
innocen|ce ['inəsəns] inocência *f*; **~t** *adj* inocente
innovation [ˌinə'veiʃən] inovação *f*
innumerable [i'nju:mərəbl] inumerável
inoculate [i'nɔkjuleit] *v/t* inocular
inoffensive [ˌinə'fensiv] inofensivo
inopportune [in'ɔpətju:n] inoportuno
inquest ['inkwest] investigação *f* judicial
inquietude [in'kwaiitju:d] inquietação *f*
inquir|e [in'kwaiə] *v/t, v/i* inquirir, perguntar; **~e into** indagar, pesquisar; **~y** (*pl* **-ries**) inquérito *m*, pesquisa *f*
inquisitive [in'kwizitiv] curioso, inquiridor
inroad ['inrəud] incursão *f*
insan|e [in'sein] demente, louco; **~ity** [-'sæniti] loucura *f*, demência *f*
inscribe [in'skraib] *v/t* inscrever
inscription [in'skripʃən] inscrição *f*
insect ['insekt] inse(c)to *m*; **~icide** [-'sektisaid] inse(c)ticida *m*
insecure [ˌinsi'kjuə] inseguro
insensible [in'sensəbl] imperceptível
inseparable [in'sepərəbl] inseparável
insert [in'sə:t] *v/t* introduzir, inserir
inside ['in'said] *adj, s* interior *m*; *adv* dentro; *prp* dentro de; **~ out** do avesso, às avessas
insight ['insait] penetração *f*; compreensão *f*
insignificant [ˌinsig'nifikənt] insignificante
insincere [ˌinsin'siə] insincero
insinuate [in'sinjueit] *v/t* insinuar
insipid [in'sipid] insípido
insist [in'sist] (**on**) *v/i* insistir (em); **~ence** insistência *f*
insolen|ce ['insələns] insolência *f*; **~t** insolente
insoluble [in'sɔljubl] insolúvel

insolvent [in'sɔlvənt] insolvente

insomnia [in'sɔmniə] insónia *f*

insomuch as [ˌinsəu'mʌtʃ əz] a tal ponto que

inspect [in'spekt] *v/t* inspe(c)cionar; revistar; **~ion** [-ʃən] inspe(c)ção *f*; revista *f*; **~or** revisor *m*; inspe(c)tor *m*

inspiration [ˌinspə'reiʃən] inspiração *f*

inspire [in'spaiə] *v/t* inspirar

install [in'stɔːl] *v/t* instalar; **~ation** [ˌ-stə'leiʃən] instalação *f*

insta(l)lment [in'stɔːlmənt] prestação *f*; episódio *m*

instance ['instəns] *s* instância *f*; exemplo *m*, caso *m*; **for ~** por exemplo

instant ['instənt] *s* instante *m*; *adj* imediato; instantâneo; **~aneous** [-'teinjəs] instantâneo

instead [in'sted] *adv* em vez disso; **~ of** em vez de, em lugar de

instop ['instep] peito *m* do pé

instigate ['instigeit] *v/t* instigar

instinct ['instiŋkt] *s* instinto *m*; **~ive** [-'stiŋktiv] instintivo

institut|e ['institjuːt] *s* instituto *m*; *v/t* instituir, estabelecer; **~ion** [-'tjuːʃən] instituição *f*

instruct [in'strʌkt] *v/t* instruir, ensinar; **~ion** instrução *f*; **~ive** instrutivo; **~or** instrutor *m*

instrument ['instrumənt] instrumento *m*

insubordinate [ˌinsə'bɔːdənit] insubordinado

insufferable [in'sʌfərəbl] insuportável

insufficient [ˌinsə'fiʃənt] insuficiente

insular ['insjulə] insular

insulat|e ['insjuleit] *v/t* isolar; **~or** isolador *m*

insult [in'sʌlt] *v/t* insultar; ['insʌlt] *s* insulto *m*

insuperable [in'sjuːpərəbl] insuperável

insupportable [ˌinsə'pɔːtəbl] insuportável

insur|ance [in'ʃuərəns] seguro *m*; **~ance company** companhia *f* de seguros; **~ance policy** apólice *f* de seguro; **~e** *v/t* segurar

insurgent [in'səːdʒənt] *adj* insurgente

insurmountable [ˌinsə'mauntəbl] insuperável

insurrection [ˌinsə'rekʃən] insurreição *f*

intact [in'tækt] inta(c)to

integrate ['intəgreit] *v/t*, *v/i* integrar(-se)

integration [ˌinti'greiʃən] integração *f*

integrity [in'tegriti] integridade *f*

intellect ['intilekt] intelecto *m*; **~ual** [ˌ-'lektjuəl] *adj*, *s* intelectual *m*, *f*

intellig|ence [in'telidʒəns] inteligência *f*; **~ent** inteligente; **~ible** inteligível

intemperate [in'tempərit] intemperado, desenfreado

intend [in'tend] *v/t* tencionar;

~ed *s* prometido *m*, futuro *m*
inten|se [in'tens] intenso; **~sity** intensidade *f*; **~sive** intensivo
intent [in'tent] *s* intento *m*; *adj* atento; **~ion** intenção *f*
interact [ˌintər'ækt] *v/i* inter-a(c)tuar-se
intercede [ˌintə'si:d] *v/i* interceder
intercept [ˌintə'sept] *v/t* interceptar
intercession [ˌintə'seʃən] intercessão *f*
interchange ['intə'tʃeindʒ] *s* intercâmbio *m*; [ˌintə'tʃeindʒ] *v/t* trocar, (inter)cambiar; **~able** permutável
intercourse ['intəkɔ:s] trato *m*, relações *f/pl*; relações *f/pl* sexuais
interdict [ˌintə'dikt] *v/t* interdizer, interditar
interest ['intrist] *s* interesse *m*; juro(s) *m* (*pl*); *v/t* interessar; **~ed** *adj* interessado; **~ing** interessante
interfer|e [ˌintə'fiə] *v/i* interferir; intrometer-se; **~ence** interferência *f*
interior [in'tiəriə] *adj*, *s* interior *m*
interlude ['inte(:)lu:d] interlúdio *m*; intervalo *m*; entremez *m*
intermedia|ry [ˌintə'mi:djəri] *adj*, *s* (*pl* **-ries**) intermediário *m*; **~te** intermédio
interminable [in'tə:minəbl] interminável
intermingle [ˌintə'miŋgl] *v/t*, *v/i* misturar(-se), entremear
intermittent [ˌintə'mitənt] intermitente
intern [in'tə:n] *v/t* internar, encarcerar
internal [in'tə:nl] interno, interior, intestino
international [ˌintə'næʃənl] *adj* internacional
Internet ['intənet] *s* Internet
interpose [ˌintə'pəuz] *v/t*, *v/i* interpor(-se); intervir
interpret [in'tə:prit] *v/t* interpretar; **~ation** [-'teiʃən] interpretação *f*; **~er** intérprete *m*, *f*
interrogate [in'terəgeit] *v/t* interrogar
interrogat|ion [inˌterə'geiʃən] interrogação *f*; **~ive** [ˌ-tə'rɔgətiv] *adj* interrogativo; **~or** [in'terəgeitə] interrogador *m*
interrupt [ˌintə'rʌpt] *v/t*, *v/i* interromper; atalhar; **~ion** interrupção *f*
interval ['intəvəl] intervalo *m*
interven|e [ˌintə'vi:n] *v/t* intervir; **~tion** [-'venʃən] intervenção *f*
interview ['intəvju:] *s* entrevista *f*; *v/t* entrevistar
intestine [in'testin] intestino *m*
intima|cy ['intiməsi] intimidade *f*; **~te** ['-mit] *adj* íntimo; *v/t* ['-meit] dar a entender, insinuar
intimidate [in'timideit] *v/t* intimidar
into ['intu, 'intə] em; para, para dentro de
intoler|able [in'tɔlərəbl] into-

lerável; ~**ant** intolerante
intoxicate [in'tɔksikeit] *v/t* embriagar; intoxicar
intractable [in'træktəbl] intratável
intrepid [in'trepid] intrépido
intricate ['intrikit] intrincado
intrigue [in'tri:g] *s* enredo *m*, intriga *f*; *v/t, v/i* intrigar
introduc|e [ˌintrə'dju:s] *v/t* apresentar; ~**e into** introduzir; ~**tion** [ˌ-'dʌkʃən] apresentação *f*; introdução *f*; ~**tory** introdutório
introvert ['intrəuvə:t] introvertido *m*
intru|de [in'tru:d] *v/t, v/i* introduzir(-se), intrometer(-se); ~**der** intruso *m*; ~**sion** [-ʒən] intrusão *f*
intuition [ˌintju'iʃən] intuição *f*
invad|e [in'veid] *v/t* invadir; ~**er** invasor *m*
invalid [in'vælid] *adj* nulo, inválido; ['invəli:d] *s* inválido *m*
invaluable [in'væljuəbl] inestimável
invariable [in'vɛəriəbl] invariável
invasion [in'veiʒən] invasão *f*
invective [in'vektiv] invectiva *f*
invent [in'vent] *v/t* inventar; ~**ion** invento *m*, invenção *f*; ~**ive** inventivo; ~**or** inventor *m, f*
inventory [in'ventri] (*pl* **-ries**) inventário *m*
inverse ['in'və:s] *adj, s* inverso *m*
invert [in'və:t] *v/t* inverter; ~**ed commas** *pl* aspas *f/pl*
invest [in'vest] *v/t, v/i* investir
investigate [in'vestigeit] *v/t, v/i* investigar, indagar
investigation [inˌvesti'geiʃən] investigação *f*, inquérito *m*
investment [in'vestmənt] investimento *m*
invigorate [in'vigəreit] *v/t* revigorar
invincible [in'vinsəbl] invencível
invisible [in'vizəbl] invisível
invit|ation [ˌinvi'teiʃən] convite *m*; ~**e** [-'vait] *v/t* convidar; ~**ing** [-'vaitiŋ] *adj* convidativo
invoice ['invɔis] *s* fa(c)tura *f*
invoke [in'vəuk] *v/t* invocar
involuntary [in'vɔləntəri] involuntário
involve [in'vɔlv] *v/t* envolver, implicar; ~**d** *adj* envolvido, implicado; complicado
invulnerable [in'vʌlnərəbl] invulnerável
inward ['inwəd] *adj* interior, íntimo; ~**s** para dentro
iodin(e) ['aiədi:n] iodo *m*
Irish ['aiəriʃ] *adj, s* irlandês *m*; ~**man** (*pl* **-men**) irlandês *m*
irksome ['ə:ksəm] fastidioso, cansativo
iron ['aiən] *s* ferro *m*; *adj* de ferro; férreo; *v/t, v/i* passar a ferro
ironic(al) [ai'rɔnik(əl)] irónico
irony ['aiərəni] ironia *f*
irradiate [i'reidieit] *v/t* irradiar
irrational [i'ræʃənl] irracional
irrefutable [i'refjutəbl] irrefutável, incontestável

irregular [i'regjulə] irregular
irrelevant [i'relivənt] irrelevante
irreparable [i'repərəbl] irreparável
irreproachable [ˌiri'prəutʃəbl] irrepreensível
irresistible [ˌiri'zistəbl] irresistível
irresolute [i'rezəluːt] irresoluto
irresponsible [ˌiris'pɔnsəbl] irresponsável
irretrievable [ˌiri'triːvəbl] irrecuperável, irreparável
irreverent [i'revərənt] irreverente
irrevocable [i'revəkəbl] irrevocável, irreparável
irrigat|e ['irigeit] *v/t* irrigar; **~ion** [-'geiʃən] irrigação
irrita|ble ['iritəbl] irritável, irascível; **~nt** irritante; **~te** ['-teit] *v/t* irritar; **~tion** [ˌ-'teiʃən] irritação *f*
is [iz, əz] *3rd sg pres of* **be** é; está; fica
island ['ailənd] ilha *f*; **~er** ilhéu *m*, insulano *m*
isolat|e ['aisəleit] *v/t* isolar; **~ion** [-'leiʃən] isolação *f*
issue ['iʃuː] *v/t* distribuir; publicar; emitir; *s* distribuição *f*; tiragem *f*, edição *f*; **~ from** provir, brotar
isthmus ['isməs] istmo *m*
it [it] *pron* ele, ela, o, a, isto, isso; **that's ~** é tudo; isso, assim
Italian [i'tæljən] *adj*, *s* italiano *m*
itch [itʃ] *s* prurido *m*, comichão *f*; desejo *m*, ânsia *f*; *v/i* prurir; ter comichão
item ['aitəm] *s* item *m*, rubrica *f*; *adv* item, também
itinerary [ai'tinərəri] (*pl* **-ries**) itinerário *m*
its [its] *poss pron* seu, sua, seus, suas; dele, dela
itself [it'self] *pron* se; ele mesmo, ela mesmo; **by ~** sozinho; **in ~** em si mesmo
ivory ['aivəri] marfim *m*
ivy ['aivi] hera *f*

J

jabber ['dʒæbə] *v/i* papaguear, palrar; *s* tagarelice *f*
jack [dʒæk] *s* MEC macaco *m*; **≗ of all trades** pau *m* para toda obra; *v/t* **~ up** levantar com macaco
jackal ['dʒækɔːl] chacal *m*
jackdaw ['dʒækdɔː] gralha *f*
jacket ['dʒækit] casaco *m* curto; jaqueta *f*
jad|e [dʒeid] jade *f*; rocim *m*; **~ed** estafado
jagged ['dʒægid] *adj* entalhado, denteado
jaguar ['dʒægjuə] jaguar *m*
jail [dʒeil] *s* cadeia *f*, prisão *f*; **~er** carcereiro *m*
jam [dʒæm] *s* compota *f*; engar-

rafamento *m*, congestionamento *m*; aperto *m*; *v/t*, *v/i* empurrar; interferir com; entalar; esmagar, comprimir, apertar
janitor ['dʒænitə] *US* porteiro *m*
January ['dʒænjuəri] Janeiro *m*
Japanese [ˌdʒæpə'niːz] *adj*, *s* japonês (*m*)
jar [dʒɑː] *s* frasco *m*; pote *m*, jarro *m*, cântaro *m*; vibração *f*, choque *m*, sacudidela *f*; *v/t* sacudir, chocar; *v/i* vibrar, ranger
jargon ['dʒɑːgən] jargão *m*, calão *m*, gíria *f*
jasmin(e) ['dʒæsmin] jasmim *m*
jaundice ['dʒɔːndis] icterícia *f*
jaunt [dʒɔːnt] *s* passeata *f*, volta *f*; **~y** animado, airoso
javelin ['dʒævlin] dardo *m*
jaw [dʒɔː] *s* maxila *f*, maxilar *m*; queixada *f*; **~s** garras *f/pl*
jay [dʒei] gaio *m*
jealous ['dʒeləs] cioso, zeloso; ciumento; **~y** ciúme *m*
jeer [dʒiə] *s* escárnio *m*; *v/i*, *v/t* **~ at** escarnecer
jelly ['dʒeli] geleia *f*; **~fish** medusa *f*, alforreca *f*
jeopard|ize ['dʒepədaiz] *v/t* arriscar, comprometer; **~y** perigo *m*, risco *m*
jerk [dʒəːk] *s* sacudidela *f*; *v/t* sacudir; **~y** espasmódico
jersey ['dʒəːzi] jérsei *m*
jest [dʒest] *s* gracejo *m*; *v/i* gracejar
jet [dʒet] *s* jacto *m*; avião *m* a ja(c)to; MIN azeviche *m*; **~ lag** *s* jet lag *m*
jettison ['dʒetisn] *v/t* alijar
jetty ['dʒeti] (*pl* **-ties**) molhe *m*, quebra-mar *m*
Jew [dʒuː] judeu *m*
jewel ['dʒuːəl] jóia *f*; **~(l)er** joalheiro *m*; **~(le)ry** joalharia *f*, jóias *f/pl*
Jewish ['dʒuːiʃ] judeu, judaico
jingle ['dʒiŋgl] *s* tinido *m*; *v/t*, *v/i* tinir
job [dʒɔb] trabalho *m*; emprego *m*; tarefa *f*; **out of a ~** desempregado
jockey ['dʒɔki] *s* jóquei *m*
jocular ['dʒɔkjulə] jovial
jog [dʒɔg] *v/t*, *v/i* sacudir, empurrar
join [dʒɔin] *v/t*, *v/i* juntar(-se) (a), unir(-se) (a)
joiner ['dʒɔinə] marceneiro *m*
joint [dʒɔint] *s* junção *f*; juntura *f*, junta *f*; articulação *f*; quarto *m* de carne; *adj* comum; unido; **~ account** conta *f* comum; **~-stock company** sociedade *f* anónima
joke [dʒəuk] *s* piada *f*, brincadeira *f*, gracejo *m*; *v/i* gracejar, brincar, galhofar; **no ~** é (a) sério, não é brincadeira
joker ['dʒəukə] brincalhão *m*
jolly ['dʒɔli] *adj* afável, alegre; *adv* muito; *v/t* animar
jolt [dʒəult] *s* solavanco *m*, sacudidela *f*; *v/t*, *v/i* ir aos solavancos; sacudir
jostle ['dʒɔsl] *v/t*, *v/i* acotovelar

(-se)
jot [dʒɔt] *s* ponta *f*, mínimo *m*; *v/t* ~ **down** anotar, apontar
journal ['dʒə:nl] jornal *m*; diário *m*; periódico *m*; **~ism** ['-izəm] jornalismo; **~ist** jornalista *m*, *f*
journey ['dʒə:ni] *s* viagem *f*; *v/i* viajar
jovial ['dʒəuvjəl] jovial
joy [dʒɔi] alegria *f*; **~ful** alegre
jubil|ation [ˌdʒu:bi'leiʃən] júbilo *m*; **~ee** ['dʒu:bili:] jubileu *m*
judge [dʒʌdʒ] *s* juiz *m*; *v/t*, *v/i* julgar
judg(e)ment ['dʒʌdʒmənt] julgamento *m*; juízo *m*; sentença *f*
judic|ial ['dʒu(:)'diʃəl] judicial; **~iary** *adj* judiciário; **~ious** judicioso
judo ['dʒu:dəu] judo *m*, jiu-jitsu *m*
jug [dʒʌg] *s* cântaro *m*, jarro *m*, *Braz* moringa *f*
juggl|e ['dʒʌgl] *v/t*, *v/i* fazer prestidigitação; **~er** prestidigitador *m*; **~ery** prestidigitação *f*
juic|e [dʒu:s] *s* sumo *m*, suco *m*; **~y** suculento, sumarento
July [dʒu'lai] Julho *m*
jumble ['dʒʌmbl] *v/t*, *v/i* misturar, confundir; *s* salgalhada *f*, trapalhada *f*
jump [dʒʌmp] *s* salto *m*; pulo *m*; *v/t*, *v/i* saltar, pular, galgar
junct|ion ['dʒʌŋkʃən] junção *f*; entroncamento *m*; **~ure** ['-tʃə] conjuntura *f*
June [dʒu:n] Junho *m*
jungle ['dʒʌŋgl] selva *f*
junior ['dʒu:niə] *adj*, *s* júnior *m*
junk [dʒʌŋk] *s* sucata *f*; refugo *m*; ~ **food** comida *f* de plástico
juror ['dʒuərə] jurado *m*
jury ['dʒuəri] (*pl* **-ries**) júri *m*
just [dʒʌst] *adj* justo; *adv* meramente, só; justamente; há pouco; agora mesmo; **have ~ ...** acabar de ...; **~ now** agora mesmo
justice ['dʒʌstis] justiça *f*
justify ['dʒʌstifai] *v/t* justificar
jut out [dʒʌt] *v/i* salientar-se, proje(c)tarse
juvenile ['dʒu:vinail] juvenil
juxtapos|e ['dʒʌkstəpəuz] *v/t* justapor; **~ition** [-pə'ziʃən] justaposição *f*

K

kangaroo [ˌkæŋgə'ru:] canguru *m*
keel [ki:l] *s* quilha *f*
keen [ki:n] *adj* afiado, agudo, penetrante; veemente, ardente, entusiasta; astuto; **be ~ on** gostar muito de; **~ness** agudeza *f*; entusiasmo *m*
keep [ki:p] *v/t*, *v/i* continuar, ficar; guardar; dirigir, manejar; cumprir; deter, demorar; manter, conservar(-se); **~ back**

reter; ~ **from** impedir, impossibilitar; ~ **off** manter(-se) afastado, afastar(-se); ~ **on** continuar; seguir; ~ **out** excluir, afastar; ~ **to** seguir; ficar; restringir-se, limitar-se; ~ **up** manter(-se); ~ **up with** acompanhar, não ficar atrás

keep|er ['ki:pə] guardião *m*; guarda *m*; **~ing** guarda *f*; conservação *f*; **in safe ~ing** a salvo; **~sake** recordação *f*, lembrança *f*

kennel ['kenl] canil *m*

kerchief ['kə:tʃif] lenço *m* de cabeça

kernel ['kə:nl] miolo *m*; cerne *m*; núcleo *m*

kettle ['ketl] chaleira *f*; **~-drum** timbale *m*

key [ki:] *s* chave *f*; tecla *f*; MUS clave *f*; **~hole** buraco *m* de fechadura; **~note** *s* nota *f* tónica; **~stone** chave *f* de abóbada

kick [kik] *s* pontapé *m*; chuto *m*, chute *m*; coice *m*; estímulo *m*, energia *f*; *v/t*, *v/i* dar pontapés (a/em); escoucear; chutar; ~ **the bucket** esticar o pernil; **~-off** *s* pontapé *m* de saída; ~ **out** pôr na rua

kid [kid] *s* cabrito *m*; criança *f*, miúdo *m*, garoto *m*; pele *f* de cabrito, pelica *f*; *v/t*, *v/i* brincar, caçoar, pegar com alguém; ~ **gloves** luvas *f/pl* de pelica

kidnap ['kidnæp] *v/t* raptar, sequestrar; **~per** raptor *m*

kidney ['kidni] rim *m*; ~ **bean** feijão *m*

kill [kil] *v/t*, *v/i* matar; **~er** assassino *m*; **~ing** *adj* assassino, mortal; cansativo, exaustivo

kiln [kiln] forno *m*, fornalha *f*

kilo ['ki:ləu] quilo *m*

kilogram(me) ['kiləgræm] quilograma *m*

kilometre ['kilə,mi:tə] quilómetro *m*

kilt [kilt] saiote *m* escocês

kin [kin] parentes *m/pl*

kind [kaind] *adj* bondoso, amável; *s* espécie *f*, género *m* qualidade *f*; ~ **of** bastante; como que

kindle ['kindl] *v/t*, *v/i* acender (-se)

kind|ly ['kaindli] *adj* bondoso, amável; *adv* amavelmente; **~ness** bondade *f*, amabilidade *f*

kindred ['kindrid] *s* parentela *f*, família *f*; *adj* aparentado; congénere

king [kiŋ] rei *m*; **~dom** ['-dəm] reino *m*; **~ly** real

kink [kiŋk] retorcimento *m*; *fig* mania *f*

kinship ['kinʃip] parentesco *m*

kiosk [ki'ɔsk] quiosque *m*

kipper ['kipə] arenque *m* salgado defumado

kiss [kis] *s* beijo *m*; *v/t* beijar

kit [kit] indumentária *f*, equipamento *m*

kitchen ['kitʃin] cozinha *f*; **~ette** [kitʃi'net] conzinha *f* pequena

kite [kait] milhafre *m*; papagaio *m* de papel

kitten ['kitn] gatinho *m*, bichano *m*
kleptomaniac [ˌkleptəu'meiniæk] cleptomaníaco *m*
knack [næk] jeito *m*, habilidade *f*
knave [neiv] valete *m*
knead [ni:d] *v/t*, *v/i* amassar; massajar
knee [ni:] *s* joelho *m*; **~-cap** *s* joelheira *f*; rótula *f*; **~l** [ni:l] *v/i* ajoelhar(-se)
knell [nel] dobre *m* a finados
knickers ['nikəz] *s/pl* cuecas *f/pl*
knick-knack ['niknæk] bugiganga *f*
knife [naif] *s* (*pl* **knives** [-vz]) faca *f*; navalha *f*; *v/t* apunhalar, esfaquear
knight [nait] *s* cavaleiro *m*; cavalo *m* (*chess*); *v/t* armar cavaleiro
knit [nit] *v/t*, *v/i* tricotar; **~ting** *s* tricô *m*
knob [nɔb] protuberância *f*; puxador *m*; castão *m*; maçaneta *f*
knock [nɔk] *s* pancada *f*; golpe *m*; *v/t*, *v/i* bater; golpear; **~ down** *v/t* atropelar; abater, derrubar; **~er** batente *m*, aldraba *f*; **~ out** *v/t* pôr fora de combate; **~-out** *s* nocaute *m*, fora *m* de combate
knoll [nəul] outeiro *m*, morro *m*
knot [nɔt] *s* nó *m*; laço *m*, vínculo *m*; grupo *m*; *v/t*, *v/i* dar um nó, laçar; **~ty** nodoso; *fig* emaranhado
know [nəu] *v/t*, *v/i* saber; conhecer; **you ~** sabe; **~ about** saber, estar informado; **~-how** perícia *f*, técnica *f*; **~ing** *adj* conhecedor, entendido; **there's no ~ing** não há meio de saber; **~ingly** cientemente; intencionalmente; **~ledge** ['nɔlidʒ] saber *m*; conhecimento *m*, conhecimentos *m/pl*; **to one's ~ledge** que se saiba
known [nəun] *adj* conhecido; **make it ~ that** dar a conhecer que
knuckle ['nʌkl] *s* nó *m* do dedo; *v/i* **~ under** submeter-se

L

label ['leibl] *s* etiqueta *f*, rótulo *m*; *v/t* pôr etiqueta em, rotular; classificar
laboratory [lə'bɔrətəri] (*pl* **-ries**) laboratório *m*
laborious [lə'bɔ:riəs] laborioso; árduo
labo(u)r ['leibə] *s* trabalho *m*, lida *f*, labor *m*, faina *f*; dores *f/pl* de parto; *v/i* trabalhar, esforçar-se, afanar-se; estar em trabalho de parto; **~er** operário *m*, trabalhador *m*, jornaleiro *m*; **≗ Party** Partido *m* Trabalhista
lace [leis] *s* renda *f*; galão *m*;

atacador *m*; *v/t* apertar, atar
lack [læk] *s* falta *f*, míngua *f*; *v/t* carecer de, faltar; **for ~ of** por falta de, à míngua de
lacking ['lækiŋ] *adj* falto, deficiente; **be ~ in** ter falta de
laconic [lə'kɔnik] lacónico
lacquer ['lækə] *s* laca *f*
lad [læd] rapaz *m*, moço *m*, garoto *m*
ladder ['lædə] *s* escadote *m*; escada *f* de mão; malha *f* caída
laden ['leidn] *adj* carregado
Ladies ['leidiz] Senhoras *f/pl*
ladle ['leidl] *s* concha *f*, caço *m*
lady ['leidi] (*pl* **-dies**) senhora *f*; dama *f*, **~ of the house** dona *f* da casa; **~bird** joaninha *f*; **~killer** conquistador *m*, galanteador *m*; **~like** senhoril, elegante
lag [læg] *v/i* ficar atrás, demorar-se
lager ['lɑ:gə] cerveja *f* de reserva
lagoon [lə'gu:n] laguna *f*
lair [lɛə] covil *m*, toca *f*
lake [leik] lago *m*
lamb [læm] *s* anho *m*, cordeiro *m*
lame [leim] *adj* coxo, manco; fraco, pouco convincente; *v/t* aleijar, estropiar
lament [lə'ment] *s* lamento *m*; *v/t*, *v/i* lamentar(-se); **~able** ['læməntəbl] lamentável; **~ation** [ˌlæmən'teiʃən] lamentação *f*
lamp [læmp] candeeiro *m*; lâmpada *f*; lampião *m*; **~post** poste *m* de iluminação
lamprey ['læmpri] lampreia *f*
lamp-shade ['læmpʃəid] abaju(r) *m*, quebra-luz *m*
lance [lɑ:ns] *s* lança *f*; *v/t* lancetar; **~t** ['-sit] lanceta *f*
land [lænd] *s* terra *f*; solo *m*; país *m*; *v/t*, *v/i* desembarcar; AVIA aterrar; **~ing** desembarque *m*; AVIA aterragem *f*; ARCH patamar *m*; **~lady** senhoria *f*, proprietária *f*; estalajadeira *f*; **~lord** senhorio *m*, proprietário *m*; estalajadeiro *m*; **~mark** marco *m*, limite *m*, baliza *f*; **~scape** *s* paisagem *f*; **~slide** desmoronamento *m*
lane [lein] beco *m*; azinhaga *f*
language ['læŋgwidʒ] língua *f*, idioma *m*; linguagem *f*
languid ['læŋgwid] lânguido
languish ['læŋgwiʃ] *v/i* e(n)languescer, languir
lank [læŋk] corredio; magro, esgrouviado; **~y** esgalgado
lantern ['læntən] lanterna *f*
lap [læp] *s* colo *m*, regaço *m*; *v/t* sorver, lamber
lapel [lə'pel] lapela *f*
lapse [læps] *s* lapso *m*; *v/i* decorrer; decair; cair em erro; caducar, prescrever
laptop ['læptɔp] *s* computador *m* portátil
lard [lɑ:d] *s* banha *f*, toucinho *m*; *v/t* untar; lardear; **~er** despensa *f*
large [lɑ:dʒ] grande; vasto, amplo; extenso, largo; volumoso, espaçoso; abundante, copioso; **at ~** em liberdade, à solta;

~ly largamente, grandemente; em grande parte
lark [lɑ:k] *s* cotovia *f*, calhandra *f*; brincadeira *f*, partida *f*
larynx ['læriŋks] laringe *f*
lash [læʃ] *s* látego *m*, açoite *m*, chicote *m*; chicotada *f*; *v/t*, *v/i* açoitar; espicaçar
lass [læs] rapariga *f*, moça *f*, garota *f*
last [lɑ:st] *adv* da última vez; em último lugar, por/no fim; *s* forma *f*, molde *m*; *v/i* durar; *adj* último, derradeiro; passado; **at ~** por fim; **~, but not least** o último, mas não o menos importante; **~ but one** penúltimo; **the ~ straw** a última gota; **~ week** a semana passada; **the ~ word** a última palavra; o último grito
lasting ['lɑ:stiŋ] *adj* duradoiro
lastly ['lɑ:stli] finalmente, por fim
latch [lætʃ] *s* aldrava *f*, trinco *m*, fecho *m*; **~key** chave *f* de trinco
late [leit] *adv* tarde; *adj* último, recente; atrasado; defunto; tarde; tardio; **be ~** chegar tarde; **~ly** ultimamente, recentemente, há pouco; **~r on** mais tarde; **at the ~st** o mais tardar
lathe [leið] torno *m*
lather ['lɑ:ðə] *s* espuma *f* de sabão; *v/t* ensaboar
Latin ['lætin] *s* latim *m*; *adj* latino
latitude ['lætitju:d] latitude *f*
latter ['lætə] este último; **~ly** ultimamente, há pouco
lattice ['lætis] gelosia *f*, rótula *f*
laudable ['lɔ:dəbl] louvável
laugh [lɑ:f] *s* riso *m*; gargalhada *f*; risota *f*; *v/i* rir(-se); **~ at** rir-se de; **~able** risível, ridículo; divertido; **burst out ~ing** desatar a rir
laughter ['lɑ:ftə] risada *f*, riso *m*; gargalhada *f*
launch [lɔ:ntʃ] *s* lancha *f*, chalupa *f*; *v/t* lançar à agua; lançar, arremessar; encetar
laundry ['lɔ:ndri] (*pl* **-dries**) lavandaria *f*
laurel ['lɔrəl] loureiro *m*, louro *m*
lava ['lɑ:və] lava *f*
lavatory ['lævətəri] (*pl* **-ries**) retrete *f*; instalações *f/pl* sanitárias, privada *f*
lavender ['lævində] *s* alfazema *f*
lavish ['læviʃ] *adj* generoso, pródigo; *v/t* **~ on** prodigalizar
law [lɔ:] lei *f*; direito *m*; **go to ~** litigar, demandar, recorrer à justiça; **~-breaker** transgressor *m* da lei; **~court** tribunal *m*; **~ful** legal, legítimo
lawn [lɔ:n] relvado *m*
lawsuit ['lɔ:sju:t] processo *m*
lawyer ['lɔ:jə] advogado *m*, jurisconsulto *m*
lax [læks] negligente; lasso, frouxo, solto; **~ative** ['-ətiv] *s* laxante *m*; *adj* laxativo
lay [lei] *v/t* pôr, meter, colocar; **~ aside** pôr de lado; **~ down** pôr, depor, assentar; **~ out** *v/t* planear, fazer o proje(c)to de; ex-

por, estender; gastar, desembolsar; ~ **the table** pôr a mesa; ~ **up** guardar, armazenar; ficar de cama, guardar o leito
layer ['leiə] *s* camada *f*; poedeira *f*
layman ['leimən] leigo *m*
layout ['leiaut] *s* plano *m*, planta *f*, esquema *f*
laz|iness ['leizinis] preguiça *f*; **~y** preguiçoso, indolente
lead [led] *s* chumbo *m*
lead [li:d] *s* primazia *f*, dianteira *f*; ELECT cabo *m* condutor; papel *m* principal; mão *f*; trela *f*; *v/t*, *v/i* conduzir, dirigir, guiar; levar (a); jogar de mão, ser mão; **take the** ~ tomar a iniciativa; tomar a dianteira, assumir o comando
leaden ['ledn] de chumbo, pesado, plúmbeo
lead|er ['li:də] chefe *m*, *f*; artigo *m* de fundo; **~ing** *adj* principal, primeiro; **~ing article** artigo *m* de fundo
leaf [li:f] *s* (*pl* **leaves** [-vz]) folha *f*; **~let** folheto *m*; panfleto *m*
league [li:g] *s* liga *f*; *v/t*, *v/i* coligar(-se)
leak [li:k] *s* fenda *f*, abertura *f*; fuga *f*, escape *m*; *v/t*, *v/i* fazer água, meter água; verter, pingar; ~ **out** tornar-se público, transpirar; **~age** fuga *f*; derrame *m*; divulgação *f*
lean [li:n] *adj* magro; *v/t*, *v/i* apoiar(-se), encostar(-se), inclinar(-se); ~ (**up**)**on** depender, apoiar-se; ~ **out of** debruçar-se em; **~ing** *s* inclinação *f*, propensão *f*
leap [li:p] *s* salto *m*, pulo *m*; *v/t*, *v/i* saltar, pular; **~-year** ano *m* bissexto
learn [lə:n] *v/t*, *v/i* aprender; saber, ser informado
learned ['lə:nid] *adj* douto, erudito
learn|er ['lə:nə] aprendiz *m*, aluno *m*; **~ing** *s* erudição *f*, saber *m*
lease [li:s] *s* arrendamento *m*; *v/t* arrendar
least [li:st] *adv* o menos; *adj* o menor; o menos; o mínimo; **at** ~ pelo menos; **not in the** ~ de maneira nenhuma
leather ['leðə] *s* couro *m*, coiro *m*, pele *f*, cabedal *m*; *adj* de coiro; **~y** semelhante ao coiro; rijo
leave [li:v] *s* licença *f*, permissão *f*, despedida *f*; *v/t*, *v/i* deixar; partir, ir-se embora, sair; **take** ~ (**of**) despedir-se (de); partir (de); ~ **behind** deixar ficar; ~ **off** deixar de
lectur|e ['lektʃə] *s* prele(c)ção *f*; conferência *f*; repreensão *f*; *v/t*, *v/i* **~e** dar cursos; dar uma conferência; repreender; **~er** lente *m*, *f*, leitor *m*; conferencista *m*, *f*
ledge [ledʒ] borda *f*; saliência *f*
ledger ['ledʒə] livro-mestre, *m*; livro-razão *m*
leech [li:tʃ] sanguessuga *f*
leek [li:k] alho-porro *m*

leer [liə] (**at**) *v/i* olhar de soslaio (para)
left [left] *s* esquerda *f*; *adj* esquerdo; **to the ~** à esquerda; **~-handed** canhoto
left-luggage office ['left 'lʌgidʒ 'ɔfis] depósito *m* de volumes/bagagens
leg [leg] *s* perna *f*; pé *m*; pata *f*; **pull someone's ~** entrar com alguém, fazer alguém de tolo
legacy ['legəsi] (*pl* **-cies**) legado *m*
legal ['liːgəl] legal; **~ize** *v/t* legalizar
legation [li'geiʃən] legação *f*
legend ['ledʒənd] lenda *f*; **~ary** lendário
legible ['ledʒəbl] legível
legion ['liːdʒən] legião *f*
legislation [ˌledʒis'leiʃən] legislação *f*
legislator ['ledʒisleitə] legislador *m*
legitimate [li'dʒitimit] *adj* legítimo
leisure ['leʒə] lazer *m*, vagar *m*; **at ~** à vontade, com vagar; **~d** desocupado; **~ly** *adj* vagaroso
lemon ['lemən] limão *m*; **~ade** [ˌ-'neid] limonada *f*; **~squash** limonada *f*; **~-tree** limoeiro *m*
lend [lend] *v/t* emprestar; **~ a hand** dar uma ajuda
length [leŋθ] comprimento *m*; duração *f*; **at ~** afinal, por fim; pormenorizadamente, detalhadamente; **~en** *v/t*, *v/i* alongar, estender, prolongar; **~y** longo, prolongado
lenient ['liːnjənt] suave, compassivo
lens [lenz] lente *f*
Lent [lent] *s* quaresma *f*
lentil ['lentil] *s* lentilha *f*
leopard ['lepəd] leopardo *m*
leper ['lepə] leproso *m*
leprosy ['leprəsi] lepra *f*
less [les] *adj* menor; menos; *adv* menos; **~ and ~** cada vez menos
less|en ['lesn] *v/t*, *v/i* diminuir; **~er** *adj* menor, mais pequeno
lesson ['lesn] lição *f*; aula *f*
lest [lest] para que não; com medo de que
let [let] *v/t* deixar, permitir; alugar; **~ alone** quanto mais; sem falar de; **~ alone** deixar em paz; **~ be** deixar à vontade, não interferir; **~ down** baixar; soltar; desiludir, abandonar; **~ go** (**of**) largar; **~ in** admitir; **~ off** descarregar, disparar; perdoar; **~ on** revelar, divulgar; **~ out** deixar escapar; deixar sair; alugar; alargar; **~ us/~'s go** vamos
letter ['letə] *s* carta *f*; **by ~** por carta; por escrito; **to the ~** à letra, à risca; **~-box** marco *m* do correio; caixa *f* do correio; **~ head** cabeçalho *m*; **~s** *s/pl* (as) letras *f/pl*
lettuce ['letis] alface *f*
level ['levl] *s* nível *m*; *v/t*, *v/i* nivelar; *adj* horizontal, plano, liso, raso; **~ crossing** passagem *f* de nível
lever ['liːvə] *s* alavanca *f*

levy ['levi] *v/t* arrecadar; recrutar; *s* (*pl* **-vies**) arrecadação *f*; recrutamento *m*

liab|ility [ˌlaiə'biliti] (*pl* **-ties**) responsabilidade *f*; *pl* COM passivo *m*; **~le** ['-bl] responsável; **~le to** sujeito a; propenso a; **~le to duty** sujeito a direitos alfandegários

liar ['laiə] mentiroso *m*, aldrabão *m*

libel ['laibəl] *s* libelo *m*; difamação *f*

liberal ['libərəl] *adj* liberal; generoso; **~ism** liberalismo *m*

liberate ['libəreit] (**from**) *v/t* libertar (de), livrar (de)

liberty ['libəti] liberdade *f*; **at ~** livre, desocupado; em liberdade

librarian [lai'breəriən] bibliotecário *m*

library ['laibrəri] (*pl* **-ries**) biblioteca *f*

licence ['laisəns] *s* licença *f*; permissão *f*

license ['laisəns] *s v/t* permitir; autorizar

lick [lik] *s* lambidela *f*, lambedura *f*; *v/t* lamber

lid [lid] tempa *f*; pálpebra *f*

lie [lai] *s* mentira *f*; *v/i* mentir

lie [lai] *v/i* jazer; estar deitado; estar situado, situar-se; existir, encontrar-se; conservar-se, permanecer; **~ down** deitar-se, descansar; submeter-se, tolerar; **~ in** deixar-se ficar na cama

lieutenant [lef'tenənt, *US* luː-] tenente *m*

life [laif] (*pl* **lives** [laivz]) vida *f*; **~ assurance** seguro *m* de vida; **~belt** cinto *m* de salvação; **~boat** barco *m* salvavidas; **~guard** salva-vidas *m*; guarda *m* pessoal; **~-jacket** colete *m* de salvação; **~less** morto, inanimado; **~long** vitalício, perpétuo; **~ support** suporte *m* de vida; **~time** existência *f*, vida *f*

lift [lift] *s* boleia *f*, *Braz* corona *f*; elevador *m*, ascensor *m*; *v/t*, *v/i* levantar(-se), erguer(-se); tirar, roubar

ligature ['ligətʃuə] ligadura *f*

light [lait] *s* luz *f*; lume *m*; claridade *f*, clarão *m*; *fig* ponto *m* de vista; *v/t*, *v/i* iluminar(-se); acender(-se); alumiar(-se); *adj* leve, ligeiro; claro; **~en** *v/t*, *v/i* aclarar(-se); relampejar; aliviar, aligeirar; **~er** isqueiro *m*; **~-headed** delirante; estouvado, decabeça-no-ar; **~-hearted** alegre; **~house** farol *m*; **~ing** *s* iluminação *f*; **~ness** ligeireza *f*

lightning ['laitniŋ] relâmpago *m*; **~-conductor** pára-raios *m*

like [laik] *prp* como; *s* igual *m*; semelhante *m*; *v/t* gostar de; querer; *adj* semelhante, igual, parecido; **how do you ~ ...?** que tal the parece ...?; **feel ~** ter vontade de, estar/sentir-se disposto a; **look ~** parecer, estar com cara/aspecto de; **~lihood** ['-lihud] verosimilhança

f; probabilidade *f*; **~ly** *adj* verosímil, provável; **~ness** semelhança *f*; **~wise** outrossim, do mesmo modo
liking ['laikiŋ] *s* gosto *m*, inclinação *f*; predile(c)ção *f*
lilac ['lailək] *s* BOT lilás *m*
lily ['lili] (*pl* **-lies**) lírio *m*
limb [lim] membro *m*
lime [laim] *s* cal *f*; tília *f*; **~-juice** sumo *m* de lima; **~light** ribalta *f*
limit ['limit] *s* limite *m*; *v/t* limitar; **~ation** [-'teiʃən] limitação *f*; **~less** sem limites, ilimitado
limp [limp] *v/i* coxear, manquejar; *s* coxeadura *f*; *adj* débil, mole
limy ['laimi] calcáreo; viscoso
line [lain] *s* linha *f*; fila *f*, fileira *f*; ruga *f*, vinco *m*; *v/t* alinhar (-se); riscar, traçar linhas (em); forrar
lineage ['liniidʒ] linhagem *f*
linen ['linin] *s* linho *m*; roupa *f* branca
liner ['lainə] vapor *m* de carreira, paquete *m*; transatlântico *m*
linesman ['lainzmən] (*pl* **-men**) juiz *m* de linha
linger ['liŋgə] *v/i* demorar-se, tardar, hesitar; definhar-se, arrastar-se
lining ['lainiŋ] *s* forro *m*
link [liŋk] *s* elo *m*; enlace *m*; COMP ligação *f*; *v/t*, *v/i* ligar, unir(-se)
links [liŋks] *s/pl* dunas *f/pl*; campo *m* de golfe
lion ['laiən] leão *m*; **~ess** leoa *f*
lip [lip] beiço *m*, lábio *m*; **~stick** batom *m*, bâton *m*
liposuction [lipə'sʌkʃən] *s* lipoaspiração *f*
liquefy ['likwifai] *v/t*, *v/i* liquefazer(-se)
liqueur [li'kjuə] licor *m*
liquid ['likwid] *s*, *adj* líquido *m*; **~ate** *v/t* liquidar; **~ation** [-'deiʃən] liquidação *f*
liquor ['likə] bebida *f* alcoólica; **~ice** ['-ris] regoliz *m*, alcaçuz *m*
lisp [lisp] *v/t*, *v/i* ciciar; *s* cicio *m*
list [list] *s* lista *f*, rol *m*; MAR inclinação *f*; *v/t* registar; *v/i* MAR inclinar-se
listen ['lisn] (to) *v/i* escutar; **~er** ouvinte *m*, *f*; **~ in** ouvir rádio; pôr-se à escuta
literal ['litərəl] *adj* literal; **~ly** ao pé da letra
literary ['litərəri] literário
literature ['litərətʃə] literatura *f*
litre ['li:tə] litro *m*
litter ['litə] *s* lixo *m*; liteira *f*; ninhada *f*; **~ bin** cesto *m* dos papéis
little ['litl] *s* pouco *m*; *adv* pouco; *adj* pequeno; **a ~ (bit)** um bocado, um pouco; **~ by ~** aos poucos; **~ finger** mindinho *m*
live [laiv] *adj* vivo; carregado; dire(c)to; [liv] *v/t*, *v/i* viver; morar; **~ on** alimentar-se de, sustentar-se de
livelihood ['laivlihud] sustento *m*, subsistência *f*

lively ['laivli] animado, vivo, vivaz
liver ['livə] fígado *m*
livery ['livəri] *s* libré *f*
live-stock ['laivstɔk] gado *m*
livid ['livid] lívido; zangadíssimo
living ['liviŋ] *adj* vivo; *s* subsistência *f*; vida *f*; **~-room** sala *f* de estar
lizard ['lizəd] lagarto *m*
load [ləud] *s* carga *f*; fardo *m*; *v/t* carregar
loaf [ləuf] *s* (*pl* **loaves** [-vz]) *s* pão *m*, *v/i* mandriar, preguiçar
loam [ləum] marga *f*
loan [ləun] *s* empréstimo *m*; *v/t* emprestar
loath [ləuθ] relutante; **~e** [ləuð] *v/t* detestar; **~some** ['-ðsəm] repugnante
lobby ['lɔbi] *s* (*pl* **-bies**) vestíbulo *m*; grupo *m* de representantes; *v/t*, *v/i* influenciar, intrigar
lobe [ləub] lóbulo *m*, lobo *m*
lobster ['lɔbstə] lagosta *f*
local ['ləukəl] *adj* local; *s* habitante *m*, *f* local; taberna *f* (local); **~ity** [-'kæliti] (*pl* **-ties**) localidade *f*; **~ize** *v/t* localizar
locate [ləu'keit] *v/t* localizar, situar; instalar, estabelecer
lock [lɔk] *s* fechadura *f*; anel *m* de cabelo; esclusa *f*, comporta *f*; *v/t* trancar, travar; fechar à chave; **~et** medalhão *m*; **~jaw** tétano *m*
locomotive ['ləukə,məutiv] *s* locomotiva *f*
locust ['ləukəst] gafanhoto *m*
lodg|e [lɔdʒ] *v/t*, *v/i* alojar(-se), hospedar(-se); **~er** hóspede *m*, *f*, inquilino *m*; **~ing** *s* alojamento *m*; **~ings** *s/pl* aposentos *m/pl*
loft [lɔft] *s* sótão *m*; palheiro *m*; **~y** elevado; altivo
log [lɔg] *s* toro *m*, cepo *m*; diário *m* de bordo; **~ in** *v/i* COMP fazer login; **~ on** *v/i* COMP fazer log-on; **~ out** *v/i* COMP fazer log-out
logic ['lɔdʒik] lógica *f*; **~al** lógico
loin [lɔin] lombo *m*
loiter ['lɔitə] *v/i* demorar-se, tardar; vadiar
lonely ['ləunli] solitário
long [lɔŋ] *adv* muito (tempo); *adj* comprido, longo, extenso; largo, muito; *v/i* desejar, ansiar; **as/so ~ as** enquanto; desde que; **before ~** em breve; **for ~** por muito tempo; **in the ~ run** COM o tempo, no fim de tudo; **no/any ~er** já não, não ... mais; **~ for** ansiar, suspirar por; **so ~** até à vista; até logo; **~ing** *s* anelo *m*, anseio *m*; **~itude** ['lɔndʒitju:d] longitude *f*
look [luk] *s* olhar *m*, olhadela *f*; aspecto *m*, ar *m*, aparência *f*; *v/i* **~** olhar; parecer; **~ after** cuidar de; tomar conta de; **~ at** olhar para; considerar, examinar; **~ for** buscar, procurar; **~ forward to** estar ansioso por; **~ in** dar uma saltada a; ver televisão; **~ into** examinar, investigar; **~ out** *v/i* ter cuidado,

acautelar-se; ~ **up** procurar, consultar
looker-on ['lukər'ɔn] espectador *m*
look-out ['luk'aut] *s* vigilância *f*, atalaia *f*
loom [lu:m] *s* tear *m*; *v/i* assomar, levantar-se
loop [lu:p] volta *f*, curva *f*; presilha *f*; **~-hole** seteira *f*; *fig* evasiva *f*
loos|e [lu:s] *adj* frouxo; móvel; solto; *v/t* afrouxar; soltar; desatar; **~en** ['-ən] *v/t*, *v/i* soltar (-se); desapertar
loot [lu:t] *s* pilhagem *f*, saque *m*
lord [lɔ:d] *s* lorde *m*, senhor *m*
Lord [lɔ:d] *s* Senhor *m*, Deus *m*; *int* meu Deus!; **~ Mayor** prefeito *m*, Lorde-maior *m*; **♀ ly** senhoril
lorry ['lɔri] (*pl* **-ries**) camião *m*, *Braz* caminhão *m*
lose [lu:z] *v/t*, *v/i* perder
loss [lɔs] perda *f*
lot [lɔt] lote *m*; sorte *f*, fortuna *f*; quota-parte *f*; **a ~ of** muito
lotion ['ləuʃən] loção *f*
lottery ['lɔtəri] (*pl* **-ries**) lotaria *f*
loud [laud] *adj* alto, forte, ruidoso; vistoso, berrante; **~speaker** alto-falante *m*
lounge [laundʒ] *s* salão *m*; *v/i* recostar-se
louse [laus] *s* (*pl* **lice** [lais]) piolho *m*
lovable ['lʌvəbl] amável
love [lʌv] *v/t*, *v/i* amar, querer, adorar; *s* amor *m*; **in ~ with** enamorado de; **~ affair** ['lʌvə] aventura *f* amorosa, caso *m* de amor; **~ly** *adj* belo, lindo; **~r** amante *m*, *f*
loving ['lʌviŋ] *adj* afe(c)tuoso, terno, amoroso
low [ləu] *adj* baixo; profundo; fraco; vulgar; **~er** *adj* inferior; *v/t*, *v/i* abaixar; diminuir, reduzir; humilhar; **~ fat** baixo em gorduras
low|-necked ['ləu'nekt] decotado; **~-spirited** desanimado; **~ water** vazante *f*
loyal ['lɔiəl] leal, fiel; **~ty** lealdade *f*, fidelidade *f*
lozenge ['lɔzindʒ] losango *m*; pastilha *f*
lubricate ['lu:brikeit] *v/t* lubrificar
lucid ['lu:sid] lúcido
luck [lʌk] fortuna *f*, sorte *f*; **be in ~** estar com sorte; **worse ~** tanto pior, infelizmente; **~ily** felizmente; **~y** afortunado, ditoso; propício
lucrative ['lu:krətiv] lucrativo
ludicrous ['lu:dikrəs] ridículo; lúdicro
luggage ['lʌgidʒ] bagagem *f*; **~-rack** rede *f*
lukewarm ['lu:kwɔ:m] tépido, morno; indiferente
lull [lʌl] *s* calmaria *f*; *v/t*, *v/i* embalar; acalentar
lullaby ['lʌləbai] (*pl* **-bies**) canção *f* de embalar/de ninar
lumber ['lʌmbə] *s* trastes *m/pl* velhos; *v/i* arrastar-se pesadamente

luminous ['lu:minəs] luminoso
lump [lʌmp] *s* pedaço *m*, massa *f*, bloco *m*; **~ of sugar** torrão *m* de açúcar; **~ in the throat** nó *m* na garganta
lunatic ['lu:nətik] *adj* lunático
lunch [lʌntʃ] *s* almoço *m*; *v/t*, *v/i* almoçar; dar de almoçar (a)
lung [lʌŋ] pulmão *m*
lurch [lə:tʃ] *v/i* andar aos bordos; guinar; *s* guinada *f*
lure [ljuə] *s* engodo *m*; *v/t* tentar, engodar, aliciar
lurk [lə:k] *v/i* esconder-se; emboscar-se
luscious ['lʌʃəs] delicioso, saboroso
lust [lʌst] *s* luxúria *f*; **~ful** luxurioso
lustre ['lʌstə] brilho *m*, resplendor *m*
lute [l(j)u:t] *s* alaúde *m*
luxur|ious [lʌg'zjuəriəs] luxuoso; **~y** ['lʌkʃəri] (*pl* **-ries**) luxo *m*
lye [lai] lixívia *f*
lynch [lintʃ] *v/t* linchar
lynx [liŋks] lince *m*
lyric ['lirik] *adj* lírico; *s* poema *m* lírico; **~al** lírico; **~s** *s/pl* MUS letra *f*

M

macaroni [ˌmækə'rəuni] macarrão *m*
macaroon [ˌmækə'ru:n] bolo *m* de amêndoa
machine [mə'ʃi:n] *s* máquina *f*; **~gun** metralhadora *f*; **~ry** maquinaria *f*; mecanismo *m*, maquinismo *m*
mackerel ['mækrəl] cavala *f*
mackintosh ['mækintɔʃ] impermeável *m*
mad [mæd] louco, doido; **like ~** furiosamente; intensamente
madam ['mædəm] (minha) senhora *f*
madden ['mædn] *v/t* enlouquecer; irritar
made [meid] *adj* feito, fabricado
madman ['mædmən] louco *m*
madness ['mædnis] loucura *f*, demência *f*
magazine [ˌmægə'zi:n] revista *f*, magazine *m*; carretel *m*
maggot ['mægət] gusano *m*, verme *m*
magic ['mædʒik] *s* magia *f*; *adj* mágico; **~al** mágico; **~ian** [mə'dʒiʃən] mágico *m*
magistrate ['mædʒistreit] magistrado *m*
magnanimous [mæg'næniməs] magnânimo
magnet ['mægnit] magnete *m*, íman *m*, *Braz* ímã *m*; **~ize** *v/t* imanizar, magnetizar
magnificent [mæg'nifisnt] magnífico
magnify ['mægnifai] *v/t* aumentar; exagerar

magnitude ['mægnitju:d] magnitude *f*
magpie ['mægpai] pega *f*
mahogany [mə'hɔgəni] mogno *m*
maid [meid] criada *f*; **~en** *adj* primeiro, inaugural; virgem; solteira; **~servant** criada *f*
mail [meil] *s* correio *m*; correspondência *f*; *v/t* deitar ao correio; **~-bag** saco *m* do correio; **~-box** caixa *f* do correio; marco *m*; do correio
maim [meim] *v/t* estropiar, mutilar
main [mein] *adj* principal, maior; *s* tubo *m* principal; **~land** terra *f* firme, continente *m*; **~ly** mormente, principalmente, sobretudo
maintain [mein'tein] *v/t* manter; sustentar; defender, afirmar
maintenance ['meintənəns] manutenção *f*
maize [meiz] milho *m*
majest|ic [mə'dʒestik] majestoso; **~y** ['mædʒisti] (*pl* **-ties**) majestade *f*
major ['meidʒə] *adj* maior, principal; *s* major *m*; **~ity** [mə'dʒɔriti] *s* (*pl* **-ties**) maioria *f*
make [meik] *s* marca *f*; fabrico *m*; *v/t* fazer; ganhar; fabricar; **~ believe** fingir; **~ haste** aviar-se, apressar-se; **~ it** conseguir; **~ love** fazer amor; **~ money** ganhar dinheiro; **~ out** decifrar; **~ sure of** assegurar-se de, certificar-se; **~-believe** *s* simulacro *m*; *adj* fictício; **~ up** *v/t*, *v/i* fazer as pazes; pintar(-se), maquilhar(-se); completar
maker ['meikə] fabricante *m*
makeshift ['meikʃift] *s* substituto *m*; *adj* provisório
make|-up ['meikʌp] *s* maquil(h)agem *f*; caracterização *f*; composição *f*
male [meil] *adj* másculo; masculino; macho
malic|e ['mælis] malícia *f*; **~e afore-thought** JUR premeditação *f*; **~ious** [mə'liʃəs] malicioso
malignant [mə'lignənt] maligno
mallet ['mælit] malho *m*, maço *m*
malt [mɔ:lt] *s* malte *m*
mammal ['mæməl] mamífero *m*
mammy ['mæmi] (*pl* **-mies**) mamã(e); *US* aia *f* preta
man [mæn] *s* (*pl* **men** [men]) homem *m*; varão *m*; *v/t* tripular; guarnecer; equipar; **~ and wife** marido *m* e mulher *f*; **to a ~** todos, sem exce(p)ção, unanimemente
manag|e ['mænidʒ] *v/t*, *v/i* administrar, gerir; conseguir, lograr; **~ement** gerência *f*, administração *f*; **~er** gerente *m*
mane [mein] crina *f*
manganese [ˌmæŋgə'ni:z] manganês *m*
manger ['meindʒə] manjedoura *f*

mangle ['mæŋgl] *s* calandra *f*; *v/t* calandrar; mutilar
mango ['mæŋgəu] manga *f*
manhood ['mænhud] virilidade *f*; idade *f* viril
mania ['meinjə] mania *f*
manifest ['mænifest] *adj* manifesto; *v/t* manifestar
manifold ['mænifəuld] *adj* múltiplo
manipulate [mə'nipjuleit] *v/t* manipular
mankind [mæn'kaind] humanidade *f*
manly ['mænli] viril; varonil
manner ['mænə] maneira *f*, modo *m*; **~ism** maneirismo *m*; **~s** maneiras *f/pl*, modos *m/pl*
manor ['mænə] solar *m*
manpower ['mæn,pauə] mão-de-obra *f*
mansion ['mænʃən] palacete *m*
manslaughter ['mæn,slɔːtə] homicídio *m* involuntário
mantelpiece ['mæntlpiːs] prateleira *f* da lareira
manual ['mænjuəl] *s*, *adj* manual *m*
manufactur|e [,mænju'fæktʃə] *s* fabricação *f*; *v/t* fabricar; **~er** fabricante *m*, *f*
manure [mə'njuə] *s* estrume *m*, adubo *m*; *v/t* estrumar
manuscript ['mænjuskript] manuscrito *m*
many ['meni] muitos, muitas
map [mæp] *s* mapa *m*; planta *f*; *v/t* traçar um mapa
maple ['meipl] BOT bordo *m*
marauder [mə'rɔːdə] saqueador *m*
marble ['mɑːbl] mármore *m*
March [mɑːtʃ] Março *m*
march [mɑːtʃ] *s* marcha *f*; *v/i* marchar
mare [mεə] égua *f*
margarine [,mɑːdʒə'riːn] margarina *f*
margin ['mɑːdʒin] margem *f*
marigold ['mærigəuld] malmequer *m*
marine [mə'riːn] *adj* marítimo; marinho; *s* marinha *f*; fuzileiro *m* naval
mark [mɑːk] *s* marca *f*; sinal *m*; nota *f*, ponto *m*; *v/t* marcar; assinalar; classificar; **~ed** *adj* marcado; marcante
market ['mɑːkit] *s* mercado *m*; *v/t*, *v/i* pôr à venda; ir às compras; **~ing** *s* compra *f*, venda *f*; **~-place** praça *f*, mercado *m*
marmalade ['mɑːməleid] compota *f*/doce *m* de laranja
maroon [mə'ruːn] *v/t* abandonar; *adj* castanho-avermelhado
marqu|ess, **~is** ['mɑːkwis] marquês *m*
marriage ['mæridʒ] casamento *m*
married ['mærid] *adj* casado
marry ['mæri] *v/t*, *v/i* casar(-se)
marsh [mɑːʃ] pântano *m*
marshal ['mɑːʃəl] *s* marechal *m*
marshy ['mɑːʃi] pantanoso
marten ['mɑːtin] marta *f*
martial ['mɑːʃəl] marcial
martyr ['mɑːtə] *s* mártir *m*, *f*;

~dom martírio *m*
marvel ['mɑːvəl] *s* maravilha *f*; *v/i* **~ at** estranhar, admirar-se; **~(l)ous** maravilhoso
marzipan [ˌmɑːzi'pæn] maçapão *m*
mascara [mæs'kɑːrə] rimel *m*
mascot ['mæskət] mascote *f*
masculine ['mæskjulin] *adj*, *s* masculino *m*
mash [mæʃ] *v/t* esmagar, triturar; **~ed potatoes** puré *m* de batata
mask [mɑːsk] *s* máscara *f*; *v/t* mascarar; disfarçar; **~ed ball** baile *m* de máscaras
mason ['meisn] pedreiro *m*; mação *m*; **~ry** alvenaria *f*; maçonaria *f*
mass [mæs] *s* massa *f*; ECCL missa *f*
massacre ['mæsəkə] *s* massacre *m*
mass|age ['mæsɑːʒ] *v/t* massajar, dar massagens a; *s* massagem *f*; **~eur** [mæ'səː] massagista *m*, *f*
massive ['mæsiv] maciço
mast [mɑːst] mastro *m*
master ['mɑːstə] *s* mestre *m*; dono *m*, senhor *m*, amo *m*; patrão; *v/t* dominar; **~ly** magistral; **~piece** obra-prima *f*; **~y** mestria *f*; domínio *m*
mat [mæt] *s* tapete *m*; esteira *f*, capacho *m*
match [mætʃ] *s* fósforo *m*; desafio *m*, partida *f*; igual *m*; *v/t*, *v/i* igualar(-se); condizer; competir; **~-box** caixa *f* de fósforos; **~less** incomparável, sem igual
mate [meit] *s* camarada *m*, *f*, companheiro *m*; *v/t*, *v/i* acasalar(-se)
material [mə'tiəriəl] *adj* material; *s* fazenda *f*, tecido *m*; matéria *f*; material *m*; **~ist** *adj*, *s* materialista *m*, *f*; **~ize** *v/t*, *v/i* materializar(-se)
maternal [mə'təːnl] maternal
mathematics [ˌmæθi'mætiks] matemática *f*
matrimony ['mætriməni] matrimónio *m*
matron ['meitrən] enfermeira-chefe *f*
matter ['mætə] *s* matéria *f*; caso *m*, assunto *m*; *v/i* importar; **what's the ~?** o que há?, que aconteceu?; o que é isso?; o que tem?; **a ~ of** uma questão de; **as a ~ of fact** na realidade, de fa(c)to; **~-of-fact** realista, terra-a-terra
mattress ['mætris] colchão *m*
matur|e [mə'tjuə] *adj* maduro; *v/t*, *v/i* amadurecer; **~ity** maturidade *f*; madureza *f*
maximum ['mæksiməm] *adj*, *s* máximo *m*
May [mei] Maio *m*
may [mei] *v/aux* poder, ser possível; ter licença
maybe ['meibiː] talvez, acaso, quiçá
mayor [mɛə] presidente *m* da câmara, prefeito *m*
maze [meiz] labirinto *m*
me [miː, mi] me; mim
meadow ['medəu] prado *m*

meagre ['mi:gə] magro, macilento; escasso; insuficiente
meal [mi:l] refeição *f*; farinha *f*; **~time** horas *f/pl* da refeição
mean [mi:n] *v/t* significar, querer dizer; pensar, propor-se; adj. mau, mesquinho, ruim; vil, baixo; médio; *s* média *f*; meio *m*, meio termo *m*
meander [mi'ændə] *v/i* colear, serpentear
meaning ['mi:niŋ] *s* significado *m*, significação *f*; sentido *m*
means [mi:nz] *s* meio *m*; recursos *m/pl*; **by all ~** certamente, sem dúvida; **by no ~** de modo nenhum; **by ~ of** por meio de
mean|time ['mi:n'taim], **~while** entretanto, no entanto
measles ['mi:zlz] sarampo *m*
measure ['meʒə] *s* medida *f*; **made to ~** feito à medida; *v/t*, *v/i* medir; **~d** *adj* comedido, ponderado; **~ment** medição *f*
meat [mi:t] carne *f*; **~ ball** almôndega *f*
mechanic [mi'kænik] mecânico *m*; **~al** mecânico; maquinal; **~ally** maquinalmente; **~s** mecânica *f*
mechanism ['mekənizəm] mecanismo *m*
medal ['medl] medalha *f*
meddle ['medl] *v/i* meter-se, intrometer-se
mediat|e ['mi:dieit] *v/i* servir de intermediário / medianeiro, mediar; **~ion** [-'eiʃən] mediação *f*; **~or** mediador *m*
medica|l ['medikəl] *adj* médico; medicinal; **~ment** [me'dikəmənt] medicamento *m*
medicin|al [me'disinl] medicinal; **~e** ['-sin] medicamento *m*, remédio *m*; medicina *f*
medieval [ˌmedi'i:vəl] medieval
mediocr|e ['mi:diəukə] medíocre; **~ity** [-'ɔkriti] mediocridade *f*
meditat|e ['mediteit] *v/i* meditar; **~ion** [-'teiʃən] meditação *f*; **~ive** ['-tətiv] meditativo
Mediterranean [ˌmeditə'reinjən] *adj* mediterrâneo
medium ['mi:djəm] *s* médio *m*; *adj* mediano, médio
medley ['medli] mistura *f*; miscelânea *f*; mixórdia *f*
meek [mi:k] manso, humilde, meigo
meet [mi:t] *v/t*, *v/i* encontrar (-se); travar conhecimento, conhecer(-se); satisfazer; reunir-se; *s* reunião *f*; **make ends ~** equilibrar receitas e despesas; **~ with** topar COM, encontrar; *US* reunir-se COM; **~ing** reunião *f*; encontro *m*
melancholy ['melənkəli] *s* melancolia *f*; *adj* melancólico
mellow ['meləu] *adj* maduro; suave, brando
melody ['melədi] (*pl* **-dies**) melodia *f*
melt [melt] *v/t*, *v/i* derreter(-se), fundir(-se)
member ['membə] membro *m*
memoirs ['memwa:z] memó-

rias *f/pl*
memorial [mi'mɔːriəl] *adj* comemorativo; *s* monumento *m* comemorativo
memory ['meməri] (*pl* **-ries**) memória *f*; recordação *f*, lembrança *f*
menace ['menəs] *s* ameaça *f*
mend [mend] *v/t*, *v/i* reparar; remendar, consertar
mental ['mentl] mental; **~ity** [-'tæliti] mentalidade *f*
mention ['menʃən] *s* alusão *f*, menção *f*; *v/t* fazer menção de, mencionar
menu ['menjuː] ementa *f*, *Braz* cardápio *m*
mercenary ['məːsinəri] *adj* mercenário
merchant ['məːtʃənt] comerciante *m*, *f*, negociante *m*, *f*
merci|ful ['məːsiful] clemente, misericordioso; **~less** cruel, desalmado
mercury ['məːkjuri] mercúrio *m*, azougue *m*
mercy ['məːsi] (*pl* **-cies**) misericórdia *f*; **at the ~ of** à mercê de
mere [miə] *adj* simples, mero
merg|e [məːdʒ] *v/t*, *v/i* fundir (-se), unir(-se); **~er** COM fusão *f*
meridian [mə'ridiən] meridiano
merit ['merit] *s* mérito *m*; *v/t* merecer
mer|maid ['məːmeid] sereia *f*; **~man** tritão *m*
merry ['meri] jovial, divertido, alegre; **make ~** divertir-se; **♀ Christmas!** Boas Festas! Feliz Natal!; **~-go-round** carrocel *m*
mesh [meʃ] *s* malha *f*
mess [mes] *s* messe *f*; apuros *m/pl*, dificuldades *f/pl*; confusão *f*; desordem *f*, porcaria *f*, trapalhada *f*
message ['mesidʒ] mensagem *f*
messenger ['mesindʒə] mensageiro *m*
metal ['metl] *s* metal *m*; **~lic** [mi'tælik] metálico
method ['meθəd] método *m*; **~ical** [mi'θɔdikəl] metódico
metre ['miːtə] metro *m*
metropolitan [ˌmetrə'pɔlitən] *adj* metropolitano
mew [mjuː] *v/i* miar; *s* miadela *f*, miado *m*
miaow [mi(ː)'au] *v/i* miar; *s* miau *m*
mice [mais] *pl of* **mouse**
microchip ['maikrə tʃip] *s* COMP microchip *m*
microphone ['maikrəfəun] microfone *m*
midday ['middei] meio-dia *m*
middle ['midl] *s* meio *m*; *adj* do meio, médio, mediano; **in the ~ of** no meio de; **~ age** idade *f* madura; **~-aged** de meia idade; **♀ Ages** *s/pl* Idade *f* Média
middling ['midliŋ] *adj* médio; meão; medíocre
midget ['midʒit] anão *m*
midnight ['midnait] meia-noite *f*
midshipman ['midʃipmən] aspirante *m* de marinha
midsummer ['midˌsʌmə] sols-

tício *m* do verão, pleno verão *m*; ≈ **Day** dia *m* de São João
midway ['mid'wei] *adv* a meio do caminho
midwife ['midwaif] (*pl* **-wives**) ['-waivz] parteira *f*
might [mait] *s* poder *m*, força *f* pujança *f*; **~y** *adv* extremamente, muito
migraine [miː'grein] enxaqueca *f*
mild [maild] *adj* brando; manso, suave, meigo
mildew ['mildjuː] *s* míldio *m*; bolor *m*, mofo *m*
mile [mail] milha *f*; **~stone** marco *m* miliário, pedra *f* miliária
military ['militəri] *adj* militar
militia [mi'liʃə] milícia *f*
milk [milk] *s* leite *m*; *v/t*, *v/i* ordenhar; **~man** leiteiro *m*; **~-shake** batido *m* de leite; **~y** leitoso; ≈**y Way** Via *f* Láctea
mill [mil] *v/t* moer; esfarelar; *s* moinho *m*; fábrica *f*; **~er** moleiro *m*
millet ['milit] painço *m*
milliner ['milinə] chapeleira *f*
million ['miljən] *s* milhão *m*; **~aire** [ˌ-'nɛə] milionário *m*
milt [milt] láctea *f*
mimic ['mimik] *adj* mímico; *v/t* imitar, remedar
mince [mins] *s* carne *f* picada; *v/t* picar; **~meat** *US* picado *m* de carne; recheio *m* de fruta; **~ pie** pastel *m* de recheio de frutas
mind [maind] *s* mente *f*; espírito *m*; *v/t*, *v/i*; cuidar de, olhar por; importar-se; ocupar-se; prestar atenção a, notar; **call/bring to ~** trazer à memória; **change one' ~** mudar de opinião; **make up one' ~** decidir-se, tomar uma resolução; **never ~** não faz mal, não importa; **to one' ~** na sua opinião, a seu ver; **would you ~ ...?** importa(va)-se de ...?; **~ed** *adj* disposto, inclinado
mine [main] *pron* (o) meu, (a) minha, (os) meus, (as) minhas; *s* mina *f*; *v/t*, *v/i* minar; minerar
miner ['mainə] mineiro *m*
mineral ['minərəl] *adj*, *s* mineral *m*
mingle ['miŋgl] *v/t* mesclar, misturar
mining ['mainiŋ] *s* exploração *f* de minas
minister ['ministə] *s* ministro *m*; **~ial** [ˌ-'tiəriəl] ministerial
ministry ['ministri] (*pl* **-ries**) ministério *m*; sacerdócio *m*
mink [miŋk] (pele *f* de) marta *f*
minor ['mainə] *adj* menor; secundário; *s* menor *m*, *f*; **~ity** [-'nɔriti] (*pl* **-ties**) minoria; menoridade *f*
minster ['minstə] basílica *f*, sé *f*
minstrel ['minstrəl] menestrel *m*; jogral *m*
mint [mint] *s* BOT hortelã *f*, menta *f*; casa *f* da moeda; *v/t* cunhar.
mint sauce molho *m* de hortelã
minus ['mainəs] *prp* menos; *adj* negativo
minute ['minit] *s* minuto *m*; mi-

nuta *f*, nota *f*; [mai'nju:t] *adj* minucioso; minúsculo, diminuto; **~s** *s/pl* a(c)tas *f/pl*
mirac|le ['mirəkl] milagre *m*; **~ulous** [-'rækjuləs] milagroso
mirage ['mirɑ:ʒ] miragem *f*
mirror ['mirə] *s* espelho *m*; *v/t* espelhar
misapprehension ['mis,æpri'henʃən] mal-entendido *m*, equívoco *m*
misbehavio(u)r ['misbi'heivjə] má conduta *f*, mau comportamento *m*
miscalculation ['mis,kælkju'leiʃən] erro *m* de cálculo
miscarr|iage [,mis'kəridʒ] aborto *m*; **~y** *v/i* abortar
miscellaneous [,misi'leinjəs] variado, vário, misto
mischief ['mistʃif] mal *m*, dano *m*; travessura *f*, diabrura *f*
mischievous ['mistʃivəs] travesso, brincalhão
misdemeano(u)r [,misdi'mi:nə] delito *m*
miser ['maizə] sovina *m*, *f*, avaro *m*
miserable ['mizərəbl] desgraçado, infeliz; miserável
misery ['mizəri] miséria *f*, desgraça *f*
misfortune [mis'fɔ:tʃən] infortúnio *m*, desventura *f*
misgiving [mis'giviŋ] apreensão *m*, receio *m*
misgovern ['mis'gʌvən] *v/t* governar mal, desgovernar
misguided ['mis'gaidid] *adj* extraviado, desencaminhado
mishap ['mishæp] azar *m*, revés *m*, contratempo *m*
misinterpret ['misin'tə:prit] *v/t* interpretar mal
misjudge ['mis'dʒʌdʒ] *v/t* julgar mal, fazer mau juízo de
mislay [mis'lei] *v/t* perder, extraviar
mislead [mis'li:d] *v/t* enganar, desencaminhar
misprint ['mis'print] *s* erro *m* tipográfico
misrule ['mis'ru:l] *s* má administração *f*
miss [mis] *s* menina *f*; moça *f*; senhora *f*; *Braz* senhorita *f*
miss [mis] *v/t*, *v/i* falhar, errar; perder; faltar a; sentir a falta de; *s* falhanço *m*, falha *f*
misshapen ['mis'ʃeipən] disforme
missile ['misail] projé(c)til *m*
missing ['misiŋ] *adj* perdido; extraviado; ausente
mission ['miʃən] missão *f*; **~ary** ['-nəri] (*pl* **-ries**) missionário *m*
mist [mist] *s* névoa *f*, neblina *f*
mistake [mis'teik] *s* erro *m*; equívoco *m*; *v/t* enganar-se, equivocar-se; confundir; **by ~** por engano; **~n** [-'teikən] enganado, equivocado; errado, erróneo
mister ['mistə] senhor *m*
mistletoe ['misltəu] visco *m*
mistress ['mistris] dona *f*, senhora *f*; professora *f*; amante *f*
mistrust ['mis'trʌst] *v/t* desconfiar de; *s* desconfiança *f*

misty ['misti] nebuloso, enevoado
misunderstand ['misʌndə'stænd] *v/t* entender mal, compreender mal; **~ing** *s* malentendido *m*, equívoco *m*; desinteligência *f*
misuse ['mis'ju:z] *v/t* abusar de; maltratar; ['-'ju:s] *s* abuso *m*; mau trato *m*
mite [mait] criancinha *f*; migalha *f*
mitigate ['mitigeit] *v/t* mitigar
mitten ['mitn] mitene *f*
mix [miks] *v/t*, *v/i* mesclar, misturar(-se); imiscuir-se; **~ed** *adj* misto; misturado; **~ up** confundir, atrapalhar; **~ed up in** metido em, implicado em; confuso; **~er** batedeira *f*; **~ture** ['-tʃə] mistura *f*, mescla *f*
moan [məun] *v/i* gemer; *s* gemido *m*
mob [mɔb] *s* multidão *f*, populaça *f*, turba *f*, gentalha *f*
mobil|e ['məubail] *adj* móvel; **~ity** [-'biliti] mobilidade *f*
mock [mɔk] *adj* simulado, falso; *v/t* mofar de, zombar de; **~ery** zombaria *f*
mode [məud] modo *m*; moda *f*
model ['mɔdl] *s* modelo *m*; *fashion* maneca *f*; *v/t* modelar; *adj* modelar
moderat|e ['mɔdərit] *adj* moderado; *v/t*, *v/i* moderar; **~ion** [,-'reiʃən] moderação *f*
modern ['mɔdən] *adj* moderno; **~ize** *v/t*, *v/i* modernizar(-se)
modest ['mɔdist] modesto; **~y** modéstia *f*
modify ['mɔdifai] *v/t* modificar
Mohammedan [məu'hæmidən] *adj*, *s* maometano *m*
moist [mɔist] (h)úmido; **~en** ['-sn] *v/t*, *v/i* (h)umedecer; **~ure** ['-tʃə] (h)umidade *f*
molar ['məulə] *adj* molar
mole [məul] lunar *m*; *zoo* toupeira *f*; MAR molhe *m*
molecule ['mɔlikju:l] molécula *f*
molest [məu'lest] *v/t* molestar; **~ation** [-'teiʃən] molestação *f*
moment ['məumənt] momento *m*; **at the ~** de/neste momento; **~ary** momentâneo
monarch ['mɔnək] monarca *m*; **~y** monarquia *f*
monastery ['mɔnəstəri] (*pl* **-ries**) mosteiro *m*
Monday ['mʌndi] segunda-feira *f*
money ['mʌni] dinheiro *m*; **~ed** abastado; **~-lender** prestamista *m*, *f*; **~ order** vale *m* postal
mongrel ['mʌŋgrəl] *adj* mestiço, híbrido
monk [mʌŋk] monge *m*
monkey ['mʌŋki] *s* macaco *m*
mono|gram ['mɔnəgræm] monograma *m*; **~log(ue)** ['-lɔg] monólogo *m*; **~mania** [-nəu'meinjə] monomania *f*; **~poly** [mə'nɔpəli] monopólio *m*; **~tonous** [mə'nɔtənəs] monótono; **~tony** [mə'nɔtni] monotonia *f*
monster ['mɔnstə] monstro *m*
monstrous ['mɔnstrəs] mons-

truoso
month [mʌnθ] mês *m*; **~ly** *adj* mensal; *adv* mensalmente
monument ['mɔnjumənt] monumento *m*; **~al** [-'mentl] monumental
moo [mu:] *v/t* mugir
mood [mu:d] disposição *f*, humor *m*; modo *m*; **~y** mal-humorado
moon [mu:n] *s* lua *f*; **~light** *s* luar *m*; **~shine** devaneio *m*, disparate *m*, *Braz* bobagem *f*
moor [muə] *s* charneca *f*; *v/t* amarrar, atracar
Moor [muə] mouro *m*; **~ish** mourisco, mouro
mop [mɔp] *s* esfregão *m*; *v/t* esfregar
moral ['mɔrəl] *adj*, *s* moral *f*; **~e** [mə'rɑ:l] moral *m*; **~ity** [mə'ræliti] moralidade *f*; **~s** moral *f*, ética *f*
morass [mə'ræs] pântano *m*
morbid ['mɔ:bid] mórbido
more [mɔ:] *adj*, *adv* mais; **~ and ~** cada vez mais; **~ or less** mais ou menos; **the ~..., the ~** quanto mais ..., (tanto) mais; **~over** além do mais, além disso
morguee [mɔ:g] morgue *f*
morning ['mɔ:niŋ] manhã *f*; **tomorrow ~** amanhã de manhã
morose [mə'rəus] tacituro, sorumbático
morphine ['mɔ:fi:n] morfina *f*
morsel ['mɔ:səl] bocado *m*, bocadinho *m*
mortal ['mɔ:tl] *s*, *adj* mortal *m*; **~ity** [-'tæliti] mortalidade *f*
mortar ['mɔ:tə] *s* argamassa *f*; MIL morteiro *m*; almofariz *m*
mortgage ['mɔ:gidʒ] *s* hipoteca *f*; *v/t* hipotecar
mortify ['mɔ:tifai] *v/t* mortificar
mortuary ['mɔ:tjuəri] (*pl* **-ries**) necrotério *m*
mosaic [mə'zeiik] *s* mosaico *m*
Moslem ['mɔzləm] *adj*, *s* muçulmano *m*
mosque [mɔsk] mesquita *f*
mosquito [mə'ski:təu] (*pl* **-toes**) mosquito *m*
moss [mɔs] musgo *m*; **~y** musgoso
most [məust] *s* o máximo; *adj* o(s) mais; a maior parte de; *adv* o mais; muito, sumamente; **at (the) ~** quando muito; **for the ~ part** na grande maioria; na sua maior parte; **make the ~ of** tirar o melhor partido/proveito de; **~ly** principalmente; na maior parte das vezes
moth [mɔθ] traça *f*; **~-eaten** roído pela traça
mother ['mʌðə] *s* mãe *f*; **~ country** pátria *f*; **~-in-law** sogra *f*; **~ly** maternal; **~ of pearl** madrepérola *f*, nácar *m*; **~ tongue** língua *f* materna
motion ['məuʃən] *v/t*, *v/i* acenar, gesticular; fazer sinal (para); *s* movimento *m*; moção *f*, proposta *f*; **~less** imóvel
motiva|te ['məutiveit] *v/t* motivar; **~tion** [-'veiʃən] motivação *f*
motive ['məutiv] *s* motivo *m*;

adj motor, motriz
motley ['mɔtli] *adj* variegado
motor ['məutə] *s* motor *m*; **~boat** gasolina; *m*, lancha *f*; **~-car** carro *m*, automóvel *m*; **~cycle** motocicleta *f*; **~ist** motorista *m*, *f*, automobilista *m*, *f*; **~way** *GB* auto-estrada *f*
mottled ['mɔtld] *adj* mosqueado, sarapintado
motto ['mɔtəu] moto *m*, divisa *f*
mo(u)ld [məuld] *s* molde *m*; forma *f*; bolor *m*, mofo *m*; *v/t* moldar; **~y** bolorento
mount [maunt] *v/t*, *v/i* montar, subir
mountain ['mauntin] montanha *f*, serra *f*; **~eer** [ˌ-'niə] alpinista *m*, *f*; **~eering** alpinismo *m*; **~ous** montanhoso
mourn [mɔ:n] *v/t*, *v/i* lamentar (-se), carpir(-se), deplorar, estar de luto; **~ful** triste, choroso; **~ing** luto *m*
mouse [maus] (*pl* **mice** [mais]) rato *m*, *Braz* camundongo *m*; COMP mouse *m*, rato *m*; **~-trap** ratoeira *f*
m(o)ustache [məs'tɑ:ʃ] bigode *m*
mouth [mauθ] *s* boca *f*; foz *f*; *v/t*, *v/i* declamar; **shut your ~!** cale a boca; **~ful** trago *m*, bocado *m*; **~piece** bocal *m*; porta-voz *m*
movabe ['mu:vəbl] móvel, movediço
move [mu:v] *v/t*, *v/i* mover(-se), avançar; mudar de casa; mexer-se; comover; *s* jogada *f*, lance *m*; movimento *m*; mudança *f*
movement ['mu:vmənt] movimento *m*
movies ['mu:viz] *s/pl fam* cinema *m*
moving ['mu:viŋ] *adj* comovente, movediço
mow [məu] *v/t* segar, ceifar
Mr. ['mistə] *abbr of* **mister**
Mrs. ['misiz] senhora *f*
much [mʌtʃ] *adj* muito; *adv* muito; **as ~ as** tanto como; **how ~?** quanto? **so ~** tanto; **so ~ the better** tanto melhor; **so ~ the worse** tanto pior; **too ~** demais, muito, demasiado; **very ~** muitíssimo
mud [mʌd] lama *f*, lodo *m*; **~dy** lamacento, lodoso; **~guard** AUTO guarda lamas *m*
muff [mʌf] *s* regalo *m*
muffle ['mʌfl] *v/t* abafar; embuçar; tapar
mug [mʌg] *s* caneca *f*; simplório *m*; fuça *f*; *v/t* assaltar; **~ up** decorar, empinar, picar; **~gy** abafado, mormacento
mulberry ['mʌlbəri] (*pl* **-ries**) amora *f*; **~ tree** amoreira *f*
mule [mju:l] mula *f*
mull [mʌl] *v/t*: **~ wine** preparar vinho quente
multiple ['mʌltipl] *adj* multíplice, múltiplo; *s* múltiplo *m*
multiplex *cinema* multiplex
multi|plication [ˌmʌltipli'keiʃən] multiplicação *f*; **~ply** ['-plai] *v/t*, *v/i* multiplicar(-se)
multitude ['mʌltitju:d] multi-

dão *f*
mumble ['mʌmbl] *v/t, v/i* murmurar, falar entre dentes
mummy ['mʌmi] (*pl* **-mies**) mamã *f, Braz* mamãe *f*; múmia *f*
mumps [mʌmps] papeira *f, Braz* caxumba *f*
munch [mʌntʃ] *v/t* mastigar
municipal [mju(:)'nisipəl] municipal
murder ['mə:də] *s* assassínio *m*; *v/t* assassinar; **~er** assassino *m*; **~ous** assassino
murmur ['mə:mə] *s* murmúrio *m*; *v/t, v/i* murmurar
musc|le ['mʌsl] músculo *m*; **~ular** ['mʌskjulə] musculoso; muscular
muse [mju:z] *v/i* meditar, cismar
museum [mju(:)'ziəm] museu *m*
mushroom ['mʌʃrum] cogumelo *m*
music ['mju:zik] música *f*; **~al** *adj* musical; **~ian** [-'ziʃən] músico *m*
musk [mʌsk] almíscar *m*
musket ['mʌskit] mosquete *m*; **~eer** [ˌ-'tiə] mosqueteiro *m*
Muslim ['mʌzlim] *adj, s* muçulmano *m*
muslin ['mʌzlin] musselina *f*
mussel ['mʌsl] mexilhão *m*
must [mʌst] *v/aux* dever, ter que, ter de; *s* mosto *m*; obrigação *f*, dever *m*, necessidade *f*
mustard ['mʌstəd] mostarda *f*
muster ['mʌstə] *s* chamada *f*; *v/t* reunir; fazer a chamada de
musty ['mʌsti] bafiento, mofoso
mutable ['mju:təbl] mudável; **~tion** [-'teiʃən] mutação *f*
mute [mju:t] *adj, s* mudo *m*
mutilat|e ['mju:tileit] *v/t* mutilar; **~ion** [-'leiʃən] mutilação *f*
mutin|eer [ˌmju:ti'niə] amotinador *m*; **~ous** amotinado, sedicioso; **~y** *s* (*pl* **-nies**) motim *m*
mutter ['mʌtə] *v/t, v/i* resmungar
mutton ['mʌtn] carne *f* de carneiro
mutual ['mju:tjuəl] mutual, mútuo, recíproco
muzzle ['mʌzl] *s* focinho *m*; açaime *m*, focinheira *f*; *v/t* açaimar
my [mai] *adj* meu(s), minhas(s); *int* caramba!; **~ dear** meu caro
myrtle ['mə:tl] mirto *m*
myself [mai'self] eu mesmo; mim mesmo; me; **(all) by ~** sozinho
myster|ious [mis'tiəriəs] misterioso; **~y** ['-təri] (*pl* **-ries**) mistério *m*
mystify ['mistifai] *v/t* mistificar
myth [miθ] mito *m*

N

nag [næg] *s* rocim *m*; *v/t*, *v/i* chatear, aborrecer
nail [neil] *s* unha *f*; prego *m*; *v/t* cravar, pregar
naïve [nɑː'iːv] ingénuo
naked ['neikid] nu, despido; **~ eye** olho *m* nu; **~ truth** verdade *f* nua e crua; **~ness** nudez *f*
name [neim] *s* nome *m*; nomeada *f*; *v/t* denominar; dar nome a; designar, nomear; **by ~** de/pelo nome; **~ly** a saber; **~sake** homónico *m*, *Braz* xará *m*, *f*
nap [næp] *v/i* dormitar, *Braz* cochilar; *s* sesta *f*, soneca *f*, *Braz* cochilo *m*; **have a ~** fazer sesta, dormitar; **be caught ~ping** ser apanhado desprevenido
nape [neip] nuca *f*
napkin ['næpkin] guardanapo *m*; **~ ring** argola *f* de guardanapo
nappy ['næpi] (*pl* **-pies**) fralda *f*, cueiro *m*
narcissus [nɑː'sisəs] narciso *m*
narcotic [nɑː'kɔtik] *adj*, *s* narcótico *m*
narrat|e [næ'reit] *v/t* narrar; **~ion** narração *f*; **~ive** ['-rətiv] *s* narrativa *f*; **~or** narrador *m*
narrow ['nærəu] *adj* estreito; apertado; restrito, limitado; *v/t*, *v/i* estreitar(-se); limitar, restringir; **~-minded** tacanho; **~ness** estreiteza *f*; **~s** *s/pl* estreitamento *m*, estreito *m*
nasty ['nɑːsti] desagradável; nojento; sério, grave; grosseiro, repugnante
nation ['neiʃən] nação *f*
national ['næʃənl] *adj* nacional; **~ism** nacionalismo *m*; **~ist** *adj*, *s* nacionalista *m*, *f*; **~ity** [ˌ-'næliti] (*pl* **-ties**) nacionalidade *f*; **~ize** *v/t* nacionalizar
native ['neitiv] *adj* natural; nativo; *s* indígena *m*, *f*; **2 American** *adj*, *s* americano *adj*, *m* nativo; índio/a *adj*, *m/f*
natural ['nætʃrəl] *adj* natural; **~ist** naturalista *m*, *f*; **~ize** *v/t* naturalizar
nature ['neitʃə] natureza *f*
naughty ['nɔːti] traquinas, mau, travesso
nausea ['nɔːsjə] náusea *f*, enjoo *m*; **~te** ['-sieit] *v/t* nausear
nautical ['nɔːtikəl] náutico
naval ['neivəl] naval
nave [neiv] ARCH nave *f*
navel ['neivəl] umbigo *m*
navig|able ['nævigəbl] navegável; **~ate** ['-geit] *v/t*, *v/i* navegar; **~ation** [-'geiʃən] navegação *f*; náutica *f*; **~ator** ['-geitə] navegador *m*
navy ['neivi] (*pl* **-vies**) marinha *f*; **~ blue** *s* azul-marinho *m*
nay [nei] *s* voto *m* negativo
near [niə] *adj* próximo; *adv* perto; *prp* perto de; **~by** *adv* per-

tinho; *adj* próximo; **~ly** quase; **~ness** proximidade *f*
neat [niːt] limpo, asseado; elegante, claro; porreiro; puro, não diluído
nebulous ['nebjuləs] nebuloso
necessaries ['nesisəriz] *s/pl* necessário *m*
necessary ['nesisəri] necessário, preciso, essencial
necessit|ate [ni'sesiteit] *v/t* necessitar; **~y** (*pl* **-ties**) necessidade *f*
neck [nek] *s* pescoço *m*; gargalo *m*; **~ or nothing** tudo ou nada; **~lace** ['-lis] colar *m*
need [niːd] *v/t* precisar (de), necessitar (de); *s* necessidade *f*, falta *f*
needle [niːdl, 'niːdl] *s* agulha *f*; **~ in a haystack** agulha *f* em palheiro
need|less ['niːdlis] desnecessário; **~y** indigente
negation [ni'geiʃən] negação *f*
negative ['negətiv] *adj* negativo; *s* negativa *f*; negativo *m*
neglect [ni'glekt] *v/t* negligenciar, descuidar; *s* descuido *m*; **~ful** descuidado
negligen|ce ['neglidʒəns] negligência *f*; **~t** negligente
negotia|ble [niˌgəuʃjəbl] negociável; **~te** [-ʃieit] *v/t*, *v/i* negociar
negress ['niːgris] negra *f*
negro ['niːgrəu] *neg!* negro *m*
neigh [nei] *v/i* rinchar, relinchar
neighbo(u)r ['neibə] *s* vizinho *m*; **~hood** vizinhança *f*; **~ing** vizinho
neither ['naiðə] *conj* nem; *adv* também não, tão-pouco; *adj* nenhum, nem um nem outro; **~...nor** nem ... nem
nephew ['nevjuː] sobrinho *m*
nerv|e [nəːv] *s* nervo *m*; **~ous** nervoso
nest [nest] *s* ninho *m*
nestle ['nesl] *v/t*, *v/i* aninhar (-se), aconchegar-se
net [net] *s* rede *f*; COMP Internet, net; *v/t* apanhar à rede, pescar; *adj* líquido, livre
nettle ['netl] *s* urtiga *f*; *v/t* irritar, picar
network ['netwəːk] rede *f*
neutral ['njuːtrəl] *adj* neutro, neutral; **~ity** [-'træliti] neutralidade *f*
never ['nevə] nunca, jamais; **~theless** contudo, todavia
new [njuː] novo; **~-born** recém-nascido; **~comer** recém-chegado *m*; **~ly** recentemente; novamente; **~ly wed** *s* recém-casado *m*
news [njuːz] *s/pl* notícias *f/pl*; **~paper** jornal *m*
newt [njuːt] tritão *m*
New Year's Day dia *m* de Ano Novo
next [nekst] *adj* próximo; seguinte; *adv* depois, em seguida; **(the) ~ day** o dia seguinte; **~ door** *adv* do lado; **~ to** *prp* a seguir a; junto a; *adv* quase
nib [nib] bico *m*, aparo *m*
nibble ['nibl] *v/t*, *v/i* mordiscar
nice [nais] bom; gentil; bonito;

fino, su(b)til
nick [nik] *s* corte *m*, entalhe *m*; **in the ~ of time** a tempo, no momento oportuno
nickel ['nikl] *s* níquel *m*; moeda *f* de 5 cêntimos
nickname ['nikneim] *s* alcunha *f*
niece [ni:s] sobrinha *f*
niggardly ['nigədli] mesquinho
night [nait] noite *f*; **at ~** à/de noite; **~-club** cabaré *m*; **~ cup** última bebida *f*; **~-dress**, **~-gown** camisa *f* de dormir, *Braz* camisola *f*
nightingale ['aitiŋgeil] rouxinol *m*
nightly ['naitli] *adj* no(c)turno
nightmare ['naitmεə] pesadelo *m*
nightpoint [naitpɔint] *s US* casa *f* noturna; boate *f*
nil [nil] nada *m*, zero *m*
nimble ['nimbl] ágil
nine [nain] nove
nine|teen ['nain'ti:n] dezanove; **~ty** noventa
ninth [nainθ] nono
nip [nip] *s* beliscão *m*; dentada *f*; *v/t*, *v/i* abocanhar; beliscar
nipple ['nipl] mamilo *m*; bico *m*, chupeta *f*
nitre ['naitə] nitro *m*, salitre *m*
nitrogen ['naitrədʒen] nitrogénio *m*, azoto *m*
no [nəu] *adv* não; *adj* nenhum a; **~ longer**, **~ more** já não, não ... mais
nobility [nəu'biliti] nobreza *f*
noble ['nəubl] *adj s* nobre *m*
nobody ['nəubədi] *pron* ninguém; *s* zé-ninguém *m*, joão-ninguém *m*
nod [nɔd] *v/t*, *v/i* acenar com a cabeça, inclinar a cabeça; cabecear; *s* aceno *m*
nois|e [nɔiz] ruído *m*, barulho *m*; **~eless** ['-lis] silencioso; **~y** ruidoso, barulhento
nominal ['nɔminl] nominal
nominat|e ['nɔmineit] *v/t* nomear, designar; **~ion** [-'neiʃən] nomeação *f*; **~ive** ['-nətiv] *adj*, *s* nominativo s
nonchalant ['nɔnʃələnt] indiferente, despreocupado
nondescript ['nɔndiskript] indefinível
none [nʌn] *pron* nenhum a; *adv* de modo algum; **~ the less** nem por isso, não obstante
nonentity [nɔ'nentiti] (*pl* **-ties**) nulidade *f*
nonplus ['nɔn'plʌs] *v/t* confundir
nonsens|e ['nɔnsəns] disparate *m*, asneira *f*, *Braz* bobagem *f*; **~ical** absurdo
non-stop ['nɔn'stɔp] dire(c)to, sem escala, ininterrupto
noodles ['nu:dlz] *s/pl* massa *f*
noon [nu:n] meio-dia *m*
no one ninguém
noose [nu:s] nó *m*, laço *m*
nor [nɔ:] nem
norm [nɔ:m] norma *f*
normal ['nɔ:məl] normal
north [nɔ:θ] *s* norte *m*; **~-east** *s* nordeste *m*; **~ern** ['-ðən] setentrional, do norte; **~west** *s* nor-

oeste *m*
nose [nəuz] *s* nariz *m*
nostril ['nɔstril] narina *f*
nosy ['nəuzi] curioso, indiscreto
not [nɔt] não; **~ a** nem um/-a; **~ at all** de maneira nenhuma
notary ['nəutəri] (*pl* **-ries**) notário *m*
notch [nɔtʃ] *s* entalhe *m*, encaixe *m*; *v/t* entalhar
note [nəut] *v/t* notar, tomar nota de; *s* nota *f*; apontamento *m*; bilhete *m*; **take ~ of** prestar atenção a, tomar nota de; **~-book** agenda *f*; caderno *m* de apontamentos; **~d** ['nəutid] *adj* notável; **~-paper** papel *m* de carta; **~worthy** notável, digno de nota
nothing ['nʌθiŋ] *pron*, *s* nada *m*; **for ~** de graça, grátis; para nada; **~ ... but** apenas, só; **~ doing!** nada feito!
notice ['nəutis] *v/t*, *v/i* reparar em, notar; *s* nota *f*; aviso *m*; **~ to quit** aviso *m* de despejo; **~able** perceptível; notável
notion ['nəuʃən] noção *f*
notorious [nəu'tɔ:riəs] notório
notwithstanding [,nɔtwiθ-'stændiŋ] *prp* não obstante
nought [nɔ:t] zero *m*
noun [naun] substantivo *m*
nourish ['nʌriʃ] *v/t* nutrir, alimentar; **~ing** nutritivo; **~ment** alimentação *f*; alimento *m*
novel ['nɔvəl] *s* novela *f*, romance *m*; *adj* novo, original; **~ty** (*pl* **-ties**) novidade *f*; inovação *f*
November [nəu'vembə] Novembro *m*
now [nau] *adv* agora; já; *s* agora *m*; *int* ora! qual!; **just ~** há pouco, agora mesmo; **~ and then/again** de vez em quando; **~adays** ['-ədeiz] hoje em dia
nowhere ['nəuwεə] em parte alguma
noxious ['nɔkʃəs] nocivo
nuclear ['nju:kliə] nuclear
nude [nju:d] *adj*, *s* nu *m*
nudge [nʌdʒ] *s* cotovelada *f*, *Braz* cutucada *f*; *v/t* acotovelar, *Braz* cutucar
nudism ['nju:dizəm] nudismo *m*
nugget ['nʌgit] pepita *f*
nuisance ['nju:səns] maçada *f*, incómodo *m*, aborrecimento *m*
null [nʌl] nulo; **~ and void** sem efeito/validade
numb [nʌm] *adj* entorpecido
number ['nʌmbə] *s* número *m*; *v/t* numerar, contar; **~ plate** place *f* de matrícula
numerous ['nju:mərəs] numeroso
nun [nʌn] monja *f*, freira *f*
nunnery ['nʌnəri] (*pl* **-ries**) convento *m*
nurse [nə:s] *s* ama *f*; enfermeira *f*; *v/t*, *v/i* amamentar; mamar; tratar de; **~ry** infantário *m*, *Braz* berçário *m*; **~ry rhyme** rima *f* infantil; **~ school** jardim-escola *m* de infância *m*
nut [nʌt] *s* noz *f*; MEC porca *f*; **~cracker** quebra-nozes *m*

nutri|ment ['nju:trimənt] alimento *m*; **~tion** [-'triʃən] nutrição *f*
nuts [nʌts] *adj* doido, louco; **~** about/over louco por
nylon ['nailən] náilon *m*; **~s** *s/pl* meias *f/pl* de náilon

O

oak [əuk] carvalho *m*
oar [ɔ:] remo *m*, **~sman** remador *m*
oasis [əu'eisis] (*pl* **-ses** [-si:z]) oásis *m*
oath [əuθ] juramento *m*; **take an ~** prestar juramento
oats [əuts] *s/pl* aveia *f*
obedien|ce [ə'bi:djəns] obediência *f*; **~t** obediente
obey [əˌbei] *v/t, v/i* obedecer
obituary [əˌbitjuəri] (*pl* **-ries**) *s* necrologia *f*; *adj* obituário
object ['ɔbdʒikt] *s* obje(c)to *m*; fim *m*, obje(c)tivo *m*; GRAM complemento *m*; [əb'dʒekt] *v/t, v/i* **~(to)** opor-se (a); obje(c)tar; **~ion** [əb'dʒekʃən] obje(c)ção *f*; **~ionable** [-ʃnəbl] censurável; **~ive** [əb'dʒektiv] *adj*, *s* obje(c)tivo *m*
obligat|ion [ˌɔbli'geiʃən] obrigação *f*; **~ory** [ɔ'bligətəri] obrigatório
oblig|e [əˌblaidʒ] *v/t* obrigar, forçar; **much ~ed** muito obrigado; **~ing** *adj* serviçal, prestável
oblique [ə'bli:k] *adj* oblíquo
obliterate [əˌblitəreit] *v/t* obliterar
oblivi|on [əˌbliviən] oblívio *m*, esquecimento *m*; **~ous** esquecido; distraído
obnoxious [əb'nɔkʃəs] ofensivo, odioso
obscene [ɔb'si:n] obsceno
obscur|e [əb'skjuə] *adj* obscuro; *v/t* obscurecer; **~ity** (*pl* **-ties**) obscuridade *f*
observ|able [əb'zə:vəbl] observável; **~ant** observador; **~ation** [-'veiʃən] observação *f*; **~tory** [-təri] (*pl* **-ries**) observatório *m*
observ|e [əb'zə:v] *v/t* observar; **~er** [-və] observador *m*
obsess [əb'ses] *v/t* atormentar; **~ion** obsessão *f*
obsolete ['ɔbsəli:t] obsoleto
obstacle ['ɔbstəkl] obstáculo *m*
obstina|cy ['ɔbstinəsi] obstinação *f*; **~te** ['-nit] obstinado
obstruct [əb'strʌkt] *v/t* obstruir; tapar; **~ion** obstrução *f*; **~ive** obstrutivo
obtain [əb'tein] *v/t* obter; **~able** conseguível
obtrusive [əb'tru:siv] intruso; importuno
obviate ['ɔbvieit] *v/t* obviar, evitar
obvious ['ɔbviəs] óbvio

occasion [ə'keiʒən] *s* ocasião *f*; caso *m*, assunto *m*; *v/t* ocasionar; **~al** casual, ocasional, fortuito
occult [ɔ'kʌlt] oculto; encoberto
occup|ant ['ɔkjupənt] ocupante *m*, *f*; **~y** ['-pai] *v/t* ocupar; **be ~ied in doing** estar ocupado a fazer
occur [ə'kəː] *v/i* ocorrer, acontecer, suceder; **~ to** ocorrer, vir à ideia; **~rence** [ə'kʌrəns] ocorrência *f*, acontecimento *m*
ocean ['əuʃən] oceano *m*
o'clock [ə'klɔk] horas *f/pl*: **at three ~** às três horas
October [ɔk'təubə] Outubro *m*
oculist ['ɔkjulist] oculista *m*, *f* oftalmologista *m*, *f*
odd [ɔd] ímpar, desirmanado; estranho; **~s** *s/pl* diferença *f*; vantagem *f*; probabilidades *f/pl*; **at ~s (with)** de ponta; **~s and ends** bugigangas *f/pl*
odious ['əudjəs] odioso, detestável
odo(u)r ['əudə] odor *m*; aroma *m*; **in bad ~ with** em desfavor; **~less** inodoro
of [ɔv, əv] de; **all ~ a sudden** de repente; **all ~ us** todos nós; **~ late** ultimanente
off [ɔf] *prp* de; fora de; longe de; *adv* embora; afastado; distante; *adj* desligado; anulado, cancelado; livre; **be ~!** fora daqui! vai-te embora!; **better ~** melhor servido; **well ~** em boa situação financeira
offence [ə'fens] ofensa *f*; delito *m*; **take ~ (at something)** ter ressentimento
offend [ə'fend] *v/t* ofender; *v/i* transgredir; **~er** transgressor *m*, delinquente *m*, *f*
offensive [ə'fensiv] *adj* ofensivo; *s* ofensiva *f*
offer ['ɔfə] *v/t*, *v/i* oferecer(-se); apresentar; sacrificar; *s* oferecimento *m*, oferta *f*; **~ing** *s* oferta *f*; oferenda *f*
offhand [ˌɔf'hænd] *adv* de improviso, de pronto; *adj* improvisado; brusco
offic|e ['ɔfis] emprego *m*; cargo *m*; ministério *m*; escritório *m*; oficina *f*; **~er** oficial *m*; funcionário *m*; polícia *m*
official [ə'fiʃəl] *adj* oficial
officious [ə'fiʃəs] intrometido
offside ['ɔf'said] *adj* fora-de-jogo
offspring ['ɔfspriŋ] prole *f*, descendência *f*
often ['ɔːfn] amiúde, muitas vezes
oil [ɔil] *s* óleo *m*; azeite *m*; petróleo *m*; **~cloth** oleado *m*, encerado *m*; **~-painting** pintura *f* a óleo; **~-well** poço *m* de petróleo; **~y** oleoso; gorduroso
ointment ['ɔintmənt] unguento *m* pomada *f*
okay, OK [əu'kei] *adv* está bem; em ordem; *adj* corre(c)to, exa(c)to
old [əuld] velho, antigo, idoso; **how ~ are you?** quantos anos

tem/tens?; ~ **age** velhice *f*; ~ **age pension** subsídio *m* da velhice; ~**-fashioned** *adj* antiquado, fora de moda; ~**-timer** veterano *m*

olive ['ɔliv] azeitona *f*

Olympic games [ə'limpik geimz] jogos *s/pl* Olímpicos

omelet(te) ['ɔmlit] omelete *f*, omeleta *f*

omen ['əumən] agoiro *m*, presságio *m*

ominous ['ɔminəs] ominoso, agoirento

omission [əu'miʃən] omissão *f*

omit [əu'mit] *v/t* omitir

on [ɔn] *adj* aceso, ligado; *prp* em, esobre, em cima de; *adv* em cima; em diante; para a frente; **and so** ~ e assim por diante, etc.; ~ **and** ~ sem cessar

once [wʌns] *conj* uma vez que; *s* uma vez, ocasião *f*; *adv* uma vez; outrora; **all at** ~ de repente; **at** ~ em seguida, imediatamente; ~ **more** mais uma vez; ~ **upon a time there was ...** era uma vez ...

one [wʌn] *pron* um; se, alguém, a gente, uma pessoa; *adj* um, uma; um único, um só; ~ **by** ~ um a um; ~ **another** uns aos outros

oneself [wʌn'self] se; si, si mesmo, si próprio

one-way ['wʌnwei] de uma só mão, de sentido único

onion ['ʌnjən] cebola *f*

online *adj* ['ɔnlain] em linha, online; ~ **banking** *s* acesso ao banco pela Internet; ~ **dating** *s* marcar encontros amorosos pela Internet; ~ **shopping** *s* (fazer) compras em linha

onlooker ['ɔn,lukə] espectador *m*

only ['əunli] *adj* único, só; *adv* somente, só, unicamente; *conj* mas, porém

onset ['ɔnset] investida *f*, arremetida *f*

onto ['ɔntu, -tə] para, para cima de

onward ['ɔwəd] para a frente, para diante; ~**s** em, diante

ooze [u:z] *v/t*, *v/i* emanar

opal ['əupəl] ópala *f*

opaque [əu'peik] opaco

open ['əupən] *adj* aberto; *s* ar livre *m*; *v/t*, *v/i* inaugurar; abrir (-se); começar; ~**ing** *adj* inicial; *s* abertura *f*; começo *m*; inauguração *f*; ~**ing night** estreia *f*

opera ['ɔpərə] ópera *f*; ~**-glasses** *s/pl* binóculo *m*; ~**-house** teatro *m*, ópera *f*

operat|e ['ɔpəreit] *v/t*, *v/i* operar; funcionar, trabalhar; ~**ion** [-'reiʃən] funcionamento *m*, a(c)ção *f*, manobras *f/pl*; operação *f*; ~**or** telegrafista *m*, *f*; operário *m*, mecânico *m*

opinion [ə'pinjən] opinião *f*

opponent [ə'pəunənt] adversário *m*

opportunity [,ɔpə'tju:niti] (*pl* **-ties**) oportunidade *f*

oppose [ə'pəuz] *v/t* opor-se a

opposit|e ['ɔpəzit] *adj* oposto; contrário; *s* contrário *m*; *prp* em frente de, defronte; **~ion** [-'ziʃən] oposição *f*
oppress [ə'pres] *v/t* oprimir; afligir; **~ion** [ə'preʃən] opressão *f*; **~ive** opressivo; **~or** opressor *m*
optic|ian [ɔp'tiʃən] ó(p)tico *m*, oculista *m*, *f*; **~s** ó(p)tica *f*
optimism ['ɔptimizəm] o(p)timismo *m*
option ['ɔpʃən] opção *f*; **~al** facultativo
opulent ['ɔpjulənt] opulento
or [ɔː] ou; quer; seja; **either ... ~ ...** ou ... ou; **~ else** senão
orange ['ɔrindʒ] *s* laranja *f*; *adj* cor-de-laranja; **~ade** [ˌ-eid] laranjada *f*
orator ['ɔrətə] orador *m*
orbit ['ɔːbit] *s* órbita *f*
orchard ['ɔːtʃəd] pomar *m*
orchestra ['ɔːkistrə] orquestra *f*
ordain [ɔː'dein] *v/t* ordenar
ordeal [ɔː'diːl] provação *f*, prova *f*
order ['ɔːdə] *v/t*, *v/i* ordenar; encomendar, mandar vir; receitar; *s* ordem *f*; regra *f*; mandado *m*; **in ~ to** para; **out of ~** avariado, estragado; **~ly** *adj* ordenado; *s* plantão *m*, ordenança *f*
ordinance ['ɔːdinəns] decreto *m*
ordinary ['ɔːdnri] ordinário
ore [ɔː] minério *m*
organ ['ɔːgən] órgão *m*; **~ic** [-'gænik] orgânico; **~ization** [-ai'zeiʃən] organização *f*; **~ize** *v/t*, *v/i* organizar(-se); **~izer** organizador *m*
orient|al [ˌɔːri'entl] oriental; **~ate** ['-teit] *v/t*, *v/i* orientar(-se)
origin ['ɔridʒin] origem *f*
origin|al [ə'ridʒənl] *adj*, *s* original *m*; **~ality** [-'næliti] originalidade *f*; **~ate** [-eit] *v/t*, *v/i* originar(-se)
ornament ['ɔːnəment] *s* ornamento *m*; *v/t* ornamentar
ornate [ɔː'neit] ornamentado
orphan ['ɔːfən] *s* órfão *m*; **~age** orfanato *m*
oscillate ['ɔsileit] *v/i* oscilar
ostentatious [ˌɔsten'teiʃəs] pomposo, ostentoso
ostrich ['ɔstritʃ] avestruz *m*
other ['ʌðə] outro; diferente; **each ~** um ao outro; **every ~ day** dia sim, dia não; **~ than** a não ser; **~wise** doutra maneira, aliás, caso contrário
ought [ɔːt] *v/aux* dever; **you ~ to** devias
ounce [auns] onça *f*
our ['auə] nosso(s), nossa(s); **~s** o(s) nosso(s), a(s) nossa(s); **~selves** nos; nós mesmos
oust [aust] *v/t* desapossar, desalojar
out [aut] *adv*, *prp* fora; *adj* ausente, fora de casa; **~ of breath** sem fôlego; **~ with it!** desembuche!; **~ you go!** fora!; **~ of** fora de; para fora de; de
out|balance [aut'bæləns] *v/t* exceder; **~bid** *v/t* cobrir o lan-

ço de; **~break** erupção *f*; **~burst** explosão *f*; acesso *m*; **~cast** *s* proscrito *m*; **~cry** clamor *m*; **~do** *v/t* exceder; **~door** exterior; **~doors** *adv* ao ar livre, fora de casa
outer ['autə] exterior
out|fit ['autfit] *s* equipamento *m*; vestuário *m*; **~grow** *v/t* crescer mais que; passar a idade de; não caber em
outing ['autiŋ] *s* excursão *f*, passeio *m*
out|last [aut'lɑːst] *v/t* durar mais que, sobreviver a; **~lay** *s* gastos *m/pl*, despesas *f/pl*; **~let** saída *f*; escoadouro *m*; **~line** *v/t* delinear, esboçar; *s* contorno *m*; **~number** *v/t* exceder em número; **~-of-date** antiquado; **~patient** doente *m* externo; **~put** produção *f*
outrage ['autreidʒ] *s* ultraje *m* afronta *f*; *v/t* ultrajar; **~ous** ultrajante
out|right ['autrait] *adj* absoluto, total, completo; [-'rait] *adv* completamente; num instante; sem rodeios, francamente; **~run** *v/t* deixar atrás, passar, alcançar; **~shine** *v/t* eclipsar; **~side** *s* exterior *m*; *adv* fora, lá fora; *prp* fora de; **~sider** forasteiro *m*, intruso *m*; **~skirts** *s/pl* arrabaldes *m/pl*, cercanias *f/pl*; **~source** *v/t* subcontratar; **~spoken** franco; **~standing** saliente, proeminente; pendente, a cobrar; **~ward** *adj* exterior, externo; **~ward(s)** *adv* para fora; **~weigh** *v/t* prevalecer sobre; pesar mais que; **~wit** *v/t* exceder em astúcia
oven ['ʌvn] forno *m*
over ['əuvə] *adj* acabado; passado; *adv* acima, por cima, em cima; *prp* sobre; por cima de; através de; acerca de; (**all**) **~ again** outra vez; **~!** fim!; **~ and ~** repetidas vezes; **~ there** lá, acolá; para lá; **~act** *v/t*, *v/i* exagerar; **~alls** *s/pl* fato *m* de macaco, *Braz* macacão *m*; **~balance** *v/t*, *v/i* perder o equilíbrio; **~board** ao MAR; **~burden** *v/t* sobrecarregar; **~coat** sobretudo *m*; **-~come** *v/t*, *v/i* vencer, superar; **~crowded** apinhado; abarrotado; **~do** *v/t* exagerar; **~done** *adj* passado demais; **~due** atrasado; COM vencido; **~flow** *s* transbordamento *m*; *v/t*, *v/i* transbordar; **~grown** coberto; **~head** *adv* ao alto, *adj* suspenso, aéreo; geral; **~heads** *s/pl* despesas *f/pl* gerais; **~hear** *v/t* ouvir por acaso; **~look** *v/t* dominar; omitir; **~night** *adv* de noite; de um dia para outro; **~power** *v/t* subjugar, superar; **~seas** *adj* ultramarino; **~see** *v/t*, *v/i* vigiar, fiscalizar; **~seer** inspe(c)tor *m*, superintendente *m*; **~shoe** galocha *f*; **~shoot** *v/t*, *v/i* ir além de, ultrapassar; **~sight** inadvertência *f*; **~sleep** *v/i* dormir demais; **~take** *v/t*, *v/i* ultrapassar, alcançar; **~tax** *v/t* sobrecarregar de impostos;

~**throw** *v/t* derrubar; subverter; ~**time** *s* horas *f/pl* extraordinárias; ~**turn** *v/t, v/i* derrubar, entornar; emborcar; ~**-weening** pretensioso, arrogante; ~**weight** *s* excesso *m* de peso; ~**whelm** *v/t* acabrunhar; ~**work** *s* excesso *m* de trabalho
owe [əu] *v/t* dever
owing ['əuiŋ] *adj* devido; ~ **to** devido a, por causa de
owl [aul] mocho *m*, coruja *f*
own [əun] *adj* próprio; *v/t, v/i* possuir; admitir; ~ **up** confessar; ~**er** proprietário *m*, dono *m*; ~**ership** propriedade *f*
ox [ɔks] (*pl* **oxen** ['-ən]) boi *m*
oxygen ['ɔksidʒən] oxigénio *m*
oyster ['ɔistə] ostra *f*
ozone ['əuzəun] ozone *m*, ozônio *m*; ~ **hole** buraco *m* da camada de ozônio

P

pace [peis] *v/t, v/i* andar a passo; *s* passo *m*; passada *f*; **keep ~ with** acompanhar, manter-se no mesmo andamento
pacific [pə'sifik] pacífico
pacifist ['pæsifist] pacifista *m, f*
pacify ['pæsifai] *v/t* pacificar; acalmar
pack [pæk] *s* fardo *m*; pacote *m*; embrulho *m*; baralho *m*; matilha *f*; súcia *f*; *v/t, v/i* empacotar; enfardar, enfardelar; arrumar, fazer as malas; ~ **off** despachar; ~**age** *s* embrulho *m*, pacote *m*; ~**et** ['-it] maço *m*; pacote *m*; MAR paquete *m*; ~**ing** *s* acondicionamento *m*
pact [pækt] pacto *m*
pad [pæd] *s* caneleira *f*; almofada *f*; bloco *m*; *v/t* forrar, acolchoar
paddle ['pædl] *s* remo *m*; pá *f*; *v/t, v/i* remar; chapinhar, patinhar
paddock ['pædək] recinto *m*, cercado *m*
padlock ['pædlɔk] *s* cadeado *m*; *v/t, v/i* fechar a cadeado
pagan ['peigən] *adj, s* pagão *m*; ~**ism** paganismo *m*
page [peidʒ] *s* página *f*; paquete *m*, moço *m* de recados; *v/t* paginar; chamar em voz alta
pageant ['pædʒənt] cortejo *m*, desfile *m*
pail [peil] balde *m*
pain [pein] *s* dor *f*, sofrimento *m*; *v/t* angustiar; entristecer; ~**ful** doloroso; ~**less** sem dor; ~**staking** cuidadoso
paint [peint] *s* pintura *f*; tinta *f*; *v/t, v/i* pintar; ~**er** pintor *m*; ~**ing** *s* quadro *m*; pintura *f*
pair [pɛə] *s* par *m*; casal *m*; parelha *f*, *v/t, v/i* emparelhar(-se); acasalar(-se); **in ~s** aos pares; ~ **of scales** balança *f*
pajamas [pə'dʒɑːməz] *s/pl US*

pijama *m*
pal [pæl] amigo *m*, camarada *m*, *Braz* capanga *m*
palace ['pælis] palácio *m*
palat|able ['pælətəbl] saboroso; **~al** *adj* palatal
palate ['pælit] paladar *m*
pale [peil] *adj* pálido; *v/i* empalidecer; **~ness** palidez *f*
palette ['pælit] paleta *f*
paling ['peiliŋ] *s* cerca *f*, paliçada *f*
palliative ['pæliətiv] *adj* paliativo
pall|id ['pælid] pálido; **~or** palidez *f*, palor *m*
palm [pɑːm] *s* palma *f*; **~-tree** palmeira *f*
palpable ['pælpəbl] palpável
paltry ['pɔːltri] insignificante, miserável
pan [pæn] *s* panela *f*; **~cake** *s* panqueca *f*
pane [pein] vidraça *f*
panel ['pænl] *s* painel *m*; caixilho *m*, almofada *f*; lista *f* de jurados, júri *m*
pang [pæŋ] angústia *f*, ânsia *f*
panic ['pænik] *s* pânico *m*; *v/t*, *v/i* aterrorizar(-se), encher(-se) de pânico
pansy ['pænzi] (*pl* **-sies**) amor-perfeito *m*
pant [pænt] *v/i* arfar, arquejar
panties ['pæntiz] *s/pl* cuecas *f/pl*, calcinhas *f/pl*
pantry ['pæntri] (*pl* **-ries**) despensa *f*, copa *f*
pants [pænts] *s/pl* ceroulas *f/pl*; calças *f/pl*; cuecas *f/pl*
pap [pæp] papa *f*, mingau *m*; teta *f*
papa [pə'pɑː] papá *m*, *Braz* papai *m*
paparazzi [pæpə'rætsiː] *s/pl* os paparazzi *m/pl*
paper ['peipə] *s* papel *m*; jornal *m*; prova *f*, exercício *m* escrito; dissertação *f*; *v/t* forrar de papel; **~back** brochura *f*; **~-money** papel-moeda *m*; **~s** *s/pl* documentos *m/pl*
parachute ['pærəʃuːt] *s* pára-quedas *m*
parade [pə'reid] *s* parada *f*, revista *f*; *v/t*, *v/i* alardear; passar revista (a); desfilar
paradise ['pærədais] paraíso *m*
paragraph ['pærəgrɑːf] *s* parágrafo *m*
parallel ['pærəlel] *adj* paralelo; *s* paralela *f*
paraly|se ['pærəlaiz] *v/t* paralisar; **~sis** [pə'rælisis] paralisia *f*; **~tic** [ˌ-'litik] *adj*, *s* paralítico *m*
paramount ['pærəmaunt] superior, supremo
parcel ['pɑːsl] *s* pacote *m*, embrulho *m*; parcela *f*, lote *m*; *v/t* **~ up** empacotar
parch [pɑːtʃ] *v/t*, *v/i* tostar; torrar; ressecar
parchment ['pɑːtʃmənt] pergaminho *m*
pardon ['pɑːdn] *s* perdão *m*; *v/t* perdoar, desculpar; **I beg your ~**, **~ me** desculpe(-me); **~?** como (disse)?; **~able** perdoável
pare [pɛə] *v/t* aparar, cortar

parent ['pɛərənt] pai *m*, mãe *f*; **~age** origem *f*; paternidade *f*; **~al** paternal, maternal; dos pais; **~s** *s/pl* pais *m/pl*

parings ['pɛəriŋz] *s/pl* aparas *f/pl*, restos *m/pl*

parish ['pæriʃ] paróquia *f*, freguesia *f*

parity ['pæriti] paridade *f*, igualdade *f*

park [pɑːk] *s* parque *m*; *v/t*, *v/i* estacionar; **~ing** *s* estacionamento *m*; **~ing lot** *US* parque *m* de estacionamento

parliament ['pɑːləmənt] parlamento *m*; **~ary** [-'mentəri] parlamentar

parquet ['pɑːkei] parquete *m*

parrot ['pærət] papagaio *m*

parsley ['pɑːsli] salsa *f*

parsnip ['pɑːsnip] pastinaca *f*

parson ['pɑːsn] cura *m*, pároco *m*

part [pɑːt] *s* parte *f*; THEAT papel *m*; *v/t*, *v/i* repartir, dividir; separar-se; partir; **for my ~** quanto a mim, cá por mim, eu cá; **for the most ~** na maioria dos casos, geralmente; **play a ~** representar, fingir

partial ['pɑːʃəl] parcial; **~ity** [ˌ-ʃi'æliti] parcialidade *f*

participate [pɑː'tisipeit] *v/i* participar

particle ['pɑːtikl] partícula *f*

particular [pə'tikjulə] *s* pormenor *m*, particularidade *f*; *adj* particular, singular; especial; **~ity** [-'læriti] particularidade *f*; **~ize** *v/t*, *v/i* particularizar; **~ly** particularmente; especialmente

parting ['pɑːtiŋ] *s* separação *f*; despedida *f*; risca *f* de cabelo; *adj* de despedida

partisan [ˌpɑːti'zæn] partidário *m*

partition [pɑː'tiʃən] *s* divisão *f*, partição *f*; tabique *m*; *v/t* dividir, repartir

partly ['pɑːtli] em parte, parcialmente

partner ['pɑːtnə] *s* sócio *m*; parceiro *m*; companheiro *m*; **be ~s with** ser parceiro de; **~ship** sociedade *f*, associação *f*

partridge ['pɑːtridʒ] perdiz *f*

part-time [ˌpɑːt'taim] *adj* de meio dia, de meio tempo

party ['pɑːti] (*pl* **-ties**) partido *m*; reunião *f*, festa *f*; grupo *m*

pass [pɑːs] *s* passagem *f*; passe *m*; desfiladeiro *m*; *v/t*, *v/i* passar (**through** por); **~ away** morrer; **~ by** passar por; ignorar; **~ on** prosseguir; passar adiante; morrer; **~ out** desmaiar

pass|able ['pɑːsəbl] passável; transitável; aceitável; navegável; **~age** ['pæsidʒ] passagem *f*; corredor *m*; viagem *f*, travessia *f*

passenger ['pæsindʒə] passageiro *m*

passer-by ['pɑːsə'bai] (*pl* **passers-by**) transeunte *m*

passing ['pɑːsiŋ] *s* passagem; *adj* passageiro; passante

passion ['pæʃən] paixão *f*; có-

lera *f*; **~ate** ['-it] apaixonado; ardente
passive ['pæsiv] *adj* passivo; *s* passiva *f*; **~ smoking** fumo *m* passivo
pass|key ['pɑːskiː] chave *f* mestra; **~port** passaporte *m*; **~word** santo-e-senha *m*, palavra *f* de passe
past [pɑːst] *s* passado *m*; *adj* passado; decorrido, último; *prp* depois de; além de; fora de; **half ~ two** duas e meia
paste [peist] *s* pasta *f*, massa *f*; grude *m*, cola *f*; *v/t* colar, pegar
pastime ['pɑːstaim] passatempo *m*
pastry ['peistri] *(pl* **-ries***)* massas *f/pl*, folhados *m/pl*, pastelaria *f*; **~-cook** pasteleiro *m*
pasture ['pɑːstʃə] *s* pasto *m*, pastagem *f*; *v/t* pastar, apascentar
pat [pæt] *s* palmadinha *f*; afago *m*; *v/t* afagar; dar palmadas a; *adj* oportuno
patch [pætʃ] *s* remendo *m*; *v/t* remendar
patent ['peitənt] *s* patente *f*; *v/t* patentear; obter uma patente para; *adj* manifesto, patente
patern|al [pə'tɜːnl] paternal; **~ity** paternidade *f*
path [pɑːθ] caminho *m*, senda *f*, vereda *f*
patien|ce ['peiʃəns] paciência *f*; **~t** *adj*, *s* paciente *m*, *f*
patriotic [ˌpætri'ɔtik] patriótico
patrol [pə'trəul] *s* patrulha *f*; *v/t* patrulhar
patron ['peitrən] patrono *m*, prote(c)tor *m*; **~age** ['pætrənidʒ] patrocínio *m*; patronato *m*
pattern ['pætən] *s* modelo *m*; amostra *f*; padrão *m*; desenho *m*; *v/t* modelar
paunch [pɔːntʃ] pança *f*
pause [pɔːz] *s* pausa *f*, *v/i* fazer pausa
pave [peiv] *v/t* pavimentar, calcetar; **~ment** passeio *m*; pavimento *m*
paw [pɔː] *s* pata *f*
pawn [pɔːn] *s* peão *m* de xadrez; penhor *m*; *v/t* empenhar; **~broker** penhorista *m*, *f*; **~shop** casa *f* de penhores
pay [pei] *v/t*, *v/i* render, dar lucro; pagar; *s* paga *f*, salário *m*, soldo *m*; **~ attention** prestar atenção; **~ back** restituir, devolver; **~ off** liquidar; dar resultado; **~ one's respects** apresentar seus respeitos; **~ a visit** fazer uma visita; **~able** pagável; **~ment** pagamento *m*
pea [piː] ervilha *f*
peace [piːs] paz *f*; tranquilidade *f*; **~ful** pacífico; tranquilo; **~maker** pacificador *m*
peach [piːtʃ] *s* pêssego *m*
pea|cock ['piːkɔk] pavão *m*; **~hen** pavoa *f*
peak [piːk] *s* pico *m*, cume *m*, cimo *m*; **~ed** *adj* macilento, doentio; pontiagudo, pontudo; **~ hours** *f/pl* horas *f/pl* de ponta

peal [piːl] *s* repique *m* de sinos; *v/i* repicar
peanut ['piːnʌt] amendoim *m*
pear [pɛə] pêra *f*
pearl [pəːl] *s* pérola *f*
peasant ['pezənt] camponês *m*, lavrador *m*
peat [piːt] turfa *f*
pebble ['pebl] seixo *m*, calhau *m*
peck [pek] *s* bicada *f*; *v/t*, *v/i* debicar; bicar, dar bicadas a; picar
peculiar [pi'kjuːljə] peculiar; singular; **~ity** [-li'æriti] peculiaridade *f*; singularidade *f*
pedal ['pedl] *s* pedal *m*; *v/t*, *v/i* pedalar
pedestal ['pedistl] pedestal *m*, peanha *f*
pedestrian [pi'destriən] *s* peão *m*; *adj* pedestre; prosaico, vulgar; **~ crossing** passagem *f* para peões; **~ precinct** zona *f* para peões
pedigree ['pedigriː] genealogia *f*, linhagem *f*
pedlar, *US* **pedler** ['pedlə] bufarinheiro *m*, *Braz* mascate *m*
peel [piːl] *s* casca *f*, pele *f*; *v/t*, *v/i* descascar, pelar
peep [piːp] *s* espiadela *f*, espreitadela *f*; *v/i* espiar, espreitar
peer [piə] *s* par *m*, nobre *m*; igual *m*, *f*; *v/i* espreitar, olhar; **~age** pariato *m*; **~less** incomparável, sem par
peevish ['piːviʃ] impertinente, rabugento
peg [peg] *s* cavilha *f*; grampo *m*, mola *f*; pretexto *m*
pelican ['pelikən] pelicano *m*
pelt [pelt] *s* pele *f*, couro *m*; *v/t*, *v/i* encher, crivar; bater, malhar; cair; apedrejar, lapidar
pen [pen] *s* caneta *f*; pena *f*
penal ['piːnl] penal; **~ servitude** trabalhos *m/pl* forçados; **~ty** ['penlti] (*pl* **-ties**) penalidade *f*
penance ['penəns] penitência *f*
pence [pens] *pl of* **penny**
pencil ['pensl] *s* lápis *m*
pend|ant ['pendənt] pendente *m*; **~ing** *adj* pendente; *prp* até
pendulum ['pendjuləm] pêndulo *m*
penetra|te ['penitreit] *v/t*, *v/i* penetrar; **~tion** [-'treiʃən] penetração *f*
penguin ['peŋgwin] pinguim *m*
peninsula [pi'ninsjulə] península *f*; **~r** peninsular
peniten|ce ['penitəns] penitência *f*; **~t** *adj*, *s* penitente *m*, *f*
pennant ['penənt] flâmula *f*, galhardete *m*
penniless ['penilis] sem vintém
penny ['peni] (*pl* **pennies** *or* **pence**) péni *m*; **a pretty ~** uma soma considerável; **~ royal** poejo *m*; **turn an honest ~** ganhar dinheiro honestamente
pension ['penʃən] *s* pensão *f*; **~ off** aposentar, reformar
pensive ['pensiv] pensativo
penthouse ['penthaus] apartamento *m* acima do telhado
people ['piːpl] *s* povo *m*; pessoas *f/pl*, gente *f*; vulgo *m*;

v/t povoar

pepper ['pepə] *s* pimenta *f*; **~mint** hortelã-pimenta *f*; **~ pot** pimenteiro *m*

per [pəː] por

perambulator ['præmbjuleitə] carrinho *m* de criança

perceive [pə'siːv] *v/t* perceber, compreender; notar, ver

percentage [pə'sentidʒ] percentagem *f*

perception [pə'sepʃən] percepção *f*

perch [pəːtʃ] *s zoo* perca *f*; poleiro *m*; vara *f*; *v/t*, *v/i* empoleirar(-se)

peremptory [pə'remptəri] peremptório

perfect ['pəːfikt] *adj* perfeito; [pə'fekt] *v/t* aperfeiçoar; **~ion** [pə'fekʃən] perfeição *f*

perforate ['pəːfəreit] *v/t*, *v/i* perfurar

perform [pə'fɔːm] *v/t*, *v/i* representar; executar; **~ance** representação *f*; execução *f*

perfume ['pəːfjuːm] *s* perfume *m*; [pə'fjuːm] *v/t* perfumar

perhaps [pə'hæps] talvez, quiçá

peril ['peril] perigo *m*; **~ous** perigoso

perimeter [pə'rimitə] perímetro *m*

period ['piəriəd] *s* período *m*; época *f*; termo *m*; GRAM ponto *m*; **~ic** [ˌ-'ɔdik] periódico; **~ical** [ˌ-'ɔdikəl] *s* revista *f*

perish ['periʃ] *v/t*, *v/i* perecer; **~able** perecível

perjury ['pəːdʒəri] perjúrio *m*

perm [pəːm] *s* permanente *f*; *v/t* fazer uma permanente a

permanen|ce ['pəːmənəns] permanência; **~t** permanente

permission [pə'miʃən] permissão *f*, licença *f*

permit [pə'mit] *v/t*, *v/i* permitir; ['pəːmit] *s* permissão *f*, licença *f*

pernicious [pəː'niʃəs] pernicioso

perpendicular [ˌpəːpən'dikjulə] *adj*, *s* perpendicular *f*

perpetua|l [pə'petjuəl] perpétuo; **~te** [-eit] *v/t* perpetuar

perplex [pə'pleks] *v/t* embaraçar; confundir; deixar perplexo; **~ed** *adj* perplexo; **~ity** (*pl* **-ties**) perplexidade *f*

persecut|e ['pəːsikjuːt] *v/t* perseguir; **~ion** [-'kjuːʃən] perseguição *f*; **~or** perseguidor *m*

persever|ance [ˌpəːsi'viərəns] perseverança *f*; **~e** *v/i* perseverar

Persian ['pəːʃən] *adj*, *s* persa *m*, *f*

persist [pə'sist] *v/i* persistir; **~ence** persistência *f*; **~ent** persistente

person ['peːsn] pessoa *f*; **~age** personagem *f*; **~al** pessoal; **~ality** [ˌ-sə'næliti] (*pl* **-ties**) personalidade *f*

personify [pə'sɔnifai] *v/t* personificar

personnel [ˌpəːsə'nel] pessoal *m*

perspective [pə'spektiv] pers-

pectiva *f*
perspicacious [ˌpəːspiˈkeiʃəs] perspicaz
perspir|ation [ˌpəːspəˈreiʃən] suor *m*, transpiração *f*; **~e** [pəˈspaiə] *v/i* suar, transpirar
persua|de [pəˈsweid] *v/t* persuadir; **~sion** [-ʒən] persuasão *f*; **~sive** [-siv] persuasivo
pert [pəːt] espevitado, vivo; impertinente
peruse [pəˈruːz] *v/t* ler atentamente
Peruvian [pəˈruːvjən] *adj*, *s* peruano (*m*)
pervade [pəːˈveid] *v/t* penetrar, impregnar
perverse [pəˈvəːs] perverso
pervert [ˈpəːvəːt] *s* invertido *m*; [pəˈvəːt] *v/t* perverter
pessimis|m [ˈpesimizəm] pessimismo *m*; **~t** pessimista *m*, *f*; **~tic** [-ˈmistik] pessimista
pest [pest] peste *f*
pester [ˈpestə] *v/t*, *v/i* maçar, ralar, incomodar
pet [pet] *s* animal *m* de estimação; favorito *m*; *v/t* acariciar, afagar, amimar
petal [ˈpetl] pétala *f*
petition [piˈtiʃən] *s* petição *f*; súplica *f*; requerimento *m*; *v/t*, *v/i* peticionar, requerer; suplicar
petrify [ˈpetrifai] *v/t*, *v/i* petrificar(-se)
petrol [ˈpetrəl] gasolina *f*; **~eum** [piˈtrəuljəm] petróleo *m*
petticoat [ˈpetikəut] combinação *f*; saiote *m*
petty [ˈpeti] trivial; mesquinho
petulan|ce [ˈpetjuləns] petulância *f*; **~t** petulante
petunia [piˈtjuːnjə] petúnia *f*
pew [pjuː] banco *m* de igreja
pewter [ˈpjuːtə] peltre *m*, liga *f* de estanho
phantom [ˈfæntəm] fantasma *m*
phase [feiz] *s* fase *f*
pheasant [ˈfeznt] faisão *m*
phenomen|al [fiˈnɔminl] fenomenal; **~on** (*pl* **-ena**) fenómeno *m*
philanthrop|ist [fiˈlænθrəpist] filantropo *m*; **~y** filantropia *f*
philosoph|er [fiˈlɔsəfə] filósofo *m*; **~y** filosofia *f*
phone [fəun] *s* telefone *m*; *v/t*, *v/i* telefonar; **~card** cartão *m* telefónico
phonograph [ˈfəunəgrɑːf] *US* = **record player**
photograph [ˈfəutəgrɑːf] *v/t* fotografar; *s* fotografia *f*; **~er** [fəˈtɔgrəfə] fotógrafo *m*; **~ic** [ˌ-ˈgræfik] fotográfico; **~y** [fəˈtɔgrəfi] fotografia *f*
phrase [freiz] MUS frase *f*; expressão *f*; locução *f*; **~ology** [ˌ-ziˈɔlədʒi] fraseologia *f*
phrenetic [friˈnetik] frenético
physic|al [ˈfizikəl] físico; **~ian** [-ˈziʃən] médico *m*; **~ist** [ˈ-sist] físico *m*; **~s** física *f*
piano [piˈænəu] *s* piano *m*
pick [pik] *v/t* apanhar; colher; escolher, eleger; palitar; *s* picareta *f*, picão *m*; escolha *f*; escol *m*; palito *m*; **~ up** *v/t*, *v/i*

captar, sintonizar; apanhar; recolher; recuperar
picket ['pikit] *s* estaca *f*; MIL piquete *m*; *v/t, v/i* cercar de estacas; estacionar piquetes
pickle ['pikl] *s* salmoura *f*; escabeche *m*; conservas *f/pl* de vinagre; *fig* apuro *m*; *v/t* salgar; pôr em salmoura
pick|pocket ['pik,pɔkit] carteirista *m, f Braz* batedor *m* de carteiras; **~-up** *s* captador *m* sonoro
picnic ['piknik] *s* piquenique *m*
pictorial [pik'tɔ:riəl] *adj* ilustrado
picture ['piktʃə] *s* quadro *m*; pintura *f*; gravura *f*; ilustração *f*, imagem *f*; retrato *m*; filme *m*, fita *f*; *v/t* imaginar; retratar, pintar; **~s** *s/pl* cinema *f*
picturesque [,piktʃə'resk] pitoresco
pie [pai] pastel *m*, empada *f*
piece [pi:s] *s* bocado *m*, pedaço *m*; retalho *m*; peça *f*
pier [piə] quebra-mar *m*, molhe *m*
pierc|e [piəs] *v/t, v/i* penetrar, furar; **~ing** *adj* cortante; penetrante
piety ['paiəti] piedade *f*
pig [pig] porco *m*
pigeon ['pidʒin] pombo *m*; **~-hole** *s* buraco *m* de pombal
pigmy ['pigmi] pigmeu *m*
pigsty ['pigstai] pocilga *f*, chiqueiro *m*
pike [paik] *s* ZOO lúcio *m*
pilchard ['piltʃəd] sardinha *f*
pile [pail] *s* montão *m*, pilha *f*; *v/t* empilhar
pilfer ['pilfə] v/t, v/i furtar, surripiar; **~er** ratoneiro *m*, larápio *m*
pilgrim ['pilgrim] peregrino *m*; **~age** peregrinação *f*
pill [pil] pílula *f*; comprimido *m*
pillage ['pilidʒ] *s* pilhagem *f*; *v/t* saquear
pillar ['pilə] pilar *m*; **~-box** marco *m* postal
pillory ['piləri] (*pl* **-ries**) *s* pelourinho *m*; *v/t* expor
pillow ['piləu] *s* travesseiro *m*; almofada *f*; **~-case** fronha *f*
pilot ['pailət] *s* piloto *m*; *v/t* pilotar
pimp [pimp] *s* alcoviteiro *m*
pimple ['pimpəl] borbulha *f*
pin [pin] *s* alfinete *m*; cavilha *f*; *v/t* pregar; prender, imobilizar
PIN number ['pin,nʌmbə] *s* número *m* de código PIN
pincers ['pinsəz] *s/pl* turquês *f*, *Braz* torquês *f*; ZOO pinça *f*, tenaz *f*
pinch [pintʃ] *v/t, v/i* beliscar; *s* beliscão *m*; pitada *f*
pine [pain] *s* pinheiro *m*; pinho *m*; *v/i* definhar-se; ansiar
pine|apple ['painæpl] ananás *m*; **~-cone** pinha *f*
ping-pong ['piŋpɔŋ] pingue--pongue *m*
pink [piŋk] *adj* cor-de-rosa; *s* cravo *m*
pinnacle ['pinəkl] pináculo *m*
pint [paint] pinta *f*, quartilho *m*
pioneer [,paiə'niə] *s* pioneiro *m*

pious ['paiəs] pio, piedoso
pipe [paip] *s* cachimbo *m*; cano *m*, tubo *m*; **~line** oleoduto *m*
pirate ['paiərit] *s* pirata *m*
pistol ['pistl] pistola *f*
pit [pit] *s* fosso *m*, buraco *m*, cova *f*; mina *f*
pitch [pitʃ] *s* piche *m*, breu *m*, resina *f*; tom *m*; grau *m*; *v/t, v/i* armar, montar; arrojar, lançar, arremessar; **~er** jarro *m*, cântaro *m*, bilha *f*; arrojador *m*; **~fork** *s* forquilha *f*, forcado *m*
piteous ['pitiəs] lastimoso
pitfall ['pitfɔ:l] cilada *f*, armadilha *f*; rasteira *f*, dificuldade *f*
pith [piθ] seiva *f*; medula *f*; *fig* âmago *m*
pitiless ['pitilis] desapiedado
pity ['piti] *s* compaixão *f*, piedade *f*; *v/t* condoer-se de, compadecer-se de; **what a ~!** que pena!
placard ['plækɑ:d] *s* cartaz *m*
place [pleis] *s* lugar *m*, sítio *m*; *v/t* pôr, meter, colocar; **in ~ of** em lugar/vez de; **take ~** ter lugar, realizar-se
placid ['plæsid] plácido
plague [pleig] *s* peste *f*, praga *f*; *v/t* atormentar, afligir
plaice [pleis] solha *f*, solho *m*
plaid [plæd] manta *f* escocesa em xadrez
plain [plein] *adj* claro, evidente; *adj* simples, franco, sincero; *s* planície *f*; **in ~ clothes** à paisana
plaint [pleint] queixa *f*
plait [plæt] *s* trança *f*; *v/t* entrançar
plan [plæn] *s* plano *m*, proje(c)to *m*; planta *f*; *v/t, v/i* planear; proje(c)tar
plane [plein] *s* plano *m*; plaina *f*; aeroplano *m*, avião *m*; *v/t, v/i* planar; aplainar
planet ['plænit] planeta *m*
plank [plæŋk] *s* prancha *f*
plant [plɑ:nt] *s* BOT planta *f*; MEC instalação *f*; *v/t* plantar, semear; **~ation** [-'teiʃən] plantação *f*; **~er** plantador *m*
plaster ['plɑ:stə] *s* emplastro *m*; **~ of Paris** gesso-de-Paris *m*
plastic ['plæstik] *s* plástico
plate [pleit] *s* prato *m*; chapa *f*, folha *f*, lâmina *f*; baixela *f* de prata *f*; *v/t* chapear; blindar
plateau ['plætəu] planalto *m*
platform ['plætfɔ:m] linha *f*, cais *m*; plataforma *f*; estrado *m*, tribuna *f*
platinum ['plætinəm] platina *f*
play [plei] *v/t, v/i* brincar; jogar; THEAT representar, desempenhar; tocar; *s* brincadeira *f*; jogo *m*; recreio *m*; THEAT peça *f* teatral; **~bill** programa *m*; **~boy** estroina *m*, farrista *m*; **~er** jogador *m*; **~ful** brincalhão; **~goer** frequentador *m* de teatros; **~ground** pátio *m* de recreio; **~wright** dramaturgo *m*
plea [pli:] alegação *f*, pretexto *m*; JUR contestação *f*; rogo *m*, súplica *f*
plead [pli:d] *v/t, v/i* rogar, supli-

car; JUR pleitear; ~ **guilty** confessar-se culpado
pleasant ['pleznt] agradável, prazenteiro, ameno
pleas|e [pli:z] *int* faz favor; *v/t, v/i* agradar, deleitar, contentar; **if you ~e** faça favor; **~ed** *adj* satisfeito; **~ing** *adj* agradável; **~ure** ['pleʒə] prazer *m*
pleat [pli:t] *s* prega *f*, dobra *f*
pledge [pledʒ] *s* penhor *m*, fiança *f*; garantia *f*; promessa *f*; *v/t* empenhar
plentiful ['plentiful] abundante, copioso
plenty ['plenti] *adv* bastante; *adj* abundante; *s* abundância *f*, plenitude *f*; ~ **of ...** muito ...
pliable ['plaiəbl] flexível
pliers ['plaiəz] *s/pl* alicate *m*
plight [plait] *s* apuro *m*, aperto *m*; *condição f*
plot [plɔt] *s* enredo *m*, trama *f*; lote *m*, parcela *f* de terreno; *v/t, v/i* tramar, urdir; conspirar
plough [plau] *s* arado *m*, charrua *f*; *v/t, v/i* lavrar; **~man** lavrador *m*; **~share** relha *f*
pluck [plʌk] *v/t, v/i* dedilhar; arrancar; depenar; *s* coragem *f*
plug [plʌg] *s* ficha *f*, tomada *f*; batoque *m*, bujão *m*, bucha *f*; *v/t* tapar, rolhar; obturar; ~ **in** ligar
plum [plʌm] ameixa *f*
plumb [plʌm] *s* sonda *f*, prumo *m*; *adj* a prumo; *v/t* sondar; **~er** canalizador *m*; picheleiro *m*
plume [plu:m] *s* pluma *f*; penacho *m*
plump [plʌmp] *s* baque *m*; *adj* roliço, rechonchudo
plum pudding [ˌplʌm'pudiŋ] pudim *m* de Natal; **~-tree** ameixeira *f*
plunder ['plʌndə] *v/t, v/i* saquear, pilhar; *s* pilhagem *f*, saque *m*
plunge [plʌndʒ] *v/t, v/i* mergulhar; precipitar(-se), lançar(-se); *s* mergulho *m*
plural ['pluərəl] *adj, s* plural *m*
plus [plʌs] *prp* mais
plush [plʌʃ] *s* pelúcia *f*
ply [plai] *v/t* fazer carreira
pneumatic [nju(:)'mætik] pneumático
pneumonia [nju(:)'məunjə] pneumonia *f*
poach [pəutʃ] *v/t, v/i* caçar ilegalmente, pescar ilicitamente; escalfar; **~er** ladrão *m* de caça
pocket ['pɔkit] *s* algibeira *f*, bolso *m*; *v/t* embolsar, meter ao bolso
pod [pɔd] *s* vagem *f*
poem ['pəuim] poema *m*
poet ['pəuit] poeta *m*; **~ic** [-'etik] poético; **~ry** poesia *f*
point [pɔint] *s* ponto *m*; ponta *f*; questão *f*, assunto *m*; ~ **of view** ponto *m* de vista; *v/t, v/i* apontar; afiar; indicar; **come/get to the** ~ vir ao caso
pointer ['pɔintə] indicador *m*; ponteiro *m*; perdigueiro *m*
pointsman ['pɔintsmən] agulheiro *m*, guarda-agulhas *m*
poise [pɔiz] *s* equilíbrio *m*; porte *m*; *v/t* equilibrar

poison ['pɔizn] *s* peçonha *f*; veneno *m*; *v/t* envenenar; intoxicar; **~ous** venenoso
poker ['pəukə] póquer *m*; atiçador *m*
polar ['pəulə] polar
pole [pəul] *s* vara *f*, pau *m*, varapau *m*; estaca *f*; pólo *m*; **♀** *s adj* polaco *m*, *Braz* polomês *m*
police [pə'li:s] polícia *f*; **~man** polícia *m*, *Braz* policial *m*; **~-station** esquadra *f* da polícia, *Braz* delegacia *f* de polícia; **~woman** mulher-polícia *f*
policy ['pɔlisi] (*pl* **-cies**) política *f*; apólice *f*
polish ['pɔliʃ] *v/t* polir; *s* lustro *m*; verniz *m*; graxa *f*
Polish ['pəuliʃ] *adj*, *s* polaco *m*
polite [pə'lait] cortês; **~ness** cortesia *f*
politic|al [pə'litikəl] político; **~ian** [ˌpɔli'tiʃən] político *m*; **~s** ['pɔlitiks] política *f*
poll [pəul] *s* votação *f*; lista *f* eleitoral; escrutínio *m*; **~ tax** capitação *f*
pollu|te [pə'lu:t] *v/t* poluir; **~tion** poluição *f*
polo ['pəuləu] pólo *m*
pomp [pɔmp] pompa *f*
pond [pɔnd] tanque *m*, charco *m*
ponder ['pɔndə] *v/t*, *v/i* (**on**, **over**) ponderar, meditar; **~ous** pesado, ponderoso
pontoon [pɔn'tu:n] pontão *m*; **~-bridge** ponte *f* de barcas
pony ['pəuni] (*pl* **-nies**) pónei *m*, garrano *m*
poodle ['pu:dl] cão *m* de água
pool [pu:l] *s* poça *f*, charco *m*; tanque *m*; *v/t* partilhar
poor [puə] pobre; **~ health** má saúde *f*; **~ly** *adv* pobremente; **~ness** pobreza *f*
pop [pɔp] *s* estalo *m*, estoiro *m*; gasosa *f*; *v/t*, *v/i* estoirar; estalar; dar uma saltada
popcorn ['pɔpkɔ:n] pipocas *f/pl*
pope [pəup] papa *m*
poplar ['pɔplə] choupo *m*, álamo *m*
poppy ['pɔpi] (*pl* **-pies**) papoula *f*
popul|ar ['pɔpjulə] popular; **~arity** [ˌ-'læriti] popularidade *f*; **~arize** ['-raiz] *v/t* popularizar
popul|ate ['pɔpjuleit] *v/t* povoar; **~ation** [-'leiʃən] população *f*; **~ous** populoso
porcelain ['pɔ:səlin] porcelana *f*
porch [pɔ:tʃ] pórtico *m*; alpendre *m*
pore [pɔ:] *s* poro *m*; *v/i* **~ over** estudar com atenção
pork [pɔ:k] carne *f* de porco
porous ['pɔ:rəs] poroso
porpoise ['pɔ:pəs] toninha *f*, porco-marinho *m*
porridge ['pɔridʒ] papa *f* de aveia, *Braz* mingau *m* de aveia
port [pɔ:t] porto *m*
portable ['pɔ:təbl] portátil
portal ['pɔ:tl] portal *m*
porter ['pɔ:tə] bagageiro *m*; carregador *m*; porteiro *m*

portfolio [pɔːt'fəuljəu] pasta *f*
porthole ['pɔːthəul] MAR vigia *f*, portinhola *f*
portion ['pɔːʃən] *s* porção *f*
portly ['pɔːtli] corpulento
portrait ['pɔːtrit] retrato *m*
portray [pɔː'trei] *v/t* retratar
Portuguese [ˌpɔːtju'giːz] *adj*, *s* português *m*
pose [pəuz] *s* pose *f*; *v/t*, *v/i* posar; pôr
position [pə'ziʃən] *s* posição *f*; *v/t* colocar
positive ['pɔzətiv] *adj* positivo
possess [pə'zes] *v/t* possuir; **~ed** *adj* possesso; **~ion** posse *f*; possessão *f*
possib|ility [ˌpɔsə'biliti] (*pl* **-ties**) possibilidade *f*; **~le** ['-bl] *adj*, *s* possível *m*; **~ly** possivelmente; talvez
post [pəust] *s* poste *m*; emprego *m*; correio *m*; posto *m*; *v/t* deitar ao correio; postar, estacionar; **~age** franquia *f*, porte *m*; **~age stamp** selo *m* postal; **~al** postal; **~box** apartado *m*, caixa *f* postal; **~card** bilhete *m* postal
poster ['pəustə] cartaz *m*
posterity [pɔs'teriti] posteridade *f*
post|man ['pəustmən] carteiro *m*; **~mark** *s* carimbo *m* postal; *v/t* carimbar
post|office ['pəustˌɔfis] correio *m*; **~-paid** franco de porte
postpone [pəust'pəun] *v/t* adiar; pospor; **~ment** adiamento *m*
postscript ['pəusskript] pós-escrito *m*
posture ['pɔstʃə] *s* postura *f*, atitude *f*
post-war ['pəust'wɔː] do pós-guerra
pot [pɔt] *s* pote *m*; panela *f*
potato [pə'teitəu] batata *f*
potency ['pəutənsi] potência *f*
potent ['pəutənt] potente; poderoso; **~ate** ['-eit] potentado *m*; **~ial** [pə'tenʃəl] *adj*, *s* potencial *m*
potter ['pɔtə] *s* oleiro *m*; **~y** (*pl* **-ries**) olaria *f*
pouch [pautʃ] saco *m*, bolsa *f*; cartucheira *f*; papo *m*
poultice ['pəultis] cataplasma *m*
poultry ['pəultri] criação *f*, aves *f/pl* domésticas
pounce [pauns] *v/i*: **~on** lançar-se sobre
pound [paund] *s* libra *f*; *v/t*, *v/i* martelar; bater, esmagar
pour [pɔː] *v/t*, *v/i* verter, derramar(-se); deitar; precipitar(-se), lançar(-se); jorrar; chover a potes
pout [paut] *v/t*, *v/i* amuar, fazer beiço
poverty ['pɔvəti] pobreza *f*
powder ['paudə] *s* pó *m*; pólvora *f*; *v/t* polvilhar; empoar
power ['pauə] *s* poder *m*; potência *f*; **~ful** poderoso, potente
practic|able ['præktikəbl] praticável; **~al** *adj* prático; **~e** ['-tis] clientela *f*; prática *f*; ensaio *m*; clínica *f*; treino *m*
practise ['præktis] *v/t* praticar;

treinar(-se); exercitar; **~d** *adj* experiente, experimentado

practitioner [præ'ktiʃnə] profissional *m*; MED facultativo *m*

prairie ['prɛəri] pradaria *f*

praise [preiz] *v/t* louvar, elogiar; *s* louvor *m*, elogio *m*; **~worthy** louvável

pram [præm] carrinho *m* de criança

prank [præŋk] partida *f*, travessura *f*

prawn [prɔːn] *s* gamba *f*, *Braz* pitu *m*

pray [prei] *v/t*, *v/i* rezar; **~er** [prɛə] oração *f*, reza *f*; **~er-book** livro *m* de orações

preach [priːtʃ] *v/t*, *v/i* pregar

precarious [pri'kɛəriəs] precário

preced|e [pri'siːd] *v/t*, *v/i* preceder; **~ence** ['presidəns] precedência *f*; **~ent** ['presidənt] precedente *m*; **~ing** [-'siːdiŋ] *adj* precedente

precept ['priːsept] preceito *m*

precinct ['priːsiŋkt] recinto *m*; **~s** *s/pl* imediações *f/pl*

precious ['preʃəs] *adj* precioso

precipice ['presipis] precipício *m*

precipi|tate [pri'sipiteit] *v/t*, *v/i* precipitar(-se); [-tit] *adj* precipitado; **~tous** escarpado, íngreme

precis|e [pri'sais] preciso, exa(c)to; **~ion** [-'siʒən] precisão *f*, exa(c)tidão *f*

precursor [pri'kəːsə] precursor *m*

predecessor ['priːdisesə] antecessor *m*, predecessor *m*

predestination [pri(ː)desti'neiʃən] predestinação *f*

predict [pri'dikt] *v/t* predizer, prognosticar

predominant [pri'dɔminənt] predominante

prefabricate [priː'fæbrikeit] *v/t* prefabricar

preface ['prefis] *s* prefácio *m*; *v/t* prefaciar

prefer [pri'fəː] *v/t* preferir; **~able** ['prefərəbl] preferível; **~ence** ['prefərəns] preferência *f*; **~ential** [,prefə'renʃəl] preferencial; **~ment** promoção *f*

prefix ['priːfiks] *s* prefixo *m*

pregnant ['pregnənt] pregnante; grávida

prejudice ['predʒudis] *s* preconceito *m*; *v/t* predispor

prelate ['prelit] prelado *m*

preliminar|ies [pri'liminəriz] *s/pl* preliminares *m/pl*; **~y** *adj* preliminar

prelude ['preljuːd] prelúdio *m*

premature [,premə'tjuə] prematuro

premeditate [priː'mediteit] *v/t* premeditar

premier ['premiə] *s* primeiro ministro *m*

premise ['premis] *s* premissa *f*; **~s** *s/pl* propriedade *f*

premium ['priːmjəm] prémio *m*

preoccup|ied [priː'ɔkjupaid] *adj* preocupado, absorto; **~y**

v/t preocupar
prepare [pri'pɛə] *v/t*, *v/i* preparar(-se)
prepay ['priː'pei] *v/t* pagar adiantado
preposition [ˌprepə'ziʃən] preposição *f*
prepossessing [ˌpriːpə'zesiŋ] *adj* atraente
preposterous [pri'pɔstərəs] absurdo, despropositado
prerogative [pri'rɔgətiv] prerrogativa *f*
prescribe [pris'kraib] *v/t*, *v/i* MED receitar; prescrever
prescription [pris'kripʃən] prescrição *f*; MED receita *f*
presence ['prezns] presença *f*; **~ of mind** presença *f* de espírito
present ['preznt] *adj*, *s* presente *m*; [pri'zent] *v/t* apresentar; oferecer; **at ~** presentemente, de momento; **for the ~** por agora, por enquanto; **~ly** daqui a pouco; *US* presentemente
preserve [pri'zəːv] *v/t* conservar; preservar; *s* conserva *f*, compota *f*; tapada *f*, coutada *f*
presid|e [pri'zaid] *v/i* presidir; **~ent** ['prezidənt] presidente *m*; **~ential** [ˌprezi'denʃəl] presidencial
press [pres] *v/t*, *v/i* carregar em; apressar(-se); comprimir, apertar; prensar, espremer; estreitar, abraçar; *s* prensa *f*; imprensa *f*; lagar *m*; prelo *m*; **~ing** *adj* urgente; **~ure** ['-ʃə] *s* pressão *f*
prestige [pres'tiːʒ] prestígio *m*
presume [pri'zjuːm] *v/t*, *v/i* presumir, supor
presumpt|ion [pri'zʌmpʃən] presunção *f*; **~uous** presunçoso, presumido
pretence [pri'tens] pretensão *f*; pretexto *m*
preten|d [pri'tend] *v/t*, *v/i* simular, fingir; pretender; pretextar; **~tious** [-ʃəs] pretensioso
pretext ['priːtekst] pretexto *m*
pretty ['priti] *adj* bonito, lindo; *adv* bastante
prevail [pri'veil] *v/i* prevalecer; **~ on** convencer
prevent [pri'vent] *v/t* impedir; evitar; **~ from** impedir de; **~ion** [-ʃən] prevenção *f*; impedimento *m*; **~ive** preventivo
preview ['priːvjuː] *s film* trailer *m*
previous ['priːvjəs] anterior, prévio
pre-war ['priː'wɔː] de antes da guerra
prey [prei] *s* presa *f*; **of ~** de rapina
price [prais] *s* preço *m*; *v/t* apreçar; **~less** inestimável
prick [prik] *s* picada *f*, picadura *f*; *v/t*, *v/i* picar; **~ up one's ears** apurar o ouvido
pride [praid] *s* orgulho *m*
priest [priːst] padre *m*, sacerdote *m*; **~hood** sacerdócio *m*
prim [prim] afe(c)tado; empertigado
primary ['praiməri] *adj* primário

prime [praim] *s*, *adj* primeiro, sumo; ~ **minister** primeiroministro *m*; ~**-number** número *m* primo
primer ['praimə] cartilha *f*, manual *m*
primitive ['primitiv] *adj*, *s* primitivo *m*
primrose ['primrəuz] prímula *f*, primavera *f*
prince [prins] príncipe *m*
princess [prin'ses] princesa *f*
principal ['prinsəpəl] *adj* principal; *s* dire(c)tor *m*, reitor *m*; COM capital *m*
principle ['prinsəpl] princípio *m*; **in** ~ em princípio; **on** ~ por princípio
print [print] *s* impressão *f*; estampa *f*, gravura *f*; tipografia *f*; *v/t* imprimir; estampar; **out of** ~ esgotado; ~**ed matter** impressos *m/pl*; ~**er** impressor *m*; tipógrafo *m*; ~**ing** *s* imprensa *f*; impressão *m*; tiragem *f*
prior ['praiə] *adj* anterior, precedente, prévio; ~ **to** antes de; ~**ity** [-'ɔriti] (*pl* **-ties**) prioridade *f*
prison ['prizn] cadeia *f*, prisão *f*; ~**er** prisioneiro *m*
privacy ['privəsi] isolamento *m*, retiro *m*; intimidade *f*; segredo *m*, reserva *f*
private ['praivit] *adj* privado; particular
privation [prai'veiʃən] privação *f*
privileg|e ['privilidʒ] privilégio *m*; ~**ed** privilegiado
prize [praiz] *s* prémio *m*; *v/t* estimar
probab|le ['prɔbəbl] *adj* provável; ~**ly** provavelmente
probation [prə'beiʃən] JUR liberdade *f* condicional; estágio *m*
problem ['prɔbləm] problema *m*
proceed [prə'si:d] *v/i* proceder; prosseguir; ~**ings** *s/pl* a(c)ta *f*, minuta *f*; procedimento *m*; processo *m*; debate *m*; ~**s** ['prəusi:dz] *s/pl* produto *m*, rendimento *m*
process ['prəuses] *s* processo *m*, método *m*
procession [prə'seʃən] procissão *f*
proclaim [prə'kleim] *v/t* proclamar
proclamation [ˌprɔklə'meiʃən] proclamação *f*
procure [prə'kjuə] *v/t* obter; alcovitar
prodigious [prəˌdidʒəs] prodigioso
produce [prə'dju:s] *v/t*, *v/i* exibir, apresentar; pôr em cena; produzir; ['prɔdju:s] *s* produto *m*; ~**r** produtor *m*
product ['prɔdʌkt] produto *m*; ~**ion** [prə'dʌkʃən] produção *f*; ~**ive** [prə'dʌktiv] produtivo
profess [prə'fes] *v/t* professar; ~**ion** profissão *f*; ~**ional** *adj* profissional
professor [prə'fesə] catedrático *m*; ~**ship** cátedra *f*
proficien|cy [prə'fiʃənsi] profi-

ciência *f*; **~t** proficiente
profile ['prəufail] *s* perfil *m*
profit ['prɔfit] *s* lucro *m*; proveito *m*; **~ by/from** *v/t* tirar proveito de; **~able** proveitoso; **~eer** [-'tiə] aproveitador *m*, explorador *m*
profound [prə'faund] profundo
profundity [prə'fʌnditi] (*pl* **-ties**) profundeza *f*, profundidade *f*
profuse [prə'fju:s] profuso, abundante
progenitor [prəu'dʒənitə] progenitor *m*
prognosis [prɔg'nəusis] prognóstico *m*
program(me) ['prəugræm] *s* programa *m*
progress ['prəugres] *s* progresso *m*; [prəu'gres] *v/i* progredir; **~ion** [prəu'greʃən] progressão *f*; **~ive** [prəu'gresiv] *adj* progressivo; *s* progressista *m*, *f*
prohibit [prə'hibit] *v/t* proibir; **~ion** [ˌprəui'biʃən] proibição *f*; **~ive** [-'hibitiv] proibitivo; **~ory** proibitório
project ['prɔdʒekt] *s* proje(c)to *m*; [prə'dʒekt] *v/t*, *v/i* proje(c)tar; **~ile** ['-tail] projé(c)til; **~ion** [prə'dʒekʃən] proje(c)ção *f*; **~or** proje(c)tor *m*
prolog(ue) ['prəulɔg] prólogo *m*
prolong [prə'lɔŋ] *v/t* prolongar
prominent ['prɔminənt] proeminente; eminente
promis|e ['prɔmis] *v/t*, *v/i* prometer; *s* promessa *f*; **~ing** prometedor; **~sory** ['-səri] promissório
promontory ['prɔməntri] (*pl* **-ries**) promontório *m*
promot|e [prə'məut] *v/t* promover; **~ion** promoção *f*
prompt [prɔmpt] *adj* pronto, expedito; pontual; *v/t*, *v/i* incitar, instigar; servir de ponto a; **~er** THEAT ponto *m*
prone [prəun] propenso
prong [prɔŋ] *s* dente *m* de garfo; ponta *f*
pronoun ['prəunaun] pronome *m*
pronounc|e [prə'nauns] *v/t* pronunciar; declarar; **~ed** *adj* acentuado, marcado; vincado; nítido
pronunciation [prəˌnʌnsi'eiʃən] pronúncia *f*
proof [pru:f] *s* prova *f*; *adj*: ... **~** à prova de; *v/t* impermeabilizar
prop [prɔp] *s* amparo *m*; estaca *f*, esteio *m*; *v/t* sustentar; apoiar
propaga|te ['prɔpəgeit] *v/t*, *v/i* propagar(-se); **~tion** [-'geiʃən] propagação *f*
propel [prə'pel] *v/t* impelir, propulsar; **~ler** propulsor *m*; hélice *f*
proper ['prɔpə] próprio, conveniente, decente; oportuno, apropriado; **~ty** (*pl* **-ties**) propriedade *f*; bens *m/pl*
prophe|cy ['prɔfisi] (*pl* **-cies**) profecia *f*, vaticínio *m*; **~sy**

['-sai] *v/t, v/i* profetizar; **~t** profeta *m*; **~tic** [prə'fetik] profético

propitious [prə'piʃəs] propício

proportion [prə'pɔːʃən] *s* proporção *f*; **~al** proporcional

propos|al [prə'pəuzəl] proposta *f*; **~e** *v/t* propor; **~er** proponente *m*; **~ition** [ˌprɔpə'ziʃən] proposicão *f*

propriet|or [prə'praiətə] proprietário *m*; **~y** decência *f*, conveniência *f*

pros|aic [prəu'zeiik] prosaico; **~e** [prəuz] prosa *f*

prosecut|e ['prɔsikjuːt] *v/t, v/i* JUR processar; **~ion** acusação *f*; **~or** demandante *m, f*; promotor *m* da acusação

prospect ['prɔspekt] *s* perspectiva *f*, expectativa *f*; [prəs'pekt] *v/t, v/i* explorar; **~or** [-'spektə] prospe(c)tor *m*, *Braz* garimpeiro *m*

prosper ['prɔspə] *v/i* prosperar; **~ity** [-'periti] prosperidade *f*; **~ous** próspero

prostitution [ˌprɔsti'tjuːʃən] prostituição *f*

prostrate [prɔs'treit] *v/t* prostrar; ['-] *adj* prosternado; prostrado

protect [prə'tekt] *v/t* proteger; **~ion** prote(c)ção *f*; **~ive** prote(c)tivo; **~or** prote(c)tor *m*

protest [prə'test] *v/t, v/i* protestar; ['prəutest] *s* protesto *m*

Protestant ['prɔtistənt] *s* protestante *m, f*; **≗ism** protestantismo *m*

protract [prə'trækt] *v/t* prolongar, protelar; **~or** transferidor *m*

protrude [prə'truːd] *v/t, v/i* ressaltar, sobressair

proud [praud] *adj* orgulhoso

prove [pruːv] *v/t* provar, demonstrar

proverb ['prɔvəb] provérbio *m*

provid|e [prə'vaid] *v/t* prover, abastecer; **~ed (that)** contanto que, desde que

providen|ce ['prɔvidəns] providência *f*; **~t** previdente; prudente

provinc|e ['prɔvins] província *f*; **~ial** [prə'vinʃəl] *s* provinciano *m*; *adj* provincial

provision [prə'viʒən] *s* provisão *f*, abastecimento *m*; cláusula *f*, estipulação *f*; **~al** provisório

provoca|tion ['prɔvə'keiʃən] provocação *f*; **~tive** [prəvɔkətiv] provocativo

provoke [prə'vəuk] *v/t* provocar

prowl [praul] *v/t, v/i* rondar

proxy ['prɔksi] (*pl* **-xies**) procuração *f*; procurador *m*

prude [pruːd] pudico, afe(c)tado

pruden|ce ['pruːdəns] prudência *f*; **~t** prudente

prune [pruːn] *s* ameixa *f* seca; *v/t* podar, desbastar

Prussian ['prʌʃən] *adj, s* prussiano *m*

psalm [saːm] salmo *m*; **~ist** salmista *m*

psychia|trist [sai'kaiətrist] psiquiatra *m, f*; **~try** psiquiatria *f*
psycholog|ical [ˌsaikə'lɔdʒikəl] psicológico; **~ist** [-'kɔlədʒist] psicólogo *m*; **~y** [-'kɔlədʒi] psicologia *f*
pub [pʌb] cervejaria *f*, taberna *f*
puberty ['pju:bəti] puberdade *f*
public ['pʌblik] *adj, s* público *m*; **~ation** [-'keiʃən] publicação *f*; **~house** taberna *f*, cervejaria *f*; **~ity** [-'lisiti] publicidade *f*; **~ize** ['-saiz] *v/t* propalar, divulgar; **~ school** *GB* colégio *m*, internato *m*; *US* escola *f* pública
publish ['pʌbliʃ] *v/t, v/i* publicar, editar; **~er** editor *m*
pucker ['pʌkə] *v/t, v/i* enrugar, franzir
pudding ['pudiŋ] pudim *m*
puddle ['pʌdl] *s* poça *f*, charco *m*
puff [pʌf] *s* baforada *f*, sopro *m*; *v/t, v/i* soprar; ofegar, arfar
pull [pul] *s* arranco *m*, puxão *m*; *v/t* puxar; arrancar; **~ down** demolir
pullet ['pulit] frango *m*
pulley ['puli] roldana *f*
pullover ['pulˌəuvə] pulóver *m*, camisola *f*
pulp [pʌlp] *s* polpa *f*
pulpit ['pulpit] púlpito *m*
puls|ate [pʌl'seit] *v/i* pulsar; **~ation** [-'seiʃən] pulsação *f*; **~e** *s* pulso *m*
pumice(-stone) ['pʌmis(stəun)] pedra-pomes *f*
pump [pʌmp] *s* bomba *f*; *v/t* dar à bomba
pumpkin ['pʌmpkin] abóbora *f*
pun [pʌn] *s* trocadilho *m*, calembur *m*
punch [pʌntʃ] *s* soco *m*, murro *m*; ponche *m*; perfurador *m*, punção *m*; *v/t, v/i* perfurar; esmurrar
punctual ['pʌŋktjuəl] pontual; **~ity** [ˌ-'æliti] pontualidade *f*
punctuation [ˌpʌŋktju'eiʃən] pontuação *f*
puncture ['pʌŋktʃə] *s* furo *m*; *v/t, v/i* furar
punish ['pʌniʃ] *v/t* punir, castigar; **~able** punível; **~ment** castigo *m*
puny ['pju:ni] débil, fraco; insignificante
pupil ['pju:pl] ANAT pupila *f*; aluno *m*, pupilo *m*
puppet ['pʌpit] marionete *f*, fantoche *m*
puppy ['pʌpi] cachorrinho *m*
purchase ['pə:tʃəs] *v/t* comprar; *s* compra *f*
pure [pjuə] puro
puri|fy ['pjuərifai] *v/t* purificar; **~tan** *adj, s* puritano *m*; **~ty** pureza *f*
purple ['pə:pl] *s* púrpura *f*; *adj* purpúreo, purpurino
purpose ['pə:pəs] *s* propósito *m*, tenção *f*; **on ~** de propósito
purr [pə:] *s* ronrom *m*; *v/i* ronronar
purs|e [pə:s] *s* porta-moedas *m*, bolsa *f*; **~er** MAR comissário *m* de bordo
pursu|e [pə'sju:] *v/t* perseguir;

~er perseguidor *m*; **~it** [-'sju:t] perseguição *f*; a(c)tividade *f*, ocupação *f*
purvey [pə:'vei] *v/t* prover, abastecer
pus [pʌs] MED pus *m*
push [puʃ] *v/t*, *v/i* empurrar; *s* impulso *m*; empurrão *m*; **get the ~** ser posto na rua; **~ up** forçar a alta; fazer subir
pussy ['pusi] (*pl* **-sies**) bichano *m*
put [put] *v/t*, *v/i* pôr, botar, colocar, meter; **~ down** reprimir; pousar; **~ off** adiar; **~ on** calçar; vestir; **~ out** apagar; **~ up with** aguentar, suportar, tolerar
putrefy ['pju:trifai] *v/t*, *v/i* putrefazer, apodrecer
putrid ['pju:trid] pútrido
putty ['pʌti] poteia *f*
puzzl|e ['pʌzl] *s* quebra-cabeça *m*, *s* enigma *m*; embaraço *m*, perplexidade *f*; *v/t*, *v/i* embaraçar, confundir; **crossword ~** palavras *f/pl* cruzadas
pygmy ['pigmi] (*pl* **-mies**) pigmeu *m*
pyjamas [pə'dʒɑ:məz] *s/pl* pijama *m*
pyramid ['pirəmid] pirâmide *f*
pyre ['paiə] pira *f* funerária
python ['paiθən] pitão *m*

Q

quack [kwæk] *v/i* grasnar; *s* grasnido *m*; charlatão *m*; **~ery** charlatanismo *m*
quadrangle ['kwɔdræŋgl] quadrângulo *m*; pátio *m*
quadrant ['kwɔdrənt] quadrante *m*
quadruped ['kwɔdruped] *s*, *adj* quadrúpede *m*
quadruple ['kwɔdrupl] *adj*, *s* quádruplo *m*
quagmire ['kwægmaiə] tremedal *m*, pântano *m*
quail [kweil] *s* codorniz *f*
quaint [kweint] estranho, pitoresco
quake [kweik] *s* tremor *m* de terra; *v/i* tremer
quali|fication [ˌkwɔlifi'keiʃən] aptidão *f*, capacidade *f*; qualificação *f*; **~fied** ['-faid] *adj* qualificado, habilitado; **~fy** ['-fai] *v/t*, *v/i* habilitar(-se); qualificar; **~ty** (*pl* **-ties**) qualidade *f*
qualm [kwɔ:m] escrúpulo *m*; receio *m*
quandary ['kwɔndəri] (*pl* **-ries**) dilema *m*
quantity ['kwɔntiti] (*pl* **-ties**) quantidade *f*
quarantine ['kwɔrənti:n] *s* quarentena *f*
quarrel ['kwɔrəl] *s* disputa *f*, altercação *f*; *v/i* disputar, discutir, brigar; **~some** brigão
quarry ['kwɔri] *s* (*pl* **-ries**) pedreira *f*; *v/t*, *v/i* extrair de pe-

dreira

quarter ['kwɔːtə] *s* quarto *m*, quarta parte *f*; trimestre *m*; quarteirão *m*, bairro *m*; *v/t* esquartejar; aquartelar; **~ly** *adj* trimestral; *s* publicação *f* trimestral; **~s** *pl* alojamento *m*; **from all ~s** de todas as dire(c)ções

quartet(te) [kwɔː'tet] quarteto *m*

quartz [kwɔːts] quartzo *m*

quash [kwɔʃ] *v/t* suprimir, anular

quaver ['kweivə] *v/i* tremer, tremular; *s* MUS colcheia *f*

quay [kiː] cais *m*

queen [kwiːn] *s* rainha *f*

queer [kwiə] *adj* estranho, singular, curioso

quench [kwentʃ] *v/t* apagar; mitigar, matar

querulous ['kweruləs] queixoso

query ['kwiəri] *s* (*pl* **-ries**) pergunta *f*; *v/t* inquirir, perguntar; duvidar de

question ['kwestʃən] *s* pergunta *f*; questão *f*; problema *m*; *v/t* interrogar; duvidar de; **ask a ~** fazer uma pergunta; **in ~** em questão; **out of the ~** fora de questão; impossível; **~able** contestável; **~-mark** ponto *m* de interrogação

questionnaire [ˌkwestiə'nɛə] questionário *m*

queue [kjuː] *s* fila *f*, bicha *f*; *v/i* fazer bicha

quibble ['kwibl] *s* argúcia *f*; *v/i* sofismar

quick [kwik] *adv* depressa; *adj* rápido; pronto; *s* âmago *m*; sabugo *m*, medula *f*; **~en** *v/t* acelerar; **~lime** cal *f* viva; **~ly** depressa; **~ness** rapidez *f*; **~sand** areia *f* movediça; **~-witted** perspicaz, esperto

quiet ['kwaiət] *adj* calmo, sossegado, *adj* tranquilo; *s* tranquilidade *f*; calma *f*; **~(en)** *v/t*, *v/i* acalmar, aquietar; **~ude** quietação *f*; quietude *f*

quill [kwil] pena *f*; tubo *m* de pena

quilt [kwilt] colcha *f*

quince [kwins] marmelo *m*

quinsy ['kwinzi] angina *f*

quire ['kwaiə] mão *f* de papel

quit [kwit] *adj* quite, livre; *v/t*, *v/i* deixar, abandonar; **notice to ~** aviso *m* de despejo

quite [kwait] completamente, totalmente; bastante; muito; **~ a/an ...** realmente um/uma ...; **~ (so)** exa(c)tamente

quiver ['kwivə] *v/i* tremer, vibrar; *s* tremor *m*; aljava *f*

quiz [kwiz] *v/t* interrogar; *s* interrogatório *m*; **~zical** motejador, zombador

quoit [kɔit] malha *f*, conca *f*

quota ['kwəutə] quota *f*

quotation [kwəu'teiʃən] citação *f*; COM cotação *f*; **~-marks** aspas *f/pl*

quote [kwəut] *v/t*, *v/i* citar; COM cotizar

quotient ['kwəuʃənt] quociente *m*

R

rabbi ['ræbai] rabino *m*
rabbit ['ræbit] *s* coelho *m*
rabble ['ræbl] turba *f*; ralé *f*, populaça *f*
rabid ['ræbid] rábido; furioso
rabies ['reibi:z] raiva *f*
race [reis] *s* raça *f*; carreira *f*, corrida *f*; corrente *f* de água; competição *f*; *v/t*, *v/i* correr; fazer uma corrida; competir; **~-course** hipódromo *m*; **~-track** pista *f* de corridas
racial ['reiʃəl] racial; **~ism** racismo *m*
racism ['reisizəm] *US* racismo *m*
rack [ræk] *s* grade *f*; cabide *m*; prateleira *f*, rede *f*; MEC cremalheira *f*; *v/t* torturar; **~ one's brains** quebrar a cabeça
racket ['rækit] barafunda *f*, barulho *m*; raqueta *f*
racy ['reisi] vigoroso
radar ['reidə] radar *m*
radiant ['reidjənt] radiante
radiat|e ['reidieit] *v/t* irradiar; iluminar; **~ion** [-'eiʃən] irradiação *f*; **~or** radiador *m*
radical ['rædikəl] radical
radio ['reidiəu] *s* rádio *f*; **~ (set)** (aparelho *m* de) rádio *m*
radio|-active ['reidiəu'æktiv] radioa(c)tivo; **~graphy** [,-'ɔgrəfi] radiografia *f*
radish ['rædiʃ] rabanete *m*
radius ['reidiəs] (*pl* **-dii** [-diai]) raio *m*; ANAT rádio *m*
raffle ['ræfl] *s* rifa *f*, sorteio *m*
raft [rɑ:ft] *s* jangada *f*, balsa *f*
rafter ['rɑ:ftə] barrote *m*, viga *f*
rag [ræg] *s* farrapo *m*, trapo *m*
rage [reidʒ] *s* raiva *f*, furor *m*, fúria *f*; *v/i* enfurecer-se, encolerizar-se; **(all) the ~** à moda
ragged ['rægid] *adj* esfarrapado
raid [reid] *s* ataque *m*, incursão *f*; *v/t*, *v/i* atacar, invadir
rail [reil] *s* carril *m*; corrimão *m*, balaustrada *f*; *v/i* **~ (at)** injuriar, invectivar; **by ~** por caminho de ferro; **~ing** *s* grade *f*; **~road**, *GB* **~way** caminho *m* de ferro, *Braz* estrada *f* de ferro
rain [rein] *s* chuva *f*; *v/i* chover; **~ cats and dogs** chover a cântaros; **~bow** ['-bəu] arco-íris *m*; **~coat** impermeável *m*; **~drop** pingo *m* de chuva; **~y** chuvoso
raise [reiz] *v/t* levantar, erguer; elevar, aumentar; provocar; cultivar, produzir; criar
raisin ['reizn] passa *f*, uva *f* seca
rake [reik] *s* ancinho *m*; *v/t*, *v/i* limpar com o ancinho; revolver
rally ['ræli] *v/t*, *v/i* reunir(-se); reanimar(-se); *s* (*pl* **-lies**) rali *m*; reunião *f*
ram [ræm] *s* carneiro *m*; *v/t* cal-

car; abalroar, chocar
ramble ['ræmbl] *s* excursão *f*, passeio *m*; *v/i* vaguear, deambular; divagar
ramify ['ræmifai] *v/t*, *v/i* ramificar(-se)
ramp [ræmp] rampa *f*
ranch [rɑːntʃ, ræntʃ] rancho *m*, fazenda *f*; **~er** rancheiro *m*
rancid ['rænsid] rançoso
ranco(u)r ['ræŋkə] rancor *m*
random ['rændəm] *adj* casual, fortuito; **at ~** à toa, ao acaso
range [reindʒ] *s* cordilheira *f*; extensão *f*, alcance *m*; classe *f*, ordem *f*; série *f*, gama *f*, escala *f*; *v/t*, *v/i* percorrer; arranjar, alinhar; estender-se, ir
rank [ræŋk] *s* posto *m*; linha *f*, fileira *f*; classe *f*, ordem *f*; *adj* luxuriante, viçoso; rançoso; *v/t*, *v/i* ordenar, classificar
ransack ['rænsæk] *v/t* saquear, pilhar
ransom ['rænsəm] *s* resgate *m*; *v/t* resgatar
rap [ræp] *s* pancada *f*; música *f* rap; *v/t* bater
rapac|ious [rə'peiʃəs] rapace; **~ity** [-'pæsiti] rapacidade *f*
rape [reip] *s* estupro *m*, violação *f*; *v/t* violar
rapid ['ræpid] *adj*, *s* rápido *m*; **~ity** [rə'piditi] rapidez *f*
rapt [ræpt] arrebatado, extasiado; **~ure** ['-tʃə] arrebatamento *m*, êxtase *m*; **~urous** ['-tʃərəs] extático
rar|e [rɛə] raro; mal passado, meio cru; **~efy** ['-rifai] *v/t* rarefazer
rarity ['rɛəriti] (*pl* **-ties**) raridade *f*
rascal ['rɑːskəl] maroto *m*, velhaco *m*
rash [ræʃ] *adj* temerário; precipitado, imprudente; *s* erupção *f*
rasher ['ræʃə] tira *f* de toucinho
rasp [rɑːsp] *s* grosa *f*, lima *f* grossa; *v/t* grosar
raspberry ['rɑːzbəri] (*pl* **-ries**) framboesa *f*
rat [ræt] *s* ratazana *f*
rate [reit] *s* velocidade *f*, marcha *f*; preço *m*, valor *m*; taxa *f*; tarifa *f*; *v/t*, *v/i* estimar, avaliar; **at any ~** em todo o caso; **at this/that ~** nesse caso, desta forma; **~ of exchange** taxa *f* de câmbio
rather ['rɑːðə] *adv* antes; um tanto
ratio ['reiʃiəu] razão *f*, proporção *f*
ration ['ræʃən] *s* ração *f*; *v/t* racionar
rational ['ræʃənl] racional; **~ism** ['ræʃnəlizəm] racionalismo *m*
rattle ['rætl] *s* matraca *f*, cegarrega *f*; guizo *m*; *v/t*, *v/i* matraquear, chocalhar; agitar(-se)
rattlesnake ['rætlsneik] cobra *f* cascável
ravage ['rævidʒ] *v/t* devastar; **~s** ['-iz] *s/pl* estragos *m/pl*
rave [reiv] *v/i* delirar
raven ['reivn] corvo *m*
ravine [rə'viːn] barranco *m*, ra-

vina *f*
raw [rɔː] *adj* cru; bruto; inexperiente; **~ material** matéria-prima *f*
ray [rei] raio *m*; zoo (ar)raia *f*
razor ['reizə] navalha *f*; máquina *f* de barbear
reach [riːtʃ] *v/t, v/i* alcançar; chegar a; entregar, passar; *s* alcance *m*; **out of ~** fora do alcance
react [ri'ækt] *v/i* reagir; **~ion** rea(c)ção *f*; **~ionary** [-ʃnəri] *adj, s* (*pl* **-rics**) rea(c)cionário *m*; **~or** rea(c)tor *m*
read [riːd] *v/t, v/i* ler; estudar; **~able** legível; fácil de ler; **~er** leitor *m*
readi|ly ['redili] prontamente; de boa vontade; **~ness** prontidão *f*, presteza *f*; boa vontade *f*
reading ['riːdiŋ] *s* leitura *f*
readjust ['riːə'dʒʌst] *v/t, v/i* reajustar
ready ['redi] *adj* pronto, preparado; **~-made** já feito, pronto a vestir
real [riəl] *adj* real, verdadeiro; genuíno, autêntico; **~ism** realismo *m*; **~ist** realista *m, f*; **~istic** realista; **~ity** [ri'æliti] (*pl* **-ties**) realidade *f*
reali|zation [ˌriəlai'zeiʃən] realização *f*; compreensão *f*; **~ze** ['-laiz] *v/t* realizar; fazer ideia, dar-se conta de
really ['riəli] realmente, na verdade, deveras
reanimate [riː'ænimeit] *v/t* reanimar
reap [riːp] *v/t, v/i* ceifar, segar; **~er** segadora *f* mecânica
reappear ['riːə'piə] *v/i* reaparecer
rear [riə] *s* traseiro *m*; retaguarda *f*; *v/t, v/i* criar; empinar-se
rearrange ['riːə'reindʒ] *v/t* arranjar de novo
reason ['riːzn] *s* razão *f*, motivo *m*; *v/t, v/i* raciocinar; persuadir; debater; **~ with** discutir; **without rhyme or ~** sem tom nem som; **~able** razoável; **~ing** *s* raciocínio *m*
reassure [ˌriːə'ʃuə] *v/t* tranquilizar
rebel ['rebl] *s, adj* rebelde *m, f*; [ri'bel] *v/i* rebelar-se, revoltar-se; **~lion** [ri'beljən] rebelião *f*, sublevação *f*; **~lious** [ri'beljəs] rebelde
rebound [ri'baund] *v/i* ressaltar; *s* ressalto *m*
rebuff [ri'bʌf] *s* recusa *f*; *v/t* repelir
rebuild ['riː'bild] *v/t* reconstruir
rebuke [ri'bjuːk] *v/t* repreender, admoestar; *s* repreensão *f*, censura *f*
recall [ri'kɔːl] *v/t* recordar; revogar; *s* revocação *f*; **beyond/past ~** irrevogável; esquecido
recapitulate [ˌriːkə'pitjuleit] *v/t, v/i* recapitular
recast ['riː'kɑːst] *v/t* refundir
recede [ri'siːd] *v/i* retirar-se; recuar
receipt [ri'siːt] *s* recibo *m*; recepção *f*; **acknowledge ~ of**

acusar a recepção de
receiv|e [ri'si:v] *v/t* receber; **~er** receptor *m*; auscultador *m*, *Braz* fone *m*
recent ['ri:sənt] recente; **~ly** recentemente
reception [ri'sepʃən] recepção *f*; acolhimento *m*
recess [ri'ses] *s* férias *f/pl*; nicho *m*; suspensão *f*; **~ion** [-'seʃən] depressão *f*, baixa *f* de produção
recipe ['resipi] receita *f*
reciprocal [ri'siprəkəl] recíproco
recital [ri'saitl] recital *m*, récita *f*
recite [ri'sait] *v/t*, *v/i* recitar
reckless ['reklis] estouvado, temerário
reckon ['rekən] *v/t*, *v/i* calcular, contar; considerar, julgar; **~ing** *s* cálculo *m*; **day of ~ing** dia *m* do ajuste de contas
reclaim [ri'kleim] *v/t* reclamar, reivindicar; reformar; recuperar, conquistar
recline [ri'klain] *v/t*, *v/i* reclinar(-se), recostar(-se)
recognition [ˌrekəg'niʃən] reconhecimento *m*
recognize ['rekəgnaiz] *v/t* reconhecer
recoil [ri'kɔil] *v/i* recuar
recollect [ˌrekə'lekt] *v/t* recordar, lembrar-se de
recommend [ˌrekə'mend] *v/t* recomendar; **~ation** [-'deiʃən] recomendação *f*
recompense ['rekəmpens] *s* recompensa *f*; *v/t* recompensar
reconcile ['rekənsail] *v/t* reconciliar, conciliar
reconsider ['ri:kən'sidə] *v/t*, *v/i* reconsiderar
reconstruct ['ri:kəns'trʌkt] *v/t* reconstruir; **~ion** reconstrução *f*
record [ri'kɔ:d] *v/t* regist(r)ar; gravar; ['rekɔ:d] *s* recorde *m*; disco *m*; regist(r)o *m*; **off the ~** confidencial; **on ~** registado; **~er** regist(r)ador *m*; MUS flautim *m*; **~ing** *s* gravação *f*; **~ player** gira-discos *m*
recourse [ri'kɔ:s] recurso *m*
recover [ri'kʌvə] *v/t*, *v/i* recuperar, recobrar; restabelecer-se; **~y** recuperação *f*; restabelecimento *m*
recreation [ˌrekri'eiʃən] recreio *m*
recruit [ri'kru:t] *s* recruta *m*
rectangle ['rekˌtæŋgl] re(c)tângulo *m*
rectify ['rektifai] *v/t* re(c)tificar
rector ['rektə] reitor *m*; ECCL cura *m*; **~y** presbitério *m*
recur [ri'kə:] *v/i* repetir-se; **~ to** ocorrer; recorrer a; **~rence** [-'kʌrəns] repetição *f*
red [red] *adj* vermelho, encarnado; **~ wine** vinho *m* tinto
redd|en ['redn] *v/t*, *v/i* avermelhar; corar, ruborizar-se; **~ish** avermelhado
redeem [ri'di:m] *v/t* remir, redimir; COM amortizar; **Ωer** Redentor *m*

redemption [ri'dempʃən] redenção *f*; COM amortização *f*
redness ['rednis] vermelhidão *f*
redouble [ri'dʌbl] *v/t, v/i* redobrar
reduce [ri'djuːs] *v/t* reduzir, diminuir, rebaixar
reduction [ri'dʌkʃən] redução *f*; COM rebaixa *f*
redundant [ri'dʌndənt] redundante
re-echo [ri(ː)'ekəu] *v/i* ressoar
reed [riːd] cana *f*, caniço *m*; flauta *f* de cana
reef [riːf] *s* recife *m*; *v/t* rizar
reek [riːk] *v/i* fumegar; **~of** cheirar a, feder a
reel [riːl] *s* carretel *m*, bobina *f*; dança *f* escocesa; *v/t* bobinar, dobar; *v/i* cambalear
reentry [riː'entri] (*pl* **-ries**) reentrada *f*
refer [ri'fəː]: **~to** *v/t* referir-se a; recorrer a
referee [ˌrefə'riː] *s* árbitro *m*; *v/t, v/i* arbitrar
reference ['refrəns] referência *f*; recomendação *f*; consulta *f*; **~ book** livro *m* de consulta
refill [ˌriː'fil] *v/t* encher de novo; ['riːfil] *s* recarga *f*
refine [ri'fain] *v/t* refinar; **~ry** refinaria *f*
reflect [ri'flekt] *v/t, v/i* refle(c)tir; **~ion** [-ʃən] reflexão *f*
reflex ['riːfleks] reflexo *m*
reform [ri'fɔːm] *v/t, v/i* corrigir(-se), melhorar(-se); reformar; *s* reforma *f*; **≗ation** [ˌrefə'meiʃən] Reforma *f*
refrain [ri'frein] *s* refrão *m*, estribilho *m*; *v/i* refrear-se, abster-se
refresh [ri'freʃ] *v/t* refrescar; **~ing** *adj* refrescante; **~ment** refresco *m*
refrigera|te [ri'fridʒəreit] *v/t* refrigerar; **~tion** [-'reiʃən] refrigeração *f*; **~tor** refrigerador *m*, frigorífico *m*, geladeira *f*
refuel [ˌriː'fjuːəl] *v/t, v/i* reabastecer(-se) de combustível
refuge ['refjuːdʒ] refúgio *m*; **~e** [ˌ-'dʒi] refugiado *m*
refund [ri'fʌnd] *v/t* reembolsar
refusal [ri'fjuːzəl] recusa *f*
refuse [ri'fjuːz] *v/t, v/i* recusar; rejeitar; ['refjuːs] *s* lixo *m*, entulho *m*
regain [ri'gein] *v/t* recuperar; recobrar; readquirir
regal ['riːgəl] real, régio
regard [ri'gɑːd] *s* consideração *f*, respeito *m*; *v/t* considerar; respeitar, acatar; **with ~ to** a respeito de, quanto a; **~s** *s/pl* cumprimentos *m/pl*, saudações *f/pl*; **with kind ~s** com os melhores cumprimentos
regency ['riːdʒənsi] regência *f*
regent ['riːdʒənt] *s* regente *m, f*
regiment ['redʒimənt] *s* regimento *m*
region ['riːdʒən] região *f*
register ['redʒistə] *s* regist(r)o *m*; *v/t, v/i* regist(r)ar; inscrever(-se), matricular(-se)
registra|r [ˌredʒis'trɑː] regist(r)ador *m*, arquivista *m, f*

registry ['redʒistri] (*pl* **-tries**) arquivo *m*, cartório *m*
regret[ri'gret] *s* pena *f*, pesar *m*; *v/t* lamentar; **~s** *s/pl* desculpas *f/pl*; **~table** lamentável
regular ['regjulə] *adj* regular; **~ity** [ˌ-'lærity] regularidade *f*; **~ize** *v/t* regularizar; **~ly** regularmente
regulat|e ['regjuleit] *v/t* regular; acertar; **~ion** [-'leiʃən] regulamento *m*; regulação *f*
rehears|al [ri'hə:səl] *s* ensaio *m*; **~e** *v/t*, *v/i* ensaiar
reign [rein] *s* reinado *m*; *v/i* reinar
reimburse [ˌri:im'bə:s] *v/t* reembolsar
rein [rein] rédea *f*
reindeer['reindiə] rena *f*, rangífer *m*
reinforce [ˌri:in'fɔ:s] *v/t* reforçar; **~ment** reforço *m*
reiterate [ri:'itəreit] *v/t* reiterar
reject [ri'dʒekt] *v/t* rejeitar; **~ion** [-ʃən] rejeição *f*
rejoic|e [ri'dʒɔis] *v/i* regozijar-se; **~ing** *s* regozijo *m*
rejoin ['ri:'dʒɔin] *v/t* reunir; **~der** réplica *f*
rejuvenate [ri'dʒu:vineit] *v/t*, *v/i* rejuvenescer
rekindle ['ri:'kindl] *v/t*, *v/i* reacender(-se)
relapse[ri'læps] *v/i* recair, reincidir; *s* MED recaída *f*, recidiva *f*
relate [ri'leit] *v/t* relatar; relacionar
relation [ri'leiʃən] relato *m*; relação *f*; parente *m*
relative ['relətiv] *adj* relativo; *s* parente *m*
relax [ri'læks] *v/t*, *v/i* relaxar, afrouxar; descansar, repousar; **~ation** [ˌri:læk'seiʃən] relaxamento *m*; afrouxamento *m*; descanso *m*
relay [ri'lei] *s* posta *f*, muda *f*; substituição *f*; *v/t* substituir; retransmitir; **~ race** corrida *f* de estafetas, *Braz* corrida *f* de revezamento
release [ri'li:s] *v/t* soltar, desprender; *s* soltura *f*
relegate ['religeit] *v/t* relegar
relent [ri'lent] *v/i* abrandar-se; ceder; **~less** implacável
relevant ['relivənt] relevante; pertinente
reliable[ri'laiəbl] resistente; seguro, de confiança
reliance [ri'laiəns] confiança *f*
relic ['relik] relíquia *f*
relief[ri'li:f] alívio *m*; auxílio *m*, socorro *m*; relevo *m*; revezamento *m*
relieve[ri'li:v] *v/t* aliviar; socorrer; render
religi|on [ri'lidʒən] religião *f*; **~ous** *adj*, *s* religioso *m*
relinquish[ri'liŋkwiʃ] *v/t* abandonar
relish['reliʃ] *v/t* saborear; *s* gosto *m*; sabor *m*; tempero *m*
reluctant [ri'lʌktənt] relutante
rely [ri'lai] **on** *v/i* confiar em, contar com
remain [ri'mein] *v/i* ficar, permanecer; **~der** *s* restante *m*, resto *m*; **~s** restos *m/pl*

remark [ri'mɑːk] *v/t* observar; *s* observação *f*; **~able** notável
remedy ['remidi] *s* (*pl* **-dies**) remédio *m*; *v/t* remediar
rememb|er [ri'membə] *v/t* lembrar-se de; ter presente; **~rance** lembrança *f*, recordação *f*
remind [ri'maind] *v/t* (fazer) lembrar; **~ of** fazer lembrar; **~er** advertência *f*
remit [ri'mit] *v/t*, *v/i* remeter, enviar; remitir, perdoar; **~tance** remessa *f* de dinheiro
remnant ['remnənt] resto *m*
remodel [ˌriː'mɔdl] *v/t* remodelar
remonstrate ['remənstreit] (**with**) *v/i* protestar
remorse [ri'mɔːs] remorso *m*; **~less** sem remorso; desapiedado
remote [ri'məut] *adj* remoto; **~ control** *s* aparelho *m* de controle remoto
removal [ri'muːvəl] mudança *f*; **~ van** camioneta *f* de mudanças
remove [ri'muːv] *v/t* remover, afastar
render ['rendə] *v/t* tornar; executar, representar; **~ing** *s* versão *f*; interpretação *f*
renew [ri'njuː] *v/t* renovar
renounce [ri'nauns] *v/t* renunciar a
renovate ['renəveit] *v/t* renovar
renown [ri'naun] renome *m*, fama *f*; **~ed** famoso
rent [rent] *s* rasgão *m*, fenda *f*; renda *f*, aluguer *m*; *v/t* alugar
reopen [riː'əupən] *v/t*, *v/i* reabrir
repair [ri'pɛə] *s* reparação *f*, conserto *m*; *v/t*, *v/i* reparar, consertar
reparation [ˌrepə'reiʃən] reparação *f*
repartee [ˌrepɑː'tiː] réplica *f*
repay [riː'pei] *v/t* pagar; compensar; reembolsar; **~ment** reembolso *m*
repeat [ri'piːt] *v/t* repetir; **~edly** repetidas vezes
repel [ri'pel] *v/t* repelir
repent [ri'pent] *v/t* **~ of** *v/i* arrepender-se de; **~ance** arrependimento *m*
repetition [ˌrepi'tiʃən] repetição *f*
replace [ri'pleis] *v/t* substituir; repor; **~ment** substituição *f*
replenish [ri'pleniʃ] *v/t* reabastecer
reply [ri'plai] *v/t*, *v/i* responder; *s* resposta *f*
report [ri'pɔːt] *v/t*, *v/i* relatar; fazer a reportagem de; contar; denunciar; comparecer; *s* relatório *m*; reportagem *f*; **~er** repórter *m*, *f*
repose [ri'pəuz] *s* repouso *m*, descanso *m*; *v/t*, *v/i* repousar, descansar
reprehensible [ˌrepri'hensəbl] repreensível
represent [ˌrepri'zent] *v/t* representar; **~ative** *adj* representativo; *s* representante *m*, *f*
repress [ri'pres] *v/t* reprimir;

~ion repressão *f*
reprieve [ri'pri:v] *s* suspensão *f* de pena; v/t suspender a pena de morte de ...
reprimand ['reprimɑ:nd] *v/t* repreender, admoestar; *s* repreensão *f*, reprimenda *f*
reprint ['ri:'print] *v/t*, *v/i* reimprimir; *s* reimpressão *f*
reproach [ri'prəutʃ] *v/t* exprobrar, censurar, repreender; *s* censura *f*, increpação *f*
reproduce [ˌri:prə'dju:s] *v/t*, *v/i* reproduzir(-se)
reproduction [ˌri:prə'dʌkʃən] reprodução *f*
reproof [ri'pru:f] *s* reprovação *f*, increpação *f*
reprove [ri'pru:v] *v/t* reprovar, censurar
reptile ['reptail] réptil *m*
republic [ri'pʌblik] república *f*; **~an** *adj*, *s* republicano *m*
repugnan|ce [ri'pʌgnəns] repugnância *f*; **~t** repugnante
repuls|e [ri'pʌls] *v/t* repelir; *s* repulsa *f*, recusa *f*; revés *m*; **~ion** [-ʃən] repulsa *f*; repulsão *f*; **~ive** repelente
reput|able ['repjutəbl] honroso, honrado; **~ation** [-'teiʃən] reputação *f*
repute [ri'pju:t] fama *f*, reputação *f*; **of bad/evil ~** de má fama *f*; **~d to be ...** ter fama de ser ...
request [ri'kwest] *s* petição *f*, pedido *m*; *v/t* rogar, pedir
require [ri'kwaiə] *v/t* requerer, necessitar, exigir
requisite ['rekwizit] *s* requisito *m*, *adj* necessário, preciso, requerido
requite [ri'kwait] *v/t* retribuir
rescue ['reskju:] *v/t* salvar; *s* salvamento *m*, salvação *f*
research [ri'sə:tʃ] *s* investigação *f*, pesquisa *f*; *v/t*, *v/i* investigar
resembl|ance [ri'zembləns] semelhança *f*, parecença *f*; **~e** *v/t* parecer-se com, assemelhar-se a
resent [ri'zent] *v/t* ressentir(-se de); **~ful** ressentido; **~ment** ressentimento *m*
reservation [ˌrezə'veiʃən] reservação *f*, reserva *f*
reserv|e [ri'zə:v] *v/t* reservar; **~ed** *adj* reservado; retraído
reservoir ['rezəvwɑ:] reservatório *m*; depósito *m*
resid|e [ri'zaid] *v/i* residir; **~ence** ['rezidəns] residência *f*; **~ent** ['rezidənt] *s*, *adj* residente *m*, *f*
resign [ri'zain] *v/t*, *v/i* demitir-se; **~ation** [ˌrezig'neiʃən] demissão *f*; **~ed** *adj* resignado
resist [ri'zist] *v/t*, *v/i* resistir (a); **~ance** resistência *f*; **~ant** resistente
resolut|e ['rezəlu:t] resoluto; **~ion** [ˌ-'lu:ʃən] resolução *f*, decisão *f*
resolve [ri'zɔlv] *v/t* resolver
resort [ri'zɔ:t] *s* estância *f*; lugar *m*; recurso *m*; **in the last ~** em último recurso; **~ to** *v/t* recorrer a

resound [ri'zaund] *v/i* ressoar, retumbar
resource [ri'sɔːs] recurso *m*; **~ful** expedito; **~s** *s/pl* recursos *m/pl*
respect [ris'pekt] *v/t* respeitar; *s* respeito *m*; **with ~ to** com respeito a; **out of ~ for** em atenção a; **~able** respeitável; **~ful** respeitoso
respective [ris'pektiv] respectivo
respite ['respait] pausa *f*, folga *f*, descanso *m*
resplendent [ris'plendənt] resplandecente
respond [ris'pɔnd] *v/i* responder; **~ to** reagir a
responsi|bility [risˌpɔnsə'biliti] (*pl* **-ties**) responsabilidade *f*; **~ble** [-'pɔnsəbl] (**for**) responsável (por); **~ve** [-'pɔnsiv] sensível
rest [rest] *v/i* descansar; *s* descanso *m*; resto *m*
restaurant ['restərɔnt] restaurante *m*
rest|ful ['restful] repousado, sossegado; **~less** inquieto, desassossegado
restor|ation [ˌrestə'reiʃən] restauração *f*; restituição *f*; **~e** [ri'stɔː] *v/t* restaurar; restabelecer; restituir
restrain [ri'strein] restauro *m*; *v/t* refrear, reprimir, conter; **~t** constrangimento *m*
restrict [ris'trikt] *v/t* restringir; **~ion** restrição *f*
result [ri'zʌlt] *s* resultado *m*; *v/i* resultar; **~ant** resultante
resume [ri'zjuːm] *v/t*, *v/i* retomar; reatar, recomeçar
resurrection [ˌrezə'rekʃən] ressurreição *f*
retail ['riːteil] *s* COM retalho *m*, *Braz* varejo *m*; *v/t* vender a retalho
retain [ri'tein] *v/t* reter, guardar, conservar; **~er** pagamento *m* adiantado
retaliate [ri'tælieit] *v/i* retaliar, revidar
retir|e [ri'taiə] *v/t*, *v/i* retirar (-se); reformar-se; **~ed** *adj* reformado; retirado, afastado; **~ement** reforma *f*
retort [ri'tɔːt] *v/t*, *v/i* retorquir, replicar; *s* réplica *f*; CHEM retorta *f*
retouch [ˌriː'tʌtʃ] *v/t* retocar
retrace [ri'treis] *v/t* rememorar, referir; **~ one's steps** retroceder
retract [ri'trækt] *v/t*, *v/i* recolher; retra(c)tar(-se)
retreat [ri'triːt] *v/i* retirar-se; bater em retirada; *s* retirada *f*
retribution [ˌretri'bjuːʃən] justo castigo *m*
retrieve [ri'triːv] *v/t* recuperar, recobrar
retrospect ['retrəspekt] retrospecto *m*
return [ri'təːn] *v/t*, *v/i* devolver, restituir; voltar, regressar; *s* volta *f*, regresso *m*; devolução *f*, restituição *f*; **by ~** na volta do correio; **in ~ (for)** em paga de; em troca de; **~ ticket** bilhete *m*

de ida e volta; **many happy ~s (of the day)!** muitos parabéns! felicitações cordiais!
reunion [riː'juːniən] reunião *f*
revaluation [riːˌvæljuː'eiʃən] nova avaliação *f*
reveal [ri'viːl] *v/t* revelar, desvendar, descobrir
revelry ['revəlri] (*pl* **-ries**) festança *f*, folia *f*
revenge [ri'vendʒ] *s* desforra *f*; vingança *f*; *v/t* vingar; **~ful** vingativo
revenue ['revinjuː] rendimento *m*, receita *f*
revere [ri'viə] *v/t* venerar
reverse [ri'vəːs] *v/t*, *v/i* fazer marcha-atrás; inverter; *s* reverso *m*, contrário *m*; inverso *m*; revés *m*, contratempo *m*; **~ gear** engrenagem *f* de inversão de marcha
review [ri'vjuː] *s* revista *f*; crítica *f*; *v/t* rever; passar revista a; criticar
revis|e [ri'vaiz] *v/t*, *v/i* rever, reler; **~ion** [-'viʒən] revisão *f*
reviv|al [ri'vaivəl] renascimento *m*; **~e** *v/t*, *v/i* reanimar; restabelecer; voltar a si
revoke [ri'vəuk] *v/t* revogar
revolt [ri'vəult] *s* revolta *f*; *v/t*, *v/i* repugnar; revoltar(-se)
revolution [ˌrevə'luːʃən] revolução *f*; **~ary** [ˌ-ʃnəri] *adj*, *s* revolucionário *m*; **~ize** [ˌ-ʃnaiz] *v/t* revolucionar
revolve [ri'vɔlv] *v/t*, *v/i* rodar, girar; voltear, revolver
revolver [ri'vɔlvə] revólver *m*
revolving [ri'vɔlviŋ] *adj* giratório, rotativo
revulsion [ri'vʌlʃən] aversão *f*
reward [ri'wɔːd] *s* recompensa *f*; *v/t* recompensar
rheumatism ['ruːmətizəm] reumatismo *m*
rhubarb ['ruːbɑːb] ruibarbo *m*
rhyme [raim] *s* rima *f*; *v/t*, *v/i* rimar
rhythm ['riðəm] ritmo *m*; **~ic** rítmico
rib [rib] *s* costela *f*
ribbon ['ribən] fita *f*
rice [rais] arroz *m*
rich [ritʃ] rico; substancial; **the ~** os ricos; **~ly** ricamente; **~ness** riqueza *f*
ricket|s ['rikits] *s/pl* raquitismo *m*; **~y** instável, frágil, vacilante
rid [rid] **of** *v/t* desembaraçar de, livrar de; **get ~ of** desembaraçar-se de, livrar-se de
riddle ['ridl] *s* enigma *m*, adivinha *f*; crivo *m*, joeira *f*
rid|e [raid] *v/t*, *v/i* cavalgar, montar; ir, andar; *s* passeio *m*; **~er** cavaleiro *m*; amazona *f*
ridge [ridʒ] *s* cume *m*, espinhaço *m*
ridicul|e ['ridikjuːl] *s* ridículo *m*; *v/t* ridicularizar; **~ous** [-'dikjuləs] ridículo
riding ['raidiŋ] *s* equitação *f*
rifle ['raifl] *s* carabina *f*, espingarda *f*; *v/t* pilhar
rigging ['rigiŋ] NAUT cordame *m*
right [rait] *adj* direito; corre(c)to, justo; verdadeiro; *adv* justamente, bem; *s* direito *m*; jus-

tiça *f*; direita *f*; bem *m*; *v/t* endireitar; **all ~** está bem; **be ~** ter razão; **(quite) ~ in the head** em seu juízo; **~ you are!**, **~ oh!** certo!, perfeitamente, pois sim; **~ away** já, imediatamente; **~ful** legítimo; **~ly** convenientemente; justamente; **~s** *s/pl* direitos *m/pl*

rigid ['ridʒid] rígido; **~ity** [-'dʒiditi] rigidez *f*

rigo|rous ['rigərəs] rigoroso; **~(u)r** rigor *m*

rim [rim] *s* borda *f*; AUTO aro *m*

rind [raind] casca *f*

ring [riŋ] *s* anel *m*; argola *f*; círculo *m*; aro *m*; ringue *m*, arena *f*; toque *m* de campainha; *v/t*, *v/i* tocar; repicar; tinir; soar; telefonar; **~ up** telefonar

rink [riŋk] ringue *m*, pista *f* de patinagem

rinse [rins] *v/t* enxaguar

riot ['raiət] *v/i* amotinar-se; *s* tumulto *m*, motim *m*; **~er** amotinador *m*; **~ous** sedicioso; desenfreado

rip [rip] *v/t*, *v/i* rasgar(-se); *s* rasgão *m*

rip|e [raip] maduro; **~en** *v/t*, *v/i* amadurecer

ripple ['ripl] *s* ondulação *f*, encapeladura *f*; *v/t*, *v/i* encapelar-se; murmurar

rise [raiz] *v/i* levantar-se, erguerse; surgir; elevar-se; sublevarse; aumentar; nascer; subir; *s* aumento *m*; elevação *f*; subida *f*; rampa *f*; origem *f*

rising ['raiziŋ] *s* sublevação *f*; *prp* cerca de

risk [risk] *s* risco *m*; *v/t* arriscar; **run a ~** correr um risco; **~y** arriscado

ritual ['ritjuəl] *adj*, *s* ritual *m*

rival ['raivəl] *adj*, *s* rival *m*, *f*; **~ry** rivalidade *f*

river ['rivə] rio *m*; **~side** *s* margem *f* do rio; *adj* ribeirinho, marginal

rivet ['rivit] *s* rebite *m*; *v/t* rebitar

roach [rəutʃ] *zoo* leucisco *m*; barata *f*

road [rəud] estrada *f*; **on the ~** de viagem, de passagem; **~side** *s* beira *f* da estrada; **~way** pista *f* de rodagem

roam [rəum] *v/t*, *v/i* vaguear, deambular

roar [rɔː] *v/i* rugir; *s* rugido *m*

roast [rəust] *s* assado *m*, carne *f* assada; *v/t*, *v/i* torrar; assar; **~beef** rosbife *m*

rob [rɔb] *v/t* roubar; **~ber** ladrão *m*; **~bery** (*pl* **-ries**) roubo *m*

robe [rəub] *s* veste *f*; manto *m*; túnica *f*

robot ['rəubɔt] autómato *m*, robote *m*

robust [rə'bʌst] robusto

rock [rɔk] *s* rocha *f*, rochedo *m*; roca *f*; *v/t*, *v/i* embalar, acalentar; balançar-se

rocket ['rɔkit] *s* foguete *m*

rocking-chair ['rɔkiŋtʃεə] cadeira *f* de balanço/balouço

rocky ['rɔki] rochoso

rod [rɔd] vara *f*, verga *f*

rodent ['rəudənt] roedor *m*

roe [rəu] ova *f* de peixe; **~-deer** corça *f*
rogu|e [rəug] *s* velhaco *m*; **~ery** velhacaria *f*
role [rəul] papel *m*
roll [rəul] *s* rolo *m*; pãozinho *m*; rol *m*, lista *f*; *v/t*, *v/i* rodar; rolar; enrolar; **~ up** arregaçar; enrolar(-se); chegar, aparecer; **~er** rolo *m*; cilindro *m*; **~er skate** *s* patim *m* de rodas; **~ing** *adj* ondulado; rolante; **~ing-pin** rolo *m* da massa
Roman ['rəumən] *adj*, *s* romano *m*; **♀ ce** [rə'mæns] *s* romance *m*; *adj* românico
romantic [rə'mæntik] *adj*, *s* romântico *m*; **~ism** [-sizəm] romantismo *m*
romp [rɔmp] *s* jogo *m* barulhento; *v/i* brincar doidamente
roof [ru:f] *s* telhado *m*; **~ of the mouth** céu *m* da boca, paladar *m*
rook [ruk] *s* gralha *f*; torre *f* (*chess*); *v/t* trapacear
room [rum] *s* quarto *m*, sala *f*; lugar *m*, espaço *m*; **~y** espaçoso
roost [ru:st] *s* poleiro *m*; *v/i* empoleirar-se; **~er** galo *m*
root [ru:t] *s* raiz *f*; *v/t*, *v/i* criar raízes, enraizar; **~ out** erradicar, exterminar; achar; **~ed** *adj* arraigado; enraizado; especado
rope [rəup] *s* corda *f*; cabo *m*; fio *m*; *v/t* amarrar com corda
rosary ['rəuzəri] (*pl* **-ries**) rosário *m*
ros|e [rəuz] *s* rosa *f*; **~ebud** botão *m* de rosa *f*; **~emary** rosmarinho *m*; **~y** róseo, rosado
rot [rɔt] *v/t*, *v/i* apodrecer; *s* podridão *f*, putrefa(c)ção *f*
rotary ['rəutəri] *adj* rotativo, giratório
rotate [rəu'teit] *v/t*, *v/i* girar, rodar
rotten ['rɔtn] podre; corru(p)to; choco; mau, ruim
rouge [ru:ʒ] *s* ruge *m*
rough [rʌf] *adj* rude, grosseiro; áspero; agitado, bravo; borrascoso, tempestuoso; duro, brutal; aproximado, geral; tosco; *v/t* **~ it** passar trabalhos; **~ly** aproximadamente; bruscamente
round [raund] *adj* redondo; arredondado; *s* circuito *m*; rodela *f*, fatia *f*; rodada *f*; ronda *f*; *prp* ao redor de, em torno de; *adv* à roda; *v/t*, *v/i* arredondar(-se); dobrar; **~about** *s* carrocel *m*; *adj* vago, indire(c)to; **~ish** arredondado; **~ness** redondeza *f*; **~-shouldered** curvado; **~ trip** *s* viagem *f* de ida e volta; curva *f*, volta *f*, giro *m*
rouse [rauz] *v/t* despertar; animar, sacudir
route [ru:t] *s* rota *f*, rumo *m*; caminho *m*
routine [ru:'ti:n] *s* rotina *f*; *adj* rotineiro
rove [rəuv] *v/t*, *v/i* vaguear
row [rəu] *v/t*, *v/i* remar; *s* fileira *f*, fila *f*
row [rau] *s* barulho *m*; rixa *f*; *v/i*

brigar, disputar-se
rowdy ['raudi] *adj* barulhento, turbulento
royal ['rɔiəl] *adj* real, régio; **~ist** *adj, s* realista *m, f*, monárquico *m*; **~ty** (*pl* **-ties**) realeza *f*; direitos *m/pl* de autor
rub [rʌb] *v/t, v/i* esfregar; **~ber** ['-ə] borracha *f*; galocha *f*
rubbish ['rʌbiʃ] *s* entulho *m*, lixo *m*; disparate *m*, *Braz* bobagem *f*
rubble ['rʌbl] cascalho *m*
ruby ['ru:bi] rubi(m) *m*
rucksack ['rʌksæk] mochila *f*
rudder ['rʌdə] leme *m*
ruddy ['rʌdi] *adj* corado, rosado
rude [ru:d] rude, grosseiro; descortês, malcriado
ruffle ['rʌfl] *v/t, v/i* encrespar; irritar(-se); eriçar
rug [rʌg] manta *f* de viagem; tapete *m*
rugby ['rʌgbi] râguebi *m*
rugged ['rʌgid] duro, austero
ruin [ruin] *s* ruína *f*; *v/t* arruinar; **~ous** ruinoso
rule [ru:l] *s* regra *f*; governo *m*, mando *m*; régua *f*; *v/t, v/i* decidir, decretar; reger, governar; **~ out** excluir; **~r** ['-ə] governante *m*; régua *f*
rum [rʌm] rum *m*
Rumanian [ru(:)'meinjən] *adj, s* romeno *m*
rumble ['rʌmbl] *s* rumor *m*, ruído *m*; estrondo *m*; *v/i* retumbar; estrondear
ruminate ['ru:mineit] *v/i* ruminar; magicar, meditar
rumo(u)r ['ru:mə] boato *m*
rump [rʌmp] alcatra *f*
rumple ['rʌmpl] *v/t* amarrotar; desgrenhar
run [rʌn] *s* corrida *f*; marcha *f*; percurso *m*; traje(c)to *m*; série *f*, sequência *f*; *v/t, v/i* dirigir, administrar; correr; circular; andar, funcionar; fazer carreira; **in the long ~** com o decorrer do tempo; **~ after** correr atrás de; andar atrás de; **~-away** *adj, s* fugitivo *m*; **~ away** fugir; **~ back** voltar, retroceder; **~ into** espetar; esbarrar(-se) com; **~ on** continuar; **~ out** esgotar-se; **~ out of** esgotar, não ter mais; **~ to** chegar, montar a; **~ up** *v/t* hastear; acumular; **~ner** corredor *m*; **~ning** *s* corrida *f*; *adj* corrente; consecutivo; contínuo
runway ['rʌnwei] pista *f* de descolagem
rupture ['rʌptʃə] *s* rompimento *m*, ruptura *f*; hérnia *f*; *v/t, v/i* romper(-se)
rural ['ruərəl] rural
rush [rʌʃ] *s* investida *f*, acometida *f*; pressa *f*; torrente *f*; tropel *m*; BOT junco *m*; *v/t, v/i* precipitar(-se); investir, acometer; apressar-se, lançar-se; **~-hour** hora *f* de ponta
Russian ['rʌʃən] *adj, s* russo *m*
rust [rʌst] *s* ferrugem *f*; *v/t, v/i* enferrujar(-se)
rustic ['rʌstik] *adj* rústico; *s* camponês *m*
rustle ['rʌsl] *s* sussurro *m*; *v/t, v/i*

farfalhar, sussurrar
rusty ['rʌsti] ferrugento, enferrujado
rut [rʌt] *s* sulco *m*, trilho *m*
ruthless ['ru:θlis] desapiedado, implacável, cruel; **~ness** crueldade *f*, implacabilidade *f*
rye [rai] centeio *m*

S

sable ['seibl] *s* zibelina *f*; pele *f* de marta-zibelina
sabotage ['sæbətɑ:ʒ] *s* sabotagem *f*; *v/t* sabotar
sabre ['seibə] *s* sabre *m*
sack [sæk] *s* saco *m*, saca *f*; saque *m*; *v/t* saquear; demitir; **get the ~** ser despedido, ser posto na rua; **give the ~** despedir, pôr na rua; **hit the ~** ir deitar-se
sacrament ['sækrəmənt] sacramento *m*
sacred ['seikrid] sagrado
sacri|fice ['sækrifais] *v/t*, *v/i* sacrificar; *s* sacrifício *m*; **~legious** [ˌ-'lidʒəs] sacrílego; **~sty** ['-sti] (*pl* **-ties**) sacristia *f*
sad [sæd] triste; **~den** *v/t*, *v/i* entristecer(-se)
saddl|e ['sædl] *s* sela *f*; selim *m*; *v/t* selar; **~er** seleiro *m*
sadness ['sædnis] tristeza *f*
safe [seif] *s* cofre *m*; *adj* salvo; seguro; **~ and sound** são e salvo; **~ conduct** salvo-conduto *m*; **~guard** *s* salvaguarda *f*; *v/t* proteger, salvaguardar
safety ['seifti] segurança *f*; **~-belt** cinto *m* de segurança; **~-pin** alfinete *m* de segurança; **~ razor** gilete *f*; **~-valve** válvula *f* de segurança
saffron ['sæfrən] açafrão *m*
sag [sæg] *v/i* vergar, ceder; baixar
sagacity [sə'gæsiti] sagacidade *f*
sage [seidʒ] *s* sábio *m*; BOT salva *f*
sago ['seigəu] sagu *m*
sail [seil] *v/t*, *v/i* navegar; velejar; *s* vela *f*; veleiro *m*; **set ~** fazer-se à vela; **~ing** *s* navegação *f*; **~ing-boat** barco *m* à vela, veleiro *m*; **~or** marinheiro *m*
saint [seint] santo *m*
sake [seik]: **for the ~ of** por causa de, por amor de; **for my ~** por mim; **for God's ~** por amor de Deus; **for the ~ of appearances** para salvar as aparências
salad ['sæləd] salada *f*; **~ dressing** tempero *m* para salada
salary ['sæləri] (*pl* **-ries**) ordenado *m*
sale [seil] venda *f*; leilão *m*; saldo *m*, liquidação *f*; **on ~** à venda; **~able** vendável, vendível
sales|man ['seilzmən] (*pl* **-men**) caixeiro *m*, vendedor *m*; **~woman** vendedora *f*
salient ['seiljənt] *adj* saliente

saliva [sə'laivə] saliva *f*
sallow ['sæləu] *adj* pálido, amarelado
sally ['sæli] (*pl* **-lies**) MIL saída *f*; dito *m* espirituoso
salmon ['sæmən] salmão *m*
saloon [sə'lu:n] salão *m*; bar *m*
salt [sɔ:lt] *s* sal *m*; *v/t* salgar
saltpetre ['sɔ:ltpi:tə] salitre *m*
salty ['sɔ:lti] salgado
salu|tary ['sæljutəri] salutar; **~tation** [ˌ-'teiʃən] saudação *f*; **~te** [sə'lu:t] *v/t* saudar; *s* saudação *f*; salva *f*
salvage ['sælvidʒ] *s* salvados *m/pl*; salvamento *m*; *v/t* salvar
salvation [sæl'veiʃən] salvação *f*
salve [sa:v] *s* unguento *m*, pomada *f*, emplastro *m*
same [seim] *adj* mesmo; idêntico, igual; *pron* o mesmo; *adv* do mesmo modo; **all the ~** ainda assim, apesar disso; **~ to you!** igualmente!
sample ['sa:mpl] *s* amostra *f*; *v/t* provar
sanatorium [ˌsænə'tɔ:riəm] sanatório *m*
sanctify ['sæŋktifai] *v/t* santificar
sanction ['sæŋkʃən] ['-ʃən] *s* sanção *f*; aprovação *f*; *v/t* sancionar
sanct|ity ['sæŋktiti] (*pl* **-ties**) santidade *f*; **~uary** ['-tjuəri] (*pl* **-ries**) santuário *m*
sand [sænd] *s* areia *f*
sandal ['sændl] sandália *f*
sand|bank ['sændbæŋk] banco *m* de areia; **~paper** *v/t* lixar; *s* lixa *f*
sandwich ['sænwidʒ] *s* anduíche *f*, sande *f*
sandy ['sændi] arenoso
sane [sein] são, sensato
sanit|ary ['sænitəri] sanitário; higiénico; **~ary towel/napkin** penso *m* higiénico; **~ation** [ˌ-'teiʃən] saneamento *m*; **~y** razão *f*
Santa Claus [sæntə 'klɔ:z] Pai Natal *m*, *Braz* Papai *m* Noel
sap [sæp] *s* seiva *f*
sapper ['sæpə] sapador *m*
sapphire ['sæfaiə] safira *f*
sarcas|m ['sa:kæzəm] sarcasmo *m*; **~tic** [-'kæstik] sarcástico
sardine [sa:'di:n] sardinha *f*
sardonic [sa:'dɔnik] sardónico
sash [sæʃ] cinto *m*, faixa *f*; cai-xilho *m*
Satan ['seitən] Satanás *m*; **≗ic** [sə'tænik] satânico
satchel ['sætʃəl] sacola *f*, pasta *f*
satellite ['sætəlait] satélite *m*; **~ dish** antenta *f* parabólica
sat|iate ['seiʃieit] *v/t* saciar; **~iety** [sə'taiəti] saciedade *f*
satin ['sætin] cetim *m*
satis|faction [ˌsætis'fækʃən] satisfação *f*; **~factory** satisfatório; **~fy** ['sætisfai] *v/t*, *v/i* satisfazer
Saturday ['sætədi] sábado *m*
sauc|e [sɔ:s] *s* molho *m*; **~epan** caçarola *f*; **~er** pires *m*
saucy ['sɔ:si] impertinente,

atrevido
saunter ['sɔ:ntə] *v/i* vaguear, saracotear; *s* passeio *m*
sausage ['sɔsidʒ] salsicha *f*
savage ['sævidʒ] *adj, s* selvagem *m, f*; **~ry** selvajaria *f*
save [seiv] *v/t, v/i* salvar; poupar, economizar; *prp* salvo, exce(p)to
savings ['seiviŋz] *s/pl* economias *f/pl*; **~-bank** caixa *f* económica
savio(u)r ['seivjə] salvador *m*
savo(u)r ['seivə] *s* sabor; *v/t* saborear; **~y** *adj* saboroso; *s* petisco *m*
savoy [sə'vɔi] sabóia *f*
saw [sɔ:] *s* serra *f*; *v/t, v/i* serrar; **~dust** serradura *f*; **~yer** serrador *m*
Saxon ['sæksn] *adj, s* saxão *m*
saxophone ['sæksəfəun] saxofone *m*
say [sei] *v/t, v/i* dizer; **that is to ~** quer dizer; **you don't ~ (so)!** não me diga!; **you said it** assim o diz, tu o dizes; **~ing** *s* dito *m*; rifão *m*
scab [skæb] *s* escara *f*, crosta *f*
scabbard ['skæbəd] bainha *f*
scaffold ['skæfəld] cadafalso *m*, patíbulo *m*; andaime *m*; **~ing** andaime *m*
scald [skɔ:ld] *v/t, v/i* escaldar
scale [skeil] *s* escala *f*; escama *f*; balança *f*; *v/t* escalar, trepar por
scalp [skælp] *s* escalpo *m*; couro *m* cabeludo; *v/t* escalpar
scalpel ['skælpəl] escalpelo *m*
scan [skæn] *v/t* esquadrinhar; escandir; COMP digitalizar; *s* COMP digitalização *f*
scanner ['skænə] *s* COMP scanner *m*
scandal ['skændl] escândalo *m*; maledicência *f*; **~ize** *v/t* escandalizar; **~ous** escandaloso
Scandinavian [ˌskændi'neivjən] *adj, s* escandinavo *m*
scant [skænt] *adj* escasso
scanty ['skænti] exíguo
scapegoat ['skeipgəut] bode *m* expiatório
scar [skɑ:] *s* cicatriz *f*; *v/t, v/i* cicatrizar
scarc|e [skɛəs] *adj* raro, escasso; **~ely** apenas, mal; **~ity** escassez *f*
scare [skɛə] *v/t, v/i* assustar (-se), espantar, amedrontar; **~ away** afugentar; **~crow** [-krəu] espantalho *m*
scarf [skɑ:f] cachecol *m*; lenço *m* de pescoço
scarlet ['skɑ:lit] *s, adj* escarlate *m*
scatter ['skætə] *v/t, v/i* espalhar; dispersar-se
scavenge ['skævindʒ] *v/t, v/i* vasculhar
scene [si:n] cena *f*; espe(c)táculo *m*; cenário *m*; vista *f*
scenery ['si:nəri] cenário *m*; panorama *m*
scent [sent] *s* cheiro *m*, aroma *m*, perfume *m*; faro *m*; pista *f*, rasto *m*; *v/t* cheirar; farejar; perfumar
sceptical ['skeptikəl] céptico

schedule ['ʃedjuːl] *s* horário *m*, plano *m*; *v/t* marcar
scheme ['skiːm] *s* esquema *m*, proje(c)to *m*, plano *m*
scholar ['skɔlə] erudito *m*; sábio *m*; bolseiro *m*, bolsista *m*, *f*; **~ly** erudito; **~ship** erudição *f*; bolsa *f* de estudos
school [skuːl] *v/t* treinar, adestrar; disciplinar; *s* escola *f*; colégio *m*; **~boy** aluno *m*; **~fellow** condiscípulo *m*; **~girl** aluna *f*; **~ing** *s* instrução *f*; educação *f*; **~mate** companheiro *m* de escola
schooner ['skuːnə] escuna *f*
sciatica [sai'ætikə] ciática *f*
scien|ce ['saiəns] ciência *f*; **~tific** [ˌ-'tifik] científico; **~tist** ['-tist] cientista *m*, *f*
scissors ['sizəz] *s/pl* tesoura *f*
scoff [skɔf] *v/i* caçoar, zombar; *s* zombaria *f*
scold [skəuld] *v/t*, *v/i* ralhar, repreender
scoop [skuːp] *s* colherão *m*; alcatruz *m*; *v/t* vazar, despejar; escavar
scooter ['skuːtə] trotinete *f*, *Braz* patinete *m*; motoreta *f*
scope [skəup] alcance *m*, extensão *f*; espaço *m*; esfera *f*, campo *m*; **give ~ to** dar largas a
scorch [skɔːtʃ] *v/t*, *v/i* queimar, chamuscar; *s* queimadura *f*
score [skɔː] *s* contagem *f*, marcação *f*; vintena *f*; MUS partitura *f*; *v/t* riscar, cortar; marcar; MUS orquestrar
scorn [skɔːn] *s* desprezo *m*, desdém *m*; *v/t* desprezar, desdenhar; **~ful** desdenhoso
Scotch [skɔtʃ] *adj* escocês; *s* uísque *m*
scot-free ['skɔt'friː] impune
Scottish ['skɔtiʃ] escocês
scoundrel ['skaundrəl] velhaco *m*, patife *m*
scour ['skauə] *v/t* esfregar, arear; **~ for** percorrer
scourge [skəːdʒ] *s* açoute *m*; *v/t* açoutar
scout [skaut] *v/t*, *v/i* espiar, patrulhar; sentinela *f* avançada; escuteiro *m*, *Braz* escoteiro *m*
scowl [skaul] *v/i* franzir a testa, fazer carranca; *s* carranca *f*
scraggy ['skrægi] escanifrado, macilento
scramble ['skræmbl] *s* escalada *f*; luta *f*, disputa *f*; *v/t*, *v/i* trepar; disputar, lutar; **~d eggs** ovos *m/pl* mexidos
scrap [skræp] *s* pedaço *m*, fragmento *m*
scrap|e [skreip] *v/t* raspar; *s* raspadela *f*; aperto *m*, dificuldade *f*; **~e together/up** juntar, poupar; **~er** raspador *m*
scratch [skrætʃ] *v/t*, *v/i* arranhar(-se); coçar; esgaravatar; *s* arranhão *m*, arranhadura *f*
scrawl [skrɔːl] *s* rabisco *m*, gatafunho *m*; *v/t*, *v/i* rabiscar, garatujar
scream [skriːm] *v/t*, *v/i*, gritar; *s* grito *m*
screech [skriːtʃ] *s* guincho *m*; *v/t*, *v/i* guinchar; chiar

screen [skriːn] *s* tela *f*, écran *m*; biombo *m*; guarda-fogo *m*; *v/t* proteger, defender; abrigar; encobrir; proje(c)tar, exibir

screw [skruː] *s* parafuso *m*; NAUT hélice *f*; *v/t* aparafusar; **~driver** chave *f* de parafuso

scribble ['skribl] *v/t*, *v/i* escrevinhar, rabiscar; *s* rabisco *m*, garatuja *f*

script [skript] escrita *f*; texto *m*, manuscrito *m*

Scripture ['skriptʃə] escritura *f* sagrada

scrub [skrʌb] *v/t*, *v/i* esfregar; *s* mato *m*; **~bing-brush** escova *f* de esfrega

scruffy ['skrʌfi] desmazelado, sujo

scrup|le ['skruːpl] *s* escrúpulo *m*; **~ulous** ['-pjuləs] escrupuloso

scrutin|eer [ˌskruːti'niə] escrutinador *m*; **~ize** ['-naiz] *v/t* escrutar, esquadrinhar; escrutinar; **~y** (*pl* **-nies**) exame *m*; escrutínio *m*

scuffle ['skʌfl] *s* rixa *f*, bulha *f*, tumulto *m*

scull [skʌl] *s* remo *m*; *v/i* remar

sculpt|or ['skʌlptə] escultor *m*; **~ure** ['-tʃə] *s* escultura *f*; *v/t*, *v/i* esculpir

scum [skʌm] escuma *f*

scurf [skəːf] caspa *f*

scurry ['skʌri] *v/i* escapulir-se; apressar-se

scurvy ['skəːvi] *s* MED escorbuto *m*; *adj* vil, ruim, desprezível

scuttle ['skʌtl] *s* balde *m*; *v/t* meter a pique; *v/i* escapar, fugir

scythe [saið] *s* gadanha *f*, segadeira *f*

sea [siː] mar *m*; **at ~** no mar, no mar alto; desnorteado, confuso; **~board** litoral *m*; **~food** mariscos *m/pl*; **~-gull** gaivota *f*

seal [siːl] *s* selo *m*, sinete *m*, carimbo *m*; ZOO foca *f*; *v/t* selar; lacrar

sea|level ['siː'levl] nível *m* do mar

seam [siːm] *s* costura *f*

seaman ['siːmən] (*pl* **-men** [-men]) marinheiro *m*

search [səːtʃ] *v/t*, *v/i* investigar; buscar, procurar; *s* procura *f*, busca *f*, pesquisa *f*; **in ~ of** em busca de, à procura de; **~ing** *adj* penetrante; **-light** holofote *m*

sea|shell ['siːʃel] concha *f*; **~-shore** costa *f*, beira-mar *f*

seasick ['siːsik] enjoado

seaside ['siː'said] praia *f*, beira-mar *f*; **~ resort** estância *f* balnear

season ['siːzn] *s* estação *f*; temporada *f*; tempo *m*; ocasião *f*; *v/t* temperar, condimentar; **in ~** na época; **out of ~** fora de estação, fora de época; **~ing** *s* tempero *m*, condimento *m*; **~ ticket** bilhete *m* de assinatura

seat [siːt] *s* assento *m*; fundilhos *m/pl*; sede *f*; lugar *m*; *v/t* sentar; ter lugares para; **have/take a ~** sentar-se; **~ belt** cinto *m* de segurança

seaweed ['si:wi:d] alga *f* marinha

seclu|ded [si'klu:did] *adj* retirado; **~sion** [-ʒən] retiro *m*; separação *f*

second ['sekənd] *s* segundo *m*; padrinho *m*; *adj* segundo; **on ~ thoughts** pensando melhor; *v/t* secundar, apoiar; **~ary** secundário; **~ class** *s* segunda classe *f*; **~-hand** *adj* em/de segunda mão

secrecy ['si:krisi] segredo *m*, sigilo *m*

secret ['si:krit] *s* segredo *m*; *adj* secreto; **in ~** em segredo; **~ariat** [ˌsekrə'tɛəriət] secretariado *m*; **~ary** ['sekrətri] (*pl* **-ries**) secretário *m*, secretária *f*

secretion [si'kri:ʃən] secreção *f*

secretive ['si:kritiv] reservado, calado

sect [sekt] seita *f*; **~arian** [-'tɛəriən] *adj*, *s* sectário *m*

section ['sekʃən] *s* se(c)ção *f*

sector ['sektə] se(c)tor *m*

secular ['sekjulə] secular, profano; **~ize** ['-raiz] *v/t* secularizar

secure [si'kjuə] *adj* seguro; certo; firme; *v/t* assegurar; pôr no seguro; prender, amarrar

security [si'kjuəriti] (*pl* **-ties**) segurança *f*; garantia *f*, penhor *m*, fiança *f*; *pl* títulos *m/pl*, valores *m/pl*

sedat|e [si'deit] *adj* sereno, calmo, sossegado; **~ive** ['sedətiv] *s*, *adj* sedativo *m*, calmante *m*

sedentary ['sedntəri] sedentário

sediment ['sedimənt] sedimento *m*

seduc|e [si'dju:s] *v/t* seduzir; **~er** sedutor *m*; **~tion** [-'dʌkʃən] sedução *f*; **~tive** [-'dʌktiv] sedutor

see [si:] *s* sé *f*, sede *f* pontifical; *v/t*, *v/i* ver; acompanhar; compreender; **~ you later!** até à vista! **let me ~** deixe-me ver; **you ~** como vê; **~ about** tratar de; **~ off** *v/t* ir despedirse de, ir dizer adeus a

seed [si:d] *s* semente *f*

seeing [si:iŋ] *conj* (**that**) visto (que)

seek [si:k] *v/t* procurar, buscar

seem [si:m] *v/i* parecer; **~ing** *adj* aparente; **~ly** decente, decoroso

seesaw ['si:sɔ:] *s* arre-burrinho *m*, *Braz* gangorra *f*

seethe [si:ð] *v/i* ferver; fervilhar

segregat|e ['segrigeit] *v/t*, *v/i* segregar; **~ed** *adj* segregado, separado

seiz|e [si:z] *v/t* agarrar; apreender; **~ure** ['-ʒə] apreensão *f*; MED ataque *m*

seldom ['seldəm] raras vezes, raramente

select [si'lekt] *v/t* escolher; *adj* sele(c)to, escolhido; **~ion** [-'lekʃən] sele(c)ção *f*, escolha *f*

self [self] *s* (*pl* **-selves**) [selvz]) ego *m*, eu *m*; pessoa *f*; *pron* mesmo, próprio

self|-command ['selfkə-'mɑːnd] autodomínio *m*; **~-confident** seguro de si; **~-control** autodomínio *m*; **~-denial** abnegação *f*; **~-government** autonomia *f*; **~-importance** presunção *f*
selfish ['selfiʃ] egoísta; **~ness** egoísmo *m*
self|-made ['self'meid] feito por si; **~-possession** sangue-frio *m*; **~-respect** respeito *m* próprio, dignidade *f*; **~-sacrifice** abnegação *f*; **~-sufficient** auto-suficiente; **~-willed** teimoso, voluntarioso
sell [sel] *v/t*, *v/i* vender(-se); **~ off** liquidar; **~ out** esgotar, liquidar; **~er** vendedor *m*
semblance ['sembləns] aparência *f*, semelhança *f*
semicolon ['semi'kəulən] ponto *m* e vírgula *f*
seminary ['seminəri] (*pl* **-ries**) seminário *m*
semolina [ˌsemə'liːnə] sémola *f*
senat|e ['senit] senado *m*; **~or** ['-ətə] senador *m*
send [send] *v/t*, *v/i* enviar, mandar; transmitir, emitir
sender ['sendə] remetente *m*, *f*
senil|e ['siːnail] senil; **~ity** [si'niliti] senilidade *f*
senior ['siːnjə] *adj* sénior, mais velho; mais antigo; **~ity** [ˌ-ni'ɔriti] antiguidade *f*
sensation [sen'seiʃən] sensação *f*; **~al** sensacional
sense [sens] *s* sentido *m*; juízo *m*, senso *m*; sentimento *m*; *v/t* perceber; pressentir, sentir; **~less** insensato; sem sentidos, desmaiado
sensib|ility [ˌsensi'biliti] sensibilidade *f*; **~le** ['-əbl] sensato
sens|itive ['sensitiv] sensível; sensitivo, impressionável; **~ual** ['-sjuəl] sensual
sentence ['sentəns] *s* frase *f*; sentença *f*, julgamento *m*
sentiment ['sentimənt] sentimento *m*; **~al** [-'mentl] sentimental
sentry ['sentri] (*pl* **-ries**) sentinela *f*; **~ box** guarita *f*
separat|e ['sepəreit] *v/t*, *v/i* separar(-se); ['sepərit] *adj* separado; **~ion** [ˌ-'reiʃən] separação *f*
September [sep'tembə] Setembro *m*
septic ['septik] séptico
sequel ['siːkwəl] consequência *f*
sequence ['siːkwens] sequência *f*, série *f*, sucessão *f*
serene [si'riːn] sereno
sergeant ['sɑːdʒənt] sargento *m*
seri|al ['siəriəl] *adj* serial, em série; *s* folhetim *m*; **~es** ['-riːz] série *f*
serious ['siəriəs] serio; **~ly** a sério; **~ness** gravidade *f*
sermon ['səːmən] sermão *m*
serpent ['səːpənt] serpente *f*
serum ['siərəm] soro *m*
servant ['səːvənt] criado *m*
serve [səːv] *v/t*, *v/i* servir
service ['səːvis] *s* serviço *m*; **~a-**

ble útil
serviette [ˌsəːvi'et] guardanapo *m*
servile ['səːvail] servil
session ['seʃən] sessão *f*
set [set] *s* jogo *m*, cole(c)ção *f*, série *f*; aparelho *m*; círculo *m*, grupo *m*; cenário *m*; *v/t*, *v/i* colocar, pôr, meter; solidificar-se; pôr-se; acertar, regular; *adj* marcado, fixo; decidido, determinado; prescrito; ~ **fire to** deitar fogo a; ~ **the table** pôr a mesa; ~ **down** pousar; anotar, pôr por escrito; deixar; ~ **off** abalar, partir; realçar; ~**back** *s* revés *m*, contratempo *m*
settee [se'tiː] sofá *m*
setting ['setiŋ] *s* fundo *m*, cenário *m*; pôr *m*, ocaso *m*; engaste *m*; montagem *f*
settle ['setl] *v/t*, *v/i* colocar, fixar(-se); liquidar, pagar; ajustar; pousar; fixar residência; estabelecer-se; ~**ment** estabelecimento *m*; povoado *m*; ~**r** colono *m*
seven ['sevn] sete; ~ **hundred** setecentos; ~**teen** dezassete; ~**th** ['-θ] sétimo; ~**ty** setenta
sever ['sevə] *v/t*, *v/i* separar, cortar
several ['sevərəl] *adj*, *pron* vários
sever|e [si'viə] severo; ~**ity** [-'veriti] severidade *f*
sew [səu] *v/t*, *v/i* coser, costurar
sewer ['sjuːə] cano *m* de esgoto
sewing ['səuiŋ] *s* costura *f*; ~**-machine** máquina *f* de costura
sex [seks] sexo *m*
sexton ['sekstən] sacristão *m*
sexual ['seksjuəl] sexual
shabby ['ʃæbi] coçado; mal vestido; mesquinho
shade [ʃeid] *s* sombra *f*; matiz *m*; *v/t* sombrear; matizar; **in the** ~ à sombra
shadow ['ʃædəu] *s* sombra *f*; *v/t* sombrear; seguir, perseguir; **in, under the** ~ **of** à sombra de; ~**y** sombrio, tenebroso; vago
shady ['ʃeidi] sombrio, sombreado, umbroso; *fig* suspeito
shaft [ʃɑːft] *s* haste *f*; fuste *m*; eixo *m*, veio *m*; raio *m*, feixe *m*
shaggy ['ʃægi] hirsuto; cabeludo
shake [ʃeik] *v/t*, *v/i* abanar; abalar, tremer; sacudir, agitar; apertar; *s* abalo *m*, estremecimento *m*; sacudidela *f*; vibração *f*; aperto *m*; batido *m*; ~ **hands (with someone)** apertar a(s) mão(s) (a alguém); ~ **one's head** abanar a cabeça
shaky ['ʃeiki] trémulo, vacilante
shall [ʃæl, ʃəl] *v/aux* dever, ter de; ~ **we go?** vamos?; ~ **I get you a chair?** quer que lhe vá buscar uma cadeira?
shallow ['ʃæləu] *adj* raso; baixo, pouco profundo; *fig* superficial, trivial
sham [ʃæm] *s* impostura *f*; *adj* falso, fingido, postiço
shambles ['ʃæmblz] *s* campo

m de batalha; matadoiro *m*; barafunda *f*
shame [ʃeim] *s* vergonha *f*; **what a ~!** que pena!; **~ful** vergonhoso; **~less** impúdico, imodesto, desavergonhado
shampoo [ʃæm'pu:] *s* champô *m*, *Braz* xampu *m*
shape [ʃeip] *s* forma *f*, figura *f*, contorno *m*; *v/t* formar, dar forma a
share [ʃɛə] *s* parte *f*, porção *f*; COM a(c)ção *f*; relha *f*; *v/t*, *v/i* repartir, distribuir; participar de, compartilhar
shark [ʃɑ:k] ZOO tubarão *m*
sharp [ʃɑ:p] *adj* agudo; aguçado, afiado; penetrante; astuto; acre; mordaz; picante; nítido, distinto; brusco; *adv* em ponto; **~en** *v/t*, *v/i* afiar, aguçar; **~ener** afia-lápis *m*, afiador *m*; **~ness** agudeza; perspicácia *f*; mordacidade *f*
shatter ['ʃætə] *v/t*, *v/i* estilhaçar; esmigalhar; despedaçar (-se)
shav|e [ʃeiv] *v/t*, *v/i* fazer a barba; barbear(-se); **~ing-brush** pincel *m* de barba; **~ing--cream** creme *m* para a barba; **~ing--stick** sabão *m* de barba
shawl [ʃɔ:l] xa(i)le *m*
she [ʃi:, ʃi] *pron* ela; *s* fêmea *f*; menina *f*
sheaf [ʃi:f] (*pl* **sheaves** [ʃi:vz]) molho *m*, feixe *m*
shear [ʃiə] *v/t* tosquiar; **~s** [-z] *s/pl* tesoira *f* grande
sheath [ʃi:θ] bainha *f*, estojo *m*; **~e** [-ð] *v/t* embainhar
shed [ʃed] *v/t*, *v/i* deixar cair, largar, mudar; derramar; *s* alpendre *m*, barracão *m*
sheep [ʃi:p] ovelha *f*, carneiro *m*; **~-fold** aprisco *m*, ovil *m*; **~ish** acanhado
sheer [ʃiə] *adj* fino; simples, puro; escarpado, íngreme
sheet [ʃi:t] folha *f*; lâmina *f*; lençol *m*
shelf [ʃelf] (*pl* **shelves** [ʃelvz]) prateleira *f*; estante *f*
shell [ʃel] *s* casca *f*; concha *f*; MIL bomba *f*, granada *f*; *v/t*, *v/i* descascar; bombardear
shellfish ['ʃel,fiʃ] marisco *m*
shelter ['ʃeltə] *s* abrigo *m*; amparo *m*; asilo *m*, refúgio *m*; *v/t*, *v/i* abrigar(-se), resguardar, amparar
shepherd ['ʃepəd] *s* pastor *m*
sherbet ['ʃə:bət] sorvete *m*
sheriff ['ʃerif] xerife *m*
sherry ['ʃeri] xerez *m*, vinho *m* de Xerez
shield [ʃi:ld] *s* escudo *m*; *v/t* amparar, proteger
shift [ʃift] *s* mudança *f*, desvio *m*; turno *m*; ardil *m*; *v/t*, *v/i* mudar; empurrar; mover(-se); **~ for oneself** governar a sua vida sozinho; **~y** ardiloso, astuto
shilling ['ʃiliŋ] xelim *m*
shin [ʃin] *s* canela *f* da perna
shine [ʃain] *v/i* brilhar; *v/t* dar lustre a; *s* brilho *m*
shingle ['ʃiŋgl] *v/t* cobrir com ripas; *s* ripa *f*; seixo *m*
shiny ['ʃaini] lustroso; brilhan-

te, cintilante

ship [ʃip] *s* navio *m*, embarcação *f*, barco *m*; **~ment** embarque *m*; carregamento *m*; **~ping** *s* navegação *f*; marinha *f* mercante; **~wreck** *s* naufrágio *m*; *v/t* naufragar; **~yard** estaleiro *m*

shirk [ʃə:k] *v/t*, *v/i* fugir (a), esquivar-se (a)

shirt [ʃə:t] camisa *f*; **in one's ~-sleeves** em mangas de camisa

shiver ['ʃivə] *v/i* tiritar; *s* calafrio *m*, arrepio *m*

shoal [ʃəul] cardume *m*; baixio *m*

shock [ʃɔk] *s* choque *m*, encontrão *m*; *v/t*, *v/i* chocar(-se); dar choque (a); assustar(-se); **~-absorber** AUTO amortecedor *m*; **~ing** *adj* chocante; péssimo

shoe [ʃu:] *s* sapato *m*; *v/t* calçar; ferrar; **~black** engraxador *m*, *Braz* engraxate *m*; **~horn** calçadeira *f*; **~-lace** atacador *m*; **~maker** sapateiro *m*; **~-shop** sapataria *f*

shoot [ʃu:t] *v/t*, *v/i* matar a tiro, caçar; filmar; tirar um instantâneo (de); fuzilar; disparar, atirar, fazer fogo; chutar

shooting ['ʃu:tiŋ] *s* caça *f*; tiros *m/pl*, tiroteio *m*; **~ star** estrela *f* cadente

shop [ʃɔp] *s* loja *f*; armazém *m*; *v/i* ir às compras, fazer compras; **~-assistant** empregado *m*, vendedor *m*; **~keeper** lojista *m*, *f*; **~-lifter** ladrão *m* de lojas

shopping ['ʃɔpiŋ] *s* compras *f/pl*; **go ~** ir às compras; **~ centre** centro *m* comercial

shop-|steward ['ʃɔp,stjuəd] representante *m*, *f* sindicalista; **~-window** montra *f*

shore [ʃɔ:] *s* praia *f*; costa *f*; **on ~** em terra

short [ʃɔ:t] *adv* de repente; bruscamente; *adj* curto, breve; **in ~** em suma, em resumo; **~age** falta *f*; **~ circuit** *s* curto-circuito *m*; **~coming** defeito *m*, falta *f*; **~ cut** atalho *m*; **~en** *v/t*, *v/i* encurtar; **~hand** taquigrafia *f*, estenografia *f*; **~ly** brevemente, em breve; **~s** *s/pl* calções *m/pl*; **~-sighted** míope

shot [ʃɔt] *s* tiro *m*; bom atirador *m*; inje(c)ção *f*; tentativa *f*; foto *f*, instantâneo *m*; remate *m*, pontapé *m*

should [ʃəd, ʃud] *v/aux* **I ~ like** queria, gostaria

shoulder ['ʃəuldə] *s* ombro *m*; espádua *f*; *v/t* empurrar com os ombros; pôr ao ombro; arcar com, assumir; **~-blade** omoplata *f*

shout [ʃaut] *s* grito *m*; *v/t*, *v/i* gritar; **~ing** *s* gritaria *f*

shove [ʃʌv] *v/t*, *v/i* empurrar; *s* empurrão *m*

shovel ['ʃʌvl] *s* pá *f*

show [ʃəu] *v/t*, *v/i* mostrar(-se); indicar, assinalar; revelar; *s* espe(c)táculo *m*; exposição *f*; **~ off** *v/i* realçar; exibir-se; **~ up** *v/t*, *v/i* desmascarar; aparecer; **~-case** mostruário *m*

shower ['ʃauə] *s* aguaceiro *m*; ducha *f*, chuveiro *m*; duche *m*; *v/i* tomar um duche; chover
showing ['ʃəuiŋ] *s* exibição *f*, demonstração *f*
showy ['ʃəui] vistoso
shred [ʃred] *v/t* retalhar; *s* retalho *m*
shrew [ʃru:] megera *f*, víbora *f*; *zoo* musaranho *m*
shrewd [ʃru:d] astuto, perspicaz
shriek [ʃri:k] *v/t*, *v/i* guinchar; *s* guincho *m*
shrill [ʃril] penetrante; estridente
shrimp [ʃrimp] camarão *m*
shrine [ʃrain] *s* relicário *m*; santuário *m*
shrink [ʃriŋk] *v/t*, *v/i* encolher (-se)
shrivel ['ʃrivəl] *v/t*, *v/i* enrugar (-se)
shroud [ʃraud] *s* mortalha *f*
Shrove Tuesday [ˌʃrəuv'tju:zdi] Terça-Feira *f* de Entrudo
shrub [ʃrʌb] arbusto *m*
shrug [ʃrʌg] *v/t*, *v/i* encolher os ombros; *s* encolhimento *m* de ombros
shudder ['ʃʌdə] *s* tremor *m*, arrepio *m*; *v/i* tremer, estremecer
shuffle ['ʃʌfl] *v/t*, *v/i* baralhar; arrastar os pés; *s* arrasto *m* de pés
shun [ʃʌn] *v/t* evitar
shunt [ʃʌnt] *v/t* desviar, manobrar
shut [ʃʌt] *v/t*, *v/i* cerrar, tapar; fechar(-se); *adj* fechado; **~ter** *s* gelosia *f*, postigo *m*; obturador *m*
shuttle ['ʃʌtl] *s* lançadeira *f*; **~cock** volante *m*
shut up *v/i* calar-se
shy [ʃai] *adj* tímido, acanhado; **~ness** timidez *f*
sick [sik] doente; enjoado; **~ of** farto de; **~ening** ['-niŋ] nauseabundo, repugnante
sickle ['sikl] foice *f*, foicinha *f*
sick|ly ['sikli] doentio, débil, fraco; **~ness** doença *f*; náusea *f*, enjoo *m*
side [said] *adj* lateral; secundário; suplementar; *v/i* (**with**) tomar o partido (de); *s* lado *m*; ilharga *f*, flanco *m*; costado *m*; margem *f*, borda *f*; **~ by ~** lado a lado
side|board ['saidbɔ:d] aparador *m*; **~long** *adj* de esguelha, de lado; **~walk** passeio *m*; **~way(s)** *adv* lateralmente, de lado
siding ['saidiŋ] *s* ramal *m*, desvio *m*
sidle ['saidl] *v/i* (**up to**) aproximar-se (de)
siege [si:dʒ] cerco *m*, sítio *m*
sieve [siv] *s* peneira *f*, crivo *m*; *v/t* peneirar
sift [sift] *v/t*, *v/i* examinar, esquadrinhar; joeirar, peneirar
sigh [sai] *s* suspiro *m*; *v/i* suspirar
sight [sait] *v/t* avistar; *s* vista *f*, visão *f*; cena *f*, espe(c)táculo *m*; **at first ~** à primeira vista; **by ~** de vista; **in ~ of** à vista

de; **catch ~ of** avistar; **out of ~** fora do alcance da vista; **lose ~ of** perder de vista

sight|ly ['saitli] agradável à vista; **~seeing** visita *f* a lugares de interesse

sign [sain] *v/t, v/i* assinar; *s* sinal *m*, marca *f*; indício *m*, indicação *f*; signo *m*

signal ['signl] *s* sinal *m*; *v/t* fazer sinais (de); sinalizar

signature ['signitʃə] assinatura *f*

signboard ['sainbɔ:d] tabuleta *f*

signet ['signit] sinete *m*

signific|ance [sig'nifikəns] significação *f*; **~ant** significante

signify ['signifai] *v/t* significar

signpost ['sainpəust] poste *m* indicador

silen|ce ['sailəns] *s* silêncio *m*; *v/t* fazer calar; **~cer** AUTO silenciador *m*; **~t** *adj* silencioso

silk [silk] seda *f*; **~worm** bicho-da-seda *m*; **~y** sedoso

sill [sil] peitoril *m*

silly ['sili] *adj* estúpido, tolo, bobo

silver ['silvə] *s* prata *f*; *adj* de prata, prateado; **~smith** ourives *m* de prata

similar ['similə] parecido, semelhante; **~ity** [,-'læriti] semelhança *f*

simmer ['simə] *v/t, v/i* ferver a fogo lento

simper ['simpə] *s* sorriso *m* afe(c)tado

simple ['simpl] *adj* simples; singelo

simpl|icity [sim'plisiti] simplicidade *f*; **~ify** ['simplifai] *v/t* simplificar; **~y** ['simpli] simplesmente

simulate ['simjuleit] *v/t* simular

simultaneous [,siməl'teinjəs] simultâneo

sin [sin] *v/i* pecar; *s* pecado *m*

since [sins] *adv* desde então; *prp* desde; *conj* desde que; já que, visto que; **long ~** há muito

sincer|e [sin'siə] sincero; **~ity** [-'seriti] sinceridade *f*

sinew ['sinju:] tendão *m*; **~y** duro, cheio de nervos

sinful ['sinfəl] pecaminoso; pecador

sing [siŋ] *v/t, v/i* cantar

singe [sindʒ] *v/t* chamuscar

singer ['siŋə] cantor *m*

single ['siŋgl] *adj* solteiro; só, único; simples; de ida; individual **~ file** fila *f* indiana; **~-minded** sincero, franco

singular ['siŋgjulə] *adj, s* singular *m*; **~ity** [,-'læriti] singularidade *f*

sinister ['sinistə] sinistro

sink [siŋk] *s* lava-louça *m*, pia *f*; *v/t, v/i* afundar(-se); pôr a pique; ir a pique

sinner ['sinə] pecador *m*

sinuous ['sinjuəs] sinuoso

sip [sip] *v/t, v/i* sorver; *s* sorvo *m*

siphon ['saifən] *s* sifão *m*

sir [sə:] senhor *m*

siren ['saiərin] sereia *f*; sirena *f*

sirloin ['sə:lɔin] lombo *m* de vaca
sister ['sistə] irmã *f*; **~-in-law** cunhada *f*
sit [sit] *v/t, v/i* sentar(-se); estar sentado; pousar, empoleirar-se; ficar/estar situado; reunir-se em sessão; posar; chocar; **~ up** *v/t, v/i* ficar até tarde, deitar-se tarde; endireitar-se
site [sait] *s* local *m*, sítio *m*; terreno *m*
sitting ['sitiŋ] *adj* sentado; *s* sessão *f*; **~-room** sala *f* de estar
situat|ed ['sitjueitid] *adj* situado, sito, colocado; **~ion** situação *f*
six [siks] seis; **~ hundred** seiscentos; **~teen** ['-'ti:n] dezasseis; **~th** [-θ] sexto; **~ty** sessenta
size [saiz] *s* tamanho *m*; medida *f*, número *m*
sizzle ['sizl] *v/i* chiar
skate [skeit] *s* patim *m*; *zoo* arraia *f*; *v/i* patinar; andar de patins
skating-rink ['skeitiŋriŋk] recinto *m* de patinagem
skeleton ['skelitn] esqueleto *m*
sketch [sketʃ] *s* esboço *m*, bosquejo *m*; *v/t, v/i* esboçar, bosquejar
ski [ski:] *s* esqui *m*; *v/i* esquiar, andar de esqui
skid [skid] *v/i* derrapar; *s* derrapagem *f*
skil(l)ful ['skilful] destro, hábil
skill [skil] perícia *f*, destreza *f*, habilidade *f*; **~ed** *adj* perito, especializado
skim [skim] *v/t* roçar; escumar; desnatar; tirar a nata a
skin [skin] *s* pele *f*; casca *f*; *v/t* esfolar; descascar; **~-deep** superficial; **~flint** sovina *m, f*; **~ny** magro, descarnado
skip [skip] *v/t, v/i* saltar, pular; omitir; *s* salto *m*, pulo *m*
skirmish ['skə:miʃ] *s* escaramuça *f*; *v/i* escaramuçar
skirt [skə:t] *s* saia *f*; *v/t* costear, marginar
skittles ['skitlz] *s* jogo *m* da bola aos pinos, *Braz* jogo *m* de boliche
skull [skʌl] crânio *m*
sky [skai] *s* (*pl* **skies**) céu *m*; **~-blue** azul-celeste; **~lark** *s* cotovia *f*; **~light** clarabóia *f*; **~scraper** arranha-céus *m*
slab [slæb] chapa *f*, laje *f*; tábua *f*, prancha *f*
slack [slæk] *v/i* mandriar; *adj* frouxo, lasso, bambo; negligente; **~en** *v/t, v/i* afrouxar; relaxar; diminuir; **~s** *s/pl* calças *f/pl*
slag [slæg] escória *f*
slake [sleik] *v/t* mitigar, satisfazer
slam [slæm] *v/t, v/i* bater, fechar com violência; *s* pancada *f*, batimento *m*; capote *m*
slander ['slɑ:ndə] *v/t* difamar, caluniar; *s* calúnia *f*, difamação *f*
slang [slæŋ] *s* calão *m*, gíria *f*
slant [slɑ:nt] *s* inclinação *f*; *v/t, v/i* inclinar(-se)
slap [slæp] *s* palmada *f*, bofeta-

da *f*; *v/t* esbofetear
slash [slæʃ] *s* cutilada *f*; *v/t*, *v/i* acutilar, retalhar
slate [sleit] *s* lousa *f*; ardósia *f*; telha *f*; *v/t* censurar
slaughter ['slɔ:tə] *s* matança *f*, carnificina *f*; *v/t* matar, massacrar; abater; **~-house** matadoiro *m*, açougue *m*
slave [sleiv] *s* escravo *m*; **~ry** escravidão *f*
Slavic ['slævik] *adj* eslavo
sled(ge) [sled(ʒ)] *s* trenó *m*; *v/i* andar de trenó
sleek [sli:k] *adj* liso, macio
sleep [sli:p] *s* sono *m*; *v/i* dormir; **go to ~** adormecer; **~ing-bag** saco *m* de dormir; **~less** sem dormir; **~-walker** sonâmbulo *m*; **~y** sonolento, amodorrado, com sono
sleet [sli:t] *s* pedrisco *m*
sleeve [sli:v] manga *f*; **laugh up one's ~** rir-se à socapa
sleigh [slei] *s* trenó *m* de cavalo
slender ['slendə] franzino, esbelto, fino
slice [slais] *s* fatia *f*; *v/t* cortar em fatias
slick [slik] *adj* escorregadio; manhoso
slide [slaid] *v/t*, *v/i* resvalar, deslizar, escorregar; esgueirar-se; *s* diapositivo *m*; resvaladouro *m*
sliding ['slaidiŋ] *adj* corrediço, corredio
slight [slait] *adj* leve, ligeiro; pequeno, curto; fraco; *s* afronta *f*; *v/t* desprezar, desdenhar; **~ly** levemente
slim [slim] *adj* diminuto; franzino, esbelto; *v/i* emagrecer
slim|e [slaim] limo *m*; **~y** limoso
sling [sliŋ] *s* funda *f*; tiracolo *m*; *v/t* suspender; arrojar, atirar, arremessar
slip [slip] *s* escorregadela *f*; combinação *f*; deslize *m*, lapso *m*; tira *f* de papel; *v/i* escorregar, resvalar; escapulir-se; enfiar
slipper ['slipə] chinelo *m*, chinela *f*
slippery ['slipəri] escorregadio
slit [slit] *s* fenda *f*; *v/t* fender
slobber ['slɔbə] *s* baba *f*; *v/t*, *v/i* babar(-se)
sloe [sləu] abrunho *m*
slogan ['sləugən] divisa *f*, lema *m*
slope [sləup] *s* inclinação *f*; *s* ladeira *f*, rampa *f*, declive *m*; *v/i* inclinar-se; **~ off** escapulir-se
sloppy ['slɔpi] desmazelado; piegas, lamecha
slot [slɔt] *s* ranhura *f*
sloth [sləuθ] *zoo* preguiça *f*
slot-machine ['slɔtmə͵ʃi:n] automático *m*
slouch [slautʃ] *v/i* andar curvado
slough [slau] *s* lamaçal *m*
slovenly ['slʌvnli] desleixado
slow [sləu] *adj* lento, vagaroso; atrasado; *v/t*, *v/i* abrandar, afrouxar a velocidade **~ly** devagar, vagarosamente; **~ness** lentidão *f*
slug [slʌg] *s* *zoo* lesma *f*

sluice [slu:s] *s* comporta *f*
slum [slʌm] *s* bairro *m* da lata, *Braz* favela *f*
slur [slə:] mancha *f*, desdoiro *m*; *v/t* arrastar, engolir (*as palavras*); MUS modular
slush [slʌʃ] lama *f*; neve *f* lamacenta
sly [slai] astuto; dissimulado, manhoso
smack [smæk] *s* estalo *m*; pancada *f*, palmada *f*; sabor *m*, gosto *m*; beijoca *f*; *v/t* espancar; estalar
small [smɔ:l] *adj* pequeno; miúdo, ténue, exíguo; **~ change** troco *m* miúdo; **~ hours** altas horas *f/pl* da noite; **~ness** pequenez *f*
smallpox ['smɔ:lpɔks] varíola *f*
smalls [smɔ:lz] *s/pl* roupa *f* miúda
small talk [smɔ:l 'tɔ:k] conversa *f* banal
smart [sma:t] *adj* vivo, hábil, engenhoso; elegante; inteligente; *v/i* picar; doer; **~ness** elegância *f*
smash [smæʃ] *v/t*, *v/i* esmagar (-se); quebrar, espatifar; *s* colisão *f*, acidente *m*; **~ing** *adj* formidável, bestial
smear [smiə] *v/t*, *v/i* cobrir, untar; caluniar; *s* mancha *f*, nódoa *f*; difamação *f*
smell [smel] *s* odor *m*, cheiro *m*, aroma *m*; olfa(c)to *m*; *v/t*, *v/i* cheirar
smelt [smelt] *v/t* fundir
smil|e [smail] *v/t*, *v/i* sorrir; *s* sorriso *m*; **~ing** *adj* sorridente, risonho
smirk [smə:k] *s* sorriso *m* afe(c)tado; *v/i* sorrir afe(c)tadamente
smith [smiθ] forjador *m*; **~y** ['-ði] forja *f*
smitten ['smitn] enamorado, apaixonado
smog [smɔg] nevoeiro *m* de fumos
smoke [sməuk] *s* fumo *m*; fumaça *f*; *v/t*, *v/i* fumar; fumegar; **~-free** de não fumador; **~less** sem fumo, sem fumaça
smok|er ['sməukə] fumador *m*, fumista *m*, *f*; **~ing** *s* fumar *m*; **no ~ing** é proibido fumar; **~y** fumegante, fumarento
smooth [smu:ð] *adj* macio; liso, plano
smother ['smʌðə] *v/t*, *v/i* abafar, sufocar
smo(u)lder ['sməuldə] *v/i* arder sem chama; estar latente
smudge [smʌdʒ] *s* mancha *f*, nódoa *f*; borrão *m*; *v/t* manchar; borrar
smuggl|e ['smʌgl] *v/t* passar em contrabando; fazer contrabando; **~er** contrabandista *m*, *f*; **~ing** *s* contrabando *m*
smut [smʌt] *s* farrusca *f*, mascarra *f*; obscenidade *f*; **~ty** sujo, tisnado; obsceno
snack [snæk] *s* refeição *f* ligeira
snag [snæg] *s* empecilho *m*, obstáculo *m*
snail [sneil] caracol *m*; **at a ~'s pace** como um caracol

snake [sneik] *s* cobra *f*
snap [snæp] *s* estalo *m*, estalido *m*; *v/t*, *v/i* abocanhar; tirar um instantâneo (de); romper, quebrar; (fazer) estalar; **~pish** resmungão; **~shot** instantâneo *m*
snare [snɛə] *s* laço *m*, armadilha *f*; cilada *f*
snarl [snɑ:l] *v/t*, *v/i* rosnar; resmungar; *s* rosnadura *f*
snatch [snætʃ] *s* bocado *m*; *v/t*, *v/i* arrebatar
sneak [sni:k] *s* delator *m*
sneaker ['sni:kə] alpergatas *f/pl*; sapatos *m/pl* de ginástica
sneer [sniə] *v/i* mofar, zombar; *s* riso *m* zombador
sneeze [sni:z] *v/i* espirrar; *s* espirro *m*
sniff [snif] *s* fungad(el)a *f*; *v/i* farejar; cheirar; fungar; **~ at** torcer o nariz, desdenhar
snip [snip] *v/t*, *v/i* cortar; *s* tesourada *f*
snipe [snaip] *s* narceja *f*
snob [snɔb] snobe *m*, *Braz* esnobe *m*
snoop [snu:p] *v/i* meter o nariz em, bisbilhotar
snooze [snu:z] *s* soneca *f*; *v/i* dormitar
snore [snɔ:] *v/i* ressonar, roncar; *s* ronco *m*
snort [snɔ:t] *v/i* bufar
snout [snaut] focinho *m*
snow [snəu] *s* neve *f*; *v/i* nevar; **~-storm** nevasca *f*; **~y** nevoso
snub [snʌb] *v/t* desprezar, ignorar; *s* desdenho *m*; **~-nosed** de nariz chato
snuff [snʌf] *s* rapé *m*
snug [snʌg] *adj* aconchegado, agasalhado; cómodo, confortável
so [səu] *adv* assim; portanto, por isso; tão; tanto; *conj* para que; de maneira que; **~ as to** de maneira a; **~ long!** adeus!, até logo!; **~ then** com que então; **~ much** tanto; **and ~ on** e assim por diante; **I hope ~** espero que sim; **I think ~** creio que sim
soak [səuk] *v/t*, *v/i* embeber (-se), ensopar(-se), encharcar (-se)
soap [səup] *s* sabão *m*; sabonete *m*; *v/t* ensaboar
soar [sɔ:] *v/i* elevar-se, remontar-se
sob [sɔb] *s* soluço *m*; *v/i* soluçar
sober ['səubə] *adj* sóbrio; *v/t*, *v/i* moderar; **~ up** desembriagar-se
sobriety [səu'braiəti] sobriedade *f*
so-called ['səu'kɔ:ld] assim chamado
soccer ['sɔkə] futebol *m*
sociable ['səuʃəbl] sociável
social ['səuʃəl] social; **~ist** *adj*, *s* socialista *m*, *f*; **~ize** *v/t* socializar
society [sə'saiəti] (*pl* **-ties**) sociedade *f*
sociology [ˌsəusi'ɔlədʒi] sociologia *f*
sock [sɔk] *s* soquete *m*, meia *f*, peúga *f*

socket ['sɔkit] encaixe *m*; órbita *f*; alvéolo *m*; ELECT tomada *f*
sod [sɔd] *s* céspede *m*, torrão *m*
soda ['səudə] soda *f*
sodden ['sɔdn] ensopado, encharcado
sofa ['səufə] sofá *m*
soft [sɔft] mole, macio, tenro; brando, suave; flexível. **~en** ['sɔfn] *v/t*, *v/i* amaciar, amolecer; enternecer; suavizar; **~ness** macieza *f*, doçura *f*; suavidade *f*
soil [sɔil] *s* solo *m*, terra *f*; *v/t*, *v/i* sujar, manchar
solace ['sɔləs] *s* consolação *f*
solder ['sɔldə] *v/t* soldar
soldier ['səuldʒə] *s* soldado *m*
sole [səul] *adj* só, único; *s* sola *f*; planta *f* do pé; ZOO linguado *m*
solemn ['sɔləm] solene; **~ity** [sə'lemniti] (*pl* **-ties**) solenidade *f*
solicit [sə'lisit] *v/t*, *v/i* pedir, solicitar; **~or** procurador *m*
solicit|ous [sə'lisitəs] solícito; ansioso; **~ude** [-tju:d] ansiedade *f*
solid ['sɔlid] sólido
solidarity ['sɔli'dæriti] solidariedade *f*
solidity [sə'liditi] solidez *f*
solitary ['sɔlitəri] *adj* solitário
solitude ['sɔlitju:d] solidão *f*
solo ['səuləu] *s* MUS solo *m*
sol|uble ['sɔljubl] solúvel; **~ution** [sə'lu∫ən] solução *f*
solve [sɔlv] *v/t* resolver
solvent ['sɔlvənt] *adj* solvente
sombre ['sɔmbə] sombrio
some [sʌm] *adj* um pouco de; um, uma; certo, certa; algun(s), alguma(s), uns, umas; *pron* algum(s), alguma(s); um pouco, certa quantidade; *adv* um tanto; **~body**, **~one** alguém; **~how** de algum modo
somersault ['sʌməsɔ:lt] *s* cambalhota *f*; salto *m* mortal
some|thing ['sʌmθiŋ] *adv* algo, um tanto; *pron* alguma coisa; qualquer coisa; **~time** *adv* algum dia; outrora, antigamente; **~times** às/por vezes; **~what** um tanto, algo; **~where** nalgum sítio, algures
somnambul|ism [sɔm'næmbjulizəm] sonambulismo *m*; **~ist** sonâmbulo *m*
son [sʌn] filho *m*
song [sɔŋ] canção *f*
son-in-law ['sʌninlɔ:] genro *m*
sonorous [sə'nɔ:rəs] sonoro
soon [su:n] em breve; **the ~er the better** quanto mais depressa melhor; **no ~er ... than** mal; **~er or later** mais cedo ou mais tarde
soot [sut] *s* fuligem *f*
soothe [su:ð] *v/t* acalmar; aliviar
sophisticated [sə'fistikeitid] *adj* sofisticado
sorcer|er ['sɔ:sərə] feiticeiro *m*; **~ess** feiticeira *f*; **~y** feitiçaria *f*
sordid ['sɔ:did] sórdido; **~ness** sordidez *f*
sore [sɔ:] *adj* inflamado; dorido; magoado; *s* úlcera *f*, chaga *f*

sorrow ['sɔrəu] *s* pesar *m*, tristeza *f*, dor *f*; **~ful** pesaroso, triste
sorry ['sɔri] *adj* triste, desconsolado; **~!** desculpe!, sinto muito; **be/feel ~ for** ter/sentir pena de
sort [sɔːt] *s* gênero *m*, espécie *f*; *v/t* classificar; sele(c)cionar; separar
sot [sɔt] bêbedo *m*
soul [səul] *s* alma *f*; **~ful** sentimental
sound [saund] *adj* são, sadio; bom, sólido; profundo; *s* som *m*; *v/t*, *v/i* tocar; sondar; MED auscultar; soar, ressoar
soup [suːp] sopa *f*
sour ['sauə] *adj* azedo; *v/t*, *v/i* azedar
source [sɔːs] fonte *f*, origem *f*, manancial *m*
souse [saus] *v/t* pôr de escabeche; ensopar, empapar
south [sauθ] *s* sul *m*; *adv* ao sul; *adj* do sul, meridional; **~ward(s)** ['-wəd(s)] *adv* para o sul
souther|ly ['sʌðəli] meridional; **~n** meridional, do sul
south-west ['sauθ'west] *s* sudoeste *m*
souvenir ['suːvəniə] lembrança *f*
sovereign ['sɔvrin] *adj*, *s* soberano *m*; **~ty** ['-rənti] soberania *f*
sow [sau] *s* porca *f*; [səu] *v/t*, *v/i* semear
spa [spɑː] estância *f* termal
space [speis] *s* espaço *m*; *v/t* espaçar; **~-ship** nave *f* espacial
spacious ['speiʃəs] espaçoso
spade [speid] *s* pá *f*; espadas *f/pl*
spam [spæm] *s* COMP spam
span [spæn] *s* período *m*, espaço *m*; envergadura *f*; palmo *m*; *v/t* atravessar; abarcar, cobrir
spangle ['spæŋgl] *s* lentejoula *f*
Spaniard ['spænjəd] espanhol *m*
spaniel ['spænjəl] sabujo *m*
Spanish ['spæniʃ] *adj*, *s* espanhol *m*
spank [spæŋk] *v/t* espancar
spanner ['spænə] chave *f* de parafusos
spare [spɛə] *v/t* dispensar, passar sem; poupar; dispor de; *adj* magro; de sobra, sobresselente, de reserva; sóbrio, frugal; disponível
spark [spɑːk] *s* centelha *f*, fagulha *f*, faísca *f*, chispa *f*; **~ing-plug** AUTO vela *f* de ignição; **~le** ['-l] *v/i* cintilar, faiscar
sparrow ['spærəu] pardal *m*
sparse [spɑːs] escasso; ralo; raro
spasm ['spæzəm] espasmo *m*
spatter ['spætə] *v/t* salpicar; *s* salpico *m*
speak [spiːk] *v/t*, *v/i* falar; **so to ~** por assim dizer; **~ one's mind** falar com franqueza; **~ for** falar por; **~ out** falar abertamente; **~ up** falar alto; **~er** orador *m*; presidente *m*

spear [spiə] *s* lança *f*
special ['speʃəl] *adj* especial; **~ist** especialista *m, f*; **~(i)ty** [ˌ-ʃi'æliti] (*pl* **-ties**) especialidade *f*; **~ize** *v/i* especializar-se
species ['spi:ʃi:z] espécie *f*
specific [spi'sifik] *adj* específico
specify ['spesifai] *v/t* especificar
specimen ['spesimin] exemplar *m*, espécime *m*
speck [spek] ponto *m*; mancha *f*; partícula *f*; **~le** pinta *f*, salpico *m*
spectac|le ['spektəkl] espe(c)táculo *m*; **~les** *s/pl* óculos *m/pl*; **~ular** [-'tækjulə] *adj* espe(c)tacular
spectator [spek'teitə] espectador *m*
speculate ['spekjuleit] *v/t, v/i* especular
speculation [ˌspekju'leiʃən] especulação *f*
speech [spi:tʃ] maneira *f* de falar; palavra *f*, fala *f*; discurso *m*; **~less** sem fala
speed [spi:d] *s* velocidade *f*; rapidez *f*; *v/i* seguir a grande velocidade; acelerar; **~-dial button** TEL botão *m* de marcação rápida; **~ limit** limite *m* de velocidade; **~ometer** [-'dɔmitə] conta-quilómetros *m*, velocímetro *m*; **~y** veloz, rápido
spell [spel] *v/t, v/i* soletrar; escrever; *s* encanto *m*, feitiço *m*; **~bound** encantado, fascinado; **~checker** COMP verificador *m* ortográfico; **~ing** *s* ortografia *f*
spend [spend] *v/t, v/i* passar; despender, gastar; consumir; **~thrift** esbanjador *m*, perdulário *m*, pródigo *m*
spent [spent] *adj* gasto; esgotado, estafado
sperm [spə:m] esperma *m*
sphere [sfiə] esfera *f*
spice [spais] *s* especiaria *f*
spick and span [ˌspikən'spæn] novo em folha, flamante
spicy ['spaisi] condimentado; apimentado
spider ['spaidə] aranha *f*
spike [spaik] *s* espigão *m*; ponta *f*; cavilha *f*
spill [spil] *v/t, v/i* derramar, entornar; *s* queda *f*
spin [spin] *v/t, v/i* tecer, fiar; rodar, girar; *s* giro *m*, volta *f*
spinach ['spinidʒ] espinafre *m*
spinal ['spainl] espinhal
spindle ['spindl] fuso *m*
spine [spain] espinha *f* dorsal
spinning-wheel ['spiniŋwi:l] roda *f* de fiar
spinster ['spinstə] solteirona *f*
spiral ['spaiərəl] *adj* (em) espiral; *s* espiral *f*
spire ['spaiə] flecha *f*, agulha *f*
spirit ['spirit] *s* espírito *m*; ânimo *m*; energia *f*; **~ed** *adj* animado, vivaz; fogoso, brioso; **~less** sem ânimo, sem vigor; **~ual** ['-tjuəl] *adj* espiritual; **~ualism** [spi'ritjuəlizəm] espiritismo *m*; **~ualist** espírita *m, f*
spit [spit] *s* cuspe *m*; espeto *m*;

v/t, v/i espetar; cuspir
spite [spait] *s* rancor *m*, despeito *m*; **in ~ of** apesar de, a despeito de; **~ful** vingativo, malévolo
spittle ['spitl] escarro *m*
splash [splæʃ] *v/t, v/i* patinhar, chapinhar; salpicar; *s* salpico *m*; chape *m*
spleen [spli:n] baço *m*; mau humor *m*
splend|id ['splendid] esplêndido; **~o(u)r** esplendor *m*
splint [splint] tala *f*
splinter ['splintə] *s* lasca *f*, estilhaço *m*; *v/t, v/i* estilhaçar(-se)
split [split] *v/t, v/i* separar-se; fender; *s* fenda *f*, greta *f*
spoil [spɔil] *v/t, v/i* estragar (-se); (a)mimar; **~t child** mimalho *m*; **~s** *s/pl* emolumentos *m/pl*
spoke [spəuk] *s* raio *m*
spokesman ['spəuksmən] (*pl* **-men** ['-men]) porta-voz *m, f*, representante *m, f*
sponge [spʌndʒ] *s* esponja *f*; *v/t* lavar com esponja
sponsor ['spɔnsə] *s* patrocinador *m*; fiador *m*; padrinho *m*; *v/t* promover, patrocinar
spontaneous [spɔn'teinjəs] espontâneo
spook [spu:k] *s* fantasma *m*
spool [spu:l] bobina *f*; carretel *m*; rolo *m*
spoon [spu:n] *s* colher *f*; **~ful** colherada *f*
sporadic [spə'rædik] esporádico
sport [spɔ:t] *s* desporto *m*, *Braz* esporte *m*; *v/t* ostentar; **~ing** *adj* desportivo, *Braz* esportivo; **~ive** brincalhão; **~sman** desportista *m*, *Braz* esportista *m*
spot [spɔt] *s* sítio *m*, lugar *m*; ponto *m*; mancha *f*, nódoa *f*; *v/t, v/i* manchar(-se); enodoar, sujar; notar, reconhecer; **~light** *s* holofote *m*; publicidade *f*
spout [spaut] *s* jacto *m*, jorro *m*; goteira *f*; bico *m*; *v/t, v/i* jorrar; declamar
sprain [sprein] *v/t* torcer; *s* torcedura *f*, entorse *f*
sprat [spræt] espadilha *f*
sprawl [sprɔ:l] *v/i* estender-se; estatelar-se
spray [sprei] *s* borrifo *m*; espuma *f*; pulverizador *m*, vaporizador *m*; *v/t* borrifar; pulverizar
spread [spred] *v/t, v/i* espalhar (-se); abrir; estender(-se); propagar(-se); *s* extensão *f*; envergadura *f*
sprig [sprig] vergôntea *f*, raminho *m*
sprightly ['spraitli] esperto, vivo, alegre
spring [spriŋ] *s* primavera *f*; mola *f*; pulo *m*, salto *m*; fonte *f*; *v/i* pular, saltar, galgar; **~-board** trampolim *m*
sprinkle ['spriŋkl] *s* chuvisco *m*; *v/t, v/i* chuviscar; aspergir, borrifar
sprint [sprint] *v/i* correr a toda a

velocidade
sprout [spraut] *s* renovo *m*, grelo *m*; couve-de-bruxelas *f*; *v/t*, *v/i* grelar, brotar
spruce [spru:s] *adj* elegante, janota
spur [spə:] *s* espora *f*; *v/t* esporear
spurt [spə:t] *v/i* esguichar; *s* esguicho *m*; arranco *m*; esforço *m*
spy [spai] *s* (*pl* **spies**) espia *m, f*, espião *m*; *v/i* espiar; espreitar; descortinar, notar
squabble ['skwɔbl] *s* briga *f*, rixa *f*; *v/i* brigar, bulhar
squadron ['skwɔdrən] esquadrão *m*; NAUT esquadra *f*
squalid ['skwɔlid] esquálido, sujo
squall [skwɔ:l] *s* berro *m*; ventania *f*, pé *m* de vento
squalor ['skwɔlə] sordidez *f*
squander ['skwɔndə] *v/t* esbanjar, malgastar
square [skwɛə] *s* quadrado *m*; praça *f*; *adj* quadrado, *v/t* quadrar, esquadr(i)ar; ajustar
squash [skwɔʃ] *s* suco *m*, sumo *m*; *v/t*, *v/i* espremer, esmagar; achatar
squat [skwɔt] *v/i* agachar-se, acocorar-se; *adj* atarracado
squeak [skwi:k] *s* chiadeira *f*; grito *m*, chio *m*; *v/i* chiar, ranger
squeal [skwi:l] *v/i* guinchar; *s* guincho *m*
squeamish ['skwi:miʃ] melindroso
squeeze [skwi:z] *v/t*, *v/i* comprimir; espremer; apertar; *s* apertão *m*
squid [skwid] lula *f*, calamar *m*
squint [skwint] *s* estrabismo *m*; *v/i* piscar os olhos
squire ['skwaiə] *s* escudeiro *m*
squirm [skwə:m] *v/i* contorcer--se
squirrel ['skwirəl] esquilo *m*
squirt [skwə:t] *v/t*, *v/i* esguichar; *s* esguicho *m*
stab [stæb] *v/t*, *v/i* apunhalar; *s* punhalada *f*
stabil|ity [stə'biliti] estabilidade *f*; **~ize** ['steibilaiz] *v/t*, *v/i* estabilizar
stable ['steibl] *s* estrebaria *f*, cavalariça *f*; *adj* estável
stack [stæk] *s* montão *m*; pilha *f*; *v/t* amontoar; empilhar
stadium ['steidiəm] estádio *m*
staff [sta:f] *s* MIL estado-maior *m*; corpo *m* docente, pessoal *m*; bordão *m*; bastão *m*; vara *f*; MUS pauta *f*
stag [stæg] veado *m*, cervo *m*
stage [steidʒ] *s* THEAT palco *m*; fase *f*; etapa *f*, *v/t* encenar, pôr em cena; organizar, preparar; representar; **~-coach** diligência *f*
stagger ['stægə] *v/i* titubear, cambalear; alternar; *s* cambaleio *m*
stagna|nt ['stægnənt] estagnante; **~te** ['-neit] *v/i* estagnar-se
staid [steid] grave, sério
stain [stein] *s* mancha *f*, nódoa

f; *v/t*, *v/i* manchar; tingir, pintar; **~ed glass** vitral *m*; **~less** inoxidável

stair [stɛə] degrau *m*; **~case** escadaria *f*; **~s** *s/pl* escada *f*

stake [steik] *s* estaca *f*, poste *m*; pelourinho *m*; aposta *f*; *v/t* marcar com estacas; apostar, arriscar; **at ~** em jogo, em risco

stale [steil] rançoso; seco, duro; velho, antiquado

stalk [stɔ:k] *s* haste *f*, talo *m*; pé *m*

stall [stɔ:l] *s* pesebre *m*; tenda *f*, barraca *f*; THEAT poltrona *f*; *v/t*, *v/i* parar, deixar de trabalhar

stallion ['stæljən] garanhão *m*

stalwart ['stɔ:lwət] *adj* resoluto, decidido

stammer ['stæmə] *v/t*, *v/i* gaguejar; tartamudear; *s* gaguez *f*

stamp [stæmp] selo *m*; estampilha *f*; cunho *m*; carimbo *m*; *v/t*, *v/i* selar, pôr selo em; estampar, imprimir; carimbar; bater com os pés

stanch [stɑ:ntʃ] *v/t* estancar

stand [stænd] *v/t*, *v/i* estar de/em pé; estar, estar situado; levantar-se, erguer-se, pôr(-se) de/em pé; colocar; aguentar, suportar; ficar; **~ by** *v/t*, *v/i* manter(-se); dar apoio a; estar de lado; **~ for** significar, representar; permitir, tolerar; **~ up** *v/t* resistir; *s* resistência *f*, defesa *f*; posição *f*, opinião *f*; estante *f*; praça *f* de táxis; tribuna *f*; bancada *f*; sítio *m*, posto *m*; tenda *f*, barraca *f*

standard ['stændəd] *s* padrão *m*; nível *m*; critério *m*, medida *f*; norma *f*; estandarte *m*, bandeira *f*; *adj* normal, clássico, oficial; **~ize** *v/t* estandardizar

standby ['stændbai] *s* reserva *f*

standing ['stændiŋ] *adj* permanente; em pé; *s* posição *f*, reputação *f*; **of ten years' ~** com dez anos de exercício; **of long ~** de longa data

stand|offish [stænd'ɔ:fiʃ] retraído, reservado; **~point** ponto *m* de vista; **~still** paragem *f*; imobilização *f*

star [stɑ:] *s* estrela *f*; astro *m*; *v/t*, *v/i* marcar com asteriscos; representar

starboard ['stɑ:bəd] estibordo *m*

starch [stɑ:tʃ] *s* amido *m*; goma *f*; fécula *f*; *v/t* engomar

stare [stɛə] *s* olhar *m* fixo; *v/i* fitar, olhar fixamente

stark [stɑ:k] *adj* completo, total; rígido

starling ['stɑ:liŋ] estorninho *m*

start [stɑ:t] *v/t*, *v/i* começar, principiar; estremecer; partir, iniciar viagem; *s* partida *f*; início *m*, começo *m*, princípio *m*; estremecimento *m*

startl|e ['stɑ:tl] *v/t* assustar, alarmar; **~ing** *adj* alarmante

starvation [stɑ:'veiʃən] fome *f*; inanição *f*

starve [stɑ:v] *v/t*, *v/i* passar fome; morrer de fome

state [steit] *s* estado *m*, condi-

ção *f*; estado *m*, nação *f*; pompa *f*; *v/t* declarar, expor; JUR depor, asseverar
stately ['steitli] augusto, majestoso
statement ['steitmənt] declaração *f*; relatório *m*; COM balanço *m*
statesman ['steitsmən] estadista *m*, homem *m* de estado
static ['stætik] *adj* estático
station ['steiʃən] *s* estação *f*; *v/t* estacionar, postar; **~ary** estacionário, fixo
station|er ['steiʃner] dono *m* de papelaria; **~ery** ['steiʃnri] artigos *m/pl* de escritório
statistic|al [stə'tistikəl] estatístico; **~s** estatística *f*
statue ['stætju:] estátua *f*
statute ['stætju:t] estatuto *m*
sta(u)nch [sta:ntʃ (stɔ:ntʃ)] *v/t* estancar; *adj* dedicado, leal
stay [stei] *s* NAUT estai *m*; estada *f*, estadia *f*; *v/i* ficar, permanecer, demorar-se
stead|fast ['stedfəst] constante, firme; **~y** *adj* firme; seguro, estável
steak [steik] bife *m*
steal [sti:l] *v/t*, *v/i* roubar, furtar
stealth [stelθ] recato *m*; **by ~** às furtadelas, às escondidas; **~y** furtivo, clandestino
steam [sti:m] *s* vapor *m*; *v/t*, *v/i* fumegar; cozinhar a vapor; deitar vapor; **~er** (navio *m* a) vapor *m*
steel [sti:l] *s* aço *m*; *v/t* acerar, revestir de aço; fortalecer-se, endurecer
steep [sti:p] *adj* escarpado, íngreme; exorbitante, excessivo
steeple ['sti:pl] torre *f*, campanário *m*
steeplechase ['sti:plitʃeis] corrida *f* de obstáculos
steer [stiə] *s* novilho *m*; *v/t*, *v/i* conduzir, dirigir, guiar; **~ing-wheel** volante *m*
stem [stem] *s* haste *f*, talo *m*; *v/t* represar; deter, conter
stench [stentʃ] fedor *m*
step [step] *s* passo *m*, passada *f*; degrau *m*; medida *f*; *v/i* dar um passo, andar, caminhar
step|daughter ['step,dɔ:tə] enteada *f*; **~father** padrasto *m*
step-ladder ['step,lædə] escadote *m*
stepmother ['step,mʌðə] madrasta *f*
stepping-stone ['steping stəun] alpondra *f*, passadeira *f*
stepson ['stepsən] enteado *m*
stereo ['stiəriəu] *adj* estereofónico
steril|e ['sterail] estéril; **~ity** [-'riliti] esterilidade *f*; **~ize** ['-rilaiz] *v/t* esterilizar
sterling ['stə:liŋ] *adj* esterlino; puro, nobre, verdadeiro
stern [stə:n] *adj* severo, austero; *s* popa *f*
stew [stju:] *s* guisado *m*, estufado *m*; *v/t*, *v/i* guisar, estufar
steward ['stjuəd] *s* despenseiro *m*; administrador *m*; criado *m* de bordo; hospedeiro *m* de bordo, acromoço *m*; **~ess** hos-

pedeira *f* de bordo, aeromoça *f*
stick [stik] *s* pau *m*, vara *f*; bengala *f*; *v/t, v/i* espetar; colar; encravar; cravar; afixar; atolar-se; deter-se; aderir; **~er** etiqueta *f* aderente; **~ to** manter-se fiel a; **~y** pegajoso, viscoso; desagradável, difícil
stiff [stif] *adj* rígido, teso; formal; **~en** *v/t, v/i* endurecer (-se); entesar(-se); **~ness** rigidez *f*, dureza *f*
stifle ['staifl] *v/t, v/i* sufocar; extinguir, suprimir; abafar
stigma ['stigmə] estigma *m*
still [stil] *adj* imóvel; calmo; sereno, tranquilo; *s* tranquilidade *f*, silêncio *m*; alambique *m*; *adv* ainda; todavia, contudo; *v/t* acalmar, sossegar; **~ life** natureza *f* morta; **~ness** calma *f*, silêncio *m*
stilt [stilt] anda *f*; **~ed** afe(c)tado, pomposo
stimulate ['stimjuleit] *v/t* estimular
sting [stiŋ] *v/t, v/i* arder, doer; picar, dar ferroadas em; *s* picada *f*, ferroada *f*
stingy ['stindʒi] avaro, avarento, mesquinho
stink [stiŋk] *s* fedor *m*; *v/i* feder, tresandar
stint [stint] *s* tarefa *f*
stipulate ['stipjuleit] *v/t* estipular
stir [stəː] *v/t, v/i* excitar, instigar; agitar, sacudir; bater, mexer; mover(-se); bulir; *s* rebuliço *m*; excitação *f*; agitação *f*, comoção *f*; **~ring** *adj* excitante; arrebatador; emocionante
stirrup ['stirəp] estribo *m*
stitch [stitʃ] *s* ponto *m*; MED pontada *f*; *v/t, v/i* coser, dar pontos (a)
stock [stɔk] *s* estoque *m*, sortido *m*; linhagem *f*, estirpe *f*; caldo *m*; COM a(c)ções *f/pl*; sortimento *m*; gado *m*; tronco *m*, cepo *m*; *v/t* fornecer, prover; sortir; acumular; **out of ~** esgotado; **~ade** [-'keid] estacada *f*; **~broker** corretor *m*; **~ exchange** bolsa *f* de valores
stocking ['stɔkiŋ] *s* meia *f*
stock|-jobber ['stɔkˌdʒɔbə] agiota *m*
stock-taking ['stɔkˌteikiŋ] inventário *m*
stocky ['stɔki] atarracado
stodgy ['stɔdʒi] indigesto; maçador, monótono
stoic ['stəuik] *adj, s* estóico *m*
stoke [stəuk] *v/t* atiçar
stole [stəul] *s* estola *f*
stolid ['stɔlid] estólido, impassível
stomach ['stʌmək] *s* estômago *m*
stone [stəun] *s* pedra *f*; gema *f*, pedra *f* preciosa; caroço *m*; MED cálculo *m*; 14 arráteis; *v/t* apedrejar; lapidar; descaroçar
stony ['stəuni] pedregoso; duro, cruel
stool [stuːl] tamborete *m*, escabelo *m*, mocho *m*
stoop [stuːp] *v/t, v/i* inclinar-se,

abaixar-se
stop [stɔp] *v/t, v/i* obstruir, tapar; parar, deter(-se); *s* paragem *f*, *Braz* parada *f*; ponto *m*; **~per** tampão *m*, rolha *f*, bucha *f*
storage ['stɔːridʒ] armazenagem *f*
store [stɔː] *v/t* armazenar, acumular; *s* abundância *f*; armazém *m*; depósito *m*; **~house** mina *f*, tesouro *m*; armazém *m*; **~-keeper** lojista *m*; **~-room** despensa *f*
stor(e)y ['stɔːri] andar *m*, pavimento *m*
stork [stɔːk] cegonha *f*
storm [stɔːm] *s* tempestade *f*, tormenta *f*; borrasca *f*; *v/t, v/i* vociferar; assaltar, atacar; **~y** tempestuoso, violento
story ['stɔːri] (*pl* **-ries**) história *f*, conto *m*; **~-book** livro *m* de histórias
stout [staut] *adj* corpulento; firme, sólido; intrépido; *s* cerveja *f* preta forte
stove [stəuv] *s* fogão *m*; estufa *f*
stow [stəu] *v/t* guardar, arrumar; **~away** *s* passageiro *m* clandestino
straddle ['strædl] *v/t, v/i* escarranchar-se, escanchar-se; escarrapachar
straight [streit] *adv* a direito, em linha re(c)ta; dire(c)tamente, imediatamente; sem rodeios; *adj* re(c)to; dire(c)to; honesto; em ordem; **~ away** imediatamente, já; **~en** *v/t* endireitar; arrumar; pôr em ordem; **~forward** [-'fɔːwəd] franco; claro
strain [strein] *v/t, v/i* forçar; torcer; estender; coar; esforçar-se; **~er** coador *m*
strait [streit] estreito *m*
strand [strænd] *s* fio *m*, fibra *f*; *v/t* encalhar; perder-se; **~ed** *adj* abandonado, perdido
strang|e [streindʒ] estranho; **~er** desconhecido *m*, forasteiro *m*
strangle ['strængl] *v/t* estrangular
strap [stræp] *s* correia *f*, tira *f*; alça *f*; *v/t* segurar com correia; amarrar; açoitar com uma correia; **~ping** *adj* robusto, forte, rijo
stratagem ['strætidʒəm] estratagema *m*
strateg|ic [strə'tiːdʒik] estratégico; **~ist** ['strætidʒist] estrategista *m*; **~y** ['strætidʒi] estratégia *f*
straw [strɔː] palha *f*
strawberry ['strɔːbəri] (*pl* **-ries**) morango *m*
stray [strei] *v/i* extraviar-se, perder-se; divagar; *adj* extraviado, desgarrado; *s* pessoa *f ou* animal *m* desgarrado
streak ['striːk] *s* listra *f*, risco *m*; *v/t, v/i* correr; listrar, riscar; **~y** listrado
stream [striːm] *s* corrente *f*; torrente *f*; riacho *m*, regato *m*; fluxo *m*, jacto *m*; *v/i* correr, fluir; afluir; jorrar, brotar

street [striːt] rua *f*; **~car** *US* (carro *m*) elé(c)trico *m*, *Braz* bonde *m*
strength [streŋθ] força *f*; vigor *m*, energia *f*; **~en** *v/t*, *v/i* fortificar(-se); fortalecer(-se)
strenuous ['strenjuəs] enérgico; intenso, agitado
stress [stres] *s* ênfase *f*; acento *m* tónico; pressão *f*, tensão *f*; *v/t* acentuar; realçar, frisar
stretch [stretʃ] *v/t*, *v/i* esticar (-se), estirar(-se); estender (-se); espreguiçar-se; *s* estiramento *m*; extensão *f*; trecho *m*; elasticidade *f*; período *m*, espaço *m*; re(c)ta *f* de chegada
stretcher ['stretʃə] maca *f*
strew [struː] *v/t* espalhar, espargir
stricken ['strikən] *adj* ferido; atacado, acometido
strict [strikt] estrito, rigoroso; severo
stride [straid] *v/i* andar a passos largos; *s* passo *m* largo, passada *f*
strife [straif] contenda *f*
strik|e [straik] *v/t*, *v/i* dar na vista, chamar a atenção; ocorrer; golpear, bater; tocar; fazer greve; *s* greve *f*; **~er** grevista *m*, *f*
striking ['straikiŋ] *adj* notável, impressionante
string [striŋ] *s* cordão *m*, cordel *m*, fio *m*, barbante *m*; MUS corda *f*; réstia *f*; chorrilho *m*
stringy ['striŋi] fibroso
strip [strip] *s* faixa *f*, tira *f*; *v/t*, *v/i* despojar; despir(-se)
stripe [straip] risca *f*, listra *f*
strive [straiv] *v/i* esforçar-se
stroke [strəuk] *s* golpe *m*, pancada *f*; rasgo *m*; braçada *f*; remada *f*; afago *m*; *v/t* acariciar, afagar
stroll [strəul] *s* volta *f*, passeio *m*; *v/i* passear, dar uma volta
strong [strɔŋ] forte, poderoso, vigoroso; **~hold** forte *m*, fortaleza *f*; cidadela *f*
structure ['strʌktʃə] *s* estrutura *f*
struggle ['strʌgl] *s* luta *f*; *v/i* lutar
strut [strʌt] *v/i* pavonear-se, empertigar-se
stub [stʌb] *s* ponta *f*, coto *m*; talão *m*, canhoto *m*
stubble ['stʌbl] restolho *m*; barba *f* hirsuta
stubborn ['stʌbən] teimoso, obstinado, cabeçudo
stuck-up ['stʌk'ʌp] *adj* presumido, vaidoso
stud [stʌd] *s* botão *m* de camisa; coudelaria *f*; tacha *f*; *v/t* tachonar
student ['stjuːdənt] estudante *m*, *f*
studied ['stʌdid] *adj* estudado, premeditado
studio ['stjuːdiəu] estúdio *m*
studious ['stjuːdjəs] estudioso
study ['stʌdi] *v/t*, *v/i* estudar; *s* (*pl* **-dies**) gabinete *m*; escritório *m*; estudo *m*
stuff [stʌf] *v/t*, *v/i* empanturrar-se; rechear; encher, atulhar; *s*

matéria *f*, material *m*; fazenda *f*
stuffing ['stʌfiŋ] *s* recheiro *m*
stuffy ['stʌfi] abafado; enfadonho
stumble ['stʌmbl] *v/i* tropeçar
stump [stʌmp] toco *m*, cepo *m*; coto *m*
stun [stʌn] *v/t* aturdir, atordoar; **~ning** *adj* formidável, esplêndido
stunt [stʌnt] *s* proeza *f*, façanha *f*
stupefy ['stju:pifai] *v/t* embasbacar
stupendous [stju(:)'pendəs] estupendo
stupid ['stju:pid] palerma, estúpido; **~ity** [-'pıditi] estupidez *f*
stupor ['stju:pə] estupor *m*
sturdy ['stə:di] robusto, vigoroso
sturgeon ['stə:dʒən] esturjão *m*
stutter ['stʌtə] *v/i* gaguejar; *s* gaguez *f*
sty [stai] (*pl* **-sties**) pocilga *f*, chiqueiro *m*
styl|e [stail] *s* estilo *m*; elegância *f*; **~ish** elegante, à moda
suave [swɑ:v] suave
subdue [səb'dju:] *v/t* subjugar, submeter; suavizar
subject ['sʌbdʒikt] *s* assunto *m*; sujeito *m*; sú(b)dito *m*; matéria *f*; *adj* sujeito; propenso; dominado; **~to** ['sʌbdʒikt tə] *prp* conforme, dependente; [səb'dʒekt] *v/t* sujeitar; **~ion** [səb'dʒekʃən] sujeição *f*; **~ive** [səb'dʒektiv] subje(c)tivo
subjugate ['sʌbdʒugeit] *v/t* subjugar
subjunctive [səb'dʒʌŋktiv] *s* conjuntivo *m*, subjuntivo
sublet ['sʌb'let] *v/t*, *v/i* subalugar, sublocar
sublime [sə'blaim] sublime
submarine [ˌsʌbmə'ri:n] *adj*, *s* submarino *m*
submerge [səb'mə:dʒ] *v/t*, *v/i* submergir(-se)
submission [səb'miʃən] submissão *f*
submit [səb'mit] *v/t*, *v/i* submeter(-se)
subordinate [sə'bɔ:dnit] *adj*, *s* subordinado *m*; *v/t* subordinar
subscrib|e [səb'skraib] *v/t*, *v/i* subscrever, assinar; **~er** assinante *m*, *f*; subscritor *m*
subscription [səb'skripʃən] subscrição *f*; assinatura *f*
subsequent ['sʌbsikwənt] subsequente
subsid|e [səb'said] *v/i* acalmar, assentar; aluir, abater-se; **~ence** derrocada *f*, aluimento *m*
subsid|iary [səb'sidiəri] *adj* subsidiário; **~ize** ['sʌbsidaiz] *v/t* subsidiar; **~y** (*pl* **-dies**) subsídio *m*
subsist [səb'sist] *v/i* subsistir, sustentar-se
substan|ce ['sʌbstəns] substância *f*; **~tial** [səb'stænʃəl] substancial
substitut|e ['sʌbstitju:t] *v/t*

substituir; *s* substituto *m*; **~ion** [-'tjuːʃən] substituição *f*
subterranean [ˌsʌbtə'reinjən] subterrâneo
subtle ['sʌtl] su(b)til
subtract [səb'trækt] *v/t* subtrair; **~ion** subtra(c)ção *f*
suburb ['sʌbəːb] subúrbio *m*; **~an** [sə'bəːbən] suburbano
subway ['sʌbwei] passagem *f* subterrânea; *US* metropolitano *m*
succeed [sək'siːd] *v/t*, *v/i* ter êxito; suceder a
success [sək'ses] sucesso *m*, êxito *m*; **~ful** feliz, próspero; **~ion** sucessão *f*, série *f*; **~ive** sucessivo; **~or** sucessor *m*
succinct [sək'siŋkt] sucinto
succulent ['sʌkjulənt] *adj* suculento
succumb [sə'kʌm] *v/i* sucumbir
such [sʌtʃ] tal; assim; **~ a** tal, semelhante; **~ as** tal como
suck [sʌk] *v/t*, *v/i* chuchar; mamar; chupar; sugar; **~le** *v/t* amamentar, dar de mamar a
sudden ['sʌdn] repentino, súbito; brusco; **all of a ~** de repente/súbito
sue [sjuː] *v/t* processar
suède [sweid] camurça *f*
suet ['sjuit] sebo *m*
suffer ['sʌfə] *v/t*, *v/i* sofrer, padecer; aguentar; **~er** sofredor *m*, vítima *f*; **~ing** *s* sofrimento *m*
suffice [sə'fais] *v/i* bastar
sufficien|cy [sə'fiʃənsi] suficiência *f*; **~t** suficiente
suffix ['sʌfiks] sufixo *m*
suffocat|e ['sʌfəkeit] *v/t*, *v/i* sufocar(-se); **~ion** [-'keiʃən] sufocação *f*
suffrage ['sʌfridʒ] sufrágio *m*
sugar ['ʃugə] *s* açúcar *m*; *v/t* açucarar; **~-beet** beterraba *f*; **~-cane** cana-de-açúcar *f*; **~y** açucarado
suggest [sə'dʒest] *v/t* sugerir; **~ion** sugestão *f*; **~ive** sugestivo
suicide ['sjuisaid] suicídio *m*; suicida *m*, *f*; **commit ~** suicidar-se
suit [sjuːt] *s* fato *m*, *Braz* terno *m*; fato *m* de saia e casaco; naipe *m*; *jur* pleito *m*; *v/t*, *v/i* convir; adaptar, ajustar; assentar, ficar bem
suitable ['sjuːtəbl] conveniente, apto, próprio, idóneo
suitcase ['sjuːtkeis] mala *f*
suite [swiːt] apartamento *m*; jogo *m* de móveis
suitor ['sjuːtə] litigante *m*, *f*
sulk [sʌlk] *v/i* amuar
sulky ['sʌlki] *adj* amuado
sullen ['sʌlən] carrancudo, rabugento; sombrio
sulphur ['sʌlfə] enxofre *m*
sultry ['sʌltri] abafadiço, abrasador
sum [sʌm] soma *f*, total *m*; **in ~** em suma
summarize ['sʌməraiz] *v/t* resumir
summary ['sʌməri] *s* (*pl* **-ries**) resumo *m*, sumário *m*
summer ['sʌmə] verão *m*, estio

m; ~ **time** hora *f* de verão
summit ['sʌmit] cimo *m*, cume *m*
summon ['sʌmən] *v/t* convocar; jur notificar; **~s** ['-z] *s* notificação *f*
sumptuous ['sʌmptjuəs] sumptuoso, *Braz* suntuoso
sun [sʌn] *s* sol *m*; *v/t* apanhar sol; **~-bathe** *v/i* tomar banhos de sol; **~-blind** toldo *m*; veneziana *f*; **~burnt** queimado, bronzeado; **♀ day** domingo *m*
sundry ['sʌndri] diversos
sun-flower ['sʌnˌflauə] girassol *m*
sunken ['sʌŋkən] *adj* submerso; encovado, fundo; cavado
sunny ['sʌni] soalheiro; radiante
sun|rise ['sʌnraiz] nascer *m* do sol; **~set** pôr *m* do sol; **~shade** guarda-sol *m*; **~shine** luz *m* do sol, sol *m*; **~stroke** insolação *f*
superb [sju(:)'pə:b] magnífico, soberbo
super|ficial [ˌsju:pə'fiʃəl] superficial; **~fine** superfino; **~fluity** superfluidade *f*; **~fluous** supérfluo; **~human** sobre-humano; **~impose** *v/t* sobrepor; **~intendent** superintendente *m*
superior [sju:'piəriə] *adj* superior; **~ity** [-'ɔriti] superioridade *f*
superlative [sju:'pə:lətiv] *adj*, *s* superlativo *m*
super|man ['sju:pəmæn] superhomem *m*; **~natural** sobrenatural; **~numerary** *adj* supranumerário; **~sede** *v/t* substituir; **~stition** superstição *f*; **~stitious** supersticioso; **~vise** *v/t*, *v/i* vigiar, fiscalizar; **~visor** fiscal *m*
supper ['sʌpə] jantar *m*, ceia *f*; **have ~** jantar, cear
supple ['sʌpl] flexível
supplement ['sʌplimənt] *s* suplemento *m*; **~ary** [-'mentəri] suplementar
supplier [sə'plaiə] fornecedor *m*
supply [sə'plai] *v/t* fornecer, prover, abastecer; suprir; *s* provisão *f*, fornecimento *m*, abastecimento *m*
support [sə'pɔ:t] *s* sustento *m*, manutenção *f*; apoio *m*; *v/t* sustentar, manter; apoiar
suppos|e [sə'pəuz] *v/t* supor; julgar, crer; *conj* se, caso; que tal se; **~ed** *adj* suposto; pretenso; **~edly** supostamente, provavelmente
supposing [sə'pəuziŋ] *conj* se, caso, suponhamos
supposition [ˌsʌpə'ziʃən] suposição *f*; hipótese *f*, conje(c)tura *f*
suppress [sə'pres] *v/t* suprimir
supreme [sju(:)'pri:m] supremo
sure [ʃuə] *adj* seguro, certo; *adv* claro, sem dúvida; **make ~ of/that** verificar, assegurar-se; **for ~** de certeza; **~ enough** de fa(c)to; **~ly** com certeza; com segurança; **~ty** caução *f*; fiador

m

surf [sə:f] *s* ressaca *f*; *v/t* **~ the net** COMP navegar na Net
surface ['sə:fis] *s* superfície *f*
surg|eon ['sə:dʒən] cirurgião *m*; **~ery** consultório *m*; cirurgia *f*; **~ical** cirúrgico
surly ['sə:li] carrancudo, rabugento
surmise [sə:'maiz] *v/t*, *v/i* supor, suspeitar; ['--] *s* suposição *f*; suspeita *f*
surmount [sə:'maunt] *v/t* superar
surname ['sə:neim] apelido *m*
surpass [sə:'pɑ:s] *v/t* sobrepujar, exceder
surpris|e [sə'praiz] *v/t* surpreender; *s* surpresa *f*; **~ing** *adj* surpreendente
surrender [sə'rendə] *v/t*, *v/i* render(-se), entregar(-se); capitular; *s* rendição *f*, capitulação *f*
surreptitious [ˌsʌrəp'tiʃəs] sub-reptício
surround [sə'raund] *v/t* circundar, rodear, cercar; **~ings** *s/pl* ambiente *m*, meio *m*
survey [sə'vei] *v/t* estudar, examinar; medir; ['sə:vei] *s* estudo *m*, inspe(c)ção *f*
survival [sə'vaivəl] sobrevivência *f*
surviv|e [sə'vaiv] *v/t*, *v/i* sobreviver (a); **~or** sobrevivente *m*, *f*
susceptible [sə'septəbl] susce(p)tível; sensível
suspect [səs'pekt] *v/t* suspeitar; ['sʌspekt] *s*, *adj* suspeito *m*
suspend [səs'pend] *v/t* suspender
suspense [səs'pens] expe(c)tativa *f*, incerteza *f*, ansiedade *f*
suspension [səs'penʃən] suspensão *f*; **~-bridge** ponte *f* pênsil
suspic|ion [səs'piʃən] suspeita *f*; **~ious** suspeitoso; suspeito
sustain [səs'tein] *v/t* sustentar, suster, manter; suportar, sofrer
sustenance ['sʌstinəns] subsistência *f*, alimento *m*
SUV [sʌv] *s* (= **sports utility vehicle**) SUV *m*
swagger ['swægə] *v/i* pavonear-se; bazofiar; *s* pavonada *f*
swallow ['swɔləu] *v/t* tragar, engolir
swallow ['swɔləu] *s* ZOO andorinha *f*; trago *m*
swamp [swɔmp] *s* brejo *m*, pântano *m*, paúl *m*
swan [swɔn] *s* cisne *m*
swarm [swɔ:m] *s* enxame *m*; *v/i* enxamear; fervilhar, pulular
swarthy ['swɔ:ði] moreno, trigueiro
sway [swei] *s* balanço *m*; *v/t*, *v/i* balançar(-se)
swear [swɛə] *v/t*, *v/i* jurar; blasfemar, praguejar
sweat [swet] *s* suor *m*; *v/i* suar
sweater ['swetə] suéter *m*
Swed|e [swi:d] sueco *m*; **~ish** *adj*, *s* sueco *m*
sweep [swi:p] *v/t* varrer, vasculhar; *s* extensão *f*; curva *f*; ges-

to *m*; limpa-chaminés *m*; varredela *f*; **~ing** *adj* extenso, vasto

sweepings ['swi:piŋz] *s/pl* lixo *m*

sweet [swi:t] *adj* doce; suave; encantador, gentil; *s* rebuçado *m*; doce *m*, guloseima *f*; **~en** *v/t*, *v/i* adoçar(-se); açucarar; **~heart** querido *m*, querida *f*; **~ness** doçura *f*; suavidade *f*; encanto *m*

swell [swel] *adj* porreiro, formidável; *v/t*, *v/i* inchar(-se); intumescer, distender; **~ing** *s* inchação *f*, intumescência *f*

swelter ['sweltə] *v/i* abafar

swerve [swə:v] *v/t*, *v/i* guinar, desviar(-se); *s* desvio *m*, guinada *f*

swift [swift] *adj* veloz, rápido

swim [swim] *v/t*, *v/i* nadar; **~ across** atravessar a nado; **~mer** nadador *m*; **~ming** *s* natação *f*; **~ming-pool** piscina *f*

swindl|e ['swindl] *v/t* lograr, calotear; **~er** caloteiro *m*

swine [swain] suíno *m*

swing [swiŋ] *v/t*, *v/i* balançarse, baloiçar(-se); *s* baloiço *m*; balanço *m*

swirl [swə:l] *s* turbilhão *m*, torvelinho *m*, redemoinho *m*, *v/i* redemoinhar

Swiss [swis] *adj*, *s* suíço *m*

switch [switʃ] *s* chibata *f*; interruptor *m*, comutador *m*; *v/t* açoutar; comutar; **~ off** desligar; **~ on** ligar; **~board** quadro *m* de distribuição

swollen ['swəulən] *adj* inchado

swoop [swu:p] *s* batida *f*, investida *f*; *v/i* precipitar-se, picar

sword [sɔ:d] espada *f*

syllable ['siləbl] sílabo *f*

symbol ['simbəl] símbolo *m*

symbolic [sim'bɔlik] simbólico

symmetry ['simitri] simetria *f*

sympath|etic [ˌsimpə'θetik] simpatizante; **~ize** ['-aiz] *v/i* simpatizar; **~y** ['-θi] simpatia *f*; compaixão *f*; compreensão *f*; solidariedade *f*

symphony ['simfəni] (*pl* **-nies**) sinfonia *f*

symptom ['simptəm] sintoma *m*

synchronize ['siŋkrənaiz] *v/t*, *v/i* sincronizar

syndicate ['sindikit] *s* sindicato *m*

synonym ['sinənim] sinónimo *m*; **~ous** [-'nɔniməs] sinónimo

syringe ['sirindʒ] *s* seringa *f*

syrup ['sirəp] xarope *m*, calda *f*

system ['sistim] sistema *m*; **~atic** [ˌ-'mætik] sistemático; **~atize** ['-ətaiz] *v/t* sistematizar, reduzir a sistema

T

tab [tæb] presilha *f*; alça *f*, aselha *f*
table ['teibl] *s* mesa *f*; **~-cloth** toalha *f* de mesa; **~-spoon** colher *f*
tablet ['tæblit] comprimido *m*; tablete *f*, barra *f*
tacit ['tæsit] tácito; **~urn** ['-ə:n] taciturno
tack [tæk] *s* brocha *f*, tacha *f*; NAUT bordada *f*; *v/t*, *v/i* alinhavar; pregar COM tachas; NAUT bordejar, virar de bordo
tackle ['tækl] *s* equipamento *m*, aparelhagem *f*; NAUT cordoalha *f*; intercepção *f*; *v/t*, *v/i* atacar, enfrentar; interceptar, derrubar
tact [tækt] ta(c)to *m*, discernimento *m*, jeito *m*, diplomacia *f*; **~ful** com/de ta(c)to, diplomático; **~ile** ['-ail] tá(c)til; **~less** sem ta(c)to
taffeta ['tæfitə] tafetá *m*
tag [tæg] *s* etiqueta *f*; agulheta *f*; estribilho *m*; *v/t* etiquetar
tail [teil] *s* cauda *f*, rabo *m*; **~coat** fraque *m*; **~-light** farol *m* da retaguarda
tailor ['teilə] *s* alfaiate *m*; **well ~ed** bem cortado; **~-made** feito á/sob medida; **~'s** (shop) alfaiataria *f*
taint [teint] *s* mácula *f*, mancha *f*; *v/t* macular, manchar; corromper; poluir
take [teik] *v/t* tomar; pegar em; receber; levar; conduzir, guiar; tirar; alugar; **~ a chance** arriscar a sorte, aproveitar a oportunidade; **~ to one's heels/legs** dar às canelas; **~ aback** tomar de surpresa; **~ in** alojar; encurtar; **~ off** despir, tirar; levantar voo, descolar; **~off** *s* descolagem *f*; caricatura *f*; **~ on** empregar; aceitar; **~ out** arrancar; levar a sair, convidar; **~ over** tomar posse de; **~ to** passar a gostar de; simpatizar COM; entregar-se a; **~ up** dedicar-se a; ocupar; seguir
taking ['teikiŋ] *adj* atraente; *s* **~ over** *idéia* adoção *f*
tale [teil] conto *m*, história *f*
talent ['tælənt] talento *m*; **~ed** talentoso
talisman ['tælizmən] talismã *m*
talk [tɔ:k] *s* conversa *f*; palestra *f*; discurso *m*; fala *f*; *v/t*, *v/i* falar, conversar; tagarelar; **~ative** ['-ətiv] loquaz, falador; **~er** conversador *m*
tall [tɔ:l] alto
tallow ['tæləu] sebo *m*
tally ['tæli] *v/t*, *v/i* condizer, corresponder (a)
tame [teim] *adj* manso, domesticado; *v/t* domesticar, amansar, domar
tamper ['tæmpə]: **~ with** mexer

em; forçar; manipular
tan [tæn] *v/t, v/i* bronzear(-se); curtir; *s* cor *f* bronzeada, tom *m* queimado
tangerine [ˌtændʒəˈriːn] tangerina *f*
tangible [ˈtændʒəbl] tangível, palpável
tangle [ˈtæŋgl] *s* nó *m*, emaranhamento *m*; *v/t, v/i* emaranhar(-se)
tank [tæŋk] reservatório *m*, cisterna *f*; tanque *m*
tankard [ˈtæŋkəd] caneca *f*; pichel *m*
tanner [ˈtænə] curtidor *m*; **~y** curtume *m*
tantalize [ˌtæntəlaiz] *v/t* tantalizar
tantamount [ˈtæntəmaunt] igual, equivalente
tap [tæp] *s* pancadinha *f*, golpe *m* leve; torneira *f*; *v/t, v/i* bater ao de leve
tape [teip] *s* fita *f*, banda *f*
taper [ˈteipə] *s* círio *m*; pavio *m*; *v/t, v/i* afilar(-se), terminar-se em ponta
tape-|recorder [ˈteipriˌkɔːdə] gravador *m*; **~-recording** gravação *f*
tapestry [ˈtæpistri] (*pl* **-ries**) tapeçaria *f*
tapeworm [ˈteipwəːm] bicha *f* solitária
tar [tɑː] *s* alcatrão *m*; *v/t* alcatroar
tare [tɛə] COM tara *f*
target [ˈtɑːgit] alvo *m*
tariff [ˈtærif] tarifa *f*
tarmac [ˈtɑːmæk] *s* pista *f* macadamizada
tarnish [ˈtɑːniʃ] *v/t, v/i* empanar(-se), deslustrar
tart [tɑːt] *adj* acre, ácido, azedo; mordaz; *s* torta *f*, pastel *m*
Tartar [ˈtɑːtə] tártaro *m*
task [tɑːsk] tarefa *f*
tassel [ˈtæsəl] borla *f*
tast|e [teist] *s* gosto *m*; sabor *m*; *v/t* provar, saborear; **~eful** gostoso; com bom gosto; **~eless** sem gosto, insípido; de mau gosto; **~y** saboroso
ta-ta [ˈtæˈtɑː] adeusinho
tatter [ˈtætə] trapo *m*, farrapo *m*, andrajo *m*; **~ed** esfarrapado
tattle [ˈtætl] *s* tagarelice *f*; *v/i* tagarelar
tattoo [təˈtuː] *s* tatuagem *f*; MIL toque *m* de recolher; *v/t* tatuar
taunt [tɔːnt] *s* insulto *m*; troça *f*; *v/t* escarnecer, mofar(-se) de
tax [tæks] *s* taxa *f*, imposto *m*; encargo *m*; esforço *m*; *v/t, v/i* sobrecarregar, pôr à prova; lançar impostos sobre
taxi [ˈtæksi] *s* táxi *m*, *v/t, v/i* deslizar, rolar; **~meter** taxímetro *m*; **~-rank/ ~-stand** praça *f* de táxis, *Braz* ponto *m* de estacionamento de táxis
taxpayer [ˈtæksˌpeiə] contribuinte *m, f*
tea [tiː] chá *m*
teach [tiːtʃ] *v/t, v/i* ensinar, instruir; **~er** professor *m*; **~ing** *s* ensinamento *m*; ensino *m*, instrução *f*

tea|-cosy ['tiːˌkəuzi] abafador *m*; **~cup** chávena *f*
team [tiːm] equipa *f*, equipe *f*
teapot ['tiːpɔt] bule *m*
tear [tɛə] *s* rasgão *m*; *v/t* rasgar
tear [tiə] *s* lágrima *f*; **~ful** lacrimoso
tease [tiːz] *v/t*, *v/i* gozar COM, entrar COM, arreliar, *Braz* cacetear
tea-spoon ['tiːspuːn] colher *f* de chá
teat [tiːt] teta *f*
techni|cal ['teknikəl] técnico; **~cian** [-'niʃən] técnico *m*; **~que** [-'niːk] técnica *f*
tedious ['tiːdjəs] fastidioso, maçador
teem [tiːm] *v/i* chover a potes; **~ with rain** chover a cântaros
teenager ['tiːneidʒə] jovem *m*, *f* adolescente
teens [tiːnz] *s/pl* idade *f* de 13 a 19 anos; **he's still in his ~** ainda não chegou aos vinte anos
teeth [tiːθ] *pl of* **tooth**; **~e** [-ð] *v/i* criar dentes, começar a ter dentes
teetota(l)ler [tiː'təutlə] abstémio *m*
tele|gram ['teligræm] telegrama *m*; **~graph** ['-grɑːf] *s* telégrafo *m*; *v/t*, *v/i* telegrafar; **~graphic** [ˌ-'græfik] telegráfico; **~pathy** [ti'lepəθi] telepatia *f*; **~phone** *s* telefone *m*; *v/t*, *v/i* telefonar; **~phone booth** cabine *f* telefónica; **~phone directory** lista *f* telefónica; **~phone exchange** central *f* telefónica; **~phonist** [-'lefənist] telefonista *m*, *f*; **~phony** [ti'lefəni] telefonia *f*; **~scope** ['-skəup] telescópio *m*; **~scopic** [ˌ-s'kɔpik] telescópico; **~vision** ['-ˌviʒən] televisão *f*
tell [tel] *v/t*, *v/i* contar, relatar; dizer, informar; **~ lies** dizer mentiras; **~ the truth** dizer a verdade; **~er** pagador *m*, caixa *m*; escrutinador *m*; **~ing** *adj* eficaz; notável; **~tale** *adj* traiçoeiro; *s* mexeriqueiro *m*
temper ['tempə] *s* génio *m*, humor *m*; índole *f*; mau génio *m*, mau humor; têmpera *f*; *v/t* temperar; **lose one's ~** perder a calma; **~ament** temperamento *m*; **~amental** caprichoso; **~ance** temperança *f*; **~ate** ['-rit] temperado; moderado, sóbrio; **~ature** ['-ritʃə] temperatura *f*
tempest ['tempist] tempestade *f*
temple ['templ] templo *m*; ANAT fonte *f*
temporary ['tempərəri] temporário
tempt [tempt] *v/t* tentar, induzir; **~ation** [-'teiʃən] tentação *f*; **~er** sedutor *m*; **~ing** *adj* tentador; **~ress** sedutora *f*
ten [ten] dez
ten|able ['tenəbl] sustentável, defensável; **~acious** [ti'neiʃəs] tenaz; **~acity** [ti'næsiti] tenacidade *f*; **~ant** ['tenənt] *s* inquilino *m*, locatário *m*
tend [tend] *v/t* guardar, velar; *v/i*

tender; **~ency** (*pl* **-cies**) tendência *f*
tender ['tendə] *s* tênder *m*; encarregado *m*; oferta *f*, proposta *f*; *adj* tenro; terno; brando; delicado; **~ness** delicadeza *f*; ternura *f*; brandura *f*
tendon ['tendən] tendão *m*
tenement ['tenimənt] habitação *f*, casa *f*
tennis ['tenis] ténis *m*
tenor ['tenə] MUS tenor *m*; teor *m*
tens|e [tens] *s* tempo *m*; *adj* tenso; teso, esticado; **~ion** ['tenʃən] tensão *f*
tent [tent] tenda *f*
tentacle ['tentəkl] tentáculo *m*
tenth [tenθ] décimo
tenuous ['tenjuəs] ténue
tepid ['tepid] tépido
term [təːm] *s* termo *m*; prazo *m*; período *m*, *v/t* nomear, chamar
terminal ['təːminl] *adj* terminal; *s* término *m*; estação *f* terminal
termin|ate ['təːmineit] *v/t* terminar; **~ation** [-'neiʃən] terminação *f*
terminology [təːmi'nɔlədʒi] terminologia *f*
terminus ['təːminəs] estação *f* terminal, término *m*
terrace ['terəs] *s* terraço *m*; socalco *m*
terrestrial [ti'restriəl] terrestre
terrible ['terəbl] terrível
terrific [tə'rifik] estupendo
terrify ['terifai] *v/t* assustar, aterrorizar
territory ['teritəri] (*pl* **-ries**) território *m*
terror ['terə] terror *m*; **~ism** terrorismo *m*; **~ist** *adj*, *s* terrorista *m*, *f*; **~ize** *v/t* aterrorizar
terse [təːs] conciso
test [test] *s* prova *f*; ensaio *m*; teste *m*; análise *f*, exame *m*; *v/t* pôr à prova; examinar
testament ['testəmənt] testamento *m*
testify ['testifai] *v/t*, *v/i* atestar, testemunhar; depor
testimon|ial [ˌtesti'məunjəl] atestado *m*, certificado *m*; **~y** ['-əni] testemunho *m*, depoimento *m*
testy ['testi] irascível
text [tekst] texto *m*; TEL SMS *m*; *v/t* enviar um SMS a; **~ message** *s* TEL mensagem *m* SMS
text|ile ['tekstail] *s* tecido *m*; *adj* têxtil; **~ual** ['tekstjuəl] textual
texture ['tekstʃə] (con)textura *f*
than [ðæn, ðən] *conj* que, do que
thank [θæŋk] *v/t* agradecer; **~ you** obrigado; **~ heaven!** graças aos céus! **~ful** agradecido, grato; **~less** ingrato, desagradecido; **~s** *s/pl* agradecimentos *m/pl*
thanksgiving ['θæŋksˌgiviŋ] a(c)ção *f* de graças
that [ðæt] (*pl* **those** [ðəuz]) *adj*, *pron* aquele, aquela, esse, essa, *pron* aquilo; isso; que, o qual; *conj* que
thatch [θætʃ] *s* colmo *m*

thaw [θɔː] *s* degelo *m*; *v/t, v/i* degelar, descongelar
the [ðiː, ðə] *art* o, a, os, as; *adv* ~ ... ~ quanto ..., tanto
theatr|e ['θiətə] teatro *m*; **~ical** [θi'ætrikəl] teatral
theft [θeft] roubo *m*
their [ðɛə, ðɛr] seu, sua, seus, suas; deles, delas; **~s** [-z] o seu, a sua, os seus, as suas; o deles, o delas
them [ðem, ðəm] os, as; eles, elas; lhes
theme [θiːm] tema *m*, assunto *m*; MUS motivo *m*
themselves [ðəm'selvz] *pron/ /pl* se; eles mesmos, elas mesmas, a si mesmos, a si mesmas
then [ðen] *adv* então; ora; depois; *adj* de então
thenceforth ['ðens'fɔːθ] desde então
theolog|ian [θiə'ləudʒjən] teólogo *m*; **~y** [θi'ɔlədʒi] teologia *f*
theorem ['θiərəm] teorema *m*
theoretical [θiə'retikəl] teórico
theory ['θiəri] (*pl* **-ries**) teoria *f*
there [ðɛə] *adv* ali, acolá, lá, aí; *int* ora toma!, então!; ~ **you are!** ora aí está
there|about(s) ['ðɛərəbauts] nas cercanias; por aí, mais ou menos; **~fore** portanto, por isso, por conseguinte; **~upon** nisso; por isso
therm|al ['θəːməl] *adj* termal, térmico; **~ometer** [-'mɔmitə] termómetro *m*
these [ðiːz] *pl* estes, estas
thesis ['θiːsis] (*pl* **-ses** ['-siːz]) tese *f*
they [ðei] eles, elas
thick [θik] *adj* espesso, denso; grosso; cerrado; **~en** *v/t, v/i* engrossar, tornar(-se) espesso; complicar-se; **~ness** espessura *f*; densidade *f*; grossura *f*
thief [θiːf] (*pl* **thieves** [θiːvz]) gatuno *m*, ladrão *m*
thieve [θiːv] *v/t, v/i* roubar, furtar
thigh [θai] coxa *f*
thimble ['θimbl] dedal *m*
thin [θin] *adj* delgado, fino, ténue; magro, franzino; ralo; escasso; *v/t, v/i* adelgaçar, afinar; rarefazer
thing [θiŋ] coisa *f*
think [θiŋk] *v/t, v/i* pensar; crer, julgar; meditar; ~ **of** pensar em; achar; ~ **over** repensar, pensar bem; **~er** pensador *m*; **~ing** *s* pensamento *m*; opinião *f*; *adj* pensante; refle(c)tido
third [θəːd] *adj* terceiro; *s* terço *m*
thirst [θəːst] *s* sede *f*; **~y** sedento, sequioso
thir|teen ['θəː'tiːn] *adj* treze; **~ty** *adj* trinta
this [ðis] (*pl* **these** [ðiːz]) *pron* este, esta; isto; *pron* este, esta; *adv* assim (tão)
thistle ['θisl] cardo *m*
thorn [θɔːn] espinho *m*
thorough ['θʌrə] esmerado; inteiro, completo, cabal; **~bred** ['-bred] *s* puro-sangue *m*; **~fare** passagem *f*; via *f* pública;

~ly inteiramente; **~ness** esmero *m*
those [ðəuz] *pl of* **that** esses, essas; aqueles, aquelas
though [ðəu] *conj* ainda que, posto que, embora; *adv* contudo; **as ~** como se
thought [θɔːt] *s* pensamento *m*; **~ful** atento, cuidadoso, pensativo; **~less** desatento, irrefle(c)tido
thousand ['θauzənd] *adj* mil; milhar; **~th** ['-tθ] milésimo
thraldom ['θrɔːldəm] escravidão *f*
thrash [θræʃ] *v/t* bater, sovar, espancar
thread [θred] *s* fio *m*, linha *f*; *v/t* enfiar
threat [θret] ameaça *f*; **~en** *v/t* ameaçar
three [θriː] *adj* três; **~ hundred** trezentos
thresh [θreʃ] *v/t*, *v/i* malhar, debulhar; **~ing-floor** eira *f*; **~ing-machine** debulhadora *f*
threshold ['θreʃhəuld] limiar *m*, soleira *f*
thrifty ['θrifti] económico, poupado
thrill [θril] *s* emoção *f* viva, estremecimento *m*; *v/t* emocionar; estremecer; **~er** romance *m* policial; **~ing** *adj* emocionante
thriv|e [θraiv] *v/i* medrar, prosperar; **~ing** *adj* próspero, florescente
throat [θrəut] garganta *f*
throb [θrɔb] *v/i* latejar, palpitar
throne [θrəun] trono *m*
throng [θrɔŋ] *s* multidão *f*, tropel *m*; *v/t* apinhar(-se), acorrer
through [θruː] *prp* por; através de; durante; por intermédio de; *adv* completamente; totalmente; de um lado a outro, do princípio ao fim; *adj* dire(c)to; completo, terminado; **~out** *prp* durante todo; por todo; *adv* por/em toda a parte; completamente
throw [θrəu] *v/t*, *v/i* deitar; lançar, atirar, arremessar; *s* lanço *m*, arremesso *m*; **~ away** deitar fora, jogar fora; **~ out** rejeitar; **~ up** abandonar, renunciar a; vomitar
thrush [θrʌʃ] tordo *m*
thrust [θrʌst] *s* empurrão *m*; investida *f*; *v/t* empurrar, impelir
thud [θʌd] *s* baque *m*
thumb [θʌm] *s* polegar *m*; *v/t* folhear
thump [θʌmp] *s* pancada *f*, soco *m*; baque *m*; *v/t*, *v/i* martelar, bater em; esmurrar, dar socos a
thunder ['θʌndə] *s* trovão *m*; *v/i* trovejar; **~bolt** raio *m*; **~storm** trovoada *f*; **~struck** estupefa(c)to, assombrado
Thursday ['θəːzdi] quinta-feira *f*
thus [ðʌs] assim
thwart [θwɔːt] *v/t* frustrar; *s* banco *m* de remador
tick [tik] *v/t*, *v/i* fazer tiquetaque; marcar, pôr visto em; *s* sinal *m* de visto; tiquetaque *m*

ticket ['tikit] *s* bilhete *m*; etiqueta *f*, rótulo *m*; *US* lista *f* de chapa; **~-collector** revisor *m*

tickl|e ['tikl] *v/t* fazer cócegas a; **~ish** coceguento; delicado, melindroso

tide [taid] maré *f*; **high ~** maré *f* alta; **low ~** maré *f* baixa, baixa-mar *f*

tidy ['taidi] *adj* asseado, arrumado; *v/t* assear, arrumar

tie [tai] *s* gravata *f*; empate *m*; *v/t*, *v/i* empatar; dar nó/laço (a); atar, ligar; amarrar, NAUT atracar

tier [tiə] camada *f*; bancada *f*; fileira *f*, fila *f*

tiger ['taigə] tigre *m*

tight [tait] *adj* apertado; teso, entesado; *adv* firmemente; bem; **~en** *v/t*, *v/i* apertar; entesar

tights [taits] *s/pl* calças *f/pl* justas

tigress ['taigris] tigre *m* fêmea

tile [tail] *s* telha *f*; ladrilho *m*; azulejo *m*; *v/t* ladrilhar; telhar; cobrir COM azulejos

till [til] *prp* até; *conj* até que; *s* gaveta *f* da caixa; *v/t* lavrar, cultivar; **~age** lavoura *f*; **~er** lavrador *m*; NAUT cana *f* do leme

tilt [tilt] *v/t*, *v/i* inclinar(-se), virar(-se)

timber ['timbə] *s* madeira *f*

time [taim] *s* tempo *m*; vez *f*, ocasião *f*; hora *f*; horas *f/pl*; época *f*; estação *f*; MUS compasso *m*; *v/t* marcar o tempo; cronometrar; estar marcado; regular, acertar; **at ~s** às vezes; **from ~ to ~** de vez em quando; **in ~** a tempo; a compasso; **in no ~** num instante; **on ~** a horas, pontualmente

time|less ['taimlis] sem fim; eterno; intemporal; **~ly** oportuno; **~s** *prp* vezes; **~-table** *s* horário *m*

tim|id ['timid] tímido; **~idity** [-'miditi] timidez *f*; **~orous** ['-ərəs] medroso, timorato, temeroso

tin [tin] *s* estanho *m*; lata *f*; *v/t* conservar em latas, enlatar

tincture ['tiŋktʃə] tintura *f*

tinfoil ['tin'fɔil] folha *f* de estanho

tinge [tindʒ] *v/t* tingir; *s* matiz *m*

tingl|e ['tiŋkl] *v/i* formigar; **~ing** formigueiro *m*

tinkle ['tiŋgl] *v/t*, *v/i* tinir, tilintar; *s* tinido *m*

tin-opener ['tinəup:nə] abre-latas *m*

tint [tint] *s* cor *m*, tom *m*, tinta *f*; *v/t* pintar (*o cabelo*)

tiny ['taini] minúsculo; **~ tot** pequenino *m*, criancinha *f*

tip [tip] *s* ponta *f*, extremidade *f*; gorjeta *f*; palpite *m*; conselho *m*; sugestão *f*; *v/t*, *v/i* dar palpite, sugerir; inclinar(-se); tombar, virar(-se); tocar levemente em; dar gorjeta (a)

tipsy ['tipsi] tocado, alegre

tiptoe ['tiptəu] *v/i* andar em bicos de pés; **on ~** na ponta dos pés

tire ['taiə] *v/t*, *v/i* cansar(-se); **~**

out estafar; **~d** *adj* cansado, fatigado; **~less** incansável, infatigável; **~some** enfadonho, maçador, *Braz* maçante
tissue ['tisju:, 'tiʃu:] tecido *m*; lenço *m* de papel; **~-paper** papel *m* de seda
tit [tit] zoo chapim *m*; ANAT teta *f*
titbit ['titbit] pitéu *m*, gulodice *f*
title ['taitl] título *m*
to [tu:, tu, tə] *prp* até; a, para; com; de; *adv* a si; **it's 5 minutes ~ 4** são 4 menos 5
toad [təud] sapo *m*
to and fro ['tu ən' frəu] *adj* de vaivém; *s* vaivém *m*; **~ ~ ~** *adv* de um lado para o outro
toast [təust] *s* torrada *f*; brinde *m*, saúde *f*; *v/t* torrar, tostar; beber à saúde de, brindar a; **~er** torradeira *f*
tobacco [tə'bækəu] tabaco *m*
toboggan [tə'bɔgən] *s* tobogã *m*
today [tə'dei] *adv* hoje
toe [təu] *s* dedo *m* de pé
toffee ['tɔfi] caramelo *m*, *Braz* bala *f* de leite, tofé *m*
together [tə'geðə] juntos, juntas
toil [tɔil] *s* lida *f*, faina *f*; *v/i* lidar, moirejar
toilet ['tɔilit] casa *f* de banho, *Braz* privada *f*; retrete *f*, *Braz* bacia *f* sanitária; **~-paper** papel *m* higiénico; **~ soap** sabonete *m*
token ['təukən] sinal *m*, marca *f*, recordação *f*
tolera|ble ['tɔlərəbəl] tolerável; **~nce** tolerância *f*; **~nt** tolerante
tolerate ['tɔləreit] *v/t* tolerar
toll [təul] *s* peagem *f*; portagem *f*, *Braz* pedágio *m*; *v/t*, *v/i* tocar, dobrar; **~-gate** barreira *f* onde se paga portagem
tomato [tə'mɑ:təu] tomate *m*
tomb [tu:m] túmulo *m*, sepulcro *m*
tom-cat ['tɔmkæt] gato *m*
tomorrow [tə'mɔrəu] *adv* amanhã *f*; **~ week** de amanhã a oito dias
ton [tʌn] tonelada *f*
tone [təun] *s* tom *m*; som *m*; timbre *m*
tongs [tɔŋz] *s/pl* pinça *f*, tenaz *f*
tongue [tʌŋ] língua *f*; **hold one's ~** calar a boca; **~-tied** calado; **~-twister** trava-línguas *m*
tonight [tə'nait] *adv* hoje à noite, esta noite
tonsil ['tɔnsl] amígdala *f*; **~litis** [,-i'laitis] amigdalite *f*
too [tu:] demasiado, demais; também
tool [tu:l] *s* instrumento *m*, ferramenta *f*
tooth [tu:θ] (*pl* **teeth** [ti:θ]) dente *m*; **~ and nail** COM unhas e dentes; **~ache** dor *f* de dentes; **~-brush** escova *f* de dentes; **~-paste** pasta *f* dentífrica
top [tɔp] *s* cimo *m*, cume *m*, topo *m*; copa *f*; pitorra *f*, pião *m*; tampo *m*; *adj* superior; primeiro, principal; *v/t* cobrir, co-

roar; chegar ao topo; sobrepujar, exceder; **at ~ speed** a toda a velocidade; **from ~ to bottom** de alto a baixo; **on ~ of** ainda por cima
topic ['tɔpik] tópico *m*; **~al** a(c)tual
top|mast ['tɔpma:st, -məst] mastaréu *m*; **~sail** gávea *f*
topsyturvy ['tɔpsi'tə:vi] *adv* às avessas, de pernas para o ar
torch [tɔ:ʃ] tocha *f*, archote *m*, facho *m*; lâmpada *f* eléctrica, *Braz* farolete *m*
torment ['tɔ:ment] *s* tormento *m*; [-'ment] vt/ atormentar
tornado [tɔ:'neidəu] tornado *m*
torpedo [tɔ:'pi:dəu] *s* torpedo *m*; *v/t* torpedear; **~-boat** torpedeiro *m*
torp|id ['tɔ:pid] entorpecido; **~or** torpor *m*
torrent ['tɔrənt] torrente *f*, caudal *m*; **~ial** [-'renʃəl] torrencial
tortoise ['tɔ:təs] tartaruga *f*
torture ['tɔ:tʃə] *s* tortura; *v/t* torturar
toss [tɔs] *s* sacudid(el)a *f*, abanadela *f*; meneio *m*; arremesso *m*; *v/t*, *v/i* atirar ao ar; sacudir, abanar; arrojar, lançar
total ['təutl] *s*, *adj* total *m*; *v/t* totalizar; montar a; **~itarian** [-ˌtæli'tεəriən] totalitário; **~ity** [-'tæliti] totalidade *f*
totem ['təutəm] totem *m*
totter ['tɔtə] *v/i* titubear, cambalear
touch [tʌtʃ] *s* ta(c)to *m*; toque *m*, apalpadela *f*; conta(c)to *m*, ligação *f*, relação *f*; retoque *m*; *v/t*, *v/i* tocar, apalpar; chepar a; comover; **~ up** retocar; **~y** irascível; melindroso
tough [tʌf] *adj* rijo, forte, duro; penoso, difícil; **~en** *v/t*, *v/i* endurecer, enrijecer; **~ness** dureza *f*, rijeza *f*
tour [tuə] *s* volta *f*; viagem *f*; giro *m*; *v/t* viajar por, percorrer; **~ism** turismo *m*; **~ist** turista *m*, *f*; **~istic** [-'ristik] turístico
tow [təu] *v/t* rebocar; *s* estopa *f*; reboque *m*; **in ~** a reboque
toward(s) [tə'wɔ:d(z)] para; para com
towel ['tauəl] *s* toalha *f*
tower ['tauə] *s* torre *f*; *v/i* erguer-se, elevar-se; estar sobranceiro
town [taun] cidade *f*; centro *m*, baixa *f*; **~ hall** câmara *f* municipal, prefeitura *f*
toy [tɔi] *s* brinquedo *m*
trace [treis] *s* traço *m*; rasto *m*, pista *f*; *v/t* seguir a pista de, descobrir; traçar, delinear
track [træk] *s* rasto *m*, vestígio *m*; trilho *m*; pista *f*; caminho *m*; *v/t* seguir a pista de
tract [trækt] extensão *f*; opúsculo *m*; **~ion** ['-kʃən] tra(c)ção *f*; **~or** tra(c)tor *m*
trade [treid] *s* comércio *m*, negócio *m*, tráfico *m*; *v/t*, *v/i* negociar, comerciar; **~-mark** marca *f* registada; **~ union** sindicato *m*
tradition [trə'diʃən] tradição *f*; **~al** tradicional

traffic ['træfik] *s* tráfego *m*, trânsito *m*; tráfico *m*; **~ in** *v/t* traficar; **~light/signal** semáforo *m*, sinal *m* luminoso

tragedy ['trædʒidi] (*pl* **-dies**) tragédia *f*

tragic ['trædʒik] trágico

trail [treil] *s* vereda *f*, picada *f*; pista *f*, rasto *m*, pegada *f*; *v/t*, *v/i* seguir a pista de; arrastar (-se); **~er**

train [trein] *s* comboio *m*, *Braz* trem *m*; comitiva *f*, séquito *m*; série *f*; *v/t*, *v/i* preparar(-se), formar(-se), estudar; treinar; exercitar

train|er ['treinə] instrutor *m*; treinador *m*; domador *m*; **~ing** *s* instrução *f*, educação *f*, ensino *m*; treino *m*

trait [treit] feição *f*, traço *m*

traitor ['treitə] traidor *m*

trajectory [trə'dʒektəri] (*pl* **-ries**) traje(c)tória *f*

tram(-car) ['træm(kaː)] (carro *m*) eléctrico *m*, *Braz* bonde *m*

tramp [træmp] *s* vagabundo *m*, vadio *m*; tropel *m*, tropeada *f*; caminhada *f*; *v/t*, *v/i* pisar; palmilhar

trample ['træmpl] *v/t*, *v/i* esmagar, pisar, calcar

trance [traːns] transe *m*, êxtase *m*

tranquil ['træŋkwil] tranquilo; **~(l)ity** [-'kwiliti] tranquilidade *f*; **~(l)ize** *v/t* tranquilizar-se

transact [træn'zækt] *v/t* executar, levar a cabo; **~ion** [-'zækʃən] transa(c)ção *f*

transatlantic ['trænzət'læntik] transatlântico

transcend [træn'send] *v/t* transcender; ultrapassar, exceder

transcribe [træns'kraib] *v/t* transcrever

transfer [træns'fəː] *v/t*, *v/i* transferir; trasladar; **~able** [-'fəːrəbl] transferível; **~ence** transferência *f*

trans|figure [træns'figə] *v/t* transfigurar; **~form** *v/t* transformar; **~formation** transformação *f*; **~fusion** [-'fjuːʒən] transfusão *f*

transgress [træns'gres] *v/t* transgredir; **~ion** [-'greʃən] transgressão *f*, violação *f*

transient ['trænziənt] *adj* transitório, passageiro

trancistor [træn'zistə] transistor *m*

transitive ['trænsitiv] *adj* transitivo

translat|able [træns'leitəbl] traduzível; **~e (into)** *v/t*, *v/i* traduzir (para)

translation [træns'leiʃən] tradução *f*; **certified ~** tradução autorizada

translator tradutor *m*

transmission [trænz'miʃən] transmissão *f*

transmit [trænz'mit] *v/t* transmitir

transmute [trænz'mjuːt] *v/t* transmutar

transparent [træn'speərənt] transparente

transpire [træns'paiə] *v/t, v/i* transpirar; tornar-se conhecido
transplant [træns'plaːnt] *v/t* transplantar
transport [træns'pɔːt] *v/t* transportar; ['-] *s* transporte *m*
transpose [træns'pəuz] *v/t* transpor; MUS transportar
trap [træp] *s* armadilha *f*; cilada *f*; *v/t* apanhar no laço
trapeze [trə'piːz] trapézio *m*
trash [træʃ] refugo *m*; bagatela *f*; lixo *m*
travel ['trævl] *s* viagem *f*; *v/i* viajar; **~ agency/bureau** agência *f* de viagens; **~(l)er** viajante *m, f*; caixeiro *m* viajante; **~(l)er's cheque** cheque *m* de viagem
traverse ['trævə(ː)s] *v/t* atravessar, cruzar
travesty ['trævisti] (*pl* **-ties**) paródia *f*
trawler ['trɔːlə] barco *m* de arrasto, traineira *f*
tray [treil] tabuleiro *m*, bandeja *f*
treacher|ous ['tretʃərəs] traiçoeiro; **~y** perfídia *f*, traição *f*
treacle ['triːkl] melaço *m*
tread [tred] *v/t* pisar, calcar; seguir, trilhar; *s* piso *m*; passo *m*
treadle ['tredl] *s* pedal *m*
treason ['triːzn] traição *f*
treasur|e ['treʒə] *s* tesouro *m*; *v/t* entesourar; prezar; **~er** tesoureiro *m*; **~y** tesouraria *f*
treat [triːt] *s* regalo *m*, festim *m*; *v/t* tratar; regalar
treatise [triːtiz] tratado *m*, dissertação *f*
treatment ['triːtmənt] tratamento *m*
treaty ['triːti] (*pl* **-ties**) tratado *m*
treble ['trebl] *v/t, v/i* triplicar (-se); *s* MUS tiple *f*; *adj* triplo
tree [triː] *s* árvore *f*
trefoil ['trefɔil] trevo *m*
tremble ['trembl] *v/i* tremer
tremendous [tri'mendəs] tremendo; estupendo
trem|or ['tremə] tremura *f*; tremor *m*; **~ulous** ['-juləs] trémulo
trench [trentʃ] *s* MIL trincheira *f*; fosso *m*, vala *f*
trend [trend] *s* inclinação *f*, tendência *f*
trespass ['trespəs] *v/i* entrar ilegalmente; **~er** intruso *m*
trestle ['tresl] cavalete *m*
trial ['traiəl] prova *f*, ensaio *m*; *jur* processo *m*, julgamento *m*; tentativa *f*; **on ~** à prova
triang|le ['traiæŋgl] triângulo *m*; **~ular** [-'æŋgjulə] triangular
tribe [traib] tribo *f*
tribunal [trai'bjuːnl] tribunal *m*
tribut|ary ['tribjutəri] *s* (*pl* **-ries**) tributário *m*; afluente *m*; **~e** ['-uːt] tributo *m*; homenagem *f*
trick [trik] *s* artifício *m*, artimanha *f*; partida *f*; fraude *f*, embuste *m*; ardil *m*; truque *m*; *v/t* enganar, iludir, lograr; **~ery** velhacaria *f*, trapaça *f*
trickle ['trikl] *v/i* gotejar, escor-

rer; *s* fio *m* de água
tricky ['triki] astucioso; complicado, intricado
trifle ['traifl] ninharia *f*, bagatela *f*; **a ~** um pouco, um tudo nada
trifling ['traifliŋ] *adj* trivial, insignificante
trigger ['trigə] *s* gatilho *m*
trill [tril] *s* trilo *m*, trinado *m*; *v/t*, *v/i* trinar
trim [trim] *s* condição *f*, estado *m*; *v/t* adaptar, ajustar; enfeitar; aparar; *adj* garboso, catita
trimming ['trimiŋ] Trindade *f*
trinket ['triŋkit] berloque *m*
trip [trip] *s* viagem *f*, excursão *f*, passeio *m*; *v/t*, *v/i* (fazer) tropeçar
tripe [traip] tripas *f/pl*
triple ['tripl] *adj* triplo, tríplice
tripod ['traipɔd] tripé *m*
trite [trait] banal, comum
triumph ['traiəmf] *s* triunfo *m*; *v/i* triunfar; **~al** [-'ʌmfənt] triunfante
trolley ['trɔli] trólei *m*; *US* carro *m* eléctrico, *Braz* bonde *m*
troop [tru:p] *s* grupo *m*, bando *m*; tropa *f*
trophy ['trəufi] (*pl* **-phies**) troféu *m*
tropic|al ['trɔpikəl] tropical; **~s** *s/pl* trópicos *m/pl*
trot [trɔt] *s* trote *m*; *v/t*, *v/i* trotar
trouble ['trʌbl] *s* incómodo *m*; moléstia *f*, inconveniente *m*; trabalho *m*; preocupação *f*, arrelia *f*; dificuldade *f*, dissabor *m*; *v/t*, *v/i* preocupar-se; afligir, molestar, incomodar(-se); **~some** enfadonho
trough [trɔf] gamela *f*
trousers ['trauzəz] *s/pl* calças *f/pl*
trout [traut] truta *f*
trowel ['trauəl] trolha *f*
truant ['tru:ənt] gazeteiro *m*; **play ~** fazer gazeta
truce [tru:s] trégua *f*
truck [trʌk] camião *m*, *Braz* caminhão *m*
trudge [trʌdʒ] *v/i* arrastar-se, andar a custo
true [tru:] *adj* verdadeiro; justo; seguro, certo; genuíno
truffle ['trʌfl] túbera *f*, trufa *f*
truism ['tru(:)izəm] truísmo *m*
truly ['tru:li] verdadeiramente; sinceramente; realmente, na verdade
trump [trʌmp] *s* trunfo *m*; *v/t* trunfar
trumpet ['trʌmpit] *s* trombeta *f*; **~er** trombeteiro *m*
truncheon ['trʌntʃən] cassetête *m*, cacete *m*
trunk [trʌŋk] tromba *f*, tronco *m*; torso *m*; baú *m*
trunk call ['trʌŋkkɔ:l] chamada *f* interurbana
truss [trʌs] *s* MED funda *f*; *v/t* atar
trust [trʌst] *s* confiança *f*; fé *f*; crédito *m*; depósito *m*; *v/t* fiar-se em, confiar em
trustee [trʌs'ti:] depositário *m*, consignatário *m*
trustworthy ['trʌst,wə:ði] digno de confiança

truth [truːθ] verdade *f*; **~ful** verídico; sincero
try [trai] *v/t*, *v/i* experimentar, provar, tentar; pôr à prova; julgar; *s* tentativa *f*; **~ on** provar
tub [tʌb] tina *f*
tube [tjuːb] tubo *m*, cano *m*; bisnaga *f*; *GB* metro *m*, *Braz* trem *m* subterrâneo
tuberculosis [tju(ː),bəːkju'ləusis] tuberculose *f*
tuck [tʌk] *s* dobra *f*, prega *f*; *v/t* meter, esconder; **~ in** cobrir, agasalhar
Tuesday ['tjuːzdi] terça-feira *f*
tuft [tʌft] tufo *m*
tug [tʌg] *s* arranco *m*, puxão *m*; *v/t*, *v/i* arrastar; puxar; **~boat** rebocador *m*
tulip ['tjuːlip] tulipa *f*
tumble ['tʌmbl] *v/i* cair, rolar; tombar; dar um trambolhão; dar cambalhotas; *s* queda *f*, tombo *m*
tumbler ['tʌmblə], copo *m*; acrobata *m*
tummy ['tʌmi] estômago *m*; barriga *f*
tumo(u)r ['rjuːmə] tumor *m*
tumult ['tjuːmʌlt] tumulto *m*; **~uous** [-'mʌltjuəs] tumultuoso
tune [tjuːn] *s* toada *f*; *v/t* afinar; **out of ~** desafinado
tunic ['tjuːnik] túnica *f*
tunnel ['tʌnl] *s* túnel *m*
turban ['təːbən] turbante *m*
turbid ['təːbid] turvo
turbine ['təːbin] turbina *f*
turbot ['təːbət] rodovalho *m*
turbulen|ce ['təːbjuləns] turbulência *f*; **~t** turbulento
tureen [tə'riːn] terrina *f*, sopeira *f*
turf [təːf] *s* relvado *m*
Turk [təːk] turco *m*
turkey ['təːki] peru *m*
Turkish ['təːkiʃ] *adj*, *s* turco *m*
turmoil ['təːmɔil] barafunda *f*, atrapalhação *f*
turn [təːn] *s* volta *f*; vez *f*; turno *m*; curva *f*; mudança *f*, transformação; *v/t*, *v/i* transformar(-se); virar, revirar; torcer; converter, mudar; voltar(-se); **~ away** recusar ver; mandar embora; **~ back** voltar; **~ down** baixar; rejeitar; **~ in** ir deitar-se; apresentar, entregar
turn|off *v/t*, *v/i* fechar; desligar, apagar; **~ on** abrir; ligar; depender de; **~ out** expulsar; vir a ser, tornar-se; confirmar-se, verificar-se; **~ to** dirigir-se a, voltar-se para; **~ up** aparecer, suceder
turncoat ['təːnkəut] vira-casaca *m*
turning ['təːniŋ] *s* curva *f*, esquina *f*
turnip ['təːnip] nabo *m*
turtle ['təːtl] tartaruga *f*; **~-dove** rola *f*
tusk [tʌsk] presa *f*
tutor ['tjuːtə] *s* tutor *m*; preceptor *m*
twang [twæŋ] *v/t*, *v/i* vibrar; *s* som *m* agudo; som *m* fanhoso
tweezers ['twiːzəz] *s/pl* pinça *f*
twelfth [twelfθ] *adj* décimo se-

gundo; duodécimo
twelve [twelv] *adj* doze
twent|ieth ['twentiiθ] *adj* vigésimo
twenty ['twenti] vinte
twice [twais] duas vezes
twig [twig] *s* rebento *m*, broto *m*
twilight ['twailait] crepúsculo *m*
twill [twil] tecido *m* com velos em diagonal
twin [twin] *s* gémeo *m*
twine [twain] *s* guita *f*, cordel *m*, retrós *m*; *v/t* enlaçar; torcer
twinkle ['twiŋkl] *s* centelha *f*, vislumbre *m*; *v/i* cintilar; piscar
twirl [twəːl] *v/t*, *v/i* girar, voltear; torcer, enrolar
twist [twist] *v/t*, *v/i* torcer(-se); retorcer
twitch [twitʃ] *s* contra(c)ção *f*; espasmo *m*; *v/t*, *v/i* contorcer (-se); contrair-se
twitter ['twitə] *s* gorjeio *m*; *v/i* trinar, gorjear, chilrear
two [tuː] *adj* dois, duas; **put ~ and ~ together** tirar as suas conclusões
type [taip] *s* tipo *m*; *v/t*, *v/i* escrever à máquina
typewriter ['taipraitə] máquina *f* de escrever
typhoon [tai'fuːn] tufão *m*
typical ['tipikəl] típico
typist ['taipist] dactilógrafo *m*
typography [tai'pɔgrəfi] tipografia *f*
tyran|ny ['tirəni] (*pl* **-nies**) tirania *f*; **~t** ['taiərənt] tirano *m*
tyre ['taiə] pneumático *m*, pneu *m*
tyro ['taiərəu] novato *m*, noviço *m*

U

udder ['ʌdə] úbere *m*
ugly ['ʌgli] feio
ulcer ['ʌlsə] úlcera *f*
ulterior [ʌl'tiəriə] ulterior
ultimate ['ʌltimit] último, final
umbrella [ʌm'brelə] guarda-chuva *m*, chapéu-de-chuva *m*; guarda-sol *m*
umpire ['ʌmpaiə] *s* árbitro *m*; *v/t*, *v/i* arbitrar
unabashed ['ʌnə'bæʃt] impassível; descarado
unabated ['ʌnə'beitid] sem diminuição, constante
unable ['ʌn'eibl] incapaz; impossibilitado; **be ~** não poder
unabridged ['ʌnə'bridʒd] integral, completo
unacceptable ['ʌnək'septəbl] inaceitável
unaccustomed ['ʌnə'kʌstəmd] não usual; não habituado; desacostumado
unadvised ['ʌnəd'vaizd] inconsiderado, irrefle(c)tido
unaffected ['ʌnə'fektid] desafe(c)tado, sincero, natural
unalterable [ʌn'ɔːltərəbl] inal-

terável

unanimity [ˌjuːnəˈnimiti] unanimidade *f*

unanswerable [ʌnˈɑːnsərəbl] incontestável, irrespondível

unapproachable [ˌʌnəˈprəutʃəbl] inabordável

unarmed [ˈʌnˈɑːmd] desarmado, inerme

unasked [ʌnˈɑːskt] espontâneo; não solicitado

unassuming [ˈʌnəˈsjuːmiŋ] despretensioso, modesto

unavailing [ˈʌnəˈveiliŋ] vão; ineficaz

unawares [ˈʌnəˈwɛəz] inesperadamente; de surpresa

unbar [ˈʌnˈbɑː] *v/t* destrancar

unbearable [ʌnˈbɛərəbl] intolerável, insuportável

unbelievable [ˌʌnbiˈliːvəbəl] incrível

unbelieving [ˈʌnbiːliːviŋ] incrédulo, descrente

unblind [ˈʌnˈbaind] *v/t* desatar

unborn [ˈʌnˈbɔːn] por nascer

unbounded [ʌnˈbaundid] ilimitado, infinito; imenso

unburden [ʌnˈbəːdn] *v/t* descarregar; desabafar; aliviar

unbuttoned [ˈʌnˈbʌtnd] desabotoado

uncanny [ʌnˈkæni] estranho, esquisito

uncertain [ʌnˈsəːtn] incerto, duvidoso; indeciso, irresoluto; variável; **~ty** incerteza *f*

unchecked [ˈʌnˈtʃekt] desenfreado; não controlado

uncle [ˈʌŋkl] tio *m*

uncomfortable [ʌnˈkʌmfətəbl] desconfortável, incómodo; desagradável; constrangido

uncommitted [ˈʌnkəˈmitid] não comprometido; sem compromissos

unconcerned [ˈʌnkənˈsəːnd] indiferente, despreocupado

unconscious [ʌnˈkɔnʃəs] *adj, s* inconsciente *m, f*; **~ness** inconsciência *f*

unconsidered [ˈʌnkənˈsidəd] irrefle(c)tido, inconsiderado

uncouple [ˈʌnˈkʌpl] *v/t* desengatar; soltar

uncouth [ʌnˈkuːθ] grosseiro, rude

uncover [ʌnˈkʌvə] descobrir

uncritical [ˈʌnˈkritikəl] não crítico

uncut [ˈʌnˈkʌt] sem cortes, completo; não talhado; não cortado

undaunted [ʌnˈdɔːntid] intrépido, denodado

undeceive [ˈʌndiˈsiːv] *v/t* desenganar, desiludir

undecided [ˈʌndiˈsaidid] indeciso

undeniable [ˌʌndiˈnaiəbl] inegável

under [ˈʌndə] *prp* debaixo de, sob; abaixo de; COM menos de; por baixo de; inferior a; *adv* debaixo, em baixo; por baixo; **~age** menor; **~clothing** roupa *f* de baixo, roupa *f* interior; **~current** subcorrente *f*; tendência *f* oculta; **~done**

mal passado; **~estimate** *v/t* subestimar; **~go** *v/t* sofrer, passar por; **~ground** *s* metropolitano *m*; *adj* subterrâneo; **~hand** clandestino; **~line** *v/t* sublinhar; **~ling** subalterno *m*; **~mine** *v/t* minar, solapar; **~neath** *prp* debaixo de, por baixo de; *adv* debaixo, em baixo, por baixo; **~pants** *s/pl* cuecas *f/pl*, ceroulas *f/pl*; **~stand** *v/t*, *v/i* entender, compreender, perceber; **~standing** *s* compreensão *f*; entendimento *m*; **~statement** atenuação *f*, afirmação *f* atenuada; **~take** *v/t* empreender; tomar a seu cargo, encarregar-se de; comprometer-se a; **~taker** agente *m* funerário; **~taking** *s* empresa *f*
under|wear ['ʌndəwɛə] roupa *f* interior; **~weight** *adj* com peso a menos
undesirable ['ʌndi'zaiərəbl] *adj* indesejável
undeveloped ['ʌndi'veləpt] não desenvolvido
undies ['ʌndi:z] *s/pl* roupa *f* interior de senhora
undo ['ʌn'du:] *v/t* desfazer; desatar
undoubted [ʌn'dautid] indubitável
undress ['ʌn'dres] *v/t*, *v/i* despir(-se)
undue [ˌʌn'dju:] indevido; excessivo
undulat|e ['ʌndjuleit] *v/i* ondular, ondear; **~ion** ondulação *f*
unearthly [ʌn'ə:θli] sobrenatural
uneas|iness [ʌn'i:zinis] inquietude *f*; **~y** inquieto
uneducated ['ʌn'edʒukeitid] ignorante, inculto
unemploy|ed ['ʌnim'plɔid] desempregado; **~ment** desemprego *m*, falta *f* de trabalho
unequal ['ʌn'i:kwəl] desigual; **be ~ to the task** não estar à altura da tarefa; **~(l)ed** sem igual, inigualável
unequivocal ['ʌni'kwivəkəl] inequívoco
uneven ['ʌn'i:vən] irregular; desigual; ímpar; acidentado
unexampled [ˌʌnig'zɑ:mpld] sem igual, sem exemplo
unexpected ['ʌniks'pektid] inesperado, imprevisto
unfailing [ʌn'feiliŋ] infalível; incansável
unfair ['ʌn'fɛə] injusto, desleal; parcial
unfaltering [ʌn'fɔ:ltəriŋ] inabalável; firme
unfavo(u)rable ['ʌn'feivərəbl] desfavorável, adverso
unfit ['ʌn'fit] *adj* inadequado, impróprio; incapacitado
unfold ['ʌn'fəuld] *v/t* desdobrar
unforeseen ['ʌnfɔ:'si:n] imprevisto
unforgettable ['ʌnfə'getəbəl] inesquecível
unfortunate [ʌn'fɔ:tʃnit] *adj* infeliz, desgraçado; **~ly** infelizmente
unfriendly ['ʌn'frendli] hostil

unfurnished ['ʌn'fəːniʃt] desmobilado
ungainly [ʌn'geinli] sem graça, tosco, desajeitado
ungodly [ʌn'gɔdli] ímpio; malvado, terrível
ungracious ['ʌn'greiʃəs] indelicado, rude
ungrateful [ʌn'greitful] ingrato
unguarded ['ʌn'gɑːdid] incauto, descuidado
unhapp|iness [ʌn'hæpinis] infelicidade *f*; **~y** triste; infeliz
unhealthy [ʌn'helθi] insalubre; doentio
unheard ['ʌn'həːd] não ouvido; **~-of** inaudito
unhook ['ʌn'huk] *v/t* desenganchar; desacolchetar
unhoped for [ʌn'həuptfɔː] inesperado
uniform ['juːnifɔːm] *s, adj* uniforme *m*; **~ity** uniformidade *f*
unify ['juːnifai] *v/t* unificar
unilateral ['juːni'lætərəl] unilateral
uninhabitable ['ʌnin'hæbitəbəl] inabitável
uninterrupted ['ʌnintə'rʌptid] ininterrupto
union ['juːnjən] sindicato *m*; união *f*
unit ['juːnit] unidade *f*; **~e** [-'nait] *v/t, v/i* unir(-se); **~y** ['juːniti] (*pl* **-ties**) unidade *f*
univers|al [ˌjuːni'vəːsəl] universal; **~e** ['-vəːs] universo *m*; **~ity** [ˌ-'vəːsiti] (*pl* **-ties**) universidade *f*
unjust ['ʌn'dʒʌst] injusto
unkempt ['ʌn'kempt] despenteado, desgrenhado
unkind [ʌn'kaind] indelicado, grosseiro; cruel
unknow|ing ['ʌn'nəuiŋ] desconhecedor, sem o saber; **~n** *adj* desconhecido
unlawful ['ʌn'lɔːful] ilícito
unless [ən'les] a menos que, a não ser que, senão
unlike ['ʌn'laik] *adj* diferente, distinto; **~lihood** inverosimilitude *f*, inverosimilhança *f*; **~ly** inverosímil, pouco provável
unlimited [ʌn'limitid] ilimitado
unload ['ʌn'ləud] *v/t, v/i* descarregar
unlock ['ʌn'lɔk] *v/t* abrir com chave
unloosen [ʌn'luːsən] *v/t* desapertar
unlucky [ʌn'lʌki] desventurado, infeliz
unmannerly [ʌn'mænəli] descortês, malcriado
unmarried ['ʌn'mærid] solteiro
unmask ['ʌn'maːsk] *v/t* desmascarar
unmatched ['ʌn'mætʃt] incomparável, sem par
unmentionable [ʌn'menʃnəbl] não mencionável
unmindful [ʌn'maindful] descuidado
unmistakable ['ʌnmis'teikəbl] evidente, manifesto; inequívoco
unmoved ['ʌn'muːvd] impassí-

vel, insensível; firme

unnatural [ʌn'nætʃrəl] desnatural; desnaturado

unnecessary [ʌn'nesisəri] desnecessário

unnerve ['ʌn'nəːv] *v/t* desalentar

unnoticed ['ʌn'nəutist] despercebido

unobserved ['ʌnəb'zəːvd] despercebido, inobservado

unobtrusive ['ʌnəb'truːsiv] comedido, discreto

unpack ['ʌn'pæk] *v/t, v/i* desfazer as malas; desembrulhar

unparalleled [ʌn'pærəleld] sem paralelo

unpleasant [ʌn'pleznt] desagradável

unpopular ['ʌn'pɔpjulə] impopular

unpractised [ʌn'præktist] inexperiente, sem prática

unprejudiced [ʌn'predʒudist] imparcial

unprincipled [ʌn'prinsəpld] sem princípios

unprovoked ['ʌnprə'vəukt] não provocado

unpublished ['ʌn'pʌbliʃt] inédito

unquestionable [ʌn'kwestʃənəbəl] inquestionável, incontestável

unravel [ʌn'rævəl] *v/t, v/i* deslindar(-se); desemaranhar(-se)

unreason|able [ʌn'riːznəbl] pouco razoável; desarrazoado; **~ing** irracional, cego

unrelenting ['ʌnri'lentiŋ] inexorável

unrest ['ʌn'rest] inquietação *f*, agitação *f*

unrestrained ['ʌnri'streind] desenfreado

unriva(l)led [ʌn'raivəld] incomparável, sem rival

unroll ['ʌn'rəul] *v/t, v/i* desenrolar(-se)

unruffled ['ʌn'rʌfld] sereno, tranquilo, calmo

unruly [ʌn'ruːli] rebelde, indisciplinado

unsaid ['ʌn'sed] *adj* não dito, não proferido

unscathed ['ʌn'skeiðd] incólume, ileso

unscrupulous [ʌn'skruːpjuləs] pouco escrupuloso; sem escrúpulos

unseemly [ʌn'siːmli] inconveniente, impróprio

unseen ['ʌn'siːn] *adj* despercebido

unserviceable ['ʌn'səːvisəbl] imprestável

unsettle ['ʌn'setl] *v/t* perturbar; desarranjar, transtornar; **~d** *adj* variável, instável, incerto

unsightly [ʌn'saitli] feio

unskilled ['ʌn'skild] não especializado

unso|ciable [ʌn'səuʃəbl] insociável; **~cial** insocial

unsound ['ʌn'saund] infundado, erróneo; instável; defeituoso; doentio

unspeakable [ʌn'spiːkəbl] indizível

unstable ['ʌn'steibl] instável
unsteady ['ʌn'stedi] inconstante; vacilante
unstudied ['ʌn'stʌdid] natural
unsuitable ['ʌn'sju:təbl] impróprio, inconveniente
untangle ['ʌn'tæŋgl] *v/t* desembaraçar, des(e)maranhar
unthankful ['ʌn'θæŋkful] ingrato, mal-agradecido
unthink|able [ʌn'θiŋkəbl] inconcebível, impensável; **~ing** irrefle(c)tido
unthought-of [ʌn'θɔ:t-ɔv] inesperado, imprevisto
untidy [ʌn'taidi] desordenado
untie ['ʌn'tai] *v/t* desatar
until [ən'til] *prp* até; *conj* até que
untimely [ʌn'taimli] inoportuno; prematuro
untiring [ʌn'taiəriŋ] incansável, infatigável
untold ['ʌn'təuld] incalculável, incontável; não contado, por contar
untruth ['ʌn'tru:θ] falsidade *f*
unusual [ʌn'ju:ʒuəl] invulgar, insólito
unutterable [ʌn'ʌtərəbl] completo, chapado; indizível, inexprimível
unveil [ʌn'veil] *v/t* descobrir, desvendar
unwarranted ['ʌn'wɔrəntid] injustificado
unwell ['ʌn'wel] indisposto
unwholesome ['ʌn'həulsəm] insalubre
unwilling ['ʌn'wiliŋ] de má vontade, pouco disposto
unwind ['ʌn'waind] *v/t*, *v/i* desenrolar(-se)
unwise ['ʌn'waiz] desajuizado, insensato
unwitting [ʌn'witiŋ] involuntário; inconsciente
unwonted [ʌn'wəuntid] inusitado
unworthy [ʌn'wə:ði] indigno
unwrap ['ʌn'ræp] *v/t* desembrulhar
unwritten ['ʌn'ritn] não escrito, oral, verbal, tradicional
up [ʌp] *adj* ascendente; levantado; *adv* acima, para cima; em pé; *prp* por … acima; **be ~** acontecer, haver; **what's ~?** que foi? que há?; **~ and down** para cima e para baixo; **~ there** lá em cima
upbringing ['ʌpbriŋiŋ] *s* educação *f*, formação *f*
upcountry ['ʌp'kʌntri] *adj* interior
uphill ['ʌp'hil] *adj fig* difícil, árduo; ascendente; *adv* para cima; colina acima
uphold [ʌp'həuld] *v/t* sustentar, manter
upholster|er [ʌp'həulstərə] estofador *m*; **~y** tapeçaria *f*
upon [ə'pɔn] em, sobre
upper ['ʌpə] *adj* superior; **~most** o mais alto
upright ['ʌp'rait] *adj* vertical, direito; em/de pé; justo, íntegro, honesto; *adv* direito
uprising [ʌp'raiziŋ] sublevação *f*

uproar ['ʌprɔː] algazarra *f*, tumulto *m*, barulho *m*
upset ['ʌpset] *s* transtorno *m*; [-'set] *v/t* derrubar, derramar; transtornar, perturbar; *adj* perturbado, transtornado; preocupado; desarranjado
upside down ['ʌpsaid'daun] de pernas para o ar
upstairs ['ʌp'stɛəz] *adv* lá em cima
upstart ['ʌpstɑːt] novo-rico *m*, filho *m* da sorte
upstream ['ʌp'striːm] *adj*, *adv* rio acima
up to ['ʌp tu] até; à altura, bastante bom, bem; **be ~ ~ someone** caber a alguém; **be/get ~ ~ do s.th.** estar a fazer a/c. **~ ~ date** moderno, em dia
upward(s) ['ʌpwəd(z)] *adv* para cima
urban ['əːbən] urbano; **~e** [-'bein] cortês
urchin ['əːtʃin] gaiato *m*, brejeiro *m*, garoto *m*, *Braz* moleque *m*
urg|e [əːdʒ] *s* impulso *m*, desejo *m*, ânsia *f*; *v/t* incitar; insistir em; urgir, instar; **~ency** urgência *f*; **~ent** urgente
urin|ate ['juərineit] *v/i* urinar; **~e** urina *f*
urn [əːn] urna *f*
us [ʌs, əs, s] nós, nos
usage ['juːzidʒ] emprego *m*, uso *m*, prática *f*
use [juːs] *s* uso *m*; [juːz] *v/t* usar, empregar, fazer uso de; **~d** [juːzd] usado; **~d** [juːst]: **~d to** habituado a, acostumado a; **~ful** útil; **~fulness** utilidade *f*; **~less** inútil; **~lessness** inutilidade *f*
user ['juːsə] *s* usuário *m*; **~ account** *s* COMP conta *f* do usuário
usher ['ʌʃə] *v/t* introduzir, anunciar; **~ette** [ˌ-'ret] arrumadora *f*, indicadora *f*
usual ['juːʒuəl] costumado, usual, habitual; **as ~** como de costume
usurer ['juːʒərə] usurário *m*
usurp [juː'zəːp] *v/t* usurpar; **~er** usurpador *m*
usury ['juːʒuri] usura *f*
utensil [ju(ː)'tensl] utensílio *m*
utility [ju(ː)'tiliti] (*pl* **-ties**) utilidade *f*; benefício *m*; serviço *m* público
utilize ['juːtilaiz] *v/t* utilizar
utmost ['ʌtməust] *adj* máximo, extremo; **do one's ~** fazer todo o possível
utopia [juː'təupjə] utopia *f*; **~n** utópico
utter ['ʌtə] *adj* completo, total; *v/t* proferir, pronunciar; soltar; passar; **~ance** articulação *f*, expressão *f*; **~most** extremo
uvula ['juːvjulə] úvula *f*

V

vacan|cy ['veikənsi] (*pl* **-cies**) vaga *f*, vacatura *f*, vacância *f*; **~t** vago, livre, desocupado; vazio
vacate [və'keit] *v/t* evacuar, deixar
vacation [və'keiʃən] *s* férias *f/pl*
vaccinate ['væksineit] *v/t* vacinar
vacillat|e ['væsileit] *v/i* vacilar; **~ion** [-'leiʃən] vacilação *f*
vacuum ['vækjuəm] *s* vácuo *m*, vazio *m*; **~-cleaner** aspirador *m*
vagabond ['vægəbənd] vagabundo *m*
vagary ['veigəri] (*pl* **-ries**) capricho *m*, veneta *f*
vague [veig] vago, impreciso
vain [vein] vão; vaidoso, **in ~** em vão
valet ['vælit] *s* criado *m* de quarto
valid ['vælid] válido; **~ity** [və'liditi] validade *f*
valley ['væli] vale *m*
valuable ['væljuəbl] valioso, de valor, precioso; **~s** ['-z] *s/pl* obje(c)tos *m/pl* de valor
valu|e ['vælju:] *s* valor *m*; *v/t* avaliar; **~eless** sem valor; **~er** ['-juə] avaliador *m*
valve [vælv] válvula *f*
van [væn] furgoneta *f*; vagão *m*; furgão *m*
vane [vein] cata-vento *m*, grimpa *f*
vanilla [və'nilə] baunilha *f*
vanish ['væniʃ] *v/i* desaparecer, desvanecer-se; dissipar-se
vanity ['væniti] (*pl* **-ties**) vaidade *f*; **~ case** bols(inh)a *f* de maquiagem
vaporize ['veipəraiz] *v/t*, *v/i* vaporizar(-se)
vapo(u)r ['veipə] vapor *m*
vari|able ['vɛəriəbl] *adj* variável; **~ance** desacordo *m*, desavença *f*; **at ~ance with** em desacordo com; **~ant** *s* variante *f*; **~ation** [-'eiʃən] variação *f*
variety [və'raiəti] (*pl* **-ties**) variedade *f*
various ['vɛəriəs] vários, diversos
varnish ['vɑ:niʃ] *s* verniz *m*; *v/t* envernizar
vary ['vɛəri] *v/t*, *v/i* variar
vase [vɑ:z] vaso *m*
vast [vɑ:st] vasto, imenso; **~ness** vastidão *f*, imensidade *f*
vat [væt] tonel *m*, tina *f*
vault [vɔ:lt] *s* abóbada *f*; salto *m* à vara; *v/t*, *v/i* saltar à vara
veal [vi:l] (carne *f* de) vitela *f*
vegeta|ble ['vedʒitəbl] *adj* vegetal; *s* legume *m*, hortaliça *f*; **~rian** [ˌ-'tɛriən] vegetariano; **~te** ['-teit] *v/i* vegetar; **~tion** [ˌ-'teiʃən] vegetação *f*
vehement ['vi:imənt] veemente

vehicle ['vi:ikl] veículo *m*
veil [veil] *s* véu *m*; *v/t* velar
vein [vein] veia *f*; veio *m*; estado *m* de espírito
velocity [vi'lɔsiti] velocidade *f*
velvet ['velvit] veludo *m*; **~een** belbutina *f*; **~y** aveludado
vend [vend] *v/t* vender; **~ing-machine** distribuidor *m* automático; **~or** vendedor *m*
venerable ['venərəbəl] venerável
venerate ['venəreit] *v/t* venerar
venereal [vi'niəriəl] venéreo
Venetian [vi'ni:ʃən] veneziano; **♀ blind** veneziana *f*, persiana *f*
vengeance ['vendʒəns] vingança *f*
venison ['venzn] carne *f* de veado
venom ['venəm] veneno *m*; **~ous** venenoso
vent [vent] *s* respiradouro *m*; *v/t* desafogar, desabafar
ventilat|e ['ventileit] *v/t* ventilar; **~ion** [-'leiʃən] ventilação *f*; **~or** ventilador *m*
ventriloquist [ven'triləkwist] ventríloquo *m*
venture ['ventʃə] *s* especulação *f*; *v/t*, *v/i* aventurar(-se), arriscar(-se)
veranda(h) [və'rændə] varanda *f*
verb [və:b] verbo *m*
verbal ['və:bəl] *adj* verbal; literal
verbose [və:'bəus] prolixo, verboso
verge [və:dʒ] *s* borda *f*, beira *f*; **on the ~ of** à beira de, prestes a
verify ['verifai] *v/t* verificar
veritable ['veritəbl] verdadeiro
vermicelli [,və:mi'seli] aletria *f*
vermin ['və:min] vérmina *f*
verm(o)uth ['və:məθ] vermute *m*
versatil|e ['və:sətail] versátil; **~ity** versatilidade *f*
vers|e [və:s] verso *m*; estrofe *f*; **~ify** ['-sifai] *v/t* versificar; **~ion** ['-ʃən] versão *f*
vertical ['və:tikəl] *adj* vertical
vertigo ['və:tigəu] vertigem *f*
very ['veri] *adv* muito; *adj* mesmo; **~ good** muito bom; muito bem; **~ well** muito bem; **the ~ idea** mas que ideia
vessel ['vesl] vaso *m*, recipiente *m*; navio *m*
vest [vest] *s US* colete *m*; *GB* camisola *f* interior
vestibule ['vestibju:l] vestíbulo *m*
vestige ['vestidʒ] vestígio *m*
vestry ['vestri] (*pl* **-tries**) sacristia *f*
vet [vet] *s* veterinário *m*
veteran ['vetərən] *adj*, *s* veterano *m*
veterinary ['vetərinəri] veterinário
veto ['vi:təu] *s* veto *m*; *v/t* vetar
vex [veks] *v/t* vexar; molestar; **~ation** [-k'seiʃən] contrariedade *f*; vexame *m*; **~atious** [-k'seifəs] vexatório; molesto
via ['vaiə] via, por (via de)
viable ['vaiəbl] viável
viaduct ['vaiədʌkt] viaduto *m*

vibrat|e [vai'breit] *v/t, v/i* vibrar; **~ion** vibração *f*
vicar ['vikə] vigário *m*; cura *m*; **~age** vicariato *m*
vice [vais] *s* vício *m*
vice versa ['vaisi'və:sə] vice-versa
vicinity [vi'siniti] (*pl* **-ties**) vizinhança *f*
vicious ['viʃəs] mau, malvado
vicissitude [vi'sisitju:d] vicissitude *f*
victim ['viktim] vítima *f*; **~ize** *v/t* vitimar
victorious [vik'tɔ:riəs] vitorioso; **~y** ['-təri] (*pl* **-ries**) vitória *f*
vie [vai] *v/i* rivalizar, competir
view [vju:] *s* vista *f*; *v/t* ver, observar; considerar, ponderar; **in ~** em vista; **in ~ of** devido a, em vista de; **on ~** em exposição; **~er** telespectador *m*
vigil ['vidʒil] vigília *f*; **~ance** vigilância *f*; **~ant** vigilante
vigorous ['vigərəs] vigoroso
vigo(u)r ['vigə] vigor *m*
vil|e [vail] vil; abje(c)to; **~ify** ['vilifai] *v/t* vilipendiar, aviltar
villa ['vilə] vila *f*, vivenda *f*
villag|e ['vilidʒ] aldeia *f*, povoação; **~er** aldeão *m*
villain ['vilən] celerado *m*, vilão *m*
vindic|ate ['vindikeit] *v/t* vindicar, justificar; **~ation** [-'keiʃən] vindicação *f*, justificação *f*; **~tive** vingativo
vine [vain] vinha *f*, videira *f*
vinegar ['vinigə] vinagre *m*
vint|age ['vintidʒ] *s* vindima *f*; **~ner** ['-nə] negociante *m* de vinhos, vinhateiro *m*
viola [vi'əulə] viola *f*
violat|e ['vaiəleit] *v/t* violar; **~ion** [-'leiʃən] violação *f*
violen|ce ['vaiələns] violência *f*; **~t** violento
violet ['vaiəlit] *adj*, *s* violeta *f*
viol|in [ˌvaiə'lin] violino *m*; **~inist** violinista *m, f*; **~oncello** [ˌ-lən'tʃeləu] violoncelo *m*
viper ['vaipə] víbora *f*
virgin ['və:dʒin] virgem *f*; **~al** virginal; **~ity** [-'dʒiniti] virgindade *f*
viril|e ['virail] viril; **~ity** [-'riliti] virilidade *f*
virtu|al ['və:tjuəl] virtual; **~e** ['-tju:] virtude *f*; **~osity** [ˌ-'ɔsiti] virtuosidade *f*; **~oso** [ˌ-'əuzəu] virtuose *m*; **~ous** ['-tjuəs] virtuoso
virulen|ce ['viruləns] virulência *f*; **~t** virulento
virus ['vaiərəs] vírus *m*; COMP vírus *m*
visa ['vi:zə] *s* visto *m*
viscount ['vaikaunt] visconde *m*; **~ess** viscondessa *f*
viscous ['viskəs] viscoso
visib|ility [ˌvizi'biliti] visibilidade *f*; **~le** ['vizibl] visível
vision ['viʒən] visão *f*; **~ary** *adj*, *s* visionário *m*
visit ['vizit] *s* visita *f*; *v/t*, *v/i* visitar; **~or** visita *f*, visitante *m, f*
visor ['vaizə] viseira *f*
vista ['vistə] perspectiva *f*
visual ['vizjuəl] visual; **~ize** *v/t* imaginar, visualizar

vital ['vaitl] vital; **~ity** [-'tæliti] vitalidade *f*; **~ize** *v/t* vitalizar
vitamin(e) ['vitəmin] vitamina *f*
vitriol ['vitriəl] acrimónia *f*; vitríolo *m*; **~ic** [ˌ-'ɔlik] vitriólico; cáustico, acerbo
vituperation [viˌtjuːpə'reiʃən] vituperação *f*, vitupério *m*
vivaci|ous [vi'veiʃəs] vivaz, vivo, animado; **~ty** [-'væsiti] vivacidade *f*
vivid ['vivid] vívido; brilhante, intenso; **~ness** vivacidade *f*
vixen ['viksn] raposa *f* fêmea; megera *f*
voc|abulary [və'kæbjuləri] (*pl* **-ries**) vocabulário *m*; **~al** ['vəukəl] *adj* vocal; **~alist** ['vəukəlist] vocalista *m, f*
vocation [vəu'keiʃən] vocação *f*
vociferous [vəu'sifərəs] vociferante
vogue [vəug] voga *f*, moda *f*
voice [vɔis] *s* voz *f*; *v/t* exprimir, formular; sonorizar; **~ mail** *s* TEL correio *m* do voz
void [vɔid] *adj* vazio; sem efeito, nulo; *s* vazio *m*, vácuo *m*; *v/t* invalidar, anular
volatile ['vɔlətail] volátil
volcan|ic [vɔl'kænik] vulcânico; **~o** [-'keinəu] (*pl* **-noes**) vulcão *m*
volley ['vɔli] *s* descarga *f*, salva *f*; **~-ball** vol(e)ibol *m*
volt [vəult] vóltio *m*; **~age** voltagem *f*
voluble ['vɔljubl] volúvel
volum|e ['vɔljum] volume *m*; **~inous** [və'ljuːminəs] volum(in)oso
volunt|ary ['vɔləntəri] *adj* voluntário; **~eer** [ˌ-'tiə] *s* voluntário *m*; *v/i* oferecer(-se); apresentar-se como voluntário
voluptuous [və'lʌptjuəs] voluptuoso
vomit ['vɔmit] *s* vómito *m*; *v/t*, *v/i* vomitar
vorac|ious [və'reiʃəs] voraz; **~ity** [-'ræsiti] voracidade *f*
vot|e [vəut] *s* voto *m*; *v/i* votar; **~er** votante *m, f*, eleitor *m*
vouch ['vautʃ]: **~ for** *v/i* garantir, responder por; **~er** senha *f*, talão *m*; vale *m*; **~safe** *v/t* conceder
vow [vau] *s* voto *m*; *v/t* fazer voto, jurar; consagrar
vowel ['vauəl] vogal *f*
voyag|e ['vɔidʒ] *s* viagem *f* por mar; **~er** viajante *m, f*, navegante *m*
vulgar ['vʌlgə] grosseiro; vulgar; **~ity** [-'gæriti] grosseria *f*, grossaria *f*
vulnerable ['vʌlnərəbl] vulnerável
vulture ['vʌltʃə] abutre *m*

W

wad [wɔd] *s* maço *m*; chumaço *m*; bucha *f*
waddle ['wɔdl] *v/i* bambolear (-se), gingar
wad|e [weid] *v/i* patinhar; vadear, passar a vau; **~ers** *s/pl* botas *f/pl* altas e impermeáveis
wafer ['weifə] ECCL hóstia *f*; bolacha *f*; obreia *f*
wag [wæg] *s* folgazão *m*, gracejador *m*; *v/t, v/i* abanar, agitar, sacudir
wage [weidʒ] salário *m*; *v/t* empreender, empenhar-se em; **~-earner** assalariado *m*; **~r** *s* aposta *f*; *v/t, v/i* apostar; **~s** *s/pl* salário *m*
waggish ['wægiʃ] pilhérico, folgazão, gracejador
waggle ['wægl] *v/t, v/i* menear (-se), abanar
wa(g)gon ['wægən] carroça *f*; vagão *m*; **~er** carreteiro *m*, carroceiro *m*
wagtail ['wægteil] alvéloa *f*
wail [weil] *s* lamentação *f*; vagido *m*; *v/i* lamentar-se; choramingar
wainscot ['weinskət] lambril *m*
waist [weist] cintura *f*, cinta *f*; **~coat** colete *m*
wait [weit] *s* espera *f*; *v/t, v/i* esperar, aguardar; ficar; **~ at table** servir à mesa; **~er** criado *m* de mesa
waiting-room ['weitiŋ-ru:m] sala *f* de espera
waitress ['weitris] criada *f* de mesa, *Braz* garçonete *f*
wake [weik] *v/t, v/i* despertar, acordar; *s* esteira *f*, sulco *m*; vigília *f*, velório *m*; **~ful** acordado, desperto; insone; vigilante
walk [wɔ:k] *s* passeio *m*, volta *f*; alameda *f*; andar *m*; caminhada *f*; *v/t, v/i* andar, caminhar, passear, ir a pé; **~er** caminhante *m, f*
walkie-talkie ['wɔ:ki'tɔ:ki] transmissor-receptor *m* portátil
walking ['wɔ:kiŋ] *adj* ambulante; a pé; para andar; **~-stick** bengala *f*, bastão *m*
wall [wɔ:l] *s* muro *m*; muralha *f*; parede *f*; *v/t* murar; emparedar; entaipar
wallet ['wɔlit] carteira *f* de bolso
wallow ['wɔləu] *v/i* chafurdar; espojar-se
walnut ['wɔ:lnət] noz *f*
walrus ['wɔ:lrəs] morsa *f*
waltz [wɔ:ls] *s* valsa *f*; *v/i* valsar
wand [wɔnd] vara *f*, varinha *f*
wander ['wɔndə] *v/t, v/i* vaguear, errar, vadiar; delirar; divagar, desviar-se de; **~er** viandante *m, f*, viajante *m, f*; **~ing** *adj* errante; nómada
want [wɔnt] *v/t* querer, desejar;

precisar (de), necessitar (de); *s* carência *f*, falta *f*, necessidade *f*; **~ing** *adj* falho (de), falto (de); *prp* sem

war [wɔː] *s* guerra *f*

warble ['wɔːbl] *v/i* gorjear, trinar; *s* gorjeio *m*, trinado *m*

ward [wɔːd] *s* pupilo *m*, tutelado *m*; enfermaria *f*; quarteirão *m*, bairro *m*; **~en** guarda *m*; dire(c)tor *m*, administrador *m*; **~er** carcereiro *m*

wardrobe ['wɔːdrəub] guarda-roupa *m*

warehouse ['wɛəhaus] armazém *m*

warlike ['wɔːlaik] bélico, belicoso, marcial

warm [wɔːm] *s* quente *m*, aquecimento *m*; *adj* quente; caloroso; ardente; *v/t, v/i* aquecer (-se), esquentar

warmth [wɔːmθ] calor *m*

warn [wɔːn] *v/t, v/i* prevenir, avisar

warning ['wɔːniŋ] *s* aviso *m*, advertência *f*

warp [wɔːp] *v/t, v/i* empenar

warrant ['wɔrənt] *v/t* justificar; garantir; **~y** (*pl* **-ties**) garantia *f*

warren ['wɔrən] lura *f*, coelheira *f*

warrior ['wɔriə] guerreiro *m*

wart [wɔːt] verruga *f*

wary ['wɛəri] cauteloso, circunspecto, prudente

was [wɔz, wəz] *1. a 3. sg past of* **be**

wash [wɔʃ] *s* lavagem *f*; *v/t, v/i* lavar(-se); **~out** *s* fiasco *m*; **~ up** lavar a louça; lançar à praia; **~able** lavável; **~-basin** lavatório *m*; **~erwoman** lavadeira *f*; **~-house** lavadoiro *m*; **~ing** *s* roupa *f* lavada/suja; **~ing-machine** máquina *f* de lavar roupa; **~ing-up** *s* lavagem *f* da louça; **~y** débil, fraco

wasp [wɔsp] vespa *f*

waste [weist] *adj* inculto; vago; perdido; inútil; *s* desperdício *m*; estrago *m*; desgaste *m*; perda *f*; *v/t, v/i* gastar; desperdiçar, estragar, esbanjar; perder; **~ away** definhar-se; **~ful** esbanjador; **~-paper basket** cesto *m* dos papéis

watch [wɔtʃ] *v/t, v/i* observar, olhar; ver, assistir a; vigiar; *s* relógio *m*; vigilância *f*; vigia *f*, guarda *f*; ronda *f*; **~ for** esperar por; **~ out** ter cuidado, estar alerta; **~ful** vigilante; **~fulness** vigilância *f*; **~-maker** relojoeiro *m*

water ['wɔːtə] *s* água *f*; *v/t, v/i* molhar; banhar; regar; aguar; **~ down** aguar, diluir; atenuar; **~-colo(u)r** aguarela *f*; **~-cress** ['-kres] agrião *m*

water|fall ['wɔːtəfɔːl] cascata *f*, catarata *f*, queda *f* de água; **~ing can** regador *m*; **~-level** nível *m* de água; **~-line** linha *f* de flutuação; **~-mill** moinho *m* de água, azenha *f*; **~-power** força *f* hidráulica; **~proof** *adj*, *s* impermeável *m*; **~shed** linha *f* divisória das águas; **~tight** es-

tanque; inequívoco; **~works** obras *f/pl* hidráulicas
watery ['wɔːtəri] aguado, aquoso; (h)úmido; encharcado
watt [wɔt] vátio *m*
wattle ['wɔtl] *s* caniçada *f*
wave [weiv] *s* vaga *f*, onda *f*; aceno *m*, gesto *m*; *v/t, v/i* ondear; agitar; ondular; acenar; tremular
waver ['weivə] *v/i* hesitar, vacilar
wax [wæks] *s* cera *f*; *v/t* encerar; **~en** de cera
way [wei] *s* caminho *m*; modo *m*, maneira *f*, meio *m*; **by the ~** a propósito; **by ~ of** por via de; para servir de; **in a ~** de certo modo; **in no ~** de nenhum modo; **on the ~ (to)** a caminho(de); **this ~** por aqui; **that ~** por ali; **give ~** ceder; desmoronar-se; **make ~** abrir caminho; **~lay** *v/t* armar ciladas a; **~ward** caprichoso, cabeçudo
we [wiː, wi] nós
weak [wiːk] fraco; débil; deficiente; **~en** *v/t, v/i* enfraquecer; **~ness** fraqueza *f*, debilidade *f*; fraco *m*
wealth [welθ] riqueza *f*; abundância *f*; **~y** rico, abastado
wean [wiːn] *v/t* desmamar
weapon ['wepən] arma *f*
wear [wɛə] *s* uso *m*; desgaste *m*; vestuário *m*; *v/t, v/i* usar, vestir, trazer; desgastar, gastar(-se), consumir-se; **~ out** gastar-se; esgotar-se, estafar-se; **~ and tear** desgaste *m*; **~ away** desgastar; **~ing** *adj* cansativo, fatigante
wear|isome ['wiərisəm] cansativo, enfadonho, maçador; **~y** *adj* exausto, estafado; estafante
weasel ['wiːzl] *s* doninha *f*
weather ['weðə] *s* tempo *m* atmosférico; *v/t* resistir a, aguentar; **~-forecast** boletim *m* metereológico
weav|e [wiːv] *v/t, v/i* tramar, urdir; tecer; **~er** tecelão *m*
web [web] teia *f*
wedding ['wediŋ] *s* casamento *m*; **~-ring** aliança *f*
wedge [wedʒ] *s* cunha *f*; *v/t* rachar com cunha
wedlock ['wedlɔk] casamento *m*, matrimónio *m*
Wednesday ['wenzdi] quarta-feira *f*
wee [wiː] *adj* diminuto, minúsculo; *v/i* fazer chichi
weed [wiːd] *s* erva *f* daninha; *v/t, v/i* arrancar as ervas daninhas, sachar; **~y** débil
week [wiːk] semana *f*; **last ~** a semana passada; **next ~** na próxima semana; **~-day** dia *m* útil; **~-end** *s* fim *m* de semana; **~ly** *s* semanário *m*; *adj* semanal
weep [wiːp] *v/t, v/i* chorar; **~ing willow** chorão *m*
weigh [wei] *v/t* pesar; **~ anchor** zarpar, levantar âncora
weight [weit] *s* peso *m*; **~y** pesado; grave, importante

weir [wiə] represa *f*, açude *m*
weird [wiəd] esquisito, estranho; misterioso, fantástico
welcome ['welkəm] *adj* bem-vindo; *s* boas-vindas *f/pl*; *v/t* dar as boas-vindas a; receber, acolher
weld [weld] *v/t*, *v/i* soldar; caldear
welfare ['welfɛə] bem-estar *m*
well [wel] *s* poço *m*; *v/i* manar, brotar; *adj* bom, bem, de/ /com saúde; *adv* bem; *int* ora, bem; **as ~ as** assim como; **~-being** bem-estar *m*; **~-bred** bem-criado, bem-educado; **~-done** bem passado; **~-known** bem conhecido; **~-meaning** bem-intencionado
Welsh [welʃ] *adj* galês
went [went] *past of* **go**
were [wəː, wə] *past pl of* **be**
west [west] *s* oeste *m*, ocidente *m*; *adj*, **~ern** ocidental, do oeste
wet [wet] *adj* molhado; (h)úmido; chuvoso; *v/t* molhar; (h)umedecer
whale [weil] baleia *f*; **~r** pescador *m* de baleias; baleeiro *m*
wharf [wɔːf] cais *m*, desembarcadouro *m*
what [wɔt] *pron* que, o que; qual; quê; *adj* que; **~** (...) **for?** para quê? **~ if ...?** que tal se ...? e se ...?; **~ the ...?** mas que ...?; **~ever**, **~soever** *pron*, *adj* qualquer que; tudo o que, tanto quanto; seja o que for; qualquer que seja
wheat [wiːt] trigo *m*
wheel [wiːl] *s* roda *f*; *v/t*, *v/i* voltar-se; rolar, fazer rodar; **~-barrow** carrinho *m* de mão
whelp [welp] *s* cachorrinho *m*
when [wen] *adv*, *pron* quando; *conj* quando, no tempo em que
whenever [wen'evə] *adv*, *conj* sempre que
where [wɛə] *adv* onde; aonde; **~abouts** *s* paradeiro *m*; *adv* onde, em que lugar; **~as** [wɛər'æz] porquanto, ao passo que; **~upon** ao que, depois do que
wherever [wɛə'revə] *adv*, *conj* onde quer que (seja); para onde quer que
wherry ['weri] (*pl* **-ries**) bote *m*
whet [wet] *v/t* estimular; afiar
whether ['weðə] se; quer, ou
whey [wei] soro *m* do leite
which [witʃ] *pron* que, o qual, o que; que?, qual?; **~ever** [-'tʃevə] qualquer que; seja qual for
whiff [wif] *s* baforada *f*
while [wail] *conj* enquanto; ao passo que; *s* pouco *m*, espaço *m* de tempo; **a ~** um pouco; **once in a ~** de vez em quando; **~ away** *v/t* passar, matar
whilst [wailst] ao passo que
whim [wim] capricho *m*, veneta *f*
whimper ['wimpə] *v/i* choramingar
whimsical ['wimzikəl] caprichoso

whimsy ['wimzi] extravagância *f*
whine [wain] *s* ganido *m*; *v/i* lamuriar, choramingar; ganir
whinny ['wini] *v/i* relinchar
whip [wip] *s* chicote *m*; *v/t* chicotear; bater; **~ping** açoite *m*, surra *f*
whirl [wəːl] *s* rodopio *m*; *s* turbilhão *m*; *v/i* turbilhonar; rodopiar; **~pool** remoinho *m*; **~-wind** turbilhão *m*
whir(r) [wəː] *v/i* zunir, zumbir; *s* zumbido *m*
whisk [wisk] *v/t* sacudir; bater; *s* batedor *m*; sacudidela *f*
whiskers ['wiskəz] *s/pl* suíças *f/pl*
whisk(e)y ['wiski] uísque *m*
whisper ['wispə] *v/t*, *v/i* cochichar; *s* cochicho *m*
whistle ['wisl] *v/t*, *v/i* assobiar, apitar; silvar; *s* assobio *m*, silvo *m*; apito *m*
white [wait] *adj*, *s* branco *m*; **~n** *v/t*, *v/i* branquear, embranquecer; **~ness** brancura *f*; **~wash** *s* cal *f*; *v/t* caiar
whitlow ['witləu] panarício *m*
Whitsun(tide) ['witsən(taid)] Pentecostes *m*
whittle ['witl] *v/t* aparar, cortar, talhar
whiz(z) [wiz] *v/i* zunir; silvar
who [huː, hu] quem; que; o que, o qual; **~ever** quem quer que seja
whole [həul] *adj* todo; inteiro; integral; inta(c)to; completo; total; *s* todo *m*; total *m*, totalidade *f*; **~sale** *adj*, *adv* em massa; COM por atacado; **~some** são, sadio, salutar
whom [huːm] *pron* quem; que; o que, o qual
whoop [huːp] *s* vaia *f*, grito *m*, apupo *m*; *v/i* vaiar, gritar, apupar; **~ing-cough** coqueluche *f*
whose [huːz] *pron* cujo; de quem, do qual
why [wai] *adv* porquê?; porque ...?; por que; *int* quê!; ora! bem!
wick [wik] mecha *f*, pavio *m*
wicked ['wikid] mau, ruim, malvado
wicker ['wikə] vime *m*
wicket ['wikit] postigo *m*, portinhola *f*
wide [waid] *adj* largo, amplo, grande, vasto, imenso; **~ly** amplamente; **~n** *v/t*, *v/i* alargar(-se), estender(-se); dilatar(-se); **~spread** muito divulgado, muito comum
widow ['widəu] viúva *f*; **~er** viúvo *m*; **~hood** viuvez *f*
width [widθ] largura *f*
wield [wiːld] *v/t* manejar
wife [waif] (*pl* **wives** [-vz]) mulher *f*, esposa *f*
wig [wig] peruca *f*, cabeleira *f* postiça
wild [waild] *adj* selvagem; feroz, bravo, bravio; silvestre; deserto, inculto; **~ boar** javali *m*; **~erness** ['wildənis] lugar *m* selvagem; ermo *m*; **~ly** descontroladamente
wil(l)ful ['wilful] voluntarioso;

intencional
will [wil] *s* vontade *f*; testamento *m*; *v/t* legar, testar; *v/aux* desejar; querer; **at ~** à vontade; **where there's a ~, there's a way** querer é poder; **~ing** *adj* disposto, pronto; voluntário; **~ingly** de boa vontade
willow ['wiləu] salgueiro *m*
wilt [wilt] *v/t, v/i* murchar
wily ['waili] ardiloso, manhoso, astucioso
win [win] *s* vitória *f*; *v/t, v/i* ganhar, vencer
wince [wins] *v/i* estremecer; *s* estremecimento *m*
wind [wind] *s* vento *m*; flatulência *f*; fôlego *m*; **get ~ of** ouvir dizer
wind [waind] *v/t* enrolar(-se); serpentear; dar corda a; içar, levantar; *s* rotação *f*, volta *f*
winding ['waindiŋ] *adj* sinuoso, tortuoso; *s* volta *f*, dobra *f*; sinuosidade *f*; ELECT enrolamento *m*
windlass ['windləs] molinete *m*, bolinete *m*
windmill ['win,mil] moinho *m* de vento
window ['windəu] janela *f*; **~-pane** vidraça *f*, vidro *m*; **~sill** peitoril *m*
windpipe ['windpaip] traqueia *f*
wind-screen ['windskri:n] pára-brisas *m*; **~ wiper** limpa-pára-brisas *m*
windy ['windi] ventoso
wine [wain] *s* vinho *m*
wing [wiŋ] *s* asa *f*; ala *f*, flanco *m*; **~ed** *adj* alado
wink [wiŋk] *s* piscadela *f*, pestanejo *m*; *v/t, v/i* piscar, pestanejar
winner ['winə] vencedor *m*
winning ['winiŋ] *adj* cativante
winnings ['winiŋz] *s/pl* ganhos *m/pl*, lucros *m/pl*
winsome ['winsəm] agradável, encantador
win|ter ['wintə] *s* inverno *m*; *v/i* passar o inverno; **~try** ['-tri] invernal, invernoso
wipe [waip] *s* limpadela *f*; esfregadela *f*; *v/t* limpar; enxugar; esfregar; **~ off** saldar, pagar; **~ up** limpar
wire ['waiə] *s* fio *m*; arame *m*; *US* telegrama *m*; *v/t* pôr instalação elé(c)trica em; telegrafar
wireless ['waiəlis] *adj* sem fio(s); **~ phone** telefone *m* sem fios
wiry ['waiəri] magro
wisdom ['wizdəm] sabedoria *f*, sagacidade *f*
wise [waiz] *adj* sábio, sagaz
wish [wiʃ] *s* desejo *m*; vontade *f*; anelo *m*; *v/t, v/i* desejar, anelar, querer, ter vontade de
wistful ['wistful] ansioso, anelante; saudoso
wit [wit] *s* espírito *m*; graça *f*, finura *f*; engenho *m*
witch [witʃ] feiticeira *f*, bruxa *f*
with [wið] com
withdraw [wið'drɔ:] *v/t, v/i* retirar(-se); **~al** retirada *f*
wither ['wiðə] *v/t, v/i* murchar,

secar

withhold [wið'həuld] *v/t* reter, deter; impedir; negar, recusar

within [wi'ðin] *prp* dentro de; no espaço de

without [wi'ðaut] *prp* sem

withstand [wið'stænd] *v/t* resistir a

witness ['witnis] *v/t* testemunhar; presenciar, assistir a; *s* testemunha *f*; **bear ~ to** testificar, testemunhar

witty ['witi] espirituoso, engraçado

wizard ['wizəd] feiticeiro *m*

woe [wəu] dor *f*; desgraça *f*, calamidade *f*; **~ful** triste; lamentável

wolf [wulf] *s* (*pl* **wolves** [-vz]) lobo *m*; *v/t* devorar

woman ['wumən] (*pl* **women** ['wimin]) mulher *f*; **~ly** feminino

womb [wu:m] útero *m*, matriz *f*; ventre *m*; *fig* entranhas *f/pl*

wonder ['wʌndə] *s* admiração *f*; assombro *m*, espanto *m*; prodígio *m*, maravilha *f*; *v/i* espantar-se, maravilhar-se; estranhar; perguntar a si mesmo; querer saber; **~ful** maravilhoso

wont [wəunt] *s* costume *m*

woo [wu:] *v/t* granjear, conquistar

wood [wud] *s* bosque *m*, mata *f*; mato *m*; madeira *f*; lenha *f*; *adj* de madeira; **~en** de madeira; **~pecker** pica-pau *m*; **~work** carpintaria *f*; madeira *f* trabalhada

wool [wul] lã *f*; **~(l)en** de lã; **~ly** *s* malha *f* de lã; *adj* confuso, vago; lanoso

word [wə:d] *s* palavra *f*; termo *m*, vocábulo *m*; letra *f*, texto *m*; *v/t* exprimir; redigir; **~ing** *s* reda(c)ção *f*, fraseologia *f*; **~y** verboso

work [wə:k] *s* obra *f*; trabalho *m*; emprego *m*; *v/t*, *v/i* trabalhar; andar, funcionar; manobrar, operar; explorar; lavrar, talhar; **~able** realizável; manejável, manobrável; **~day** dia *m* útil; **~er** operário *m* trabalhador *m*; **~ing** *adj* trabalhador; de trabalho; admissível; **~man** trabalhador *m*, operário *m*; artífice *m*; **~manship** artesanato *m*; mão-de-obra *f*; **~s** *s* fábrica *f*; mecanismo *m*; **~shop** oficina *f*

world [wə:ld] mundo *m*; **~liness** mundanidade *f*; **~ly** mundano; **~-power** potência *f* mundial; **~ war** guerra *f* mundial; **~-wide** *adj* mundial

worm [wə:m] *s* verme *m*, bicho *m*; lombriga *f*

worn-out ['wɔ:n'aut] *adj* gasto, usado; coçado; alquebrado; fatigado

worried ['wʌrid] *adj* preocupado, inquieto

worry ['wʌri] *s* (*pl* **-ries**) preocupação *f*, ânsia *f*, ansiedade *f*; *v/t*, *v/i* ralar, atormentar; preocupar(-se), arreliar-se

wors|e [wə:s] *adv*, *adj* pior; **~en**

v/t, *v/i* piorar
worship ['wəːʃip] *v/t* adorar, venerar; *s* adoração *f*, veneração *f*
worst [wəːst] *adj* péssimo; o pior; *adv* da pior maneira, pior
worsted ['wustid] fio *m* de lã
worth [wəːθ] *s* valor *m*; *adj* que vale a pena; merecedor, digno; **be ~** valer, merecer; **~less** sem valor; **~while** que vale a pena; **~y** ['-ði] *adj* digno, merecedor
wound [wuːnd] *s* ferida *f*, ferimento *m*, chaga *f*; *v/t* ferir
wrangle ['ræŋgl] *s* disputa *f*; *v/i* disputar
wrap [ræp] *v/t* envolver, embrulhar; **keep under ~s** *s/pl* manter em segredo
wrapper ['ræpə] invólucro *m*
wreath [riːθ] grinalda *f*, coroa *f*; **~e** [-ð] *v/t* engrinaldar; cingir
wreck [rek] *s* MAR naufrágio *m*, ruína *f*, destruição *f*; *v/t* arruinar, destruir; naufragar
wren [ren] carriça *f*
wrench [rentʃ] *s* torcedura *f*; arranco *m*, puxão *m*; chave *f* inglesa; *v/t* arrancar; deslocar, torcer
wrest [rest] *v/t* arrebatar, arrancar; desvirtuar, distorcer
wrestle ['resl] *v/i* lutar; **~r** lutador *m*
wretch [retʃ] infeliz *m*, *f*, desgraçado *m*; patife *m*
wretched ['retʃid] infeliz, desgraçado, miserável; **~ness** miséria *f*
wriggle ['rigl] *v/i* torcer-se, menear-se
wring [riŋ] *v/t* torcer, retorcer
wrinkle ['riŋkl] *s* ruga *f*; *v/t*, *v/i* enrugar(-se)
wrist [rist] pulso *m*, munheca *f*
writ [rit] *s* mandado *m*; escritura *f*
write [rait] *v/t*, *v/i* escrever; **~ down** anotar, pôr por escrito; **~ off** eliminar, anular; **~ out** redigir; preencher, passar
writer ['raitə] escritor *m*
writhe [raið] *v/i* contorcer-se
writing ['raitiŋ] *s* escrita *f*; caligrafia *f*, letra *f*; **in ~** por escrito; **~-desk** escrivaninha *f*, secretária *f*; **~ paper** papel *m*, de carta; **~s** *s/pl* escrito *m*, obra *f*
wrong [rɔŋ] *adj* falso, errado, erróneo, incorre(c)to; enganado; **~ side** avesso *m*; *s* injúria *f*, agravo *m*; dano *m*; injustiça *f*; mal *m*; *adv* mal, erradamente; *v/t* afrontar, ofender, injuriar; **be ~** não ter razão; **~doing** má a(c)ção *f*; **~ful** injusto; ilegal
wry [rai] forçado; de esguelha

X, Y

X-mas ['krisməs] = **Christmas**
X-ray ['eks'rei] *s* raio *m* X; *v/t* radiografar, examinar ao raio X
xylophone ['zailəfəun] xilofone *m*
yacht [jɔt] iate *m*; **~ing** *s* navegação *f* em iate
yak [jæk] *s* iaque *m*
yam [jæm] inhame *m*
Yank(ee) ['jæŋk(i)] ianque *m, f*, americano *m* do norte
yap [jæp] *v/i* latir
yard [jɑːd] jarda *f*; pátio *m*; **~-arm** ponta *f* da verga, lais *m*
yarn [jɑːn] *s* fio *m*; patranha *f*
yawn [jɔːn] *v/i* bocejar; *s* bocejo *m*
yeah [jeː, jæ] sim
year [jəː] ano *m*; **calendar** ~ ano civil; **leap** ~ ano bissexto; **school** ~ ano le(c)tivo; **~ly** *adv* anualmente; *adj* anual
yearn [jəːn] *v/i* suspirar, ansiar
yearning ['jəːniŋ] *s* ânsia *f*; saudade *f*
years [jiəz] *s/pl* idade *f*, anos *m/pl*
yeast [jiːst] fermento *m*; levedura *f*
yell [jel] *s* berro *m*, grito *m*; *v/i* berrar, gritar; vociferar
yellow ['jeləu] *adj*, *s* amarelo *m*; *v/t*, *v/i* amarelecer
yelp [jelp] *s* ganido *m*; *v/i* ganir
yes [jes] *adv* sim
yesterday ['jestədi] *adv* ontem
yet [jet] *conj* mas, contudo; *adv* ainda; já
yew [juː] teixo *m*
yield [jiːld] *s* produção *f*; rendimento *m*; *v/t*, *v/i* produzir, render; ceder; **~ing** *adj* submisso, fraco; moldável
yogh(o)urt ['jəugəːt] iogurte *m*
yoke [jəuk] *s* canga *f*, jugo *m*; *v/t* jungir; emparelhar
yokel ['jəukəl] saloio *m*, labrego *m*, *Braz* caipira *m*
yolk [jəuk] gema *f* de ovo
yon(der) ['jɔn(də)] acolá
you [juː, ju, jə] tu; vós; você; o senhor; te, vos; o, a; lhe, lhes; ti; se, a gente
young [jʌŋ] *adj* jovem, novo; *s/pl* jovens *m/pl*; cria *f*; **~er** mais novo; **~ster** ['-stə] menino *m*, jovem *m*
your [jɔː] teu(s), tua(s); seu(s), sua(s); vosso(s), vossa(s); do(s) senhor(es), da(s) senhora(s)
yours [jɔːz] o(s) teu(s), a(s) tua(s); seu(s), sua(s); vosso(s), vossa(s); do(s) senhor(es), da(s) senhora(s), de você(s); ~ **truly** atenciosamente, respeitosamente
yourself [jə'self] (*pl* **-selves** ['selvz]) te, se; a ti/si mesmo; você mesmo, o senhor mesmo, tu próprio; (**all**) **by** ~ sòzinho, sem ajuda

youth [juːθ] mocidade *f*, juventude *f*; moço *m*, jovem *m*; **~ful** jovem, juvenil; **~ hostel** albergue *m* da juventude

Z

zap [zæp] *v/t fam* (*delete*) apagar; (*kill*) despachar; (*hit*) bater; (*send*) mandar
zeal [ziːl] zelo *m*; **~ot** ['zelət] fanático *m*; **~ous** ['zeləs] zeloso
zebra ['ziːbrə] zebra *f*; **~ crossing** passadeira *f* para peões
zenith ['zeniθ] zénite *m*; apogeu *m*, auge *m*
zeppelin ['zepəlin] zepelim *m*
zero ['ziərəu] zero *m*
zest [zest] ardor *m*, gosto *m*
zigzag ['zigzæg] *s* ziguezague *m*; *v/i* ziguezaguear
zinc [zɪŋk] zinco *m*
Zionism ['zaiənizəm] sionismo *m*
zip [zip] *s*, **zip-fastener** fecho *m* de correr; silvo *m*; *fig* vitalidade *f*, energia *f*
zither ['ziðə] cítara *f*
zodiac ['zəudiæk] zodíaco *m*
zone [zəun] *s* zona *f*
zoo [zuː] jardim *m* zoológico
zoolog|ical [ˌzəuə'lɔdʒikəl] zoológico; **~ist** [-'ɔlədʒist] zoólogo *m*; **~y** [-'ɔlədʒi] zoologia *f*
zoom [zuːm] *s* subida *f* vertical; **~ lens** obje(c)tiva *f* de foco variável
Zulu ['zuːluː] *adj* zulo

Cardinal and ordinal numbers

Numerais cardinais e ordinais

0 nought *zero*
1 one *um, uma*
2 two *dois, duas*
3 three *três*
4 four *quatro*
5 five *cinco*
6 six *seis*
7 seven *sete*
8 eight *oito*
9 nine *nove*
10 ten *dez*
11 eleven *onze*
12 twelve *doze*
13 thirteen *treze*
14 fourteen *catorze*
15 fifteen *quinze*
16 sixteen *dezasseis*
17 seventeen *dezassete*
18 eighteen *dezoito*
19 nineteen *dezanove*
20 twenty *vinte*
21 twenty-one *vinte-e-um (-uma)*
23 twenty-three *vinte-e-três*
30 thirty *trinta*
40 forty *quarenta*
50 fifty *cinqüenta*
60 sixty *sessenta*
70 seventy *setenta*
80 eighty *oitenta*
90 ninety *noventa*
100 a hundred *cem*
101 a/one hundred and one *cento e um/uma*
200 two hundred *duzentos, -as*
300 three hundred *trezentos, -as*
400 four hundred *quatrocentos, -as*
500 five hundred *quinhentos, -as*
600 six hundred *seiscentos, -as*
700 seven hundred *setecentos, -as*
800 eight hundred *oitocentos, -as*
900 nine hundred *novecentos, -as*
1000 a thousand *mil*
1000 000 a million *um milhão*
1st first *primeiro, -a*
2nd second *segundo, -a*
3rd third *terceiro, -a*
4th fourth *quarto, -a*
5th fifth *quinto, -a*
6th sixth *sexto, -a*
7th seventh *sétimo, -a*
8th eighth *oitavo, -a*
9th ninth *nono, -a*
10th tenth *décimo, -a*